MOON

BAJA

JENNIFER KRAMER

31652002990738

D1009881

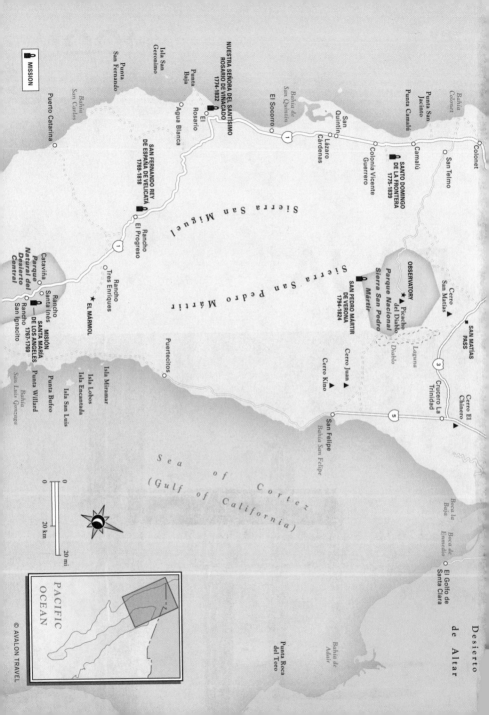

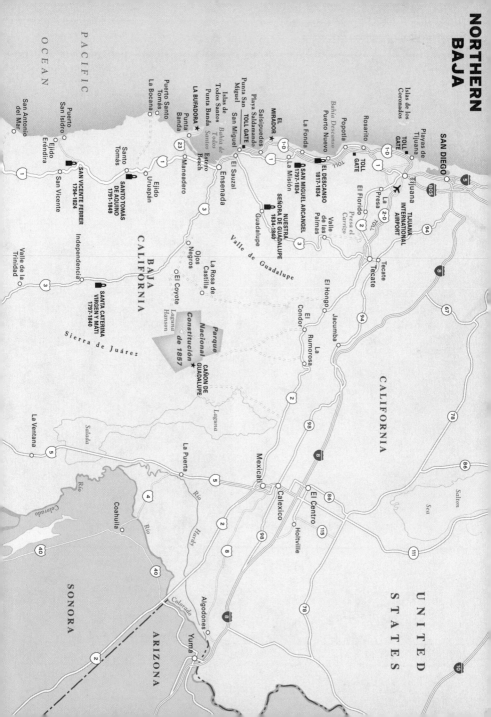

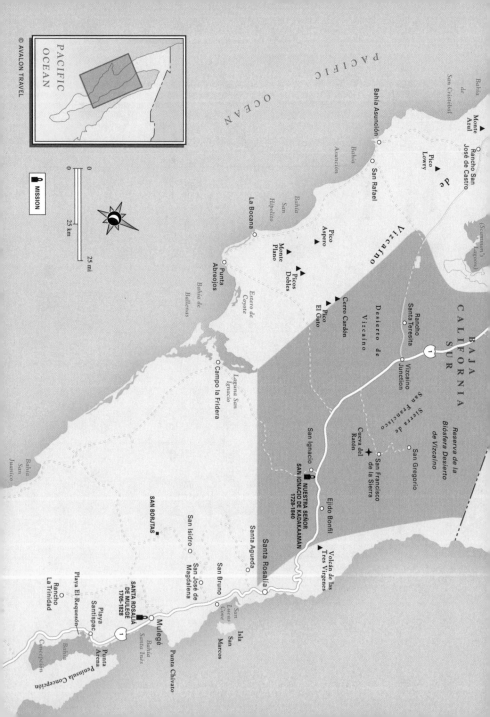

© AVALON TRAVEL

PACIFIC OCEAN

MISSION

0
0
25 km
25 mi

PACIFIC OCEAN

BAJA CALIFORNIA SUR

▲ Monte Azul
Rancho San José de Castro
▲ Pico Lowry
Bahía Asunción
San Rafael
Bahía de San Cristóbal
Bahía de San Hipólito
Bahía Asunción
La Bocana
▲ Pico Aspero
▲ Monte Plano
▲ Picos Dobles
▲ Pico El Gato
▲ Cerro Cardón
Punta Abreojos
Estero de Coyote
Bahía de Ballenas
Campo la Frídera
Laguna San Ignacio

Desierto de Vizcaíno

Sierra de San Francisco

Reserva de la Biósfera Desierto de Vizcaíno

Rancho Santa Teresita
Vizcaíno Junction
Cueva del Ratón
★ San Francisco de la Sierra
San Gregorio

San Ignacio
NUESTRA SEÑOR SAN IGNACIO DE KADAKAAMAN 1728-1840
Ejido Bonfil
Santa Águeda
Santa Rosalía
▲ Volcán de las Tres Vírgenes

SAN BORJITAS ■

San Isidro
San José de Magdalena
San Bruno
Mulegé
SANTA ROSALÍA DE MULEGÉ 1705-1828 ■
Santa Inés
Punta Santispac
Punta Arena
Punta Chivato
Rancho La Trinidad
Playa El Requesón
Playa Santispac
Península Concepción
Bahía Concepción
Bahía San Juanico

San Lucas
San Marcos
Isla San Marcos

1

1

Isla
Cedros

Pico Gill

Cerro de
Cedros

Cedros

Isla
Natividad

Punta Eugenia

Bahía
Tortugas

Bahía
Thurloe

Pico
Veracruz

Península

To Islas San Benito

Sebastián Vizcaíno

Playa
Malarrimo

Bahía de

Laguna
Ojo de
Liebre

Parque Natural
de la Ballena Gris

Guerrero
Negro

★ EAGLE MONUMENT

Estero de San José

Morro Santo Domingo

Laguna Manuela

Ejido
Morelos

Jesús María

Punta Rosarito

Bahía
Santa Rosalillita

Punta Santa Rosalillita

Bahía
Santa María

Punta Negra

Punta María

Punta Cono

Parador
Punta Prieta

Punta
Prieta

Rosarito

Nuevo Chapala

Laguna
Chapala

Valle
del
Desierto
Central

Valle de los Cirios

Parque
Natural

Rancho
San Ignacio

Punta Final

Bahía de
Calamajué

Sierra de la Asamblea

SAN FRANCISCO
BORJA
1762-1818

San Borja

Bahía de los
Ángeles

BAJA CALIFORNIA

Parque
Natural
del Desierto
Central

El Arco

1

10

SANTA GERTRUDIS
1752-1822

San
Francisquito

Isla
Coronado

Bahía de
los Ángeles

Bahía de
las Ánimas

Bahía
San
Rafael

Bahía San Francisquito

Bahía Santa Teresa

Isla
San
Lorenzo

Isla
Las Ánimas

Isla
Salsipuedes

Isla Raza

Isla Partida

Canal de
Ballenas

Isla
de la
Guarda

Canal de

Isla
Ángel

Parque Natural
Isla Ángel de la Guarda

Sea of California (Gulf of California)

Mar de Cortez

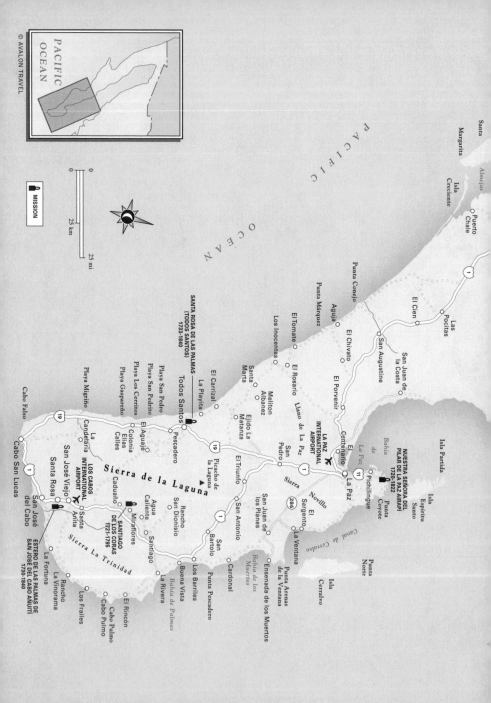

© AVALON TRAVEL

PACIFIC OCEAN

🏛 MISSION

0   25 km
0   25 mi

PACIFIC OCEAN

Santa
Margarita

Isla
Creciente

Puerto
Chale

Las
Pocitas

El Cien

Isla
Espíritu
Santo

Isla Partida

Punta
Conejo

Aguja

Punta Márquez

El Tomate

Los Inocentes

El Chivato

El Porvenir

San Augustine

San Juan de
la Costa

NUESTRA SEÑORA DEL
PILAR DE LA PAZ AIRAPI
1720–1822

SANTA ROSA DE LAS PALMAS
(TODOS SANTOS)
1733–1840

El Carrizal

El Rosario

Santa
Marta

Meliton
Albañez

Ejido La
Matanza

Llano de La Paz

LA PAZ
INTERNATIONAL
AIRPORT

Pichilingue

Punta
Coyote

Bahía de La Paz

Playa Migriño

Playa Las Cerritos

Playa Gaspareño

Playa San Pedro

Playa San Pedrito

El Aguaje

Colonia
Elías
Calles

El Pescadero

Todos Santos

La Playita

Picacho de
la Laguna

El Triunfo

San
Pedro

La
Candelaria

LOS CABOS
INTERNATIONAL
AIRPORT

Sierra de la Laguna

Caduaño

Miraflores

Agua
Caliente

Rancho
San Dionisio

Santiago

SANTIAGO
DE LOS CORAS
1721–1795

San Juan de
los Planes

San Antonio

Sierra

El
Sargento

Novillo

La Paz

Centenario

El Triunfo

Punta Arenas
de la Ventana

La Ventana

Cabo Falso

Cabo San Lucas

Santa Rosa

San José Viejo

San José
del Cabo

Santa
Anita

ESTERO DE LAS PALMAS DE
SAN JOSÉ DEL CABO AÑUTI
1730–1840

La Fortuna

La Vinorama

Rancho

Los Frailes

El Rincón

Cabo Pulmo

Cabo Pulmo

San
Bartolo

Los Barriles

Buena Vista

La Rivera

Punta Pescadero

Cardonal

Ensenada de los Muertos

Bahía de los
Muertos

Bahía de Palmas

Sierra La Trinidad

Isla
Cerralvo

Canal de Cerralvo

Punta
Norte

Magdalena

Punta
Entrada

Isla

Punta
Entrada

Isla
Magdalena

Puerto San
Carlos

Bahía
Bahía
Magdalena

Puerto
Cancún

Santa Rita

23

Llano   de   Magdalena

Puerto
López Mateos

Ciudad
Constitución

Ciudad
Insurgentes

Llano de
Magdalena

SAN LUIS GONZAGA
1740-1768

San Luis
Gonzaga

NUESTRA SEÑORA DE
LOS DOLORES DEL SUR
1721-1818

Sierra   de   la   Giganta

Cerro
Guillermo

Agua
Verde

Puerto
Agua Verde

Agua Verde

Isla San
Francisco

Isla
San
José

Isla
Santa
Cruz

Isla
Santa
Catalina

Punta San Juanico

Bahía
San Juanico

Santo
Domingo

Isla
Santo
Domingo

Boca de las Animas

La
Purísima

San
Isidro

LA PURÍSIMA
CONCEPCIÓN DE CADEGOMÓ
1720-1822

San José de
Comondú

B A J A

C A L I F O R N I A

S U R

San Javier

Rancho
Las Parras

SAN FRANCISCO
XAVIER DE
VIGGÉ-BIAUNDÓ
1699-1817

SAN JUAN BAUTISTA
MALIBAT (LIGÜÍ)
1705-1721

Ensenada Blanca

Isla Danzante

Isla
Monserrate

Puerto
Escondido

Nopoló

Loreto

NUESTRA SEÑORA
DE LORETO DE CONCHÓ
1697-1829

Loreto Bay National
Marine Park

Isla del
Carmen

Isla Coronado

SAN BRUNO
1683-1685

SAN JOSÉ DE COMONDÚ
1708-1827

1

1

Isla San Ildefonso

Sea   of   Cortez
(Gulf of California)

SOUTHERN
BAJA

Contents

Baja

Baja California is a land rich with cultural treasures, natural landscapes, and exhilarating adventures. With its dramatic terrain ranging from picturesque turquoise waters and white-sand beaches to rugged desert mountain ranges, it's a region that leaves a long-lasting impression on those who journey through it. Baja shares the same warm and colorful culture of the rest of Mexico, but due to its isolated peninsular geography, it has a spirit and manner unique to itself.

In the north are the cities of Tijuana and Ensenada, leading an exciting culinary movement with bourgeoning wine region and craft beer industry. In the south, Los Cabos offers luxury resorts, world-class golf courses, chic art galleries, and upscale restaurants. In between are colorful deserts, picturesque mountain ranges, and unspoiled coastlines. A few fishing villages and small colonial towns are nestled within these glories of nature. This is the Baja that adventurers seek out. This is where surfers find perfect waves without the crowds, anthropologists view rarely seen cave paintings, anglers come to catch large yellowtail by the dozens, historians to study the first Spanish missions, and divers experience what Jacques Cousteau called "the world's aquarium"—the Sea of Cortez.

Clockwise from top left: a tour boat in Cabo Pulmo; palapa at Los Frailes Beach; sunset from Las Animas Bajas in San José del Cabo; artisan shopping in Loreto; mariachi statues on the roof of Hotel California; Agua Verde.

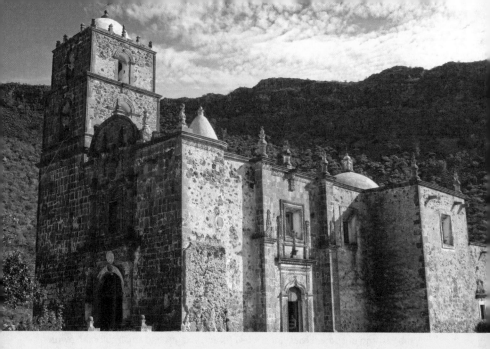

A road trip is the perfect way to explore and discover the peninsula. Cruise down Mexico 1 with the endless cactus deserts as a backdrop and the warm Baja breeze in your face. Encounter small seaside villages where local fishers will invite you to join them in a home-cooked meal of fresh-caught lobster. Enjoy a *cerveza* from the comfort of a hammock with the breezes of the Pacific erasing all cares. Take a *panga* ride out to encounter a pod of dolphins that swim and jump alongside the boat. Watch vibrant sunsets over the ocean followed by bonfires on the beach with a blanket of stars overhead.

Even though it's practically in their backyard, most people in the United States aren't aware of the special treasures that Baja has to offer beyond margaritas and mariachis. Bring an open mind and a sense of adventure— Baja awaits.

Clockwise from top left: Misión San Francisco Xavier de Viggé-Biaundó; Chileno Bay is one of Los Cabos' best beaches; Plaza de los Mariachis in Cabo San Lucas; San Borjitas cave paintings.

If You Have...

FOUR DAYS

Northern Baja is a popular destination for long weekends because of the beaches, incredible culinary scene, and Mexico's wine country. Tijuana, Rosarito, Ensenada, Valle de Guadalupe, and Tecate (or any combination of these) all make for quick and easy road trips. In Baja Sur, Loreto, La Paz, and Los Cabos are easy to reach by plane for perfect four-day escapes.

SEVEN DAYS

With a full week, take a road trip to Bahía de los Ángeles to relax and swim with the whale sharks. Southern Baja can be fully explored by flying into Los Cabos and taking the cape loop around the East Cape, La Paz, and the West Cape.

THREE WEEKS

Three weeks is a comfortable amount of time to explore most of what the peninsula has to offer from the U.S. border to the tip of the peninsula and back again. Stop at all the towns along Mexico 1, explore the Spanish missions, take advantage of the beautiful beaches along the way, and save some time to relax.

Planning Your Trip

Where to Go

Tijuana, Ensenada, and Valle de Guadalupe

Tijuana is going through a cultural renaissance with **exquisite restaurants, craft breweries, and art galleries** taking over the spaces where the nightclubs and bars used to be. Down the Pacific coast, Ensenada also draws **foodies** to its high-end **restaurants,** famous **street carts,** and **fish taco stands.** Ensenada's Ruta del Vino takes travelers into the Valle de Guadalupe, popular for its charming boutique **wineries** and *campestre* restaurants.

Mexicali, San Felipe, and the Sierra de Juárez

Mexicali, the capital of Baja California Norte, is a tranquil city with a bourgeoning **craft beer** scene and Mexico's largest **Chinatown,** La Chinesca. Travelers head to the nearby Sierra de Juárez to enjoy **hot springs** in the Cañon de Guadalupe. Down the coast is the Sea of Cortez

village of San Felipe where tourists and expats **fish** and relax. Visit the giant cardón cacti in the Valle de los Gigantes or **camp** at Bahía San Luis Gonzaga.

San Quintín and Bahía de los Ángeles

The Sierra de San Pedro Mártir is a **high mountain range** and home to the **National Observatory** and the condor release program. In the Valle de los Cirios, the desert starts to open up and cacti and *cirios* (the odd-looking boojum trees) take over the landscape. Expats and tourists head over to Bahía de los Ángeles to **fish and relax.**

Guerrero Negro and El Vizcaíno

Guerrero Negro marks the state line between Baja California Norte and Baja California Sur. In the winter, travelers make their own migration to have friendly encounters with the **gray whales**

11/23/2022

Item(s) Checked Out

TITLE	Baja / Jennifer
BARCODE	31652002990738
DUE DATE	**12-14-22**

Total Items This Session: 1

You saved $22.00 by visiting the library today!

Books are just the beginning.

Use your library card to access ebooks, audiobooks, and magazines. Plus, you can check out Wi-Fi hotspots and Chromebooks, learn a new language and get free museum passes.

Terminal #   204

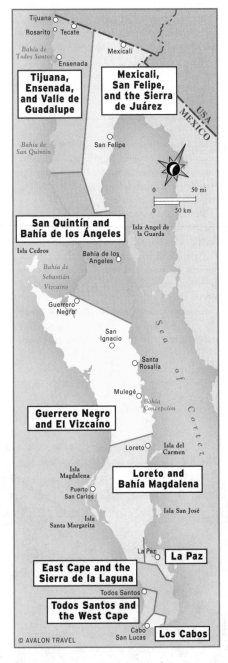

at the nearby Laguna Ojo de Liebre. From colonial **mission towns** to incredible **rock art** sites, and **fishing** off the coast of the Vizcaíno peninsula, this is an area ripe for exploration.

Loreto and Bahía Magdalena

The clear waters and **white-sand beaches** of Bahía Concepción lure **snorkelers, kayakers, campers, and RVers.** Just south, Loreto is a charming colonial town, home to California's **first mission** and an offshore **marine reserve.** Bahía Magdalena is popular with **water sports** fanatics, **gray whale** watchers, and nature enthusiasts.

La Paz

La Paz centers on the beautiful *malecón* that wraps around the bay where strolling locals and tourists to enjoy the views, **restaurants, hotels, and shops.** But its main draws are the **beaches** and the **islands. Snorkel** with **sea lions,** swim with **whale sharks,** or enjoy deserted beaches.

East Cape and the Sierra de la Laguna

The East Cape is home to beaches, world-class **diving,** offshore **fishing,** charming towns, and the **lush peaks** of the Sierra de la Laguna. Los Barriles attracts **kiteboarders and windsurfers,** while the off-the-grid town of Cabo Pulmo draws divers and snorkelers with its **coral reef** teeming with marinelife.

Los Cabos

The most-recognized and **most-visited** location in all of Baja, Los Cabos refers to the region comprising the two cities of **San José del Cabo** and **Cabo San Lucas** and **the corridor** that connects them. This is a Baja completely different from the rest of the peninsula. **Luxury, relaxation, and fun** are the focus here. **Yachts** fill the marinas, and **all-inclusive resorts** line the beaches. **Dance clubs** and **bars** are busy until the wee hours of the morning.

Todos Santos and the West Cape

Up the coast from Los Cabos, Todos Santos is a charming colonial town of **bohemian art galleries, upscale restaurants,** and **chic** **boutique hotels.** Surf spots, beautiful beaches, and the nearby El Pescadero community draw tourists looking for a humbler **alternative to Cabo.**

Know Before You Go

High and Low Seasons

The best season for visiting Baja depends on the region you will be visiting and the activities you hope to participate in. The farther south you go, the warmer the temperatures and the higher the humidity. Temperatures are warmer on the Sea of Cortez than on the Pacific side of the peninsula.

Winter is the **high season** for visiting **Baja California Sur** with the holidays around Christmas and New Year's Day being the busiest weeks of the year, especially in **Los Cabos.** Snowbirds head to Baja Sur and the Sea of Cortez in the winter, as do kiteboarders and windsurfers in search of El Norte winds. **Whale** **season** from January to April makes the areas around Guerrero Negro, San Ignacio, and Bahía Magdalena extremely busy. Expect to pay the most for accommodations at this time and make arrangements in advance.

Winter has been considered more of a **low season** for tourism in **northern Baja** on the Pacific side around **Ensenada** and **Rosarito.** The temperatures are pleasant here year-round so businesses will still be open during the winter, but you'll get cheaper rates on hotel rooms.

Summer is **low season** for **Baja California Sur** and **the Sea of Cortez** as temperatures and **humidity** are so high that many places

ocean views from the hammock in the beachside palapa at Villa Santa Cruz, Todos Santos

Visitors enjoy sunbathing on the rocks and swimming in the pools at Cañon de la Zorra.

close down for July, August, and September. Any hotels that stay open will be cheap, but restaurants and other attractions are likely to be shuttered in towns like Loreto, La Paz, and Todos Santos. Anglers, divers, and surfers still flock to southern Baja in the summer because the fish are plentiful, the waters are warm, and the surf is good. **Hurricane season** is from June-October, so travelers to Baja California Sur should be aware of the risk of tropical storms. Northern Baja California is not affected by hurricane season.

Summer is **high season** for visiting **northern Baja** along the coast around **Ensenada** and **Rosarito.** Hotel rates will be the most expensive during summer weekends. The coast can experience the marine layer during early summer with "May Gray" and "June Gloom."

Spring and fall are generally considered the **best seasons for traveling in Baja** as the weather is pleasant anywhere on the peninsula.

Passports and Visas

Passports are required to visit Baja California. Non-Mexican citizens must also obtain a *forma migratoria múltiple* **(FMM) tourist permit** in order to travel in Mexico. If you are flying into Baja from outside of Mexico, this will be included in your ticket. If crossing by land, you can obtain your permit at the border crossing.

Transportation

Many travelers explore Baja by car. **Mexican auto insurance** is required by law, so don't forget to purchase it before you leave on your trip. It's best to reserve a **rental car** for use during your trip if you are flying into Baja, unless you plan on spending most of your time at a resort in Los Cabos.

Classic Baja Road Trip

One of the most popular ways to explore the peninsula is on a road trip down the transpeninsular highway. Driving the full length of Mexico 1 from Tijuana to Cabo is a rite of passage memorable for its diverse landscapes, scenic small towns, historical and archaeological sites, and friendly people.

Day 1
86 MI (140 KM)
2.5 HOURS
Drive across the **U.S./Mexico border** in Tijuana and down the Pacific coast along **Mexico 1.** Enjoy the impressive Pacific views from the highway as you cruise into the port town of **Ensenada.** Check into **Corona Hotel & Spa** in town or **Las Rosas** just north of town, where you'll enjoy sweeping **ocean views.** Head to the heart of Ensenada to the **Mercado de Mariscos** where you can browse the fresh fish and enjoy a **fish taco** from any of the **stands** outside. From here go for a stroll along the harbor to see the fishing boats and cruise ships that dock in Ensenada.

Two blocks east of the harbor, **López Mateos (Calle Primera)** is the main street in Ensenada where you can do some **shopping** and have **dinner.** Cap off your evening with a **margarita** at Ensenada's oldest bar, **Hussong's Cantina.**

Side Trips
Drive 30 minutes inland, heading east on Mexico 3, from Ensenada to the nearby Valle de Guadalupe wine region and spend the day **wine-tasting** at boutique wineries and eating **farm-to-table cuisine** at outdoor *campestre* restaurants. Spend a night in the valley at **La Villa del Valle** or **Bruma** so you can fully take advantage of the relaxing atmosphere and some of the **120 wineries** now in the area. Or, south of Ensenada at **San Telmo**, turn off of Mexico 1 at Km. 140 and head east into the **Sierra de San Pedro Mártir** to enjoy a different landscape of **high peaks** and **pine trees.** Enjoy a night or two in the foothills of the sierra at a working ranch like **Rancho Meling** and visit the

the Tuscan-style villa at La Villa del Valle B&B

National Observatory, hike among the pine trees in the national park, and do some **stargazing** at night.

Day 2
229 MI (370 KM)
5 HOURS

Get an early start from Ensenada to continue south on Mexico 1 through **San Quintín** and into the **central desert,** what many consider to be the **heart of Baja.** Take a short detour to see the **sea lions** at **La Lobera** before heading to **El Rosario** to enjoy a **lobster burrito** for lunch at **Mama Espinoza's.** Don't forget to fill up the gas tank in El Rosario. Continue south and stay the night amid the cacti and boulders in the heart of the *desierto central* in Cataviña at the **Hotel Misión Cataviña.**

Side Trip

Take two days to visit **Bahía de los Ángeles.** Turn off of Mexico 1 at kilometer 280 and drive 65 kilometers (on a paved road) east to the Sea of Cortez. Spend some time **relaxing** along the bay, check out the local **Museo de Naturaleza y Cultura,** or head out with a local *panguero* to spend the day fishing or exploring marinelife. Campers will enjoy a rustic stay on the beach at **Camp Archelon,** or get a room at **Costa del Sol.** If it's late summer or early fall, ask around with local *pangueros* or at Villa Bahia about going out in a boat to **swim with the whale sharks.** History buffs shouldn't miss a day trip to **Misión San Francisco de Borja Adac,** a beautiful stone mission nearby.

Day 3
236 MI (380 KM)
5 HOURS

Take an hour to check out the **cave paintings** at **Cataviña** before getting on the road to head south. When you cross the state line at **Guerrero Negro,** stop in town to take a tour of the **saltworks factory** and grab some **fish or shrimp tacos** for lunch at **Tacos el Muelle.** Continue south to the colonial oasis town of **San Ignacio** and check into **Hotel La Huerta.** Enjoy an evening walk around the small town to check out the **colonial architecture, the plaza,** and **the mission** before dinner at **Tootsie's Bar & Grill.**

Cardón cacti provide a beautiful backdrop for road trips down the peninsula.

Side Trip

If it's **gray whale** season (Jan.-Apr.), make advanced arrangements to have a friendly encounter with these mammoth sea mammals. Both **Guerrero Negro** and **Laguna San Ignacio** are annual **winter** destinations for the gray whales, who come to the shallow and warm waters of Baja California to breed and calve. Visitors go out in small *pangas* to have **up close encounters** with the gray whales where they can pet and even kiss the whales in the wild. Guerrero Negro whale-watching can be done in one day, while Laguna San Ignacio usually requires a multiday stop.

Day 4
86 MI (140 KM)
2 HOURS

Stop in the morning at a local **Tortillería La Misión** to stock up on fresh **handmade tortillas** before heading out of town. When you get to the Sea of Cortez and the mining town of **Santa Rosalía**, stop in town to find **Iglesia de Santa Bárbara,** a church designed by Gustave Eiffel. Line up with the locals for a **chile relleno taco** at **Tacos el Faro Verde** before continuing on to the

oasis town of Mulegé. Spend the afternoon visiting the beautiful stone **Misión Santa Rosalía de Mulegé,** perched on a hilltop overlooking the palm trees, river, and town. Check into **Hotel Hacienda** in town or **Hotel Serenidad** just south of town.

Day 5
83 MI (135 KM)
2 HOURS

Enjoy a beach day along the **white sand beaches** and **crystal waters** of Bahía Concepción. Spend the morning **kayaking** or **snorkeling** at **Playa Santispac**, or just **sunbathe** and enjoy the beautiful setting. Grab a **burger** and a **beer** at **Playa Buenaventura** before you leave this beautiful bay. Then continue south to **Loreto** and check into your hotel at **Las Cabañas de Loreto** or **Coco Cabañas**.

Day 6
24 MI (39 KM)
1.5 HOURS

Get an early start and drive into the **mountains** for a **day trip** from Loreto to the village

the clear waters of Bahía Concepción

Best Baja Beaches

Playa Santispac is one of the most popular beaches on Bahía Concepción for snowbirds and RVers.

With 3,000 kilometers of coastline, Baja has plenty of beaches from secluded hangouts to popular sands buzzing with activity. The waves of the Pacific and the tranquility of the Sea of Cortez attract visitors who come to surf, kiteboard, kayak, or just relax.

ROSARITO

You don't need to go too far south of the border to find great beaches. Just an hour from San Diego, Rosarito has a number of lovely white sand beaches, including the expansive and bustling beach right in town. Surfing, swimming, horse and camel rides, fishing from the pier, and ultralight plane rides all happen here.

ENSENADA

In town, Playa Hermosa is one of the most beautiful spots (hence the name, *hermosa*, meaning beautiful). It's a great beginner surf spot and nice for swimming and relaxing. South of town, the tranquil Playa Estero is great for sunbathing and enjoying a horseback ride.

BAHÍA CONCEPCIÓN

On the Sea of Cortez, the turquoise bays and white sand beaches of Bahía Concepción are the things tropical dreams are made of. The series of bays provides plenty of options like the popular Playa Santispac or unique Playa El Requesón.

They're all beautiful spots and great for swimming, kayaking, snorkeling, and camping.

LA PAZ

La Paz is home to a number of beautiful Sea of Cortez beaches. Just south of town, visitors can drive to Playa Balandra and Playa El Tecolote. Both have shallow clear waters and white sandy beaches. Even more fun is to take a boat ride out to explore the beaches of the islands offshore where you'll get to enjoy beautiful deserted beaches with bright turquoise waters.

THE WEST CAPE

Todos Santos has a number of stunning beaches, but the currents and waves are strong and make most of them great for surfing, but not safe for swimming. Playa Los Cerritos, south of Todos Santos in El Pescadero was once touted as one of the best beaches in Baja, but some complain that it's become too busy and commercial in recent years.

LOS CABOS

Cabo San Lucas, San José del Cabo, and the corridor in between, are all home to some of the most beautiful beaches in Baja. Be careful, as swimming is not safe at many of the beaches. At popular tourist beaches like Lover's Beach (near the land's end arch) and Playa Chileno (on the corridor), swimming and snorkeling are allowed and encouraged.

of **San Javier.** Check out the **mission,** see the 300+-year-old **olive trees** and have **lunch** at **La Palapa** restaurant. Head back to Loreto and spend the evening around the town **plaza,** visiting the **Loreto mission,** enjoying **two-for-one margarita happy hour** along the plaza, and savoring dinner at any of the restaurants in town.

Day 7
267 MI (430 KM)
5.5 HOURS

Drive south to the colonial artist town of **Todos Santos.** Stroll around the historic district and have dinner at any of the **quaint restaurants** in town like **Café Santa Fe** or **Los Adobes de Todos Santos.** Stay along the beach at the stunning **Villa Santa Cruz** where you can spend your evening **stargazing** from the **hot tub** or enjoying a **rooftop bonfire.**

Day 8
46 MI (75 KM)
1 HOUR

Go for a **morning walk** along one of the beautiful **Todos Santos beaches** before driving south for an hour on Mexico 1 to **Los Cabos.** Stay in the **historic district** in **San José del Cabo** at **Casa Natalia** where you'll be right in heart of town with its bustling plaza and vibrant art galleries. Head out to enjoy a relaxing **dinner and drinks** at any of the restaurants along **Boulevard Mijares.**

Day 9
49 MI (80 KM)
1 HOUR

Get out of the bustle of Los Cabos and head northeast on Mexico 1 to the **tranquil East Cape.** Stop in the foothills of the **Sierra de la Laguna** in the small town of **Santiago** to explore some of the nearby **natural hot springs** or the impressive **waterfall** at the **Cañon de la Zorra.** Spend the night along the Sea of Cortez in the town of **Los Barriles** or nearby **Buena Vista** where you can enjoy **family-friendly beachfront accommodations** at places like **Rancho Leonero** or **Hotel Buena Vista.**

Todos Santos town plaza

Marine Adventures

Getting outside and up close with nature is one of the lures of the peninsula. While there are plenty of opportunities for spontaneous encounters with a pod of dolphins or for divers to encounter giant manta rays, there are a few specific interactions that visitors come to the peninsula to experience.

GRAY WHALE ENCOUNTERS

There are three spots in Baja California Sur where the gray whales come every winter—Laguna San Ignacio, Laguna Ojo de Liebre, and Bahía Magdalena. Visitors go out into the lagoons in small fishing boats, and up close encounters with the gentle giants are extremely common. There's nothing quite like getting to kiss a baby gray whale in the wild from a *panga*. Prime season for gray whale watching is late January through early April.

SWIMMING WITH WHALE SHARKS

There are a few spots along the Sea of Cortez where the whale shark can be found. As the largest fish in the sea, growing up to 18 meters, these gentle creatures can be a delight to experience. August to October, they are present in Bahía de los Ángeles, and in recent years, they've been found year-round in La Paz.

SNORKELING WITH SEA LIONS

There are various sea lion colonies on the peninsula, but Los Islotes off of Isla Espíritu Santo in La Paz is probably the most well-known. Boats take visitors out to swim, snorkel, and dive with the sea

gray whale-watching in Guerrero Negro's Laguna Ojo de Liebre

lions. The islands are also home to a host of other marine and wildlife.

GREAT WHITE SHARK CAGE DIVING

Isla Guadalupe, off the Pacific coast of Baja, is known as one of the premier spots for cage diving with great white sharks. Live-aboard trips leave from San Diego and Ensenada.

Side Trip

Divers and **snorkelers** will want to spend a few days in **Cabo Pulmo,** exploring one of only three **coral reefs** in North America. Snorkelers can head to **Los Arbolitos** to snorkel right from the beach while divers can take a boat from town to get to the best spots. Stay at **Baja Bungalows** for comfortable and relaxed accommodations.

Day 10

65 MI (105 KM)

1.5 HOURS

On your drive north to La Paz along Mexico 1, stop to explore the old mining town of **El Triunfo** where you can walk around the mining grounds up to the lookout and have **brunch** at **Caffé El Triunfo.** Continue on to La Paz and spend your

Crystal clear waters and white sand attract travelers to Playa El Tecolote.

afternoon out at **Playa Balandra** or **Playa El Tecolote,** taking advantage of some of the city's best beaches. Stay in town at a **B&B** or along the beach at **Costa Baja.**

Day 11

Spend the day in La Paz going out on a boat to **Isla Espíritu Santo** where you'll have a chance to **swim and snorkel** with sea lions, whales, tropical fish, and other marinelife. In the evening, grab a bite at one of the **restaurants along the** *malecón* and go for a **stroll** along **the promenade** after dinner.

Day 12-13

683 MI (1,100 KM)
13 HOURS

Spend two days driving north back up Mexico 1, stopping to spend more time or stay the night in any towns you missed on the way down. Plan on your last night being at **Baja Cactus** in El Rosario or **Hotel Misión Santa Maria** in San Quintín.

Day 14

220 MI (355 KM)
5 HOURS

Just north of Ensenada, turn off of Mexico 1 and head east on the northern branch of Mexico 3 to the *Pueblo Mágico* town of Tecate. Stop in Tecate to take a rest, listen to the **mariachis** on the plaza, and enjoy one last **taco.** Be sure to swing by the famous **El Mejor Pan de Tecate** to fill up a tray of pastries and baked goods before crossing back into the United States.

Alternative Northbound Route

Those with **four-wheel drive** vehicles can take the Mexico 5 north from Laguna Chapala to spend your last two days on the road along the northern Sea of Cortez. The route is **unpaved** for the first 40 kilometers (24 mi.) after turning off of Mexico 1. Stop in for a **beer** at **Coco's Corner,** relax at **Bahía San Luis Gonzaga,** visit the giant cardón cacti in the **Valle de los Gigantes,** and spend the night in the fishing town of **San Felipe.** Head up Mexico 5 to cross back into the United States through the Mexicali/ Calexico border.

The Northern Route: Tijuana to Tecate

The northern coastal border region is one of the most fascinating and culturally interesting on the peninsula. The beautiful beaches and countryside provide the perfect backdrop for an incredible culinary scene, world-class wine region, and bourgeoning craft beer industry.

Day 1
18 MI (30 KM)
1 HOUR

Get an early start to cross south at the **San Ysidro border** into **Tijuana.** Head to the **Mercado Hidalgo** to explore its stalls of **fresh produce, regional spices,** and **local artisan goods.** Tijuana has some of the best **street food** in the world, so get some *birria* at nearby **Tacos Fito,** or enjoy street tacos at **Las Ahumaderas.** After lunch, catch an exhibit at **CECUT cultural center.** For dinner, try out a nice restaurant like **La Justina** or **Verde y Crema** to get a taste of Tijuana's incredible **culinary scene.** If you like **craft beer,** cap off your night at **Plaza Fiesta,** Tijuana's collection of craft beer **tasting rooms.**

Day 2
65 MI (105 KM)
1.5 HOURS

Head to **breakfast** at the original **Food Garden** and then drive down the coast along Mexico 1 to Ensenada. Check out the **Mercado de Mariscos** and grab one of Ensenada's famous **fish tacos** at one of the stalls outside the market, or walk over to **Muelle 3** for incredible **ceviche** and **fresh seafood.** Spend the afternoon shopping and taking in the sights on López Mateos (Calle Primera). Enjoy **dinner** at one of Ensenada's prime **restaurants** like **Boules** or **Manzanilla.** After dinner, stop in at the long-established **Hussong's Cantina** for a beer or margarita.

Mercado Hidalgo in Tijuana

Mercado de Mariscos in Ensenada

Baja's mountain ranges boast lush waterfalls, snowcapped peaks—and fewer visitors.

SIERRA DE JUÁREZ

The Sierra de Juárez is home to the Cañon de Guadalupe hot springs, nestled into a palm oasis. At higher elevations, there are pine trees and camping areas like Laguna Hanson.

SIERRA DE SAN PEDRO MÁRTIR

The northern range of the Sierra de San Pedro Mártir is a rich area with pine trees, snow-capped peaks, and California Condors that are being re-introduced into the wild. The Parque Nacional here is home to Picacho del Diablo (the highest mountain on the peninsula), the National Astronomical Observatory, and plenty of hiking trails. In the foothills there are working ranches, where guests can stay in charmingbut rustic accommodations.

SIERRA DE SAN FRANCISCO

These mountains are home to some of the most incredible rock art sites in North America. You'll need to make arrangements for guides and tours in advance, as most of the best cave paintings require multiday excursions camping and on pack animal.

The Sierra de San Pedro Mártir is home to the highest peaks in Baja.

Tours leave from the small mountain town of San Francisco.

SIERRA DE LA LAGUNA

There are no accommodations in Sierra de Laguna, but nearby towns like Miraflores and Santiago in the foothills provide easy access to the hiking, hot springs, and waterfalls that lure travelers to the area. Multiday hiking trip excursions depart from the West Cape to reach the now dried-up *laguna* that the range is named for.

Day 3

18 MI (30 KM)

30 MINUTES

Grab a breakfast featuring local cheeses and other products at Casa Marcelo before driving east to the Valle de Guadalupe. Stop in at the new Museo de la Vid y el Vino to learn about the history of winemaking and the valley. Enjoy lunch alfresco at the *campestre* Finca Altozano and visit a winery like Las Nubes

to enjoy your wine with beautiful views. Enjoy a gourmet six-course dinner while looking out at the garden at the famous Corazón de Tierra restaurant.

Day 4

Enjoy a hearty breakfast of *huevos con machaca* at La Cocina de Doña Esthela before heading off for a day of wine-tasting at boutique wineries like Vena Cava, Pijoan, or Lechuza.

Enjoy a Mexican-style late **lunch/early dinner** at **Malva**. Then catch **sunset** with incredible dramatic ocean views at the **cliff-top Bar Bura** at **Cuatrocuatros**.

Day 5
49 MI (80 KM)
1 HOUR
Drive north on Mexico 3 to the *Pueblo Mágico* **town of Tecate** and grab some **fresh baked goods** for breakfast at **El Mejor Pan de Tecate**. Head to the **Museo Comunitario de Tecate** to learn about the **history and culture** of the region. Grab a **carne asada taco** for a quick bite at **Taqueria Los Amigos** and enjoy a stroll around the town plaza, savoring the shade of the mature trees and listening to the **mariachis**. If you want to have a drink before dinner, head to the local's spot **Bar Diana**, right on the plaza, for a **beer or margarita**. Then go to **El Lugar de Nos** to enjoy a memorable meal before crossing back to San Diego through the laid-back Tecate border crossing.

The Cabo Loop

For those who visit the Los Cabos area but want to see and experience more of the natural beauty and adventure of Baja California, this fun road trip explores the Cape area of Baja California Sur.

Day 1
Fly into **Los Cabos International Airport** and **rent a car** at one of the stands in the airport. Drive the 15 minutes south from the airport to the town of San José del Cabo and check into one of the **hotels along the beach** or in the historic town center. Walk around town to take in the **plaza, historic district**, and **art galleries**. **Bird-watchers** will want to check out the nearby **Estero San José**. For **dinner**, drive just out of town on the Camino Cabo Este (East Cape Road) to **Flora's Field Kitchen** for a gourmet **farm-to-table** dinner.

Day 2
55 MI (90 KM)
1.5 HOURS
Head over to the **East Cape** town of **Cabo Pulmo** where **divers and snorkelers** will enjoy exploring the **coral reef** just offshore. Snorkelers can swim out from the beach at **Los Arbolitos** or **Los Frailes**, and divers will enjoy taking a boat out to get to remoter spots. Enjoy **dinner and drinks** at the casual **La Palapa** restaurant looking out at the water. Stay in one of Cabo Pulmo's casual **eco-lodging** accommodations.

Alternate Trip
35 MI (55 KM)
45 MINUTES
For those not interested in diving or snorkeling, explore more of what the East Cape has to offer with the **hot springs** of Santa Rita and the Cañon de la Zorra **waterfall**, both **accessed from the town of Santiago**. Spend the night in **Los Barriles** or **Buena Vista** on the coast.

Day 3
93 MI (150 KM)
2.5 HOURS
Get an early start driving north on Mexico 1 to La Paz. Spend a few hours in the small old mining town of **El Triunfo** where you can walk along the mine ruins and grab some **baked goods** at **Caffé El Triunfo**. When you get to La Paz, drive out to the **scenic beaches** at **Playa Balandra** or **Playa El Tecolote**. Enjoy **ceviche** and **beers** with your toes in the sand at **restaurant bar El Tecolote**.

Day 4
Take a break from driving today and book a **boat excursion** out to the La Paz islands, especially

Lover's Beach is one of the top beaches in Cabo San Lucas.

Isla Espíritu Santo. Dive with sea lions, swim with whale sharks, or just enjoy the beautiful island and beach views from the boat. When you get back to La Paz, enjoy a **stroll** along the **lively** *malecón*.

Day 5

49 MI (80 KM)

1 HOUR

Head southwest on Mexico 1 to Mexico 19 to the **West Cape** to the colonial artist town of **Todos Santos** and check into the charming **Villa Santa Cruz** or **La Bohemia Hotel Pequeño**. Spend some time walking around the **historical center of town** to check out the **colonial architecture, shops, and restaurants**. Splurge for an incredible meal of **fish carpaccio** and **lobster ravioli** at **Café Santa Fe**.

Day 6

46 MI (75 KM)

1 HOUR

Drive south on Mexico 19 to **Cabo San Lucas** and hop on a **water taxi** to check out the famous **El Arco or Land's End Arch** and to go to **Lover's Beach**. Spend the afternoon here **snorkeling, swimming,** and **sunbathing**. At night, head out to **Cabo Wabo Cantina** or somewhere else along the strip to take in a bit of Cabo's legendary **nightlife**.

Day 7

Spend your last morning enjoying one of Cabo's indulgent treats—a round of **golf**, a **massage** at the spa, a morning **surf**, or **sipping a margarita poolside**.

Four-Day Getaways

Baja has a wealth of options if you're looking for a quick getaway. Whether you're out for a weekend road trip or a quick flight to a unique destination, the peninsula has an adventure waiting for you.

La Ruta del Vino

DAY 1

75 MI (120 KM)

2 HOURS

Drive across the San Diego/Tijuana border at San Ysidro and keep going two hours south to arrive at the **Valle de Guadalupe**. Check into your intimate **B&B** at **La Villa del Valle** or **Terra del Valle**. Start your explorations in the valley with a quick visit to the **Museo de la Vid y el Vino** to learn about wine and the history of the region. Check out a few **wineries** like **Clos de Tres Cantos, Vena Cava,** or **Las Nubes**. Enjoy a **six-course gourmet meal** at Chef Diego Hernandez's **Corazón de Tierra**.

DAY 2

Have breakfast at your B&B before heading out to your first **winery** such as **Lechuza** or **Viñas de Garza**. Then enjoy a **lunch** of octopus, brussels sprouts, or lamb *birria* at Javier Plascencia's *campestre* restaurant, Finca Altozano. Leave yourself enough time before or after your lunch reservation to enjoy a glass of wine atop one of the **giant wine barrel lookouts** perched around the property. After lunch, enjoy another wine-tasting at a **boutique winery** like **Pijoan** or **Villa Montefiori**. For **sunset,** head to the **cliff-top Bar Bura** at Cuatrocuatros where you'll bask in stunning **Pacific Ocean views.**

DAY 3

40 MI (65 KM)

1.5 HOURS

Get and early start and drive south out of Valle de Guadalupe to the **Antigua Ruta del Vino**

Finca Altozano is one of the Valle de Guadalupe's campestre restaurants.

the Museo de la Vid y el Vino

Fish tacos are one of Baja's most well-known street foods.

Northern Baja has turned into a globally recognized culinary hot spot with its fresh and flavorful food, growing craft beer scene, and popular wine region. Here's where to go to find what.

TIJUANA STREET FOOD

From excellent fine dining to some of the best **street food** in the world, Tijuana is leading Baja California's culinary movement. Alongside chefs like Javier Plascencia and Miguel Angel Guerrero with **gourmet restaurants,** are **taco stands** and *mariscos* **street carts** that have been around for 30 years. There are a few independent *cervecerías* (breweries) that have their own tasting rooms, and the old Plaza Fiesta mall has reinvented itself as a collection of small beer tasting rooms, drawing breweries from Mexicali, Ensenada, and Tijuana to open up shop there.

MEXICALI BREWS

The capital of the state of Baja California is growing as a destination for beer lovers. **Craft breweries** like **Urbana, Legion, Big Bad Brewing Co.,** **Fauna,** and **Cucapá** are joined along by **beer bars** like **The Show** and **El Sume.**

ENSENADA SEAFOOD

Seafood reigns supreme in Ensenada from **fish tacos** and **ceviche tostadas** sold at street carts to nice sit-down restaurants like **Manzanilla** or **Boules.** **La Guerrerense** serves up fresh *mariscos* and has been called the best street cart in the world by Anthony Bourdain. There's also a growing craft brewery scene in Ensenada with more and more breweries and tasting rooms opening.

VALLE DE GUADALUPE WINE

Just inland from the town of Ensenada is Mexico's bourgeoning wine region. There are **over 100 wineries** and a growing number of *campestre* restaurants where the food is cooked over wood fires. The result is a region being recognized worldwide for its rustic but charming atmosphere, beautiful **boutique wineries,** and gourmet restaurants like **Finca Altozano** and **Corazón de Tierra.**

in **Valle de la Grulla.** Savor **wine-tastings** at **MD Vinos** and **Palafox.** Then head to the **Valle de Santo Tomás** to visit the first winery in Baja California, **Bodegas de Santo Tomás,** established in 1888. Return to the Valle de Guadalupe to have an unforgettable **dinner** in a serene **open-air setting at Malva.**

DAY 4
50 MI (80 KM)
1 HOUR

For your last morning, enjoy a delicious **homemade Mexican breakfast** like **huevos rancheros** or *huevos con machaca* at the famous **La Cocina de Doña Esthela.** Enjoy one last wine-tasting at **Chateau Camou** or **Monte Xanic** on your way up the Mexico 3 heading to Tecate. Grab some **baked goods** at **El Mejor Pan de Tecate** before crossing back over the border to the United States.

San Felipe

DAY 1
125 MI (200 KM)
2 HOURS

Cross the U.S. Mexico border in Calexico/Mexicali and drive the two hours down Mexico 5 to arrive at the **fishing village** of **San Felipe.** Enjoy some **fish tacos** at **Taqueria y Mariscos Adriana** or any of the spots in town. Walk along the *malecón* to enjoy the bustle of the beach and the town. At the south end of the *malecón*, climb up the **Shrine of the Virgin Guadalupe** lookout to get **sweeping views of the bay** and town. Have **dinner** at the **Taco Factory** or the adjoining **Bajamar Seafood and Steak House.**

DAY 2

Arrange with one of the local *pangueros* to spend a day **fishing** out at **Isla Konsag** ("The Rock"). Those who don't enjoy angling will still have fun checking out the **sealife** like **sea lions and marine birds.** Enjoy a **seafood dinner** at **Mariscos La Vaquita.** Make sure to order some of San Felipe's famous **shrimp.**

DAY 3
120 MI (195 KM)
3 HOURS

Get an early start and drive south on Mexico 5 to take your photo with the **enormous cardón** cacti in the **Valle de los Gigantes.** Then continue south to check out the picturesque **Bahía San Luis Gonzaga** where you can have a **beer** on the deck at **Alfonsina's** to enjoy the peaceful bay. For those with **four-wheel drive,** continue south on Mexico 5 after the pavement ends to get to the quirky and endearing **Coco's Corner** where you can throw back a cold beer with Coco.

DAY 4
125 MI (200 KM)
2 HOURS

Drive north up Mexico 5 to the border town of Mexicali. Spend the afternoon checking out the city's excellent **craft beer** scene at places like **Urbana, Legion, The Show,** or **Cucapá.** Cross back over the easygoing Mexicali/Calexico border back to the United States.

Loreto

DAY 1

Fly from Los Angeles or Tijuana (you can use the convenient Cross Border Xpress pedestrian bridge from San Diego) into the **Loreto International Airport.** Check into a place in town with a convenient **walking location** like **Las Cabañas de Loreto** or **Coco Cabañas.** Spend the day walking along the *malecón* and then around the **historical town plaza.** Don't miss seeing the **Loreto mission,** the first mission established in both Alta and Baja California. Enjoy **dinner** as an outdoor meal at the charming **Mi Loreto.**

DAY 2
25 MI (40 KM)
1 HOUR

Rent a car or join an organized tour to enjoy a **scenic drive** through the **Sierra de la Giganta** to get to the town of **San Javier** and

Loreto's plaza is the heart of the town.

visit one of the most beautiful **missions** on the Baja peninsula. Don't miss taking a walk behind the mission to see the **300+-year-old olive tree.** Enjoy **lunch at La Palapa** and buy some **damiana liquor** at one of the small shops. Head back to town and enjoy **dinner** at the casual local's spot **Asadero Super Burro.**

DAY 3

Take a boat out **fishing** or to visit the beautiful islands in the protected **Bay of Loreto National Marine Park.** When you get back on shore, catch **two-for-one happy hour** exotic margaritas at **Agave** or any of the places along the plaza. Have your **freshly caught fish** specially prepared for you at any of the many restaurants in town that will do so for you, such as **La Palapa.**

DAY 4

Spend your last morning **golfing** at one of the courses south of town, or grab a copy of *Hiking Loreto* and go explore the area. Have **lunch** at **Orlando's Mexican Cocina** or get a **craft beer** at **El Zopilote** before heading to the airport.

Tijuana, Ensenada, and Valle de Guadalupe

Look for ★ to find recommended sights, activities, dining, and lodging.

Highlights

★ **Avenida Revolución:** Tijuana's busy avenue buzzes with restaurants, breweries, shops, bars, the city's famous *pasajes,* and arch (page 39).

★ **Centro Cultural Tijuana (CECUT):** Catch an art exhibition or an IMAX show at Tijuana's impressive cultural center (page 41).

★ **Craft Breweries:** Tijuana's craft brewery scene echoes the one just over the border in San Diego and is gaining a strong following from both Mexicans and Norteños (page 44).

★ **Plaza Parque Hidalgo:** Sit in the shade of the tall trees while listening to Mariachi bands and taking in the daily bustle of Tecate (page 53).

★ **Rosarito Beach:** The expansive and beautiful beach draws tourists ready to relax or have fun (page 61).

★ **Mercado de Mariscos:** The bustling fish market in Ensenada is a wonderful place to taste a famous fish taco (page 74).

★ **Avenida López Mateos in Ensenada:** The main tourist drag in Ensenada is bursting with shops, restaurants, and bars (page 75).

★ **La Bufadora:** A trip to Ensenada isn't complete without a visit to the natural sea geyser that shoots water up to 30 meters into the air (page 78).

© AVALON TRAVEL

★ **La Ruta del Vino:** Spend the day exploring Mexico's highly acclaimed wine region, now home to over 110 wineries (page 87).

Northwestern Baja, the gateway to the peninsula, has a unique flavor.

The influence of the United States just over the border can be felt everywhere as the region balances the two cultures with a subtle finesse. Here, you'll find a thriving culinary scene whose food, craft beer, and wine are being recognized worldwide. The gritty cityscape of Tijuana is balanced by the serene Valle de Guadalupe wine region. While many road-trippers skip this region to get farther south, just as many come across the border with it as their final destination.

The five regions that define this area: Tijuana, Tecate, Rosarito, Ensenada, and Valle de Guadalupe, are as different from each other as they are from the rest of the peninsula. Tijuana is the big city (the largest on the entire peninsula) with a population of 1.7 million. The infamous party town of yore has reinvented itself in recent years as a culinary and cultural destination that should not be missed. Creative types and entrepreneurs are turning old vacant dance clubs into tech offices, art galleries, and craft breweries. Regional chefs are leading a food movement emulated around the world by renowned chefs like Rick Bayless and Anthony Bourdain.

To the east of Tijuana, the tranquil border town of Tecate is a newly designated *Pueblo Mágico*. The small town is centered in the mountains and ranch land dominating the region. Down the coast past Tijuana on Mexico 1 is the beach town of Rosarito, a popular destination for tourists looking to enjoy a weekend of margaritas at sunset, feasting on seafood, and relaxing. An hour south of Rosarito, the port town of Ensenada is a destination for road-trippers as well as for the cruise travelers that come into port multiple days a week. There's also a sophisticated culinary scene here with exceptional restaurants and new craft breweries.

Just east of Ensenada, the Valle de Guadalupe is now home to over 120 wineries and quickly becoming the big tourist draw for the entire state. The restaurants have followed the wineries, and many of the well-known chefs from Tijuana and Ensenada have opened their own *campestre* restaurants in the valley. While the valley has grown incredibly in the past few years and is gaining worldwide recognition, it remains a tranquil destination with dirt roads, small boutique wineries, and rustic accommodations setting the tone for this intimate region.

Previous: The drive on the toll road from Rosarito to Ensenada offers striking views of the Pacific; The Valle de Guadalupe is Mexico's premier wine region. **Above:** Avenida Revolución in Tijuana.

Tijuana, Rosarito, and Tecate

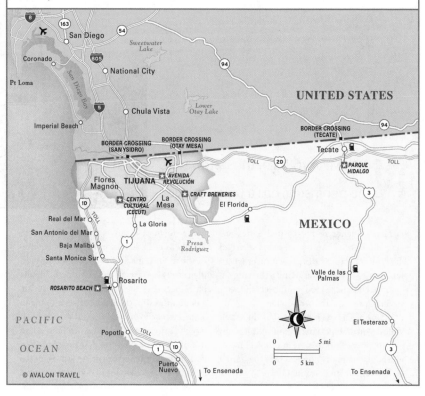

PLANNING YOUR TIME

Because Tijuana and Tecate are just across the border from the United States, Southern Californians frequently explore these two border cities as day trips. Rosarito, Ensenada, and Valle de Guadalupe are best reserved for full weekend trips, since they're farther south. A convenient way to see this entire region is to make a loop, starting in Tijuana, driving down the coast on Mexico 1 to Rosarito, and then carrying on to Ensenada. From here, head east to the Valle de Guadalupe on Mexico 3 and then continue up through Tecate to cross back into the United States. Give yourself a week to thoroughly enjoy the full loop.

GETTING THERE
Border Crossing

There are three border crossings in this region, two in Tijuana and one in Tecate. The San Ysidro border crossing in Tijuana is the world's busiest with 50 million people crossing every year. If you don't have an expedited crossing via SENTRI, Ready Lane, or Fast Pass, expect long lines heading northbound whether you are crossing by car or on foot. Still in Tijuana but farther east is the Otay Mesa crossing. This border crossing is generally less busy and more relaxed than San Ysidro. Even more tranquil and usually with the shortest wait, is the Tecate border

Best Accommodations

★ **Grand Hotel Tijuana:** Visitors can look forward to clean, modern rooms, an on-site restaurant, pool, and whirpool tub (page 49).

★ **Rancho La Puerta:** Guests come to the historic ranch in Tecate for a fitness and spa retreat (page 58).

★ **Las Rosas:** Watch the stunning view of waves crashing onto the shore right in front of this Ensenada hotel (page 85).

★ **La Villa del Valle:** This Tuscan-style villa nestled into the Valle the Guadalupe gives guests a dose of luxury in Baja's rustic wine region (page 98).

★ **Cuatrocuatros:** Chic glamping and dramatic Pacific views draw guests to this spot just outside of the Valle de Guadalupe (page 99).

crossing. There are no expedited lanes here, but northbound car crossings can be a quarter of the wait compared to San Ysidro, and there's rarely any wait at all for northbound pedestrians.

Car

Many travelers choose to explore this region by driving their own car across the border, since everything is so close to Southern California. If you'll be traveling outside of Tecate or Tijuana, having a car is the only way to easily and thoroughly sample all that the region has to offer. Don't forget to get the mandatory Mexican auto insurance before driving south.

MEXICAN CAR INSURANCE

Mexican law requires all drivers to have Mexican auto insurance when operating a vehicle in Mexico. Even if you have U.S. auto insurance that covers you while in Mexico,

Tijuana is a border city home to 1.7 million people.

Best Restaurants

★ **Misión 19:** Chef Javier Plascencia's sleek upscale restaurant in Tijuana offers some of the best dining in Baja (page 48).

★ **La Justina:** This gastropub on Avenida Revolución in Tijuana serves well-crafted food and cocktails (page 48).

★ **El Lugar de Nos:** Delicious food is served in a welcoming and eclectic setting at this Tecate restaurant (page 56).

★ **La Guerrerense:** Anthony Bourdain once called this Ensenada seafood spot "The best street cart in the world" (page 82).

★ **Corazón de Tierra:** Chef Diego Hernandez brings farm-to-table foods to a heightened sophistication in this beautiful restaurant in the Valle de Guadalupe (page 94).

★ **Finca Altozano:** Chef Javier Plascencia's *campestre* restaurant brings his flavorful food to alfresco dining overlooking the vineyards in Valle de Guadalupe (page 95).

you must still get Mexican auto insurance because Mexico does not recognize U.S. insurance. This is not a matter that Mexican officials take lightly. If you get into an accident and do not have Mexican auto insurance, it's likely that you will go to jail. Liability is the minimum that's required by law, but you may want to get the full coverage so that your own car and the passengers inside will be taken care of in case of an accident as well.

Air

The only commercial airport in this region is Tijuana's General Abelardo L. Rodríguez International Airport (TIJ). There are rental car facilities as well as taxis at the airport. Uber is also available to pick up passengers at the airport. For those coming from San Diego and flying out of the Tijuana airport, the new Cross Border Xpress pedestrian bridge (www.crossborderxpress.com) allows ticketed passengers to park in San Diego and walk across the bridge directly to the Tijuana airport (US$12, one-way).

Bus

There are bus services between Tijuana, Tecate, Rosarito, and Ensenada as well as to other cities and parts of the peninsula. **Autobuses de la Baja California** (ABC, tel. 664/104-7400, www.abc.com.mx) and **Aguila** (Mex. tel. toll-free 800/026-8931, www.autobusesaguila.com) are two of the largest bus companies that operate along the entire peninsula.

Tijuana

With a gritty honesty and buzzing energy, Tijuana is both the largest city on the Baja peninsula and also the most misunderstood. The raw vitality of Tijuana hits you as soon as you cross the border from San Diego, and it's something that people either love or hate. The city is full of neglected buildings punctuated with graffiti and street art and avenues crazed with disorderly traffic. It's also a city brimming with world-class art and culture, fascinating history, and incredible cuisine—from street carts to fine dining.

Tijuana first came to the attention of Americans during Prohibition when it was a playground for Norteños indulging in the drinking and gambling that were outlawed on the other side of the border. Tijuana maintained its party city image over the years, in later decades crawling with college students and young members of the U.S. military who came to take advantage of the young drinking

Pasaje Rodriguez

age, dance clubs, bars, and anything-goes attitude.

All of that has changed. When the violence of the drug wars started ramping up in Mexico the late 2000s, the tourists stopped coming to Tijuana. One by one the businesses that relied on tourism shuttered their doors, and the city grew quiet. But then something beautiful happened. A cultural renaissance took place as the Tijuanenses rebuilt their city as a mecca for chefs, artists, and entrepreneurs. Businesses converted to art galleries, craft breweries, and high-tech offices. New restaurants started opening each week with unbelievably creative and delicious local cuisine. And the tourists eventually began to return as well. With its new culinary and cultural reputation, Tijuana is now drawing trendsetting crowds from both sides of the border.

SIGHTS
★ Avenida Revolución

A trip to Tijuana isn't complete without spending time on one of the city's most famous streets: **Avenida Revolución,** running though in Zona Centro, Tijuana's downtown area. The large avenue anchors the tourist zone and stays busy night and day with locals and visitors who come to take advantage of many of the great restaurants, bars, breweries, and shops that Tijuana has to offer. While the street was once home to all of the dance clubs and nightlife of the city, most of those businesses have become artisanal restaurants, craft breweries, art galleries, and Tijuana's famous *pasajes.* The *pasajes* are enclosed alleyways supporting small art galleries, cafes, bars, and shops. Pasajes Rodriguez and Gomez are the two most well-known, located across the street from one another on Revolución between Calles 3 and 4. They're covered in colorful street art and attract a young bohemian crowd.

While many of the more touristy signs

Tijuana

© AVALON TRAVEL

0   0.5 km
0   0.5 mi

UNITED STATES

CALIFORNIA

BAJA CALIFORNIA

To San Diego

To Rosarito, Ensenada, and Playas de Tijuana via toll road

To Rosarito and Ensenada via free road

To Hotel la Mesa Inn, Tecate, and Mexicali

To Terminal de Autobuses

To Abelardo L. Rodríguez International Airport

CALLE 1 (ARTICULO 123)
CALLE 2 (B. JUÁREZ)
CALLE 3
CALLE 4 (D. MIRON)
CALLE 5
CALLE 6
CALLE 7
CALLE 8
CALLE 9
CALLE 10
CALLE 11 (PE CALLES)

AV INTERNACIONAL
AV H
AV G
AV F
AV MUTUALISMO
AV MARTINEZ
AV NIÑOS HEROES
AV CONSTITUCION
AV REVOLUCION
AV NEGRETE
AV OCAMPO
AV PASEO DE LOS HEROES
AV PIO PICO
AV QUINTANA ROO

Parque Guerrero
CATEDRAL GUADALUPE
TIJUANA ARCH
MERCADO DE ARTESANIAS
"SEE AVENIDA REVOLUCION MAP"
CERVEZA TIJUANA
POST OFFICE

BLVD FUNDADORES
BLVD AGUA CALIENTE
AV B. JUÁREZ
AV 16 DE SEPTIEMBRE
AV SANTA MARIA
CUAUHTEMOC

HOTEL PALACIO AZTECA
PLAZA FIESTA
MONUMENTO A CUAUHTEMOC
MONUMENTO A LA RAZA
CENTRO CULTURAL TIJUANA
BANAMEX
BANCOMER
CALIMAX
MEXICANA AIRLINES
MONUMENTO A ABRAHAM LINCOLN
MARISCOS LOS ARCOS
HOTEL REAL DEL RIO
BABYROCK
HOTEL LUCERNA
MONUMENTO A GENERAL IGNACIO ZARAGOZA
HOTEL HACIENDA DEL RIO
LA DIFERENCIA
TANGALOO
FIESTA INN
GRAND HOTEL TIJUANA
TIJUANA COUNTRY CLUB
U.S. CONSULATE

PLAZA RIO TIJUANA
ZONA RIO
PEDESTRIAN BRIDGE
VIA PONIENTE
VIA ORIENTE
AV PASEO DE TIJUANA
AV INDEPENDENCIA
PEDESTRIAN BRIDGE
PALACIO MUNICIPAL
MONUMENTO A PADRE MIGUEL HIDALGO
MONUMENTO A DIANA LA CAZADORA
PUEBLO AMIGO INN
PLAZA PUEBLO AMIGO
RAILROAD STATION
HOTEL CAMINO REAL
DEPORTIVAS
AV P KINO
CALLE 16

TOURIST INFORMATION
PEDESTRIAN BRIDGE
MEXICAN CUSTOMS
U.S. CUSTOMS
TIJUANA TROLLEY
SHUTTLE BUSES TO TIJUANA

Tijuana Río

RIVIERA
TABOADA
RODRIGUEZ
BLVD AGUA CALIENTE
AV G SALINAS
TAPACHULA
ESTADIO CALIENTE
BLVD DIAZ ORDAZ
CARRETERA AEROPUERTO

Avenida Revolución

TIJUANA ARCH
CALLE 1
CANACO OFFICE
(ARTICULO 123)
TOURIST INFORMATION
TIJUANA WAX MUSEUM
CENTRAL DE AUTOBUSES
HARD ROCK CAFÉ
PEDESTRIAN WALKWAY (BARS)
BITAL
CALLE 2
(B. JUÁREZ)
BANAMEX
AV
AV
AV
CALLE 3
(CARRILLO PUERTO)
IGUANAS RANAS
SANBORNS CAFÉ
CALLE 4
(D. MIRON)
BAR SAN MARCOS
CONSTITUCIÓN
REVOLUCIÓN
MADERO
CAESAR'S SPORTS BAR & GRILL
HOTEL CAESAR
CALLE 5
(E. ZAPATA)
TILLY'S 5TH AVE
CALLE 6
(F. MAGON)
TERMINAL TURÍSTICA TIJUANA
MARGARITA VILLAGE
CALLE 7
(GALEANA)
TIA JUANA TILLY'S
HOTEL LA VILLA DE ZARAGOZA
CALLE 8
(HIDALGO)
POLICE STATION
SANBORNS RESTAURANT/ DEPARTMENT STORE
FIRE STATION
BANCOMER
CALLE 9
(ZARAGOZA)
SCALE NOT AVAILABLE
CALIMAX
CALLE 10
(SARABIA)
© AVALON TRAVEL

of Tijuana's past are slowly disappearing, you'll still spot the town's famous **zonkeys** on Revolución. These donkeys, painted with black and white stripes to look like zebras, have been ready and waiting for photo ops with tourists since 1914.

Tijuana Arch

At the northern end of Avenida Revolución is a landmark visible from most parts of Tijuana. The large **Tijuana Arch** similar to the one that graces the skyline of St. Louis was built to celebrate the new millennium in 2000 and has since become one of the city's most recognized landmarks.

Zona Rio

The **Zona Rio neighborhood** is a fashionable middle-class area where many of Tijuana's restaurants, bars, and shops are located. The large Paseo de los Héroes is the heart of the neighborhood. The CECUT, Mercado Hidalgo, Plaza Río shopping mall, and Plaza Fiesta beer tasting rooms all call this street home.

★ Centro Cultural Tijuana (CECUT)

Tijuana's **Centro Cultural Tijuana (CECUT)** (Paseo de los Héroes 9350, tel. 664/687-9600, www.cecut.gob.mx, 9am-9pm daily, US$3) is a distinct landmark with the large spherical planetarium (that now functions as an IMAX theater) in front. The large cultural center houses permanent and temporary exhibitions, art galleries, a 1,000-seat performing arts theater, IMAX theater, café, bookstore, and shops. World-class rotating exhibitions feature art and photography by local and visiting artists. Many of Tijuana's large events and festivals take place at CECUT. On Sunday there's free admission to everything except the IMAX theater and the concert hall.

Mercado Hidalgo

Since 1955, restaurateurs and other Tijuanenses have been buying their produce at Tijuana's best market: **Mercado Hidalgo**

(Sanchez Taboada 9351, tel. 664/684-0485, www.mercadomiguelhidalgo.com, 6am-6pm daily). It's a popular spot for travelers to come browse the regional produce and products and eat at some of the nearby taco stands. Peruse the stands full of piles of dried chilies, local spices, regional cheeses, and fresh fruits and vegetables. When you're hungry, grab a tamale, *chicharrón, carnitas,* or taco from any of the stands in the market. Just outside the market on the surrounding streets are a number of famous taco, *birria,* and seafood stands as well. There's parking in the center of the market (US$1).

Spectator Sports

Tijuana has three professional sports teams. Arguably the most popular is its *fútbol* (soccer) team, **Club Tijuana Xoloitzcuintles de Caliente** (www.xolos.com), nicknamed the Xolos. The 33,000-seat stadium, Estadio Caliente (Boulevard Agua Calinete) fills with spirited fans and the entire city is abuzz when there's a game. Tijuana's baseball team, the **Toros** (www.torosdetijuana.com, tickets US$2-7)), play in the Mexican league. And their basketball team, the **Zonkeys** (www. tijuanazonkeys.com.mx) play at **Tijuana Auditorio Fausto Gutiérrez Moreno**

(Boulevard Gustavo Díaz Ordaz, tel. 664/321-6385, tickets US$8-24).

Recognized for its colorful costumes and masks, **Lucha Libre** (www.facebook.com/LuchaLibreDeTijuana) wrestling takes place at the Auditorio Municipal Fausto Gutierrez Moreno, Tijuana's municipal auditorium on Friday nights. The controversial **bullfighting** has many advocates pushing to ban it permanently from the city, but attempts to do so have failed thus far. The season takes place each summer at the bullring in Playas de Tijuana.

ORGANIZED TOURS

The growing interest in Tijuana has sparked a growing number of tours leading unique culinary and activity-based excursions to the city (most tour operators in Tijuana will accommodate visitors departing from San Diego or visitors who are already in Tijuana). Tijuana is a large city that can feel daunting to navigate on your own, so many people choose to visit for the day with an organized tour. **Turista Libre** (www.turistalibre.com) attracts a young crowd who enjoy visiting destinations tourists normally don't make it to on their own such as water parks, sporting events, and markets. **Baja Test Kitchen** (www.bajatestkitchen.

CECUT

com) focuses on Tijuana's culinary side with food, beer, and wine tours for private tours or groups of 2-20 people. Their "Tijuana Bites" tour samples the best and most famous food of the city from taco stands to fine dining.

Let's Go Clandestino (www.letsgoclandestino.net) leads monthly group tours to Tijuana and surrounding areas with a focus on the region's food and drinks.

ENTERTAINMENT AND EVENTS
Events
Tijuana is a city that thrives on festivals and events. Almost every weekend brings culinary fests, art fairs, beer festivals, and concerts. The State Tourism website **www.discoverbajacalifornia.com** is a great resource for Tijuana events. The **Baja Culinary Fest** (www.bajaculinaryfest.com) in October is a series of dinners, workshops, and parties, highlighting Tijuana's bourgeoning culinary scene. **Entijuanarte** (www.entijuanarte.org) is a large cultural and art fest that takes place every fall at CECUT with art booths, live entertainment, food, and drinks.

Nightlife
Just the name Tijuana carries connotations of its past notoriety for dance clubs, tequila shots, and drunk college students. You won't find much of that anymore as in the past decade, many of the dance clubs have closed and the city has reinvented itself with and a more cultured and respectable nightlife scene.

In Zona Centro, **Calle Sexta** (Sixth Street) off of Revolución is where many of the bars can be found. **Dandy del Sur** (Calle Sexta, tel. 664/688-0052, 10am-3am daily) here is where you'll get a downright local dive bar experience. Across the street is **La Mezcalera** (Calle Sexta 8267, tel. 664/688-0384, 6pm-2am Tues.-Sat.), where local hipsters go to sip on mescal.

A few blocks away near the arch on Revolución, the historic **Bar Nelson** (Ave. Revolución 721, tel. 664/685-8988, 11am-2am daily) is a retro spot for cocktails. Try the "Especial," a salt-rimmed highball with lime, white rum 7Up, and Coca-Cola.

Downstairs from Javier Plascencia's Misión 19 restaurant, is **Bar 20** (tel. 664/634-2493, 3pm-12am Mon.-Thur., 3pm-2am Fri.-Sat.) offering craft cocktails. Sip on cocktails like the "Mezcalero" or "Sangria 20" in the sleek and swanky setting.

For those still looking for the large dance clubs that used to dominate Zona Centro,

Mercado Hidalgo

Las Pulgas (Revolución 1127, tel. 664/685-9594, www.laspulgas.info, 4pm-6am daily) is located on Revolución between Calles 7 and 8. The club has been one of the top spots for nightlife in Tijuana since 1988.

The lively **Sótano Suizo** (Paseo de los Héroes 9415, tel. 664/684-8834, www.sotanosuizo.com, 1pm-2am Tues.-Sun.) in Plaza Fiesta in Zona Rio is a fun spot for beers or cocktails. If you order their famously huge half-meter hot dog, be ready to share it with a friend (or two!).

★ Craft Breweries

Tijuana is one of three locations on the peninsula where the craft beer scene is gaining popularity (the other two spots are Mexicali and Ensenada). It's no wonder, since the city borders San Diego, considered to be the craft beer capital of the United States.

The beer scene here consists of very small microbreweries, many too small to have their own tasting rooms. Enter Tijuana's **Plaza Fiesta** (Paseo de los Héroes 10001, tel. 664/200-2960, www.facebook.com/plazafiestatijuana), an old defunct mall that sat basically deserted for a number of years until microbreweries started moving in to provide folks with a way to sample their output. Breweries from Tijuana, Mexicali, and Ensenada have tasting rooms in Plaza Fiesta, making this the go-to spot in northern Baja to get a taste of Baja's craft beer scene. Breweries like Border Psycho, Fauna, Tres B, Insurgente, and Mamut currently have tasting rooms in Plaza Fiesta. There are no set hours, but most breweries open around 5 or 6pm in the evening.

Mamut (Calle 3 8161, tel. 664/685-0137, www.mamutcerveza.com, 10am-11pm Mon.-Thurs., 10am-midnight Fri.-Sat.) is one of Tijuana's breweries to have its own tasting room outside of Plaza Fiesta. One part of the brewery in Pasaje Rodríguez, and the other part (with a separate entrance) is on the second floor of the outside block with an outdoor patio open to the downtown buzz of Tijuana. They have a large assortment of tasty craft

Dandy del Sur is one of Tijuana's most popular dive bars.

beers that they brew as well as housemade pizzas and other snacks. They've recently added a new mescal bar.

Just down the street from Mamut is **Norte Brewing Co.** (Calle 4ta, tel. 664/638-4891, 2pm-10pm Mon.-Wed., 2pm-midnight Thurs.-Sat.), a new craft brewery featuring bold beers and epic views of Tijuana. The brewery is housed in what was once a strip club, and names of beers such as "Escort," "Cougar," and "Penthouse" reflect the location's past. The brewery can be difficult to find—it's on the fifth level of the Foreign Club parking structure. Entrance to the parking structure is on Calle 4 between Revolución and Constitución.

For a craft beer experience in a bar setting, **BCB Tasting Room** (Orizaba 3003-E5, no tel. , www.bajacraftbeers.com, 12:30pm-midnight Mon.-Thurs., 1:30pm-1:30am Fri.-Sat.) has an impressive 42 beers on top and about 300 more in bottle. The industrial but intimate space features local craft beers from both Baja and San Diego.

Cervecería Tijuana (Blvd. Fundadores 2951, tel. 664/638-8662, www.tjbeer.com) is a large facility producing craft beer that's now shipped around the world. La Taberna, adjacent to the brewery, is a Czech-inspired tavern where you'll find the beers available, as well as food and live music.

SHOPPING

For artisan crafts and souvenirs, **Avenida Revolución** has a number of small shops as well as a collection of stalls down near the arch. Don't be afraid to bargain for a lower price. Tijuana's large **Plaza Río Mall** (Ave. Paseo de los Héroes 96 and 98, www.plazariotijuana.com.mx) in Zona Rio has a Sears, Cinépolis movie theater, and a number of specialty stores.

The **Mercado de Artesanías** (Between Negrete and Ocampo north of Calle 2) is an area of shops where you can find artisan goods for prices cheaper than what you'll pay at the souvenir stands. Leather shoes, colorful talavera pottery, glassware, home decor items, and other arts and crafts are all available here.

Plaza Fiesta has grown into a beer mecca.

For a tasty treat that also makes a great gift, **Venus Chocolates** (Tapacula #5-A, tel. 664/972-9338, 10am-9pm Mon.-Fri., 10am-8pm Sat., 11am-7pm Sun.) in the Hipódromo neighborhood, specializes in exquisite truffles in various flavors indicative of the region (tequila, chile, mezcal, wine from the Valle de Guadalupe) as well as other confections.

Mercado Hidalgo (Sanchez Taboada 9351, tel. 664/684-0485, 6am-6pm daily, www.mercadomiguelhidalgo.com) not only provides an entertaining way to spend the afternoon exploring one of the city's best markets, but is also a great place to buy fresh produce, local spices, regional cheeses, and souvenirs like pottery, serving ware, and glassware.

FOOD

Tijuana has the best food in Baja and is quickly turning into a world-recognized culinary destination. From fine dining to street food, there are plenty of savory options for every budget.

Mexican

The chic **Verde y Crema** (Orizaba 3034, tel. 664/681-2366, www.verdeycrema.com, 1pm-10pm Tues., Wed., Sun., 1pm-11pm Thurs.-Sat., US$9-13) is the Tijuana restaurant of Chef Jair Tellez, who also has the famous Laja restaurant in the Valle de Guadalupe. The menu changes on a regular basis depending on what's fresh and available but features foods like tacos, tostadas, and sliders with fresh and unique ingredients and flavors. The main dining area downstairs is refreshingly breezy with large open-air windows, and the service is incredibly warm and helpful.

For A traditional Mexican breakfast, locals head to **La Espadaña** (Blvd. Sánchez Taboada 10813, tel. 664/634-1488, www.espadana.com.mx, 7:30am-10:30pm daily, US$8-11). From traditional posole and *huevos ahogados* to American-style omelettes and hotcakes, the menu is extensive. Breakfast is served daily until 1pm. Don't miss the famous *café de olla*—Mexico's traditional preparation of coffee with cinnamon and sugar. They also serve lunch and dinner. Dishes include traditional Mexican plates as well as chicken and steaks (no seafood).

Another traditional Mexican restaurant near La Espadaña is **La Diferencia** (Blvd. Sánchez Taboada 10521, tel. 664/634-7078, 8am-10:30pm Mon.-Sat., 8am-6pm Sun., mains US$8-13). Guests dine in a hacienda-style courtyard surrounding a fountain with Talavera pottery. The traditional Mexican decor creates a welcoming ambience and the perfect setting for dishes like *chilaquiles,* chicken mole, and *arrachera* with cactus. The off-street parking and a family-friendly environment make this a comfortable spot for groups of locals and tourists.

For innovative contemporary Mexican dining, **IPA'A Cocina Mexicana** (Plaza MARUB, Ave. Rio Tijuana 2554, tel. 664/681-7440, www.ipaa.mx, 1:30pm-5:30pm and 7pm-10pm Tues.-Wed. 1:30pm-5:30pm and 7pm-11:30pm Thurs.-Sat., US$13-20) offers a high-end experience. Diners can order à la carte or there's a five- or seven-course option. The sleek and modern setting and friendly staff create an inviting ambience.

For a unique taco experience in a sit-down restaurant, **Kokopelli** (Cuauhtémoc Sur and Sánchez Taboada, tel. 664/674-4906, www.

Baja Med

You may hear the term "Baja Med" in reference to the emergent **culinary movement** in Baja California. The term is actually trademarked by Tijuana chef **Miguel Angel Guerrero.** It's his way of describing the fusion of fresh regional Baja ingredients, Mexican flavors, and a twist of Mediterranean and Asian influence.

kokopelli.mx, 11am-9pm daily, tacos US$2-3) serves tacos with a unique twist on traditional flavors and ingredients. In addition to savory seafood tacos like octopus with melted cheese and pesto, vegetarians will enjoy options like the portobello taco with goat cheese and spinach. The intimate and funky setting creates a hip and casual vibe. Valet parking is available.

Seafood

For fresh ceviche and seafood, another one of Javier Plascencia's restaurants fits the bill. **Erizo** (Ave. Sonora 3808, 664/686-2895, www.erizobaja.com, 11am-9pm daily, US$3-8) is an open and airy restaurant with a nautical beach feel with boats, oars, and surfboards serving

souvenir shopping off of Avenida Revolución

serving up *al pastor* tacos at Las Ahumaderas

as decor. The menu is full of various tostadas, tacos, and ceviches like the special green shrimp ceviche—shrimp with serrano chile, tomatillo, cilantro, chives, and avocado. They also serve mixology cocktails and craft beer.

If the weather is warm, sit out on the front patio at **La Corriente Cevicheria Nais** (Calle 6 at Ave. Madero, tel. 664/685-0555, 11am-10pm daily, US$3-10). This hip and casual spot serves great *mariscos.* Order the special red snapper tostada, ahi tuna tostada, or the taco "Kalifornia" with shrimp stuffed into a chile, served in a taco.

Antojitos and Street Food

Founded in 1960, **Las Ahumaderas** (Guillermo Prieto 9770) is a series of six taco stands next to each other. Also called "Taco Alley," this is a classic stop for those looking for a taste of street tacos. Carne asada and *adobada* (*al pastor*) are the favorites. Grab a seat at the counter and enjoy the experience.

For *birria,* there are two places near Mercado Hidalgo that are local favorites.

One is **Tacos Fito** (Francisco Javier Mina 14, 5:30am-1pm daily), specializing in both beef *birria* and *tripa.* The other is **Tacos Rio** (Calle Guadalupe Victoria, 3am-2pm daily) also serving beef *birria.*

Don't miss the tacos *adobada* at **Tacos El Franc** (Blvd. Sánchez Taboada, Calle 8, tel. 667/142-2955). A specialty here is the *suadero* tacos—a smooth meat taken from between the belly and the leg. Near Tacos El Franc is **Mariscos Ruben** (Calle 8 and Quintana Roo), a food truck serving delicious Sonoran-style seafood cocktails.

El Tío Pepe (Garcia Glez 9937, tel. 664/971-0279) is a great spot to get a *torta ahogada* (a *torta* covered in a chile sauce), a specialty from Guadalajara. They also serve *birria* tacos and *carnitas.*

Taqueria Hipodromo (Ave. Hipodromo 14, tel. 664/686-5275, 8:30am-2am daily) has been serving up carne asada tacos and *mulitas* (two tortillas with cheese and taco filling inside) since 1971. It's a favorite late-night spot since they stay open until 2am.

Best known for their shrimp *enchilados* (chilied) tacos, **Mariscos el Mazateño** (Calzada Tecnologico 473-E, tel. 664/607-1377, 7am-8pm daily) also serves up great marlin tacos and tostadas. It can be a trek to the Tomas Aquino neighborhood location, but many foodies think it's worth it.

Serving up *tortas* since 1964, **Tortas Wash Mobile** (tel. 664/255-2349, 9am-9pm Mon.-Sat.) is a must for anyone who loves street food. The juicy steak sandwiches are available at their cart on Avenida Jalisco or their stand in Hipodromo.

Colectivos

Over the past number of years, *colectivos,* collections of food stalls or food trucks have become popular in Tijuana.

The most well-known of these *colectivos* is **Food Garden** (Blvd. Rodolfo Sánchez Taboada 10650, tel. 664/634-3527, www.foodgarden.mx, 9am-9pm Mon.-Thurs., 9am-11pm Fri.-Sat., 9am-7pm Sun.), an array of stands from well-established restaurants around the city. The food stalls line the courtyard where guests dine alfresco. The rich and savory *chilaquiles* with white or avocado sauce from the Los Chilaquiles stand are a local favorite. Vegetarians will love the tacos or veggie burgers from Veggie Smalls. There's now a second location of Food Garden in the **Plaza Río Mall** (tel. 664/634-1087). There are different stands in each location of Food Garden, so it's worth it to check out both.

Just off of Revolución is **Colectivo 9** (Ave. Revolución, tel. 664/123-1234, www.colectivo9.com, 1pm-8pm Tues.-Thurs., 1pm-midnight Fri.-Sat., 1pm-8pm Sun.), a gathering of nine food stalls. They have an eclectic assortment of food from burgers to Asian food to empanadas. The *colectivo* can be easy to miss, as it's down a narrow *pasaje*. Watch for the entrance on the west side of the street between Calles 6 and 7.

Telefónica Gastro Park (Ave. Melchor Ocampo 2036, no tel., 8am-9pm daily) hosts a collection of food trucks. Seating is outdoors here, and diners can choose from options like risotto and fish from the Creta truck, or homemade sausages from Humo. Craft beer is also available from the beer bar.

International

Chef Miguel Angel Guerrero brings specialties like oyster shooters, carpaccio, *machacas,* and grilled octopus to guests at **La Querencia** (Ave. Escuadrón 201 3110, tel. 664/972-9935, www.laquerenciatj.com, 1pm-11pm Mon.-Thurs., 1pm-midnight Fri.-Sat., US$9-14). The sleek setting features touches of stainless steel, wood, brick, and taxidermy for an eclectic feel. Another one of Chef Angel Guerrero's restaurants is **El Taller** (Ave. Rio Yaqui 296, tel. 664/686-3383, www.eltallerbajamed.com, 11am-11pm Mon.-Thurs., 11am-midnight Fri.-Sat., 11am-10pm Sun., mains US$9-16). The building used to be a garage, and the industrial decor matches the history of the building. Craft pizza, steaks, and fresh fish are on the menu, along with a nice wine selection.

Many people may not know that Tijuana is the original home of the Caesar salad. While the exact details of the story depend on which person you ask, there's no doubt that the salad was invented at **Caesar's Restaurante Bar** (Revolución between Calles 4 and 5, tel. 664/685-1927, www.caesarstijuana.com, mains US$15-19) where it's still prepared tableside today. Other dishes like steak, seafood, and pastas are served in this upscale bistro setting. Owned by the Plascencia family today, this institution is worth a stop for a drink at the beautiful large bar or to enjoy one of Tijuana's most famous dishes.

In the heart of Revolución, the chic ★ **La Justina** (Revolución between Calles 3 and 4, tel. 664/638-4936, 1pm-midnight Tues.-Thurs., 1pm-2am Fri.-Sat., mains US$7-12) is a welcome and fresh gastropub culinary experience. Everything on the menu is handcrafted and well executed from the cocktails to the seasonally changing menu featuring dishes such as bone marrow, pork buns, and fresh seafood. The small and intimate space is filled with upcycled industrial materials that create the chic atmosphere—wooden tables and chairs, exposed brick walls, rope chandeliers, and hanging Edison bulbs. Weekend evenings they get really busy with hip Tijuanenses coming in for craft cocktails and dinner.

For some of the best fine dining in Baja, foodies head to ★ **Misión 19** (Misión San Javier 10643, tel. 664/634-2493, www.mision19.com, mains US$20). Housed in one of Tijuana's most upscale high-rise buildings, the sleek setting and sweeping city views set the scene for the sophisticated menu. Filet mignon, pork belly, bone marrow, octopus, tripe tacos—all are made with fresh ingredients and carefully crafted into savory treats. Reservations should be made in advance for this special dining experience.

ACCOMMODATIONS

Because of the number of business travelers who come to the city, there are upscale hotels in Tijuana, and the prices are very affordable. It's possible to stay in nice

The Plascencia Dynasty

Caesar's is where the Caesar salad was first invented.

Ask any Tijuanense who the most influential family in the Tijuana restaurant business is, and they are likely to respond with one name: Plascencia. Starting the empire in 1969 with their Italian restaurant, Giuseppis, the Plascencia family has expanded into multiple locations including Caesar's, Villa Saverios, and Casa Plascencia. Son Javier Plascencia is considered Baja California's most-recognized chef and independently manages his own string of popular restaurants including Misión 19 and Erizo in Tijuana, as well as Finca Altozano in the Valle de Guadalupe and Bracero in San Diego.

accommodations—even by U.S. standards— for under $100 a night.

Under US$50

For budget accommodations, **Aqua Rio Hotel** (Ave. Constitución 1618, tel. 664/685-1914, www.aquariohotel.com, US$40) offers nice clean rooms with granite floors, modern bathrooms, flat-screen TVs, wireless Internet, and air-conditioning. Free coffee and fruit are available in the lobby. The hotel is walking distance to Revolución, but away from most of the noise of downtown.

The only hostel in Tijuana, **Hostal Pangea Tijuana** (8250 Calle 1ra, tel. 664/379-1818, www.pangeatijuana.wordpress.com, US$10) functions as a multipurpose community space that also features two restaurants, a café, bar, and multiple stages. The fun and funky place

is often used as a venue for events such as music festivals, concerts, and dance lessons. The hostel offers shared rooms (private rooms are currently not available) with hot showers and access to the kitchen.

US$50-100

The upscale ★ **Grand Hotel Tijuana** (Agua Caliente 4558, tel. 664/681-7000, toll-free U.S. tel. 866/472-6385, www.grandhoteltj.com, US$75) features large, clean, and modern rooms. Amenities include a pool and Jacuzzi, as well as self-parking for US$1. The restaurant has a breakfast buffet in the mornings, and the hotel is located within walking distance of many other great restaurants. There's a bar in the lobby with live music on the weekends. Their special "Grand Care" rooms are equipped with hospital beds, wheelchairs, and shower chairs for those visiting Tijuana for medical tourism.

Guests will find friendly staff and large comfortable rooms at **Hotel Ticuan** (Ave. Miguel Hidalgo 8190, tel. 664/685-8078, www. hotelticuan.mx, US$95). A free breakfast is included in your stay (but only for one guest per room). Once you park your car in the secured parking garage, you can easily walk to restaurants and stores from this convenient hotel. Because of the central location, rooms that face Avenida Revolución can be noisy, especially on the weekends with music from the clubs. Ask for a room away from Revolución for a quieter experience.

Close to the cultural center and Plaza Río Mall, **Hotel Real del Rio Tijuana** (José María Velazco 1409, tel. 664/634-3100, www. realdelrio.com, $60-80) is a sleek hotel with modern rooms, a gym, and outdoor terrace. A modern restaurant and bar are located in the lobby of the hotel.

Palacio Azteca Hotel (Blvd. Cuauhtémoc Sur 213, tel. 664/681-8100, www.hotelpalacio-azteca.com, US$85) has clean spacious rooms with nice bathrooms, minibars, and air-conditioning. There's a restaurant and bar and business center. The sleek **Pueblo Amigo Plaza & Casino** (Via Oriente 9211, tel. 664/624-2700, www.hotelpuebloamigo.com, US$89) is attached to the Caliente Casino. The location is close to the border and has a friendly and accommodating staff.

For a good option near Rodriguez airport, **Fiesta Inn Tijuana Otay** (Rampa Aeropuerto 16000, tel. 664/979-1900, www.fiestainn.com, US$70-90) has large rooms with comfortable beds and nice sheets. There's a pool, gym, restaurant, and 24-hour room service.

US$100-150

Those looking for the nicest accommodations in town will want to stay at the new **Hyatt Place Tijuana** (Agua Caliente 10488, tel. 664/900-1234, www.tijuana.place.hyatt. com, US$109-119). With 145 rooms, the hotel features all of the modern and convenient amenities that you would expect from Hyatt. Guests will enjoy plush, comfortable beds, friendly staff, a nice buffet breakfast, a 24-hour gym, and a convenient location. There's secure underground parking that's free with your stay.

Although it's smaller than the location in Mexicali, **Lucerna Tijuana** (Paseo de los Héroes 10902, tel. 664/633-3900, www.hoteleslucerna.com, US$135) is up-to-par with the same amenities and service. Rooms are well appointed, the grounds are well maintained, and amenities include a nice pool area and gym. The hotel has a bar and two restaurants in addition to 24-hour room service. They are currently renovating parts of the property.

Travelers will find a hotel up to U.S. standards with Mexican hospitality at **Marriott Tijuana** (Agua Caliente 11553, tel. 664/622-6600, www.marriott.com, US$125). The staff is welcoming and friendly, and rooms are clean and modern with fast wireless Internet. There's an outdoor pool and a fitness center. A restaurant and café are located on-site.

With a sister location in San Diego, the soon-to-open Tijuana **One Bunk** (Ave. Revolución 716, U.S. tel. 858/972-2865, www. onebunk.com) will provide boutique accommodations in the heart of Revolución. One Bunk aims to give travelers a curated stay meant to bridge the Tijuana/San Diego border lifestyle.

INFORMATION AND SERVICES

Tijuana is a large city with all of the major conveniences you would find anywhere in the world. Many businesses will accept U.S. dollars, but you'll get a better exchange rate by using pesos. There are ATMs, banks, and exchange houses all around the city.

Tourism Assistance

On Avenida Revolución, there's an office for **Baja State Tourism** (Ave. Revolución 686-1, between Calles 2 and 3, 664/682-3367, www. discoverbajacalifornia.com) with brochures and information about Tijuana and the northern state of Baja California. Tourists can call 078 on any phone for 24/7 bilingual assistance in northern Baja.

Foreign Consulates

The **U.S. Consulate** (Paseo de la Culturas, Mesa de Otay, tel. 664/977-2000, 7:30am-4:15pm Mon.-Fri., after-hours emergency U.S. tel. 619/692-2154) is in Tijuana near the airport and can help with lost passports, visa issues, or emergency services. They can also assist with notaries, births and deaths of U.S. citizens, and arrests of U.S. citizens in Baja. The **Canadian Consulate** (Germán Gedovius 10411-101, tel. 664/684-0461, tjuna@international.gc.ca, 9:30am-12:30pm Mon.-Fri.) helps Canadian citizens with passport issues and other emergency situations that may arise while traveling.

GETTING THERE
Car

Tijuana has two border crossings, San Ysidro in the heart of Tijuana and Otay Mesa farther east. San Ysidro is open 24 hours a day and the busiest land port of entry in the world. Southbound crossings by car are relatively quick and easy. If you are crossing northbound back to the United States at San Ysidro, expect a long border wait. Otay Mesa generally has a shorter northbound wait than San Ysidro, but travelers should still expect multiple hours at peak times. For more information as well as wait times for either border, refer to the **U.S. Customs and Border Protection website** at www.cbp.gov.

On Foot

Many San Diego residents park in San Diego and cross San Ysidro by foot to explore Tijuana for the day. Those crossing by foot at the San Ysidro El Chaparral border crossing will need to fill out a *forma migratoria multiple* (FMM) tourist permit. Visitors staying for seven days or less can get an FMM for free; stays over seven days require a payment of US$24. The paid FMMs are valid for up to 180 days. Once in Tijuana, it's easy to get around by Uber or taxi. Zona Centro and Avenida Revolución are best explored on foot and provide lots of options for food, shopping, and entertainment.

Air

Tijuana's **General Abelardo L. Rodríguez International Airport** (TIJ, tel. 664/607-8200, www.tijuana-airport.com) is about 10 kilometers east of downtown in Otay Mesa. Many domestic and international flights arrive at the airport. There are car rentals and Uber and taxi service at the airport.

The new **Cross Border Xpress** (www.crossborderxpress.com) pedestrian bridge now makes it possible for ticketed passengers flying out of Tijuana to park in San Diego and walk across a pedestrian bridge to get to the airport (and vice versa). Tickets for the bridge are available for US$12 one-way and can be purchased on-site or in advance through their website.

Bus

The **Central de Autobuses de Tijuana** (tel. 664/621-2982) is on Lazaro Cardenas at Blvd Arroyo Alamar south of the airport. Large bus lines such as Greyhound, **Autobuses de la Baja California** (ABC, tel. 664/104-7400, www.abc.com.mx), and **Aguila** (tel. 800/824-8452, www.autobusesaguila.com) run services out of Tijuana.

GETTING AROUND

Tijuana is a large city but has pockets that are easily walkable. Zona Centro and Avenida Revolución are best explored on foot since there are enough things to see and places to eat and drink to keep you occupied for a full day. If you aren't experienced at driving in large cities in developing countries, you may find it stressful to get yourself around Tijuana. Luckily, **Uber** (www.uber.com) has come to the city, providing a safe and easy way to get from place to place. Download the app before you travel. Taxis are also available. **Taxi B-Seguro** (tel. 664/687-1010) is one of the largest taxi companies with white and orange taxis all over the city.

PLAYAS DE TIJUANA

Separated geographically from the rest of the city, the community of Playas de Tijuana is situated on the beach on the west side of town. It's a peaceful area, with a very different vibe from the rest of the city. The large beach stretches out in the background with small restaurants and cafés on the boardwalk looking out at the Pacific. Behind the boardwalk, the Plaza Monumental Bullring by the Sea sits quiet for most of the year except when the bullfights take place certain summer weekends.

Sights
BOARDWALK

South of the international border fence, the boardwalk heads along the beach with colorful street art and a string of cafés, bars, restaurants, on one side and the Pacific ocean on the other.

EL PARQUE DE LA AMISTAD

It's hard to ignore the rust-colored border fence separating Tijuana from San Diego that goes all the way into the Pacific Ocean.

El Parque de la Amistad or Friendship Park (www.friendshippark.org) sits beneath the lighthouse just adjacent the beach. The park has both a Mexico and a U.S. side. This is a spot where families and close friends reunite from either side of the fence. The park is open 24 hours on the Tijuana side, but only currently open 10am-2pm Saturday-Sunday on the U.S. side. On the Tijuana side, there's the famous "Monument 258" and a small garden.

Food and Accommodations

There are many little spots along the boardwalk that take advantage of the ocean views. Hipsters come to hang out at **Café Latitud 32** (Paseo Costero, tel. 664/609-4200, 8am-10pm daily, US$2-3) for the ocean views, funky atmosphere, and lattes. Nearby is **Sunset Lounge** (Ave. Pacifico 769, tel. 664/680-1863, www.sunsetlounge.com.mx), a restaurant and lounge with an outdoor space looking over the ocean, perfect for catching sunset with a glass of wine in hand.

La Terraza Vallarta (Del Pacifico 343, tel. 664-680-0769, US$6-8) is a *mariscos* restaurant most famous for the replica of the *Titanic* on the roof and for being visited by Anthony Bourdain on his show *No Reservations*.

The Playas de Tijuana boardwalk has cafes and restaurants looking out onto the Pacific.

The History of Friendship Park

In 1849, following the Mexican-American War, a monument was put in place to signify the new international boundary between the United States and Mexico established by the Treaty of Guadalupe Hidalgo. This location next to the Pacific Ocean, called Monument Mesa, is considered the birthplace of the border. Crossings between the two countries were largely unregulated at this time, and only the monument demarcated the difference between the United States and Mexico.

A refurbished monument was placed in this spot in 1894. This new monument was dubbed Monument 258 (there are 258 of these monuments along the 2,000-mile Mexico/U.S. border) and is the one that stands there today. Its base sits directly on the international boundary inscribed "Boundary of the United States" on one side and "Punto Límite de la Republica de México" on the other.

The border here has changed significantly over the years, from a wide-open space to a wire demarcation, to a fence, to the wall that stands there today. The park has always been a meeting place for separated friends and family who reunite and spend time together in Friendship Park despite the border that separates them.

El Yogurt Place (Cantera 360, tel. 664/680-2006, www.elyogurtplace.com, 7:30-8:30pm daily, US$4-7) has plenty of healthy and organic options for dining from granola and whole-wheat waffles for breakfast to salads and sandwiches for lunch and dinner.

For accommodations in this area, **Dali Suites** (Colina 551, tel. 664/680-6369, www.dalisuites.com, US$70) is an intimate 19-room hotel close to the beach, restaurants, and shops. The property is secure and well-maintained, and the staff members are friendly and accommodating. South of town along the coast on the way to Rosarito is **Real Del Mar** (Km. 19.5, tel. for golf 664/631-3406, tel. for hotel 664/631-3670, www.realdelmargolfresort.com) an 18-hole golf course with a 75-room hotel and a housing community.

Tecate

The small border town of Tecate is a far cry from nearby Tijuana to the west. Rather than a congested metropolis, here you'll find a tranquil town nestled into the foothills of the Sierra de Juárez. The Kumiai (Kumeyaay) were the original inhabitants of this area, and their presence is still felt strongly today through the various museums and rock art sites in the region. In the late 19th century, the ranchers came in to settle the land, and the area is still dominated by those large ranches.

Tecate was recently designated as a *Pueblo Mágico*, a "magic town" and the government is working on beautifying the town and improving infrastructure. You won't find the immediate colonial charm of Baja's other two *Pueblos Mágicos*, Loreto and Todos Santos, but if you look closely, Tecate is full of hidden gems. The plaza and Tecate brewery are must-visits for most travelers, as is a stop at El Mejor Pan de Tecate, the famous bakery. Unlike the coastal areas of northern Baja, you won't see as many tourists in Tecate, which makes it even more exciting to explore.

SIGHTS
★ Plaza Parque Hidalgo

The center of town, **Plaza Parque Hidalgo,** is just a few blocks south of the U.S. border crossing. The lovely plaza has a *zocalo* in the center surrounded by plenty of benches, mature trees, grass, and flowers. Built in 1952,

Tecate

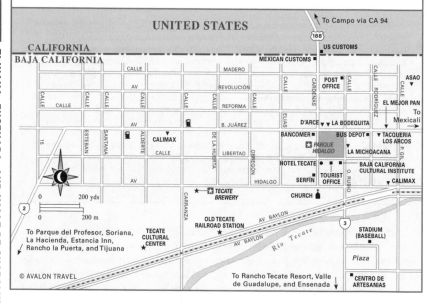

the plaza is the hub of town life and a lovely spot to sit and relax while getting a good sense of what Tecate is all about. The plaza is lined by small businesses like restaurants, banks, and Michoacan ice cream shops. On the south side of the plaza are a number of tables and chairs, shaded by the tall trees, where locals gather in the afternoons and mariachi bands are often heard serenading crowds. There's a statue of Miguel Hidalgo, who issued the call for Mexican Independence in 1810, welcoming visitors on the northeast corner of the park. Public bathrooms can be found on the south side of the plaza.

Tecate Brewery

The namesake **Tecate Brewery** (Dr. Arturo Guerra 70, tel. 656/654-9478, contacto@cuamoc.com, 10am-5pm Mon.-Fri., 10am-2pm Sat.) is hard to ignore. The large white factory with the Tecate sign on top looms over the entire town. The factory is home to a popular beer garden where visitors receive a free beer. Normally, advance arrangements can be made

for a free tour of the factory and a tasting, but the brewery is closed to the public for remodeling until 2017.

The Tecate Railroad

Tecate was once part of an important train route from San Diego, California, to Yuma, Arizona. The Tecate railroad station was built in 1915 and today is part of a small historic district right next to the Tecate Brewery. For years the **Pacific Southwest Railway Museum** (weekend U.S. tel. 619/478-9937, www.psrm.org) offered Saturday railroad trips on their "Ticket to Tecate" service from San Diego. However, in mid-2009, one of the railroad tunnels burned and collapsed so service is currently suspended. Construction efforts are still underway and the tunnel has been cleared, but the track still needs to be laid. Work is hoped to be completed by 2017.

Museo Comunitario de Tecate

In the Tecate Cultural Center, **Museo Comunitario de Tecate (Tecate**

Pueblos Mágicos

Pueblo Mágico is a designation given by Mexico's Secretary of Tourism to towns throughout the country believed to offer travelers a "magical" experience whether though natural beauty, cultural riches, or historical importance. The Baja peninsula has three *Pueblos Mágicos*: Tecate, Loreto, and Todos Santos.

Community Museum) (Calle Tláloc 400, tel. 665/521-3191, www.carem.org, 10am-5pm Wed.-Sun.) is a bilingual museum explaining the culture, history, and natural geography of the region. The permanent exhibits feature photographs, murals, artifacts, and informative signs that highlight the three periods of Tecate's history: the prehistoric era, the era of the ranchers, and contemporary times. In addition to these, there's a traditional Kumiai house, a botanical garden, and a gift shop with traditional indigenous arts for sale. Events and workshops led by local indigenous instructors include basket making, corn processing, music, language, and other arts. The museum is managed by Corredor Histórico CAREM, a Mexican nonprofit dedicated to the historical and cultural heritage of Baja California. CAREM can also offer day trips outside of Tecate to nearby sites like La Rumorosa and El Vallecito. They also host multiday organized tours all along the Baja peninsula.

Parque del Profesor

On the outskirts of the east side of town, the **Parque del Profesor** is a 10-hectare park dedicated to Profesor Edmond Szekely, the founder of Rancho La Puerta. The sports and cultural complex includes a soccer field and a plaza used for community and private events. Right next to the park and also opened by Rancho La Puerta, **Las Piedras** is an environmental center housed in buildings made to look like giant granite boulders. They have a series of workshops for children.

Parque los Encinos

Named for the large oak trees interspersed throughout the park, **Parque los Encinos** (between Encinos, Dr. Arturo Guerra, and Querétaro, 10am-8pm daily, free) is a 10-hectare park where families gather to relax and play. There are picnic areas, playgrounds, soccer fields, skate and bike ramps, and an amphitheater. Admission to the park is free.

Plaza Parque Hidalgo

Tecate Beer

Mention the word *Tecate* and most people immediately conjure up the image of the red beer can with the stylized eagle on the front. This beer is ubiquitous in Baja California as well as other parts of the world. The exported Tecate has a lower alcohol content than what is available in Mexico.

The beer-making history of Mexico was heavily influenced by German immigrants in the 19th century, who brought their Vienna-style dark beers to the region. The influence of these flavors can be seen in beers such as Negra Modelo and Dos Equis Amber. Even today, the commercial beers of Mexico are of a much higher quality than many standard beers from other parts of the world.

Tecate's story began in 1944 when Alberto Aldrete took over an old brick building. He had been operating a malt factory and making beer on the side. With his new factory, he focused on beer full-time and named his brew after the town. The Tecate facility was the first factory in Baja California. Today, Tecate is owned by Heineken and shipped all around the world for beer drinkers everywhere to enjoy.

ENTERTAINMENT AND EVENTS

Tecate doesn't have much of a nightlife scene aside from a few quiet bars that generally close early. There are a few Tecate wineries, but most don't have tasting rooms open to the public. The same goes for the local Tecate craft breweries. A few little places serve some of the local wines and beer.

Nightlife

Since 1957, **Bar Diana** (Cardenas 35, tel. 665/654-0515) has been the local watering hole and gathering spot right on the town plaza. The bar was named after a life-size bronze sculpture of the goddess of hunting that once stood in the courtyard of its patio. The statue was stolen in 1974 and never seen again, but a painting of the sculpture graces the wall behind the large wooden bar. Stop into this Tecate landmark for a cold beer or margarita.

With a healthy selection of regional craft beers on tap and in bottles, **BeerHouse Gastrobar** (Benito Juárez 683, tel. 665/122-1415) has live music and entertainment many nights.

A great way to sample some of the wines from Tecate is by visiting **Tecate Gourmet** (Carretera Tecate-Ensenada Km. 10, tel. 665/655-6095, www.tecategourmet.com,

1pm-6pm Thurs.-Sun.). The wine cave and bistro does wine-tastings of local wines and also serves paninis and salads. They make fresh preservatives that are available for purchase.

La Antigua Wine Bar (Benito Juárez 300-C, tel. 665/122-3712, 5pm-10pm Tues.-Sat.) is a small wine bar across the street from the plaza that serves regional wines, cheeses, pizzas, and paninis.

One of the few wineries with a tasting room open to the public is **Cava Garcia** (Calle Cerro Colorado 165, tel. 665/799-6175, 10am-10pm Sun.-Wed., 10am-midnight Thurs.-Sat.). The large tasting room is family-friendly. Visitors can also tour the farm to see the horses, emus, goats, and donkeys.

SHOPPING

The best place to shop for souvenirs is the **Centro de Artesanías de Tecate** (Calzada Universidad in front of Parque Adolfo López Mateos, no tel., 8:30am-6pm Mon.-Fri., 10am-3pm Sat.) where local pottery, tiles, jewelry, and other crafts may be purchased.

FOOD

At ★ **El Lugar de Nos** (Benito Juárez 384, tel. 665/521-3340, 1pm-11pm Wed.-Sat., 1pm-5pm Sun., mains US$11-18) incredibly fresh creations like rib eye pizza, *jamaica* salad, and ahi tuna tostadas are created by Chef Mariela Manzano who studied at the Culinary Art School in Tijuana and was formerly a chef at Rancho La Puerta. Mismatched tablecloths, vintage furniture, and funky art create an eclectic, charming, and comfortable atmosphere. There's an intimate and cozy feeling to the restaurant even though the space is large and there are numerous patios and courtyards. In addition to the fresh and creative food, craft cocktails and local artisanal beers round out the menu, and the staff are incredibly friendly and accommodating.

There's no written menu at **Restaurante Amores** (Adolfo de la Huerta 42, tel. 665/122-1323, restauranteamores@gmail.com, 12:30pm-9pm Tues.-Thurs., 12:30pm-10pm Fri.-Sat., 12:30pm-7pm Sun., US$15 for three courses), but guests can choose from a three-, five-, or eight-course tasting menu with several choices per course. There are only a few tables, so it's best to email in advance to make a reservation. The restaurant can be difficult to find, but look for the small sign in the window.

On the highest point of the property of the Santuario Diegueño hotel, **Asao** (Rio Yaqui 798, www.santuariodiegueno.com, 7am-11pm Mon.-Sat., 7am-8pm Sun., mains US$11-21) offers fine dining with beautiful views. The food is artfully prepared with a delicate presentation. Consulting chef Martin San Roman helped Chef Silvia Lizarraga create a menu with items like duck confit and braised short rib. The large and impressive dining room has high ceilings and huge glass sliding doors that look out onto a patio with views of the town and the surrounding hills. On warm days the sliding doors open up to create an open-flow concept between the indoor and outdoor spaces. Guests can peer into the kitchen, situated behind a wall of windows on the other side of the dining room, as well as the glassed-in wine cellar full of regional wines.

For the best tacos in town, head to **Taqueria Los Amigos** (Ortiz Rubio and Ave. Hidalgo, tel. 665/521-3851, US$1-2). The stand has been serving up tacos and quesadillas since 1980. The large space is open air with nice wooden tables and chairs. Carne asada is the specialty here, and the flour tacos and quesadillas are large and filling.

Gourmet food and coffee truck **Astratto** (Plaza Cuchuma, tel. 665/851-0747, 5pm-10pm Wed., Thurs., and Sat., 7am-1pm Mon. and Fri., US$4-5) is a favorite spot for hip locals. They serve savory gourmet *tortas* like the specialty "Astratto Sandwich," marinated

the back patio at El Lugar de Nos restaurant

beef with caramelized onions and melted cheddar cheese. This family-run operation is also known for artisanal drip and press coffees. Watch for the orange and teal food truck parked near Plaza Cuchuma.

One of Tecate's most famous attractions, **El Mejor Pan de Tecate** (Benito Juárez 331, tel. 665/654-0040, www.elmejorpandetecate.com, open 24 hours) is a must-visit bakery for most travelers passing through. The rows of freshly baked bread, pastries, cookies, and cakes will entice anyone with a sweet tooth. They're open 24 hours, so whenever you find yourself passing through town, grab a tray and tongs to fill up on goodies. There's a parking lot in the back and tables to enjoy your treats out front.

ACCOMMODATIONS

You'll find accommodations that are up to U.S. motel standards at **Estancia Inn** (Benito Juárez 1450, tel. 665/521-3066, www.estancia-inn.com.mx, US$60). There are 85 rooms set back from the street with TVs with lots of channels including a decent selection in English. There's a swimming pool, a small gym, secure parking, and a restaurant, El Mesquite, on the property.

For a budget option, **Motel La Hacienda** (Mexico 2 #861, tel. 665/654-1250, US$35) has older rooms and bathrooms but are clean and in working order. Beds are comfortable, and there are flat-screen TVs with cable.

For nice accommodations in town, travelers head to **Santuario Diegueño** (Rio Yaqui 798, tel. 665/654-4777, www.santuariodieguено.com, US$156-229). The 26 rooms are spacious and well-appointed with mini fridges, coffeemakers, wine chillers, flat-screen TVs, fast wireless access, and patios. There's a lovely pool area with a Jacuzzi, and the grounds are landscaped with regional flora. There's an event center, bar, and two restaurants on the property including the famed restaurant Asao.

Ranchos

The most famous and recognized name in Tecate is the historic ★ **Rancho La Puerta** (Mexico 2 Km. 136.5, toll-free U.S. tel. 800/443-7565, www.rancholapuerta.com, US$3,600/week). Guests book a full week here at the famous fitness and spa retreat to relax, detox, renew, and redirect. Activities reflect these principles, and a sample itinerary for the day may include hiking, stretching, yoga, art class, well-being workshops or a cooking class at their famous cooking school: **La Cocina Que Canta.** Rates start at $3,600 for the week

El Mejor Pan de Tecate

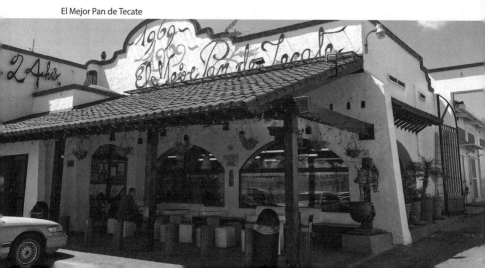

for the high season (Feb.-June). Shorter three- or four-day stays may be available as well. For those who can't commit to a longer visit, the Rancho La Puerta **Saturdays at the Ranch** are day trips to the ranch from San Diego that include activities like hiking, fitness classes, massages, and cooking demonstrations.

For rustic elegance, **Rancho Tecate Resort** (Carretera Tecate-Ensenada Km. 10, tel. 665/655-5226, www.ranchotecate. mx, US$110) is a 650-hectare ranch with 21 rooms. The lobby will give you a true ranch lodge feeling with large wrought-iron chandeliers, vaulted ceilings with wood beams, and a grand fireplace. Rooms have modern amenities like flat-screen TVs and slippers and bathrobes provided for use. There's a pool and Jacuzzi area, as well as an equestrian center.

For a trip back in time to the days of the Wild West, visit the 1,133-hectare horse ranch of **Rancho La Bellota** (Mexico 3 between Tecate and Valle de Guadalupe, tel. 646/172-7773, www.bajarancho.com, US$475/weekend). There's no electricity (except a small generator used to power the blender for margaritas), cell phone reception, TV, or Internet. Enjoy days of relaxation and trail rides on horseback like the real rancheros.

Camping and RV Parks

Perfect for families, **Rancho Ojai** (Carretera Mexicali-Tecate Km. 112, tel. 665/655-3014, www.rancho-ojai.com, US$9 for tent camping, US$25 for RV, US$62-96 for cabins) offers a range of accommodations from tent camping to RV spaces to cabins that can accommodate up to six people. There's no lack of activities for the family here. Kids will enjoy miniature golf, volleyball, basketball, soccer, bicycles, playgrounds, and a game room with pool and foosball tables. The whole family will enjoy the pool and all of the picnic areas with grills.

With tent camping and cabins, **Cañada del Sol** (Carretera Tijuana-Mexicali Km. 105,

tel. 664/634-6503, www.canadadelsol.com, US$9 pp for tent camping, US$59 for cabin) is also a popular day destination with all of the activities they have to offer. There's a pool, horseback riding, ATV riding, basketball, and playgrounds. It's US$6 to enter for just the day.

INFORMATION AND SERVICES

Gas station, markets, banks, and ATMs are interspersed throughout town. On the south side of Plaza Hidalgo is a **State Tourism Office** (1305 Andador Libertad, tel. 665/654-1095) with brochures and other regional information.

GETTING THERE AND AROUND

If you will be arriving by car from the United States, CA 188 (accessible from CA 94) leads directly to the Tecate border crossing. Tecate is a popular day trip for San Diego residents who enjoy parking their car on the U.S. side of the border (for US$5) and walking across to spend the day. Once in Mexico, visitors can walk a couple of blocks to the plaza and many shops and restaurants. Taxis are readily available for longer rides around town.

To get to Ensenada or the Valle de Guadalupe, follow the tranquil two-lane Mexico 3 that leads south to these areas. Mexico 2 heads east to Mexicali or west to Tijuana.

Tecate Border Crossing

The Tecate border is open 5am-11pm daily. This is considered one of the shortest border waits for northbound crossings. Pedestrians often have no wait, and cars will wait considerably less than at Tijuana's San Ysidro border crossing. There are no special expedited lanes for crossing here (Ready Lane or SENTRI). The northbound pedestrian crossing entrance is at Lazaro Cardenas and Callejon Madero (just east of the southbound car crossing). The northbound car crossing is east of this.

LA RUMOROSA AND VICINITY

Sights

EL VALLECITO CAVE PAINTINGS

Heading east on Mexico 2 from Tecate leads you to the dusty town of La Rumorosa. The main draw for tourists are the cave paintings of **El Vallecito** (Mexico 2 Km. 72, tel. 686/552-3591, 10am-4pm Wed.-Sun.). There are more than 18 rock art sites here, although only six may be visited by the public. Of these, El Diablito, a painting of a small red devil, is the most popular. On the winter solstice, a ray of sunlight hits the painting, and his eyes are said to illuminate. There is a two-kilometer path visitors can take to visit the five sites that are open to the public.

CAMPO ALASKA

Also of interest in La Rumorosa is **Campo Alaska** (Mexico 2 Km. 60, 686/552-3591, 9am-5pm Wed.-Sun., US$0.50). General Abelardo L. Rodríguez, governor of the state of Baja California, constructed the stone buildings as a House of Government almost 100 years ago. From 1923 to 1929 the Mexicali government offices would move to the site during the months of June to October to escape the summer heat of the city and to enjoy a cooler mountain climate. The buildings were later used as a mental hospital and a tuberculosis hospital until 1955. Today, the historical site functions as a museum related to the history of the region.

Food

If you're hungry, you can get a great steak or traditional Mexican food in town at **La Cabaña del Abuelo** (Carretera Mexicali-Tecate Km. 75, tel. 686/575-0152, www.cabanadelabuelo.com, 7am-9pm Mon.-Fri., 7am-10pm Sat.-Sun., mains US$9-18). The hearty dishes are served in an inviting mountain cabin atmosphere with friendly and attentive service.

Getting Around

Heading east from La Rumorosa on highway Mexico 2 winds you down the mountains through scenic rock formations until you reach Mexicali. The tolls on the roads from Tecate to Mexicali are the most expensive you'll find anywhere on the peninsula.

Rosarito

Down the Pacific coast, about a half-hour drive south of the border is the small beachside town of Rosarito. Weekenders flock here during the summer to enjoy the handsome and expansive beaches that offer visitors the chance to relax or enjoy a wide range of activities.

Boulevard Benito Juárez, the main tourist drag, runs parallel to the beach a few blocks inland. Here you'll find many of the major hotels, shops, and restaurants lining the newly remodeled street with palm trees down the middle. New pedestrian-only side streets off of Benito Juárez offer pedestrians wide pathways to stroll about and enjoy the central area of the town.

While Rosarito has only been its own municipality since 1995 (it was previously an extension of Tijuana), the beach town is now growing into a destination in its own right with a state center for the arts, an underwater dive park, and a convention center that have all opened within the past couple of years. While Rosarito has traditionally been a summer destination because of the beaches, there is temperate weather year-round and visitors who come in months other than summer can enjoy the town with cheaper hotel rates and smaller crowds. With its central location, Rosarito is also a great jumping-off spot for exploring Tijuana, Ensenada, and the Valle de Guadalupe.

Rosarito was once a major spring break destination, and while a few of the clubs remain, the city has undergone a transformation in recent years and now attracts a more diverse crowd. This is a popular region for expats (there are an estimated 12,000 living in the area), but it's a friendly mix of Mexicans and Norteños getting along together. Since tourism is the main draw for the region, you'll find that many of the employees in the hotels and restaurants speak excellent English. While there are options for hotels in the center of town where most of the action is, many travelers rent a condo or house on the beach somewhere in the greater Rosarito area, which includes regions like K38, La Fonda, Puerto Nuevo, and La Misión to the south.

SIGHTS
★ Rosarito Beach

One of the main draws for Rosarito is the expansive **Rosarito Beach.** Eight kilometers long and running parallel to the main street in the center of town, the beach is the center of life in Rosarito when the weather is warm. On summer weekends, it is packed with families who come to spend the day swimming, playing, and relaxing. The beach buzzes with activities like horseback riding, ultralight planes, and ATV riding. The **Rosarito Pier,**

just in front of the Rosarito Beach Hotel, is great for fishing off of and also a popular surf spot. Farther north along the beach are Club Iggy's and Papas & Beer, a couple of the large clubs left in town. Day and night these are popular spots to enjoy drinks in the sand with ocean views. There are no official parking lots for the beach, so summer weekends find the streets nearby overly crowded with beachgoers fighting for spots. If you're staying at one of the hotels in the main area of town, it's a better idea to walk. Access to the beach is gained through any of the many streets that run perpendicular to it.

CEART State Center for the Arts

Rosarito's new **Centro Estatal de las Artes or CEART** (Paseo La Cascada, tel. 661/100-6271, www.icbc.gob.mx, 9am-5pm Mon.-Fri., free admission) is a large and modern space for galleries, exhibitions, workshops, a bookstore, and a cafeteria. The vibrant Rosarito art scene is highlighted at this state center for the arts through photography, painting, sculpture, dance, music, and theater. Located south of town, the space is also used for large events and festivals. The full calendar of their many events and exhibitions can be found on

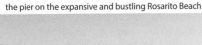

the pier on the expansive and bustling Rosarito Beach

Rosarito

To Tijuana

SECTUR

Free road

PACIFIC OCEAN

0   0.25 mi
0   0.25 km

LA FLOR DE MICHOACÁN

EJIDO MAZATLÁN SHOPPING PLAZA

AV MIRAMAR
LAUREL

QUINTA DEL MAR RESORT
QUINTA PLAZA

BLVD JUÁREZ

AV COSTA AZUL

AV MAR DEL NORTE
AV MAR MEDITERRANEO

HOTEL & RESTAURANT LOS PELICANOS
EBANO
CEDRO
ABETO
ALAMO

ROSARITO BEACH

AV MOSSEAU

SPAZIO CAFFE & CREPES
RESTAURANT LA TIA
LA CAZUELA DEL MOLE
TOURIST OFFICE
POLICE
ROBLE
ACACIAS
MERCADO DE ARTESANIAS
ORTEGA'S
EL NIDO

PAPAS & BEER
ANIMALE
IGGY'S
HOTEL FESTIVAL PLAZA
TACQUERIA LOS POBLANOS
PALMA

PINO

ROSARITO BEACH HOTEL
TAXIS TO TIJUANA

TOURIST INFORMATION

RENE'S SPORTS BAR RESTAURANT
TOLL PLAZA

BAJA STUDIOS
To Ensenada
© AVALON TRAVEL

their Facebook page at www.facebook.com/CeartRosarito.

The Coronado Islands

The four islands that can be seen offshore from Rosarito are the **Coronado Islands.** The islands are uninhabited and mostly undeveloped aside from an abandoned casino turned military base. Today, they attract mostly divers and anglers, some who come from Rosarito and others who come from San Diego. Because the islands are just 18 miles from San Diego, they're a popular day trip for anglers who come on fishing charters directly from the United States. **H&M Landing** (U.S. tel. 619/222-1144, www.hmlanding.com, US$145) operates daily fishing trips to the Coronado Islands from San Diego. If you're looking to visit the islands from Rosarito, **Rosarito Ocean Sports** (Benito Juárez 890-7, tel. 661/100-2196, www.rosaritooceansports.com) can arrange for boat tours of the islands (US$110) or scuba diving trips to the islands (US$125).

RECREATION
Surfing

There are a number of surf spots in northern Baja that receive the steep angled swells that skip even most of Southern California. In Rosarito, the best break in town is at the **Rosarito Pier**, next to the Rosarito Beach Hotel. This is a great spot for all levels of surfers, and surf lessons for beginners are available here. South of town at kilometer 38 is the famous **K38** surf spot. This is one of the most popular surf spots in northern Baja. It's a right break, but sometimes lefts can be found here as well. It's best on a mid to low tide. Farther south, at kilometer 58, near the La Fonda Restaurant and Hotel, is another one of the most popular surf spots in the region, **K58.** The wave here breaks on nearly any swell, but combo swells bring the best shape.

Diving

In November 2015 the government sank a Mexican navy battleship, the *Uribe121,* to create the **Parque Submarino Rosarito** (www.rosaritounderwaterpark.com), Rosarito's first artificial reef and underwater park. Just offshore from Puerto Nuevo, the sunken ship is divided into different areas of interest; a sculpture garden, an homage to *Titanic* (the movie was filmed at the nearby Baja Studios), replicas of prehistoric art, and a ship graveyard.

The **Coronado Islands** just offshore are also a popular destination for dive trips. There's a colony of sea lions, rocky reefs, kelp beds, and even the broken wreckage of a yacht to explore. **Rosarito Ocean Sports** (Benito Juárez 890-7, tel. 661/100-2196, www.rosaritooceansports.com) can arrange dive tours to both the Coronado Islands and the Parque Submarino. They have PADI courses as well as equipment rental. Many of the major hotels arrange for dive trips as well.

ENTERTAINMENT AND EVENTS
Nightlife

Although Rosarito used to be a mecca for the spring break crowd, the town has tamed down and grown up in recent years. Many of the large clubs have closed down with artisanal restaurants and small cafés and bars taking their place. The nightlife scene in Rosarito is more subdued with locals preferring to gather at a small bar or restaurant. The larger hotels in town have their own bars where guests can enjoy margaritas and local beers. In a nod to the growing craft beer scene in northern Baja, **Beer Nights** (Benito Juárez 748, tel. 664/507-2814, 4pm-2am daily) has artisan beers from Mexico and the United States. It's a low-key locals spot with live music on certain nights.

Those who are missing the large clubs that used to dominate the nightlife of Rosarito, can still get their fix at **Papas & Beer** (Coronado 400, tel. 661/612-0244, www.rosarito.papasandbeer.com, 10am-1am Mon.-Thurs., 10am-3am Fri.-Sun.) or **Club Iggy's** (11337 Rosarito Centro, www.clubiggys.com, 10am-9pm Mon.-Thurs., 10am-1am Fri., 10am-2am Sat., 10am-10pm Sun.). These spots right on

Rosarito Beach are popular with those who want to drink in the sand during the day and party by DJ at night.

Events

Twice a year, in spring and fall, the 80K **Rosarito Ensenada Bike Ride** (www.rosaritoensenada.com) runs from Rosarito to an ending with a big fiesta in Ensenada.

The annual **Rosarito Art Fest** (www.rosaritoartfest.com) held each Memorial Day weekend has become one of the town's most-famous events in recent years. With the bourgeoning art scene in northern Baja, the festival is a great showcase for local arts in addition to having live music and plenty of food and drinks.

Wineries

Because it's only an hour away from the Valle de Guadalupe wine region, many who stay in Rosarito take a day trip to go wine-tasting. **Baja Test Kitchen** (www.bajatestkitchen.com) will arrange for private wine tours of the Valle de Guadalupe, with door-to-door service for clients from their accommodations in Rosarito.

Rosarito has its own winery in town: **Claudius** (Blvd. Sharp 3722, tel. 661/100-0232, www.claudiusvino.com), making exceptional wines. They have a tasting room and can accommodate wine-tastings for special occasions or if you call ahead. They also have a wine school where participants go to weekly classes and end up making 25 cases of their own wine.

SHOPPING

Just south of town, if you continue on Benito Juárez—the Mexico 1 free road—you'll reach the **Popotla Artisan Corridor** with a number of artisan shops where buyers can purchase items like wrought-iron work, wooden furniture, chimeneas, and colorful Talavera ceramics.

In town just north of El Nido restaurant, the **Mercado de Artesanías** features over 100 stalls carrying Mexican souvenir arts and crafts such as blankets, silver jewelry, ceramics, and glassware. Don't be afraid to bargain for a fair price. If you prefer a more curated shopping experience, don't miss **Fausto Polanco** (Benito Juárez 2400, tel. 661/612-2271, www.faustopolanco.com.mx, 10am-6pm daily) on the north side of town. A visit to the showroom featuring hacienda-style Mexican furniture and beautifully refined rustic pieces feels almost like a trip to a museum.

There's also a small mall on the north side of town, **Pabellón Rosarito** (Carretera Libre 300, tel. 661/612-3140, 10am-10pm daily, www.pabellonrosarito.com) that has a Cinemax movie theater, Home Depot, food court, and other small specialty stores.

FOOD

Rosarito doesn't have the new culinary scene that you'll find in other northern Baja regions such as Tijuana, Ensenada, or the Valle de Guadalupe. But that doesn't mean that there isn't good food here. Rosarito has incredible traditional Mexican restaurants, tasty taco stands, and fresh seafood.

Mexican

For traditional Mexican food or steak, you can't beat any of the restaurants associated with the Perez family. The 13 Perez siblings own many of the best restaurants in town (and the youngest owns the Don Pisto liquor stores). The restaurants all have a similar authentic ranch atmosphere, savory steaks, and rich Mexican food. The original is **El Nido** (Benito Juárez 67, tel. 661/612-1430, www.elnidorosarito.com, 8am-midnight daily, mains US$7-18), which has been a mainstay on the main drag in town since 1971. Just down the street and on the beach is **Los Pelicanos** (Calle del Ebano 113, tel. 661/612-0445, www.lospelicanosrosarito.com, 7am-10pm Sun.-Thurs., 7am-midnight Fri.-Sat., mains US$6-13), which offers the best views of any of the restaurants with the expansive Rosarito Beach just out the window. With their huevos rancheros and *machaca* dishes,

this is a popular spot for locals to enjoy brunch on the weekends.

Meat lovers will want to head to **La Estancia** (Ave. Francisco Villa 316, tel. 661/613-0695, www.laestancia.mx, 7am-11:45pm Sun.-Thurs., 7am-12:45am Fri.-Sat., mains US$6-13) in the northern part of town. Steak, quail, lamb, and rabbit are specialties. The walls are adorned with taxidermy, giving the restaurant a dark cozy hunting lodge feel. Many locals pop in to have dinner at the large bar for a more casual experience. They now have a second location, **La Estancia Valle de Santa Rosa** (Km. 78, 8am-11pm Fri.-Sat., 8am-9pm Sun.), an hour south on the Mexico 1 freeway on the way to the Valle de Guadalupe. Situated in a remote location in the Santa Rosa valley, the restaurant offers much of the same menu with stunning views of the countryside.

The last of the Perez dynasty in Rosarito is **Tapanco** (Blvd. Popotla Km 31.5, tel. 661/100-6035, www.tapancorosarito.com, 8am-10pm daily, mains US$5-16), just south of town. The restaurant has expanded over the years to include an outdoor patio area and café as well as an upstairs bar called Why Not? Alfredo, the owner, is a welcome presence, greeting customers and making sure that everyone has an incredible experience. Their housemade soups, salad dressings, marmalades are always a nice touch to the meal.

Carnitas La Flor de Michoacán (Benito Juárez 291, tel. 661/612-1062, 9am-9pm Thurs.-Tues., mains US$5-8) has been serving up *carnitas* to locals in the same location since 1950. The large restaurant is a gathering place for families and groups who can come to eat *carnitas* family-style on the cheap. They have a second, smaller location, also on Benito Juárez, closer to the tourist area.

Antojitos and Street Food

The most famous taco stand in town is **Tacos El Yaqui** (Mar del Norte, Esp. La Palma, no tel. , www.tacoselyaquirosarito.com, 9am-5pm Mon.-Tues. and Thurs., 9am-7pm

Fri.-Sun., tacos US$2). They've been serving traditional Sonoran-style *arrachera* (skirt steak) *perrones* since 1984. *Perrones* are different from the usual Mexican street tacos in that they are served in a flour tortilla with beans and melted cheese in addition to the usual meat and toppings. Just off the main drag, this spot has become extremely popular with locals and tourists, so expect lines.

For more traditional street tacos, both **Tacos el Paisano** (Blvd. Benito Juarez, US$1-2) and **Tacos el Norteño** (Blvd. Benito Juarez, US$1-2) on the main drag are solid options.

The best deal in town for fish tacos is at **Mariscos Titos** (Blvd. Articulo 27, tel. 661/120-0657, www.mariscostitos.com, 7:30am-5:30pm daily), the large taco stand across from the Comercial Mexicana grocery store. For under US$1, patrons get a gigantic battered fish taco with all of the works. It's more of a locals' spot, since it's out of the tourist area of town, but the affordable and savory tacos make it worth the trek. They have a large menu with a variety of other seafood dishes on the menu as well. Just south of town, **Mariscos Popotla Jr.** (Blvd. Popotla Km. 30.29, tel. 661/100-2598, 9am-7pm daily, tacos US$1-2) is another popular option for fish tacos and *mariscos* like ceviche served in a casual setting.

For something different, **El Gaucho Argentino** (Calle Rene Ortiz Campoy 30, tel. 664/440-5984, www.elgauchoargentinorosarito.com, 10am-7pm daily, US$2-6) is an Argentinian spot serving authentic steak and sausage sandwiches (with chimichurri sauce, of course) as well as empanadas. Husband and wife owners Gerardo and Flavia are wonderful hosts and make the little shop feel like home. On Saturday they bring a grill out on the sidewalk for an Argentinian barbecue.

Rosarito has its own new *colectivo* of outdoor food stalls in front of the Hotel Festival Plaza called **Plaza Food Fest** (Benito Juárez 1207, tel. 661/612-2950, noon-8pm Sun.-Thurs., noon-11:30pm Fri.-Sat., US$5-9). Beloved Rosarito eateries such as Betuccini's

and El Gaucho have small stands here as well as a handful of other options. The Cerveceria Tinta Negra stall is one of the best spots in town to try local Baja craft beers. Patrons order from various stands and can enjoy their food at the outdoor tables as they watch the world go by along Rosarito's main drag.

International

Owned by a California native and a favorite restaurant of many of the expats who live in town, is **Susanna's** (Pueblo Plaza, tel. 661/613-1187, www.susannasinrosarito.com, 1pm-11pm Wed.-Mon., mains US$14-24). The restaurant specializes in California cuisine with fresh salads, hearty pastas, savory chicken and fish dishes, and steak. To top it off, the menu features wines from the nearby Valle de Guadalupe.

To satisfy a burger craving, **Betty's** (Blvd. Popotla Km. 28, tel. 661/116-2160, 11am-6pm Tues.-Sun, US$6-9) serves authentic Norteño-style burgers just south of town. The family-run operation uses fresh ingredients to create gourmet burgers.

When they're in the mood for Italian, hip locals head to **Betuccini's Pizzeria & Trattoria** (Blvd. Popotla Km. 28.8, tel. 661/100-6148, www.betuccinispizzeria.com, noon-11pm daily, US$9-13) where the homemade pizzas, pastas, and salads are a welcome change for those tired of Mexican food. When the weather is warm, sit on the outdoor patio where the Italian strung lights and lush setting provide a perfect backdrop for a summer meal. Another option for Italian is the new **Pasta y Basta** (Blvd. Popotla Km. 28.5, tel. 661/117-9825, 4:30pm-9:30pm Thurs.-Fri., noon-9:30pm Sat.-Sun., US$14-20) just down the road. The small and cozy restaurant is owned by a northern Italian chef and his wife.

Cafés

Spazio Café and Crepes (Rene Ortiz Campoy 24, tel. 661/613-0660, 8am-10pm daily) is a popular spot where locals pop in for lattes, crepes, and fresh salads and sandwiches.

ACCOMMODATIONS

Hotels in Rosarito tend to be expensive for the quality of accommodations you get in return. Prices go up on weekends during peak season (summer), especially in August when the town is flooded with residents of Mexicali and other inland areas who come to the coast to escape the heat. While there are no luxury hotel accommodations in Rosarito, there are a number of very nice condo and house rentals, a popular option for visitors. A few campsites and RV parks can be found south of town on the beach in the stretch between Rosarito and Ensenada.

Under US$50

The budget **Posada Don Luis Hotel** (Benito Juárez 272, tel. 661/612-1166, donluisprofile@ gmail.com, US$42) has very basic rooms but offers a small outdoor pool and off-street parking. Another budget option, **Motel Baja Del Sol Inn** (Carretera Libre Km. 26.8, tel. 661/612-0401, US$25) is just south of town with a pink and purple exterior that's hard to miss. Rooms are outdated but have all of the basic amenities.

US$50-100

The 71 rooms at **Brisas del Mar** (Benito Juárez 22, tel. 661/612-2547, www.hotelbrisas-delmar.net, US$90) have air-conditioning and heating, cable TV, wireless Internet, balconies, and room service. There's a pool and Jacuzzi in addition to a restaurant and bar. The hotel is only two blocks to the beach, and has parking in the courtyard.

Los Pelicanos (Calle del Ebano 113, tel. 661/612-0445, www.lospelicanosrosarito. com, US$60-95) is a cozy little hotel right on the beach with a lush pool and Jacuzzi area. Rooms are spacious but older and in need of an update. There's a great Mexican restaurant by the same name on-site.

With 47 rooms, **Hotel Pueblito Inn** (Benito Juárez 286, tel. 661/612-2516, www. hotelpueblitoinn.com, US$80-90) offers basic accommodations with cable TV, air-conditioning, and heating. It's in the northern part

the iconic Rosarito Beach Hotel

of town, so you'll likely need to take a cab to get down to the central tourist area where many of the restaurants, shops, and other hotels are located.

With a good location right in town, **Hotel Del Sol Inn** (Benito Juárez No. 32, tel. 661/612-2552, www.del-sol-inn.com, US$85) is walking distance to lots of restaurants and shops as well as the beach. There's a friendly staff and working wireless Internet.

A new **City Express** hotel is scheduled to open early 2017 in the Pabellon and will cater to business travelers who come to conventions in the Baja California Center.

US$100-150

The iconic ★ **Rosarito Beach Hotel** (Benito Juárez 31, tel. 661/612-1111, toll-free U.S. tel. 866/767-2748, www.rosaritobeachho-tel.com, US$100) is the most prominent landmark in Rosarito and also one of the most recognized hotels in Baja. It first opened to the public in 1925 and has been the hub of action ever since. The traditional Mexican ambience, old-world charm, and history of the hotel continue to attract most of the visitors who come to Rosarito today, whether they stay as guests or come to eat or drink in any of the restaurants or bars. Past guests have included Orson Welles, Gregory Peck, Spencer Tracy, and such ladies as Marilyn Monroe, Lana Turner, Kim Novak, and Rita Hayworth, prompting the declaration painted over the lobby entrance stating "through this door pass the most beautiful women in the world." The founder's nephew, Hugo Torres, who runs the hotel today, was the first mayor of Rosarito and more recently served a second mayoral term. He was integral in growing the town of Rosarito and turning it into a tourist destination. His entire family is actively involved in local politics and promotion.

Today, the Rosarito Beach Hotel has 500 rooms, including a new 17-story luxury condo-hotel tower built in 2008, with units available to rent as hotel rooms. These accommodations are newer and more modern than rooms in the older section of the hotel. The hotel often features special packages and deals so check their website before booking.

With its location in the heart of Rosarito, imposing size, and brightly colored carnival-themed architecture, it's hard to ignore **Hotel Festival Plaza** (Benito Juárez 1207, tel. 661/612-2950, toll-free U.S. tel. 800/453-8606, www.hotelfestivalplaza.com, US$85-110). Just look for the large building with the faux roller coaster on the facade. The hotel, once buzzing with people and energy years ago, feels somewhat neglected recently. There are plans for much-needed renovations and improvements. Rooms are basic and offer wireless access and cable TV. A small pool and Ferris wheel (no longer operational) are in the courtyard. There are a number of restaurants that rotate in an out of business on the property. With its interior courtyard and central location, the hotel is host to many of the city's art and food festivals.

Just south of town, **Castillos del Mar** (Carretera Libre Km. 29.5, tel. 661/612-1088, www.castillosdelmar.com, US$135) offers basic accommodations right on the water. Many guests feel that the price is expensive for what they get in return, with rooms and a property that could use an updating. However, the new bar, **Sunio's,** has fresh architecture and decor and beautiful beach and ocean views. They offer beers and small bites such as tacos and tostadas.

the beach at Castillos del Mar

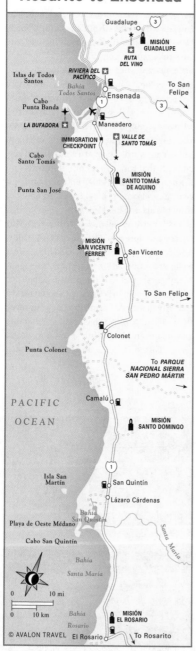

Rosarito to Ensenada

Guadalupe

MISIÓN GUADALUPE

RUTA DEL VINO

RIVIERA DEL PACÍFICO

Islas de Todos Santos

Bahía Todos Santos

Ensenada

To San Felipe

Cabo Punta Banda

LA BUFADORA

Maneadero

IMMIGRATION CHECKPOINT

VALLE DE SANTO TOMÁS

Cabo Santo Tomás

MISIÓN SANTO TOMÁS DE AQUINO

Punta San José

MISIÓN SAN VICENTE FERRER

San Vicente

To San Felipe

Colonet

Punta Colonet

To PARQUE NACIONAL SIERRA SAN PEDRO MÁRTIR

Camalú

PACIFIC OCEAN

MISIÓN SANTO DOMINGO

Isla San Martín

San Quintín

Lázaro Cárdenas

Bahía San Quintín

Playa de Oeste Médano

Cabo San Quintín

Bahía Santa María

Santa María

0   10 mi

0   10 km

Bahía Rosario

MISIÓN EL ROSARIO

© AVALON TRAVEL   El Rosario   To Rosario

Vacation Rentals

Due to an abundance of new high-rise condominiums and classic Mexican houses on the beach, renting a condo or house for the weekend is a popular choice in Rosarito.

The **Oceana Rosarito Inn** (Benito Juárez 907-24, tel. 888/849-4500, www.rosaritoinn. com) is an option right in town that can accommodate up to 10 people in their four-bedroom units. The condominium resort **La Paloma** (tel. 664/609-5555, www.rosaritolapaloma.com) is just south of town and a beautiful property right on the water with multiple swimming pools and Jacuzzis. They have units with up to three bedrooms.

South of Rosarito, **Las Gaviotas** (www. las-gaviotas.com) is a popular choice for U.S. citizens coming down for the weekend to rent a house. You may be able to find private rentals in **La Jolla Del Mar/La Jolla Real** (www. lajollareal.com) or **Club Marena** (www.club-marenrentals.com) for the most luxurious accommodations in the area.

INFORMATION AND SERVICES

Rosarito has major services like large grocery stores, banks, ATMs, and gas stations. The large structure just north of town is the **Baja California Center** (tel. 664/609-7900, www. bccenter.mx), a convention center that opened in 2013 and attracts international conferences.

Medical Resources

Rosarito has a number of hospitals and clinics. The **Hospital General de Playas de Rosarito** (Galilea Este 2200, tel. 661/612-6164) is right across from city hall. The modern facility has an emergency room, state-of-the-art facilities, and a skilled staff. They provide services at very affordable prices.

Tourist Resources

There is a **State Tourism Office** (Benito Juárez 907, tel. 661/612-5127, 8am-6pm Mon.-Fri., 9am-1pm Sat.) on the main drag downtown providing brochures and information about Rosarito.

TRANSPORTATION
Getting There

Most visitors coming to Rosarito arrive by car because the town is about a half-hour drive south from the San Ysidro border crossing in Tijuana. For those coming south over the Otay Mesa border crossing, the Boulevard 2000 connects to Mexico 1 just south of Rosarito near the fishing village of Popotla. Taxis and shuttle vans (called *colectivos* or *calafias*) make the trip from Rosarito to the San Ysidro border crossing and vice versa.

THE TOLL ROAD
AND THE FREE ROAD

There are two options for driving to Rosarito from the San Ysidro border crossing: the free road or the toll road. Most tourists take the toll road to avoid the traffic and confusion of navigating Tijuana streets and to enjoy the scenic ocean views. The toll is US$2 at each toll station. There is a station in Playas de Tijuana and another just south of Rosarito. Once you are in Rosarito, the free road, or Carretera Libre, and the toll road run parallel to each other until La Fonda where the free road turns inland and the toll road follows the coast south. The roads converge again just north of Ensenada in San Miguel where

the third and final toll station is located. It's possible to get on and off of the toll road between stations around the Rosarito area without having to pay the toll if you are driving on stretches between the stations.

Getting Around

It's easy to walk around the downtown tourist area of Rosarito. Taxis are also easy to hail along Benito Juárez in downtown. Uber, based in Tijuana, serves Rosarito as well, but allow for extra time as there may not be one immediately in the area.

ROSARITO
TO ENSENADA

Many travelers who come to the Rosarito area opt to stay somewhere south of town itself. The stretch between Rosarito and Ensenada is full of little villages and communities with plenty of options for accommodations, restaurants, and activities. Most directions are given by kilometer along this stretch. The numbers for the kilometer markings get larger as you head farther south.

Popotla Fishing Village

Those unfamiliar with the fishing village of Popotla may be initially deterred by the grimy

the Pacific fishing village of Popotla

appearance, fishy smell, and derelict buildings. Restaurant employees aggressively call out to passersby to come into their establishments, which are not much more than ramshackle buildings perched on the rocks. The weekends here are especially overwhelming when hundreds of local families converge on the small beachfront village, causing traffic to back up all the way to the highway. But herein lies the secret to Popotla, because underneath its repellent appearances, adventurous foodies swear that this is the best place to go to get the freshest seafood in the region.

There are plenty of restaurants lining the few streets that comprise the village, but be sure to make it down to the beach where the fishers bring in their fresh seafood to sell. There are a few more restaurants directly on the beach where customers can sit in the sand to enjoy a meal while they watch the day's catch coming in. Popotla specialties include the giant spider crab and *pescado zarandeado,* where the fish is butterflied, lathered with mayonnaise and ancho chile, and then grilled.

Just south of the fishing village, the **Popotla Mobile Home Park Camping & RV** (Km. 34, tel. 661/612-1502, www.popotla.mx) is a trailer park with spaces for camping (US$25) and for RVs with full hookups (US$35). The ocean views are stunning from around the property and also at the restaurant and bar. There's beach access and also a small pool.

Anyone who frequented this region in the 1980s and '90s has likely stayed or eaten at the legendary **Hotel Calafia** (Km. 35.5). Perched on a dramatic point right on the Pacific, the restaurant here was comprised of a series of terraces with stunning views. Calafia claims to be a historic mission site (it wasn't), and there are buildings in the parking lot set up to mimic an old colonial town and mission. The property today is a derelict shadow of its former glory days. While the stunning views from the point remain the same, the restaurant goes in and out of operation, and the hotel rooms are tired and outdated. The only sign of life is the new residential towers just to the north.

K38

One of northern Baja's most famous surf spots is **K38,** recognized as much for the surf as for the giant statue of Jesus up on the hill with arms outstretched toward the ocean. There's a right surf break here, but sometimes lefts can be found as well. The spot is best on a mid to low tide. Watch out for sea urchins, especially at the mouth of the river. There's another break just south at kilometer 38.5 in front of the Club Marena condo buildings.

Most surfers stay at **Robert's K38 Surf Motel** (U.S. tel. 310/613-4263, www.robertsk38.com, US$60). They have clean comfortable rooms and secure gated parking. Surfboards, kayaks, booties, and wetsuits are available to rent.

For a quick and tasty bite to eat, **K38 Fish & Shrimp Tacos** (Mexico 1, US$1.50) is at the south end of the strip of buildings on the highway and serves delicious traditional seafood tacos. The casual taco stand also serves a chipotle shrimp taco that's a unique treat. Just a few doors up, **Taco Surf** (Mexico 1, 10am-7pm daily, US$1.50) is the place to go for carne asada and *al pastor* tacos and *tortas.*

For a sit-down meal, **Baja Calypso** (Km. 38, tel. 661/613-2696, www.bajacalypso.com, 8am-10pm daily, mains US$11-19) is one of the most popular options around, especially for breakfast. Gilles Knafo, the chef and owner, serves a fusion of Moroccan, French, and Mediterranean foods. The eclectic restaurant has a cozy indoor space as well as a huge patio out back looking onto the ocean. The musician Joaquin "Quino" McWhinney, who is the lead singer for the reggae band Big Mountain, is a resident of Ensenada and frequently plays live on weekend evenings at Baja Calypso.

Puerto Nuevo Lobster Village

For years, the famous "lobster village" of northern Baja was a draw for tourists coming across the border to eat lobster served "Puerto

Baja Studios

Just north of Popotla is the famous **Baja Studios** (formerly Fox Studios) where big blockbuster hits like *Titanic, Master and Commander, All is Lost,* and the James Bond *Tomorrow Never Dies* have been filmed. The studio is home to the world's largest water tank, covering over three hectares. Unfortunately, the studios are not open to the public for tours as they were when owned by Fox. They are still actively used for filming, and it's not uncommon to see big Hollywood stars around town who are shooting at the studios and have made Rosarito their temporary home for a few months. Many of the local expats are regular extras for TV shows and movies that are filmed at the studios.

Nuevo style": split in half, fried, and served with flour tortillas, rice, and beans.

Those who have frequented Puerto Nuevo for decades remember when they would bring platters heaped with lobsters for just a few dollars each. Today, the prices have gone up considerably as the village now panders to tourists, but you can still get a lobster meal with ocean views for cheaper than you would in the United States.

Within the few square blocks that comprise the village, there are a number of restaurants, all with generally the same menu and prices. They will also all have an employee out on the street trying to lure you into their restaurant. The large **Ortega's** (www.ortegas.com) along the water on the south side of town is popular with tourists. They have both indoor and outdoor seating and of course plenty of lobsters and margaritas to keep the crowds happy. The family owns multiple restaurants in town, so chances are even if you don't eat at the large location, you'll still end up at one of the Ortega restaurants. Their other popular restaurant, **Hacienda Ortega's,** has a more intimate atmosphere and a lovely upstairs patio. It's on the north street in town.

There are also a number of artisan stalls in town, so shoppers can get their fill of silver jewelry, Mexican knickknacks, and locally made flavored tequilas.

Right next door to the village is the large **Puerto Nuevo Hotel & Villas** (Carretera Libre Km. 44.5, tel. 661/614-1488, www.puertonuevohotelyvillas.com, US$92-120). With a beautiful oceanfront location, the hotel boasts 300 rooms, indoor and outdoor pools, a spa, and restaurant.

North of the village a few kilometers, there are a few more options for accommodations. At kilometer 43, **Bobby's by the Sea** (tel. 661/614-1135, www.bobbysbytheseaatk43.com) has daily, weekly, or monthly condo and casita rentals. The charming property offers modern amenities and a restaurant and bar on the property that's popular with local expats. The housing community of **Las Gaviotas** (www.las-gaviotas.com) is a classic community for expat homes and weekend rentals for tourists.

Just north of Las Gaviotas, **Ollie's Pizza** (Km. 40.4, tel. 664/231-7946, www.olliesbrickovenpizza.com, 4pm-10pm Wed.-Sun., pizza US$9-14) is serving up some of the best artisanal brick-oven pizza in the area. Kids (of all ages) can ask to go behind the counter to don a chef hat and put the toppings on their pizza before it goes into the oven. Don't miss drizzling the homemade chile oil on your pizza.

MISIÓN EL DESCANSO

Just south of Puerto Nuevo, **Misión el Descanso** (also sometimes called San Miguel la Nueva) was established in 1810 by Padre Tomás de Ahumada after floods had destroyed the mission site in nearby La Misión. In 1830, new buildings were constructed by Padre Felix Caballero but were eventually abandoned in 1834 for the new Nuestra Señora de Guadalupe church in what is the current-day Valle de Guadalupe. An archaeological dig in 1997 revealed stone foundation ruins and a few adobe walls from the 1830 structure. Today they are preserved by INAH and partially covered by a steel awning.

Primo Tapia

The small town of Primo Tapia is mostly known to expats and tourists as the home of the housing community of Cantamar and a few restaurants that are popular with local expats.

Ruben's (Carretera Libre Km. 46.5, tel. 661/613-2371, www.rubensbaja.com, 11am-10pm Mon.-Fri., 10am-midnight Sat., 9am-10pm Sun., mains US$8-13) recently moved from its *palapa*-roofed structure to a new building just a few hundred meters south, right next to the new Pemex station. This is a popular spot for expats and tourists, especially for their Sunday brunch for US$17 per person with live music, Mexican folk dancing, and bottomless mimosas. Another popular expat spot is **Splash** (Carretera Libre Km. 52, tel. 661/614-0095, www.splashcantina.com, 9am-10pm daily), which also recently moved to a new location south of the sand dunes and north of the Halfway House. The ocean views from the second floor are superb. Happy hour

is 4-7pm Monday-Thursday with fish tacos and draft beer for US$1.25 each.

South of town, **Los Arenales sand dunes** are right on the ocean and attract motocross and 4x4 riders. The land is owned by the local *ejido*, which charges US$5 to enter. You can rent an ATV for US$35 an hour.

La Fonda/K58

Home to the famous **K58 surf spot,** the area along the ocean here is often referred to by tourists as "La Fonda" because of the namesake hotel/restaurant that has been around since the 1970s.

The place to camp here is **Alisitos K58** (Km. 58, no tel., US$15). The only things offered in terms of facilities are bathrooms (bring your own toilet paper) and outdoor showers. But the tranquil oceanfront spot and access to the waves are what keep the surfers coming back.

The restaurant at **Poco Cielo** (Km. 59, tel. 646/155-0606, www.pococielo.com, US$8-12) serves a selection of Mexican food as well as Thai food Thursday through Sunday. They also have hotel rooms available (US$85-100) all decorated in different themes.

Due to owner disputes, the famous La Fonda property is currently split into two

lobster served "Puerto Nuevo" style

separate businesses—**Gary's La Fonda** (Km. 59, tel. 646/155-0872, www.garyslafondabaja. com, US$100) and **Dmytri's La Fonda** (Km. 59, tel. 646/155-0872, dmytrislafonda@gmail. com, US$100). You can't miss the competing signs out front that seem to grow louder and more outrageous every month. Both properties offer hotel rooms, restaurants, bars, and a popular Sunday brunch with a large buffet and bottomless Bloody Marys or margaritas.

La Misión

The town of La Misión is where the free road and the toll road split. The free road heads inland here, through the small ranching town of La Misión and into the country toward the northern entrance to the Valle de Guadalupe wine region. The toll road follows the coast south on a scenic route to Ensenada.

La Misión Beach is best reached by staying on the toll road. The large and expansive beach is a popular spot for families on summer weekends, but remains empty during most of the week. There are a few *palapas* for shade as well as a number of food stalls. The waves and riptides can be fierce here so this is a good beach for relaxing, sunbathing, and taking walks, but not a good one for swimming.

If you're taking the free road through town, **Tacos Magaña** (Carretera Libre Km. 65, no tel., 6:30am-10:30pm daily, US$4-8) is a good stop for a bite to eat or a bathroom break before driving into the countryside. Their tacos are tasty, and the huge burritos are large enough for two people to share.

The adobe **Misión San Miguel Arcangel** was constructed from 1793 to 1800 under Dominican Padre Luis Sales. After severe flooding in 1809, the operation was moved to another mission in Descanso in 1810. Today, the adobe ruins are in a fenced-off area in town next to the school, just off of the free road.

South along the Coast to Ensenada

On a beautiful stretch of beach, **Clam Beach Resort** (tel. 646/155-0976, www. clambeachresort.com, US$30-65) provides an RV park with 82 sites with 50-amp full hookups. The property is newer and in good condition. Wireless Internet is available around the property, and there are bathrooms with hot showers as well as coin laundry.

Just south, **Baja Seasons** (formerly Baja Oasis, Mexico 1 Km. 72.5, tel. 646/155-4015, www.bajaseasons.net, US$40-53) is an older property that has fallen slightly into disrepair in recent years, but still offers a stunning beach location. There's a pool and wireless Internet in the clubhouse. The restaurant is open during the summer on weekends.

Golfers who are looking for a relaxing day filled with scenic views head to **Bajamar** (Mexico 1 Km. 77, U.S. tel. 619/425-0081, www.bajamar.com, golf US$94, hotel US$150). Set along five kilometers of stunning coastline, there are 27 holes divided into three courses (lakes, ocean, views) with nine holes each. Golfing rates are for 18 holes, so golfers get to choose which two courses to golf. There are also a driving range and a putting green. The property also has a beautiful hacienda-style hotel with 81 rooms set around a courtyard. Accommodations are modern with duvet covers and plasma TVs, but retain Mexican colonial charm with Saltillo tile floors and Juliet balconies. There's a heated pool and Jacuzzi as well as a spa. The restaurant on the property serves breakfast, lunch, and dinner, and the bar is a popular spot for a blended margarita after a day on the golf course. Don't miss taking a venture up to the small tower lookout. Drinks are sometimes served at the bar up on "El Mirador," but even if they aren't serving, it's worth it to see the spectacular 360-degree views.

For camping with views, **Playa Saldomando** (Mexico 1 Km. 94, tel. 646/118-5974, U.S. tel. 619/857-9242, www. playasaldamando.com, tent camping US$17 per vehicle, motor home US$19, trailer rental US$40-80) has a mile of coastal property with campsites on the beach and up on the cliffs. Tent camping and motor home camping (there are no hookups) are allowed, and trailer rentals are available.

Ensenada

Ensenada is the third largest city in Baja and sees a number of tourists from the cruise ships that dock here multiple days a week, weekenders who come down from Southern California, and road-trippers passing through. But locals know that Ensenada still retains a small Mexican pueblo feel. While it's a popular weekend destination, there are enough attractions to keep a family occupied for a week or more.

The downtown and harbor area of Ensenada is easily explored on foot, and many of Ensenada's best sights can be visited in a day just walking around this area. The *malecón* and *mercado de mariscos* are along the harbor, and just a block away is Avenida López Mateos, the main street in town, with souvenir shops and plenty of restaurants and bars.

There's a large culinary scene in Ensenada that draws foodies with its famous street carts, high-end restaurants, and everything in between. Don't miss eating fish tacos or *mariscos* (seafood) that come right out of the Pacific. There's a growing craft beer scene in Ensenada, and the Valle de Guadalupe,

Mexico's wine region, is just a half-hour drive inland.

SIGHTS
★ Mercado de Mariscos

Fishing has always been one of Ensenada's primary industries. To get an idea of the broad diversity of seafood caught in Ensenada, take a walk through the fish market. Down along the harbor, the **Mercado de Mariscos** (Miramar 16, 8am-8pm daily) hosts a number of stalls full of shrimp, tuna, mussels, abalone, and the odd-looking gooey duck clams. You may hear locals refer to the market at the *Mercado Negro,* black market, as it used to be called (the name supposedly comes from the fact that the market used to be very dirty, not because they were selling illicit goods). Try one of Ensenada's famous fish tacos at one of the many stands right outside the market.

Malecón

The best way to take in Ensenada's harbor area is to go for a walk along the *malecón,* which stretches along the water from Miramar to

The Riviera del Pacifico now serves as a cultural center for the city.

Ensenada

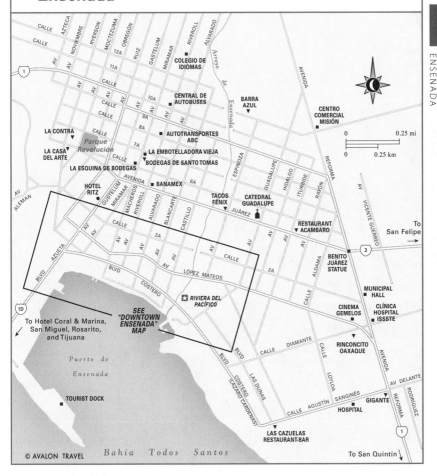

© AVALON TRAVEL

Castillo streets. The pedestrian walkway is a nice spot for checking out the fishing boats and cruise ships while doing some souvenir shopping at the stalls along the way. At the north end of the *malecón* is the fish market and at the south end is access to the cruise ship pier. Also near the south end is Parque de la Bandera, a plaza with a large Mexican flag, a water feature, and a new stage and pavilion. The plaza is often used for local festivals and events and popular with families for weekend gatherings. Just around the corner

Plaza Cívica features large gold busts of three prominent historical figures: Benito Juárez (the first president of Mexico), Padre Miguel Hidalgo (who began the Mexican Revolution), and Venustiano Carranza (the first president after the revolution).

★ Avenida López Mateos

The heart of the action in downtown Ensenada is **Avenida López Mateos** (Calle Primera). Along with souvenir stalls, shoppers will find a variety of brick-and-mortar stores selling

Downtown Ensenada

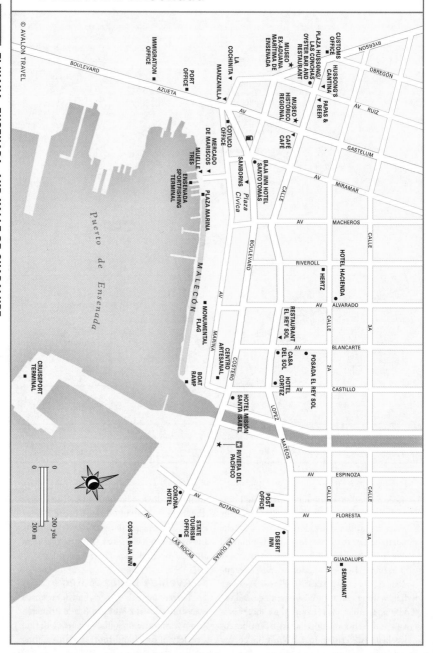

© AVALON TRAVEL

BOULEVARD

AZUETA

IMMIGRATION OFFICE

PORT OFFICE

LA COCHINITA ▼

MANZANILLA ▼

MUSEO EX-ADUANA MARÍTIMA DE ENSENADA

PLAZA HUSSONG/ LAS CONCHAS OYSTER BAR AND RESTAURANT

★ MUSEO HISTÓRICO REGIONAL

CUSTOMS OFFICE ■

HUSSONG'S CANTINA ▼

PAPAS & BEER ▼

RYVERSON

OBREGÓN

AV. RUIZ

GASTELUM

AV

MIRAMAR

CAFÉ CAFÉ ●

BAJA INN HOTEL SANTO TOMAS ●

COTUCO OFFICE ■

MERCADO DE MARISCOS ▼

MUELLE TRES ▼

ENSENADA SPORTFISHING TERMINAL

PLAZA MARINA ■

SANBORNS ▼

Plaza Cívica

CALLE

AV MACHEROS

AV

RIVEROLL

HOTEL HACIENDA ■

HERTZ ■

CALLE

3A

Puerto de Ensenada

M A L E C Ó N

BOULEVARD

AV ALVARADO

RESTAURANT EL REY SOL ▼

CASA DEL SOL ●

POSADA EL REY SOL ■

MONUMENTAL FLAG ■

CENTRO ARTESANAL ■

MARINA

COSTERO

BOAT RAMP ■

HOTEL CORTEZ

CALLE

BLANCARTE

2A

CASTILLO

LOPEZ

HOTEL MISIÓN SANTA ISABEL ■

MATEOS

CRUISEPORT TERMINAL ■

★ RIVIERA DEL PACÍFICO ✚

AV ESPINOZA

CALLE

CALLE

POST OFFICE ■

CORONA HOTEL ●

AV

ROTARIO

AV

STATE TOURISM OFFICE ■

DESERT INN ●

AV FLORESTA

3A

LAS DUNAS

LAS ROCAS

COSTA BAJA INN ●

GUADALUPE

2A

SEMARNAT ■

0   200 yds
0   200 m

The Margarita

One of Mexico's most iconic commodities is the margarita. There are variations on the drink, but it most commonly consists of fresh lime juice, tequila, and controy (Mexico's orange liquor), served with ice. When you order a margarita, you can have it blended (*liquada*) or on the rocks (*en las rocas*), with salt on the rim of the glass (*con sal*) or without (*sin sal*).

There are a number of reputed stories about where the margarita was invented. In Ensenada, both Hussong's and the Riviera del Pacifico claim to be the birthplace of the margarita.

silver jewelry, home decor items, and handicrafts from mainland Mexico. Interspersed with the shops are restaurants and bars where tourist will be beckoned in to enjoy a margarita or tequila shot. Many of the restaurants have sidewalk seating or an open-air concept, so this can be a nice spot to relax and take in the city while enjoying a bite to eat or drink. This is a great place to get a general feel for Ensenada as locals and travelers all congregate in this area to enjoy some of the best shopping, food, and drink that Ensenada offers.

Riviera del Pacifico

With its elegant Spanish architecture, the **Riviera del Pacifico** (Blvd. Lázaro Cárdenas 1421, tel. 646/176-4310, www.rivieradeensenada.com.mx) has been one of Ensenada's crowning jewels since 1930. The white building and surrounding gardens, used to be one of Ensenada's grandest hotels, when it was opened by the famous boxer Jack Dempsey. Many of Hollywood's elite, including Bing Crosby and Rita Hayworth, spent time here during Prohibition. Today, the space operates as a local cultural center and event space with an open-air theater and a number of rooms used for workshops and classes. Much of the original tile and paintings have been preserved throughout the structure. Visitors who want to see the architecture and learn more about the history of the building can go to **Bar Andaluz** (10am-2am Mon.-Sat., noon-7pm Sun.) in the main building at street level. The mural behind the bar was painted by Alfredo Ramos Martínez and is original to

the building. Both Bar Andaluz and Hussong's Cantina claim to be the original home of Mexico's iconic beverage, the margarita. Bar Andaluz has a well-known 2-for-1 margarita night on Wednesday where you can enjoy the famous cocktail inside the bar or out in the courtyard if the weather is nice. Inquire at the bar about tours of the entire property.

Museo Caracol

Just across the street from the Riviera del Pacifico is the **Caracol Museo de Ciencias y Acuario** (Calle Club Rotario No. 3, tel. 646/117-0897, www.caracol.org.mx, 9am-5pm Tues.-Fri., 10am-5pm Sat.-Sun., US$3.50, students US$2.50). This family-friendly museum focuses on a hands-on approach to science. The museum is still being completed, but there are a number of open exhibits all related to science and history of elements relating to the sky, land, or sea. The large and impressive space will eventually be home to a rooftop café, cafeteria, gift shop, and more galleries.

Chapultepec Hill Mirador

For the best views of Ensenada, head up to the *mirador* on **Chapultepec Hill** (GPS: 31.862557, -116.633984). From this spot northwest of the harbor, you'll get scenic overviews of the harbor and the bay, the Todos Santos islands, and the town. There's not much else aside from a crumbling pony wall here, but it's a nice spot to take some photos and sit and enjoy the views for a bit. You can either drive by following Calle Segunda to Miguel Alemán (park on the street in the neighborhood as there's no official parking lot), or you can spend 10 minutes hiking up from the base of the hill.

★ La Bufadora

One of Ensenada's most famous attractions is south of town by about an hour on the Punta Banda peninsula. At the end of a long and windy coastal road **La Bufadora** is a natural geyser that shoots water up to 30 meters in the air. The ocean swells come into a sea cave here, and when the water recedes, the air and water spout upward along with a thunderous noise. The blowhole shoots off about every minute or so, to the delight of bystanders who gather along viewing areas next to it. A number of shops selling Mexican souvenirs and food have lined up along the walkway that leads out to La Bufadora and the viewing areas. Don't miss the *almejas gratinadas* (au gratin clams) at one of the stalls near the blowhole if you're looking for a bite to eat. You'll need to pay about US$1.50 for parking and then walk about 700 meters along the walkway with stalls to get to La Bufadora at the end. There's no charge to see La Bufadora, but be prepared to pay a few pesos to use the bathrooms.

La Bufadora is a natural water geyser.

Hussong's Cantina

As the oldest and most famous cantina in Baja California, **Hussong's Cantina** (Ave. Ruiz 113, tel. 646/178-3210, www.cantinahussongs.com, 11am-2am Tues.-Sun.) is more than just a bar—it's an institution. Founded in 1892 by a German immigrant named John Hussong, 100 years and three generations later Hussong's is still a family-run operation. The bar has remained much the same over the years and has been visited by the likes of Marilyn Monroe, Steve McQueen, and John Wayne. Saddle on up at the long bar or grab a seat at one of the tables. Don't mind the peanut shells on the floor.

BEACHES

Ensenada has a number of picturesque Pacific beaches, great for swimming, surfing, snorkeling, and relaxing. North of town where the tollbooths are is the famous surf spot of **San Miguel.** In town, the large sandy **Playa Hermosa** is great for families and is buzzing with people on the weekends. Twelve kilometers south of town, the Río San Carlos meets the bay to create an estuary. Out here, **Estero Beach** has a more relaxing scene where visitors can enjoy horseback riding or taking it easy with fewer crowds. Near La Bufadora, **Arbolitos** is a great spot for diving, snorkeling, and kayaking among the natural caves.

RECREATION
Surfing

Ensenada is largely regarded as the birthplace of Mexican surfing, and everyone from big wave aficionados to beginners will find a place to catch a swell. Off the coast, the **Isla Todos Santos** is a challenging spot where waves can reach heights of up to 60 feet. There are five breaks on the island, and the Bog Wave Surf contest has taken place here a number of years. Along the coastline back on the peninsula, there are a series of point and beach breaks. Experienced surfers can also head to **San Miguel,** to the north of town, where they'll find one of the most famous right point breaks in Baja. Beaches like **Playa Hermosa** are perfect for beginners with the sandy bottom and gentle waves.

For those of all levels seeking surf lessons, **Surf Ensenada** (tel. 646/194-0846, U.S. tel. 619/988-2989, www.surfensenada.com) offers private and group instruction for all ages. Owner Miguel Arroyo is a fun and enthusiastic instructor as well as a great ambassador for Ensenada. He has a great team of knowledgeable and friendly instructors working with him.

Fishing

The glory days of Ensenada as a sportfishing mecca have diminished over the years due to the commercial fishing in the area, but sport anglers can still catch lingcod, calico bass, barracuda, bottom fish, bonito, and every once in a while, yellowtail. It's easy to hire at outfitter for fishing at the north end of the harbor near the fish market. **Sergio's Sportfishing Center** (tel. 646/178-2185, U.S. tel. 619/399-7224, www.sergiosfishing. com) has a variety of different-size vessels

and welcomes anglers of any experience level. They offer private deep-sea tours as well as open party trips. Their large fleet ranges from *pangas* to an 85-foot yacht.

Boating

Ensenada is an official Mexico port of entry, so boaters arriving from U.S. waters must check in with the port captain's office on Boulevard Azueta to get their FMM tourist permits and temporary importation permit for their vessel to clear customs. Most marinas in Ensenada can help you with customs clearance if you contact them in advance.

Conveniently located downtown, **Ensenada Cruiseport Village Marina** (tel. 646/178-8801, toll-free tel. 877/219-5822, www.ecpvmarina.com) has 200 slips and can accommodate oversize boats. They provide 24-hour security as well as showers, restrooms, and a laundry. They can help you with customs clearance for no additional charge. **Marina Coral** (tel. 646/175-0000, www.hotelcoral.com) located at the Hotel Coral & Marina has 350 slips and offers a range of services including a fuel dock, maintenance services, pump-out service, free wireless Internet, and use of hotel facilities like the swimming pool and spa.

Playa Hermosa

ENTERTAINMENT AND EVENTS
Nightlife

Most of Ensenada's nightlife is centered in the downtown area. Despite its fame with tourists, **Hussong's Cantina** (Ave. Ruiz 113, tel. 646/178-3210, www.cantinahussongs.com, 11am-2am Tues.-Sun.) remains a popular spot for the locals who go for the 2-for-1 drink specials (beer on Tuesday and margaritas on Saturday).

Down the block from Hussong's is **Papas & Beer** (Calle Primera, tel. 646/174-0145, www.papasandbeer.com) where people can get a taste of the club nightlife scene that used to dominate Ensenada's spring break vibe. **La Villa** (Calle Segunda between Alvarado and Riveroll, tel. 646/947-9039) is where the young locals go these days for beer specials and good music. **Ultramarino Oyster Bar** (Calle Ruiz 57, tel. 646/178-1195) is the spot to go for DJs and live music on the weekends.

For a hipper and more clandestine bar, check out **Santos en el Pacifico** (Paseo Hidalgo 6, tel. 646/175-9583, 7pm-2am Sun., Tues.-Thurs., 7pm-3am Fri.-Sat.) located on the hillside just above the downtown area. They make a variety of specialty cocktails and serve food like hamburgers and ceviche. They often have live music on the weekends. Watch for the sign of a heart and the neon "BAR" sign outside.

Breweries

For tasty craft beers and views of the Pacific, head north of town to **Agua Mala** (Mexico 1 Km. 104, tel. 646/174-6068, www.aguamala. com.mx, 2pm-midnight Tues.-Sat., 1pm-9pm Sun.). The brewery is constructed of shipping containers and the second-story bar looks directly out at the ocean, giving patrons fantastic sunset views. There are a variety of beers made in-house like the Sirena Pilsner and Astillero IPA. They serve food and often collaborate with famous chefs and restaurants in the region to create special menus offered for a limited time.

If you're just getting acquainted with Baja's craft beer scene and want to be able to try beers from various breweries in one place, on the same road just north of Agua Mala is **Baja Brews Colectivo y Jardin Cervecero** (Mexico 1 Km. 103, tel. 646/174-4528, 6pm-midnight Wed.-Thurs., 4pm-2am Fri.-Sat., noon-8pm Sun.). The converted warehouse houses seven stands, each featuring a craft brewery from Ensenada, Tijuana, or Mexicali. Beers are available by 2 oz., 10 oz., or 16 oz. servings at most of the stands. There are bars with stools at each of the beer stands as well as a number of communal tables and chairs. The back rollup door of the warehouse is open to the outside, where patrons can head out to enjoy their beer looking out at the Pacific. Le Pinche Frances, Ochentos pizzeria, and El Local by Slowburger serve food if you're hungry. There's often live music at night, and the place gets packed with locals as the evening wears on.

In town is the gastropub location of brewery **Wendlandt** (Blvd. Costero, tel. 646/178-2938, www.wendlandt.com.mx, 6pm-midnight Tues.-Sat.). Hip locals and beer-loving tourists go here to sip on beers like Hann Zomer Saison and the Harry Polanco Red Ale and enjoy gourmet pub food like artisanal pizzas. The actual brewery is in a warehouse just north of town in El Sauzal. They can accommodate brewery tours and tastings at that location only with advance notice.

South of town, looking out at Playa Hermosa, is craft brewery **Cervecería Doble C** (Blvd. Lázaro Cárdenas, tel. 664/338-4951, 4pm-10pm Wed.-Fri., 2pm-10pm Sat.). The industrial space features exposed brick, corrugated metal, and communal wooden bar tables that share the same space as the beer tanks at the end of the room. Beer lovers will enjoy their Session IPA and hoppy-flavored pale ale while looking out the large picture windows at the ocean.

Events

Ensenada hosts a number of events each year including a **Carnaval** celebration in February, the **Rosarito Ensenada Bike Ride** (www.rosaritoensenada.com) twice a year (spring and fall), and a large **beer fest.** The state tourism site, www.discoverbajacalifornia.com, has a thorough calendar of events. Perhaps Ensenada's largest event each year is the kick-off and starting line (and sometimes the finish line as well, depending on the course) of the famous **Baja 1000** (www.score-international. com) off-road race each November.

SHOPPING

Ensenada has some great artisanal and souvenir shopping along **Avenida López Mateos** (Calle Primera), where there's a good mix of touristy stands selling shot glasses and blankets and brick-and-mortar shops selling higher-end artisanal items from mainland Mexico. There are a number of souvenir stands along the harbor near the Mercado de Mariscos as well. Due to the large numbers of cruise ship tourists that Ensenada receives, there are plenty of pharmacies that can be found along Avenida López Mateos.

Los Globos (Calle Nueve and Cinco de Mayo, open daily) is a huge market where visitors can find everything from produce to meat to books to clothing to secondhand items. The market spans multiple blocks and is partially indoors, but has expanded so that other vendors can set up tents nearby. The market is open every day, but the extra stalls are there only on weekends.

FOOD
Mexican

For artisanal breakfast made with fresh local ingredients, head to **Casa Marcelo** (Ave. Riveroll between Calle 7 and 8, tel. 646/117-0293, www.casamarcelorestaurante.com, 8am-6pm Wed.-Sun, mains US$5-7). As the sister restaurant to Rancho Campana making Ramonetti cheeses and Cava de Marcelo in Ojos Negros, many of the dishes are made with the cheeses and butter from the ranch. Egg dishes are handcrafted and paired with fresh produce and local meats topped off with cheeses and butter from the ranch. They also have the cheese and butter available for sale.

Locals head to **La Hoguera** (Alvarado and Calle 11, tel. 646/209-0617, 1pm-10pm Sun. and Tues.-Thurs., 1pm-11pm Fri.-Sat., mains US$11-16) for meats grilled over a wood fire and served in a natural outdoor setting. The open-air restaurant is set within adobe walls and under the shade of trees. Enjoy grilled meats, fish, and pork, served alongside cold beers, tequila, and wine.

There's no shortage of souvenir shopping in Ensenada's downtown area.

Seafood

Seafood lovers and foodies won't want to miss **Muelle 3** (Blvd. Teniente Azueta, tel. 646/174-0318, noon-6:30pm Tues.-Sat., US$6-10) down on the pier just north of the fish market. Don't let the simple and unassuming interior fool you, this is some of the most sophisticated seafood coming out of Ensenada. Chef David Martinez takes fresh Ensenada seafood and gives it a kick of Baja and Asian flavors. The *ceviche de la casa* is a delectable mix of octopus, clams, fish, and avocado.

Popular with cruise ship passengers, **Mahi Mahi** (Paseo Hidalgo 33, tel. 646/178-3493, mahimahiens@hotmail.com, noon-10pm daily, mains US$8-12) is a large casual restaurant in town. It is conveniently located at the end of López Mateos, the prices are reasonable, and they offer an extensive seafood menu.

Antojitos and Street Food

Many locals claim that the best fish tacos in town come from the **Tacos El Fenix** (Ave. Espinoza, 8am-8pm Mon.-Sat.) food cart. They've been serving up both fish and shrimp tacos since 1970. There's no seating here; locals and foodies gather around on the sidewalk to enjoy a quick and savory bite from the cart. There are also a number of fish taco stands outside the Mercado de Mariscos. **Tacos Lily** is the stand here where Anthony Bourdain went in his TV show *No Reservations*. Another option for fish tacos farther east in town is **El Chopipo** (Diamante 449, tel. 646/177-0202, 7am-8pm daily) where they have a small stand with some tables and chairs for seating. In addition to fish and shrimp tacos, they serve ceviche tostadas.

It's been called "the best street cart in the world" by Anthony Bourdain, and ★ **La Guerrerense** (López Mateos and Alvarado, www.laguerrerense.com, 10am-4pm Wed.-Mon.) lives up to its reputation. With sophisticated flavors, she serves up ceviches and unique seafood combinations on tostadas. Don't miss the award-winning *ceviche de*

Seafood lovers will enjoy the fresh sashimi and ceviche at Muelle 3.

erizo com almeja (sea urchin with clams), or the signature *La Guerrerense ceviche,* made with orange juice. They are also in the process of opening a sit-down restaurant down the street. Just a block east of La Guerrerense is another seafood cart, **Mariscos El Guero** (Blvd. Costero and Alvarado, tel. 646/151-0008, 10-6pm daily), serving up *cocteles de mariscos* (seafood cocktails) consisting of various types of seafood in a tomato-based broth. Served chilled, this is the perfectly refreshing and delicious meal for any seafood lover.

For those looking for a taco fix at any hour, **El Trailero** (Ave. J, tel. 646/204-7678, open 24 hours) should be your destination. Located north of town in El Sauzal along Mexico 1, this mega taco stand has multiple stations serving all types of tacos—fish, *al pastor,* carne asada, *cabeza,* as well as *tortas* and *birria.*

For *birria* (a traditional meat stew often served as a taco using just the meat), locals have been heading to **Birrieria La**

Guadalajara (Calle Macheros, tel. 646/174-0388, www.birrieriaguadalajara.com, 7am-8pm daily, mains US$4-6) since it opened in 1972. The tender and savory *birria* is available in lamb, goat, beef, and pork. The large sit-down restaurant is known for quick service, affordable prices, and good food.

Colectivos

The *colectivos,* collections of different food stands in one location, are a trend that has trickled down from Tijuana to Ensenada as well. **El Callejón** (Floresta 320, tel. 646/120-8004, 1pm-10pm Tues.-Thurs., 1pm-11pm Fri.-Sat., 1pm-9pm Sun.) has a variety of stalls like pizza, sushi, Argentinian, wraps, and salads. The outdoor seating area also has a small playground for kids.

Directly across the street is the bohemian **Region Gastronómica** (Calle Veracruz and Floresta, tel. 646/204-8624, 1pm-10pm Sun.-Thurs., 1pm-11pm Fri.-Sat.) another collection of local food stands. Don't miss the **Peninsula** stall, serving up delicious Baja/Asian-inspired seafood dishes. Beer and wine are available for sale from the bar.

International

Chef Benito Molina, one of the most well-known chefs in Mexico, created **Manzanilla** (Recinto Portuario, Teniente Azueta 139, tel. 646/175-7073, www.rmanzanilla.com, 1pm-1am Wed.-Sat., 1pm-6pm Sun., mains US$12-17) along with his wife and fellow chef, Solange. As one of Ensenada's top restaurants, it boasts a chic setting and a menu with items like oysters, steaks, abalone, and quail ravioli. The restaurant is right next to the port, and the industrial feel of the area is reflected in the decor. The large converted warehouse features an eclectic detailing with a large traditional wooden bar juxtaposed to modern pink chandeliers. There's a small outdoor garden that the dining room looks out onto.

Hip locals and foodie travelers head to eat at **Boules** (Moctezuma 623, tel. 646/175-8769, mains US$9-16) where Javier Martinez (brother of Chef David Martinez at Muelle 3) serves up dishes like *queso fundido de mar* (seafood in melted cheese), crab ravioli, and *tuetano* (bone marrow) served in a gigantic bone, along with mini corn tortillas, limes, and red onions. Most seating is on the patio under the trees and strung lights. Local wines and beers round out the menu. And yes, there's boules for those who want to play an after-meal game.

The French cuisine at **El Rey Sol** (López Mateos 1000, tel. 646/178-1733, www.el-reysol.com, 7am-10:30pm daily, mains US$13-20) has been a staple of fine dining in Ensenada since 1947. Weekend brunch is a classy affair where patrons can order off the menu or feast at the buffet and listen to live piano music in the formal dining room. Don't miss the decadent pastries and baked goods they're famous for.

For rib eye or filet mignon, **Sano's Steak House** (Mexico 1 Km. 108, tel. 646/174-5145, 1pm-11pm daily, US$18-27) is a classy spot with cocktails, swanky atmosphere, friendly staff, and great steaks. For non-steak eaters, they also have a selection of pastas, fish, and chicken on the menu.

The fine dining restaurant at **Punta Morro** (Mexico 1 Km. 106, tel. 646/178-3507, www.hotelpuntamorro.com, 8am-10pm Mon.-Thurs., 8am-11pm Fri., 9am-11pm Sat., 9am-10pm Sun., mains US$17-34) is as famous for its dramatic views as for the food. Built out over the edge of the water, the bountiful windows allow for dramatic sea vistas with waves crashing onto the rocks below. Diners enjoy items like lobster enchiladas, ribs, grilled octopus, and *arrachera* steak.

Cafés

North of town on the highway, **La Flor de la Calabaza** (Zona Playitas, tel. 646/174-4092, flordelacalabaza@gmail.com, 8am-5pm Mon.-Sat., 9am-4pm Sun.) is not only a café serving up healthy, organic breakfasts and lunches, but they also operate as a local organic market.

The Birthplace of the Fish Taco

While fish tacos can be found all over the Baja peninsula, they are especially prevalent in Ensenada, a city that claims to be the original home of the delicious dish. Strips of white fish or shark are battered, fried, and served in a corn tortilla, topped off with cabbage, *crema*, salsa, and a squirt of fresh lime.

The history of the fish taco is a bit murky, and both San Felipe and Ensenada claim the title as home of the first fish taco. Ensenada asserts that the fish taco was influenced by the Japanese immigrants that came to the area in the 1920s. The fish batter for the fish taco is similar to a tempura, and the *disca,* which is used to fry the fish taco, is similar to a wok.

Fish tacos are a breakfast/lunch specialty in Baja. For the most part, you won't find fish tacos available after about 5pm.

Also serving healthy lunches and coffee is **Casa Antigua Café** (Calle Obregón 110, tel. 646/205-1433, 8am-10:30pm Mon.-Sat., 2pm-10pm Sun.) located in a historical house in a convenient spot in town. Around the corner, the tiny **Breve Café** (Calle Segunda 380, tel. 646/174-0049, 7am-9:30pm Mon.-Fri., 8am-9:30pm Sat.) is a chic espresso bar that opens up right onto the sidewalk. There are a few stools for patrons, or it's perfect for a macchiato on the go.

ACCOMMODATIONS

Peak season in Ensenada is summer, especially during the Valle de Guadalupe Vendimia season, when hotels fill up with those attending the wine harvest festival. Prices at most hotels are significantly cheaper during the week than on the weekends. Reservations should be made in advance when possible as the many festivals and events that Ensenada hosts can quickly deplete hotel inventory.

Under US$100

With a central location and large parking lot, **San Nicolas Hotel and Casino** (Ave. Guadalupe, tel. 646/176-1901, www.snhotel-casino.com, US$80-90) has 118 hotel rooms. Rooms need to be updated, but the central pool and Jacuzzi area is lovely and the poolside bar serves up good margaritas. The attached casino is a draw for those who like playing the slot machines.

It's hard to miss **Hotel Santo Tomas** (Blvd. Costero 609, tel. 646/178-3311, US$40), the brightly painted hotel in the heart of the action of Ensenada. Rooms are basic and clean and there's secure, off-street parking. Another in-town option is **Hotel Casa Del Sol** (López Mateos and Blancarte 1001, tel. 646/178-1570, www.casadelsolmexico.net, US$65). Rooms are basic, but there's a pool area and a café attached to the hotel.

Hotel Mision Santa Isabel (formerly La Pinta, Blvd. Lázao Cárdenas and Ave. Costillo, tel. 646/178-3616, www.hotelmisionsantaisabel.com, US$80) has rooms built around a courtyard with a small pool and seating areas. The Spanish hacienda architecture features tile floors and wood-beam ceilings.

North of town, **Quintas Papagayo** (Mexico 1 Km. 108, tel. 646/174-4575, www.quintaspapagayo.com, US$80) offers accommodations right on the ocean. Rooms vary from cabins, suites, studios, and chalets, with the price varying accordingly as well. The property has been around since 1947 and the rooms are clean but older and could use an update.

US$100-200

With a great in-town location, **Posada El Rey Sol** (Ave. Blancarte 130, tel. 646/178-1601, www.posadaelreysol.com, US$125) has 52 rooms, all comfortable and decorated with Mexican charm. There's a friendly staff, pool and Jacuzzi area, and free breakfast.

The famous El Rey Sol restaurant is across the street, known for its French cuisine and delicious pastries.

On the harbor, the 92-room **Corona Hotel & Spa** (Blvd. Lázaro Cárdenas 1442, tel. 646/176-0901, www.hotelcorona.com.mx, US$160) is walking distance to the downtown area. Rooms all have wireless Internet, air-conditioning heating, flat-screen TVs, and many have harbor views. There's a pool and Jacuzzi, and the Marina Spa on the property offers full spa services and has a hair salon and sauna. They have a nice remodeled bar and Los Veleros restaurant on-site.

In town, **Hotel El Cid Best Western** (López Mateos 993, tel. 646/178-2401, U.S. toll-free tel. 800/352-4305, www.hotelelcid. com.mx, US$145) has 52 rooms, decorated in Mediterranean style with Spanish charm. Rooms feature flat-screen TVs, mini-refrigerators, air-conditioning, and patios. There's no elevator, so ask for a room on a lower level if you aren't able to take stairs.

The beautiful oceanfront location draws travelers to stay north of town at ★ **Las Rosas** (Mexico 1 Km. 105.5, tel. 646/174-4310, www.lasrosas.com, US$170). The property is nicely kept and has a fabulous pool area perched right on the ocean. The infinity edge appears to drop right into the Pacific. Rooms are well appointed, and there's a spa on the property providing a range of services. Even people who aren't staying at the hotel come to have a margarita at sunset to enjoy the views, or go to Sunday brunch at the restaurant.

On Playa Estero south of town, the **Estero Beach Hotel and Resort** (Playas del Estero, tel. 646/176-6225, www.hotelesterobeach. com, US$170) has been a favorite of travelers since the 1950s. Rooms are tasteful with cable TV and private patios. The lovely pool area is set against the background of the ocean and beach. A restaurant and bar on-site are convenient since the hotel is situated far from the center of town. They also have an RV park on the property with 38 spots with full hookups (US$60/night).

Six miles east on the Mexico 3 to San Felipe is **Horsepower Ranch** (Mexico 3 Km. 9, tel. 646/151-2896, U.S. tel. 949/656-1088, www. hprbaja.com, US$150), a classic spot for off-roaders. The 40-hectare ranch has 49 rooms and is home to many pre-race parties throughout the year. Room rates include breakfast and dinner.

Over US$200

The intimate hotel at **Punta Morro** (Mexico 1 Km. 106, tel. 646/178-3507, www.hotelpuntamorro.com, US$200) is smaller in size than most of the other higher-end hotels in Ensenada. Rooms are nicely appointed, and they have a range of units from studios to three-bedroom suites, making it a great spot for families or groups to stay. The entire property has beautiful ocean views, and the restaurant attracts diners from both sides of the border who come to watch the waves crash onto the rocks as they enjoy a gourmet meal.

Some of the nicest accommodations in Ensenada can be found north of town at **Hotel Coral & Marina** (Mexico 1 Km. 103 #4321, tel. 646/175-0000, www.hotelcoral.com, US$205). With the black leather couches, modern light fixtures, and sleek modern design, the swanky vibe is something you would be more likely to find in Las Vegas or Cabo rather than Ensenada. The hotel has its own marina, indoor and outdoor pools, a covered parking area, and a grill and bar on the property.

INFORMATION AND SERVICES

Ensenada is a large city for Baja and there are a number of banks, ATMs, markets, and stores. There are plenty of gas stations and service shops.

Tourist Assistance

There's an office for **Proturismo de Ensenada** (Blvd. Lázaro Cárdenas 540, tel. 646/178-2411, 8am-8pm Mon.-Fri., 8am-6pm Sat.-Sun.) conveniently located near the fish market with a number of brochures about the area and a helpful staff that speaks English.

Emergencies

Hospital Velmar (De Las Arenas 151, tel. 646/173-4500, www.hospitalvelmar.com) is open 24 hours and can handle emergency services.

Organized Tours

Foodies won't want to visit Ensenada without taking a culinary tour of the city. **Baja Test Kitchen** (www.bajatestkitchen.com) offers an "Ensenada Eats" tour, visiting some of the cities best street food carts and breweries. They can also arrange for wine-tasting tours of the Valle de Guadalupe departing from Ensenada.

GETTING THERE

Outside of the cruise ship passengers, most visitors arriving on their own in Ensenada come by private car. Ensenada is just two hours south of San Diego and a popular weekend destination. From San Diego, travelers take Mexico 1 along the coast until arriving in town. There is bus service from other large cities in Baja through companies such as **Autobuses de la Baja California** (ABC, tel. 664/104-7400, www.abc.com.mx) and **Aguila** (tel. 800/824-8452, www.autobusesaguila.com). The **Central de Autobuses bus station** is on Calle 11 and Avenida Riveroll.

GETTING AROUND

Most everything in downtown Ensenada can be easily explored on foot. A car is necessary to visit La Bufadora or some of the restaurants and breweries north of town. Taxis can be found along López Mateos or at the bus station on Calle 11 and Avenida Riveroll. Negotiate the fare before getting in.

OJOS NEGROS

A drive out east on the southern branch of Mexico 3 (heading toward San Felipe) will bring travelers to the small dusty town of Ojos Negros. This agricultural region was named "black eyes" for all of the wells in the area that look like black eyes from up above. Just east of the town is Rancho la Campaña, better know these days as the home of Ramonetti cheeses and **La Cava de Marcelo** (Mexico 3 Km. 43, 646/117-0293, www.lacavademarcelo.com, 12:30pm-6pm Thurs.-Sun., tour and cheese tasting US$10). Since 1911, the Ramonetti family has been making cheese on the large dairy farm. Visitors can take an interesting tour of the farm to see the cows and learn about the cheese-making process. At the end of the tour, visitors go underground to have a wine and cheese tasting and to see the cheese cave, which can hold up to 10,000 wheels of cheese. They've opened a restaurant on the property, so visitors can enjoy farm-fresh food at the tables under the trees outdoors.

ISLA GUADALUPE

Isla Guadalupe is a volcanic island 350 kilometers southwest of Ensenada. It is home to one of the largest populations of great white sharks on the planet. Coupled with the large number of sharks are the clear waters with up to 45-meter visibility, which make this remote island one of the best shark destinations. Multiday live-aboard cage diving tours take place July through November. **Islander Charters** (tel. 619/224-4388, www.islander-charters.com) has vessels that depart directly from San Diego. They've been featured on National Geographic, The History Channel, and Shark Week on the Discovery Channel. **Great White Adventures** (www.greatwhite-adventures.com) and **Nautilus Explorer** (www.guadalupegreatwhitesharks.com) bus clients down to Ensenada where they depart in vessels to Isla Guadalupe.

Valle de Guadalupe

East of Ensenada, La Ruta del Vino takes travelers into Baja's rapidly growing wine region, the Valle de Guadalupe. Here, dirt roads wind through the arid valley bringing travelers to beautiful boutique wineries serving award-winning wines. Outdoor *campestre* restaurants allow diners to look out at the vineyards while enjoying gourmet farm-to-table food prepared by the best chefs in the country. Luxury B&Bs give travelers time to truly absorb the intimate tranquility and beauty of the region.

This is an area unparalleled on the rest of the peninsula, and the whole world is taking notice. In the past few years, the region has gained attention through the likes of the *New York Times, Wall Street Journal, Vogue, Condé Nast Traveler,* as well as from renowned chefs like Anthony Bourdain and Rick Bayless. It's been referred to as the "Napa of Baja" and the "Tuscany of Mexico," but anyone intimate with the Valle de Guadalupe will tell you that this is a unique place with its own rustic charm, friendly spirit, and an essence that is distinctively Mexican.

Wine has been made in this region for well over 100 years, but it's just been in the past 20 years that the new wine movement has brought so much attention to the valley. Characterized by boutique wineries producing small batches of high-quality wines, this new wine movement paved the way for a foodie movement as well. Chefs came to the valley to open *campestre* restaurants—open-air venues serving regional seafood and meats cooked on wood fires, fresh vegetables from the garden, and locally made cheeses and olive oil.

There are now over 120 wineries here. Weekends are the best for finding them all open—they are also the busiest time for tourists to visit and people from Southern California to come down. If you have flexibility with your schedule, Thursday and Friday are days when most wineries and restaurants will be open and you won't have to deal with the weekend crowds. Many restaurants and wineries are closed on Monday.

Summer has traditionally been considered the peak season for the valley, because the vineyards are full of grapes and the harvest begins in August. Coinciding with the beginning of harvest season is the Fiestas de la Vendimia, the annual wine harvest festival. For two weeks, crowds converge on the region to enjoy festivals, parties, dinners, and lots of wine. This is by far the busiest time to visit the valley, and reservations for hotels must be made nearly a year in advance. If you're unable to get a hotel in the valley, check accommodations in nearby Ensenada or Rosarito. In addition to the crowds, summer can also bring temperatures of well over 100 degrees. Now that the valley is becoming better known and restaurants and wineries are open year-round, it's more pleasant to avoid the heat and the crowds and visit in the fall or spring.

★ LA RUTA DEL VINO

La Ruta del Vino, The Wine Route, is the name given to the collection of wineries and restaurants in the Valle de Guadalupe that are now drawing visitors from all over the world. There are over 120 wineries in the Valle de Guadalupe, ranging in size from small micro wineries to large commercial wineries. Many visitors to the Valle will agree that the charm and soul of the region lies in the small and medium boutique wineries where the winemakers are often found around the property, and visitors will get a more unique and personal experience in the tasting room.

There are only three paved roads in the Valle de Guadalupe, the rest of the valley is a network of unnamed dirt roads. A day wine tasting in the Valle often requires winding along dirt roads (seemingly lost) before arriving at a stunning boutique winery or campestre restaurant with gourmet food. There

Valle de Guadalupe and the Ruta del Vino

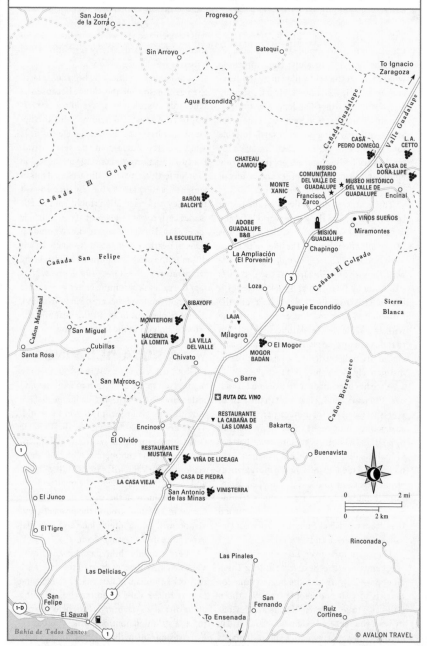

San José de la Zorra
Progreso
Sin Arroyo
Batequí
To Ignacio Zaragoza
Agua Escondida
Cañada Guadalupe
Valle Guadalupe
CASA PEDRO DOMECQ
L. A. CETTO
Cañada El Golpe
CHATEAU CAMOU
MUSEO COMUNITARIO DEL VALLE DE GUADALUPE
LA CASA DE DOÑA LUPE
MUSEO HISTÓRICO DEL VALLE DE GUADALUPE
MONTE XANIC
Francisco Zarco
Encinal
BARÓN BALCH'É
Cañada San Felipe
ADOBE GUADALUPE B&B
VIÑOS SUEÑOS
Miramontes
LA ESCUELITA
La Ampliación (El Porvenir)
MISIÓN GUADALUPE
Chapingo
Cañada El Colgado
Loza
BIBAYOFF
MONTEFIORI
LAJA
Milagros
Aguaje Escondido
Sierra Blanca
Cañón Matajanal
San Miguel
HACIENDA LA LOMITA
LA VILLA DEL VALLE
Chivato
El Mogor
MOGOR BADÁN
Santa Rosa
Cubillas
San Marcos
Barre
Cañón Borreguero
RUTA DEL VINO
Encinos
RESTAURANTE LA CABAÑA DE LAS LOMAS
Bakarta
El Olvido
RESTAURANTE MUSTAFA
VIÑA DE LICEAGA
Buenavista
CASA DE PIEDRA
LA CASA VIEJA
San Antonio de las Minas
VINISTERRA
El Junco
0   2 mi
0   2 km
El Tigre
Rinconada
Las Pinales
Las Delicias
San Felipe
San Fernando
Ruiz Cortines
El Sauzal
To Ensenada
Bahía de Todos Santos
© AVALON TRAVEL

Mexican Wines

Ninety percent of the wines from Mexico come from this region, and 96 percent of the wines that are produced here go to one place—Mexico City. There's such a demand for wines from Valle de Guadalupe in the restaurants in Mexico City that wineries have a difficult time producing enough to fulfill orders. That means there isn't much left over for distribution anywhere else, which is why Mexican wines haven't received much exposure outside of the country.

Most non-Mexican citizens are surprised to learn that Mexico has such a vibrant wine industry. While many of the varietals from this area will be familiar to U.S. citizens, other grapes that thrive in the region, such as the Spanish tempranillo and the Italian nebbiolo, may be new to some wine drinkers. In addition, many of the wines coming out of this region are blends (as opposed to monovarietals), which means that the winemakers are creating unique taste profiles that you won't find anywhere else.

The one factor that keeps Mexican wine production limited is the lack of water in the region. All of the water in the Valle de Guadalupe comes from private wells and underground rivers and aquifers, which have been at very low levels due to recent years of drought. Even those with a well on their property may not be able to use it if they don't have the water rights.

Most of the wineries in the Valle de Guadalupe are small producers, making only a few thousand cases every year. U.S. citizens crossing at the California border may only bring back one liter of alcohol per adult into the U.S. every 30 days (a wine bottle is 750 ml).

are a series of blue signs designating the turn offs from the paved roads for various wineries and restaurants. From here, you'll need to keep an eye out for any private signs that the business has put up along the road directing you to the property. Some of the individual establishments that are more difficult to find will have maps and more precise directions on their website or Facebook page. Because many of the best wineries and restaurants are tucked away out of sight from the paved roads, it's a good idea to have picked out a few wineries ahead of time that you know you'd like to visit. Calling ahead to make a reservation or to at least make sure that the winery will be able to receive you on the day that you desire is a good idea as well. Those who simply drive around the valley in hopes of stumbling across good wineries may find themselves frustrated and disappointed.

Wineries

LAS NUBES

First-time travelers, frequent visitors, and locals all find themselves enjoying the fantastic views and good wine at **Las Nubes** (tel. 646/156-8037, www.vinoslasnubesbc.com,

11am-5pm daily). Owner and winemaker Victor Segura not only creates easy-to-drink wines, but has established a welcoming environment for all guests. Perched on the northern hillside of the valley, the beautiful stone winery (all of the stones used to build it were mined from the property) offers sweeping views from the large outdoor terrace and the chic indoor tasting room. It's easy to understand where the name Las Nubes, meaning "The Clouds," came from when you're standing out on the terrace looking at the scenic vista of the valley and feeling the gentle breeze. The friendly staff, affordable tastings, large space, and good wines make this spot a favorite for many valley visitors.

BODEGAS F. RUBIO

Just east of Las Nubes, family-operated **Bodegas F. Rubio** (tel. 646/156-8046, www.bodegasfrubio.com, noon-6pm Thurs., noon-7pm Fri.-Sun.) has a nice indoor facility as well as an outdoor patio for wine-tasting. Try their montepulciano wine, an Italian red grape that isn't available anywhere else in the valley. There's a restaurant that's open on the weekends, serving well-crafted gourmet bistro fare. They open later in the day and stay open until 7pm on the weekends, so this is one of the few places in the valley to visit past 5pm once most of the other wineries have closed.

VENA CAVA

The unique architecture is part of the allure for **Vena Cava** (tel. 646/156-8053, www.venacavawine.com, 11am-5pm daily, tastings on the hour). The wine cave is dug out of the hillside and topped off with decommissioned wooden fishing boats from Ensenada. Winemaker Phil Gregory is often around the winery regaling guests with stories and talking about his winemaking process. He and his wife Eileen are the owners of four of the valley's most beloved businesses, all on the same property—Vena Cava winery, La Villa del Valle B&B, Corazón de Tierra restaurant, and TROIKa food truck. Favorite wines at Vena Cava are the tempranillo, the "Big Blend" red, and the special espumoso brut rosé (one of only two sparkling wines produced in the Valle de Guadalupe).

ALXIMIA

Looking somewhat like an adobe spaceship, **Alximia** (Camino Vecinal al Tigre Km. 3, tel. 646/127-1453, www.alximia.com, 11am-6pm daily) is a winery that comes from a family of scientists. Winemaker Alvaro Alvarez is a former mathematician, his father was an astronomer at the National Observatory in the San Pedro Mártir, and his mother was a schoolteacher. Alximia means the chemist, and the main wines produced here are named after the four elements (earth, water, air, and fire) and created by drawing on Alvaro's background in chemistry. Restaurant La Terrasse San Roman is located on the outdoor patio of the winery.

LECHUZA

Family-operated **Lechuza** (tel. 646/947-6315, www.vinoslechuza.com, open daily by appointment only) offers a tranquil setting for enjoying some of the best wines coming out of the Valle de Guadalupe. This small boutique winery takes great care in making its wines, which have become insider favorites. Appointments are required for tastings, but you'll receive personal attention as you learn directly from the family about their wines and become familiar with their process and facility.

VINOS PIJOAN

Visitors will feel comfortably at home at the intimate winery at **Vinos Pijoan** (Carretera

Vena Cava is a winery constructed of old Ensenada fishing boats from the 1920s.

El Tigre Km. 13.5, tel. 646/127-1251, www.
vinospijoan.com, 10am-4pm Mon.-Fri., 11am-
5pm Sat.-Sun.). The inviting outdoor patio
creates a serene setting for enjoying wine,
looking out onto the vineyards. Pau Pijoan,
the owner/winemaker, is often around, and
Sharon and Arturo, who work in the tasting
room, are beloved by all patrons. If they aren't
too busy, ask them for a behind-the-scenes
tour of their unique wine cave.

VIÑAS DE GARZA

Serving up wine and beautiful vineyard
views from a covered deck, **Viñas de Garza**
(Mexico 3 Km. 87, tel. 646/175-8883, www.
vinosdegarza.com, 11am-4:30pm Fri.-Sun.)
offers an intimate and picturesque wine-tasting experience.

VINÍCOLA 3 MUJERES

Vinícola 3 Mujeres (Mexico 3 Km. 87,
tel. 646/171-5674, 10am-5pm daily) was
started in 2005 by three friends who met
studying winemaking at La Escuelita. Ivette
Vaillard, Eva Cotero Altamirano, and Laura
McGregor Garcia were the first women
winemakers in the region, and today they
serve their wines in a rustic and intimate
cave.

FINCA LA CARRODILLA
AND HACIENDA LA LOMITA

The rooftop garden at **Finca La Carrodilla**
(tel. 646/156-8052, 11am-4pm Wed.-Sun.)
looks out onto the gardens and vineyards
on the property. It's the perfect setting for
enjoying their organic biodynamic wines.
Their sister winery, **Hacienda La Lomita**
(tel. 646/156-8466, www.lomita.mx, 11am-
4pm Wed.-Thurs., 11am-6pm Fri.-Sun.), also
has an outdoor restaurant, **Traslomita** (tel.
646/156-8469, 1pm-7pm Thurs.-Mon.) on
the property.

VINÍCOLA TORRES
ALEGRE Y FAMILIA

The family-run **Vinícola Torres Alegre y
Familia** (tel. 646/688-1033, www.vinicola-
torresalegreyfamilia.com, 10am-5pm daily)
takes great care in making wines from de-
stemming the grapes to ensuring the flavors are perfectly balanced without adding
chemicals. The results are superb, creating some of the most well-respected wines
coming out of the valley. Family patriarch
Victor Torres Alegre studied winemaking
in Bordeaux, France, before returning to
Mexico to help revitalize the Mexican wine
industry.

The patio at Vinos Pijoan is a serene spot for wine tasting while enjoying views of the vineyards.

CHATEAU CAMOU

Nestled into its own little corner of the valley, **Chateau Camou** (tel. 646/156-8456, www.chateau-camou.com.mx, 10am-4pm daily) uses all French grapes and French winemaking techniques. The winery has been in operation for 20 years, and it's worth it to take a tour of the facilities, which include the large barrel room where classical music is played according to a weekly schedule in order to help with the stabilization process of the wine, getting the molecules of the wine and barrel to vibrate together. Make sure you get to see the impressive bottle room, home to almost 300,000 vessels arranged in fun designs on the walls.

CLOS DE TRES CANTOS

The unique pyramid-like architecture at **Clos de Tres Cantos** (tel. 558/568-9240, www.closdetrescantos.com, 10am-5pm Wed.-Sun.) continues underground into their wine caves below. If you're looking for a one-of-a-kind experience, pay to take the tour (all tour profits go to charity) to see the cave and underground "cathedral." They have two rooms available to rent for overnight stays on the property as well.

VILLA MONTEFIORI

With an Italian winemaker and varietals, **Villa Montefiori** (tel. 646/156-8020, www.villamontefiori.mx, 11am-5pm daily) creates "Mexican wines with an Italian heart." Winemaker Paolo Paoloni started growing grapes in the Valle de Guadalupe in 1997 and today uses the most modern technology available for his production. The tasting room is set up on the second story and boasts beautiful views of the valley from an outdoor patio. The Italian restaurant Tre Galline is on the same property.

TREVISTA

The personal attention and gracious hospitality are what keep visitors coming back to **Trevista** (tel. 646/156-8027, www.trevistavineyards.com, open weekends by appointment only). Owners Hilda and James take great care in growing their grapes, making their wines, and sharing their creations with visitors. Their tempranillo is a favorite of those familiar with Valle de Guadalupe wines. With advance notification, they can accommodate groups for food prepared skillfully by Hilda herself.

BODEGAS CIELI WINERY & BREWERY

If you have a beer lover in your group, head to **Bodegas Cieli Winery & Brewery** (Mexico 3 Km. 84.7, tel. 646/185-4478, www.cieliwinery.com, 11am-9pm Thurs.-Sat., 11am-6pm Sun.) where owner Ron McCabe creates both boutique wine and excellent craft beers. Perched up on the hill, the comfortable and relaxed environment offers beautiful views of the valley from the outdoor deck. This is one of the best spots in the valley to sit and relax during sunset while enjoying a drink in the company of friends. Ron used to own an Italian restaurant in the United States, and he regularly hosts special dinners and events at the bodega.

LA CETTO

For a larger more commercial experience, **LA Cetto** (Mexico 3 Km. 73.5, tel. 646/1155-2179, www.cettowines.com, 10am-5pm daily) has been around since 1928 and is one of the oldest and biggest wineries in the region. You can take a tour of the facility to learn about the winemaking process and then do a tasting afterward.

MONTE XANIC

Monte Xanic (tel. 646/155-2080, www.montexanic.com.mx, 10am-5pm daily) is another large winery experience, with beautiful views from a newly remodeled tasting room.

EL CIELO

El Cielo (Carretera El Tigre Km. 7.5, tel. 646/688-1902, www.vinoselcielo.com, 10am-8pm Mon.-Fri., 9am-9pm Sat., 9am-8pm Sun.) offers tastings and has the restaurant

School of Wine

One of the most important factors in the recent history of the Valle de Guadalupe is the wine school, **Estación de Oficios del Porvenir,** known affectionately as **"La Escuelita."** Highly respected winemaker Hugo D'Acosta started the nonprofit school in 2004 to promote the production of boutique wine and to educate locals about winemaking traditions. The idea was to create a place where the local farmers—who, at the time, were growing grapes for the few large wineries that existed—could learn how to cultivate grapes that were good for making wine and learn how to make wine themselves. La Escuelita offered them classes at an affordable price and access to winemaking machinery. The school was pivotal in the history of the valley in creating quality Mexican wines and opening the door for new winemakers. Today, a majority of the boutique wineries in the valley have winemakers who attended La Escuelita. The school still thrives and may be found in the town of El Porvenir. You'll recognize it by the eclectic architecture that features buildings constructed from different reclaimed materials.

Latitud 32 on the property as well as a large store selling wine and other regional products.

SIGHTS
Museo de la Vid y el Vino

To learn a bit about the history of wine and the Valle de Guadalupe, stop in at the **Museo de la Vid y el Vino** (Mexico 3 Km. 81.3, tel. 646/156-8165, www.museodelvinobc.com, 9am-5pm Tues.-Sun., US$3). The large, new facility also features an art gallery, garden, and outdoor amphitheater. All of the information is in Spanish, but the museum usually has a tour guide available who can walk you through the museum (for free) in English.

Misión Nuestra Señora de Guadalupe del Norte

The last mission founded in both Alta and Baja California was the **Misión Nuestra Señora de Guadalupe,** founded in 1834. Dominican Padre Felix Caballero oversaw the mission until his death (a possible poisoning) in 1840. The last of the missions on the peninsula closed down by 1849. Not much is left of this one, aside from the ruins of the foundation walls, which have been developed into a historical park with free admission, open during daylight hours. They are just off of the northern paved road in the town of Francisco Zarco.

ENTERTAINMENT AND EVENTS

There's no nightlife in the valley, in fact, once most of the restaurants close at 5pm, you'll be hard-pressed to find much open aside from restaurants. There are a few wineries that stick around until 7pm or 8pm, but that's the extent of the nightlife. Visitors staying overnight in the Valle de Guadalupe will find that a peaceful quiet falls upon the valley in the evenings after the last wineries have shut their doors.

For stunning sunset views over the Pacific, head to **Bar Bura** (Carretera Libre Tijuana-Ensenada Km. 89, www.cabanascuatrocuatros.com.mx, noon-9pm Fri.-Sun.), located on the **Cuatrocuatros** property. Perched on the cliffs looking down at the ocean, the completely open-air bar features breathtaking views. There are some tables and covered hay bales for seating, which are arranged under the canopies. They don't have a full menu at the bar (there's a full restaurant on another part of the property), but they do serve some appetizers like ceviche. They make their own wines on the property, which they serve along with other local wines and beverages. To get to the bar, you'll need to pay an entrance fee (US$5 for cars, US$10 for vans) and park at the viewpoint; you'll then be driven in one of their vehicles up to the bar.

The famous **Fiestas de la Vendimia** (wine harvest festival) takes place over two weeks every August. Coinciding with the beginning of the harvest season, the festival is a series of private parties and dinners held at the wineries and restaurants in the valley. There are two large events that bring together most of the wineries and huge crowds—the Muestra del Vino (wine-tasting), which opens the festival, and the famous **Concurso de Paella** (paella contest), which closes the festival. Tickets for events and parties are sold at a premium (starting around US$100). The Vendimia is considered one of Ensenada's most high-society events.

FOOD

When the Valle de Guadalupe started garnering international recognition for its wine in recent years, Baja chefs began flocking to the region to open restaurants. Many of these were built in the *campestre* (country) style, characterized by outdoor seating and local ingredients cooked over fire grills. Some restaurants that are entirely outdoor seating have reduced hours in the winter season, so inquire ahead of time if visiting at that time of year.

Chef Diego Hernandez creates exquisite local food at his restaurant ★ **Corazón de Tierra** (tel. 646/156-8030, www.corazon-detierra.com, info@corazondetierra.com, lunch seatings at 1:30pm and 4:30pm, dinner seatings at 6:30pm and 8:30pm Wed.-Mon., US$65). Vegetables and herbs come from the garden on the property and meats and fish are locally sourced. There's no menu—the six courses change daily depending on what's fresh and in season. Don't skip on doing the wine pairing with the meal. The pairings perfectly complement the food for a completely unforgettable experience. Even though this is upscale dining, the restaurant feels comfortable with bright mismatched fabric chairs and wooden tables. The floor-to-ceiling windows open up when the weather is warm for a complete open-air experience looking out onto the beautiful garden where much of the food for the meal comes from. Reservations should be made in advance.

On the same property, is the food truck of Diego Hernandez, **TROIKa** (tel. 646/156-8030, 1pm-7pm Thurs.-Sun., mains US$6-10). The project is a collaboration between Chef Hernandez, Vena Cava winery (on the same property), and Wendlandt brewery. The food truck is right outside of Vena Cava winery and serves gastropub fare like sliders with bacon marmalade and beer-battered tomatillos,

The Concurso de Paella is one of the largest and best events of the annual Fiestas de la Vendimia.

suckling pig tacos, and octopus tostadas. The *campestre* setting features picnic tables set under a canopy of woven repurposed irrigation tubing.

The *campestre* of Tijuana chef Javier Plascencia is ★ **Finca Altozano** (tel. 646/156-8045, www.fincaltozano.com, 1pm-9pm Tues.-Thurs., 1pm-10pm Fri.-Sat., noon-8pm Sun., mains US$9-14) where locals and visitors go for incredible food and a casual but chic atmosphere. The open-air restaurant features tables that look out onto the vineyards. Food is cooked over a wood-fire grill that produces unforgettable flavors. Don't miss the *pulpo del pacifico,* an octopus dish made with citrus sauce and peanuts. Other standouts on the menu are the brussels sprouts grilled with aioli and parmesan cheese, and the lamb *birria.* They've turned large wine barrels into lookouts with benches at the top that are scattered around the property. Grab a glass of wine and climb the stairs to enjoy your after-meal *vino* with views of the valley.

Located at Aliximia winery, **La Terrasse San Roman** (tel. 646/196-7803, www.laterrassesanroman.com, noon-8pm Wed.-Fri., 9am-8pm Sat., 9am-6pm Sun., mains US$9-16) offers diners the opportunity to enjoy their food on the deck overlooking the vineyards.

Chef Martin San Roman has created a menu of fresh local ingredients prepared with rich and decadent sauces. Enjoy elegant dishes like duck, escargot, and New York strip steak in a casual *campestre* environment.

The original haute dining experience in the valley was Chef Jair Tellez's **Laja** (Mexico 3 Km. 83, tel. 646/155-2556, www.lajamexico.com, 1:30pm-8:30pm Wed.-Sat., 1:30pm-5:30pm Sun.). Opened in 1999, Laja was the original farm-to-table restaurant here and for decades was the only option for gourmet dining in the region. Because of this, Laja was often referenced as the "French Laundry" of the Valle de Guadalupe. Today, it remains on the list as one of the top 50 restaurants in Latin America. The fixed menu changes daily depending on what's in season and growing in the garden. The intimate restaurant is simple but elegant and sets the mood for the fresh food and local wines.

Tijuana chef Miguel Angel Guerrero brings his "BajaMed" style of food to the valley with **La Esperanza** (Mexico 3 Km. 73.5, tel. 664/143-0999, 12:30pm-9pm Wed.-Thurs., 12:30pm-10pm Fri.-Sat., 12:30pm-8pm Sun., mains US$9-15). The rustic industrial setting looks out over the vineyards and offers both indoor and outdoor seating. Because they are

Corazón de Tierra serves gourmet food that comes from the restaurant's own garden and other local sources.

located on the L.A. Cetto property, they only serve L.A. Cetto wines.

Locals and foodies head to **La Cocina de Doña Esthela** (tel. 646/156-8453, 8am-6pm Tues.-Sun., mains US$5-9) for some of the best breakfasts on the entire peninsula. The signature *machaca con huevos* is a dish that shouldn't be missed. Everything served here is made in house from the savory meat dishes to the fresh tortillas. They're also open for lunch. Doña Esthela herself is there most of the time, checking on customers to make sure they have everything they need. Don't expect a fancy setting, the operation started with Esthela serving food out of her kitchen to local patrons. They've expanded to multiple dining rooms and a large new outdoor patio space, but it still features the same warm hospitality and homemade cooking. If visiting on the weekend, go early—this has become a popular spot with locals and travelers, so long waits can now be expected on Saturday and Sunday.

Visitors have the option of dining à la carte or choosing from a seven- or 10-course experience at **Malva** (Mexico 3 Km. 96, tel. 646/155-3085, www.malvarestaurant.com, 1pm-9pm Wed.-Sun.). Chef Roberto Alcocer has an impressive background and brings his experience and creativity to all of the detailed dishes on the menu. The beautiful outdoor deck with a tall palapa roof is nestled into a grove of trees overlooking the valley, and gives the sensation of being in an exclusive tree house. They have local wines on the menu, including some from Mina Penélope, the winery on the same property.

On the property of Mogor Badan winery, **Deckman's en el Mogor** (Mexico 3 Km. 85.5, tel. 646/188-3960, www.deckmans.com, 1pm-8pm Sat.-Mon. and Wed.-Thurs., 1pm-7pm Fri.) is an outdoor *campestre* experience, set under the trees and looking out over the vineyards. Chef Drew Deckman serves sustainable local ingredients including fresh seafoods like oysters, octopus, and king crab.

Another option for *campestre* dining under the trees is **El Pinar de 3 Mujeres** (Mexico 3 Km. 87, tel. 646/101-5268, ismene.venegas@gmail.com, 1pm-6pm Fri.-Sun. from spring to fall, winter by appointment only) on the property of Tres Mujeres winery. Patrons sit under a canopy of pine trees and dine on six courses (with a choice of fish, meat, or vegetarian for the main course) from Chef Ismene.

ACCOMMODATIONS

In keeping with the intimate feeling of the area, most accommodations in Valle de

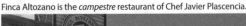

Finca Altozano is the *campestre* restaurant of Chef Javier Plascencia.

Guadalupe are small (fewer than 10 rooms) so they tend to book up quickly, especially during summer weekends and holidays. Visitors used to traveling in other parts of Baja may also be surprised to find the expensive prices. Rates are higher on weekends, so you'll be able to find cheaper rooms Sunday-Thursday. Prices peak during the Fiestas de la Vendimia in August. Be aware that many of the nice hotels require a two-night minimum stay during peak season. Even the nicest will not have televisions, and wireless Internet is often unreliable.

Under US$100

With a central location that's easy to find just off the highway, **Rancho Maria Teresa** (Mexico 3 Km. 82.5, tel. 646/688-1020, www.ranchomariateresa.com, US$62-78) has 27 rooms and two villas. The grounds are extremely lush for the area with palms and citrus trees all around. The property is large with mountain bike trails, two pools and Jacuzzis, and plenty of picnic areas with barbecues. Be aware that during the summers, the ranch doubles as a *balneario,* where families can come for the day between 9am and 6pm to enjoy the pools and picnic areas.

One of the most popular budget options

in the valley is **El Meson del Vino** (Mexico 3 Km. 88, tel. 646/151-2137, www.hotelmesondelvino.com, US$70). There are 12 basic rooms as well as a small swimming pool and a restaurant that's open for breakfast. This is one of the few properties in the valley that allows pets.

For a unique experience, **Glamping Ruta de Arte y Vino** (Tecate Km. 13, tel. 646/185-3352, rutadearteyvino@gmail.com, US$40) has five Airstreams that guests stay in for a fun, rustic experience. Camping is also allowed on the property.

US$100-200

There are four sustainable *cabañas* with a light and airy design at **Casa Mayoral** (tel. 664/257-2410, www.casamayoral.com, US$150). The cabins all have air-conditioning, large bathrooms, plenty of windows, high ceilings, and patios. Breakfast is included in your stay. There are plenty of tables and seating under the shade of tall eucalyptus trees where you can enjoy the serene setting, or grab a bike or spend some time hiking around the 10 hectares of property.

In the little town of Francisco Zarco, **Viñedos Malagon** (Calle Sexta 75, tel.

Patrons eat *al fresco* at Malva restaurant.

646/155-2102, www.vinedosmalagon.com, US$125) has a three-room bed-and-breakfast, serving some of the best breakfast in the valley. The 100-year-old ranch sits on 400 acres where they have their own vineyards and make their own wine.

There are five rooms at boutique hotel **Terra del Valle** (San José de la Zorra Road, tel. 646/117-3645, www.terradelvalle.com, US$195). The peaceful property and has wireless access throughout, and bikes are available for guests to use to visit nearby wineries and restaurants. Breakfast is served in the mornings with freshly squeezed orange juice. There's a communal grill and refrigerator for those who want to prepare their own food. The personal attention of the owners Ana and Nacho is what keeps guests returning.

Hotel Boutique Valle de Guadalupe (Camino de los Ranchos 1, tel. 646/155-2164, www.hoteldelvalledeguadalupe.com.mx, US$190-240) has a newer property, but is not necessarily well maintained. The ample grounds provide a pool, large lawns, and plenty of areas for sitting and lounging. There are free bikes that guests can use, as well as stables with horses on the grounds. The open-air **Fuego** restaurant on the second floor has views of the valley.

Over US$200

The wonderfully serene ★ **La Villa del Valle** (tel. 646/156-8007, www.lavilladelvalle.com, US$245) will make you feel like you've been transported to a residence in Tuscany. The well-curated B&B is on the same property as Corazón de Tierra restaurant, Vena Cava winery, and TROIKa food truck. Owners Phil and Eileen Gregory have created a relaxing sanctuary where guests can sip on a glass of wine while overlooking the valley or enjoy a refreshing dip in the swimming pool. Guests start their mornings with a full breakfast and spend their evenings enjoying a *botana* and a glass of wine. A complimentary wine-tasting at Vena Cava winery is included with a stay at the villa.

The chic five-room **Bruma** (Mexico 3 Km. 75, tel. 646/116-8031, www.bruma.mx, US$290) is situated on the east side of the valley on 80 hectares. The beautiful eco-architecture features stone construction and large windows to take advantage of the natural setting. Breakfast for two is included in the room rate. There's a pool and Jacuzzi, common areas, and bicycles to use.

Chef Javier Plascencia, who has Finca Altozano in the valley, brings guests **Finca la Divina** (Mexico 3 Km. 93.5, tel. 646/155-3238,

The chic eco cabins at Casa Mayoral have private decks looking out onto the valley.

www.fincaladivina.com, US$235-250), a three-bedroom home turned into a beautiful bed-and-breakfast. Common areas include a kitchen, large living room with fireplace, and an outdoor area with a pool, Jacuzzi, and barbecue. Breakfast is available in the morning for an additional US$12.

Grupo Maglen (tel. 646/120-5372, www.grupomaglen.com, US$200-250) operates three boutique properties in the valley: **Villas Maglen, El Encinal,** and **Tesela.** Each only has a handful of accommodations, but features modern and well-appointed rooms with wireless Internet, minibars, safes, coffeemakers, and room service.

The Spanish-style **Hacienda Guadalupe** (Mexico 3 Km. 81.5, tel. 646/155-2859, www.haciendaguadalupe.com, US$240) has 12 rooms that all have king-size beds with new down comforters, air-conditioning and heating, in-room safes, and Saltillo-tiled floors. There's a pool and Jacuzzi on the property as well as a good restaurant that serves breakfast, lunch, and dinner. The winery on the property, Melchum, has wine-tastings for US$9.

The eco-lofts at **Encuentro Guadalupe** (Mexico 3 Km. 75, tel. 646/155-2775, www.grupoencuentro.com.mx, recepcionencuentro@gmail.com, US$385) are individual cabins perched on the hillside each with their own terrace and fire pit. The units are simple, mixing rustic with contemporary style. As the units are located on a steep hillside, many guests find it challenging to get around from the rooms down to the reception and bar area. Some customers enjoy the rustic nature of the hotel, while others feel the price is too high for what they get in return.

Another option that's been around in the Valle de Guadalupe for a number of years is **Adobe Guadalupe** (tel. 646/155-2094, www.adobeguadalupe.com, US$275). The bed-and-breakfast also has a winery, restaurant, and food truck on the property.

Just outside of the valley, ★ **Cuatrocuatros** (El Tigre, Carretera Libre Km. 89, tel. 646/174-6789, www.cabanascuatrocuatros.com.mx, US$200-215) offers glamping in 12 platform cabana tents. The *cabañas* have air-conditioning, minibars, fireplaces, and private terraces. The impressive property offers stunning views from their bar on the cliffs overlooking the Pacific.

INFORMATION AND SERVICES

There are no ATMs in the valley. Many of the wineries do not accept credit cards, so

the view from the bar at Cuatrocuatros

be sure to get cash in Ensenada or Rosarito before arriving in the Valle de Guadalupe. There is a gas station located in the town of San Antonio de las Minas and another in Francisco Zarco.

Organized Wine Tours

Since most of the Valle de Guadalupe is unmarked dirt roads without signs, it can be challenging for first-time visitors to navigate the valley on their own. If it's your first time to the Valle de Guadalupe and you want to make the most of your experience, it's best to take an organized wine tour. This also alleviates the problem of needing a designated driver for a day of wine-tasting. **Baja Test Kitchen** (www.bajatestkitchen.com) operates single- or multiday tours that can originate in either San Diego or anywhere in northern Baja for groups of 2 to 25 people. The owners are residents of the region and have close relationships with many of the winemakers and restaurateurs in the valley, so guests get a very personal and unique experience.

GETTING THERE AND AROUND

You will need to drive or take a private vehicle to get to the wineries and restaurants in the valley. There are only three paved roads in the Valle de Guadalupe—otherwise the entire valley consists of unmarked dirt roads. The government has been better about marking wineries and restaurants—look for blue signs around the valley marking establishments. Four-wheel drive is not necessary.

Mexicali, San Felipe, and Sierra de Juárez

Look for ★ to find recommended sights, activities, dining, and lodging.

Highlights

★ **La Chinesca:** The largest Chinatown in all of Mexico, La Chinesca supports over 200 restaurants. This Chinese cuisine has absorbed some Mexican flavors and ingredients over time to synthesize a unique fare found only here (page 108).

★ **Cañon de Guadalupe:** Camp with your own private natural hot springs tub, tucked away in a palm-studded valley of the Sierra de Juárez (page 114).

★ **San Felipe *Malecón*:** Have dinner overlooking the Sea of Cortez and watch as local *pangas* come in from a day of fishing (page 118).

★ **Valle de los Gigantes:** Just south of San Felipe, this valley is filled with giant cardón cacti that can grow up to 18 meters tall (page 123).

★ **Bahía San Luis Gonzaga:** This remote bay is popular with campers, anglers, and those looking to get away from modern distractions (page 124).

The border town of Mexicali operates as the gateway to Baja California, the Sea of Cortez, and mainland Mexico.

This is a varied region, rich with natural resources. Agricultural lands surround Mexicali and farming helps to drive the local economy. The fertile lands extend south to the Río Hardy and the Colorado River Delta, home to some of the best fishing and hunting in all of Mexico. This region empties out into the top part of the Gulf of California or the Sea of Cortez. The Sea of Cortez is a 1,100-kilometer-long body of water that separates the Baja peninsula from the rest of Mexico. It's one of the most diverse seas on earth. People flock to it for the incredible fishing, diving, kayaking, snorkeling, and beautiful beaches and landscapes.

Situated along the northern part of the Sea of Cortez, the fishing village of San Felipe is just a few hours' drive from the border. The nearby beaches and seaside settlements are a popular destination for expats and travelers because of the warm winters and the relaxed pace of life. The road from San Felipe is now paved all the way south to Bahía San Luis Gonzaga, providing easy access to the region and the Sea of Cortez. What used to require

four-wheel drive and a full day of patience behind the wheel is now accessible in any vehicle in just a few hours.

Inland from the Sea of Cortez, the mountains of the Sierra de Juárez provide a different type of beauty. The range contains the Cañon de Guadalupe with hot springs nestled into rocks and shaded by palm trees. The region also lures visitors with waterfalls, hiking, swimming, and rock art sites. At a higher elevation, the Constitución de 1857 National Park shows travelers a different type of scenery not seen often in Baja with coniferous trees and large granite rock formations.

This area is perfect for a road trip, and adventure seekers will have plenty to explore. While most of Baja California is situated along Mexico 1, this northeastern region is a separate and unique pocket that's worth getting to know.

PLANNING YOUR TIME

Mexicali is about a two-hour drive from downtown San Diego and often used as a

---

Previous: the fishing village of San Felipe; Bahía San Luis Gonzaga. **Above:** Valle de los Gigantes.

Mexicali to San Felipe

← To San Diego

CALIFORNIA

UNITED STATES

MEXICO

Calexico

111

7

98

8

To Tucson

Yuma

Algodones

Cuidad Morelos

BORDER CROSSINGS

LA CHINESCA

2D

TOLL

← To Tecate

MEXICALI

2

Benito Juárez

2

6

San Luis Río Colorado

95

ARIZONA

Rio Colorado

2

To Nogales →

CAÑON DE GUADALUPE

Cañon de Guadalupe

5

Laguna Salada

Colonia La Puerta

Delta

3

Guadalupe Vitoria

RIO HARDY

Sierra de Juárez

Guardines de la Patria

Rancho Mil

Rio Colorado

Desierto del Altar

40

BAJA CALIFORNIA

SONORA

To Ensenada

3

Héroes de Independencia

La Ventana

Isla Montague

Isla Pelicano

Golfo de Santa Clara

Boca La Bahía

Bahía Ometepec

Valle La Trinidad

Lázaro Cárenas

San Matias

3

El Michoacano

El Crucero la Trinidad

5

Sierra San Felipe

Salinas Ometepec

Esteros La Ramada

Sea of Cortez (Gulf of California)

0   10 mi
0   10 km

Sierra San Pedro Mártir National Park

NATIONAL OBSERVATORY

Picacho del Diablo

SAN FELIPE MALECÓN

San Felipe

To BAHÍA SAN LUIS GONZAGA

VALLE DE LOS GIGANTES

Punta Estrella

© AVALON TRAVEL

Best Accommodations

★ **Lucerna Mexicali:** Luxuriate in resort-style accommodations within the city of Mexicali. The lush grounds feature a nice pool area, and the rooms are modern, comfortable, and outfitted with high-quality furniture (page 113).

★ **Fiesta Inn Mexicali:** This popular spot is conveniently located with comfortable, modern rooms and a delicious breakfast buffet (113).

★ **Casa la Vida:** These San Felipe vacation suites all look out over the Sea of Cortez and provide a friendly and relaxing atmosphere for a stay (page 121).

★ **Hotel Riviera Coral:** With basic amenities and clean rooms, this spot is great for travelers on a budget (121).

★ **Hacienda Don Jesus:** Just a block away from the malecon, this hacienda-style hotel has a fun pool area and ample parking (121).

gateway city for travelers heading on to mainland Mexico or to San Felipe. Many just spend a night passing through (if they stop at all), but there's enough in Mexicali to fill a weekend. As the capital of the state of Baja California, the city operates mostly on business tourism, so hotel rates drop on the weekends, providing the perfect excuse to linger over one, enjoying the unique cuisine and craft beers that the city has to offer.

The most popular weekend trip is to head to San Felipe. Most of the region along the coast down to Bahía San Luis Gonzaga can be easily explored over the course of a few days now that the road is paved all the way to Gonzaga. With a few more days, add in side trips to Cañon de Guadalupe or to the Río Hardy.

GETTING THERE
Starting Points

Many travelers to this region drive from San Diego or other parts of Southern California or Arizona. Mexicali is the easiest border crossing to use to access any of this area from the United States. Mexico 3 connects the region from Ensenada and the coast of northern Baja on the Pacific side.

CAR

The easiest way to get to this region and to get around is by car. To reach Mexicali from San Diego, take I-8 to Route 111 south where you will drive right into the Mexicali west border crossing. To reach the Mexicali east crossing, continue on the I-8 to Route 7 south.

Taking Mexico 5 south out of Mexicali will lead you directly to the Río Hardy region and then on to San Felipe and Bahía San Luis Gonzaga. Mexico 5 is paved all the way to Bahía San Luis Gonzaga. The pavement ends shortly after Gonzaga, before 5 reconnects with Mexico 1.

Fuel and Services

Gas is easy to find in Mexicali and San Felipe. It's always a good idea to fuel up before leaving any city in Baja, so fill the tank before leaving Mexicali to head over to the Sierra de Juárez or south toward the Río Hardy or San Felipe. If you are going to Río Hardy, the closest gas station is at kilometer 30 on Mexico 5. Gas prices in northern Baja fluctuate, so if you are driving down across the border, you may want to fill up in Calexico before crossing to Mexicali.

Best Restaurants

★ **Tacos del Ferrocarril:** This row of taco stands has been serving up lamb *barbacoa* and *cabeza de res* tacos since 1976 (page 112).

★ **Museo del Valle de Mexicali:** Stop in for authentic *menudo* and a mini-museum (page 111).

★ **Pekin Restaurant:** Sample from a large menu with traditional Chinese dishes as well as unique Mexican/Chinese creations like Chinese chipotle shrimp (page 110).

★ **Mariscos La Vaquita:** Lobster, seafood cocktails, and large steamed clam platters are local favorites at this San Felipe seafood restaurant (page 120).

★ **Taqueria y Mariscos Adriana:** Rumored to be the fish taco stand that inspired the Rubio's chain in the United States, this taquería has fish tacos so fresh and good it doesn't even matter if the rumors are true (page 120).

AIR

The **General Rodolfo Sánchez Taboada International Airport (MXL)** just outside of Mexicali is the only commercial airport in the region. The airport serves cities in mainland Mexico as well as a flight to La Paz, BCS. There are currently no flights outside of Mexico.

BUS

Greyhound (www.greyhound.com.mx) has service to Mexicali from San Diego and Los Angeles. Once you are in Mexicali, **Autobuses de la Baja California** (ABC, tel. 664/104-7400 or toll-free tel. 800/025-0222, www.abc.com.mx) provides regional service to San Felipe.

Mexicali

As the capital of the state of Baja California Norte, business, and not tourism, has historically been the focus for Mexicali. But that's not to say that the city doesn't have anything to offer travelers. In fact, travelers visiting Mexicali may find that they get a more authentic experience of Baja, because the city is not entirely focused on tourism.

Mexicali was founded in 1903 by a group of American, Chinese, Indian, and Japanese immigrants. The Chinese came to Mexicali as laborers in the late 1880s to install farming irrigation for the Colorado River Land Company. Today Mexicali is home to Mexico's largest Chinatown, La Chinesca. Many travelers are fascinated by the Chinese food in Mexicali that has been heavily influenced by Mexican flavors and ingredients, thereby becoming its own unique creation. Mexicali is also is becoming well known as a destination for its emerging (and high-quality) craft brewery scene.

The Mexicali metropolitan area has a population of nearly one million, but this is a big city with a small-town feel and extremely friendly people (known as *Cachanillas*). With wide streets lined with palm trees and courteous locals, Mexicali is an agreeable place. Even though it's one of the largest cities in Baja, Mexicali is easy to navigate and even to

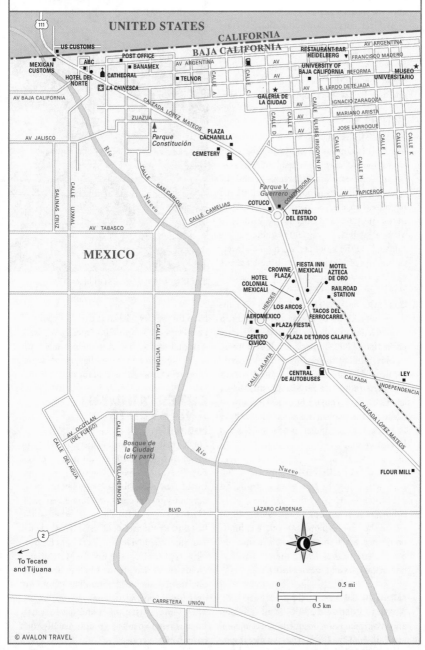

Mexicali

UNITED STATES

CALIFORNIA

BAJA CALIFORNIA

MEXICO

US CUSTOMS
MEXICAN CUSTOMS
POST OFFICE
ABC
BANAMEX
HOTEL DEL NORTE
CATHEDRAL
LA CHINESCA
TELNOR
AV ARGENTINA
AV BAJA CALIFORNIA
CALZADA LÓPEZ MATEOS
ZUAZUA
Parque Constitución
PLAZA CACHANILLA
CEMETERY
AV JALISCO
SALINAS CRUZ
CALLE UXMAL
CALLE SAN CARLOS
Río Nuevo
AV TABASCO
CALLE CAMELIAS
COTUCO
Parque V. Guerrero
COMPRESORA
TEATRO DEL ESTADO

RESTAURANT-BAR HEIDELBERG
FRANCISCO MADERO
AV ARGENTINA
UNIVERSITY OF BAJA CALIFORNIA
REFORMA
MUSEO UNIVERSITARIO
GALERÍA DE LA CIUDAD
S. LERDO DE TEJADA
IGNACIO ZARAGOZA
MARIANO ARISTA
JOSE LARROQUE
CALLE A
CALLE C
CALLE D
CALLE E
CALLE ULISE IRIGOYEN (F)
CALLE G
CALLE H
CALLE I
CALLE J
CALLE K
AV TAPICEROS

MEXICO

CROWNE PLAZA
FIESTA INN MEXICALI
MOTEL AZTECA DE ORO
HOTEL COLONIAL MEXICALI
RAILROAD STATION
HEROES
LOS ARCOS
TACOS DEL FERROCARRIL
AEROMÉXICO
PLAZA FIESTA
CENTRO CIVICO
PLAZA DE TOROS CALAFIA
CALLE VICTORIA
CALLE CALAFIA
CENTRAL DE AUTOBUSES
CALZADA
LEY
INDEPENDENCIA
CALZADA LÓPEZ MATEOS

AV OCOTLAN (DEL FUEGO)
CALLE DEL AGUA
CALLE VELLAHERMOSA
Bosque de la Ciudad (city park)
Río Nuevo
FLOUR MILL

BLVD
LÁZARO CÁRDENAS

2
To Tecate and Tijuana

CARRETERA UNIÓN

0   0.5 mi
0   0.5 km

© AVALON TRAVEL

drive in due to the fact that streets are laid out mostly on a grid system and the local drivers obey the traffic signals.

Mexicali is a pleasant destination any time of year except for the summer when temperatures can reach up to 49 degrees Celsius (120°F). You'll find that most *Cachanillas* spend the month of August on the coast of northern Baja where temperatures are cooler.

SIGHTS
★ La Chinesca

Mexicali is famous for its Chinatown, the largest in all of Mexico, called **La Chinesca.** Because of the Colorado River Delta and the agricultural lands surrounding Mexicali, the region saw an abundance of Chinese laborers in the late 1800s and early 1900s. Visitors to Mexicali will find over 200 Chinese restaurants where the food has taken on an interesting mix of Mexican and Chinese flavors and ingredients. The heart of La Chinesca is at the intersection of Calle Benito Juárez and Calle Altamarino. The region is a bit rundown but still has a buzzing energy and can be interesting to walk around. Today there are fewer than 2,000 Chinese people still living in Mexicali, but the region remains heavily influenced by Chinese culture. **The Pagoda on Plaza de Amistad** (Calle Agustín Melgar and Cristóbal Colón) is a historical monument honoring the importance of Chinese culture in Mexicali and a popular spot for tourists and locals to visit.

the old rail line in Mexicali's La Chinesca

Museo Sol del Niño

Kids will enjoy the **Museo Sol del Niño** (Alfonso Esquer Sández, 686/553-8383, www.sol.org.mx, 10am-6pm Tues.-Sun., US$3) where they can explore interactive exhibits on science, art, technology, and the environment. There's also an IMAX theater that plays documentaries and movies in 3D.

Bosque de la Ciudad

A visit to **Bosque de la Ciudad** (Ocotlán and Alvarado, www.bosquedelaciudad.com.mx, 9am-5pm Tues.-Sun., free) is a nice respite from the big city. The large park has plenty of green space, a zoo, and botanical gardens. A water park is open during the summer with large pools and waterslides that provide a welcome relief from the heat of the city.

ENTERTAINMENT AND EVENTS
Nightlife

For a great opportunity to try a variety of the craft beers that Mexicali makes, check out **The Show Beer Rock Bar** (Calzada Cuahtémoc 1326, tel. 686/244-4489, theshowbeerbar@gmail.com, 6pm-2am Tues.-Sat.). The bar is operated by the same owners as the **Big Bad Brewing Co.** (Tres B). They opened The Show to provide an opportunity for people to try beer from some of the Mexicali microbreweries that are too small to have their own tasting rooms. The Show has 15 rotating beers on tap as well as a selection of liquor. They serve artisan pizza and have a small stage where live music groups (usually rock cover bands) perform.

Chabelas

When *Cachanillas* aren't drinking *chelas* (Mexican slang for beer), you'll likely find them drinking *chabelas*. A *chabela* is a drink made by mixing beer and Clamato juice. Why Clamato juice? Clamato was invented in Mexicali at "El Acueducto" bar at Hotel Lucerna. The name Clamato is an appropriate mix of the words "clam" and "tomato" as the liquid is made from a combination of clam broth and tomato juice. The salty and savory drink is usually served with salt around the rim and a lime wedge. In other parts of Baja, you may find people drinking *micheladas*, which are a mix of beer and tomato juice.

El Sume (Calzada Justo Sierra 845, tel. 686/568-4465, www.elsume.com, 4pm-1am Mon.-Sat.) is a fun bar that's packed on weekends with young, hip *Cachanillas* looking for a relaxed place to mingle and enjoy a few quality drinks. The El Sume beer menu is large, offering tap and bottle selections from all over Mexico, the United States, and other countries. Ask them to recommend a Mexicali craft beer. There's a nice outdoor patio area as well as an indoor area with a small stage for live music and performances.

BREWERIES

Cerveza Urbana (Ave. Reforma, tel. 686/554-6012, www.cervezaurbana.com) is a brewery in an idyllic setting with a big walled-in yard and large trees with lights strung around for nighttime. Grab a seat at any of the picnic tables around the garden and enjoy your beer. Urbana has won awards for their beers overall and specifically their IPAs.

Cervecería Legion (Avenida de los Jazmines 3000, tel. 686/567/9005, 6pm-midnight Thurs.-Sat.) is a warehouse-turned-tasting room in a fun atmosphere for drinking amid the tanks and equipment where they brew the beers. They have a variety of in-house beers (including a sour beer that's particularly unique) as well as some beers from other breweries. Tasters start at about US$1.

Cerveza Fauna (tel. 686/562-6719, www. cervezafauna.com) is quickly becoming one of the brightest stars in the northern Baja beer scene. Cerveza Fauna makes beers that are well-crafted and flavorful. They are in

the process of opening a tasting room at the brewery and their beers can be found at beer bars around town like The Show and El Sume.

Cucapá (Blvd. Lopez Mateos 2301, tel. 664/625-5630, www.cucapa.com) is one of the bigger craft breweries in the region. They have a large distribution at grocery stores and convenience stores as well as their own tasting room. The name Cucapá comes from one of the indigenous tribes in the Mexicali area.

Theater

The **Teatro del Estado** (Blvd. Adolfo López Mateos, 686/557-0372) has a 1,100-person capacity and hosts many theatrical and musical productions throughout the year. Don't miss the state theater's popular Café Literario, which hosts its own popular events.

Festivals and Events

Every year for three weeks in the fall, the **Fiesta del Sol** (www.fiestasdelsol.com.mx) kicks up a huge celebration with concerts, performances, fair rides, and food and drinks to celebrate the anniversary of Mexicali.

Because so many of northern Baja's breweries are from this region, **Mexicali Beer Fests** (www.mexicali.gob.mx) are held a few times a year, usually once in the fall and again in the spring. This is a great chance to try the beers from microbreweries that are too small to have tasting rooms or distribution.

SHOPPING

Tourists looking for Mexican arts and crafts won't find a large selection available in

Mexicali. There are a few curios shops along Melgar and Avenida Reforma. There are plenty of pharmacies around the city as well as major U.S. chain stores such as Costco.

Plaza la Cachanilla (Blvd. Adolfo López Mateos, 686/553-4177) is the most famous mall in Mexicali. Nearly everything can be found in this large shopping venue, including some handcrafted pieces by Mexican artists. Locals do most of their shopping here, and tourists may find souvenirs to take home.

Sports and Recreation

Mexicali's baseball team, **Las Aguilas** (The Eagles), have their own modern stadium in the **Estadio B'Air** (also affectionately referred to as El Nido, The Nest, Calzada Cuauhtémoc, tel. 686/567-0010, www.aguilasdemexicali. mx), with a 19,500 person capacity. They play in the Mexican Pacific League and host games from October to December.

While Baja is cutting back on bullfighting as a sport, Mexicali is one of the few cities on the peninsula that still has a bullring. Bullfights take place occasionally on Sunday afternoons from October to May at the **Plaza de Toros Calafia** (www.bullfights.org). Tickets are around US$10 for adults with free admission for kids under 12.

FOOD

There are over 200 Chinese restaurants in Mexicali as well as a variety of international foods and Mexican restaurants. The city has plenty of taco stands as well as sit-down restaurants geared for the many business workers and travelers. While the food scene isn't as sophisticated as other northern Baja regions such as Tijuana or Ensenada, there are still plenty of good choices.

Most of the Chinese food in Mexicali is Cantonese style, but the food all caters to a Mexican palate and has therefore become its own unique fusion. Traditional Chinese dishes are made with a twist of Mexican flavors like jalapeño, mango, and chipotle. What's the best way to fit in as a local at a

Cervecería Legion craft brewery and tasting room

Chinese restaurant in Mexicali? Mix ketchup in with your soy sauce.

Chinese

For some of the most popular Chinese food in Mexicali, try ★ **Pekin Restaurant** (Justo Sierra 891, tel. 686/838-3127, pekin.mexicali@ gmail.com, 11am-11pm daily, mains US$6-11). They have an extensive menu with traditional Chinese dishes as well as some of their own unique Mexican/Chinese creations like Chinese chipotle shrimp. The portions are large and perfect for sharing. The space is big and can accommodate large groups and private parties. They have a second location on Centro Civico.

Serving Chinese and Baja fusion, **The Wok** (Ave. Gral. Venustiano Carranza 118, tel. 686/568-3026, www.thewokmxli.com, 1pm-10pm Mon.-Sat., mains US$9-13) creates a unique blend of the two cuisines with dishes like dumplings, egg rolls, and pork belly tacos with hoison sauce. The intimate and dark restaurant has a small bar and friendly staff.

Craft Breweries

While there is a long history of beer making in Mexico, the craft brewery scene is a new phenomenon just catching on with consumers in the last few years. Its expansion in northern Baja is echoing the rapidly growing microbrewery industry in nearby San Diego. The freshest thing about Mexicali is the brewery scene, and most of the nightlife for young people revolves around breweries and beer bars. While there are over 40 breweries in the area, the beer industry is close-knit, with the brewmasters all getting together to hang out, drink beer, and work on beer events together.

The craft beer scene is so new to Mexicali that most breweries are operated out of homes or small warehouses. There are a few that have tasting rooms, but that number is growing as the microbrewery scene takes on momentum. A great way to sample some of the local brews is to visit some of the bars that specialize in local beers, such as **The Show Beer Rock Bar** or **El Sume**. The city also holds regular beer fests a few times a year that have a huge turnout and provide a way for locals and tourists to try new offerings they wouldn't otherwise have access to.

For traditional Cantonese, **China House** (Justo Sierra and Carpinteros 1001, tel. 686/554-8805, 11am-11pm daily, mains US$8-15) serves large family-style dishes like Peking duck, orange chicken, and chow mein. The spacious restaurant can accommodate large groups and has friendly service.

Jade Express (Calle H 421, tel. 686/554-3515, 10am-10pm daily, US$4-8) is a Cantonese restaurant serving traditional Chinese dishes, dim sum, and dumplings. As the name implies, it's fast food in a casual environment.

Rincón de Panchito (Benito Juárez 1990, tel. 686/567-7718, 11am-11pm daily, mains US$7-12) doesn't offer a lot in terms of atmosphere, with a basic setting and large TVs up on the walls, but is a favorite among locals for the ramen dishes and family-style dining. Nearby **Dragón** (Benito Juárez 1830, tel. 686/566-2020, 11am-11pm daily, mains US$12) is a large restaurant with a popular duck lechón dish.

Mexican

For an authentic local spot, stop by for some *menudo* at ★ **Museo del Valle de Mexicali** (Río Amazonas 138, tel. 686-555-8108, 7am-2pm Fri.-Sun., US$5-8). *Menudo* is a traditional Mexican soup made with beef stomach in a chile-based broth, normally eaten with tortillas or other bread. The restaurant is only open on the weekends for breakfast and lunch. This rustic ranch set up as a mini museum also showcases interesting artifacts and exhibits related to the region.

For a classic Mexican breakfast, head to **La Plazita** (Calzada Justo Sierra 377, tel. 686/568-1051, 7am-10:30pm Mon.-Sat., 8am-5pm Sun., US$6-9), a little café serving up traditional Mexican egg dishes, *chilaquiles,* and also omelettes. They're also open for lunch and dinner.

Seafood

Known for their seafood cocktails, **Laguna Azul** (Calzada Independencia 823, tel. 686/565-6181, www.mariscoslagunaazul.com, 9am-8pm daily, US$6-12) has a range of seafood dishes on the menu from grilled shrimp specialties to fish filets. It's a casual dining experience without any frills—the focus here is on the food.

There are numerous **Los Arcos** (Calle Calafia 454, tel. 686/556-0903, www.restaurantlosarcos.com, 11am-10pm Sun.-Wed., 11am-11pm Thurs.-Sat. mains US$9-15) in northern Baja, and this mini chain is a favorite for locals and tourists alike. The Mexican seafood dishes and friendly atmosphere make for a pleasant eating experience.

Taco Stands and *Antojitos*

There are lots of taco stands and street food options around Mexicali, and one of the most-famous spots is ★ **Tacos del Ferrocarril** (Ferrocarril between Lopez Mateos and De la Industria), which is a row of taco stands next to the old railroad (*ferrocarril* means railroad) that began in 1976. While the railroad is long gone, the stands are still a favorite for locals craving a savory bite. The specialty lamb *barbacoa* and *cabeza de res* (beef head) will please any adventurous foodies. They open in the mornings and stay that way until late at night (around 3am).

For tacos in a more refined environment, try **El Tasajo** (Calzada Cuauhtémoc 601, tel. 686/252/5996, 4pm-midnight Mon-Wed., 4pm-4am Thurs.-Sat., tacos US$2) a taquería that specializes in New York steak meat. It's a hip and delicious taco experience.

Fans of *cabeza* (head) or *borrego* (lamb) tacos, won't be disappointed at **Tacos el Cesarín** (Calle Novena 1769, across the street from Walmart) where the meat is savory and served up in warm corn tortillas.

International

For good service and food, **Kobu** (Blvd. Benito Juárez 2220, tel. 686/564-1100, www. koburestaurant.com, 1pm-11pm Sun-Wed., 1pm-1am Thurs.-Sun., mains US$7-13) is a popular Japanese fusion restaurant. The menu features dishes from Tomahawk steak to sushi to seafood. Kobu is connected to Hotel Araiza Mexicali, and therefore it is a popular and easy dining spot for many travelers.

Serving local and sustainable ingredients, **La Cava de Qorot** (Blvd. Benito Juárez 1028, tel. 686/218-0783, noon-10pm Mon.-Sun., noon-11pm Fri.-Sat., mains US$7-12) operates on the motto *come y toma local* (eat and drink local). The meats, cheese, vegetables, wine, and beer served at this gastropub are all from the region. There's also an artisanal shop where you can purchase regional cheese, jams, breads, coffees, and salsas.

For something unique, **Heidelberg Restaurant** (Ave. Francisco I. Madero, tel. 686/554-2022, www.restauranteheidelberg. com, noon-11:30pm Mon.-Sat., bar open until 1:30am, mains US$18-32) is a German pub-themed restaurant with a cozy and rustic feeling. While there are a few German items on the menu, the selection is mostly Mexican food as well as steaks and some seafood. They also have a bar with a great selection of wine and beer.

Gastro Bar & Steakhouse (Just Sierra 1495, tel. 686/568-1655, www.gastrobar. com.mx, 1pm-midnight Mon.-Wed., 1pm-1am Thurs., 1pm-3am, Fri.-Sat., mains $16-28) has a menu that ranges from steak to pizzas and includes other comfort foods like mac 'n' cheese and pork chops. They have lots of Mexicali craft beers on tap. They're associated with the Ariaza Calafia and Convention Center down the street, so if you're staying at the hotel, you can charge meals to your room.

For the rare chance to enjoy Thai food in Baja, try **Bangkok** (Calzada Cetys 2681, Plaza Marsella, tel. 686/565-7279, www.bangkok-mexico.com.mx, noon-10pm Tues.-Thurs., noon-11pm Fri.-Sat., 1pm-7pm Sun., mains US$8-11). The menu offers a variety of traditional Thai dishes all made with fresh ingredients. The ambience is nothing special, but it's a nice sit-down restaurant with quality food.

ACCOMMODATIONS

There's a wide range of accommodations in Mexicali with cheap motels and hotels available for a quick stay and nice accommodations to appease high standards because of all of the business travelers that the city welcomes. Because of the abundance of business travelers in Mexicali, room rates drop on the weekends for the more expensive hotels. Therefore, travelers can book nice rooms for relatively low prices over a weekend. For the mid-range to high-end hotels, it's best to make reservations in advance.

Under US$50

Hotel Azteca de Oro (Calle de la Industria 600, tel. 686/557-1433, US$30) is a budget motel with fairly nice accommodations and free parking. Rooms feature air-conditioning and flat-screen TVs. The staff is friendly and speaks English.

The rooms at **Hacienda del Indio** (Blvd. Adolfo López Mateos 100, tel. 686/557-2277, www.haciendadelindio.com, US$45) all face a central courtyard. The decor is older, but there's 24-hour room service and free wireless Internet.

Steps from the Mexicali west border crossing, **Hotel del Norte** (Ave. Francisco I. Madero 205, tel. 686/552-8102, www.hoteldelnorte.com.mx, US$45) is convenient if you are crossing the border or want to be near downtown El Centro.

Hotel Regis (Blvd. Benito Juárez 2150, tel. 686/566-8801, www.hotel-regis.com, US$40) offers basic accommodations with friendly service. All rooms feature air-conditioning, free wireless Internet, and cable TV.

US$50-100

The small Mexican chain hotel **City Express Mexicali** (Blvd. Benito Juárez 1342, tel. 686/564-1650, US$58-70) has a location in Mexicali with clean, modern rooms and free breakfast. Rooms on the back of the hotel tend to be quieter as they avoid the noise of the busy boulevard.

Hotel Colonial Mexicali (Blvd. Adolfo López Mateos 1048, tel. 686/556-1312, www.hotelescolonial.com, US$45-70) has nice grounds with gardens and an outdoor swimming pool. The rooms are older, and the back rooms close to the parking lot tend to fill with groups partying until late at night. Ask for a room near the front, away from the parking lot for a quieter experience.

During the week, it's mostly business travelers staying at **The Ariaza Calafia and Convention Center** (Justo Sierra 1495, tel. 686/568-3311, www.araizahoteles.com/calafia, US$65). The hotel has nice clean rooms and a swimming pool. Request a room at the back of the hotel for a quieter experience. They are sister hotels with the Ariaza Mexicali.

US$100-150

★ **Fiesta Inn Mexicali** (Blvd. Adolfo López Mateos 1029, tel. 686/837-3300, toll-free U.S. tel. 800/343/7821, www.fiestainn.com, US$75-125) is a popular choice for business travelers for its convenient central location. There's a small pool area, and the rooms are very comfortable with modern and clean accommodations. There's a breakfast buffet as well as a hotel restaurant and bar.

Nice rooms and amenities can be expected at **Araiza Mexicali** (Blvd. Benito Juárez 2220, tel. 686/564-1100, toll-free U.S. tel. 800/026-5444, www.araizahoteles.com, US$100-129). If you think you'll have breakfast at the hotel, book to include the breakfast buffet when you reserve your room, it's cheaper than paying for it later. There are two nice pools, but rooms near the pools can be noisy. The executive wing has newer and quieter rooms.

For a less-business, more-resort feel in Mexicali, try ★ **Lucerna Mexicali** (Blvd. Benito Juárez 2151, tel. 686/564-7000, www.hoteleslucerna.com, US$90-115). The lush grounds feature a nice pool area, and the rooms are modern, comfortable, and outfitted with high-quality furniture. The staff is friendly and helpful. Skip the breakfast buffet and eat elsewhere.

INFORMATION AND SERVICES
Tourism Assistance

The **Secretary of Tourism for Mexicali** (1 Francisco Montejano St. and Blvd. Benito Juárez, 2nd fl., tel. 686/566-1277 or 686/566-1116) has maps, brochures, and other visitor information.

Money

Mexicali is home to branches of nearly every Mexican bank where travelers can withdraw pesos with their ATM card. There are also *casas de cambio* where people can exchange money both in Mexicali and in Calexico before crossing the border. Many of the nicer hotels and restaurants around town will accept credit cards.

GETTING THERE AND AROUND

U.S. Border Crossing

There are two border crossings in Mexicali—east and west. The Mexicali west border crossing is the main border crossing and open 24/7. Crossing south into Mexicali here puts you directly into El Centro, downtown Mexicali.

The Mexicali east border is recommended for travelers with RVs (there's more room than at the west border crossing) as well as for southbound travelers stopping to get an FMM tourist permit. Hunters returning to the United States with game to declare should use the Mexicali east crossing as officers will know how to process the declaration there.

Car

To get to Mexicali from San Diego, take the I-8 to Route 111 south where you will drive right into the Mexicali west border crossing. To reach the Mexicali east crossing, continue on the I-8 to Route 7 south.

For such a large city in Baja, Mexicali is relatively easy to navigate in due to the wide streets and the fact that the city is basically laid out on a grid system. Drivers in Mexicali are generally very courteous, and the traffic isn't too heavy. Be sure to watch your speed as the limits are quite low and there are a number of officers patrolling the roads. The best way to get around in Mexicali is by car as the city is extremely spread out and there are not many taxis. However, there are a few areas like El Centro and La Chinesca where you can walk around to sightsee.

Air

Mexicali's airport, the **General Rodolfo Sánchez Taboada International Airport,** is about 20 kilometers east of the city. No U.S. airlines currently service the airport, and most flights only connect to mainland Mexico, but Aéreo Calafia (www.aereocalafia.com.mx) has flights from Mexicali to La Paz in Baja California Sur.

Bus

Autobuses de la Baja California (ABC, tel. 664/104-7400, www.abc.com.mx) offers bus service to and from Tijuana as well as San Felipe. It costs about US$20 to take the bus from Mexicali to San Felipe and about US$25 for service from Mexicali to Tijuana. **Greyhound** (www.greyhound.com.mx) also has service directly to Mexicali from either San Diego or Los Angeles.

Buses within Mexicali cost less than US$1 for fare. Many of the bus routes pass through or originate at Calle Altamarino in El Centro, just past the border crossing.

Taxi

There are relatively few taxis in Mexicali, but those there are can be found around the downtown area fairly easily. Your hotel will be able to call a taxi for you, or you can call **Ecotaxi** (tel.686/562-6565) to order one yourself.

Sierra de Juárez

Driving west of Mexicali on Mexico 2, visitors will pass Laguna Salada, a vast dry salt lake, before starting to climb up into the foothills of the Sierra de Juárez. This mountain range is home to the Cañon de Guadalupe with some of the best hot springs in Baja. In the Parque Nacional Constitución de 1857, animals like bighorn sheep are a common sight.

★ CAÑON DE GUADALUPE HOT SPRINGS

Located in one of the larger canyons of the Sierra de Juárez, the **Cañon de Guadalupe** features palm-studded mountains and rocks and is one of the most popular regions because of the hot springs. The area also features hiking, rock climbing, small waterfalls, and cave painting sites. There are two options for camping and experiencing the hot springs. **Guadalupe Canyon Oasis** (Mexico 2 Km. 28, U.S. tel. 619/937-1546, www.guadalupe-canyonoasis.com, US$40-100) offers 14 individual campsites, each with its own natural hot spring tub, grill, *palapa,* and space for tent and vehicle. There are sites that can accommodate up to 16 people.

The other is **Guadalupe Canyon Hot Springs** (Mexico 2 Km. 28, tel. 686/558-5048, U.S. tel. 323/627/4671, www.guadalupecanyonhotsprings.com, US$40-100). The setup is similar with 15 individual campsites that have their own hot springs tubs in addition to *palapas,* picnic areas, and grills. Because both campsites are popular and remote, it's best to make reservations in advance. Rates are much cheaper during the week and increase on the weekends. The tubs are closed during July and August due to high temperatures.

PARQUE NACIONAL CONSTITUCIÓN DE 1857

In the highest part of the Sierra de Juárez at elevations of 1,500-1,800 meters (5,000-6,000 feet), the **Parque Nacional Constitución de 1857** (tel. 686/554-5404, pnconstitucion@ conanp.gob.mx, summer: 8am-8pm daily, winter: 8am-4pm, US$4) is one of two national parks in Baja California. With 5,000 hectares (12,355 acres) of protected nature, the park is a unique refuge for wildlife such as bobcats, foxes, coyotes, eagles, and hawks amid the coniferous trees. This is one of the few regions in Baja California where temperatures can get very low and it can snow in the winter months. The park can be accessed from the north on Mexico 2 at Km. 71, or from the south on Mexico 3 (Ensenada-San Felipe) at Km. 53. There are administration buildings at both entrances where visitors will need to register and pay the park fee. Overnight camping is included in the park fee. There are nine camping areas within the park. Cabins are available starting at US$28.

RÍO HARDY

Southeast of Mexicali, the **Río Hardy** is a 26-kilometer river believed to be an old channel of the Colorado River. The Hardy empties out into the Colorado River Delta (a UNESCO Biosphere Reserve), which then empties out into the Sea of Cortez. All activity centers around the river in this tranquil area, and travelers come to relax and enjoy activities such as kayaking, boating, and Jet

kayakers on the Río Hardy at Rancho Mil

Skiing. Hunting is also popular in the region. But keep in mind that bringing a gun into Mexico is illegal. Any accommodations that offer hunting will provide the gun, ammunition, and required permit for you.

There are a number of places along the Río Hardy to stay and enjoy the region. **Rancho Mil** (Mexico 5 Km. 58, tel. 949/466-2069, www.ranchomil.com, US$75) offers riverfront cabins in addition to a camping area in a tranquil setting and provides activities such as kayaking, hiking, and ATVing. **Campo Mosqueda** (Mexico 5 Km. 53.5, tel. 686/566-1520, www.campomosqueda.com, US$25 per car up to five people) is another riverfront spot with camping spaces, *palapas* with grills, and a restaurant. They have a day fee (US$15) to use the spaces between 8am and 7pm, and an additional fee (an extra US$10) to camp for the night. **Rancho Baja Cucapah** (Mexico 5 Km. 48.5, tel. 686/272-0648, www.bajacucapah.travel, US$75) has a wide variety of land and water activities as well as rustic cabins to rent.

San Felipe

San Felipe is a small fishing village on the Sea of Cortez that has grown into a popular spot for expats and tourists. Just 2.5 hours from the U.S. border, San Felipe is within reach for weekend travelers coming to enjoy the relaxed Baja lifestyle. Fish tacos, sunrises over the Sea of Cortez, and prolific fishing trips are the way of life in San Felipe.

The population of San Felipe is about 25,000, and half of that is expats from the United States and Canada who enjoy the warm weather and laid-back pace of life.

Many things in downtown San Felipe are within walking distance as most of the action centers around the *malecón* and surrounding streets. San Felipe is a casual town, and although there are a few bars and clubs along the *malecón,* it doesn't offer any of the glitz or glamour that some of the larger cities in Baja do.

The road is now paved all the way from San Felipe to Bahía San Luis Gonzaga passing through tiny fishing villages, settlements, and housing communities all along

the San Felipe *malecón* at sunrise

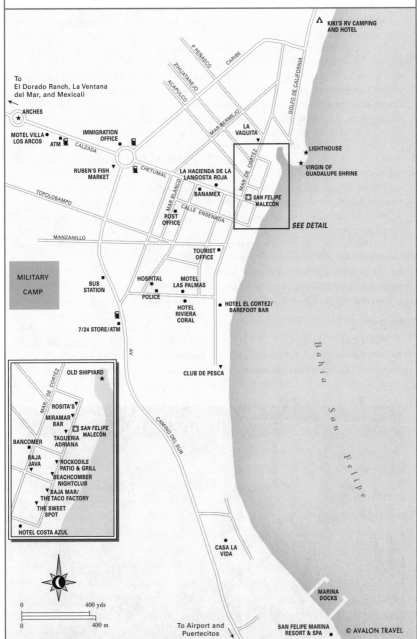

San Felipe

To
El Dorado Ranch, La Ventana
del Mar, and Mexicali

ARCHES

MOTEL VILLA
LOS ARCOS

ATM

IMMIGRATION
OFFICE

CALZADA

RUBEN'S FISH
MARKET

CHETUMAL

TOPOLOBAMPO

MANZANILLO

MILITARY
CAMP

BUS
STATION

HOSPITAL

POLICE

7/24 STORE/ATM

P PEÑASCO

ZIHUATANEJO

ACAPULCO

CARIBE

MAR BERMEJO

GOLFO DE CALIFORNIA

KIKI'S RV CAMPING
AND HOTEL

LA
VAQUITA

MAR DE CORTEZ

LIGHTHOUSE

VIRGIN OF
GUADALUPE SHRINE

LA HACIENDA DE LA
LANGOSTA ROJA

BANAMEX

MAR BLANCO

CALLE ENSENADA

POST
OFFICE

SAN FELIPE
MALECÓN

SEE DETAIL

TOURIST
OFFICE

MOTEL
LAS PALMAS

HOTEL
RIVIERA
CORAL

HOTEL EL CORTEZ/
BAREFOOT BAR

CLUB DE PESCA

AV

Bahía

San

Felipe

OLD SHIPYARD

MAR DE CORTEZ

ROSITA'S

MIRAMAR
BAR

SAN FELIPE
MALECÓN

TAQUERIA
ADRIANA

BANCOMER

BAJA
JAVA

ROCKODILE
PATIO & GRILL

BEACHCOMBER
NIGHTCLUB

BAJA MAR/
THE TACO FACTORY

THE SWEET
SPOT

HOTEL COSTA AZUL

CAMINO DEL SUR

CASA LA
VIDA

MARINA
DOCKS

0   400 yds
0   400 m

To Airport and
Puertecitos

SAN FELIPE MARINA
RESORT & SPA

© AVALON TRAVEL

the 160 kilometers down the coast. This whole area is popular because of its access to the Sea of Cortez.

Fishing is a draw for the region and, therefore, so is the seafood. Northern Baja is the original home of the fish taco, with Ensenada and San Felipe in a constant argument over which was its true birthplace. In addition to fish, San Felipe is known for its shrimp. During shrimp season, you can buy large fresh shrimp at very affordable prices. The annual shrimp festival in the fall is one of the town's main attractions. Clams are another regional draw, showing up on many menus, and visitors can go clamming on the beach.

October through June is the best time to visit San Felipe. The monsoon season begins in June and continues through September bringing temperatures of well over 37 degrees Celsius (100°F) with humidity over 90 percent. Because of this, many businesses close up during the summer months. It's best to check ahead with hotels and restaurants if you plan on traveling to San Felipe at that time of year.

SIGHTS
★ Malecón
The *malecón* is the heart of San Felipe. The promenade runs along Playa San Felipe where the *pangas* all gather. Little taco stands, restaurants, and bars line the other side of the street. The *malecón* is also the center of nightlife in San Felipe with bars and nightclubs in the area and mariachi bands playing in the evening. Drinking along the *malecón* is legal, so it makes for a great spot to grab a beer from a convenience store and stroll along the promenade to people-watch.

Shrine of the Virgin Guadalupe
One of San Felipe's most iconic landmarks is the **Shrine of the Virgin Guadalupe,** on top of a small mountain right next to the San Felipe *faro* (lighthouse). From the *malecón*, walk north across the bridge where you'll see the lighthouse and the shrine. You have to climb a lot of stairs to get to the top, but the views of San Felipe from above make the trek worthwhile.

Isla Konsag
Isla Konsag is a 45-minute boat ride from San Felipe's *malecón* (you can arrange a ride with any of the *pangueros* along the *malecón*). Referred to by locals as "The Rock," the island hosts a variety of wildlife including marine birds and a colony of sea lions. The island is a

the shrine of the Virgin Guadalupe

Save the Vaquita of the Sea of Cortez

Around San Felipe, you will hear people mentioning the *vaquitas*, which are an endangered species of porpoise only found in the Sea of Cortez. They are smaller than other dolphins with a flatter nose and darker coloring. In 2014, the estimated number of *vaquitas* alive has dropped to below 100. While the *vaquitas* have never been hunted directly, they get trapped in gill nets used to illegally fish totoaba, an endangered fish. In April 2015, President Enrique Peña Nieto announced a program to conserve and protect the *vaquita* and the totoaba. The plan includes a ban on gill nets until at least 2017. There is a *vaquita* monument in the center of the San Felipe *malecón*.

prolific fishing spot as well, so you can combine sightseeing and fishing in this one excursion. Don't expect to step onto the island (it's a steep rock formation), but taking a boat ride out to enjoy the Sea of Cortez and the wildlife is one of the best lesser-known attractions in San Felipe. For fishing, it's best to go out to the rock during slack tide so your lines don't get caught in currents.

RECREATION
Fishing

San Felipe is essentially a fishing village so angling is one of the main draws. What's available to catch depends on when and exactly where you go, but usually anglers will find sea bass, cabrilla, corbina, triggerfish, red snapper, sierra mackerel, dorado, grouper, roosterfish, amberjack, and plenty of yellowtail. Commercial fishing is currently banned in the area, but sportfishing is still allowed.

Fishing from shore is an easy option and does not require a Mexican fishing license. Serious anglers will want to go out on a boat. For day trips out to sea, the *pangas* on the beach along the *malecón* in front of Miramar Bar are available for hire. The price is about $60 per person, which will include the fee for a daily Mexican fishing license, life jackets, bait, and reels. Boats leave around 6:30am as winds pick up in the afternoon and evening. It's best to make advance arrangements, so go down at least the evening before to set up plans.

Tony Reyes Fishing Tours (Mar Bermejo 130, tel. 686/577-1120, www.tonyreyes.com)

is the most famous sportfishing operation for the region and runs popular six-day fishing trips to the Midriff Islands. They offer all-inclusive "mothership" fishing trips, where a larger boat transports the group on a 24-hour journey out to the islands. From there, anglers go out fishing each day on smaller *pangas*.

Boating

Many people bring their own boats to San Felipe. There is a launch ramp that anyone can use free of charge at the harbor, a mile south of town. There is no crane launch in San Felipe.

Golf

Las Caras de Mexico (Mexico 5 Km. 176.5, www.lascarasdemexico.com, US$20-45) is San Felipe's only golf course. The 18-hole course features ocean and mountain views and is part of El Dorado Ranch and La Ventana del Mar developments. Clubs are available for rent for US$30.

ENTERTAINMENT AND EVENTS
Nightlife

Rockodile Bar, Grill and Nightclub (Ave. Mar de Cortés, tel. 686/577-1453, noon-3am) is San Felipe's largest disco and the best bet for some exciting nightlife. Just off of the *malecón*, it's hard to miss the giant green building with the large crocodile on the front. The club has been around since 1987 and is popular for its cheap drinks and large dance floor.

Club Bar Miramar (Ave. Mar de Cortés

315, tel. 686/577-1192) is a favorite bar for local expats, who have been coming to this classic spot since the 1940s. There's a Ping-Pong table and pool tables, but most people are here to just hang out and catch up with friends.

For relaxing views and a drink, try **Barefoot Bar** (Ave. Mar de Cortés, tel. 686/577-1055) at the El Cortez hotel. The location is right on the beach so it's a great place to grab a margarita or a beer while enjoying views of the Sea of Cortez. There's live music on the weekends.

Festivals and Events

The biggest annual event is the **Score San Felipe 250** (www.score-international.com), an off-road race that takes place around February. It's a loop race, starting and ending in San Felipe.

The **San Felipe Shrimp Festival** (www.sanfelipeshrimpfestival.com) is a free event that takes place every year around November. The large celebration features food, drinks, live entertainment, and music along the *malecón*.

Springtime brings the annual **San Felipe Blues and Arts Fiesta** (www.bluesandartsfestival.sanfelipebclionsclub.com) with blues music and art booths. Tickets are $35 and proceeds benefit local charities.

SHOPPING

Most of the shopping in San Felipe is on the main street, **Avenida Mar de Cortés,** where you'll find typical Mexican trinkets and souvenirs along with street vendors selling silver jewelry. There are also a number of vendors who will walk through town selling items like hats, hammocks, jewelry, and blankets.

FOOD
Seafood

A favorite for seafood is ★ **Mariscos La Vaquita** (Ave. Mar de Cortés, tel. 686/577-2837, 11am-10pm Wed.-Mon., mains US$10-18). The large steamed clam platter is a solid contender for best dish, and lobster and other seafood dishes round out the large menu.

They have craft beers from Mexicali available as well.

Bajamar Seafood and Steak House (Ave. Mar de Cortés 100, tel. 686/221-1359, restaurantbajamar@hotmail.com, 10am-10pm Mon.-Fri., 9am-11pm Sat., 9am-10pm Sun. mains US$8-18) is on the *malecón* and a popular spot for breakfast. They serve seafood, steak, and Mexican food for lunch and dinner. Right next door and run by the same family is **Taco Factory** (*Malecón* at Chetumal, tel. 686/577-2648, tacos US$1-2), a casual outdoor restaurant under a large *palapa* roof with a bar, a variety of tacos, and famous shrimp-stuffed peppers.

Mexican

Rosita's (Ave. Mar de Cortés 381, tel. 686/540-6218, www.rositarest.com, 9am-10pm daily, mains US$6-11) is a local's favorite serving up large plates of Mexican food and seafood. At the south end of the *malecón,* this great spot has nice views and affordable prices.

A second location of the popular restaurant in Rosarito, **El Nido Steakhouse** (Ave. Mar de Cortez 348, tel. 686/577-1028, 1pm-10pm Thurs.-Tues., mains US$8-28) is a good choice for quality Mexican food and excellent steaks. The ambience is Western-inspired and feels cozy and rustic.

Taco Stands and *Antojitos*

San Felipe and Ensenada are in a constant rivalry for which city can claim to be the true home to the original fish taco. ★ **Taqueria y Mariscos Adriana** (Malecón 196, no tel., US$1-2), run by Maria Soledad for nearly 30 years, is rumored to be the fish taco stand that inspired the Rubio's fish taco chain in the United States. Like most taco stands, the facilities are bare minimum, but the fish tacos are great and shouldn't be missed.

Most towns in Baja have a popular roasted chicken spot, and for San Felipe, the **El Kikiriki** (Malecón Sur 162, no tel., US$4-7) street cart is it. The chicken comes with tortillas, rice, beans, and salsa. They also serve tacos, and the *al pastor* are a favorite of many. Grab a seat at one of the tables and watch the people go by as you enjoy your food.

Churros La Bufadora (Ave. Mar de Cortés across from Costa Azul hotel) is a great little spot to get a bag of fresh churros for under $2.

International

If you're not in the mood for seafood or Mexican food, **El Padrino Pizzeria y Restaurante** (Calzada Chetumal 125, tel. 686/163-7704, noon-10pm Wed.-Sun., US$6-8) is an option for some great Italian food. Pizzas, pastas, salads as well as steak are all on the menu. The servings are large and the location is right in town.

The **Sweet Spot Bar and Grill** (Malecón 162, tel. 686/577-6366, www.sweetspotsanfelipe.com, 1pm-midnight Thurs.-Sun., 4pm-9pm Mon., US$9-14) is owned by former San Diego Charger D'Andre White and specializes in southern-style smoked barbecue. The menu features items like pulled pork and ribs as well as seafood. The decor is cozy and inviting.

ACCOMMODATIONS

Because of the extreme heat in the summer, San Felipe is a seasonal town for tourism. Rates below are for peak season (Oct.-May) and will be cheaper during summer months.

Under US$50

For clean, budget accommodations, head to ★ **Hotel Riviera Coral** (Ave. Mar Baltico, tel. 686/577-2604, www.hotelrivieracoral.com, US$37). There are nice grounds with palm trees and a pool. The location is a little removed up on the hill, and there's no restaurant on-site. All of the rooms have air-conditioning.

Across from Hotel Riviera Coral is hacienda-style **Las Palmas** (Mar Baltico 1101, tel. 686/577-1333, www.laspalmasanfelipe.com, US$45) with small but comfortable and clean rooms. There's a basic pool and a restaurant called **Alfredo's** on-site. The hotel is

up a hill, but within walking distance to town and the beach.

US$50-100

La Hacienda de la Langosta Roja (Calzada Chetumal 125, tel. 686/577-0483. US$80) offers basic accommodations with the *malecón* and beach just a block away. In spite of its location it still stays fairly quiet. Coffee and a continental breakfast are served in the morning.

On the main street in town and walking distance to restaurants and bars, **Chapala Motel** (Ave. Mar de Cortés 142, tel. 686/577-1240, $60) is a good choice for budget travelers. There's no pool, but the hotel is one block up from the *malecón* and the beach. Because of the location, the hotel can get noisy on the weekends, so bring earplugs if you're a light sleeper.

With colorful hacienda-style architecture, ★ **Hacienda Don Jesus** (Mar Báltico 829, tel. 686/577-0080, www.donjesus.com, US$60) has 31 rooms just one block off of the *malecón*. Rooms are clean and comfortable with cable television, wireless Internet, air-conditioning, and toiletries. Kids will love the pool area, and there's a large secure parking lot.

The large **Hotel El Cortez** (Ave. Mar de Cortez, tel. 686/577-1055, www.elcortezsanfelipebaja.com, US$85) is right on the beach, just south of town and the *malecón*. The 112 rooms are a bit dated, but offer air-conditioning and a large and comfortable setting. There's a pool on the property in addition to a restaurant and the popular Barefoot Bar.

US$100-150

Some of the best accommodations in San Felipe, the vacation suites at ★ **Casa la Vida** (Misión de Santo Toman 2738, tel. 686/577-2807, toll-free U.S. tel. 800/334-3345, www.casalavida.com, US$100-135) all have ocean views and are nicely appointed. The owners, two expats, are welcoming and accommodating and will help you out with recommendations on what to do while in town. It's a clean, friendly, and relaxing atmosphere with a lovely swimming pool.

US$150-200

The **Sandollar "Condotels"** (tel. 686/123-7688, www.sanfelipesandollar.com, US$125-175) offer hotels rooms and condos for rent, as well as stand-alone houses. The accommodations are clean and modern with flat-screen TVs, wireless Internet, air-conditioning, and a location right on the Sea of Cortez. Located a little bit south of town, it's just a few minutes away from the San Felipe airport.

Vacation Rentals

There are a wide variety of units from studios up to four-bedrooms available at **Playa del Paraiso** (Ave. Mission de Loreto 130, tel. 686/577-0821, toll-free U.S. tel. 888/647-5292, www.playadelparaiso.com, US$150-300). Because it is a condo rental, there's no daily maid service or trash removal, but units are fully equipped with linens and towels. The development is still unfinished, even though construction began many years ago. There is security on the premises.

Seven miles north of town is **El Dorado Ranch** (tel. 686/576-0717, toll-free U.S. tel. 800/404-2599, www.eldoradoranch.com, US$150-200) with fully furnished and equipped rental vacation homes and condos. With over 14,000 hectares of land (the largest ranch in all of Baja), El Dorado features tennis, pickleball, and Las Caras de Mexico, San Felipe's only golf course.

Playa Bonita Condo Suites and RV Park (California 787, tel. 626/967-8977, www.sanfelipebeachcondos.com, US$125) has eight one-bedroom condos available for rent on the beach. Playa Bonita also offers RV and camping spots with small spaces for tent camping, vans, or small trailers. Spaces have a patio with a roof and a picnic table.

Camping and RV Parks

The campsite situation in San Felipe has changed dramatically in the past number of years with many of the campsites that had large spaces and RV hookups closing to make space for new developments. Camping and RVing are still popular choices for visiting San Felipe, but there are fewer available sites.

Club de Pesca (Ave. Mar de Cortés, tel. 686/577-1180, www.clubdepescarvpark.com, US$12-35) is an old favorite with locals and tourists. The beachfront location has spots featuring full hookups as well as open beach camping.

Kiki's RV Camping & Hotel (Golfo de California 80, tel. 686/577-2021, www.kiki.com.mx, US$35) is right on the beach and has space for RVs up to 9 meters. Spaces offer 30-amp outlets, sewer, and water. There are also a few hotel rooms available that start at US$65 a night. For peak season and weekends it's best to make a reservation in advance.

With 79 spaces right on the beach, **Pete's Camp El Paraiso** (Mexico 5 Km. 178, U.S. tel. 951/694-6704, www.petescamp.com, US$15 per vehicle) offers campers beautiful views in addition to services like showers, restrooms, and a restaurant and cantina on the property. Hot showers are available for an extra US$2. Reservations must be made via phone at least two weeks in advance.

INFORMATION AND SERVICES

Tourist Assistance

The **Secretary of Tourism for San Felipe** (Ave. Mar de Cortés and Calzada Chetumal 101, tel. 686/577-1865 or 686/577-1155) is located downtown. Visitors can get brochures, maps and other visitor information at this tourist office.

Money

There are ATMs throughout town (OXXOs are a good place to find them) as well as one bank, Bancomer, with an ATM to withdraw pesos. Most places will accept U.S. dollars, but often only if you have exact change or your purchase is at least 90 percent of the bill that you're paying with. Many places in San Felipe are cash only and do not accept credit cards, so travelers should definitely plan on getting pesos.

Emergencies

In the case of an emergency, the police will call a Red Cross Ambulance and you will be taken to the Red Cross facility or Mexicali for treatment. The **Red Cross** (tel. 686/577-1544) can be reached directly for ambulance services and physical exams. The **Abasalo Medical Clinic** (Calzada Chetumal, tel. 686/577-1458 or 686/573-0174 for emergency care) is where most locals go for medical care. Dr. Victor Abasalo can arrange for ground or air evacuation to San Diego if needed. The **Baja Medical Center** (178.5 Carretera Federal 5, tel. 686/576-0200) provides outpatient primary care as well as urgent care. Other emergency numbers for San Felipe are the **Police Department**, tel. 686/577-1134, and the **Fire Station**, tel. 686/577-1182.

GETTING THERE AND AROUND
Car

Most travelers visiting San Felipe drive in their own cars. Because San Felipe is about 2.5 hours from the U.S. border crossing at Calexico/Mexicali, it's a popular choice for a weekend trip for many California and Arizona residents. The Calexico/Mexicali east border is recommended for travelers with RVs as well as for those stopping to get an FMM tourist permit. The Calexico/Mexicali west border crossing has very little space for parking.

Bus

Autobuses de la Baja California (ABC, tel. 664/104-7400 or toll-free tel. 800/025-0222, www.abc.com.mx) offers bus service to San Felipe from Mexicali and Tijuana. The bus station in San Felipe is located on Airport Road near the Pemex gas station with the 7-Eleven. They open around 5:30am and close around 10:30pm, after the last bus arrives from Mexicali. It costs US$20 to take the bus from Mexicali to San Felipe, and US$45 from Tijuana. There is not a local bus system within San Felipe.

Taxi

Taxis in San Felipe are clean and reliable. You can easily catch one on Avenida Mar de Cortés or on Calzada Chetumal. If you are staying at a hotel outside of the main area of town, you can always ask your hotel to call a taxi for you. Prices are fixed, and it shouldn't cost more than US$5 to get around town.

LAGUNA PERCEBU

About 20 minutes south of San Felipe, you'll find a small lagoon and sandy beach with a small cluster of homes. The lagoon is ideal for activities live swimming or kayaking, and the beach is one of the longest and cleanest in the region with nice sandy shores. The famous **Shell Beach** is just beyond Laguna Percebu at kilometer 26, where beachcombers can walk at low tide to collect shells and enjoy the peaceful and relaxing environment.

If you're looking to camp in the area, **Rancho Percebu** (Mexico 5 Km. 21.5, tel. 686/577-2449, US$25) has *palapas,* camping sites, and a restaurant/bar. For a less-rustic experience, try **Baja Rentals** (Mexico 5 Km. 21, U.S. tel. 619/276-1430, www.bajarentals. com, US$120), a cluster of rental houses on the seaside bluff. Houses are equipped with full kitchens, cable TV, DVD players, and board games. They have kayaks for rent, an outdoor grill for barbecuing, and bonfire pits.

Just south of Percebu, you'll find **Chelos Café & Bar** (Mexico 5 Km. 35, 7am-6pm Tues.-Sun., US$4-8) a popular locals' spot for food and tequila. Located right off the highway, they have indoor and outdoor seating and serve traditional Mexican dishes at affordable prices.

★ VALLE DE LOS GIGANTES

One of the treasures of Baja California is the **Valle de los Gigantes**. The names refers to the massive cardón cacti that can grow to heights of nearly 18 meters tall and weigh up to 25 tons. Many of the cacti are over one hundred years old. These giant cardón cacti are one of the most-photographed attractions in northern Baja, and you can't take a trip to this region without getting one of your own with them. They are so unique that one cactus was transported to Spain for the World's Fair in 1992.

The turnoff is around kilometer 14 on Mexico 5 near Rancho Punta Estrella. It's US$10 per vehicle to enter the park. There's a parking area where visitors can leave their vehicles and hike around. Because of soft sand, four-wheel drive is required in order to venture farther into the park by vehicle. Temperatures can be extremely warm, so visitors are advised to bring water for walking around the park.

PUERTECITOS

Another big draw to the San Felipe region is the **Puertecitos Hot Springs.** It's $12 per vehicle to access the hot springs through Puertecitos Seaside Campo. The hot springs are located among the rocks along the coastline. High tide is the best time to visit as the ocean waters cool the hot springs down to the perfect temperature to enjoy the beautiful scenery and warm waters. Consult an online tide calendar such as **Tide Forecast** (www.tide-forecast.com) to find out the exact

time for the day you plan to visit. For US$19 you can camp for the night. Access to the hot springs is half a block past the Pemex gas station, on the left.

Cowpatty (Mexico 5 Km. 72, mscowpatty@gmail.com, noon-5pm Wed.-Sun.) is a popular open-air cantina in Puertecitos where locals and passersby stop in the afternoon for a cold beer, hot dogs, and other snacks.

★ BAHÍA SAN LUIS GONZAGA

To the north of Bahía San Luis Gonzaga is **Punta Bufeo** (Km. 135.5, tel. 555/151-9408) a spot with camping and sportfishing. The Islas Encantadas are just offshore here and anglers enjoy fishing for yellowtail and croaker around the islands.

About 12 kilometers south of Punta Bufeo at Punta Willard, **Papa Fernandez** (tel. 686/577-2492, www.papafernandez. com) offers camping, a boat launch, and a restaurant serving delicious authentic Mexican food. The settlement has been around since the late 1950s, and one of the famous clients from back in the early days was John Wayne.

Just south of Punta Willard you'll reach **Bahía San Luis Gonzaga.** The bay is

The giant cardón cacti in the Valle de los Gigantes reach heights of up to 60 feet.

actually comprised of two bays that are separated by a sand spit appearing during low tide and connecting to a small island in the bay. While the whole bay and area is referred to as Gonzaga Bay, the southern bay is technically named Ensenada de San Francisquito. This tranquil area is prime for camping, relaxing, and stargazing at night.

If you aren't camping along the beach, there's only one option in Gonzaga, **Alfonsina's** (www.alfonsinasresort.mx, US$80). Room reservations should be made at least two weeks in advance via email. Alfonsina's has a 15-room hotel as well as a decent restaurant (the shrimp burrito is a favorite), and does have a gas station. If Alfonsina's is out of gas, try **Rancho Grande** (tel. 555/151-4065, ranchogrande-baja@hotmail.com). They provide a restaurant, gas station, and mini market. They also offer *palapas* along the beach for camping.

About five kilometers southeast of Bahía San Luis Gonzaga is **Punta Final,** a cape with deserted beaches and some expat homes.

FROM BAHÍA SAN LUIS GONZAGA TO MEXICO 1

Mexico 5 after Gonzaga, heading to Laguna Chapala, has been a main topic of discussion over the past number of years. The road is only paved to kilometer 165, just past Bahía San Luis Gonzaga. Beyond that, the road to connect to Mexico 1 is unpaved and in poor condition. Roadwork is still in process, but government budget cuts have slowed progress. The road is rough and even four-wheel-drive vehicles will need to go at slow speeds to avoid the potholes and bumps.

About 35 kilometers south of Bahía San Luis Gonzaga, you'll hear the chime of hundreds of empty beer cans rattling in the wind as you come across **Coco's Corner,** a roadside institution for Baja adventurers. Coco's Corner is legendary for its setting in the middle of nowhere and its owner, Coco, who has been there for 26 years. The seemingly haphazard structure is decorated with empty beer cans and filled with off-road stickers plastered on the walls and signed underwear hanging from the ceiling. Coco has a famous book (he's filled eight of them) with the signatures of people who have passed through and a log of their vehicles. Stop for a cold beer and the opportunity to check out one of Baja's quirky desert legends. Basic camping is available as well.

Bahía San Luis Gonzaga

San Quintín and Bahía de los Ángeles

Once travelers drive south of Ensenada, the big cities of northern Baja dissipate and the adventures begin.

This is a part of Baja California where cell phone service, reliable Internet connections, and even 24-hour electricity can be hard to find at times. Many Baja adventurers believe that such factors add to the true charms and allure of the region. The focus here is on the diverse nature and wildlife and the activities that can be enjoyed are a result of those natural resources.

Surfers and anglers will want to head over to the coast for near-empty waves and yellowtail, halibut, and rock cod. The shore here is scattered with tiny fishing villages and not much else. The sea and what it has to offer those who seek it are the focus. Just inland open up the valleys of the Antigua Ruta del Vino, where Baja's wine region began well over 100 years ago. The wineries in this region offer visitors a peaceful and high-quality wine-tasting experience.

The Sierra de San Pedro Mártir offers adventurers and wildlife seekers a different side of Baja cloaked in pine trees and snowcapped mountains. The national park of the Sierra de San Pedro Mártir is home to the second largest telescope in Mexico as well as the highest mountain on the Baja California peninsula—Picacho del Diablo. This prestigious natural protected area offers nature lovers prime hiking and camping as well as the chance to view the endangered California condors that were released into the area in 2002.

Farther south, the unique and picturesque central desert is home to the protected Valle de Cirios. Here, cactus forests and rolling mountains offer road-trippers the classic Baja backdrop. For a detour off of Mexico 1, head over to the serene fishing village of Bahía de los Ángeles on the Sea of Cortez. The bay draws anglers, windsurfers, snowbirds, and those looking for the chance to swim with whale sharks in the wild.

PLANNING YOUR TIME

This region has many things to offer, and how you spend your time depends on your interests.

Surfers will want to head along the coast, exploring points from Punta Santo Tomás to

Previous: Red Mountain; the Sea of Cortez. **Above:** The *Cirios*, or Boojum Trees, fill the landscape in the Valle de los Cirios.

Look for ★ to find recommended
sights, activities, dining, and lodging.

Highlights

★ **Valle de la Grulla's Antigua Ruta del Vino:** This is where wine was first introduced by the missionaries in the late 19th century. A few beautiful wineries are still making some impressive wines today (page 131).

★ **Parque Nacional Sierra de San Pedro Mártir:** The snowcapped peaks and pine trees of this national park offer travelers a rare opportunity to experience something different from the usual desert and coastlines of the peninsula (page 136).

★ **Cataviña Cave Paintings:** See the most accessible cave paintings in Baja, just an easy hike off of Mexico 1 (page 147).

★ **Swimming with Whale Sharks:** Summer and fall bring the giant but docile whale sharks into Bahía de los Ángeles, where visitors can swim, snorkel, and kayak with the unique creatures (page 148).

Desierto Centralto Bahía de los Ángeles

El Rosario

Punta Baja

Isla San Geronimo

Bahía Rosario

Agua Blanca

1

PARQUE NACIONAL
★ SIERRA DE SAN PEDRO MÁRTIR

Puertecitos

S e a

Rancho El Progreso

o f

Punta San Fernando

MISIÓN SAN FERNANDO VELICATÁ

Rancho Tres Enriques

C o r t e z

(Gulf of California)

Bahía San Carlos

San Carlos

★ EL MÁRMOL

Isla Miramar

Isla Lobos

Isla Encantada

Puerto Catarina

CATAVIÑA CAVE PAINTINGS

Cataviña

Isla San Luis

Punta Canoas

Rancho San Ignacito

MISIÓN SANTA MARÍA

Punta Bufeo

Punta Willard

Bahía San Luis Gonzaga

Punta Final

Bahía de Calamajué

PACIFIC

OCEAN

San José de la Piedra

Nuevo Chapala

V a l l e   d e   l o s   C i r i o s

S i e r r a   d e   l a   A s a m b l e a

Punta Blanca

Parque Natural Isla Angel de la Guarda

0   20 mi

0   20 km

Punta Cono

Punta María

Bahía Santa María

Punta Negra

1

Parador Punta Prieta

Isla

Angel

de la

Punta Prieta

★ VALLE DE LA GRULLA'S ANTIGUA RUTA DEL VINO

Guarda

Punta Santa Rosalillita

Isla Coronado

C a n a l   d e   l a s   B a l l e n a s

Punta Rosarito

Rosarito

Bahía de Sebastián Vizcaíno

Bahía Santa Rosalia

Bahía de los Angeles

Bahía de los Angeles

MISIÓN SAN FRANCISCO BORJA

Bahía de las Animas

Ejido Morelos

Morro Santo Domingo

Laguna Manuela

Jesus María

★ SWIMMING WITH WHALE SHARKS

Isla Salsipuedes

Işla Las Animas

Playa Malarrimo

Peninsula   de   Vizcaíno

Laguna Ojo de Liebre

Guerrero Negro

★ EAGLE MONUMENT

Parque

Natural

del Desierto

Central

Bahía San Rafael

Isla San Lorenzo

Bahía San Franciscquito

Parque Natural de la Ballena Gris

BAJA CALIFORNIA
BAJA CALIFORNIA SUR

1

○ El Arco

San Franciscquito

MISIÓN SANTA GERTRUDIS

© AVALON TRAVEL

Best Accommodations

★ **Rancho Meling:** This serene property offers travelers a stay on an authentic working ranch in the Sierra de San Pedro Mártir (page 138).

★ **Mike's Sky Ranch:** Popular with off-roaders and dirt bikers, the ranch is easily accessible and rates include breakfast and dinner (page 138).

★ **Hotel Misión Santa María:** Situated directly on the beach in San Quintín, this hotel sits amid deserted beaches with hauntingly beautiful sand dunes and blowing winds (page 142).

★ **Baja Cactus:** With a surprisingly high level of luxury, Baja Cactus has become a famous must-stop in El Rosario (page 145).

★ **Guillermo's Hotel:** Excellent for large groups and families, this rustic hotel has large rooms and welcomes pets (page 150).

Santa Rosalillita. A week or more is needed to fully explore all of the coast, but this will also depend on how the surf is. Anglers will also have an interest in this coastal area and will want to spend at least a couple of days in San Quintín.

Those headed to Sierra de San Pedro Mártir will want to budget 3-4 days to enjoy what these mountains and the national park have to offer. Most travelers choose to stay for at least a week in Bahía de los Ángeles (many snowbirds come down for a full six months during the winter) in order to truly unwind and enjoy the region.

GETTING THERE
Starting Points
San Diego and northern Baja are the most common starting points for travel to this region. For those looking to get to the uninhabited and serene areas of the peninsula, this region will normally be the first night's stop from Southern California.

Car
Since there are no commercial airports and

very few airstrips for private planes, this part of the peninsula is best accessed by automobile. The flexibility a car provides is essential for exploring the region, as taxi service is limited.

FUEL AND SERVICES
Gas stations are available in all the big cities along Mexico 1. Make sure to get gas in El Rosario as there are no other gas stations along Mexico 1 again for another 361 kilometers until Jesus Maria just north of Guerrero Negro. Before heading into the Sierra de San Pedro Mártir, get gas in San Telmo.

Bus
Autobuses de la Baja California (ABC, tel. 664/104-7400, www.abc.com.mx) and **Aguila** (tel. 800/824-8452, www.autobusesaguila.com) have service between major towns throughout the area (excluding Bahía de los Ángeles). They stop at all of the towns from Maneadero to San Quintín, El Rosario, and Cataviña. While ABC and Aguila will take you from town to town, there aren't local bus services within towns.

Best Restaurants

★ **Jardines Restaurant:** Located next to Hotel Jardines, this restaurant serves up hearty Mexican dishes for breakfast, lunch, and dinner in a friendly atmosphere (page 140).

★ **Muelle 30:** For beautifully presented artisanal seafood dishes, Muelle 30 offers some of the best dining in San Quintín (page 141).

★ **Mama Espinoza's:** This restaurant has been a checkpoint of the Baja 1000 road race since its inception in 1967, and it continues to please road-trippers with its famous lobster burritos (page 145).

★ **Las Hamacas:** Enjoy popular Mexican breakfast dishes or fresh seafood in this casual spot with affordable prices (page 150).

Maneadero to Vicente Guerrero

This is a region of beautiful agricultural valleys with small farming towns and fishing villages along the coast. Anglers are drawn to the coast for yellowtail, rock cod, and halibut, and great waves without the crowds beckon to surfers.

There are two dirt coastal routes in this region that are popular with surfers, anglers, and adventurers. The first heads west from Santo Tomás to the sea and loops south to connect with Eréndira. The second option is to head west from Colonet over to the coast to Cuatro Casas, then down to Punta San Jacinto and wrapping around to Calamú to reconnect with Mexico 1.

The waterside is littered with small fishing villages but not many tourists. The locals are friendly, and it's not uncommon for fishers to share their lobster with you for dinner over a bonfire if you're camping on the shore.

MANEADERO

Maneadero is a small farming village with nothing much of interest for travelers aside from being notorious as the first southbound INM immigration checkpoint for cars. The checkpoint is not always open, but have your

passport and FMM tourist permit ready for inspection and you'll be on your way quickly.

Families won't want to miss **Las Cañadas Campamento** (Mexico 1 Km. 31.5, tel. 646/153-1055, www.lascanadas.com, US$9), just south of Ensenada. Zip lines, hanging bridges, waterslides, multiple swimming pools, ATV rentals, and horseback riding are enough to keep everyone busy. Many people come just for the day, but overnight camping is an option (US$16 pp) and there are also cabins (US$75) and tepees (US$38) available for rent.

★ VALLE DE LA GRULLA'S ANTIGUA RUTA DEL VINO

While the Valle de Guadalupe takes most of the spotlight when it comes to Baja wines, the much smaller and lesser-known Valle de la Grulla (located in Ejido Uruapan) is quickly making a name for itself. There are currently only a handful of wineries here, but the wines they produce are excellent, the valley is lush and beautiful, and you won't have to battle the crowds of the Valle de Guadalupe. Most of the wineries are family-run operations and offer an intimate and special experience for all who visit. There are no accommodations out here and very few options for food, but the wineries are exceptional and shouldn't be missed. Most travelers stay in Ensenada and explore Valle de la Grulla in a day trip. The turnoff for Valle de la Grulla is at kilometer 42 on Mexico 1. All wineries are marked with signs that are clear and easy to follow once turning off the highway.

Along with a few neighboring wine-producing valleys, including the Valle de Santo Tomás, this area is known as **La Antigua Ruta del Vino** or the old wine route. This is where the missionaries first introduced wine production in the late 19th century and where the Baja wine industry began.

With an impressive facility and beautiful property on an expansive 41 hectares, **MD Vinos** (tel. 646/116-6397, www.mdvinos.com, 9am-5pm daily) is well situated with vineyards, crops, stables, and areas to relax and enjoy the beautiful views. Wine-tastings take place in the main building and consist of five wines for US$6. On another part of the property, they have a picturesque picnic area where people can rent *palapas* for the day to eat, drink, and relax. Food like suckling pig, carne asada, fresh fish, and other grilled specialties is available on the weekends for US$15.

Aldo Cesar Palafox (tel. 646/174-5035, www.aldopalafox.mx, 11am-5pm Sat.-Sun.) has a beautiful and modern new tasting room and winemaking facility. Tastings consist of four exquisite wines (US$8) that are bold and complex but easy to drink. All of their grapes are grown on their property, and the views from the tasting room are of the beautiful vineyards and valley. They also have a quixotic outdoor space with shady oak trees and a small stage for events. They are only open to the public on weekends, but advance reservations can be made during the week for groups larger than six. Meals can be arranged for groups larger than 10.

At the entrance to the Valle de la Grulla just off of Mexico 1 is **Vinicola Santo Domingo** (www.cavasantodomingo.com.mx). Housed in a brick building, this family-run operation has been in business for just over 10 years. They aren't open every day, so contact them ahead of time if you want to do a wine-tasting and get a tour of the facility.

SANTO TOMÁS

South of Ensenada, travelers will encounter another wine region, Valle de Santo Tomás, with the oldest winery in Baja California anchoring the region. The agricultural valley is

Established in 1888, Bodegas de Santo Tomás is the oldest winery in Baja California.

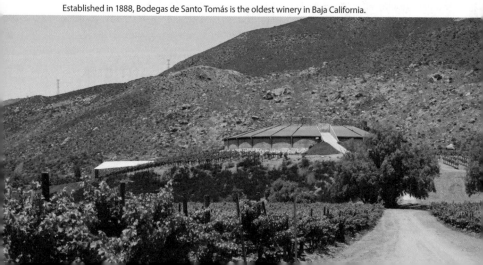

beautifully picturesque and green and lush after rains.

Misión Santo Tomás de Aquino

Misión Santo Tomás de Aquino was founded in 1791 by Dominican Padre José Loriente. The mission was relocated in 1794 and again in 1799. It was the last operating mission in California, until it was finally abandoned in 1849 when the military took over, using it as a base and capital for northern Baja California. The third (and final) site of the mission is just east of Mexico 1 as you enter Santo Tomás near the palm trees just north of El Palomar campground.

Ruins of the first two mission sites can be seen on the graded road out to La Bocana/Puerto Santo Tomás. The 1791 site has just a small section of wall remaining. Five and a half kilometers after turning onto the dirt road to La Bocana, take a road to the left and go nearly one kilometer to a clearing near the picnic area. The 1794 site is now a planted field (just a few pieces of melted adobe and rocks remain) about 1.5 kilometers east of the 1791 site, on the graded road to La Bocana.

Bodegas de Santo Tomás

The Valle de Santo Tomás is one of the five wine-producing valleys in this part of Baja California and home to the oldest winery in Baja California, the **Bodegas de Santo Tomás** (Mexico 1 Km. 49, tel. 646/174-0338, www.santo-tomas.com, 10am-5pm daily) established in 1888. They have 350 hectares where they grow 21 varietals of grapes. They have a nice tasting room set in a grove of eucalyptus trees. The wine tour they offer consists of a tasting on a tractor-pull through the vineyards and is a uniquely special experience. Regular wine-tasting in the tasting room doesn't require a reservation, but it's necessary to make advance reservations for the vineyard tractor tour. Bodegas de Santo Tomás also has tasting rooms in Ensenada and the Valle de Guadalupe.

Accommodations

El Palomar (Mexico 1 Km. 51, tel. 646/153-8002, vivepalomar@gmail.com, 7am-10pm daily, camping US$18, hotel US$35-45) has been a popular campsite, *balneario*, and picnic area for decades. *Balnearios* are swimming resorts where families can come use swimming pools and picnic areas for the day or camp for the night. There are two swimming pools as well as a small lake (swimming areas are open only in summers). In addition, El Palomar has 10 hotel rooms, a restaurant, bar, and a store directly on the highway. The store carries curios, souvenirs, and wine from Santo Tomás, as well as basic provisions and supplies.

LA BOCANA/PUERTO SANTO TOMÁS

Just south of kilometer 46 on Mexico 1, you'll see signs for the graded dirt road heading west to La Bocana and Puerto Santo Tomás. Keep veering right at the forks in the road, and you'll get to the coast. The fishing villages of La Bocana and Puerto Santo Tomás allow free camping on the beach. The point at San Jose, just north of here, is a popular surf spot as well.

About five kilometers north of La Bocana is **Puerto Santo Tomas Resort** (tel. 646/154-9415, www.puertosantotomas.com) with cabins (US$40), houses for rent (US$100-120) and camping (US$14). Bring your own beverages and food to cook, unless you've made arrangements in advance to have meals prepared for you (the food and cooks come in from Ensenada and therefore must be booked ahead of time). They can arrange for *panga* fishing trips as well.

If you head south from here on the dirt roads along the coast, you'll pass Playa Calavera, Punta Cabras (another spot for camping and surfing), and then will eventually connect with paved roads again at Eréndira.

ERÉNDIRA/PUERTO SAN ISIDRO

This region can be reached by turning off of Mexico 1 at kilometer 78 (watch for the sign for Coyote Cal's). It can also be accessed from the north via the coastal dirt roads from La Bocana.

A classic spot for Baja travelers, **Coyote Cal's** (Ejido Eréndira, tel. 646/154-4080, www.coyotecals.com) offers hotel rooms as well as tent and RV camping. There's a range of accommodations for every budget from camping (US$15) to dorm rooms (US$25) to staying in the "Crow's Nest" room (US$60). Weekly and monthly rates are also available. Family-style dinners can be had for an extra charge and must be reserved in advance. There's a game room with a pool table and table tennis where people gather to socialize. Many travelers use Coyote Cal's as a base for exploring the area.

Anglers head to **Castro's Fishing Camp** (follow signs for Castro's Campo in Eréndira, tel. 646/176-2897, www.castrosfishingplace.com, US$50-60 for cabin that sleeps 6-9 people) where they can enjoy unbridled access to deep-sea fishing. Cabins have gas-burning stoves, refrigerators, and bathrooms with hot water. Fishing charters are available for US$200 a day. The restaurant on the property serves breakfast, lunch, and dinner.

SAN VICENTE

San Vicente is a small agricultural town with a few services in the town center (including an ABC bus terminal), but not much for tourists to see except for the mission.

Misión San Vicente Ferrer

Misión San Vicente Ferrer was founded in 1780 by Dominican Padres Miguel Hidalgo and Joaquin Valero. This mission played a pivotal role because of its location along the Camino Real at the intersection of routes north to San Diego and east to Yuma. It was one of the largest and most important missions until it was abandoned in 1833. Today, Mexico's Instituto Nacional de Antropología

e Historia (INAH) has taken over the protection of the adobe remains. The mission walls have been stabilized and there are walkways around the site, which travelers can visit without having to pay an entrance fee. To find the mission, turn off of Mexico 1 onto the dirt road south of kilometer 88. The mission is just over one kilometer off of the highway.

COLONET AND SAN ANTONIO DEL MAR

The town of Colonet doesn't have much interest for tourists, but it is a good spot to get gas and gather supplies for heading out to the coast or the Sierra de San Pedro Mártir. Surfers go to the coast from here to enjoy the popular **Cuatro Casas** surf spot.

A favorite with surfers, **Cuatro Casas Hostel** (Mexico 1 Km 141, tel. 616/159-2756, www.cuatrocasashostel.com, US$50) is a funky, well-kept hostel with dorm-style rooms as well as private rooms. It is set right on the beach near some of the best surf in northern Baja. Because the hostel is a ways from town bring any supplies and provisions you may want. Breakfast and dinner are available for an extra price. In addition to the nearby surf, the property has the "showbowl"—an empty swimming pool for skateboarding. Surfboards, wetsuits, skateboards, kayaks, and bicycles are all available for rent.

With a location convenient for those passing through town in Colonet, **Hotel Paraiso Colonet** (Mexico 1 Km.131, tel. 616/165-7387, paraisocolonet@yahoo.com, US$50) is right on the highway and has 20 clean and basic rooms as well as an attached restaurant.

PUNTA SAN JACINTO AND PUNTA CAMALÚ

Punta San Jacinto is famous for its surf break nicknamed Shipwrecks (or sometimes called Freighters). The exposed point break has solid surf, especially in winter months. The nickname for the break comes from *Isla del Carmen*, a huge freighter ship that was wrecked here and sticks out of the ocean. The turnoff for Punta San Jacinto is off of Mexico 1 just south of kilometer 149.

South of Punta San Jacinto, Punta Camalú is another fishing and surfing spot. A large and imposing building on the point in Camalú, **Cueva de Pirata** (tel. 616/163-7317, www.cueva-pirata.blogspot.com, US$30-45) offers 19 rooms with basic accommodations that most surfers and fishers find to be sufficient. There's wireless access and comfortable beds. The adjoining RV site has spaces with full hookups. The seafood restaurant (open 8am-10pm daily) is frequented by those who live nearby.

The town of Camalú on Mexico 1 at kilometer 157 has a handful of markets, taco stands, and stores as well as a Pemex gas station.

VICENTE GUERRERO

The town of Vicente Guerrero is a regional agricultural hub. Tomatoes and strawberries comprise most of the crops that come from this region. A number of services are available here—gas stations, ATMs, grocery stores, and a police station.

Misión Santo Domingo

Misión Santo Domingo was a Dominican mission founded in 1775 by Padres Manuel García and Miguel Hidalgo. The indigenous people suffered from smallpox and other diseases, and the mission was closed in 1839. Ruins of adobe walls are all that's left of the mission today. To get to Misión Santo Domingo, turn off of Mexico 1 at kilometer 169 onto the graded dirt road heading east. Continue for eight kilometers north of the Santo Domingo river bridge. An old mission graveyard can be found near the ruins.

Accommodations

For accommodations in Vicente Guerrero, **Hotel Mission Inn** (Mexico 1 Km. 172.6, tel. 616/166-4400, www.hotelmissioninn. com, US$50) has modern accommodations (some of the nicest in the region) with an attached restaurant. They also offer various tour packages for exploring other destinations in the region such as the San Pedro Mártir and Cataviña.

RVers often stay at **Posada Don Diego** (Mexico 1 Km. 174, tel. 616/166-2181, www.posadadondiego.com), an RV campsite with a motel and restaurant that's been in operation since 1970. There are over 100 campsites, half of them with full hookups (US$15-18.50), and four motel rooms ($40), as well as a three-bedroom house available for rent ($110). The restaurant at Posada Don Diego was considered the first in Vicente Guerrero and serves breakfast, lunch and dinner.

Sierra de San Pedro Mártir

For nature lovers and adventure seekers, the Sierra de San Pedro Mártir offers visitors a glimpse at some uncharacteristic Baja terrain. Home to the highest peak in Baja, Pichaco del Diablo (over 3,000 meters), this is an attractive mountain region for hiking and camping. Due to the high elevation, the landscape is different here than in the rest of Baja, with pines, cypress trees, and snowcapped mountains in the winter. The diverse fauna include mule deer, bighorn sheep, cougar, bobcat, and coyote. The region also provides travelers with the rare opportunity to observe California condors in the wild because of a successful reintroduction program that released the endangered birds into the area in 2002.

With clean air and low levels of light pollution, the national park is home to the National Astronomical Observatory with the second largest telescope in all of Mexico. There are also a number of working cattle ranches in the lower-lying areas of the mountains, a few which have opened their doors to travelers looking for a serene place to stay in the area.

Parque Nacional Sierra San Pedro Mártir

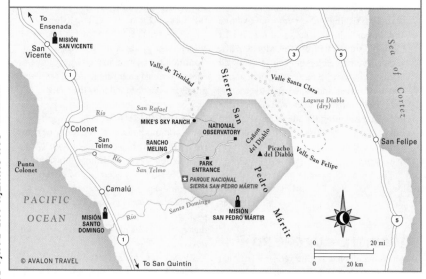

© AVALON TRAVEL

Because of the elevation, the region is very cold in the winters (the average temperature is below freezing) with a decent amount of snow. Even in summers, temperatures can dip below freezing at night.

SIGHTS

★ Parque Nacional Sierra de San Pedro Mártir

The 68,796-hectare (170,000-acre) **Parque Nacional Sierra de San Pedro Mártir** (tel. 646/172-3000, sanpedromartir@baja.gob.mx, 7am-8pm daily, US$3.50) is home to the highest peak in Baja, Pichaco del Diablo, (Devil's Peak) at 3,095 meters (10,154 feet). The park is full of pine and fir trees, snowcapped peaks, and 142 plant species, making this one of the most prestigious natural protected areas in all of Mexico.

This is a wonderful area for hiking (make sure to have GPS and topography maps) and self-contained camping. All supplies must be brought in. To arrive at the park from Mexico 1, turn east off of the highway in San Telmo at kilometer 140. Follow the signs for the "Observatorio." This will take you on another

road for 78 kilometers where you'll find the park entrance. At the park entrance is a small ranger station where you will stop to pay the park entry fee (US$3.50 per person per day) and can pick up a map of the park and get information on hiking, camping, the small cultural museum (10am-3pm Fri.-Sun.), and the observatory. For those who are staying in the small ranches in the foothills of the San Pedro Mártir, the park makes a wonderful day trip for a change of scenery and the opportunity to see the observatory and to do some hiking.

Observatorio Astronómico Nacional

The **Observatorio Astronómico Nacional** (tel. 646/174-4580, www.astrossp.unam.mx, jefatura@astrosen.unam.mx, 10am-1pm and 2pm-3pm Mon.-Fri., free tours) is home to the second largest telescope in Latin America. The San Pedro Mártir provides ideal atmospheric conditions for astronomy with clean air and very little light pollution. The observatory is regarded as one of the best places on earth to observe the planets and stars. There are three high-powered deep-space telescopes at the

the entrance to the Parque Nacional Sierra de San Pedro Mártir

is a unique chance to see these birds in their natural habitat. The birds were brought into the park in 2002 as part of a very successful reintroduction program. As of 2015 there were 28 condors in San Pedro Mártir. The condors living in the park have become used to humans and are therefore easy to observe and photograph.

Misión San Pedro Mártir de Verona

Of all of the missions in Baja California, Misión San Pedro Mártir de Verona is the highest in elevation and also the most difficult to reach. The mission was founded by the Dominicans in 1794 and stayed in operation until 1824. Only the remains of the foundation and parts of a low rock wall have survived over the years. The remains are not accessible by automobile; a two- or three-day hike or pack animal ride is required to reach the mission site. Those who venture to the mission ruins usually depart from Rancho Santa Cruz via San Isidoro to the east, or La Tasajera via La Grulla from the south.

HIKING

There are a number of marked trails throughout the **Parque Nacional Sierra de San Pedro Mártir** (tel. 646/172-3000, sanpedromartir@baja.gob.mx, 7am-8pm daily, $7.50 per vehicle) that are well maintained. Several depart from the camping area and from park roads. Hiking off-trail is also permitted in the park, but make sure to have GPS and topography maps. There are a number of beautiful ridges and vistas to enjoy. Take enough water and be aware of the altitude, which is around 2,700 meters. One popular route is the six-mile round-trip hike to El Altar. The trek features views of Picacho del Diablo, the desert of San Felipe, the Sea of Cortez, and even the coast of Sonora on a clear day.

Experienced backpackers may want to summit Picacho del Diablo. The mountain is normally approached from the eastern side on a three-day trip.

observatory. The largest, with a 2.12-meter optical lens, was built in 1975. You can take a short, free tour to see the inside of the observatory and the large telescope. Try to contact the observatory in advance about the tour. Otherwise, you can inquire at the yellow gate of the observatory (there's a telecom system here that you can use to let them know you'd like to take a tour). Since it's a working observatory, they may not be able to accommodate last-minute visitors or you may end up having to wait for a while until being able to see the observatory. There are no nighttime tours available. The view from behind the observatory is stunning with Picacho del Diablo, the Sea of Cortez to the east, and the Pacific to the west.

California Condor Lookout

Just before the entrance to the national park is a lookout where California condors congregate. You'll find some of the endangered birds perched on top of granite rocks and can watch as they soar over the valley. This

ACCOMMODATIONS
Ranchos

The most beloved spot to stay in the area is ★ **Rancho Meling** (tel. 646/120-2590, www.ranchomeling.com, US$70, meals extra). They have a plethora of activities at the ranch—swimming, basketball, horseshoes, volleyball, mountain biking, hiking, and horseback riding. The ranch, which has been in the Meling family for over 100 years, is still a working cattle ranch with a couple hundred head that roam the 4,000-hectare ranch. David Lang and his wife Sandra Meling run the ranch and have recently refurbished the rooms (which each have a potbellied stove). The quaking aspens around the property are especially beautiful in the fall against the rustic background. To get to Rancho Meling, turn off of Mexico 1 at San Telmo following the signs for the observatory. The ranch will be 50 kilometers up the road. There will be signs.

Owners Mike Wirths and Pamela Weston take care of **Baja Dark Skies** (tel. 646/116-7849, www.bajadarkskies.com, US$120 for cabin) with individual cabins available for rent. They don't provide meals and there are no restaurants nearby, so guests need to bring their own food. There's a barbecue area with a wood grill and a sink for cooking. Dry camping is also available for $10/person per day. Mike is a member of the Royal Astromony Society of Canada and has built an observatory behind the house where clients can arrange for a star-viewing. The ranch is closed January and February. To find the ranch, take the road past Rancho Meling to kilometer 67 and turn left. Four-wheel drive is advised to make it up the road.

Rancho el Coyote Meling (tel. 616/166-0086, www.ranchoelcoyote.com, US$70) is another working cattle ranch operated by a part of the Meling family (from Rancho Meling). The property has rustic but clean rooms, fire pits, and a swimming pool. They make meals for guests at the ranch, eaten in a communal dining room. Activities on the ranch include hunting for deer and quail. Turn off from Mexico 1 at kilometer 140 to get to the ranch.

the Observatorio Astronómico Nacional

For nearly 50 years, off-roaders and dirt bikers have flocked to ★ **Mike's Sky Ranch** (tel. 664/681-5514, US$45). There are 27 rooms, all around the swimming pool. Breakfast and dinner are included in the rates and are served family-style. There's a small bar that's open nightly. There are no phones (beyond the one at reception), and the power goes off at 10pm each night. The easiest access to the ranch is via Mexico 3 at kilometer 138.5, southeast of Ensenada.

Camping

Self-contained camping is permitted in the **Parque Nacional Sierra de San Pedro Mártir** (tel. 646/172-3000, sanpedromartir@baja.gob.mx, $3.50 per day, children under 6, seniors over 60, and disabled persons enter free). There is a designated camping area close to the park entrance. Services are limited, but sites feature fire pits, picnic tables, trash cans, and pit toilets. Fires are allowed at night and are recommended as temperatures can drop below freezing, even in summer months.

California Condor Reintroduction

Condors are being reintroduced into the wild in the Sierra de San Pedro Mártir.

More than ten thousand years ago, the California condor was found all along the western coast of North America from Canada to Baja California. By 1982, only 22 survived. Hunting, lead and pesticide poisoning, power line collisions, and consuming garbage led to the decimation of the population. The condors disappeared from Baja California as early as the 1950s.

In August 2002, five condors were transferred to Sierra de San Pedro Mártir as a program to reintroduce the species into the wild. The San Diego Zoo manages the recovery program, working with Mexico's National Commission for Natural Protected Areas and the U.S. Fish and Wildlife Service. As of 2015, there were 28 condors living in the San Pedro Mártir and 410 worldwide.

Condors are scavengers, not hunters, and eat carcasses. They are therefore considered to be important "cleaners of the environment." They are often found in groups and can fly 250 kilometers in a day. The largest North American land bird, the condors have a wingspan of 2.8 meters and can weight up to 25 pounds. They mate for life and lay one egg every two years.

Wood for fires is available in the park. Note that they don't allow you to bring wood into the park from the outside. There are designated day-use areas throughout the park, and campfires are not allowed in these areas.

There are also a few rustic cabins available for rent just outside the park entrance near the ranger stations. Cabins have full bathrooms, running water, electricity, gas stoves, and water heaters, but you must bring your own gas. There are also wood-burning stoves. Bring your own sheets, toilet paper, food, and drinking water. Arrangements for cabins should be made in advance by calling the park office (tel. 646/172-3000, ext. 3229, 8am-3pm).

INFORMATION

The park station at the entrance to the **Parque Nacional Sierra de San Pedro Mártir** (tel. 646/172-3000, sanpedromartir@ baja.gob.mx, 7am-8pm daily) is the best place to get information on hiking and camping in the region.

GETTING THERE AND AROUND

Private vehicles are the only way to get to and around the Sierra de San Pedro Mártir. It's about a 5.5-hour drive from San Diego. To get to the San Pedro Mártir from Mexico 1, turn east off of the road in San Telmo at kilometer 140. Follow the signs for the "Observatorio." Take this paved road for 78 kilometers to arrive at the park entrance. There are no services (gas, food, water) once you leave San Telmo, so don't forget to get gas at the station on Mexico 1 before you turn off of the highway. Rancho Meling can arrange for guided tours within the national park if you don't want to explore on your own.

San Quintín

San Quintín is popular among sportfishers and a regular overnight spot for travelers headed along Mexico 1. The town of San Quintín is nestled into a large agricultural area where strawberries and tomatoes are the main crops. There are lots of services and stores—mechanics, gas stations, hardware stores, supermarkets—along Mexico 1. Most travelers who stay in San Quintín head out to the bay or the beaches where the setting is more serene and picturesque and where most of the hotels, campsites, and some restaurants are located. The beaches flanked by sand dunes along the bay are large, picturesque, and mostly deserted.

There are technically three connected bays here: Bahía San Quintín, Bahía Falsa, and Bahía Santa Maria. There is a field of cinder cones in the ocean offshore, which make the area great for kayaking and fishing. There are many charters in the area that will take you out fishing for the day.

In the late 1800s, a British company with plans for a wheat operation settled the area. They planted crops and constructed a mill, but drought wrecked one of the first harvests, and within two decades, most of the British had left the area. The mill equipment can still be seen at The Old Mill hotel and restaurant (El Molino Viejo), and the Old English Cemetery in town has crosses and tombstones bearing British names.

RECREATION
Fishing
Sportfishing is the main reason that travelers come to stay in San Quintín. Yellowtail and rock cod are available year-round.

Dorado, white sea bass, calicos, tuna, halibut, and other species are available when in season. There are a number of options for sportfishing charter services. **Don Eddie's** (toll-free U.S. tel. 866/989-6492, www.doneddies.com) is one of the most popular choices. They also offer hunting trips, whale-watching, and diving. **Pedro's Pangas** (tel. 616/165-6040, toll-free U.S. tel. 888/568-2252, www.pedrospangas.com) launches from the Old Mill site. Boats range $220-320 per day. **K&M Sportfishing** (tel. 616/101-4714, U.S. tel. 949/370-6532, www.kmfishing.com) also launches from the Old Mill and in addition to fishing excursions, offers diving, whale-watching, and even surfing lessons.

Surfing
Surfers will find a sand bottom right point break at **Cabo San Quintín.** The spot is consistent with solid form and decent size, but the access is difficult. Take the turn off from Bahía Falsa from Mexico 1 (four-wheel drive is necessary). A better option can be to take a boat to the area. **Isla San Martin,** one of the uninhabited volcanic islands off the coast, is a spot for big-wave tow-in surfing.

FOOD
Many of the restaurants in San Quintín are attached to hotels or RV parks. There are a number of good taco stands in town along Mexico 1. Look for one with a crowd of locals.

For a modern restaurant with a fun and friendly vibe, ★ **Jardines Restaurant** (Mexico 1 Km. 1, tel. 616/165-1651, www.hotel-jardinesbaja.com, 8am-10pm

Valle and Bahía de San Quintín

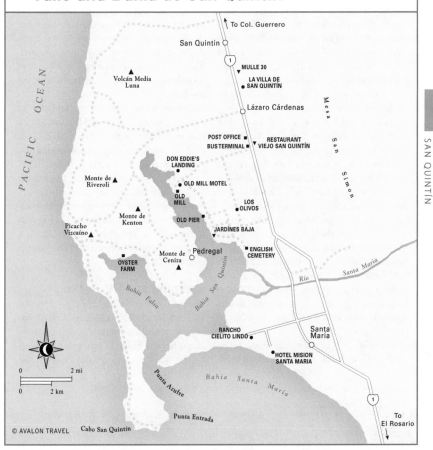

Tues.-Thurs. 8am-2am Fri.-Sun., mains US$6-13) is open for breakfast, lunch, and dinner. They serve hearty Mexican dishes as well as seafood. The bar is outfitted with large flat-screen TVs for sports, and they have a decent happy hour. They are right next door to Hotel Jardines.

The classic **Old Mill restaurant** (Mexico 1 Km. 1, tel. 616/165-6058, www.hotelold-mill.com, mains US$7-14) is on the same property as the Old Mill hotel. The property is a little run-down and in need of a remodel, but remains a popular choice for anglers

and off-roaders with the large traditional Mexican dishes and seafood specialties.

For a more artisanal food experience in San Quintín, try ★ **Muelle 30** (Mexico 1 Km. 188, Col. Las Flores, tel. 616/165-1401, aniceto60@ho-tmail.com, 11:30am-6:30pm Wed.-Mon., mains US$8-14). Located in town along Mexico 1, they specialize in seafood dishes with beautiful presentation. Ceviche, local clams, coconut shrimp, and fresh fish are among the offerings. The environment is casual with wooden tables and chairs and not much in terms of decor, but this is some of the best dining in San Quintín.

ACCOMMODATIONS

Most travelers to San Quintín choose to stay outside of town on the bay where there are a handful of hotels and campsites. This provides better and easier access to fishing and water sports as well as the beautiful beaches and sand dunes. There are a few options for hotels in town on Mexico 1 for those who are just quickly passing through and looking for a place to stay for the night.

Just off the highway in downtown San Quintín, **La Villa de San Quintín Hotel** (Km. 192 Mexico 1, tel. 616/165-1800, www.hotellavilla.biz/sanquintin, US$45) has secure off-street parking with room for trailers and boats. This newer hotel has modern and comfortable rooms that are up to U.S. standards. There is a restaurant on-site.

Rooms at the **Old Mill** (Mexico 1 Km. 1, tel. 616/165-6030, toll-free U.S. tel. 855/690-9272, www.hoteloldmill.com, US$37-42) are basic and rather rustic. Accommodations are centered around a courtyard. This no-frills joint is popular with anglers and off-roaders and can get rowdy at night. There's an attached campground.

Some of the best accommodations out on the bay are at **Hotel Jardines** (Mexico 1 Km. 1, tel. 616/165-6060, U.S. tel. 619/591-8922, www.hotel-jardinesbaja.com, US$40). The property features nice lush grounds, and the rooms are comfortable and affordable. They do allow pets in certain rooms, but its best to call in advance to make those arrangements. They have a nice restaurant with a bar next door. Free coffee and tea are available in the morning.

Formerly the Desert Inn (and the La Pinta before that), ★ **Hotel Misión Santa María** (Camino a playa Santa Maria, tel. 616/165-9008, www.hotelmisionsantamaria.com.mx, US$45) is set right on an expansive and beautiful beach. The rooms all face the beach and have recently undergone renovations. Travelers stay here for the peace and solitude and direct access to the beaches and sand dunes. There is a restaurant and bar on-site and the hotel is dog-friendly.

Camping and RV Parks

The old standby, **Cielito Lindo** (tel. 616/162-1021, www.cielitolindo.8m.com, US$12) has sites with hookups as well as tent camping sites. They also have a 13-room motel and restaurant/bar with a famous crab dinner. While

Hotel Misión Santa María in San Quintín

it was once the nicest spot in San Quintín, the property is aging and has not been well taken care of. The electricity still goes out each night around midnight.

The newest campground in San Quintín, **Los Olivos** (tel. 616/111-3205, www.losolivosrvpark.com, US$15), has spaces for tent camping as well as six pull-through RV sites with 15-amp 120-volt hookups, water, and dump stations. There are modern and clean bathrooms, fast wireless access, and a swimming pool.

Popular with the sportfishing set, **Don Eddie's** (toll-free U.S. tel. 866/989-6492, www.doneddies.com, US$15) has 20 full hookup spaces, as well as tent camping spaces. They also have a few basic rooms available starting at US$45. Fishing packages are offered that include accommodations, fishing, and food.

INFORMATION AND SERVICES

There is a **State Tourism Office** (Mexico 1 Km. 178, tel. 616/165-3645, 7am-6pm Mon.-Fri., 10am-2pm Sat.-Sun.) on Mexico 1 where you can get information and brochures about the region.

GETTING THERE AND AROUND

San Quintín is a 4.5-hour drive from San Diego and therefore a regular destination for road-trippers as a first or last night accommodations as they head south down the peninsula or are on their way home to the United States. Having a car is necessary as most of the tourist destinations and accommodations are out on the bay where there is no public transportation. There are no paved roads, addresses or formal street names in much of the area.

Autobuses de la Baja California (ABC, tel. 664/104-7400, www.abc.com.mx) has buses that stop in San Quintín, but there is no local service within town.

LA LOBERA

Just south of San Quintín, travelers will find **La Lobera,** a sea lion crater along the coast. The ceiling of a cave collapsed and created a circular space overlooking the sea and beach where sea lions enjoy sunbathing and playing. There's a viewing deck that was constructed for visitors. The coastline around La Lobera is rugged and beautiful, making the trip out to the coast here worthwhile even if just for the sights.

the coastline near La Lobera

The turnoff for La Lobera is just past kilometer 47 on Mexico 1. There will be blue signs marked La Lobera. You'll take the dirt road for 5-10 minutes (follow the power lines) to the coast where you'll find the viewing deck for La Lobera next to a three-story building.

El Rosario

El Rosario is best known as an essential fuel stop; it's the last place to gas up before heading into the central desert of the peninsula. It's also become a popular overnight stop for travelers and is home to a few beloved restaurants and hotels. Don't miss the gas station here (it's open 24/7). Even if you just filled up in San Quintín, it's a good idea to top off, as the next stop for gas along Mexico 1 is 360 kilometers away in Jesus Maria, just north of Guerrero Negro. El Rosario is the gateway to what some adventurers call the "real Baja."

SIGHTS
Misión Nuestra Señora del Rosario de Viñadaco

The mission at El Rosario was the first established in California by the Dominican order. **Misión Nuestra Señora del Rosario de Viñadaco** was founded in 1774 on a site the Cochimí referred to as Viñadaco. The mission was moved in 1802 and, by 1832, was no longer in commission. Mexican farmers moved into the valley and made use of the abandoned mission tiles and other coverings for their own homes.

There are a few adobe ruins left at both mission sites. The first is north of Mexico 1 in El Rosario. Go just over one kilometer from the gas station and turn uphill a few hundred feet. The second site is in the small village of El Rosario de Abajo across the river. Turn right where Mexico 1 makes a sharp left curve (just past Mama Espinoza's). Then turn left at the next street and cross the river. Head west, going 2.5 kilometers from Mexico 1. The ruins are on the right as you drive through El Rosario de Abajo.

Travelers stop at Mama Espinoza's for the famous lobster burritos.

FOOD AND ACCOMMODATIONS

Since 1930, ★ **Mama Espinoza's** (Mexico 1 Km. 56, tel. 616/165-8770, www.mamaespinoza.com, mains US$6-11) has been serving food to locals and travelers passing through. The restaurant is famous for their lobster burrito, and the crab quesadilla is also a unique treat (and is large enough to share). The restaurant's founder, Doña Anita or "Mama Espinoza," was a beloved Baja icon who just passed away in 2016 at the age of 109. This is a very popular spot with the off-road community. They also have 17 basic motel rooms on the same property (tel. 616/165-8615).

Baja's Best (tel. 616/165-8656, bajabest@hotmail.com, 7am-7pm daily, mains US$6-13) is a great option for breakfast, lunch, or dinner. The owner, Ed, and his family run the restaurant and offer friendly service and good food. There's also a bar. Ask them what's fresh that day and order that. They also have a few rooms available on the property (US$45).

★ **Baja Cactus** (Mexico 1 Km. 55, tel. 616/165-8850, www.bajacactus.com, motel@bajacactus.com, US$32) has earned a reputation for having unexpectedly nice accommodations for a location in the middle of the Baja peninsula. Large rooms feature hand-carved wood furniture, four-poster beds, and lovely tiled bathrooms. In-room coffeemakers and complimentary shampoos and conditioners are upscale touches not regularly seen in Baja hotels in this price range. These American-style accommodations come at incredibly reasonable prices, as you can fit a family of four into a spacious room for under US$40. Ask for one of the newer rooms at the back of the property and you won't have to listen to the trucks going by on the highway during the night. Because this is such a popular spot, it's wise to call or email and make reservations in advance.

At the south end of town, **Turista Motel** (tel. 616/165-8999, US$22) offers quiet clean rooms that are simple and inexpensive but nothing fancy. King-size beds and nice showers are a treat for travelers passing through.

LAS PINTAS

Just outside of El Rosario is the rock art site of **Las Pintas.** The petroglyphs date back over 2,000 years. The rock art at Las Pintas is less the hunting imagery found at many other sites in Baja California, and more religious

With nice rooms at affordable prices, Baja Cactus hotel is a beloved overnight stay for road trippers.

and ritual-style art, leading experts to believe that Las Pintas was a ceremonial location. Trails and passageways climb around the rocks, creating a full day's worth of exploring for those who appreciate rock art. To get to Las Pintas, drive 22 kilometers south of El Rosario to the turnoff for the graded dirt road for Punta San Carlos. Take the dirt road for 27 kilometers and then take a left and drive along the riverbed for eight kilometers. Take a left, leaving the riverbed for about half a kilometer before taking a right at the fork. In three kilometers, you'll arrive at the base of the boulders of Las Pintas. Four-wheel drive is recommended. There are no facilities and no entry fees.

EL MARMOL ONYX QUARRY

Ninety kilometers south of El Rosario is the old **El Marmol Onyx Quarry.** The deserted mine still has large slabs of onyx around the area and there's an old schoolhouse built out of blocks of cream onyx. The mine was discovered in the 1890s and stayed active until 1958. During its operation, the mine shipped onyx around the world to markets in England, Belgium, Asia, and the United States to be used for mantels, tabletops, and smaller decorative items. Watch for signs around kilometer 149 on Mexico 1. Follow the dirt road out 15 kilometers to get to El Marmol.

Valle de los Cirios

South of El Rosario, the scenery will start to change, and this is where many travelers will say that the "true Baja" begins. The towns are gone, and the cacti and mountains of the *desierto central* (central desert) seem to envelope the scenery. Aside from the lonely Mexico 1 winding through the landscape, there's no sign of civilization in sight. It's possible to drive for hours at a time without even coming across another car.

The Valle de los Cirios beginning here is a natural protected area (the second largest in all of Mexico) full of wildlife. It spans from coast to coast all the way from south of El Rosario down to the state line at Guerrero Negro. Mountain lions, red-tailed hawks, and foxes live among the *cirios* (boojum trees) and cardón cacti. Along the coast, sand dunes, reef systems, and coastal wetlands comprise the unpopulated shore.

The valley is named for the odd-looking *cirios*, a Dr. Seuss-looking tree that only grows in this part of the world between latitudes 29 and 30. The *cirios* is a member of the ocotillo family. The trunk is covered all over with small branches with tiny leaves, giving it a bizarre textured look. Sometimes there are other large branches that grow out of the trunk; other times it's just the single trunk. Some grow straight up, up to 21 meters, and others bend and loop. Flowers bloom in summer and fall.

There's a small population of the *cirios* in mainland Mexico, but otherwise the tree is only found in this region of Baja California. The Mexican name *cirios,* or wax candle, came about because of the shape of the tree. The English name boojum comes from Lewis Carroll's poem, "The Hunting of the Snark."

CATAVIÑA

In the middle of the desert, the small dusty town of Cataviña offers travelers a break from the solitude with a hotel, mini market, and nearby cave paintings. Because of the convenience and beauty of the desert location, Cataviña is a popular and easy overnight stay for road-trippers passing through. The old gas station is no longer in service, but you can buy barrel gas if you need it. The terrain around Cataviña is memorable because of the large mountains of rocks, creating a unique landscape.

★ Cataviña Cave Paintings

The **Cataviña cave paintings** are the northernmost chance along Mexico 1 to see rock art. The rock art at Cataviña is a popular spot for many travelers because of the fast access. On Mexico 1 at kilometer 176, watch for the INAH sign on the east side of the highway. You can park your car here to begin the easy 10-minute hike up the hill to the paintings. The trail is well-marked and has historical and informational signs about the region and the indigenous people. The colorful images are tucked inside a small cave and depict geometric designs, a sun, and other abstract graphic shapes. The yellow, red, and black colors were made from local minerals. The paintings are believed to have been created by the Cochimí people about 1,000 years ago. These are some of the most accessible cave paintings in Baja and provide visitors a small snippet of the rock art to be found all over the peninsula.

Misión Santa María de los Ángeles

The last of the Jesuit missions settled on the Baja California peninsula was **Misión Santa María de los Ángeles** in service from 1766 to 1774. The mission today is just adobe ruins, but it's famous for its remote and arid location.

The ruins are only 23 kilometers off of Mexico 1, but the road is considered one of the roughest four-wheel-drive trails in Baja California. Most who visit the mission these days opt to hike in or take a pack animal. Ask at Rancho Santa Inés (Mexico 1 Km. 181) about an arranged guide and mules.

La Poza de Esquadra

For those who make it to the mission and are looking for even more adventure, about a half mile downstream is a natural oasis, **La Poza de Esquadra.** The best way to access the oasis is to hike down the arroyo from the mission. Those who make it will be rewarded with a pool surrounded by large rocks and palm trees.

Accommodations

Hotel Misión Cataviña (Mexico 1 Km. 174, tel. 200/124-9123, toll-free U.S. tel. 888/205-7322, www.hotelmisioncatavina.com, US$76) is the only hotel option in Cataviña. The rooms are centered around a courtyard with a pool and are nice, but slightly overpriced. There's a bar and a restaurant open for breakfast, lunch, and dinner. The gas station in front of the hotel is no longer in service.

For RV or tent camping, head to the **Santa**

The cave paintings in Cataviña are just a short hike from Mexico 1.

Ynez RV Park (Mexico 1 Km. 191, no tel., US$8). There's not much aside from some mesquite trees for shade and a small restaurant. There are no hookups, but there are some rustic bathrooms. The caretaker is the rancher next door who will come around to collect camping fees.

Off of the highway, 26 kilometers west of Cataviña, is the rustic and secluded eco-lodge of **Geoturismo La Bocana** (tel. 664/231-3505, www.geoturismolabocana.com). The eco-lodge can accommodate up to 14 people. There are plenty of places to hike around the lodge to explore palm-filled canyons, desert flora and fauna, rock formations, fossils, and cave paintings. This is a great place to make as your base for some thorough exploring of the Valle de los Cirios. Your stay includes food, accommodations, and a guided hike. Because of the remote location, reservations should be made in advance; ask about specific driving directions when making your reservation.

Bahía de los Ángeles

A popular side trip from Mexico 1 takes visitors over to the Sea of Cortez side of the peninsula to Bahía de Los Ángeles referred to as L.A. Bay, BOLA, or just "Bahía" by the expats and regular visitors. This small fishing village has become a very popular spot for expats and travelers looking for a place to get away from everything. Fishing, boating, beachcombing, camping, and enjoying the nature are favorite activities in this small, remote town. Bahía de los Ángeles has become one of the best places in recent years to swim with the docile but large whale sharks. This is often the first time Baja road-trippers get over to the Sea of Cortez.

Cell phone service is difficult to get and wireless access can be unreliable. There are not many restaurants or services, and the town just got a gas station (two, in fact) in recent years.

There are 16 islands off the coast of Bahía de los Ángeles, the largest being Isla Ángel de la Guarda. None are inhabited, but they make for a great spots for viewing wildlife and fishing. The winds pick up in the afternoon here so plan for kayaking and fishing in the early morning when the bay is tranquil.

The warm Sea of Cortez winters attract snowbirds. Fall and spring make lovely times to visit as well, but summers are exceptionally hot and usually avoided by those who know better.

SIGHTS
Museo de Naturaleza y Cultura

The small **Museo de Naturaleza y Cultura** (no tel., 10am-1pm daily, free) is full of bilingual exhibitions representing the history and ecology of the region with mining equipment, indigenous artifacts, and examples of local marinelife and shell species. Run by American Carolina Shepard, this has become one of the top attractions in Bahía de Los Ángeles. The museum is located on the south side of town just west of the main road. Watch for signs from the main road.

★ Swimming with Whale Sharks

Whale sharks are the world's largest fish and grow up to lengths of 12 meters and can weigh over 21 tons. With extremely large mouths, whale sharks are filter feeders and no danger to humans. These docile creatures are impressive to see up close in real life. Middle of summer to early fall is the best time to visit the whale sharks in Bahía de los Ángeles, but when they come to the bay depends on the year and the weather. When they are in the bay, people can take *panga* rides out to swim or snorkel with these giant creatures.

The whale sharks mostly congregate around the southern bay of Rincón, but can be found in other areas as well. It's best to go out in the early mornings when the bay is calm to kayak, snorkel, or swim with the whale sharks. Many of the local fishing guides will take you out to see them. **Ricardo's Diving Tours** (www.scubadivingbaja.com) is able to arrange boat trips to visit with the whale sharks for a few hours. Villa Bahia (www.villa-bahia.com) offers packages with lodging and guided *panga* trips.

Wildlife in the Bay

There are a string of uninhabited islands in the bay, the largest being Isla Ángel de la Guarda, which provides protection for the bay and creates the Canal de la Ballenas. The marinelife here is incredible. All kinds of whales have been spotted—orca, finbacks, blue, sperm, humpback, and pilot whales. There are a number of marine birds such as terns, pelicans, gulls, egrets, herons, cormorants, boobies, and ospreys. You may find yourself catching sea lions sunbathing, watching manta rays jump out of the water, or boating along with a pod of dolphin—the prolific wildlife in this region is always a pleasant and incredible surprise.

RECREATION
Fishing and Boating

Inquire with your hotel or campsite to hire a boat to take out for a day of fishing. They can all make arrangements for you and many of them have their own *pangas*. **Daggett's** (tel. 200/124-9101, www.campdaggetts.info, rubendaggett@hotmail.com) north of town has two 28-foot super *pangas* available for fishing trips. Reservations on the boat fill quickly in prime fishing months, so email to make reservations ahead of time.

If you have your own boat, there's a public boat ramp in town available to use for free. Villa Vitta, Guillermo's, and Casa Diaz also have boat ramps you can use for a fee.

Kiteboarding and Windsurfing

Punta la Gringa, on the north side of the bay, is a beautiful place for kitesurfers of all levels. It's particularly good for beginners because the conditions are easy, especially on the waters between mainland and the sand spit. The best season is November-April when the "El Norte" Baja winds blow.

FOOD

There aren't a lot of restaurant options in Bahía de los Ángeles because of the small population and remote location. Many of the expats with homes in the area catch fish to cook and prepare themselves. There are a few

whale bones along the shore of the bay

Bahía de los Angeles

To Airstrip, Campo Archelón, Los Vientos Spa and Resort, and Daggett's

To Mexico 1

LA PALAPA RESTAURANT

RESTAURANT LAS HAMACAS

MOTEL LAS HAMACAS

MARKET

COSTA DEL SOL

VILLA VITTA

LA PLAYA RV PARK/ VILLA VITTA RV PARK

GCC FIELD STUDIES CENTER

GUILLERMO'S RV PARK AND RESTAURANT

Plaza

MUSEUM

SUPER XITLALI

To Canal De Las Ballenas

Bahía de los Angeles

0   200 yds
0   200 m

To Bahía San Francisco

© AVALON TRAVEL

markets in town, but major grocery shopping is done out of town in Guerrero Negro. Most of the restaurants are attached to hotels, so visitors tend to eat where they are staying. Look for signs around town, which direct visitors to these businesses.

The nicest restaurant in town is at **Costa del Sol** (Km. 66, tel. 200/124-9110, costadelsolhotel@hotmail.com, mains US$6-12), but don't expect anything fancy. The restaurant has typical Mexican plates and seafood dishes, and the crowd is mostly Americans and Canadians with many off-roaders. The restaurant has indoor seating as well as outdoor patio dining with *palapas* that are lit up with strung lights at night.

★ **Las Hamacas** (tel. 200/124-9114, 6am-9pm, mains US$5-12) has savory Mexican breakfast dishes (the huevos rancheros are particularly good) and seafood dishes for lunch and dinner. Prices are affordable, and the atmosphere is casual and comfortable. There's a large indoor area with flat-screen TVs, as well as outdoor seating. There's also a basic motel on the property.

ACCOMMODATIONS
Under US$50

Right in town and a favorite of travelers, **Costa del Sol** (Km. 66, tel. 200/124-9110, costadelsolhotel@hotmail.com, US$60) has basic rooms with 24-hour electricity and air-conditioning. There's a restaurant on-site (one of the most popular in town) that's open for breakfast, lunch, and dinner. They only have a handful of rooms and these are the most popular accommodations in town, so it's best to book in advance.

Easy to find on the main street just down from Costa del Sol, **Villa Vitta** (tel. 200/124-9103, www.villavitta.com, US$35-45) has rooms all on a single level surrounding a courtyard with a pool. Hammocks and tables with chairs are set around the courtyard in the shaded areas and provide a nice option for relaxing. The rooms are modest but clean, and they have a camping and RV site across the street.

US$50-100

In town and right on the water, ★ **Guillermo's Hotel** (tel. 200/124-9104, lucygalvan2009@hotmail.com, US$65, +US$10 per extra person) has large rooms with multiple beds (some rooms have up to five queen-size beds), making this a great place to stay for groups of family or friends. The rooms are rustic with tile floors and basic

Bahía de los Angeles and Vicinity

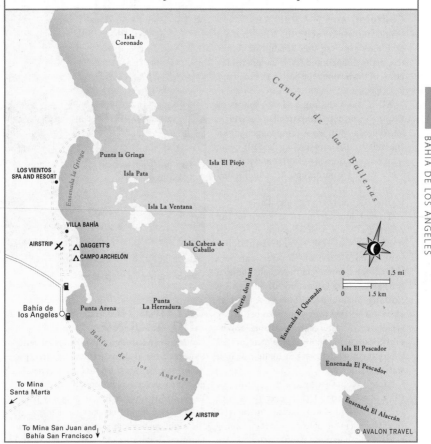

accommodations, but it's a perfect spot for anglers, and the property is pet-friendly. There's a restaurant and bar attached to the hotel, and you can also arrange for a fishing *panga*. They also have camping spaces. Cash only.

North of town, **Villa Bahia** (on road out to La Gringa, no tel., www.villabahia.com, hotelvillabahia@gmail.com, US$60-85) offers travelers a quiet and rustic escape. There's a funky common area with a barbecue pit and tables and chairs on the beach. The property

is pet-friendly, and there are dogs and cats around that belong the hotel.

US$100-150

Traditionally the nicest accommodations in Bahía de los Ángeles, **Los Vientos** (on road out to La Gringa at Km 4.5, no tel., losvientosresort@live.com, US$120) is under new ownership and underwent renovations in summer of 2015. Located north of town in a peaceful setting, they have 17 suites with bay views. William and Rosa, the new owners, are extremely hospitable and make visitors feel at home.

Camping and RV Parks

While Guillermo's and Villa Vitta in town both have camping sites in addition to hotels, many campers and RVers choose to stay north of town, along the bay on the road out to La Gringa.

All of the camping and RV spaces at **Daggett's Beach Camp** (road to La Gringa, tel. 200/124-9101, www.campdaggetts.info, rubendaggett@hotmail.com, US$10) come with views of the Sea of Cortez and *palapas*. Some also have barbecues. Air-conditioned rooms are available for rent (US$50), and fishing and boating charters are available.

Three kilometers north of town on the road to La Gringa, watch for signs for **Camp Archelon** (no tel., resendizshidalgo@yahoo.com, US$8), which offers campers *palapas* for camping on the beach. Some of the *palapas* have tables and cots. There are flushing toilets and hot showers. A few kayaks are available for campers to use. They also have two rustic cabins available for rent for US$50 a night. Camp Archelon is located where the now-defunct sea turtle research station used to be.

Many people enjoy beach camping at **Playa La Gringa,** 11 kilometers north of town. The road is only paved for the first five kilometers out of town, and it's a bumpy ride for the remaining six kilometers. There are no facilities and the location is remote, so come prepared with everything you need. This spot offers a nice opportunity to enjoy the Sea of Cortez.

INFORMATION AND SERVICES

There are now two gas stations in town as well as a few little markets and convenience stores along the main street. It's important to note that there are no ATMs in Bahía de los Ángeles and many places to not accept credit cards. Make sure to get cash before heading into town.

a sign on the way out to Villa Bahia

GETTING THERE AND AROUND

Getting to and around Bahía de los Ángeles requires a car as there are no buses that go to (or around) the town and the airstrip is no longer in service. It's possible to drive to Bahía de los Ángeles in one long day from San Diego, but most people choose to spend the night somewhere along the way in San Quintín, El Rosario, or Cataviña. If you are staying in town, it's possible to walk around to various hotels, restaurants, and the museum (the main street is nice and wide with sidewalks), but be aware that things are fairly spread out.

The turnoff for Bahía de los Ángeles from Mexico 1 is at kilometer 280. The road from Mexico 1 to Bahía de los Ángeles is now paved and in good condition.

OFF-ROAD EXCURSIONS
Las Animas

South of Bahía de los Ángeles is Bahía de Las Animas, which is only reached by boat. **Las**

Animas Baja Eco Lodge (toll-free U.S. tel. 800/221-9283, www.bajaairventures.com) run by Baja Airventures is a secluded retreat with yurts. All-inclusive packages for the resort include airfare from San Diego.

San Francisquito

An off-road adventure from Bahía de los Ángeles heads south to the remote San Francisquito, following the route that the Baja 1000 race takes. Off-roaders and motorcyclists will be rewarded with solitude and the beauty of the Sea of Cortez at **Punta San Francisquito** (sanfrancisquito@hotmail.com, US$20). Travelers can stay here in one of two rustic cabins with three single beds in each hut. Cold beer and soda are also available for those passing through.

West of San Francisquito on the way to El Arco are two other ranches that take in off-roaders. **Rancho Piedra Blanca** (ranchopiedrablanca@hotmail.com, cabin US$15) offers cabins, camping, barrel gas, and meals on the weekends. **Rancho Escondido** (cabins US$30) also has barrel gas, cold beverages, and rustic *palapa* rentals.

To get into this area, turn off from Mexico 1 about 30 kilometers south of Guerrero Negro.

Misión San Francisco de Borja Adac

The northernmost stone mission on the Baja peninsula, **Misión San Francisco de Borja Adac** was established in 1762 by the Jesuits in the Cochimí settlement of Adac, west of Bahía de los Ángeles. The mission was in operation until 1818. The stone church that stands today was built in 1801. The caretaker is a fourth generation Cochimí, and he and his family give free tours of the mission 8am-6pm daily. They are also available to give guided tours of nearby rock art sites. There's a picnic area at the mission if you want to take food and enjoy the afternoon. Don't miss the adobe ruins behind the stone church.

The mission is accessed by a scenic drive from the road out to Bahía de los Ángeles (at Km. 44) or from Mexico 1 at Rosarito.

Valle Montevideo

An interesting side trip near Mission San Borja is to Montevideo, one of the rock art sites in Baja California easily reached with four-wheel drive. These rock paintings are believed to be 10,000 years old. Abstract figures and colorful patterns are painted along the large cliff face.

From Mexico 1, take the signed turnoff for

dirt road at the southern area of Bahía de los Angeles

Mission San Borja. Drive three kilometers, turn left on a side road, and drive another nine kilometers until you reach the side of a cliff. The pictographs are along its face.

Santa Rosalillita

Once a sleepy Pacific fishing village, Santa Rosalillita received electricity, wide paved streets, and an expanded port in 2008 due to the Mexican government's plan to create the "Escalera Nautica." This failed project was intended to establish ports along both sides of the Baja California peninsula and mainland Mexico along the Sea of Cortez. Boats were to dock in Santa Rosalillita and be carried in big trucks across the peninsula over to the calmer waters of the Sea of Cortez. When the project did not take off, it left Santa Rosalillita as a ghost town marina.

While the Escalera Nautica project has come to a halt, the area is still popular for surfers and windsurfers. Punta Santa Rosalillita, a long right point break north of Santa Rosalillita, breaks pretty consistently. Farther south off of Punta Rosarito is The Wall surf break. Santa Rosalillita is a great access point for the Seven Sisters, a series of seven right point breaks starting at Punta Cono in the north and ending at Punta Rosarito with The Wall as the southernmost point. Four-wheel drive is required to reach most of the breaks.

The turnoff for Santa Rosalillita from Mexico 1 is at kilometer 38.5 where you will drive 15 kilometers on a paved road to the coast.

Paralelo 28

Just north of the city of Guerrero Negro, as you approach kilometer 128 on Mexico 1, you'll see a large Mexican flag and monument that signifies that state line between Baja California (Norte) and Baja California Sur. You'll pass through an immigration and agricultural checkpoint where you'll need to show your passport and FMM tourist permit. Fruits and vegetables are not allowed across state lines, so if you have any produce, it will likely be confiscated. They will charge US$1.50 to spray the undercarriage of your vehicle for insects. The time jumps ahead one hour as you cross from Baja California Norte into Baja California Sur.

Guerrero Negro and El Vizcaíno

Look for ★ to find recommended
sights, activities, dining, and lodging.

Highlights

★ **Saltworks:** The world's largest saltworks facility is in the town of Guerrero Negro, and visitors can tour the entire operation (page 161).

★ **Isla Cedros:** Anglers flock here for the abundant fishing of bass, sheepshead, and yellowtail (page 167).

★ **San Ignacio Colonial Plaza:** This quaint colonial square operates as the soul of this oasis town (page 170).

★ **Whale-Watching Tours:** One of Baja's most unique experiences is petting gray whales in the wild. Laguna San Ignacio is the best place to encounter these gentle giants (page 175).

★ **Sierra de San Francisco Cave Paintings:** The most impressive and well-known cave paintings on the peninsula require a multiday foot and pack-animal trek to reach (page 175).

The northern part of the state of Baja California Sur is a region of small towns, beautiful mountain ranges, the natural biosphere reserve, and the wonders of the Pacific Ocean.

This is an area for true adventurers. Fancy hotels and fine dining are not the order of the day; accommodations are basic and your best meal will often be at the local taquería. The area is mostly undeveloped and ripe for exploring. Adventurers come here to hike in uncharted areas, explore rarely seen cave paintings, surf empty waves, and experience personal encounters with gray whales.

Situated on the state line, the town of Guerrero Negro is known for having the world's largest saltworks operation and for being a prime spot for gray whale watching. Farther south, the Vizcaíno peninsula (part of the Vizcaíno Biosphere Reserve) has great spots along the Pacific for fishing, surfing, and exploring. Also inside the Vizcaíno Biosphere Reserve are the remote but world-famous cave paintings of the Sierra de San Francisco, accessible via a multiday hiking and pack animal trip into the mountains.

The nearby colonial town of San Ignacio has a lovely town plaza, complete with a stone mission. Outside of town, Laguna San Ignacio is perhaps the best spot in the world for gray whale encounters.

PLANNING YOUR TIME

Plan to stay 2-3 days in either Guerrero Negro or San Ignacio if you want to see the gray whales. You'll need at least 3-4 days for exploring the cave paintings of the Sierra de San Francisco. Visitors who venture to the Vizcaíno peninsula generally do so to relax, fish, surf, and explore the region, so you will want to dedicate a number of days to doing so. An easy overnight stay in Guerrero Negro or San Ignacio works for road-trippers anxious to get farther south.

GETTING THERE
Starting Points

Companies that arrange for all-inclusive

Previous: gray whale-watching in Guerrero Negro's Laguna Ojo de Liebre; San Ignacio's Misión Nuestra Señor San Ignacio de Kadakaamán. **Above:** rugged Sierra de San Francisco.

Guerrero Negro to Bahía Concepción and El Vizcaíno

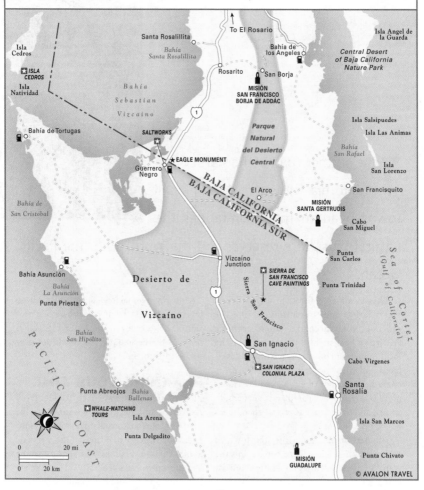

© AVALON TRAVEL

packages for fishing at Isla Cedros or whale-watching at Laguna San Ignacio will likely provide you with transportation from San Diego. Road-trippers who don't mind a very long day of driving may arrive in Guerrero Negro after a long day (about 12 hours) from San Diego. Those less interested in that many hours behind the wheel will likely have spent the night in El Rosario or San Quintín.

Car

This is an engaging area for road-trippers because of the scenic views and interesting small towns. Whether the final destination is in this region or farther south on the peninsula, most road-trippers end up staying at least one night in the area. Mexico 1 crosses from the Pacific Ocean side of the peninsula to the Sea of Cortez here, so it makes for diverse options for driving and exploring.

Best Accommodations

★ **Hotel TerraSal:** This new pet-friendly hotel in Guerrero Negro provides an affordable and convenient overnight stay for road-trippers (page 163).

★ **Halfway Inn:** With wireless internet, a restaurant and bar, this small inn is a great choice for road-trippers who want to avoid the bustle of the town (page 163).

★ **Ignacio Springs Bed & Breakfast:** Stay in a yurt along the Río San Ignacio at this unique bed-and-breakfast (page 173).

★ **Las Casitas:** If you can get one of the oceanfront *casitas*, this hotel on the bluffs overlooking the Sea of Cortez can be worth a stop in Santa Rosalía (page 180).

FUEL AND SERVICES

Gas stations are fairly plentiful with fuel available in the cities and along the way on Mexico 1. Services such as grocery stores, mechanics, hospitals, and banks, are found in the cities, which are spread out within an hour or so of each other driving on Mexico 1.

Air

There's a small airport in Guerrero Negro with regional flights to and from other cities in Baja California. If you arrange for an all-inclusive charter with airfare for a trip to Isla Cedros or whale-watching at Laguna San Ignacio, you will depart from the San Diego area.

Bus

Autobuses de la Baja California (ABC, tel. 664/104-7400, www.abc.com.mx) and **Aguila** (tel. 800/824-8452, www.autobusesaguila.com) have bus service to the major cities along Mexico 1 in this region from other spots on the peninsula.

Guerrero Negro

The state of Baja California Sur begins in Guerrero Negro, the midway point between Tijuana and Cabo. Often cold and foggy, Guerrero Negro is generally just an overnight stop for travelers to sleep, refuel, and get services while heading to other regions of the peninsula. But in the winter months, Guerrero Negro becomes a busy destination for whale-watching.

The nearby Laguna Ojo de Liebre (formerly called Scammon's Lagoon) is one of three lagoons on the Pacific gray whales migration each winter. While whale-watching is the main draw for tourism to Guerrero Negro, the town is also home to the largest open-air saltworks factory in the world where travelers can take a behind-the-scenes tour. While Guerrero Negro is a relatively large town for the region, it's still easy to navigate because one main street houses many of the banks, gas stations, restaurants, and hotels.

SIGHTS
Laguna Ojo de Liebre Whale-Watching

Laguna Ojo de Liebre (formerly known as Scammon's Lagoon) is one of three spots in Baja California gray whales migrate to every winter.

Charles Melville Scammon first came to the

Guerrero Negro

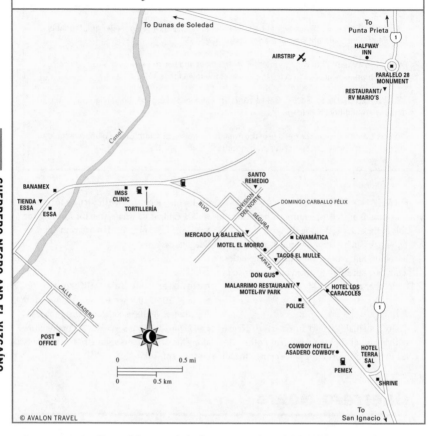

To Dunas de Soledad

To Punta Prieta

AIRSTRIP

HALFWAY INN

PARALELO 28 MONUMENT

RESTAURANT/ RV MARIO'S

Canal

BANAMEX

IMSS CLINIC

TORTILLERÍA

TIENDA ESSA

ESSA

SANTO REMEDIO

DIVISIÓN DEL NORTE

SEGURA

BLVD

DOMINGO CARBALLO FÉLIX

MERCADO LA BALLENA

MOTEL EL MORRO

LAVAMÁTICA

ZAPATA

TACOS EL MULLE

DON GUS

MALARRIMO RESTAURANT/ MOTEL-RV PARK

HOTEL LOS CARACOLES

POLICE

CALLE MADERO

POST OFFICE

0   0.5 mi
0   0.5 km

COWBOY HOTEL/ ASADERO COWBOY

HOTEL TERRA SAL

PEMEX

SHRINE

© AVALON TRAVEL

To San Ignacio

lagoon in 1857 and hunted the gray whales for oil. Over the next 18 years, whalers nearly extinguished the gray whale population in the region, but luckily the whales were able to rebound. Today, visiting with these friendly creatures is one of the most unique attractions on the peninsula. The gray whales come to the lagoon to breed and give birth every winter and have been known to engage in extremely friendly behavior with humans—coming up to boats where people can pet and kiss them. Because waters are calmer in the mornings, whale-watching excursions generally set out then.

There are two ways to do some whale-watching at Ojo de Liebre. The first option is to go through a tour operator. **Malarrimo Eco-Tours** (Blvd. Emiliano Zapata, tel. 615/157-0100, www.malarrimo.com, US$38 per adult, US$30 for children) offers four-hour tours (three hours on the water with the whales) with a bilingual guide. Reservations must be made at least one day in advance. A boxed lunch is included. The whale-watching tours through **Mario's Tours** (Mexico 1 Km 217.3, tel. 615/157-1940, www.mariostours. com, mariostours@hotmail.com, US$50) begin in their large *palapa* restaurant where they explain about the whales and their behaviors. Boats go into a northern lagoon, an area most other boats do not have access to.

Best Restaurants

★ **Tacos el Muelle:** This place is affectionately called "Tony's Tacos" for the owner who serves delicious fish and shrimp tacos every day out of his taco truck painted like a gray whale (page 162).

★ **Victor's:** Full of San Ignacio nostalgia and charm, this restaurant offers good Mexican food and excellent margaritas (page 172).

★ **Tonka's Grill:** As one of the best dining options in Santa Rosalía, Tonka's Grill offers carefully crafted meals, artisanal Baja beers, and a friendly ambience (page 178).

★ **El Muelle:** Enjoy delicious and affordable breakfast, lunch, or dinner on El Muelle's lovely outdoor patio (page 178).

★ **Panadería El Boleo:** This French bakery, which opened in 1901, offers both *boleos* and baguettes--and tasty breakfast options (page 179).

They spend three hours on the water and provide a boxed lunch. Reservations must be made in advance by calling or emailing.

The second option for whale-watching in Laguna Ojo de Liebre is to go directly to the lagoon yourself and go out on the water with a local *panguero*. The southern part of the lagoon is controlled by the **Ejido Benito Juarez** (tel. 615/157-0025, benitojuarez08@ hotmail.com, US$45), and this cooperative runs *pangas* out to see the whales. Boats leave about every half hour from 9am to 3pm and spend an hour and a half on the water. From Guerrero Negro, head south on Mexico 1 to kilometer 207.5 and turn west onto the dirt road, following signs for Ojo de Liebre to out to the lagoon. You'll pass a guard you who will take your information, and then you will eventually get to a large dirt parking lot and a beige adobe building. Around the back of the building, you will find the kiosk and dock for whale-watching. They also have camping *palapas* here that cost US$10 a night.

There are also all-inclusive gray whales trips originating from San Diego. **Baja Custom Tours** (tel. 619/886-4116, www. bajacustomtours.com, US$1,700/week all-inclusive) offers clients a unique experience whale-watching along with other interesting Baja attractions on the trip down and up the peninsula. Shari Bondy of La Bufadora Inn at Bahía Asuncion also offers whale-watching tours in Guerrero Negro through her company **Magic Whale Tours** (tel. 615/155-7197, U.S. tel. 619/906-8438, www.magicwhaletours.com). These multiday packages can be either fly-in or drive-in.

★ Saltworks

Guerrero Negro was founded in 1957 with the creation of the saltworks to supply the western United States. This evaporative saltworks is the largest open-air salt mine in the world, exporting seven million tons of salt per year for consumption in Asia, the United States, Canada, and New Zealand. Nine percent of the world's salt comes from this mine. The mine is owned and operated by ExportadoraSal, S.A. and employs 1,000 laborers, accounting for 60 percent of the town's economy.

Free tours can be arranged by going directly to **the plant** (Blvd. Emiliano Zapata, tel. 615/157-5100, www.essa.com.mx). Visitors will get to see the large lakes where the saltwater evaporates, leaving behind the salt that will be harvested. They'll also get to see the refinery where the salt is processed and separated into road salt and salt that will be used for human consumption. Watch the salt get loaded onto the conveyor belts for transport onto the barges that will take it over to Isla Cedros to be shipped out all over the world. If you don't speak Spanish, it can be easier to arrange for a tour through **Malarrimo Eco-Tours** (www.malarrimo.com) for US$10.

Dunas de Soledad

Just ten kilometers north of town, four kilometers west of Mexico 1 on a dirt road, are the impressive **Dunas de Soledad.** Mostly devoid of vegetation, these pristine and large sand dunes face the immaculate Playa Don Miguelito along the shore and are a beautiful spot for a walk or for some striking photographs. There's no entry fee to access this remote spot.

Bird Sanctuary

Bird watchers will want to take the road out to the old lighthouse and abandoned pier to the salt marshes that have been turned into the **Refugio de Aves.** The marshes attract thousands of birds migrating south in the winter as well as resident species. Ninety-five different species of birds have been counted here. Herons, sandpipers, and egrets are commonly spotted as well as ospreys (whose nests can be seen around the town). There's a small archway with a sign at the entrance to the sanctuary where visitors can park and then walk around on foot. There's no entry fee. There are a few interpretive signs with information on the birds that can be found in the area. On the weekends, families come out to the sanctuary to enjoy picnics.

FOOD

Restaurant options are limited in Guerrero Negro, so many travelers end up eating at the restaurant at their hotel as the easiest option.

The fish taco truck ★ **Tacos el Muelle** (Blvd. Emiliano Zapata at Rosaura Zapata, 10:3am-3pm daily, US$1.50) is known affectionately as "Tony's Tacos" because the owner has been serving up delicious, battered fish

the saltworks of Guerrero Negro

tacos from his truck for 22 years. You can't miss Tony's tack truck right on the main street, as it is painted like a gray whale. These delicious fish and shrimp tacos are a favorite of locals and travelers in the know. Tony is moving locations by the end of 2017 to be across from the casino.

Santo Remedio (Domingo Carballo Felix, tel. 615/157-2909, Mon-Sat 9am-11pm, Sun 6pm-11pm, mains US$7-13) is the closest thing to upscale dining in Guerrero Negro. The restaurant features a nice ambience, friendly staff, and decent food. The seafood dishes are popular (especially the coconut shrimp), and they have a good wine selection. It's located off of the main street, behind the casino.

The restaurant at **Malarrimo** (Blvd. Emiliano Zapata, tel. 615/157-0100, www.malarrimo.com, 7:30am-10pm daily, mains US$7-12) has been a popular choice for travelers for a number of decades. Seafood is the specialty here, especially the oysters and scallops. They also have a full bar.

North of town on the highway, **Mario's Palapa** (Mexico 1 Km. 217.3, tel. 615/157-1940, www.mariostours.com, 7am-9pm Mon.-Sat., 7am-2pm Sun., mains US$6-16) is a giant open-air restaurant, open for breakfast, lunch, and dinner. Meats and seafood as well as traditional Mexican dishes grace the menu. They also have tourist information and offer whale-watching tours that originate here at the *palapa*.

If you're tired of Mexican food, **Roberto's Pizza** (Avenida Industrial Salinera, tel. 615/157-0615, 11am-10pm daily, US$8-11) serves large pizzas and salads. It's a very casual and basic restaurant, with a few video arcade games and a foosball table that kids will enjoy. They'll also deliver to your hotel.

ACCOMMODATIONS

Accommodations in Guerrero Negro are basic and generally affordable. Reservations should be made in advance during whale-watching season (Jan.-Apr.), as places tend to book up. Outside of whale season, they aren't necessary.

A new hotel generating lots of buzz for Baja road-trippers is ★ **Hotel TerraSal** (Blvd. Emiliano Zapato, tel. 615/157-0133, hotelterrasal@hotmail.com, US$35). They have modern spacious rooms, a friendly staff,

and they accept dogs for an additional US$6. A large gated parking area with a guard is nice for travelers looking for a spot to park their truck and trailer without having to unhitch. The convenient location is just off of Mexico 1 before heading into town. There's a restaurant conveniently located at the hotel as well.

Malarrimo Motel & RV Park (Blvd. Emiliano Zapata, tel. 615/157-1011, www.malarrimo.com, US$35) offers standard rooms that are a bit outdated but clean with color TVs, coffeemakers, and free wireless access. They also have 45 RV sites (US$15) with full hookups and tent camping sites (US$10 per person). They have a restaurant on-site and are one of the most popular outfitters for tours of whale-watching, the saltworks, and cave paintings.

Many off-roaders and road-trippers enjoy staying at **Don Gus** (Rosaura Zapata, tel. 615/157-1611, dongushotrest@prodigy.net.mx, US$37) where the accommodations are basic and clean with hot showers. The property is dog-friendly, and they have an enclosed parking lot. There's a popular restaurant on-site as well.

Directly off of Mexico 1, just near the state line at *paralelo* 28, ★ **Halfway Inn** (formerly Desert Inn and La Pinta, Mexico 1,

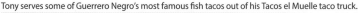

Tony serves some of Guerrero Negro's most famous fish tacos out of his Tacos el Muelle taco truck.

Gray Whale-Watching

gray whale-watching in Guerrero Negro's Laguna Ojo de Liebre

One of the most incredible natural wonders on the Baja peninsula is visiting with the gray whales that come to the warm lagoons of Baja California Sur every winter.

Every October, the gray whales of the Pacific begin a two- to three-month migration from the cold Alaskan seas to Baja California. At nearly 22,530 kilometers (14,000 mi.) round-trip, it is the longest annual migration of any mammal. The gray whales travel to the warm lagoons of Baja California Sur to mate and give birth to their calves.

From January to April, tourists travel from all over the world to visit Baja and see the gray whales. There are three locations in Baja that the gray whales migrate to each year: Ojo de Liebre (formerly Scammon's Lagoon) in Guerrero Negro, Laguna San Ignacio, and Bahía Magdalena. The shallow and protected waters of these bays provide an ideal spot for birthing and nursing calves.

Weighing up to 40 tons and measuring nearly 15 meters long, the gray whales are the gentle giants of the ocean. Seeing them in Baja is not your typical whale-watching experience. In addition to putting on a show for humans by spyhopping, breaching and spouting, the gray whales of Baja actually seek out human contact and will come right up to the whale-watching boats.

Whale-watching in this region is highly regulated and controlled. Guides are taken out in smalls groups of 6-8 people on *pangas* (small fishing boats) and are able to get up close and personal with the whales. The whales are so friendly that they will come right up and surface alongside the boats in the lagoon so that people can pet and touch them. Often mother whales will push their young calves right up to the boats so that people can pet, hug, and kiss the baby whales. It's a uniquely thrilling and unforgettable experience.

tel. 615/157-1305, hotelhalfwayinn@gmail.com, www.halfwayinnhotel.com, US$35) has 30 rooms, a restaurant and bar, and wireless Internet. This is a good option for road-trippers who don't want to hassle with going into town.

Hotel Los Caracoles (Calzada de la República, tel. 615/157-1088, www.hotelloscaracoles.com.mx, US$40) offers clean but sparse rooms, sufficient for a night's stay when passing through town. The hotel is along one of the first streets when heading into town from Mexico 1, which is another reason it's a popular spot for road-trippers passing through.

SERVICES

Guerrero Negro is the largest city in this region and has numerous banks, grocery stores, and Pemex gas stations. Tourist information can be picked up at **Mario's Restaurant and Tours** (Mexico 1 Km. 217.3, tel. 615/157-1940, www.mariostours.com, mariostours@hotmail.com), a *palapa* just north of town on the highway. There's a **Comision Nacional de Areas Naturales Protegidas (CONANP) office** (Casa de la Fauna, Ave. Profesor Domingo Carballo Félix, Esquina Ruiz Cortinez, tel. 615/157-1777, www.conanp.gob.mx, vizcaino@conanp.gob.mx) in Guerrero Negro that handles anything involving the Vizcaíno Biosphere Reserve.

GETTING THERE

Most travelers arriving in Guerrero Negro come in a private vehicle. There is also bus service to Guerrero Negro from other Baja cities with **Aguila** (tel. 800/824-8452, www.autobusesaguila.com) and **Autobuses de la Baja California** (ABC, tel. 664/104-7400, www.abc.com.mx). Those who are driving into Guerrero Negro from the north should note that Guerrero Negro is the state line dividing Baja California (Norte) and Baja California Sur at *paralelo* 28 (the 28th parallel). You will be stopped at the state line to spray the undercarriage of your car for bugs (you'll need to pay US$1.50 for this), and they will likely confiscate any fruits and vegetables that you have. You should also be prepared to show your FMM tourist permit and passport.

There is a small airstrip just north of town, and two regional airlines, **Aéreo Calafia** (www.aereocalafia.com.mx) and **Aéreo Servicio Guerrero** (www.asg.com.mx), offer service from other towns in Baja California such as Ensenada and Cabo. There are no international flights. There's a turnoff for the airstrip north of town along Mexico 1 at kilometer 124.5.

GETTING AROUND

City buses run along Boulevard Zapata and Calle Madero. Taxis will get you around town for under US$5. You can also get a taxi to take you out to the Laguna Ojo de Liebre for whale-watching. Ask for a price in advance and make sure that they wait for you at the lagoon to bring you back to town.

The Vizcaíno Peninsula

The Vizcaíno peninsula is an area rich in natural resources where anglers, surfers, and naturalists enjoy the treasures of the Pacific coastline. It's a nice side trip off of Mexico 1 that will take you off of the beaten path for a bit. A majority of the area remains untouched by development with most visitors staying along the coast where there are a few fishing villages, eco-lodges, and hotels tucked into the bays. Camping is a popular choice for accommodations in this region.

VIZCAÍNO BIOSPHERE RESERVE

Created in 1988, the **Vizcaíno Biosphere Reserve** (www.conanp.gob.mx) is the largest wildlife refuge in Latin America. At 24,930 square kilometers (9,625 sq. mi.), the biosphere reserve encompasses Guerrero Negro down to Santa Rosalía along Mexico 1 and down to Laguna San Ignacio on the Pacific Coast. The area protects the impressive flora, fauna, and cultural sites. The gray whale breeding lagoons of Ojo de Liebre and San Ignacio are included in the reserve as well as the cave paintings of the Sierra de San Francisco.

VIZCAÍNO JUNCTION

Vizcaíno is a large city with lots of services such as gas, groceries, and mechanics along Mexico 1, but it isn't much of a tourist destination. Visitors mostly know it as the junction for getting off of Mexico 1 to head west out to the Vizcaíno peninsula.

For an overnight stay in Vizcaíno, **Hotel Kadekaman** (Mexico 1 Km. 143, tel. 615/156-4112, www.kadekaman.com, US$40) offers nice remodeled rooms with wireless Internet, TVs, and a small but nice restaurant on-site. There's also a small RV park (US$10 with no hookup, US$15 for water/electricity) on the property with very nice bathrooms and showers.

MALARRIMO BEACH

On the north side of the Vizcaíno peninsula along the Bahía Vizcaíno is the beachcombing paradise of **Malarrimo Beach.** Items scattered along the beach that have washed ashore here include pieces of shipwrecks, buckets, appliances, bottles, cans of food, and more. A visit to Playa Malarrimo is not easy since there are no roads, nor is it for the faint of heart, since the winds blow fiercely, kicking up sand and moving the dunes feet at a time in a matter of hours. Treasure seekers who can't resist can visit the office of **CONANP,** the National Commission of Natural Protected Areas office (Casa de la Fauna, Ave. Profesor Domingo Carballo Félix, Esquina Ruiz Cortinez, tel. 615/157-1777, www.conanp.gob.mx, vizcaino@conanp.gob.mx) located in Guerrero Negro to get permission and see about arrangements for a boat. You will need to buy a permit for US$29 that will be valid for a year and grant you full access to the Vizcaíno Reserve as well as to all of the parks and protected areas in Mexico. There's nothing but sand dunes and flotsam out at Malarrimo, so you must bring everything in with you to camp.

BAHÍA TORTUGAS

Bahía Tortugas or Turtle Bay is a remote fishing town built on a large protected bay. The large harbor and its location halfway down the peninsula make Bahía Tortugas a popular spot for those boating down Baja. At

The Endangered Berrendo

The berrendo pronghorn (*Antilocapra americana peninsularis*) were once abundant in Baja, but now only exist within the confines of the Vizcaíno Biosphere Reserve and are in critical danger of going extinct. The pronghorn is the fastest land mammal in the Western Hemisphere and can sustain running at high speeds longer than cheetahs. It's estimated that there are only 150 berrendos left in Baja. The San Diego Zoo and Los Angeles Zoo are working to reestablish the berrendo in protected areas.

360 nautical miles from San Diego, it's a stop on the annual Baja Ha-Ha boating rally as well as a regular spot for refueling and resting for other yachters. There is very little tourist infrastructure in Bahía Tortugas as relatively few tourists visit here. To find the area, Take Mexico 1 from Guerrero Negro for 249 km until you reach Deportivo in Bahía Tortugas.

The main beach near town with the pier is generally gray and dirty, but out near the airstrip, **Playa el Playón** is a good beach for spending the day or camping. Nearby rocky points provide decent breaks for surfing.

Services in town include a bank, small grocery store, and an Internet café. There are a few small restaurants and taco stands as well as very basic accommodations such as **Motel Rendón** (Pedro Altamirano #5, tel. 615/158-0232, US$22) and **Motel Nancy** (Ave. Independencia, tel. 615/158-0056, US$25). Lobster is one of the main catches for the fishers here, so don't miss having a fresh lobster meal.

PUNTA EUGENIA

Taking the dirt road north from Bahía Tortugas for 26 kilometers, travelers will arrive at the small village of Punta Eugenia. Boats depart from here for Islas Cedros, Natividad, and San Benito. Camping is permitted along the cliffs, and there are beautiful views of the islands in the background.

★ ISLA CEDROS

One of Mexico's largest islands, **Isla Cedros** is also one of Baja's most developed islands, relatively speaking. While there is still very little here, there are a two small towns, a few smaller settlements, and some fishing eco-lodges.

The island is mostly a draw for anglers who come to catch calico bass, sheepshead, and especially yellowtail (which breed here). The other draw on Isla Cedros is for naturalists and eco-enthusiasts. The island is full of hiking areas and interesting flora such as the unique Isla Cedros pine trees and California juniper.

Travelers who choose to visit Isla Cedros mostly do so through an outfitter running all-inclusive trips ranging from four to eight days. **Cedros Outdoor Adventures** (tel. 619/793-5419, www.cedrosoutdooradventures.com) is an eco-lodge with all-inclusive packages starting at $1,695 per person for 4 days/3 nights. This includes flights, ground transportation from San Diego as well as accommodations, food, and fishing excursions. They can also provide just accommodations and food for those travelers who arrive on the island themselves.

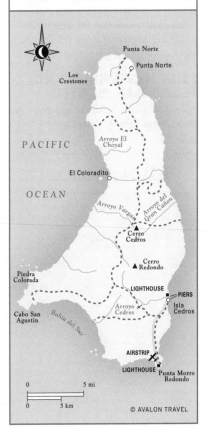

Isla Cedros

Another outfitter with all-inclusive trips is **Cedros Adventures** (U.S. tel. 619/772-7570, www.cedrosadventures.com), the first fishing resort on the island. They have American-style accommodations and four fishing boats with professional and knowledgeable captains. Trips range from four to eight days.

Visitors can get to Isla Cedros by chartered boat from Punta Eugenia or Bahía Tortugas. Flights from Guerrero Negro are available multiple times a week via **Aéreo Calafia** (www.aereocalafia.com.mx) and **Aéreo Servicio Guerrero** (www.asg.com.mx) for US$60 one-way.

Although many travelers travel to Isla Cedros from Baja California Sur, the island is actually a part of the state of Baja California (Norte) and therefore in the same time zone as the northern state an hour behind Baja Sur.

ISLA NATIVIDAD AND ISLAS SAN BENITO

Isla Natividad is known for its surf spot, Open Doors, which breaks on a south swell. To get to Isla Natividad, it's a half-hour boat trip from Punta Eugenia. Primitive camping is the only option for accommodations. **Baja Airventures** (www.bajaairventures.com) runs four-day, all-inclusive surf trips to Isla Natividad when there's a south swell.

The three barren islands of Islas San Benito lure divers with kelp beds teeming with marine wildlife. **Horizon Charters** (www.horizoncharters.com) offers multiday trips from San Diego to dive around the islands.

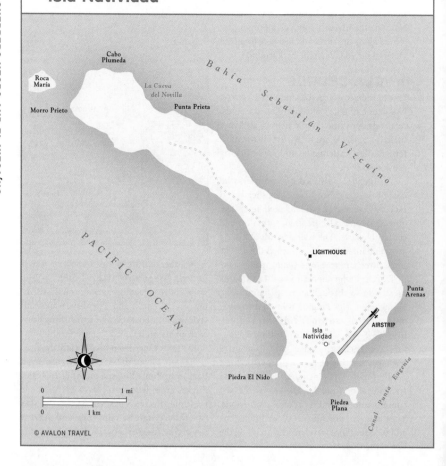

Isla Natividad

Cabo Plumeda

Roca María

La Cueva del Novilla

Morro Prieto

Punta Prieta

Bahía Sebastián Vizcaíno

PACIFIC OCEAN

LIGHTHOUSE

Punta Arenas

AIRSTRIP

Isla Natividad

Piedra El Nido

Piedra Plana

Canal Punta Eugenia

0   1 mi

0   1 km

© AVALON TRAVEL

BAHÍA ASUNCIÓN

133 kilometers southwest of Guerrero Negro (on Mexico 1) is the Pacific fishing village of Bahía Asunción, set on a sandy beach with rocks and beautiful sunset views. Sportfishing is popular here for yellowtail, dorado, halibut, sea bass, and more. There's also a small natural *bufadora* (blowhole) along the beach where the water meets the rocks to create a small geyser. The village of Asunción has grown over recent years, and there's now a gas station (with diesel) as well as a small hospital, nice grocery stores, and other services.

There are a few small restaurants in town. **Restaurant Bar Keyko** (Dom. Conocido, tel. 615/161-5837, 9am-5pm Mon., 9am-11pm Tues.-Sun., US$7-11) at the entrance to town is new. They serve traditional Mexican dishes like chiles rellenos, enchiladas, and tostadas, in addition to seafood like lobster, clams, and seafood cocktails. **El Blady's Mariscos** (no tel., Fri.-Sun., US$6-11) is a *palapa* restaurant on the beach where patrons can enjoy dishes like ceviche, shrimp, scallops, and clams with ocean views. For really good fish and shrimp tacos, locals head to **Tacos Don Ramon** (no tel., Sat.-Sun., US$1-2) across from the baseball stadium.

Shari Bondy and her husband Juan Arce operate **La Bufadora Inn** (formerly the Blowhole B&B, Mexico 1 Km. 44, tel. 615/160-0289, U.S. tel. 619/906-8438, www. bahiaasuncion.com, US$100) with six rooms and *casitas* available for rent. Sportfishing charters are available as well as trips for diving, snorkeling, and swimming with sea lions. October and November are the high season, and it's necessary to make reservations in advance as they book up quickly. They also own **Campo Sirena** (US$10-20) a full-service campground on the beach. Tent camping is an option, and there are power and water hookups for RVs.

PUNTA ABREOJOS

Punta Abreojos is a small fishing village also known as a great spot for surfing and windsurfing. To get to Abreojos, turn off of Mexico 1 just north of kilometer 97. Follow the paved road 88 kilometers to the coast. For surfers, there's a long point, and depending on tide and swell, different locations will be breaking. There's a series of surf spots favoring rights.

Hotel Chelos (tel. 615/620-4515, US$35) is in town on the main street and also features a restaurant and bar. **Casitas at the Point**

la bufadora in Bahía Asunción

(Mexico 1 Km. 97, no tel., www.casitasatthe-point.wordpress.com, US$65-89) consists of two vacation houses: a one-bedroom house and a three-bedroom house. Both are fully equipped with linens, TV, DVDs, books, magazines, complete kitchens, garages with washers and dryers, and porches looking over the estuary.

Eighteen kilometers north of Abreojos on a dirt road is La Bocana, a tiny fishing village with a few eateries and good fishing. Ask in Abreojos for the road to get to La Bocana. If you want to stay here, book a room at **Baja Bocana B&B** (tel. 615/156-0056, www.ba-jabocana.com, US$40-75), a large house with seven rooms. Owners Les and Blanca live in the house next door and are wonderful hosts who fix a nice breakfast in the mornings. Ask

them to make you a reservation at **Joaquin's Cactus Restaurant** (tel. 615/156-004, US$8-13) for a special seafood dinner. **Las Cabañas** (8am-10pm daily, US$6-10) is a restaurant and bar right on the beach with good food and great margaritas.

South of Abreojos, Estero de Coyote is a lagoon and salt marsh area that lures anglers and bird-watchers. One of the best-known accommodations for the whole region is **Campo Rene** (tel. 615/103-0008, www.camporene. com, US$30) with simple cabins and camping. They offer sportfishing, whale-watching, boating, kayaking, and surfing. There's a restaurant on-site serving seafood and traditional Mexican dishes. Although there's an airstrip here, the road is also paved all the way from Mexico 1.

San Ignacio and Vicinity

A welcome relief from the desert landscape comes in the form of the sleepy colonial town of San Ignacio, nestled into a date palm oasis. The town itself is small, but it has a beautiful mission on the plaza and some picturesque examples of colonial architecture. While the town has fallen into some disrepair and depression recently, it's still interesting to walk around the square and the surrounding streets for the beautiful buildings. It's a very small town, and visitors just looking to just a snippet of it can park on the plaza near the church and spend an hour or so tooling around the plaza, seeing the mission, and exploring a little bit of the area.

The peak season for San Ignacio is January through April because of whale-watching season. San Ignacio makes a great jumping-off point for heading out to the Laguna de San Ignacio—the best place on the peninsula to experience gray whale watching. In the heat of summer, this sleepy town gets even sleepier, with some businesses closing down completely during the off-season. Many that stay open abide by "siesta" hours, closing in the

heat of midday to reopen again later in the early evening.

Just outside of San Ignacio are the Volcán las Tres Virgenes, an area rich in hiking and exploring options, and the Sierra de San Francisco cave paintings, which are considered to be some of the best cave paintings in the world.

SIGHTS
★ San Ignacio Colonial Plaza
The heart of San Ignacio is its central plaza shaded by large Indian laurel trees. The Spanish mission, as well as a number of businesses and food stands, sit around the square. The plaza is generally sleepy during the day (especially in the off-season), but comes buzzing to life in the evenings. Festivals and town events take place here and general town life centers around the plaza. Grab a seat in the shade to take in what feels like a step back in time—the tranquil life of a small Mexican town.

Right on the town plaza, **Misión Nuestra Señor San Ignacio de Kadakaamán** is

San Ignacio

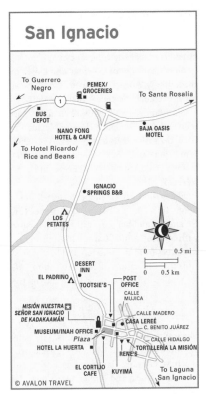

To Guerrero Negro
PEMEX/ GROCERIES
To Santa Rosalía
1
BUS DEPOT
NANO FONG HOTEL & CAFE
BAJA OASIS MOTEL
To Hotel Ricardo/ Rice and Beans
IGNACIO SPRINGS B&B
LOS PETATES
0   0.5 mi
0   0.5 km
DESERT INN
EL PADRINO
TOOTSIE'S
POST OFFICE
CALLE MUJICA
MISIÓN NUESTRA SEÑOR SAN IGNACIO DE KADAKAAMÁN
CALLE MADERO
CASA LEREÉ
C. BENITO JUÁREZ
MUSEUM/INAH OFFICE
Plaza
CALLE HIDALGO
HOTEL LA HUERTA
TORTILLERÍA LA MISIÓN
RENE'S
EL CORTIJO CAFE
KUYIMÁ
To Laguna San Ignacio
© AVALON TRAVEL

one of the most beautiful and easy-to-visit missions in the peninsula. It was founded in 1728 by Jesuit Padre Juan Bautista as the 11th mission in California. In its day, many expeditions were launched here to find new mission sites. One of these expeditions in 1746 was to the Colorado River Delta and put an end to the misconception that California was an island. The beautiful cut stone church that now stands here was started by the Jesuits and completed in 1786 by the Dominican Padre Juan Gómez. The mission was in operation here until 1840.

Next to the church, the Instituto Nacional Antropología e História (INAH) runs the small **Museo Local de San Ignacio** (no tel., 8am-6pm Mon.-Sat., free) showcasing some history of the region and information about the rock art of the Sierra de San Francisco. Inquire here to get a permit or make a booking for viewing any cave paintings in the region.

While it used to be a popular guesthouse in San Ignacio, the 1885 colonial **Casa Lereé** (20 Callejón Morelos, tel. 615/154-0158, www.casaleree.com) no longer offers rooms to rent but is still open during the days as a bookstore, photo archive, and garden. There are a few old hiking trails around San Ignacio—marked

The colonial town of San Ignacio is nestled in an oasis of palms.

with rocks painted white—that were cleared by Jane Ames, the owner of Casa Lereé. You can pick up a free map of the trails in the bookstore. The trail up to nearby Mesa de la Cruz provides a beautiful view overlooking the town.

FOOD

Restaurants are limited in San Ignacio, but a few hotels such as Desert Inn and Ricardo's Rice & Beans have their own associated restaurants. Many stand-alone restaurants are seasonal and only operate during the winter whale season. In town around the plaza, taco stands and hot dog carts are easy spots for a tasty snack in the evenings.

Toni Marcer, the owner of **Tootsie's** (11 Francisco I. Madero, tel. 615/154-0268, tootsiesbarandgrill@gmail.com, 6pm-11pm Mon.-Sat., Nov.-Apr., US$7-12), is the daughter of the owners of San Ignacio Springs B&B. This seasonal restaurant is open during whale season and located one block off of the plaza. There's a patio out back for when the weather is warm. Don't expect Mexican food here. The menu offers salads, curries, vegetarian dishes, and other north-of-the-border cuisine.

Rene's (Hidalgo, tel. 615/154-0196, 7am-10pm daily, mains US$6-10) prepares classic Mexican dishes as well as seafood cocktails. Situated a few blocks up from the town plaza, this is one of the biggest restaurants in town, but don't expect anything fancy.

Outside of the town center and closer to the highway, **Antojitos Nano Fong's** (near town entrance, no tel., 8am-11pm daily) is a small family-run business with Mexican food and cold beer. Also close to Mexico 1 is **Ricardo's Rice & Beans** (tel. 615/154-0283, 7am-11pm daily, US$5-14) restaurant and bar serving up decent food, cold beers, and good mixed drinks.

El Cortijo Cafe (11 poniente, no tel., 8am-noon, 4pm-6pm daily Jan.-Apr.) serves coffee and tea and has a beautiful garden patio with colorful animal statues. It's right across the street from the mission and lovely for a stop for a morning or late afternoon coffee while strolling around town during the whale season.

Right on the plaza, ★ **Victor's** (Hidalgo, no tel., 8am-10pm, US$4-8) serves good Mexican food at affordable prices. The walls are full of old photos from San Ignacio over the past decades. They're a good bet for breakfast, lunch, and dinner. Don't miss the margaritas.

For fresh tortillas, don't miss **Tortilleria**

The heart of San Ignacio is the town plaza.

La Mision a few doors down from Rene's restaurant, where you can buy bags of warm, freshly made flour or corn tortillas for under US$1.

ACCOMMODATIONS
Under $50

New in town, **Hotel La Huerta** (Calle Prof. Valdivia, tel. 615/154-0116, hotel.lahuertabcs@outlook.es, US$40) is a large and modern hotel by San Ignacio standards. There are amenities like flat-screen TVs and updated bathrooms, and the property is peaceful and quiet. The grounds are fairly large with a little park area and aviary cages with peacocks, pheasants, turkeys, and a number of chickens. There are 21 rooms, and they are currently building a restaurant on the property that will be opening by 2017. Just past the mission and the plaza, the location is great for walking around town. Also on the property is **Mercado La Huerta** (tel. 615/154-0016) selling food, produce, meats, dairy, ice, and supplies.

Outside the center of town on the highway, **Baja Oasis Motel** (Mexico 1 Km. 72.5, tel. 615/154-0111, bajaoasismotel@yahoo.com.mx, US$40) has 18 rooms with wireless Internet, air-conditioning, and cable TV. There's a large parking lot for keeping your car right next to your room. The sound of the nearby road may be bothersome for light sleepers.

Popular with off-roaders, **Ricardo's Rice & Beans** (tel. 615/154-0283, rice_beans@hughes.net, US$45) is located north of town near Mexico 1 and offers travelers a few basic but clean motel rooms as well as RV space with full hookups. They have a restaurant with a bar serving giant margaritas.

US$50-100

The peaceful and relaxing ★ **Ignacio Springs Bed & Breakfast** (400 meters off Mexico 1 on Río San Ignacio, tel. 615/154-0333, www.ignaciosprings.com, US$100) is outside of town on the San Ignacio river. Travelers here get the unique experience of staying in a cozy and well-appointed yurt. Owners Terry and Gary are expat Canadians who have become a well-known fixture on the peninsula. This bed-and-breakfast features wonderful homemade breakfast and provides visitors with kayaks to use on the river.

Also just outside of the center of town on the road coming into San Ignacio from Mexico 1 is the **Desert Inn** (formerly La Pinta, toll-free U.S. tel. 888/205-7322,

Tortilleria La Mision

www.desert-inn-san-ignacio.h-rez.com, US$60). Owned by FONATUR, the tourism department for Baja California Sur, this hotel features basic rooms with air-conditioning and cable TV. All of the rooms are built around a courtyard with a pool. The hotel is a bit run-down these days and has unreliable wireless access. The restaurant on-site, **Las Cazuelas** (open 6am-10pm daily), is a decent dining option.

INFORMATION AND SERVICES

San Ignacio has a Telecomm office for long-distance calls, a Western Union, and an Internet café on the plaza. There are a few small markets in town for snacks and provisions. The gas station is outside of town along Mexico 1. For tourist information and to book tours for whale-watching or cave paintings, there is a **Kuyima** (tel. 615/154-0070, www.kuyima.com) right on the town plaza.

GETTING THERE AND AROUND

The only way to get to San Ignacio is by private vehicle or bus. **Autobuses de la Baja California** (ABC, tel. 664/104-7400, www.abc.com.mx) has service to San Ignacio as does **Aguila** (tel. 800/824-8452, www.autobusesaguila.com). There's no public transportation within San Ignacio, but the town itself is so small that visitors can walk around the plaza and central area.

LAGUNA SAN IGNACIO

Of the three locations in Baja California where the gray whales make an appearance each year (Ojo de Liebre in Guerrero Negro and Bahía Magdalena being the other two), Laguna San Ignacio is regarded as the best: It's where the whales are friendlier and encounters more likely. It's never guaranteed that travelers will get to pet a gray whale, but the odds are pretty good here.

There's not much of anything out at the lagoon other than a number of *pangueros* and some basic eco-camps. Some of the tour companies will arrange to take you out to the lagoon, and some will have you drive directly to the lagoon yourself. Reservations for whale-watching must be made in advance.

Getting There

The lagoon is 53 kilometers out of town. Nearly the entire road is now paved (the last 10 kilometers or so are still unpaved), but ask about conditions in town before heading out.

a baby gray whale at Laguna San Ignacio

There are signs that are easy to follow to the lagoon from the center of town.

★ Whale-Watching Tours

The **Kuyima** (on the plaza across from the mission, tel. 615/154-0070, www.kuyima.com) office in San Ignacio can arrange for you to see the whales for a day or overnight trip. Accommodations at the lagoon consist of primitive eco-camps. You should make arrangements in advance (especially if you want to stay overnight). There are also a few other companies based out on the lagoon that lead whale-watching excursions, some originating from San Diego.

Pachico's Eco Tours (no tel., pachicosecotours@hotmail.com, www.pachicosecotours.com) has rates starting at US$230 per night. They recommend staying with them at the lagoon for at least 3-4 days in order to have the best chance for encounters with the whales. They have *cabañas* for rent and can also provide a camping area for you to bring your own tent or camper if you make arrangements in advance.

Antonio's Ecotours (tel. 615/103-3323. www.antonioecotours.com) offers a variety of affordable options for whale-watching, from day trips to camping to staying in eco-cabins at the lagoon. The staff is comprised of San Ignacio natives with decades of experience with the gray whales and incredible customer service.

With 16 solar-powered cabins, another eco-lodge option is **Baja Eco Tours** (toll-free U.S. tel. 877/506-0557, www.bajaecotours.com). They also offer all-inclusive tours (starting at $1,550) with air or bus transportation from San Diego included. They can accommodate travelers arriving at the lagoon on their own during nonpeak dates.

Both **Baja Expeditions** (tel. 612/125-3828, U.S. tel. 858/581-3311, www.bajaex.com) and **Baja Discovery** (U.S. tel. 619/328-9678, www.bajadiscovery.com) offer all-inclusive tours to Laguna San Ignacio that originate in San Diego and include transportation, eco-lodging at the lagoon, meals and drinks, activities, and whale-watching.

SIERRA DE SAN FRANCISCO
★ Cave Paintings

One of the most impressive and unique experiences in Baja California is the **cave paintings of the Sierra de San Francisco.** This UNESCO World Heritage Site encompasses some of the best-preserved and most

Sierra de San Francisco cave paintings

impressive rock art sites in the world. Four hundred sites have been recorded in the region, and most remain intact and in good condition, attributable to the dry climate and remote location. Visitors will find rock shelters and huge panels decorated with depictions of human figures as well as marine and land wildlife, painted in red, black, white, and yellow.

All visitors to the rock art must be registered with INAH, Mexico's National Institute of Anthropology and History, and have a guide. You can either book a guide directly through the **Buenaventura Hostel** (Mexico 1 Km. 115, tel. 615/156-4747, buenaventurahostal@gmail.com) in Sierra de San Francisco or you can go with a tour outfitter like **Kuyima** (tel. 615/154-0070, www.kuyima.com) on the plaza in San Ignacio. While it's possible to do day trips to see some of the rock art, in order to get the full experience and view the best sites, it's necessary to dedicate 3-4 days to visiting the cave paintings. The best rock art is only reachable by hiking and riding a pack animal while camping in the sierras.

There is a turnoff for San Francisco off of Mexico 1 at kilometer 117.5. It takes about 1.5 hours to reach San Francisco from the highway. Most travelers spend the night in San Francisco at the Buenaventura Hostel to start out early the next morning for the cave paintings.

The **Sierra de San Francisco website** (www.sierrasanfrancisco.com) has plenty of information in English about the rock art and how to book a tour. The website features the various cave painting sites and shows the levels of difficulty and the time required to visit each of the locations.

San Francisco has six different sites available for tours—El Ratón Cave, Los Cristones, El Represo, Santa Teresa Canyon, San Pablo Canyon, and Rancho San Gregorio, Casimiro, and San Gregorito. The most-photographed and well-known paintings are those of La Pintada in San Pablo Canyon. The nearby cave paintings of Santa Martha include sites of El Palmarito, El Parral Canyon, and El Torotal.

VOLCÁN LAS TRES VÍRGENES

The drive from San Ignacio south to Santa Rosalía is full of stunning scenery of large dormant volcanoes, old lava flows, cactus forests, and eventually the first glimpses of the Sea of Cortez from Mexico 1. Just outside of

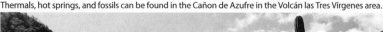
Thermals, hot springs, and fossils can be found in the Cañon de Azufre in the Volcán las Tres Vírgenes area.

Santa Rosalía, an old French mining town, has a distinct character unlike anywhere else in Baja California. The area is full of relics of old mining equipment and industrial buildings from the 1800s when the French-owned Boleo Mining Company dominated the town. With deteriorating French-style houses with wood siding, porches, and balconies overlooking the narrow streets, many parts of the town look like a Wild West movie set. One of the most famous landmarks in town is a metal church that was designed by Gustave Eiffel (of Eiffel Tower fame).

For travelers who have driven south on Mexico 1, this is their first glimpse of the Sea of Cortez. The gulf appears dramatically through mountains while you are winding into town. Although this is a city on the Sea of Cortez, Santa Rosalía is a port town rather than a beach town. The beaches are gray and unattractive and don't get much use, even by locals. But there's a nice large *malecón* that runs along the water's edge making for a lovely stroll in the evenings. The town itself is settled into a narrow, protected valley just off of the coast.

Santa Rosalía has all the potential to be one of the crowning jewels of Baja California, but unfortunately blight and apathy have kept this city from being a general tourist stop. Many travelers note that Santa Rosalía lacks the warm Mexican hospitality felt nearly everywhere else on the peninsula. But if you enjoy architecture and history, Santa Rosalía can be full of hidden gems.

Sights

The white-painted metal **Iglesia Santa Bárbara de Santa Rosalía** (Calle P. Altamirano between Constitución and Álvaro Obregón) was designed in 1884 by the famous Alexandre-Gustave Eiffel, who also designed the Eiffel Tower in Paris. The Boleo Mining Company acquired the church and had it installed in Santa Rosalía in 1897. The simple structure was originally destined for reconstruction in Africa and is made entirely of

Iglesia de Santa Bárbara de Santa Rosalía was designed by Gustave Eiffel.

San Ignacio is the Volcán las Tres Vírgenes, named for the three volcanoes there. The area is great for hiking and exploring the desert and canyons.

Eco Tour Las Tres Vírgenes (Mexico 1 Km. 32, tel. 615/152-1280, ecotourtresvirgenes@gmail.com, US$18) is the only option for lodgings in this area. The lodge has five cabins (10 rooms) that offer simple, off-the-grid accommodations with stunning views. Solar power provides the electricity and heats the water, and the Wi-Fi is on a point-to-point system and is not always reliable. The views of the expansive valley and volcanoes are breathtaking, and there's a lovely restaurant on-site. There are nearby hiking trails, and they can take you on tours to hot springs and fossils in the nearby Cañon de Azufre. To get to the eco-lodge, turn off of Mexico 1 at kilometer 31 onto the paved road. Three kilometers later, there will be a dirt road lined with white rocks to the left that will take you up the driveway to the lodge.

Santa Rosalía

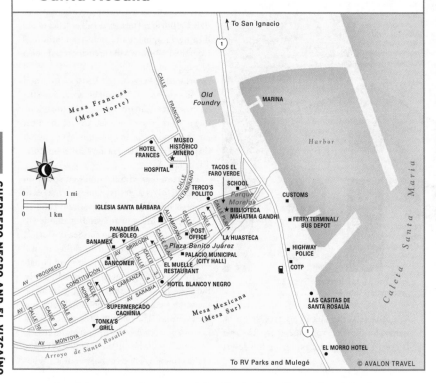

stamped steel sheet squares, for easy portability. The local community still uses the church for regular worship.

Housed in a landmark wooden building up on a mesa on the north side of town, the **Museo Histórico Minero de Santa Rosalía** (Jean Mitchell Cousteau #1, tel. 615/152-2999, 8:30am-2pm and 5pm-7pm Mon.-Sat., US$1) is a small museum with a display of mining artifacts and information on the history of Santa Rosalía.

Food

A newer restaurant, set back from the center of town, ★ **Tonka's Grill** (Avenida Vincete Guerrero, tel. 615/152-0959, 6pm-11pm Tues.-Sat., 2pm-8pm Sun., US$7-12) serves burgers, ribs, and steaks. A lot of care has been put into the design and operation of the restaurant.

The food is well-crafted, and they have artisanal Baja beers on the menu. For a location in central Baja, this is very hip dining.

Good for breakfast, lunch, or dinner, ★ **El Muelle** (Calle 9 and the Plaza, tel. 615/152-0931, 8am-11pm daily, US$9-13) is a popular spot for some decent food at reasonable prices. The service can be aloof, but the outdoor patio is a charming spot for dining in the evening.

Near the entrance of town just off the highway, **Terco's Pollitos** (Obregón at Calle Playa, tel. 615/152-0075, 8am-10pm daily, US$5-7) is known for chicken but has everything from Mexican food to seafood and meats on the menu. They've been around since 1962 and have a patio with picnic tables as well as a bar.

A few doors down from Terco's Pollitos, **La**

El Boleo Mine

In the late 1800s, local ranchers discovered copper deposits (*boleos*) in the hills of Santa Rosalía. The French Compagnie de Boleo bought the rights to the El Boleo mine in 1884 and built the town. The French company was granted a 70-year tax exemption to encourage development of this arid and undeveloped area. In 1954, when the tax exemption expired, the project went bankrupt and was sold back to the Mexican government. The mine ran under the Mexican government until the 1980s when it was closed down. El Boleo sat dormant for a number of decades until just recently. In early 2015, the mine became active again.

Huasteca (tel. 615/152-3438, US$4-8) specializes in *carnitas* and roasted chicken. This casual eatery is open for breakfast and lunch and has outdoor patio seating.

One of the best tacos stands in town is **Tacos el Faro Verde** (no tel., 8am-2:30pm Tues.-Sun), right in the little plaza near Terco's Pollitos and La Huasteca. They serve up the usual fish and shrimp tacos in addition to a unique and tasty chile relleno taco—jalapeño stuffed with cream cheese and shrimp, inside a taco. As the lines of locals will tell you, this is a don't-miss taco stop.

Open since 1901, the ★ **Panadería El Boleo** (Obregón at Calle 4, tel. 615/152-0310, 8am-9pm Mon.-Sat.) is another remnant of the French influence in Santa Rosalía. In addition to Mexican *bolillos*, the bakery also offers French baguettes. This was once considered one of the best bakeries in Mexico; unfortunately the quality has declined in recent years. But that doesn't stop locals and visitors from coming to pick up fresh baguettes in the mornings.

Accommodations

Up on the mesa north of town, **Hotel Frances** (Don Gaspar 210, tel. 615/152-2052, US$75) is an old, two-story French building with large wraparound balconies. The hotel is a bit run-down, but with lots of French colonial charm, it gives visitors the unique feeling of being on the movie set of an old western movie. There's a small pool in the courtyard, which is a relief

El Morro hotel is situated on the coast in Santa Rosalía.

in the heat of summer. The views of town and the Sea of Cortez from the second-floor balcony can be nice in the evenings.

Just south of town on the coast, ★ **Las Casitas** (Mexico 1, tel. 615/152-3023, mariahsantarosalia@hotmail.com, US$45-65) is worth the stay if you can get one of the nice oceanfront *casitas* looking out at the Sea of Cortez. They have 16 rooms in total, all with wireless Internet, Sky TV, coffeemakers, and air-conditioning. The *casitas* have patios right on the water.

Under new ownership, **El Morro** (Mexico 1 Km 1.5, tel. 615/152-0414, www.santarosaliaelmorro.com, US$35) is an expansive property with palm trees scattered around and nice views of the Sea of Cortez. While the rooms are out-of-date, they are currently in the process of being updated. There's a nice new pool, a large parking lot, free continental breakfast, and a restaurant on-site that's open 7am-10pm.

Information and Services

There are a few gas stations in town as well as a large Ley grocery store.

Santa Rosalía is one of only two locations on the peninsula (the other being La Paz) where travelers can take a ferry over to mainland Mexico. **Ferry Santa Rosalía** (tel. 800/505-5018, www.ferrysantarosalia.com)

runs routes multiple times a week between Santa Rosalía and Guaymas, Sonora.

Getting There and Around

Autobuses de la Baja California (ABC, tel. 664/104-7400, www.abc.com.mx) and **Aguila** (tel. 800/824-8452, www.autobusesaguila.com) have bus service to the city of Santa Rosalía. Most travelers arrive by car. The city itself is not large, and the downtown area can be explored easily on foot.

SAN LUCAS COVE, SAN BRUNO, AND ISLA SAN MARCOS

South of Santa Rosalía, San Lucas Cove has a small community of American-style houses, and there's also the **San Lucas Cove RV Campground** (no tel., US$10) with running water, toilets, showers, and a boat ramp for small to medium boats. A restaurant is open on the weekends.

The small fishing village of San Bruno has a harbor and paved launch ramp for boats. Just off the coast here is **Isla San Marcos** known for its gypsum mines. The island itself doesn't offer anything on land for tourists, but there are a few good diving and snorkeling spots around it. Inquire in Santa Rosalía or San Bruno for a local *panguero* who can take you out to the dive spots.

Loreto and Bahía Magdalena

Look for ★ to find recommended
sights, activities, dining, and lodging.

Highlights

★ **Misión Santa Rosalía de Mulegé:** The stone mission of Mulegé also has a lookout point with great views of the oasis town and date palm trees along the river (page 186).

★ **San Borjitas and La Trinidad Cave Paintings:** Some of the best cave paintings in this region can be reached on an easy day trip from Mulegé (page 188).

★ **Beaches of Bahía Concepción:** The clear turquoise waters and white sand beaches are a picturesque background for water sports and relaxing (page 193).

★ **Kayaking:** The protected and beautiful bay provides some of the most scenic kayaking in Baja (page 197).

★ **Misión Nuestra Señora de Loreto Conchó in Loreto:** The first Spanish mission built in California (both upper and lower) was in Loreto in 1697 (page 203).

★ **Loreto's Historic Plaza Juárez:** The heart of this *Pueblo Mágico* is the town plaza with colonial buildings, restaurants, shops, and cafés (page 204).

★ **Parque Marítimo Nacional Bahía de Loreto:** The protected islands and marine park of Loreto provide visitors a great opportunity to see wildlife and beautiful deserted islands (page 204).

★ **Sportfishing:** Anglers flock to Loreto in the summer to catch yellowtail, dorado, cabrilla, and snapper (page 204).

★ **Misión San Francisco Javier de Viggé-Biaundó at San Javier:** Nestled into the Sierra de la Giganta, crown jewel of Baja's missions is an interesting day trip from Loreto (page 212).

★ **Whale-Watching in Bahía Magdalena:** Bahía Magdalena is the southernmost spot on the peninsula for gray whale encounters each winter (page 217).

This region in the heart of the peninsula is filled with marvels of both the Sea of Cortez and the Pacific Ocean. Outdoor enthusiasts enjoy the world-class kayaking, snorkeling, fishing, whale-watching, and surfing.

Bahía Concepción is one of the most beautiful spots on the peninsula with stunning clear waters casting beautiful turquoise colors and white sand beaches. Because of the generally warm winters, snowbirds flock to the area to spend winters along this bay's shores. While summers can bring extreme heat on the Sea of Cortez, causing some seasonal businesses to shutter doors from August and September, summers will see anglers hurrying to the Loreto area for sportfishing and surfers to the waves at San Juanico Scorpion Bay.

The town of Loreto, a recently designated *Pueblo Mágico,* is the largest town in this region and has a little something to offer everyone with plenty of culture, history, fishing, and outdoor adventures. Bahía Magdalena is the southernmost spot on the peninsula for gray whale encounters, and the bay comes alive during the winter months as visitors come to hug the baby gray whales.

PLANNING YOUR TIME

It's possible to fly into Loreto to enjoy a long weekend, but there's plenty to keep you occupied for at least a week. Many travelers to Bahía Concepción come to stay for the winter, although spending a few days will grant you the time to see the beaches and enjoy some activities.

GETTING THERE
Car

Many travelers exploring this area are road-trippers from the United States who have driven down on Mexico 1. A private vehicle is required in order to fully enjoy this region, although travelers flying into Loreto who intend to just stay in town can get by without a vehicle. Those flying into Loreto can rent a car at the airport or in town. Fox (www.foxtrentacar.mx), Alamo (www.alamo.com), and Europcar (www.europcar.com) all have offices in town and at the airport. Because

---

Previous: Playa Punta Arena; sunset over the Loreto mission and plaza. **Above:** San Borjitas cave paintings.

Bahía Concepción, Loreto, and Bahía Magdalena

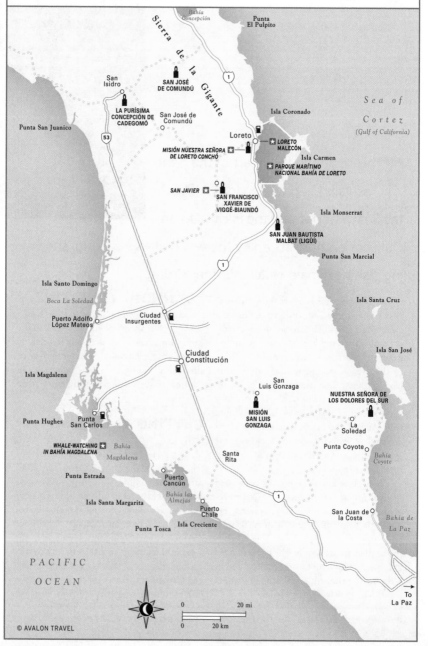

Sierra de la Gigante

Bahía Concepción

Punta El Pulpito

San Isidro

SAN JOSÉ DE COMUNDÚ

LA PURÍSIMA CONCEPCIÓN DE CADEGOMÓ

San José de Comundú

Isla Coronado

Sea of Cortez
(Gulf of California)

Loreto

LORETO MALECÓN

Punta San Juanico

53

MISIÓN NUESTRA SEÑORA DE LORETO CONCHÓ

Isla Carmen

PARQUE MARÍTIMO NACIONAL BAHÍA DE LORETO

SAN JAVIER

SAN FRANCISCO XAVIER DE VIGGÉ-BIAUNDÓ

Isla Monserrat

SAN JUAN BAUTISTA MALBAT (LIGÜÍ)

Punta San Marcial

1

Isla Santo Domingo

Boca La Soledad

Ciudad Insurgentes

Isla Santa Cruz

Puerto Adolfo López Mateos

Isla San José

Ciudad Constitución

Isla Magdalena

San Luis Gonzaga

NUESTRA SEÑORA DE LOS DOLORES DEL SUR

Punta Hughes

Punta San Carlos

MISIÓN SAN LUIS GONZAGA

La Soledad

WHALE-WATCHING IN BAHÍA MAGDALENA

Bahía Magdalena

Punta Coyote

Bahía Coyote

Punta Estrada

Santa Rita

Puerto Cancún

Bahía las Almejas

Isla Santa Margarita

Puerto Chale

San Juan de la Costa

Bahía de La Paz

Punta Tosca

Isla Creciente

PACIFIC OCEAN

To La Paz

0   20 mi

0   20 km

© AVALON TRAVEL

Best Accommodations

★ **Hotel Hacienda Mulegé:** This beautiful and historic hacienda is clean and spacious with a swimming pool and great service (page 190).

★ **Coco Cabañas:** These comfortable accommodations offer a variety of options from *cabañas* to large houses on a great location near the *malecón* and plaza (page 209).

★ **Posada del Cortes:** This boutique hotel offers luxurious rooms and is conveniently located near the *malecón* and the plaza (page 210).

★ **Las Cabañas de Loreto:** Combining all of the best comforts of home with the special perks of being on vacation, the *cabañas* are equipped with everything you would ever need on vacation (page 210).

★ **Posada de las Flores:** Full of authentic Mexican charm and accents, this colonial-style hacienda provides some of the best views in the area from its beautiful and unique rooftop (complete with a glass bottom pool) (page 211).

★ **Villa del Palmar:** The only luxury resort in the region, Villa del Palmar on Loreto Bay provides multiple swimming pools, restaurants, and a spa (page 214).

Loreto has a small inventory of cars, it can be beneficial to make a reservation in advance.

Air

Loreto has its own small commercial airport, **Loreto International Airport (LTO)**. Alaska Airlines has direct flights from Los Angeles; WestJet offers seasonal flights from Calgary (Oct.-May); and Aéreo Calafia offers flights from Tijuana and La Paz in Baja and Guaymas and Hermosillo in mainland Mexico.

Bus

Aguila (tel. 800/824-8452, www.autobusesaguila.com) and **Autobuses de la Baja California** (ABC, tel. 664/104-7400, www.abc.com.mx) offer bus services throughout the region and from other cities in Baja California. Mulegé, Loreto, Ciudad Insurgentes, and Ciudad Constitución all have multiple runs a day. Buses are large and modern with air-conditioning. Check at local bus terminals for current schedules and to purchase tickets.

Mulegé

Along Mexico 1 coming into Mulegé, the desert is suddenly replaced with palm trees and a lush green oasis. The small, but lively colonial town nestled in this haven attracts snowbirds, expats, and travelers with its Mexican charm and variety of attractions. The Río Santa Rosalía de Mulegé (now just called the Río Santa Rosalía or commonly referred to as the Mulegé River) runs through town and feeds the lush area before meeting up with the Sea of Cortez out along the beach. Up on the hill, the Misión Santa Rosalía de Mulegé is a beautiful stone structure that's easy to visit and has great views of the town and the palm-lined river. While Mulegé itself is a destination for many

Mulegé

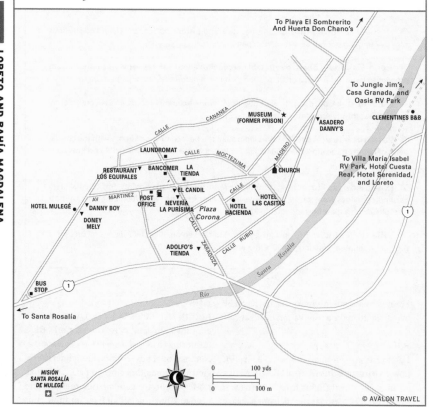

To Playa El Sombrerito
And Huerta Don Chano's

To Jungle Jim's,
Casa Granada, and
Oasis RV Park

CLEMENTINES B&B

MUSEUM
(FORMER PRISON)

ASADERO
DANNY'S

CALLE CANANEA

CALLE

CALLE MOCTEZUMA

MADERO

LAUNDROMAT

CHURCH

To Villa María Isabel
RV Park, Hotel Cuesta
Real, Hotel Serenidad,
and Loreto

RESTAURANT
LOS EQUIPALES

BANCOMER

LA
TIENDA

EL CANDIL

CALLE

HOTEL
LAS CASITAS

AV MARTINEZ

POST
OFFICE

HOTEL MULEGÉ

DANNY BOY

NEVERIA
LA PURÍSIMA

Plaza
Corona

HOTEL
HACIENDA

DONEY
MELY

CALLE ZARAGOZA

CALLE RUBIO

ADOLFO'S
TIENDA

Santa Rosalía

1

BUS
STOP

1

Río

To Santa Rosalía

MISIÓN
SANTA ROSALÍA
DE MULEGÉ

0   100 yds

0   100 m

© AVALON TRAVEL

SIGHTS
★ Misión Santa Rosalía de Mulegé

In 1705, Jesuit Padre Manuel de Basaldúa traveled north from Loreto to found a settlement for Cochimí natives living in an area they called Mulegé, meaning "large sandbar of the white mouth." The **Misión Santa Rosalía de Mulegé** is the fourth mission founded in both Baja and Alta California. The handsome stone church that now stands was constructed in 1766.

In addition to a beautiful structure, behind the mission is a lookout that gives travelers great views of the Río Santa Rosalía and of town. To get to the church, follow Calle

expats and travelers, it also serves as a great base for exploring around Bahía Concepción and the nearby La Trinidad and San Borjitas cave paintings.

The official name of the town is "Heroica Mulegé" (heroic Mulegé) as it's painted over the archway that greets visitors. The town received this name for events that took place during the Mexican-American War of 1846-1848. Americans were invading and occupying areas of Mexico (what we now know as California and New Mexico), but the people of Mulegé and the surrounding settlements gathered to defend the region, defeating the Americans and keeping the region from being occupied.

Best Restaurants

★ **El Candil:** Just off of the Mulegé plaza, El Candil features great gourmet burgers and cold beers (page 189).

★ **Hotel Serenidad:** Famous margaritas and a pig roast make this an unforgettable dining experience (page 189).

★ **Restaurant & Bar Buenaventura:** Just steps away from Bahía Concepción, travelers can enjoy cold beers and hamburgers with views of the turquoise waters (page 195).

★ **La Picazón:** This well-curated *palapa* restaurant is perfect for an afternoon of relaxing in a hammock and enjoying a margarita with views of the Sea of Cortez (page 208).

★ **Asadero Super Burro:** With savory and delicious food in a casual and fun environment, it's no wonder this eatery is a favorite of both locals and tourists (page 208).

Zaragoza (the road just south of the bridge) west and up a slight hill to the site.

Museo Histórico de Mulegé

Mulegé's **Museo Histórico** (Cananea, tel. 615/153-0056, 9am-1pm Mon.-Fri.) is located up on a hill in an old building that used to house Mulege's infamous "prison without doors." This special jail is famous for the freedom it allowed its prisoners. Instead of being held captive, prisoners were allowed to leave the prison during the day on the honor system to work in town. They just had to return to the jail by 6pm when they were called back by the sound of a conch shell being blown. Because of the town's remote location until the highway came through in the 1970s, there was no easy way for prisoners to flee. Today, the prison operates as a museum that's home to a small collection of historical artifacts as well as some information on the Mexican-American War battle that took place here.

Misión Santa Rosalía de Mulegé is located on a hill overlooking the town.

Lighthouse

The Mulegé **Lighthouse** (*El Faro*) is a great place to take in some views of the Sea of Cortez and the Río Santa Rosalía. To access the lighthouse, take Calle Playa on the north side of the Río Santa Rosalía and head east toward the Sea of Cortez. Turn to the right once you reach the Sea of Cortez.

Playa El Sombrerito

The Río Santa Rosalía empties out into the Sea of Cortez at **Playa El Sombrerito**. A large estuary is formed here where bird-watchers can spot a variety of marine birds.

★ San Borjitas and La Trinidad Cave Paintings

There are a few sets of cave paintings in the Sierra de Guadalupe, located west of Mulegé, that can be visited from town as day trips. A guide is required to visit the sites and can easily be acquired in town or at the ranches near the sites.

LA TRINIDAD

The cave paintings at **La Trinidad** are a collection of animal depictions, including a famous painting of a large orange deer with a checkerboard pattern. The deer is a recurring theme in prehistoric rock art throughout Baja, and the La Trinidad deer is known as the best example of the motif. There are two groups of paintings at La Trinidad. It's about a 45-minute hike to get to the first set and an extra hour to reach the second set. Many guides only take visitors to the first set, so inquire ahead of time when making arrangements if you want to be sure to see both. Getting to La Trinidad cave paintings used to require a rigorous excursion of swimming through gorges and multiple river crossings. Since Hurricane Odile in September 2014, the trek has been completely dry, but conditions could change at any time so be sure to inquire ahead of time. Bring plenty of your own drinking water.

Visiting the cave paintings requires a permit from INAH and hiring a local guide.

Guides can be hired from Mulegé by inquiring at your hotel or at Hotel Las Casitas. A guide form Mulegé will cost about US$45 per day. The other, and cheaper, option is to drive to Rancho La Trinidad yourself and hire a guide directly at the ranch (US$5). Rancho La Trinidad is located 29 kilometers west of Mulegé and is accessed by taking a road off of Mexico 1 just north of town at Km. 135. This road is locally called "Ice House Road" because the turn off from Mexico 1 is at the ice factory. Follow the signs for "La Trinidad." It will take about an hour and half driving from Mulegé to arrive at Rancho La Trinidad. For the sake of convenience, most travelers visiting the La Trinidad cave paintings hire a guide from Mulegé rather than driving themselves to the ranch.

SAN BORJITAS

The best-known cave paintings in the Sierra de Guadalupe are the **San Borjitas** cave paintings, which are carbon-dated to be 7,500 years old. The oldest cave paintings in North America, they are also some of the most impressive in Baja California. The canvas for the paintings is a 30-meter-long cave overhang with the ceiling containing over 80 *monos* (human figures). The feature that distinguishes San Borjitas from other sites on the peninsula is the bi-color figures with one half painted in black and the other half in red. Monos also appear at right angles to one another, another characteristic of the San Borjitas paintings.

To get to San Borjitas, visitors can hire a guide in Mulegé or out at Rancho Las Tinajas. Getting to Rancho Las Tinajas involves a rigorous 30-kilometer, 2.5-hour off-road drive through riverbeds, deep sand, and large rocks. It should not be attempted without a high-clearance, four-wheel-drive vehicle. It's advisable to hire a guide directly in Mulegé who will drive you out to the site. It is then a 20-minute hike to the cave paintings. The turnoff for Rancho Las Tinajas and the San Borjitas cave paintings is at kilometer 165 on Mexico 1.

GUIDED TOURS

For guided tours to the cave paintings in the region, **Salvador Castro Drew** (tel. 615/153-0232, cell tel. 615/103-5081, mulegetours@hotmail.com) speaks perfect English. He can customize the tours depending on what your group is interested in. His most popular tour is a hiking trip out to La Trinidad. Expect to pay around US$45 per person for the INAH permit, use of camera, and the tour, which includes lunch. Inquire at Hotel Las Casitas if you're unable to reach Salvador by phone.

Another guide in the area, **Ciro Cuesta** (tel. 615/153-0566, cell tel. 615/106-8892) speaks English and knows the area extremely well. He will be able to explain about the petroglyphs, cave paintings, and the region in general. Inquire at Hotel Cuesta Real or Hotel Hacienda if you can't reach him by phone.

RECREATION
Fishing

Las Casitas and **Hotel Serenidad** will arrange fishing charters for you out up to Punta Chivato or down to Bahía Concepción. For fishing from shore, try the south side of the estuary. Yellowtail, dorado, marlin, and even occasional sailfish are available in the area.

FOOD
Restaurants

For some of the best hamburgers in Baja, ★ **El Candil** (Ignacio Zaragoza, tel. 615/153-0305, noon-10pm Tues.-Sat., 11am-8pm, mains US$5-8) is conveniently located just off of the plaza. It's a popular spot for local Mexicans and expats with an outdoor patio as well as a large indoor area with a bar, pool table, and darts. In addition to gourmet burgers, the extensive menu has sandwiches, pizza, tacos, Mexican plates, and daily specials (the French dip sandwiches on Fridays are a local favorite). It's good food with friendly service in a fun and casual setting. They have live music occasionally.

The restaurant and bar at **Las Casitas** (Madero 50, tel. 615/153-0019, lascasitas1962@hotmail.com, 7am-10pm daily) has been feeding regulars and tourists since 1962. The colorful interior and lush tropical patio are a fun setting for enjoying traditional Mexican food, margaritas, and Baja craft beers.

The restaurant at ★ **Hotel Serenidad** (South of town off Mexico 1, follow road signs, tel. 615/153-0530, www.serenidad.com.mx, 6:30am-9:30pm daily) serves breakfast, lunch, and dinner with traditional Mexican food indoors or on the outdoor patio near the pool.

Hiring a local guide is required for access to the San Borjitas cave paintings.

The margaritas are famous among Baja aficionados for being incredibly large and strong. Locals and travelers enjoy the famous pig roast that takes place every Saturday starting at 6:30pm (US$15 pp). Call to make a reservation and enjoy all you can eat pork, ribs, tamales, beans, salad, tortillas, barbecue sauce, dessert, and one small margarita or beer.

Across the street from Hotel Mulegé, **Doney Mely's** (Moctezuma 81, tel. 615/153-0095, 7:30am-10pm Wed.-Mon., US$7-13) has been open since 1989 and serves breakfast, lunch, and dinner. Don't expect fast or friendly service, but they have decent traditional Mexican food.

For a steak dinner in a casual setting, **Los Equipales** (Moctezuma 70, tel. 615/153-0330, 7:30am-10:30pm daily, mains US$11-19) specializes in Sonoran beef and steaks. Large arched windows and tables covered in Mexican serapes help create a typically comfortable Baja setting. They're open for breakfast, lunch, and dinner, serving fresh food and hearty meals.

Taco Stands and *Antojitos*
Asadero Danny's (Romero Rubio and Madero) has great carne asada tacos or quesadillas as well as *carnitas* on Saturday.

For some of the best fish tacos in town, don't miss little taco cart **Taquitos Mulegé** right on the central plaza near the taxi stand.

Groceries
There are a handful of grocery stores and markets in town where shoppers can find a wide selection of food. The water stores have fresh-squeezed juice from local orchards when it's in season.

ACCOMMODATIONS
Under US$50
For budget accommodations, **Hotel Mulegé** (Moctezuma, tel. 615-153-0090, hotelmulege@gmail.com, US$30) has 17 basic and clean rooms with air-conditioning and wireless Internet. They sell ice in the lobby so that road-trippers and anglers can refill their coolers. There's a common area with a barbecue and picnic tables. This is a convenient in-town location offering off-street parking.

Located in one of Mulegé's oldest historic buildings from the late 17th century is ★ **Hotel Hacienda Mulegé** (Madero 3, tel. 615/153-0021, www.hotelhaciendamulege.com, US$22). In true hacienda style, the rooms are centered around a courtyard,

The Hotel Hacienda Mulegé is housed in an old colonial building.

Serenidad Pig Roast

American Don Johnson and his wife Nancy Ugalde Gorosave, a Mulegé local, have owned Hotel Serenidad since 1968, and Don's name has been synonymous with the resort ever since. The airstrip next to the hotel was at one time the main mode of transportation for visitors who would fly in to the tropical resort for sportfishing and relaxation. Guests such as John Wayne and Olivia Newton-John were once regulars at the Serenidad during its heyday in the 1970s. The famous Saturday night pig roast started in 1970 and is a weekly tradition continued to this day. A full pig is roasted and served along with other side dishes. Music, entertainment, and the famous Serenidad margaritas round out the evening.

and all have air-conditioning. There's also a swimming pool and secure parking. It's an older property, but the rooms are spacious and clean. The service is friendly, and they can help you with activities or booking tours.

Since 1962, **Las Casitas** (Madero 50, tel. 615/153-0019, lascasitas1962@hotmail.com, US$30) has been welcoming guests in their hacienda-style hotel and restaurant. Rooms haven't been updated in a while but have a charming eclectic style. The staff can help arrange excursions in the area. Local expats and travelers enjoy the traditional Mexican food and margaritas served in their restaurant and bar.

US$50-100

Famous since its heyday as a fly-in resort in the 1970s, **Hotel Serenidad** (South of town off Mexico 1, follow the road signs, tel. 615/153-0530, www.serenidad.com.mx, US$65) is still one of the best options for accommodations in Mulegé. Rooms are a bit outdated, but visitors come for the nostalgia, the margaritas, the weekly pig roast, and the refreshing pool.

By the river, **Clementine's Bed and Breakfast and Casitas** (tel. 615/153-0319, www.clementinesbaja.com, US$75-105) has four rooms in the main bed-and-breakfast, as well as six individual *casitas*. Kayaks are provided for guests who want to paddle around on the river. You'll get personalized attention here, from help with tour arrangements to recommendations on where to eat

in town. The B&B section has a shared living and cooking space.

Over US$100

South of Mulegé and just north of Bahía Concepción, **Playa Frambes Lighthouse Resort** (Mexico 1 Km. 118, no tel., http://mulege.org, US$160) has a remote setting right on the water. Guests can stay in one of three two-bedroom detached hotel suites or choose the suite in the lighthouse that's on the property. Rooms are air-conditioned during the summer. There's a nice pool area as well as kayaks, snorkeling, bocce ball, croquet, volleyball, and horseshoes available for guest use. Breakfast is served, but no other meals are offered.

Camping and RV Parks

Although it's fallen into some disrepair over the past few years, **Hotel Cuesta Real** (Mexico 1 Km. 132, tel. 615/153-0321, www.hotelcuestareal.com, US$15) offers full hookups with dump service and fresh water. Camping sites are also available as are 12 basic hotel rooms. It's on the south side of the river, as is **Villa Maria Isabel** (tel. 615/153-0246, US$20), offering 30 sites with full hookups (18 pull-throughs), showers, and a pool.

Offering both space for tent camping and lots for RVs, **Huerta Don Chano** (Calle Playa, tel. 615/153-0720, manuel_romero25@yahoo.com.mx, US$8) is on the north bank of the river, equidistant from town and the lighthouse. Pull-through RV spots have 20 amp outlets, but the water hookups are unreliable. The campsite has nice lawns and palm trees, providing lush grounds for tent camping. The Wi-Fi works well. **Hotel Serenidad** also has a handful of RV spots (US$12).

INFORMATION AND SERVICES

There are Pemex gas stations, ATMs, and a few grocery stores in Mulegé. There's no large hospital in town, but there is a health clinic, **Centro de Salud** (tel. 615/153-0298), on Francisco I Madero.

GETTING THERE AND AROUND

Loreto International Airport (LTO) is the closest commercial airport with flights from Los Angeles, Calgary, and other parts of Mexico. There's no formal bus station in Mulegé, but **Aguila** (tel. 800/824-8452, www.autobusesaguila.com) and **Autobuses de la Baja California** (ABC, tel. 664/104-7400, www.abc.com.mx) have buses that stop on Mexico 1 near the town entrance. Most visitors arrive in Mulegé by car, either on a road trip down from the United States or by renting a car in Loreto. It's easy to walk around the central part of town, but a car is needed for any excursions.

PUNTA CHIVATO

Visitors head out to Punta Chivato, southeast of Mulegé, for secluded beaches and great fishing. Services remain sparse here and most visitors coming to the area tent camp, but Punta Chivato has built up as an American housing community over the past few decades with residences ranging from modest structures to million-dollar beach mansions. Travelers spend their time here snorkeling, digging for chocolate clams, fishing, or beachcombing on Shell Beach. The road to Punta Chivato is dirt, and potholes and washboard sections should be expected.

There are a number of isolated beaches and camping areas at Punta Chivato, but there are no services, so you must be self-contained. There have been a few instances of petty theft over the years, so it's best to not leave your belongings unattended. The big hotel in Punta Chivato went through a number of owners and names before finally closing for good. There are few small hotels and restaurants, but they are very inconsistent about staying open. A few small markets sell provisions like beer, ice, meat, and gypsy gasoline. **Julia's restaurant** (no tel.) is consistently open and serves delicious and fresh seafood and handmade flour tortillas. She also sells beer, water, sodas, and firewood.

Getting There

The turnoff for Punta Chivato is at kilometer 156 on Mexico 1. From here, a 20-kilometer graded dirt road takes travelers east to Punta Chivato. The condition of the road varies, but is generally passable with a four-wheel drive, high-clearance vehicle. Inquire in Mulegé about current road conditions.

Bahía Concepción

Just south of Mulegé along Mexico 1, Bahía Concepción is a stunning example of some of the best things that Baja California Sur has to offer. The series of shallow bays feature picturesque turquoise waters and white sand beaches, like the trappings of a tropical dream. It's no wonder that Bahía Concepción is a mecca for snowbirds RVing for the winter and travelers looking to camp in tranquility for a few days. Snorkelers, divers, and kayakers are all drawn to the bay for water sports with beautiful views. Whether you choose to camp on the sandy shores of the bay or just visit for a day trip, this is a true Baja marvel to experience.

Accommodations on the bay consist mostly

Bahía Concepción

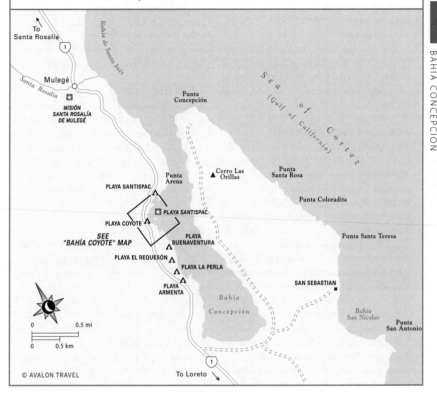

of tent or RV camping. Travelers who want to experience Bahía Concepción but stay in a hotel will need to stay in Mulegé about 30 minutes away. Expect to pay to enter most of the beaches on the bay, even if you are just visiting for the day and not staying overnight.

★ BEACHES
Northern Beaches
PLAYA LOS NARANJOS AND PLAYA PUNTA ARENA

The *palapas* at **Playa Los Naranjos** have been converted into *casitas* with communal toilets nearby. Some *casitas* have private showers. The nearby **Playa Punta Arena,** although windy in the afternoons, is a popular spot for RVers.

Bahía Coyote
Near the north end of Bahía Concepción, is a smaller bay, Bahía Coyote, which encompasses many of the most picturesque beaches of the area.

PLAYA SANTISPAC
At kilometer 113.5, **Playa Santispac** is one of the most popular beaches of Bahía Concepción. Both day-trippers and snowbirds in their RVs are attracted to Santispac because of its large size and striking beauty. There are no hookups here and the local *ejido* collects an entrance fee even for those just spending the day (US$6 for day and night, US$3 for the day). People spend their days here swimming, snorkeling, and kayaking

in the sheltered waters. There are extreme tides, which can leave sea bottoms exposed for clam digging during low tides. There's a mangrove nestled into the back of the bay with hot springs.

Right on the beach, **Ana's Restaurant** (mains US$6-9) serves breakfast, lunch, and dinner. There's often live music, and delicious cinnamon buns and empanadas come out of the brick oven.

POSADA CONCEPCIÓN

The gated community of **Posada Concepción** is located at kilometer 112 off of Mexico 1. The community is home to houses available for rent by the week or month in addition to tennis and bocce ball courts and hot springs. A hostel on the property, **Hostel Posada del Sol** (www.posadaconcepcion. net, US$20) has large dormitory rooms and private rooms, all under a *palapa* roof. There's a kitchen area, locked storage, and a common area with TVs. Guests can pay to use snorkels, kayaks, and tennis courts. The hostel and adjoining **restaurant** are run by Lucy, who makes great breakfasts, hearty lunches and dinners, as well as fresh-baked bread and treats like Bavarian cream doughnuts. The restaurant is popular with expat residents

and people camping at Playa Escondida and Playa Los Cocos.

Across from the office at Posada Concepción is a bulletin board listing local events. Visitors can park in the lot across from the tennis courts to check out the board to find out what's going on around the area.

PLAYA ESCONDIDA

Living up to its name, which means "hidden beach," **Playa Escondida** can't be seen from the highway. There's a turnoff from Mexico 1 at kilometer 111. The road has been in very rough condition for many years and is not recommended for trailers or large motor homes. If you can make it over the road, this beach has a number of sites, but no hookups.

PLAYA LOS COCOS

The little cove of Playa Los Cocos is just north of kilometer 111. There are open *palapa* structures for camping as well as pit toilets. This is usually a less crowded beach, for those looking for more solitude. There's a small lagoon with mangroves between the beach and cliffs.

PLAYA EL BURRO

There are lots of activities going on at **Playa el Burro.** At kilometer 109, the beach is home

The clear waters and white-sand beaches of Bahía Concepción lure snowbirds, kayakers, and swimmers.

Bertha's and JC's rotate with Estrella del Mar to host weekly movie nights.

PLAYA COYOTE

At kilometer 108 is the large expanse of **Playa Coyote.** There are hot springs at the south end of the beach just up from the shore. A number of nice American homes rest the shade of palm trees.

Across the highway from Playa Coyote is **Estrella del Mar** (Mexico 1 Km. 108). They have good Mexican foods (try the chiles rellenos) and an outstanding bartender serving up margaritas and other drinks. They have regular movie nights with new releases and live music on occasion, contributing to the fun atmosphere.

PLAYA SANTA BARBARA

While there's a turnoff for **Playa Santa Barbara** at kilometer 100, the beach is most easily reached by boat or even kayak. This secluded spot isn't possible to see from the highway and many people enjoy it for the seclusion and privacy.

Southern Beaches
PLAYA BUENAVENTURA

One of the best restaurants along the bay is ★ **Restaurant & Bar Buenaventura** (Mexico 1 Km. 94.5, U.S. tel. 619/663-1826, www.playabuenaventura.com, US$6-11) at Playa Buenaventura. Mark and Olivia run the place, serving hamburgers, tacos, cold beer, and margaritas. Tacos Tuesday (noon-4pm, Nov.-Apr.) is popular here—try the coconut mango shrimp tacos. There's a pool table and large indoor and outdoor spaces for hanging out. With a location right on the beach, the views are great, and even if you aren't hungry, it's worth a stop to enjoy a cold beer at one of the picnic tables outside just steps away from the turquoise waters of the bay. On the same property, and run by the same owners, is **San Buenaventura** with five hotel rooms available for rent (US$40-70) right on the water. Everything is off the grid here, so water is trucked in and rooms use candles for light.

wild horses along the southern edge of Bahía Concepción

to many local events and an occasional flea market. Directly offshore is the largest island in Bahía Concepción, Isla Bargo (which has its own secret beach on the far side). Snorkeling and kayaking are popular activities here, and this is one of the few places on the entire bay where you can get rentals and take tours. Eduardo and Sandra have a spot on the beach where they have kayak rentals as well as offer fishing and whale shark tours. **El Burro Baja Tours** (tel. 615/155-9114, www.elburrobajatours.com) is based here, offering four-hour tours around the bay that include snorkeling with whale sharks and gathering clams to enjoy.

Up in the canyons around Playa el Burro are petroglyphs of fish, turtles, and other wildlife that have been carved into the rocks. Ask around for someone to point you in the right direction for the hike.

Locals enjoy lunch or dinner at **Bertha's** restaurant on the beach as well as **JC's,** across the highway next to the firefighters. JC's has weekly live music with local bands. Both

Bahía Coyote

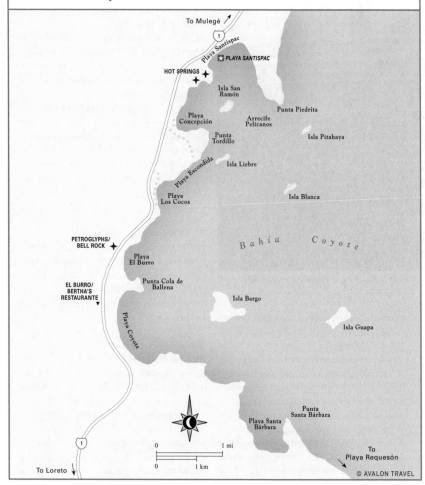

To Mulegé

Playa Santispac

PLAYA SANTISPAC

HOT SPRINGS

Isla San Ramón

Punta Piedrita

Playa Concepción

Arrecife Pelícanos

Punta Tordillo

Isla Pitahaya

Playa Escondida

Isla Liebre

Playa Los Cocos

Isla Blanca

PETROGLYPHS/ BELL ROCK

Bahía Coyote

Playa El Burro

Punta Cola de Ballena

EL BURRO/ BERTHA'S RESTAURANTE

Isla Bargo

Playa Coyote

Isla Guapa

Punta Santa Bárbara

Playa Santa Bárbara

0   1 mi

0   1 km

To Playa Requesón

To Loreto

© AVALON TRAVEL

Two houses are also available for rent (US$90), one on the beach and one off the beach but with still with water views. Camping is also an option whether in tents or RVs (no hookups). Amenities include bathrooms, hot showers, boat launch, kayaks, wireless Internet, and bonfires. Dogs are welcome.

PLAYA EL REQUESÓN

Travelers will find the turnoff for **Playa El Requesón** at kilometer 91.5. This is a popular beach for tent camping because of the unique sandbar that connects the shore to a small island. Shallow coves form on either side of the sandbar, creating a picturesque setting.

PLAYA LA PERLA AND PLAYA ARMENTA

At kilometer 91 are **Playas La Perla and Armenta.** You won't get the calm turquoise waters like you will at beaches farther north at these southernmost beaches on the bay because the waters are less protected here and the wind kicks up in the afternoon. You will, however, be likely to have the sand to yourself.

Peninsula Concepción

The large landmass on the other side of the bay from the beaches of Bahía Concepción is Peninsula Concepción. Many travelers are tempted to visit Peninsula Concepción because it's so visible from the rest of the bay; however, it remains remote and fairly inaccessible by car. There is a dirt road that goes out along the peninsula, but it can be rough and conditions can vary. You'll pass a few fishing

camps along the way but not much else. It's easier to take a boat from Punta Arena.

RECREATION
★ Kayaking

Kayaking in Bahía Concepción provides access to the small islands, secluded beaches, and remote areas that can't be reached by the road. The waters are calm and warm for most of the year. **Playa Santispac** is the best launch point because of the easy access to several islands—San Ramón, Liebre, Pithaya (Luz), and Blanca. There are very few kayak rentals in the area, so it's best to bring your own or rent one in Mulegé or Loreto.

Bahía San Juanico (Scorpion Bay)

Bahía San Juanico, also called Scorpion Bay, is arguably the most popular spot for surfing on the entire Baja peninsula. This small, remote fishing village on the Pacific has become a classic Baja surfing spot.

While the roads out to Bahía San Juanico can be treacherous, for serious surfers it's worth the hassle to get to the series of right

point breaks with seemingly endless waves. There are very few services here (no ATMS—make sure to bring pesos with you as you will need to pay cash nearly everywhere in San Juanico) and no reliable cell phone service. There are a few markets in town where provisions can be purchased and pay phones are available.

Playa El Requesón is a favorite beach for campers with its unique sandspit.

SURFING

In total, there are eight right point breaks in the area, although the first four are the most famous. The points break on south swells, which occur between March and November. On big days, a ride can last over a minute.

This isn't a commercialized tourist surfing spot—there are no surfing lessons for beginners or board rentals going on here. This is a destination for serious surfers. It's still a good spot for beginners on small days, but larger days are best reserved for the experienced.

FOOD AND ACCOMMODATIONS

The most high-end accommodations to be found in the area are at the **Scorpion Bay Hotel** (Santo Domingo Lote 14, U.S. tel. 858/551-4900, www.scorpionbayhotel.com, US$90-110) and consist of a number of *casitas* and bunkhouses. Breakfast is included with your stay, and lunch and dinner are available upon request. Surfboard rentals are available starting at $10 per day. They also have kayaks, stand-up paddleboards, and beach chairs to rent. Fishing trips can be chartered as well as trips to see local cave paintings.

The hub of social life for surfers and visitors to San Juanico is the **Scorpion Bay Cantina and Campground** (North of town at second point, www.scorpionbay.net). Most visitors tent camp here (US$9 pp) with facilities including hot showers, toilets, and trash removal. There are three sleeping *palapas* (US$45), an apartment (US$125), and a suite (US$100) for those who prefer not to tent camp. Reservations for these accommodations can be made on the website. Reservations are not taken for tent campers, who will need to check in and pay cash when they arrive. Guests gather at **The Cantina** (7:30am-10pm daily, mains US$5-11), a large *palapa* serving breakfast, lunch, and dinner daily. Wi-Fi is available for light Internet use.

In town, visitors will find markets selling basic provisions like water, ice, groceries, and gypsy gasoline. There are also a few taco stands and hot dog carts. Many visitors buy the fresh day's catch from local fishers.

GETTING THERE

Once you reach Scorpion Bay, the question you are most likely to be asked is, "which road did you take to get here?" There are three roads into San Juanico: the paved south road, the dirt east road, and the dirt north road. Varying road conditions and your comfort level with off-road adventures generally dictate which you use.

The **South Road** is now completely paved. This is the easiest, but longest route and optimal if you're towing anything or do not have four-wheel drive. Start in Ciudad Insurgentes on Mexico 1 and turn north onto Mexico 53. Drive north toward La Purísima to the Las Barrancas turnoff and follow the signs to San Juanico.

The **East Road** is a rough dirt road that is not used often and can be especially challenging if there have been recent hurricanes or rainstorms. Roads may be muddy and washed out and are prone to flash floods. If the road is passable, you will need to have four-wheel drive and spare tires with you. From Mexico 1 at El Rosarito, head west on Mexico 53 to San Isidro/La Purísima. Follow the signs to San Juanico.

The **North Road** is currently the preferred off-road option. The route is 170 kilometers from San Ignacio. In San Ignacio, drive through the town plaza and connect with the road leading south to La Fridera Fish Camp on the shore of Laguna San Ignacio. This road is paved for the first eight miles. Go left at the fish camp and proceed to Cuarenta, San Jose de Gracia, Raymundo, Cadajé, and on to San Juanico. Bear to the right, leave the graded road, and go through El Datil and Ballena via the mudflats. Do not leave the tracks on the mudflats or your vehicle will get stuck. You'll encounter steep arroyos, some with mud and flowing water. It's best to take the route when caravanning with another vehicle. Take a shovel, plywood, a tow chain, a good map and a GPS, shortwave radios, extra fuel, water, and spare tires.

La Purísima and Comondú

Heading south of Bahía Concepción, there's a turnoff of Mexico 1 at kilometer 60 to go west into the Sierra de la Giganta. The fertile valleys here are home to small ranching communities and scenic views. Tourists are not commonly seen, but are welcomed with warm Mexican hospitality when they are.

SAN ISIDRO

The small town of San Isidro consists of a few small stores, taco stands, and a church, all surrounded by orchards. It doesn't have much to offer tourists; there's more to see in La Purísima.

LA PURÍSIMA

Underground springwater helped La Purísima to develop into an area suitable for agriculture and cattle. The small village is nestled into a palm oasis surrounded by volcanic cliffs. There aren't many services here, but there is a pharmacy, tire shop, and a small market selling basic provisions.

The prominent **El Pilón** is a large rock (400 meters) relief from a hill that was eroded and a landmark for the area. An old aqueduct (over 300 years old) that was built by the missionaries runs along the cliffs on the south side of town. It played an integral part in bringing prosperity to the town.

Sights

Oasis La Purísima is a marked trail that gives views of El Pilón and other scenic vistas of the area. The trail is marked by white rocks and has informative signs along the way naming the local plants. It leads all around the terrain, offering beautiful viewpoints, following the river and up through canyons with cliff walls imprinted with hundreds of fossils. Be aware that the trail is over 20 kilometers, so if you're looking for a day hike, you'll likely end up following the trail out a bit and then doubling back.

If you get a chance to visit the local graveyard, don't miss the tomb of Loretoo de Blackman, locally referred to as **"Vampire Blackman."** Local legend has it that Blackman (a European) came to La Purísima and married a woman many years his junior. When she died shortly after of anemia, rumors started spreading that Blackman had been drinking her blood. He's also credited with the death of several miners while working at the El Boleo mine. When Blackman died in 1912, no town in Baja Sur wanted his body out of fear that he would curse it. In the end, he was buried in La Purísima, next to his young bride. Residents believe that he will come back to haunt the locals because he was not accepted by them when he was living.

Jesuit Padre Nicolás Tamarl founded the **Misión La Purísima Concepción de Cadegomó** in 1720. In 1735 it moved to a new location about 10 miles south of the original site. The mission was abandoned in 1822, and only a few traces remain of either site. They are mostly just rubble. Only some foundation stones that outline the original structure are left at the first site. The irrigation canals that were built by the missionaries can be seen in town and still function over 300 years later.

Accommodations

Cabañas la Purísima (tel. 612/141-7231, www.cabanaslapurisima.com) offers three new cabins, each of which sleeps up to four people. Air-conditioning and meals are available for an extra fee. Another option for accommodations is **Posada Del Ángel**. The owner, Quithy (pronounced Kitty), is a retired professor and an authority on La Purísima and the region. She can tell you about the history of the region and suggest activities.

COMONDÚ

The villages of San Jose de Comondú and San Miguel de Comondú are known collectively as Comondú. Located in a fertile ravine three kilometers apart, both offer travelers the feeling of stepping back in time. Each has an impressive and lively plaza surrounded by colonial buildings and basic services.

The region is rich with agriculture—fruits, vegetables, sugarcane, dates, figs, olive trees, and vineyards first planted by the missionaries. Because of these resources, the region for a long time was very prosperous and almost self-sufficient. Cattle produced meat, cheese, and butter and provided leather, which was used to make containers to export dates and raisins to mainland Mexico.

Today, these two oasis villages provide an ideal base for exploring the history, culture, and natural adventures that the region offers. The area is home to petroglyphs, cave paintings, rugged peaks, natural springs and pools, prism rock formations, and desert scenery.

Sights

The fifth mission built in California was **Misión San José de Comondú,** founded by Jesuit Padre Julián de Mayorga in 1716. There were two locations of the mission as well as two nearby *visitas* (for the missions of San Ignacio and San Javier, called San Miguel). Some have listed the *visita* for San Javier as a separate mission, but the Jesuit records are clear that it was always just a *visita*. The location is now known as San Miguel de Comondú. The remains of the original mission location are between the ranches of San Juan and La Presa. A side chapel to the main church was preserved and can be seen today in San José de Comondú.

Events

The **Festival del Vino Misional** is the major event each year taking place in November and featuring locally made wine, food, and music and art. More information can be found on their Facebook page at www.facebook.com/VinoMisionalDeBcs.

Accommodations

Located in San Miguel de Comondú, **Hacienda Don Mario** (tel. 664/134-5924, www.haciendadonmario.com, US$45) is a nice new hotel offering six rooms with air-conditioning and kitchenettes. They can help arrange for tours and sightseeing around the area.

Getting There

There are a few options for getting to this area. The easiest route is to take a paved road north from Ciudad Insurgentes (the branch of Mexico 1 that does not go to Loreto) which ends a few kilometers before La Purísima. From here, it's possible to get to San Isidro, but the road to Comondú is impassable for vehicles. To get to Comondú, return to the paved road and take the Comondú turnoff in Ejido Francisco Villa. Another more scenic route is from a turnoff of Mexico 1 at kilometer 60, south of Bahía Concepción. A third option, currently in rough condition, is accessed from the road out to San Javier from Mexico 1. The dirt road turnoff is 6.5 kilometers north of San Javier.

Loreto

Nestled between the Sea of Cortez and the peaks of the Sierra de la Giganta is the quaint, picturesque town of Loreto. The town's historic plaza, examples of colonial architecture, and California's oldest mission (in both Baja and Alta) provide a magical background for this Baja destination. Appropriately enough, Loreto was designated a *Pueblo Mágico* in 2012 (a recognition given to cities in Mexico that offer visitors a "magical" experience by reason

of their natural beauty, cultural riches, or historical relevance), and this charming town has grown into a must-see for any Baja traveler.

Loreto is a town as diverse as it is beautiful. This is a place where culture and history come alive. It's where the outdoors call to those who enjoy fishing, snorkeling, golfing, kayaking, and hiking. You can spend your morning swimming with sea lions and your afternoon exploring 300-year-old missions. History

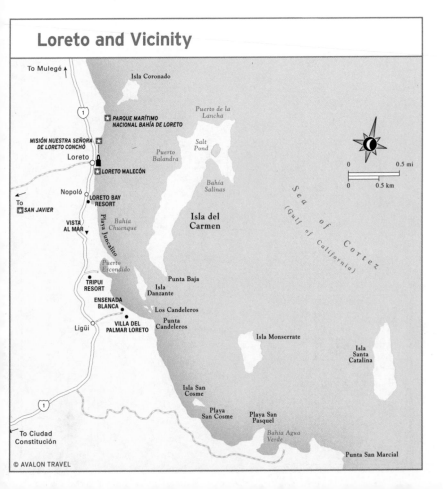

Loreto and Vicinity

Loreto

To Nopoló and
Puerto Escondido

To Mulegé

To La Picazón

To RV Parks

BASEBALL
STADIUM

PASEO PEDRO DE UGARTE

ARNES

PASEO NICOLAS TAMARAL

BUS
TERMINAL

HOTEL
SANTA FE

POST OFFICE

HACIENDA SUITES

HOTEL
ANGRA

Río

Loreto

BANAMEX

EL PESCADOR
SUPERMARKET

CALLE ALLENDE

CALLE

CALLE

CALLE

LEÓN

JUÁREZ

SALVATIERRA

BAJA CALIFORNIA

CALLE COLEGIO

CALLE MORELOS

ZARAGOZA

CABAÑAS DE LORETO

PASEO SALVATIERRA

Plaza

HIDALGO

JORDAN

CALLE PIPILA

SEE DETAIL

SUKASA

AUGIE'S

LUCIA

MITA GOURMET

MEDITERRANEO

IGUANA INN

1697

DOLPHIN DIVE CENTER

ROBLES

LA MISIÓN

CALLE AYUNTAMIENTO

CALLE

CONSTITUYENTES

ZAPATA

MISIONEROS

PINO SUÁREZ

MADERO

CARRILLO

ORLANDO'S/
LA MICHOACANA

CALLE INDEPENDENCIA

CALLE

CALLE

CALLE

CALLE

DAVIS

DESERT INN

COCO
CABANA

Playa Loreto

DE PLAYA (LÓPEZ MATEOS)

LORETO MALECÓN

CALLE MADERO

HOTEL
OASIS

Beach

Sea of Cortez
(Gulf of California)

© AVALON TRAVEL

N

0   500 yds
0   500 m

SEE DETAIL

MISIÓN NUESTRA SEÑORA
DE LORETO CONCHÓ

MI
LORETO

HOTEL
PLAZA
LORETO

LA DAMIANA
INN

P. SUÁREZ

SALVATIERRA

TOURISM
OFFICE

BANK

Plaza

MADERO

EL CABALLO
BLANCO

POSADA
DEL CORTÉS

1697

MITA GOURMET

RICHARD JACKSON'S
PHOTOGRAPHY GALLERY

POSADA DE
LAS FLORES

CAFÉ
OLÉ

ARTURO'S
SPORTFISHING

LA
PALAPA

BUDGET
RENTA-CAR

HIDALGO

CALLE PIPILA

CALLE JORDAN

buffs, outdoor adventurers, avid shoppers, and anglers will all find plenty to do here.

A boat ride will take you out to any of the five islands off the coast in the Parque Marítimo Nacional Bahía de Loreto where you can see whales and other wildlife, as well as snorkel, dive, kayak, or just enjoy the beautiful views and crystal clear waters. The nearby Sierra de la Giganta is home to the crowning jewel of all of the Baja missions, Misión San Francisco Javier de Viggé-Biaundó, and also offers hikers and backpackers a playground for exploration and discovery.

With a commercial international airport, Loreto is now an easy weekend escape from the United States or Canada. This small town becomes even sleepier in the heat of summer when high temperatures cause some small hotels and businesses in town close down. This is particularly true for the months of August and September. But there are still plenty of places that remain open to accommodate the anglers who flock to the area in June and July when the fishing is good.

SIGHTS
★ Misión Nuestra Señora de Loreto Conchó

As the first Spanish mission founded in California (both Alta and Baja California), the **Misión Nuestra Señora de Loreto Conchó** holds a special place in the history of the region. Jesuit Padre Juan Aria de Salvatierra founded the mission of Loreto at the village of Conchó on October 25, 1697. It began as a simple structure inside the presidio until the Spanish gained more acceptance by the local indigenous people. A larger adobe church was completed in 1704. Loreto was the capital and religious center of California for decades. New missions and *visitas* were built out from Loreto on a network of roads eventually known as El Camino Real. In 1740 Padre Jaime Bravo began constructing a larger church built from stone and mortar, the walls of which survive today. The entrance over the doorway to the church reads "Head and mother of the Missions of Lower and Upper California."

Directly next to the church is the **Museo de los Misiones** (tel. 613/135-0441, 9am-1pm and 1:45pm-6pm Tues.-Sun., US$3) run by INAH. The small museum has some interesting exhibits about the history of the missions and the missionaries including historic maps and artifacts from daily life during that era.

Arched tree walkways lead to the town plaza.

Malecón

While most of the action centers around the plaza and surrounding streets, Loreto has a quiet palm-lined *malecón* that runs along the beach of the Sea of Cortez and Boulevard López Mateos. It's a pleasant spot to watch the sunrise or go for a stroll. There are a number of restaurants, bars, and hotels that line the west side of the street.

★ Plaza Juárez

Loreto's lively **Plaza Juárez** is lined with colonial buildings, shops, restaurants, cafés and the *palacio municipal* (town hall). On the south side of the plaza, Paseo Salvatierra is a pedestrian walkway with a shady archway of topiary trees which runs up to the mission and then down to the *malecón*. Many of the establishments along the plaza offer 2-for-1 margaritas during happy hour, which is a wonderful opportunity to sit outside and enjoy the quiet buzz of the plaza.

★ Parque Marítimo Nacional Bahía de Loreto

The waters and five islands off the coast of Loreto form Mexico's largest marine preserve, designated a UNESCO World Heritage Site in 2005. There are over 800 species of marinelife inhabiting the Sea of Cortez, and many of them are endangered. **Eco-Alizanza de Loreto A.C.** (www.ecoalianzaloreto.org) is a local nonprofit dedicated to protecting the national marine park and the natural and cultural environment of Loreto. The five islands within the park (Coronado, Carmen, Danzante, Monserrate, and Santa Catalina) are reachable by boat trips from Loreto. Your hotel or any local tour operators can make arrangements for you to take a day trip out to the islands.

RECREATION
★ Sportfishing

Anglers have been coming to Loreto from all over the world since the 1960s. They're lured to the region for the dorado, yellowtail,

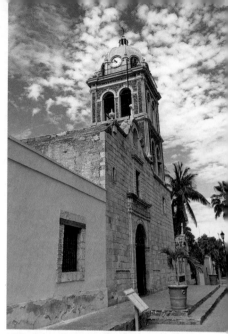

Misión Nuestra Señora de Loreto Conchó

marlin, roosterfish, yellowfin tuna, cabrilla, grouper, and sailfish. There's sportfishing year-round, but the big draw is for the summer dorado and other migratory species. Most hotels in town can arrange for a fishing charter or there are a number of independent companies.

For over 30 years, **Arturo's Sportfishing** (Calle Hidalgo, tel. 613/135-0766, www.arturosport.com) has been handling fishing charters for the area. Prices range US$240-440 depending on the size of the boat and the season. Reservations can be made online. **Loreto Fly Fishing Guide** (www.loretoflyfishingguide.com) can direct anglers to local fishing guides and captains and has local Loreto fishing reports.

Boating

The islands offshore from Loreto make for interesting and fun boat trips, with secluded beaches and bays to explore. *Panga* trips can be arranged by most hotels in Loreto. There are a few launch ramps around town for smaller boats at the north end of the *malecón*, and at the **Loreto Shores Villas and RV Park** (Colonia Zaragosa, tel. 613/135-1513, loretoshores@yahoo.com). Larger boats should anchor at the deeper and larger **Puerto Escondido marina** south of town. The **port captain** (tel. 613/133-0656) has offices in Loreto and Puerto Escondido.

Kayaking

The islands of Loreto are one of the most popular areas for kayaking in Baja, and kayakers can easily paddle out to Isla Coronado or the north end of Isla Carmen from Loreto. From Puerto Escondido, kayakers can make it to the southern or eastern shores of Isla Carmen, Isla Danzante, and Los Candeleros.

There are many options for organized multiday kayak tours in the area. Trudi Angell has been leading multiday kayak tours through her company **Paddling South** (www.tour-baja.com) since the 1980s. Also with multi-day kayaking and stand-up paddleboarding trips around the Loreto islands is **Sea Trek Baja** (www.seatrek.com). **Sea Kayak Baja Mexico** (www.seakayakbajamexico.com) has guided expeditions and will also rent kayaks for multiple days to experienced and qualified kayakers who want to create their own adventure.

Diving

Loreto attracts divers who come to explore the rock reefs, caves, seamounts, and even a few shipwrecks. There are 800 species of marinelife found in the protected waters around Loreto such as dolphins, whales, sea lions, sea turtles, and rays. Visibility usually varies from 15 to 30 meters. **Dolphin Dive Center** (tel. 613/135-1914, www.dolphindivebaja.com) handles rentals, diving tours, and certifications. They offer day trips as well as night dives and snorkeling trips.

Hiking

There's a lot of great hiking around Loreto and the Sierra de la Giganta, but there aren't many marked trails. The book *Hiking Loreto* (www.hikingloreto.com) is a valuable resource as it can guide do-it-yourself hikers on runs such as Punta El Abajo, Shell Canyon, and El Rio del Pez. It can be purchased ahead of time or in many stores in town. If you're more comfortable hiring a guide to lead you on a hike around the region, **Said Orozco** (www.loretoguide.com) is a reliable and

Coronado Island is a popular boat trip, just off the coast from Loreto.

resourceful one who can point out local plants and wildlife.

Golf

The **Loreto Bay Golf Course** (tel. 613/133-0010, www.loretobayresort.com) offers 18 holes and beautiful views of the Sierra de la Giganta and the Sea of Cortez. The course is well maintained and sets up some challenging shots, especially hole 15, which crosses the lagoon. Golfers are still awaiting the opening of the much-anticipated 18-hole **Danzante Bay Golf Course** at Villa del Palmar.

Organized Tours

Organized tours are the easiest way for most travelers to get out to the islands of Loreto and can also be a convenient way to partake in other activities and day trips around the area. For outdoor nature adventure tours, **Wild Loreto** (www.wildloreto.com) has everything from island-hopping, fishing, and whale-watching to hiking and mission tours. Likewise, **Desert and Sea Expeditions** (Calle Pino Suarez, tel. 613/135-1979, www.desertandsea.com) offers a number of day trips in the region to see cave paintings and the missions or for fishing, diving, and island excursions.

ENTERTAINMENT AND EVENTS
Bars

Right on the *malecón* with great ocean views from their second story, **Augie's** (Malecón, tel. 613/135-1224, www.augiesbarloreto.net, 11am-10pm daily) is a popular expat hangout. They have a full menu with a wide variety of food from tacos to pizza to sushi. The same folks own **Evening Shade Bar & Grill** (noon-2am Wed.-Sun.) just down the *malecón*. They're open for lunch and dinner and one of the only late-night spots in Loreto. Often events and parties will start at Augie's and move down to Evening Shade at the night wears on.

The **Giggling Dolphin Restaurant and Boat Bar** (Benito Juárez, tel. 613/109-9853) is a large open *palapa* serving seafood (they're a popular spot to take your freshly caught fish to have them prepare it for you) and beer and margaritas from a boat that's been converted to a bar.

Right on the plaza, **Agave** (tel. 613/135-2225, 7am-11pm daily) is a great place to enjoy people-watching while also enjoying two-for-one margaritas during happy hour. The margaritas are large and come in a variety of flavors from cilantro to coconut. The *pepino* (cucumber) and the *jamaica* (hibiscus) are definitely worth a try. Stay for dinner if you want to linger in the picturesque outdoor garden dining area.

Events

The anniversary of the Mission of Loreto is October 25. The **Festival of the Missions** takes place every year at the end of October to celebrate the founding of Loreto and the earliest mission in Baja and Alta California. The town honors its history with music, food, dancing, and celebrations of mass.

SHOPPING

There's no shortage of curios shops in Loreto where travelers can buy authentic Mexican souvenirs such as colorful blankets, handcrafted pottery, silver jewelry, and knick-knacks. **Conchita's Curios** (Misioneros, tel. 613/135-1054, 9am-8pm daily) has Mexican home decor items, furniture, textiles, and Talavera dishes. With a great selection of the finest crafts from Mexico, **Gecko's Curios** (Calle Hidalgo, tel. 613/135-2505, 10am-5pm Mon.-Wed., 10am-9pm Thurs.-Sat.) showcases beautiful pottery, artisanal pieces, and straw art, where colorful bits of straw are cut and placed on a wooden base one at a time to create a design. **Tony's Silver** (Salvatierra 54, tel. 613/135-1400, www.tonyssilverloreto.com) offers Talavera pottery, Huichol beadwork, metal art pieces, and silver jewelry.

The bookstore **El Caballo Blanco** (Hidalgo 85, tel. 613/116-5374) has amassed a collection of more than 10,000 used books and an extensive selection of new Baja books as well. Art supplies, pottery, art, fabrics, and handmade paper round out the offering.

Because of its prime location on the plaza, many tourists find themselves wandering through **Richard Jackson's Photography Gallery** (tel. 613/118-2207, www.soulcatchingimages.com) and buying at least some small prints to take home as a memento of beautiful Loreto. Jackson's wildlife and landscape photographs perfectly capture the beauty and essence of the region. Those who are falling even more for the beauty of Loreto, may want to stop in next door to visit his wife Jill Jackson's real estate office, **Misión Loreto Properties** (www.misionloreto.com), to check out what is on sale in the area.

FOOD
Mexican

New in town and with a prime location on the paseo off the plaza across from the mission is **Mi Loreto** (Calle Salvatierra, tel. 624/151-5894, 12:30pm-9:30pm Tues.-Sun., mains US$5-9). The small restaurant is run by a family originally from Oaxaca, and their recipes are culled from five different regions around Mexico. This gives a slightly different twist to the dishes typically found in Baja—enchiladas with mole and chiles rellenos stuffed with bananas. The ingredients are fresh, and the food is made from scratch. The seating is all outside with brightly colored decor and strung lights creating an enticing and friendly atmosphere. If the weather is cold, they have Mexican ponchos that diners can wear to stay warm.

As the name implies, **La Palapa** (Miguel Hidalgo, tel. 613/135-1101, www.restaurant-lapalapaloreto.com, noon-10pm daily, mains US$6-14) is housed under a giant open-air *palapa*. They serve traditional Mexican food as well as seafood in a fun atmosphere with colorful tablecloths. Take in your freshly caught fish to have them cook it up three different ways.

With a casual *palapa* environment just near the plaza, **Orlando's Mexican Cocina** (Madero between Juárez and Robles, tel. 613/135-1655, 7:30am-9pm Tues.-Sun., mains US$4-7) is a favorite of many Loreto locals. Breakfast, lunch, and dinner all mean authentic Mexican food at affordable prices. During happy hour (3pm-5pm), beer and margaritas are two for one. Also right off of the plaza, **Café Olé** (7am-10pm Mon.-Sat., 7am-1pm Sun., US$3-5) is a casual and affordable eatery with quick service. The savory Mexican egg dishes are a favorite for breakfast.

On the *malecón* with views of the Sea of Cortez from the second-floor patio,

Loreto has plenty of artisan shopping.

Mediterraneo (Blvd. Adolfo Lopez Mateo, tel. 613/135-2577, noon-4pm and 6pm-10pm Tues.-Sun., US$7-10) serves up good food with great views. They have everything from salad to seafood to meat on the menu. Also on the *malecón* is Los Mandiles de Santa Lucía (tel. 613/135-1846, US$6-9), popular for traditional Mexican dishes, especially breakfasts.

A mini oasis off the beaten path, ★ La Picazón (Calle Davis Norte 27, tel. 613/111-8782, www.lapicazon.com, noon-6pm Mon.-Sat., mains US$7-15) can be difficult to find, but that makes the paradise that awaits patrons all the more rewarding. On a dirt road eight kilometers north of Loreto, La Picazón is what Baja living is all about: fresh food and a relaxing and welcoming environment. The large *palapa* is in a remote location right on the Sea of Cortez, with a picturesque view of Isla Coronado just off the coast. The oasis has tables for dining, couches for lounging, and hammocks for resting. This is the type of spot where you come to while the afternoon away sipping on margaritas and enjoying wraps, seafood, burgers, and salads. Owner and chef Esmerelda is half of the reason that patrons keep frequenting La Picazón, with her warm hospitality and "mi casa es su casa" mantra.

Seafood

Located right on the plaza, Mita Gourmet (tel. 613/135-2025, www.mitagourmet.com, 9am-3pm and 5:30pm-11pm Mon.-Sat., mains US$7-15) has become favorite of many tourists and expats in Loreto. They have unique seafood dishes with bold flavors and heavy sauces. Their location and prices definitely cater to the American market.

On the *malecón,* Loreto Islas (Blvd. Adolfo López Mateos and Salvatierra, tel. 613/135-2341, www.loretoislas.com, 8am-9pm Tues.-Sun., mains US$8-13) offers nice views and good margaritas. Chef Caesar serves up shrimp, octopus, and scallops, as well as pastas. If you bring in fish you caught, they will prepare it for you and serve it with a number of savory sauces.

Taco Stands and *Antojitos*

Locals, tourists, Americans, Mexicans— everyone in Loreto eventually finds their way to ★ Asadero Super Burro (Francisco Fernández, tel. 613/135-1243, 5:30pm-midnight Thurs.-Tues.). The casual spot offers large portions, delicious food, affordable prices, friendly staff, and a fun atmosphere. They're known for their large *arrachera* meat *burros* (large burritos). Equally good are the *papas rellenas*—potatoes stuffed with meat, vegetables, and cheese.

With a colorful and inviting setting under a casual *palapa*, Almejas Concho (tel. 615/135-1452, www.almejasancholoreto.com, US$5-9) serves delicious ceviche and seafood cocktails. The specialties here are the chocolate clams and the *almejas gratinadas* (clams au gratin), grilled and stuffed with cheese, shrimp, and salsa.

For fish tacos, head to the popular El Rey del Taco (Benito Juárez, no tel., 9am-2pm, US$2-6). In addition to fish tacos, they have carne asada and *cabeza*. All of the usual taco toppings are arrayed for you to make your own tasty treat. You can order from the window that faces out onto the street or sit down inside. They close down around 2pm or whenever the food runs out, so go early.

The *paletas* at La Michoacana (Madero at Juárez, tel. 613/135-0549) are a favorite treat to satisfy a sweet tooth when the weather is warm.

International

Uruguay meets Italy at Mezzaluna (Hidalgo and Madero, no tel., 5pm-9pm, US$4-8) with homemade pasta, pizza, empanadas, and salads. The casual environment has nice wooden tables and benches with gingham tablecloths and a few tables outside on the patio as well.

Directly on the plaza, 1697 Restaurant and El Zopilote Brewing Co. (Calle Davis 13, tel. 613/135-2538, restaurantbar1697@ prodigy.net, noon-10pm Tues.-Sat.) offers a great location for people-watching, sharing a pizza, and enjoying a good craft beer. El Zopilote is Loreto's first microbrewery and the best place in town for finding craft beer. The menu features Italian and Mexican dishes and hamburgers for lunch.

For southwestern flavors, head south of town to **Sabor!** (Mexico 1 Km. 118, tel. 613/104-8568, www.saborloreto.com, 12:30pm-8pm Wed.-Sat., 10am-8pm Sun., mains US$6-11). The menu features poblano pasta, lime butter shrimp, southwestern chimichangas, and savory burgers. The rooftop dining patio gives diners views of the Sea of Cortez and the Sierra de la Giganta.

The friendly bistro-style restaurant **Pan Que Pan** (Ave. Miguel Hidalgo, 8am-6pm Tues.-Sat, 8am-3pm Sun., US$6-8) also doubles as a favorite local bakery. The menu lists homemade pastas, salads, calzones, and thincrust pizza (they also have a gluten-free option). The bakery here serves up favorites like freshly baked breads, pasties, and chocolate croissants. Go early in the morning for the baked goods before they sell out.

Groceries

The new **Super Ley** (Heroes de Independencia and Padre Kino, 7am-10pm daily) is the largest grocery store in town, although the **El Pescadero** (Salvatierra) is also a large market where shoppers can find typical groceries. Across the street from El Pescadero, **El Galivan** (Salvatierra, tel. 613/108-3437) carries specialty items like medicinal plants, seeds, spices, chilies, and gluten-free and sugar-free products.

ACCOMMODATIONS
Under US$50

Oozing with Mexican charm next to the mission, **Hostal Casa Loreto** (Misioneros 14, tel. 613/116-7014, casasabel@yahoo.com, US$21-37) has rooms with private bathrooms, wireless Internet, TV, and a full communal kitchen. The entire property bursts with the authentic ambience of old Mexico with Saltillo tiles, wood beams, brick archways, carved wood furniture, and colorful Mexican textiles.

For affordable and comfortable accommodations with a good in-town location, **Iguana**

Inn (Juárez between David and Madero, tel. 613/135-1627, www.iguanainn.com, US$40-55) offers four basic bungalows with kitchenettes, air-conditioning, and wireless Internet. The grounds feature lots of shady *palapa*-covered areas and outdoor cooking facilities.

In the center of town, a few blocks from the plaza, **Hotel Plaza Loreto** (Paseo Hidalgo 2, tel. 613/135-1731, admon.plto@gmail.com, US$40) gives guests a quiet and central location. It's a clean and decent low-budget option, but the rooms need to be updated and the wireless access doesn't always have a strong signal in the rooms. Located on the *malecón,* **Sukasa Bungalows** (tel. 613/135-0490, www.loreto.com/sukasa, US$35-60) offers comfortable and clean accommodations and personalized service. Accommodations consist of two air-conditioned bungalows, a casita, and a yurt.

Outside of the town center but close to the bus station, **Hotel Angra** (Juárez between Marquez de León and Ignacio Allende, tel. 613/135-1172, www.hotelangra.com, US$45) provides large clean rooms with king-size beds and air-conditioning. Guests will enjoy the friendly service and free continental breakfast. The property is pet-friendly, and there's a secure parking area in courtyard, which makes this hotel popular with road-trippers.

US$50-100

If you're looking for all the comforts of home while traveling, ★ **Coco Cabañas** (tel. 613/135-1729, www.cococabanasloreto.com, US$95) offers a variety of options from studio *cabañas* to two-bedroom *casitas* and three-bedroom houses. The accommodations are comfortable and all equipped with kitchens and air-conditioning. There are two pools on the property as well as common areas with barbecues. The location is excellent—near the *malecón* as well as the plaza but on a residential alley so you get peace and quiet. The property was built and is run by two American brothers, Barrett and Stephen. Stephen works on the property and gives great recommendations for restaurants and bars in town. The office can arrange for fishing and diving trips as well as an excursion to San Javier.

With seven rooms, the boutique **La Damiana Inn** (Francisco Madero #8, tel. 613/135-0356, www.ladamianainn.com, US$68-77) features colorful Mexican decor and a convenient in-town location. Air-conditioning and wireless Internet are available in all rooms. There's a full outdoor kitchen, dining area, garden, patio, and barbecue with hammocks around the property. The relaxed and friendly property also welcomes dogs.

Directly on the plaza, **Hotel 1697** (Calle Davis 13, tel. 613/135-2538, restaurant-bar1697@prodigy.net.mx, US$70) offers a few basic rooms, each with its own patio. Rooms are clean, and the staff is very friendly. Hotel guests enjoy a 15 percent discount at the adjoining **1697 Restaurant and Brewery.**

For luxury accommodations at affordable prices, head to ★ **Posada del Cortes** (Callejon Pipila 4 Sur, tel. 613/135-0258, www.posadadelcortes.com, US$68). This boutique hotel has eight rooms that are kept to high standards with orthopedic mattresses, down comforters, and tasteful decorations. The property has Mexican charm with colonial-style architecture and well-manicured grounds. Rooms have mini kitchenettes and balconies. The Posada is near the *malecón* and walking distance to the plaza and restaurants and shops.

While it was once an institution in Loreto, **Desert Inn** (formerly La Pinta, Prolongación Francisco Madero, tel. 613/135-0025, recepciondesertinn@gmail.com, US$70) has fallen into disrepair in recent years. The property, still in its prime location on the beach, has changed hands many times over the past few years and vacillates between being well-kept and run-down. At last check the grounds and pool area were nicely manicured and the rooms were clean and kept up, but there weren't many guests on property.

On the edge of town near the highway and perfect for road-trippers looking for a place to stay overnight, **Hotel Santa Fe** (Salvatierra at Ebanista, toll-free U.S. tel. 877/217-2682, www.hotelsantafeloreto.com, US$60-80) supports five floors of rooms centered around a courtyard with a nice pool area. Unless you book a suite on an upper level, your room will not have any outward-facing windows, just the glass sliding doors that open to the courtyard area. Accommodations are clean and up to modern standards with air-conditioning and wireless Internet. There's a secure parking lot at the back of the hotel.

Just down the street is **Hacienda Suites** (Salvatierra 152, tel. 613/135-1693, www.haciendasuites.com, US$70-80) with two stories of rooms looking into a large central courtyard. All rooms have air-conditioning and in-room safes. A traditional Mexican breakfast is included with your stay and served in the courtyard. Guests enjoy the pool and getting drinks at the pool bar.

US$100-150

Mixing the comforts of home with the special perks of being on vacation, ★ **Las Cabañas de Loreto** (J. Morelos, tel. 613/135-1105, www.lascabanasdeloreto.com, $110) is a wonderful spot for a long weekend or a full two-week stay. With a beautiful pool and Jacuzzi area, a large communal outdoor kitchen and dining room, and palm trees and *palapas* scattering the grounds, the property is its own mini oasis. Guests are welcomed with cold beers and a kitchenette stocked with yogurt, granola, milk, coffee, and a basket overflowing with fruit for breakfast. The individual *cabañas* have kitchenettes with everything you may need (fridge, coffeemaker, coffee grinder, blender, toaster, microwave, dishes, glasses, silverware, etc.). The rooms are spacious and have plenty of Mexican charm but are up to modern standards. There's air-conditioning, TV, and wireless Internet in all of the rooms and plenty of amenities to take advantage of outside of your room as well—bikes, coolers, beach chairs, sun hats, wetsuits, snorkels, and a library stocked with hundreds of DVDs and books are all free for guests to use and enjoy. The location of Las Cabañas is walking distance to everything in Loreto. Make sure to book in advance—this is a popular and beloved place with only four cabañas and there's a three-night minimum stay.

El Tiburon Casitas (65/69 Norte Calle Davis, tel. 613/111-1614, www.eltiburoncasitas.com, US$110) offers four *casitas* all with full kitchens and also has great common areas for guests to use. There's a pool, barbecue area, hammocks, and a central *palapa* that operates as a gathering area. Guests can rent stand-up paddleboards or use the free bikes to explore around town.

One of the oldest hotels in Loreto, **Hotel Oasis** (Baja California and Blvd. López Mateos, tel. 613/135-0211, www.hoteloasis.com, US$105-120) has lots of Mexican charm with a cobblestone terrace and *palapa* roof. The property is right on the *malecón* with 39 rooms with views of the Sea of Cortez. Rooms and pool could use an update, but the restaurant on the premises has friendly service and serves great food, especially for breakfast. Every Saturday evening, the traditional clambake takes place at the Coronado Bar at Hotel Oasis featuring *almejas tatemadas* (baked clams), barbecue ribs, live music, and happy hour.

For weekly or monthly rentals, **Villas del Santo Niño** (Salvatierra 4, tel. 613/135-1564, www.villasdelsantonino.com, US$560/ week) has studios and apartments set in lush grounds. The property has an incredible location in the heart of Loreto, just off of the plaza and a few blocks to the *malecón*. Amenities include cleaning service, use of bicycles and kayakas, and a common area with grill. Studios can hold up to two people and apartments up to four people. No children under the age of 14 are allowed.

US$150-250

Situated right on the plaza in a colonial-style hacienda, ★ **Posada de las Flores** (Avenida Salvatierra and Madero, tel. 613/135-1162, www.posadadelasflores.com, US$150)

is a beautiful hotel with lots of charm and Mexican details. Rooms face the central courtyard (if you want a room with windows that open to the outside, ask for a room overlooking the plaza). The rooftop has beautiful views of the plaza and mission and a unique rooftop glass-bottom pool that looks down into the center of the courtyard. Continental breakfast and coffee are served up on the rooftop in the mornings. There's no parking lot and no elevator—upstairs rooms are accessed by a spiral staircase.

For upscale accommodations right on the *malecón*, **La Mision Loreto** (López Mateos, tel. 613/134-0350, www.lamisionloreto.com, US$146-198) is a large hotel with 65 rooms offering the most luxurious accommodations in town. The rooms are nicely appointed with comfortable beds and terraces that look out over the Sea of Cortez. The staff is very friendly and accommodating. There's a bar and restaurant on-site as well as a serene pool area. Because of its site on the *malecón,* certain rooms can get noisy at night, so bring earplugs if you're a light sleeper.

Camping and RV Parks

Loreto Shores Villas and RV Park (Colonia Zaragosa, tel. 613/135-1513, loretoshores@ yahoo.com, US$26) offers guests full hookups, a laundry room, hot showers, and a pool. Pull-through spots don't have much privacy, but there are beautiful views and beach access. Tent camping is available for US$7.

Rivera del Mar RV Park and Camping (Madero Norte 100, tel. 613/135-0718, lanyvall@yahoo.com.mx, US$16-18) has 25 RV spaces with full hookups, 15 amp outlets, and wireless Internet. Other amenities include laundry, restrooms, barbecues, and 24-hour security. The location is walking distance to the beach and the center of town. Tent camping and pets are allowed.

Backpackers, cyclists, and tent campers head to **Casa Palmas Altas Camp** (Nicolas Bravo, tel. 613/135-0897, www.palmasaltascamp.com, US$7 pp). There's a barbecue and swimming pool on the grounds, which are located just a few blocks away from the town center. They organize events like paintings lessons, theater performances, and a farmers market, and have a work exchange program for those who qualify.

INFORMATION AND SERVICES

There are several banks and ATMs around town (one BBVA Bancomer is right on the plaza) as well as a number of gas stations. **Loreto's tourist office** (tel. 613/135-0680, 8am-8pm daily) is inside the *palacio municipal* right on the plaza.

For medical emergencies, the **Hospital de la Comunidad do Loreto** on the edge of town on Mexico 1 is open 24 hours.

SAN JAVIER

A trip to Loreto isn't complete without taking a day trip to explore the small town and mission of San Javier. Located 36 kilometers southwest of Loreto, the town is nestled into the lush and craggy Sierra de la Giganta. From Mexico 1 (turn off at Km. 118), it's a beautiful drive through scenic valleys and lava flows that are covered in lush green vegetation after rains. Glimpses of the Sea of Cortez can be caught in the distance between the mountains. The sleepy village of San Javier is a small agricultural town, with one of the most well-preserved missions on the entire Baja peninsula.

★ Misión San Francisco Javier de Viggé-Biaundó

In 1699, Padre Francisco María Piccolo founded **Misión San Francisco Javier de Viggé-Biaundó.** During a drought in 1710, the original headquarters were moved to a visiting mission site, which is where the mission remains today. The stone church you can go to now was built from 1744 to 1758 and is considered to be the crown jewel of the Baja missions because of its excellent state of preservation and the beauty of the structure. The mission features the first stained-glass windows of the peninsula and three gold-leaf altars that were shipped from mainland Mexico and reassembled on-site. The mission reportedly cost nearly a million pesos to build and was financed by profits from pearl fisheries on the Sea of Cortez.

Today, a priest comes into town to give mass for the residents every Thursday. Jorge is the caretaker of the mission and is around daily 7am-6pm to answer any questions that visitors may have. Don't visit the mission at

Misión San Francisco Javier de Viggé-Biaundó, located in the small town of San Javier outside of Loreto

San Javier without taking some time to walk around the back to explore the old gardens and stop to see the large gnarled olive tree that's over 315 years old.

Food and Services

There's an even older olive tree in town behind a row of buildings on the main street that leads up to the mission. Ask at the artisan shop **Vigeé Biandó Arts & Crafts** (8am-5pm daily) to have them point you in the right direction of the olive tree. While you're at the shop, don't forget to pick up a bottle of damiana, a sweet herbal liqueur from Mexico that's believed to be an aphrodisiac. They also have very primitive rooms for rent for US$25 a night.

The **Living Roots Community Center** (www.livingrootsbaja.org) has locally produced handcrafts like leatherwork, quilts, and baked goods for sale that are all made by local rancheros.

La Palapa restaurant (8am-5pm daily, US$4-5) is the only restaurant in town and serves breakfast and lunch as well as cold beer. The service can be slow if they're busy, but the food is all homemade Mexican dishes (tostadas, enchiladas, burritos) and very good.

Getting There

The turnoff for San Javier is on Mexico 1 at kilometer 118 on the west side of the highway (look for the Del Borracho cowboy sign). The 34-kilometer road is currently paved all the way to San Javier except for a segment between kilometers 14 and 15 where you'll find a graded dirt road. The condition is usually good but the road goes through about a dozen arroyos that can be filled with water that can get quite high, especially after rains. A high-clearance vehicle is recommended. Ask in Loreto about road conditions or about joining a guided tour if you don't want to drive yourself.

SOUTH OF LORETO
Nopoló

The planned community of Nopoló is a large real estate development that's been growing over the past number of years. Within the community are a few small cafés and restaurants and one of the region's largest and nicest hotels, **Loreto Bay Resort** (Blvd. Paseo Misión de Loreto, tel. 613/134-0460, www. loretobayresort.com, US$130-180). The hotel has 155 oceanfront rooms with modern accommodations set around nicely manicured lawns, a pool area, and a beautiful beach

The road to San Javier is a scenic drive through the Sierra de la Giganta.

with views of the bay. There's an 18-hole golf course and a spa as well as on-site restaurant and bar.

The Wine Cellar (corner of south entrance road and Paseo Misión de Loreto, tel. 613/104-5562, www.nopolowinecellar.com, 4pm-10pm Mon., Wed.-Fri., 2pm-10pm Sat.-Sun.) is a warm and welcoming place for locals and tourists to enjoy a glass or bottle of wine. They also have a full bar and serve tapas.

The local friendly coffee shop **El Corazón Café** (Paseo Misión de Loreto 162, tel. 613/113-7161, www.elcorazoncafe.com, 8am-3:30pm Mon.-Fri., 8am-1pm Sat.) serves fresh-roasted beans from Mexico's top coffee regions. Food like sandwiches and hamburgers are all freshly made, and there's also an array of baked goods like cinnamon buns and scones.

South of Nopoló on the way to Puerto Escondido is the beachside clam shop **Vista al Mar** (11am-8pm daily, mains US$5-10). In addition to clams, they have a variety of filleted fish, scallops, and shrimp served different ways. This is casual dining with plastic chairs and tables in the sand under a *palapa* roof, but having the Sea of Cortez just steps away, helps to make it an unforgettable experience.

Tripui and Puerto Escondido

Large boats that come to Loreto will end up docking at the large deep port of Puerto Escondido. The nearby Tripui RV Park has comfortably modern accommodations at **Hotel Tripui** (tel. 613/133-0818, www.tripui-hotel.com.mx, US$95). Rooms are nicely appointed, and there's a large pool area and a restaurant. Breakfast is included with your stay. There's a deal for US$350 a week that many people who have boats docked at Puerto Escondido take advantage of.

Ensenada Blanca

Forty kilometers south of Loreto, the white sand beaches of Ensenada Blanca have been taken over by the only large resort in the region—★ **Villa del Palmar** (Mexico 1 Km. 83, toll-free U.S. tel. 800/790-4187, www.villadelpalmarloreto.com, US$210-240). The sprawling grounds are wall-manicured with palm trees, hammocks, Adirondack chairs, multiple pools, and restaurants all looking out onto the Sea of Cortez. There's a spa on the property and an 18-hole golf course will be opening soon. A shuttle takes guests back and forth to Loreto. Visit their website for package deals.

Off-roaders enjoy stunning views driving out to the small beach town of Agua Verde, south of Loreto.

San Cosme and Agua Verde

For those with a high-clearance, four-wheel-drive vehicle and a sense of adventure, the off-road drive out to Agua Verde offers some of the most scenic views on the peninsula. With the ocean views of the Sea of Cortez and islands juxtaposed against the mountain views of the Sierra de la Giganta, it's a stunningly beautiful—if harrowing—drive. The road hugs mountain curves with sharp drop-offs into deep canyons.

The route passes through the small rancho town of San Cosme, before continuing out to Agua Verde. Agua Verde is a very small town with just one mini market, **abarrotes Miguelito**. Bring a cooler and enjoy a picnic lunch on the beach or be prepared to self-contain camp for a few days. The turnoff for Agua Verde from Mexico 1 is just south of kilometer 65 on the east side of the road. The drive is just over 40 kilometers and takes about 1.5-2 hours.

Ciudad Constitución and Ciudad Insurgentes

CIUDAD INSURGENTES

Ciudad Insurgentes doesn't have much to offer tourists aside from services (food, gas, and supplies), but it's an important junction and a point of departure for trips to La Purísima, Comondú, San Juanico, and Puerto López Mateos. Drivers who were counting down the kilometers from Santa Rosalía should note that the kilometer markings reset here and start over at kilometer 236.

CIUDAD CONSTITUCIÓN

You can find all of the services that you need along Mexico 1 in Constitución—gas stations, banks, grocery stores, mechanics, restaurants, cafés, and a hospital. While this isn't a typical tourist destination, there are a few hotels for those who need to spend the night.

Food

There are plenty of places to eat right along Mexico 1. Sushi restaurants, cafés, taco stands, and street food are plentiful. You may see the people lined up at **Taqueria Karen** (Mexico 1, no tel., US$3-6) for a variety of tacos including *cabeza* and *pescado*. **Birrieria Jalisco**

(Mexico 1, tel. 613/132-1077, US$4-8) is the local's choice for *birria*.

Parlante Café Restaurant and Bar (Mexico 1 and Ave. Obregón, tel. 613/132-7571, 7am-11pm Mon.-Thurs., 7am-midnight Fri.-Sat., 8am-11pm Sun., US$4-8) serves breakfast, lunch, and dinner in addition to coffee and wine. The menu has a wide variety of offerings including hamburgers, pizza, sandwiches, Italian, and traditional Mexican food. The dishes are substantial, and the ingredients are fresh.

Accommodations

One of the best hotels in town is **Hotel Oasis** (Vicente Guerrero 284, tel. 613/132-4458, www.hoteloasis.mx, US$25), a modern and clean hotel with air-conditioning and hair dryers in the rooms. There's a pool as well as a mini market and café on the property.

For cheap and reliable accommodations, **Cuatro Misiones Hotel** (tel. 613/132-0612, contacto@cuatromisiones.com, US$35) is a good choice. The rooms are small, basic, and clean, and the staff is friendly. Although the hotel is just off of the main highway, the rooms face the opposite direction so it's fairly quiet at night.

Mumai Hotel (Mexico 1 Km. 208, tel. 613/132-3052, US$32) offers newly renovated rooms with modern amenities such as flatscreen TVs and wireless Internet. There's secure parking (in a private garage), and pets are accepted. **Paraiso del Valle** (Blvd. Agustin Olachea, tel. 613/132-6206, US$22) has 22 clean and spacious rooms, all facing a central parking lot.

For RVers, the **La Pila Balneario RV Park** (tel. 613/132-0562, la_pila_campestres@hotmail.com, US$15) features pools, grassy lawns, palm trees, and 18 sites with water and electric hookups. Tent camping is also allowed. The property is south of town at kilometer 209, turn west for one kilometer.

MISIÓN SAN LUIS GONZAGA CHIRIYAQUI

Ciudad Constitución is the departure point for **Misión San Luis Gonzaga Chiriyaqui,** a Jesuit mission that started as a *visita* in 1721. The site became a full mission in 1737 under Padre Lamberto Hostell. The striking cut-stone church that survives today was finished in 1758. In 1768 the mission was abandoned, but the remaining church is still used by the small community of San Luis Gonzaga. To reach the mission, there is a turnoff from Mexico 1 about six kilometers south of Ciudad Constitución. Follow the graded dirt road 37 kilometers east to arrive at the oasis community of San Luis Gonzaga.

Bahía Magdalena

Bahía Magdalena, affectionately called "Mag Bay" by many Americans, is an area popular with water sports fanatics, whale-watchers, and nature enthusiasts. Protected by a string of barrier islands, this is the third and southernmost bay the friendly gray whales migrate to during breeding and calving season.

Whale-watching, kayaking, windsurfing, fishing, and bird-watching are all favored activities within the protected bays and mangrove swamps. The largest town along the bay, **Puerto San Carlos,** has a handful of hotels and restaurants and is a great base for whale-watching or exploring the bay.

Visitors come to Bahía Magdalena in the winter for gray whale-watching.

Bahía Magdalena

La Poza Grande
Boca de las Ánimas
Boca de Santo Domingo
Isla Santo Domingo
Santo Domingo
Colonia Purísima
Boca de Soledad
Puerto López Mateos
Isla Magdalena
Ciudad Insurgentes
To Loreto
Villa Benito Juaréz
Cabo San Lázaro
22
Punta Hughes
Bahía Santa María
Puerto San Carlos
Ciudad Constitución
Villa Morelos
WHALE-WATCHING
Puerto Magdalena
Bahía Magdalena
To Misión San Luis Gonzaga
Punta Entrada
Punta Redonda
Canal Gaviota
Bahía Almejas
Puerto Cancún
Santa Rita
Isla Santa Margarita
Puerto Chale
To La Paz
Isla Creciente
0   15 mi
0   15 km
© AVALON TRAVEL

★ WHALE-WATCHING

The third and southernmost point for friendly gray whale encounters on the peninsula is Bahía Magdalena. A string of barrier islands here protect a series of shallow bays and provide a safe area for whale breeding. Whale watching tours that depart from Mulegé, Loreto, or La Paz generally come to Bahía Magdalena.

Two port cities directly on the bay also offer whale-watching tours: Puerto San Carlos and Puerto López Mateos.

For over 18 years, family-operated **Mag**

Bay Tours (U.S. tel. 202/642-6386, www. magbaytours.com) has been leading whale-watching experiences. You can select from a day tour (US$450 per boat for five hours of whale-watching) or multiday excursions that start at $495 per person for three-day, two-night experience with whale-watching, camp accommodations, and meals included.

Magdalena Bay Whales (toll-free U.S. tel. 855/594-2537, www.magdalenabaywhales. com) is a whale camp where visitors can stay on the property and go out for whale excursions and enjoy other activities during the day. The property has a campsite with tents on platforms, a restaurant, and main *palapa*. Prices start at US$495 per person for a two-day, one-night whale experience. Meals, accommodations, whale-watching, and other activities are included.

If you want to go whale-watching for the day without an organized tour group, head to the port at López Mateos. Here you'll find a number of businesses authorized to take tourists out whale-watching. Expect to pay about US$65 per person for a few hours. If you're looking for fewer crowds, avoid weekends and plan to go out during the week.

SPORTS AND RECREATION
Fishing and Boating

July to November is the prime fishing season in this area. Anglers catch halibut, yellowtail, corvina, cabrilla, grouper, and the coveted snook. Fishing from shore here is a good way to catch halibut and spotted bay bass. Farther out at sea, anglers can catch yellowfin tuna, wahoo, billfish, and striped marlin.

Both Puerto San Carlos and Puerto López Mateos have concrete launch ramps. The ramp at Puerto San Carlos can accommodate boats up to 28 feet, but it's only usable during high tides. Hotels in town can arrange for sportfishing charters.

Kiteboarding and Windsurfing

Bahía Magdalena is home to some of the best windsurfing and kiteboarding on the Pacific

Puerto San Carlos

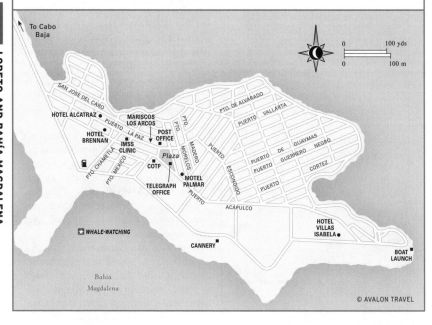

To Cabo
Baja

SAN JOSE DEL CABO

HOTEL ALCATRAZ ●
● PUERTO

HOTEL
BRENNAN
IMSS
CLINIC
PTO. CHAMETLA
PTO. MEXICO

MARISCOS
LOS ARCOS
LA PAZ
POST
OFFICE

COTP

Plaza

TELEGRAPH
OFFICE

MOTEL
PALMAR

PTO.
PTO.
MADERO
MORELOS

PTO. DE ALVARADO

PUERTO VALLARTA

PUERTO

PUERTO ESCONDIDO

PUERTO DE GUAYMAS NEGRO

PUERTO GUERRERO
CORTEZ

PUERTO

PUERTO ACAPULCO

WHALE-WATCHING

CANNERY ■

Bahía
Magdalena

HOTEL
VILLAS
ISABELA ●

BOAT ■
LAUNCH

0   100 yds
0   100 m

© AVALON TRAVEL

coast of Baja. The barrier islands protect the bay from large swells and strong winds blow year-round. Novice riders will enjoy the calm waters of the bay, while more experienced riders will want to check out the areas near the mouth of the bay where there are breakers and stronger winds. Riders should have their own equipment, as there aren't rentals or lessons here as in other areas such as La Ventana or Los Barriles.

Surfing

There are three right-hand point breaks in Bahía Santa Maria (one of the bays within Bahía Magdalena): Cuevas, Campsites, and Betadines. For beginner surfers, the estuary mouth has a sand bottom, beach break. **Mag Bay Tours** (U.S. tel. 202/642-6386, www. magbaytours.com) offers board rentals as well as surf expeditions from May to November.

South of Bahia Magdalena, Punta El Conejo is a remote point that catches north

and south swells. You can camp on the bluffs here, but you'll need to bring all of your own provisions. With the danger of flash floods in the area, camping below on the sand is not advisable. If you continue another 17 kilometers south on the coastal road, you'll come to another break, Punta Márquez.

ACCOMMODATIONS
Puerto San Carlos

One of the most popular options for accommodations in Puerto San Carlos is **Hotel Brennan** (Puerto Acapulco 47, tel. 613/136-0288, www.hotelbrennan.com.mx, US$65-80). This family-run hotel is clean, quiet, and well operated. There are 14 large and well-appointed comfortable rooms. Breakfast is available for an extra fee. You'll recognize the building by the shamrocks and green accents painted on the exterior. The theme continues with green bedspreads in all the rooms. They have daily whale-watching tours available

(US$60 per hour per boat, six people maximum per boat) as well as individual sportfishing excursions.

Hotel Villas Isabela (Calle Isla Magdalena 230, tel. 613/136-0317, www.villasisabela.com, US$65) provides simple rooms that feature satellite TV, air-conditioning, and wireless Internet. They offer room packages that include whale-watching excursions. They also offer year-round excursions to the mangroves and sand dunes, as well as having sportfishing charters, boat trips, and ecotourism excursions around Bahía Magdalena.

The 25 rooms at **Hotel Alcatraz** (Puerto La Paz 40, tel. 613/136-0017, www.hotelalcatraz.mx, US$65) are basic and on the small side, but the hotel has a nice courtyard with a lush garden. Credit cards are not accepted, payments must be made in cash. There's an adjoining **restaurant** (7am-10pm Mon.-Sat.) serving delicious seafood.

The focus is on being ecofriendly at **Hotel Villas Mar y Arena** (Carretera San Carlos Constitución Km. 57, tel. 613/136-0599, www.villasmaryarena.com, US$75-90). Accommodations consist of standard rooms as well as beachfront *cabañas* with nice patios looking over the bay. They can arrange for gray whale tours or bird-watching excursions. There's also a restaurant on-site.

Puerto López Mateos

Along Bahía Magdalena, north of Puerto San Carlos is the tiny town of Puerto López Mateos, which is reached by turning west from Ciudad Insurgentes off of Mexico 1. This is a great place for whale-watching, but doesn't have much else to offer tourists. There's free camping with pit toilets available at Playa Boca de la Soledad. You can find a few small hotels and rooms for rent during whale-watching season, but most travelers come for day and then stay in Puerto San Carlos or Ciudad Constitución. While restaurants are scarce outside of whale-watching season, there are a multitude of food stands and small restaurants that open to accommodate tourists January-April.

The rooms are small but clean and quiet at **El Camarón Feliz** (Rodriguez and Rumbo, tel. 613/131-5032, US$32). There's an on-site café as well as a restaurant, and friendly owners run the place. They can arrange whale-watching or fishing excursions for you. At **Hotel el Refugio** (Luis Echeverria and Ruiz Cortinez, tel. 613/131-5064, US$22), the rooms for rent are cheap, but sparse. They do have air-conditioning, hot water, wireless Internet, and cable TV. Some of the rooms have bathrooms that are essentially partitioned-off areas rather than separate rooms.

La Paz

As the capital of Baja California Sur, La Paz has a plethora of culture, history, beaches, and islands, and is one of the best places in Baja for water sports and fishing.

Even with so much to offer, La Paz still retains a friendly small-town feel. Downtown La Paz is centered on the beautiful *malecón* that wraps around the bay and makes for a popular spot for locals and tourists to enjoy the views and get a pulse on the city. Many locals refer to La Paz as a "real Mexican town," a comment comparing it to the more commercialized Los Cabos region.

A number of restaurants, hotels, and shops line the *malecón*, and the museums and cultural sites are just a few blocks off of the boardwalk. And while the city itself has a lot to offer, the main draw for most tourists coming to La Paz are the beaches and nearby islands. Travelers can take boat tours out to Isla Espíritu Santo where they can snorkel with sea lions, swim with whale sharks, or enjoy sandy beaches on deserted islands. There are also a number of famous beaches accessible by car from downtown La Paz—Playa El Tecolote and Playa Balandra being the most beautiful and popular with white sand and clear turquoise waters. Nearby Bahía de la Ventana is

a mecca for kiteboarders and windsurfers who come from all over the world for the warm waters and thermal winds.

La Paz is also a famous destination for scuba divers and snorkelers who visit to experience the marinelife of the Sea of Cortez around La Paz's islands and nearby reefs. Jacques Cousteau once called the Sea of Cortez "the aquarium of the world," and nowhere is that more apparent than around La Paz. Manta rays, whales, sea lions, tropical fish, dolphins, and whale sharks delight those who come in search of marinelife. Anglers also flock to the area for the roosterfish, marlin, wahoo, dorado, and tuna.

For first-time travelers to La Paz, the orientation can be slightly confusing. Because of the city's location on the bay and the Pichilingue peninsula, the water is actually to the west of the city, even though La Paz in on the east side of the peninsula. This is the only place on the Sea of Cortez where you'll get beautiful sunsets over the water.

Summers can be extremely hot and humid

Previous: La Paz's *malecón;* Workers repair *palapa* roofs at Playa Tecolote. **Above:** Fair rides during La Paz's Carnaval celebration.

Look for ★ to find recommended sights, activities, dining, and lodging.

Highlights

★ **Malecón Álvaro Obregón:** The heart of La Paz is the large *malecón* along Álvaro Obregón street with shops, restaurants, and bars on one side and beautiful white sand beaches on the other (page 226).

★ **Playa El Tecolote:** Locals and tourists come to Playa El Tecolote's turquoise waters and white sands to swim, relax, and eat and drink beachside (page 232).

★ **Isla Espíritu Santo:** The large island off the coast of La Paz is home to a colony of sea lions, whales, and other marinelife (page 233).

★ **Diving and Snorkeling:** Choose from diving shipwrecks to snorkeling with sea lions along the beaches and islands of La Paz (page 236).

★ **Sportfishing:** May through November, anglers will enjoy catching wahoo, dorado, tuna, marlin, and roosterfish (page 237).

★ **Kiteboarding and Windsurfing:** In the winter months, La Ventana draws crowds of kiteboarders and windsurfers following the El Norte winds (page 247).

La Paz and Vicinity

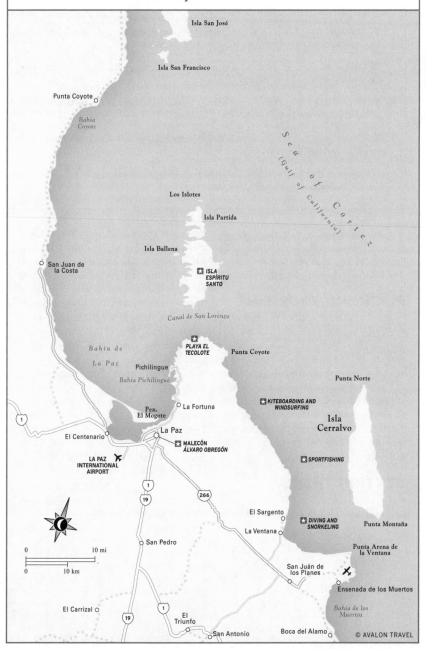

Isla San José

Isla San Francisco

Punta Coyote

Bahía Coyote

S e a   o f   C o r t e z

(Gulf of California)

Los Islotes

Isla Partida

Isla Ballena

San Juan de la Costa

✈ **ISLA ESPÍRITU SANTO**

Canal de San Lorenzo

Bahía de La Paz

➕ **PLAYA EL TECOLOTE**

Punta Coyote

Pichilingue

Bahía Pichilingue

Punta Norte

Pen. El Mogote

La Fortuna

➕ **KITEBOARDING AND WINDSURFING**

Isla Cerralvo

El Centenario

La Paz

➕ **MALECÓN ÁLVARO OBREGÓN**

(1)

LA PAZ INTERNATIONAL AIRPORT ✈

➕ **SPORTFISHING**

(1)

(19)

(266)

El Sargento

➕ **DIVING AND SNORKELING**

Punta Montaña

La Ventana

Punta Arena de la Ventana

San Pedro

0 ___ 10 mi

0 ___ 10 km

San Juán de los Planes

✈

Ensenada de los Muertos

Bahía de los Muertos

El Carrizal

(19)

(1)

El Triunfo

San Antonio

Boca del Alamo

© AVALON TRAVEL

Best Accommodations

★ **El Ángel Azul Hacienda:** Stay in an old renovated hacienda, conveniently located in town near all of the restaurants, shops, and *malecón* (page 243).

★ **Costa Baja:** This resort has well-appointed rooms, an infinity-edge pool, restaurants, and spa services on the property (page 244).

★ **Hacienda Paraiso:** This tranquil B&B has Mexican hospitality and charm in addition to personalized attention (page 244).

★ **Casa Verde Inn:** With three beautiful rooms, this small inn has modern amenities and a cozy courtyard pool (page 245).

★ **Ventana Bay Resort:** This resort offers private bungalows, a restaurant and bar, as well as a certified kiteboarding school (page 248).

here, but the rest of the year, the climate is pleasant. February is the liveliest time for La Paz with the large multiple-day Carnaval celebration that takes place along the *malecón*.

PLANNING YOUR TIME

Because La Paz is a large city with lots to offer, you'll want to allow yourself at least 3-4 days to explore the city, the beaches, and to take a boat trip out to the islands. With a week or more, you'll have plenty of time to get to know La Paz and to take day trips to surrounding places like La Ventana and El Triunfo. If you are coming to La Paz with the intention of taking the ferry over to mainland Mexico, give yourself an extra few days to sort out permits and reservations.

GETTING THERE
Air

La Paz has its own international airport, **Manuel Marquez de Leon International Airport (LAP)** (tel. 612/124-6307), 12 kilometers south of La Paz. There are currently no direct flights from the United States, but Aéreo Calafia and Volaris have direct flights from Tijuana and other cities in Baja. Some visitors fly into the **Los Cabos International Airport (SJD)** because there are more options and direct flights from the United States. Travelers who choose this option can rent a car in Cabo and drive the 2.5 hours up to La Paz.

Baja Ferries

The car and passenger ferry arrives to La Paz from Topolobampo and Mazatlán in mainland Mexico. Ferries arrive from both locations multiple times a week. Full schedule and prices can be found by contacting **Baja Ferries** (tel. 612/123-6397, toll-free tel. 800/337-7437, www.bajaferries.com).

Taking the Ferry to Mainland Mexico

The ferry travels between La Paz and mainland Mexico.

La Paz is one of only two locations in Baja (the other being Santa Rosalía) where travelers can take the ferry from the peninsula over to the mainland. **Baja Ferries** (tel. 612/123-6397, toll-free tel. 800/337-7437, www.bajaferries.com) operates car and passenger ferry routes between La Paz and Mazatlán or Topolobampo, Mexico. It's a long journey (18 hours to Mazatlán and seven hours to Topolobampo) but still more time- and cost-effective than driving up the peninsula and back down the mainland.

Ferries only depart for particular cities on certain days, so make sure to check the schedule on the Baja Ferries website ahead of time. Purchase your ticket a few days in advance from either the ferry terminal office in Pichilingue or any one of the **Baja Ferries offices** in town (Ignacio Allende 1025, tel. 612/123-6600, 8am-5pm Mon.-Fri., 8am-2pm Sat.).

When purchasing your ticket, you will need to have your passport with you. If you are also taking a vehicle on board, you should bring the vehicle to be measured and will also need to show your temporary importation permit for it. If you do not already have your temporary car import permit (which is not required for driving in Baja California, but is for mainland Mexico), you can purchase this at the ferry terminal in Pichilingue. This should be taken care of a few days in advance of ferry travel. Vehicle permits are US$48 (plus a refundable deposit which can be up to US$400, depending on the value of your vehicle) and are valid for six months. You can also start the temporary vehicle import in advance by going online to **Banjercito** (www.banjercito.com.mx).

If you are taking your vehicle on board the ferry, they will measure it to see how much it will cost. The ticket for the driver of the vehicle is included in the price of the ticket for the vehicle. Any other passengers will need to pay a separate ticket fee (US$70). These tickets will get you the standard passenger fare. This means you will get a seat on the ferry (very similar to a plane seat) in a room where they show movies. Meals served in the cafeteria are included in the ticket price. There's a deck on the ferry for passengers to enjoy the fresh sea air.

Private cabins cost an additional US$50 and sleep up to four people on bunk beds. There's a bathroom, complete with a shower with hot water and great water pressure. Cabins come with windows and without windows. Specify your preference when booking. If not all of the cabins are booked ahead of time, they will also sell cabins to passengers once on board the ferry, although the price will be more expensive.

Be aware that there is also a separate port fee (US$10) that you will need to pay in cash when you arrive to board the ferry.

Best Food

★ **El Zarape:** Visitors love the delicious, traditional Mexican food and the large buffet (240).

★ **Tio Bencho:** Enjoy from-scratch Oaxacan and Guerrero cuisine on a hip outdoor patio (240).

★ **Tacos el Estadio:** The most popular place in town for fish and shrimp tacos (241).

★ **El Rincon de la Bahía:** On the beach in La Ventana, this restaurant and bar was one of the first in the area (247).

★ **Playa Central:** This restaurant/coffee shop has live music and special events (248).

Sights

★ MALECÓN ÁLVARO OBREGÓN

The heart of La Paz is the large three-mile long *malecón* along **Álvaro Obregón** street with shops, restaurants, and bars on one side and the beautiful white sand beaches and shallow turquoise bay of the Sea of Cortez on the other. Day or night, this is a great place to stroll, do some people-watching, and get a feel for the pulse of the city. The views at sunset are stunning. Palm trees line the wide sidewalk and *palapas* dot the beach. Ornate ironwork benches painted white provide lovely places to sit while enjoying a *paleta* on a warm day. A white two-story gazebo is the focus of Plaza Malecón, which is considered the heart of the *malecón*, and the boardwalk is dotted with copper statues denoting whales, pearls, dolphins, and other representations of La Paz life. The nearby 16 de Septiembre is one of the main

palapas on the beach along La Paz's *malecón*

La Paz

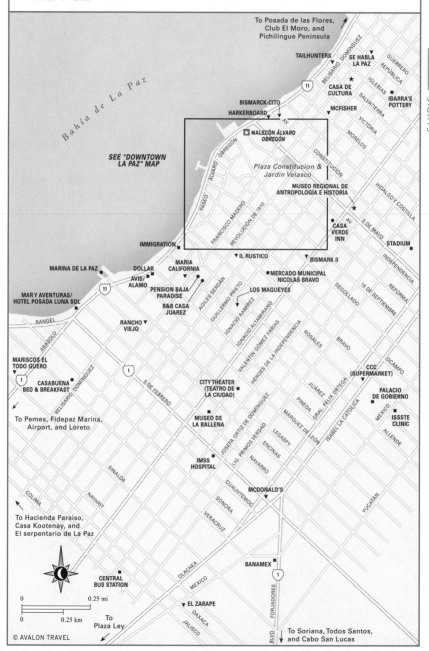

To Posada de las Flores,
Club El Moro, and
Pichilingue Peninsula

TAILHUNTERS

SE HABLA
LA PAZ

GUERRERO

REPÚBLICA

IGLESIAS

CASA DE
CULTURA

SALVATIERRA

IBARRA'S
POTTERY

BISMARCK-CITO

MCFISHER

VICTORIA

HARKERBOARD

MORELOS

★ MALECÓN ÁLVARO
OBREGÓN

CONSTITUCIÓN

Plaza Constitucion &
Jardín Velasco

HIDALGO Y COSTILLA

MUSEO REGIONAL DE
ANTROPOLOGÍA E HISTORIA

Bahía de La Paz

SEE "DOWNTOWN
LA PAZ" MAP

PASEO ÁLVARO OBREGÓN

FRANCISCO MADERO

REVOLUCIÓN DE 1910

5 DE MAYO

CASA
VERDE
INN

STADIUM

IMMIGRATION

IL RUSTICO

BISMARK II

INDEPENDENCIA

MARINA DE LA PAZ

DOLLAR

MARIA
CALIFORNIA

MERCADO MUNICIPAL
NICOLAS BRAVO

REFORMA

AVIS/
ALAMO

PENSION BAJA
PARADISE

ADILES SERDÁN

GUILLERMO PRIETO

LOS MAGUEYES

16 DE SEPTIEMBRE

MAR Y AVENTURAS/
HOTEL POSADA LUNA SOL

B&B CASA
JUAREZ

IGNACIO RAMÍREZ

DEGOLLADO

RANGEL

RANCHO
VIEJO

IGNACIO ALTAMIRANO

VALENTÍN GÓMEZ FARÍAS

ROSALES

BRAVO

OCAMPO

ABASOLO

HÉROES DE LA INDEPENDENCIA

CCC
(SUPERMARKET)

MARISCOS EL
TODO GUERO

BELISARIO DOMÍNGUEZ

JUÁREZ

GRAL. FELIX ORTEGA

PALACIO
DE GOBIERNO

CASABUENA
BED & BREAKFAST

CITY THEATER
(TEATRO DE
LA CIUDAD)

PINEDA

MARQUEZ DE LEÓN

ISABEL LA CATÓLICA

MEXICO

ISSSTE
CLINIC

5 DE FEBRERO

To Pemex, Fidepaz Marina,
Airport, and Loreto

MUSEO DE
LA BALLENA

JOSEFA ORTIZ DE DOMÍNGUEZ

ING. PRIMOS VERDAD

LEGASPY

ENCINAS

ALLENDE

SINALOA

IMSS
HOSPITAL

NAVARRO

NAYARIT

CUAUHTÉMOC

MCDONALD'S

YUCATÁN

COLIMA

To Hacienda Paraiso,
Casa Kootenay, and
El serpentario de La Paz

SONORA

VERACRUZ

OLACHEA

BANAMEX

CENTRAL
BUS STATION

MEXICO

FORJADORES

0   0.25 mi

0   0.25 km

To
Plaza Ley

EL ZARAPE

OAXACA

JALISCO

BLVD

To Soriana, Todos Santos,
and Cabo San Lucas

© AVALON TRAVEL

Downtown La Paz

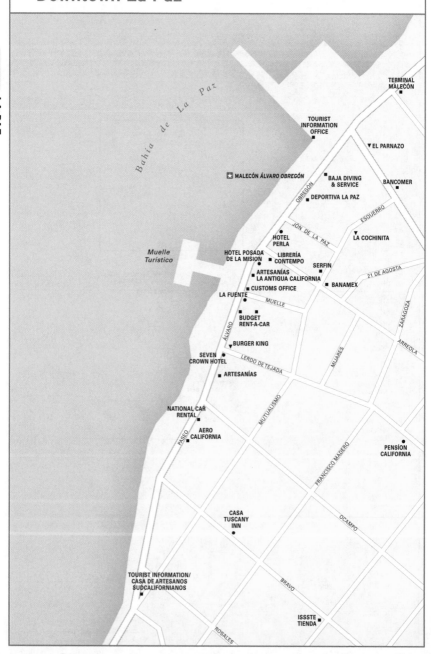

Bahía de La Paz

TERMINAL
MALECÓN

TOURIST
INFORMATION
OFFICE

▼ EL PARNAZO

MALECÓN ÁLVARO OBREGÓN

BAJA DIVING
& SERVICE

BANCOMER

OBREGÓN

DEPORTIVA LA PAZ

ESQUERRO

JÓN DE LA PAZ

LA COCHINITA

HOTEL
PERLA

Muelle
Turístico

HOTEL POSADA
DE LA MISIÓN

LIBRERÍA
CONTEMPO

SERFIN

21 DE AGOSTA

ARTESANÍAS
LA ANTIGUA CALIFORNIA

BANAMEX

CUSTOMS OFFICE

LA FUENTE

MUELLE

ZARAGOZA

ARREOLA

BUDGET
RENT-A-CAR

ÁLVARO

BURGER KING

SEVEN
CROWN HOTEL

LERDO DE TEJADA

MILARES

ARTESANÍAS

NATIONAL CAR
RENTAL

MUTUALISMO

PASEO

AERO
CALIFORNIA

PENSIÓN
CALIFORNIA

FRANCISCO MADERO

CASA
TUSCANY
INN

OCAMPO

TOURIST INFORMATION/
CASA DE ARTESANOS
SUDCALIFORNIANOS

BRAVO

ISSSTE
TIENDA

ROSALES

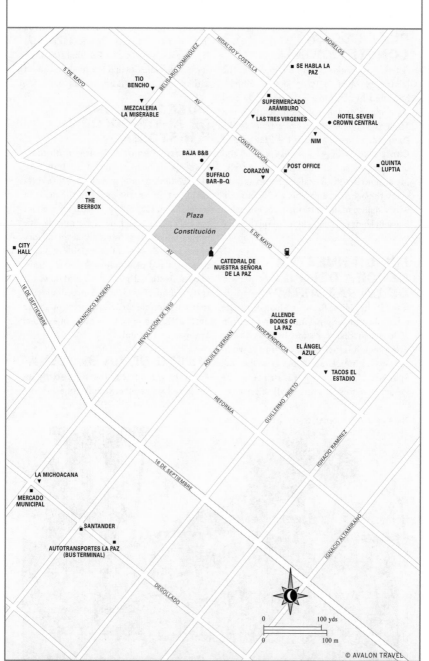

streets in La Paz and is good a stroll to check out shops, cafés, and restaurants.

PLAZA DE LA CONSTITUCIÓN

A few blocks inland from the *malecón,* the central plaza of La Paz is a square block bounded by Avenida Independencia and 5 de Mayo and Revolución de 1910 and Madero. While the center of activity for La Paz is the *malecón* and not the **Plaza de la Constitución,** the plaza is still a pleasant and quiet place to sit and relax on a day of walking around the city. Locals and tourists alike enjoy the benches, a gazebo, and a fountain with a replica of the mushroom rock found at Playa Balandra. On one side of the plaza is the Catedral de La Paz.

MISIÓN NUESTRA SEÑORA DEL PILAR DE LA PAZ AIRAPÍ

Jesuit Padres Jaime Bravo and Juan de Ugarte established the original mission in La Paz in 1720. Its success was short-lived as La Paz was a region fraught with conflict between the several indigenous tribes as well as the Spaniards. The mission was ruined in the Pericú Revolt of 1734 and finally closed and

moved to Todos Santos in 1748. The possible first mission site is marked by a plaque on the wall of the pink and white **Biblioteca de los Misioneros** on Ignacio Zaragoza (Zaragoza 31). The **Catedral de La Paz** that stands on Plaza de la Constitución is a modern church with no relation to the original mission.

MUSEO REGIONAL DE ANTROPOLOGÍA E HISTORIA

The **Museo Regional de Antropología e Historia** (Ignacio Manuel Altamirano, tel. 612/122-0162, 8am-6pm daily, US$3, an extra US$4 to take photos) is set in the heart of town and an interesting place to learn about the La Paz region and the Baja peninsula. The museum features exhibits about the history of the area, displays of Baja California cave paintings and pictographs, historic photographs, fossils dating back 60 million years, and a botanical garden. The museum is currently under construction for remodeling until 2017, and only a few areas of exhibits are open to the public.

MUSEO DE LA BALLENA

Recently remodeled, the **Museo de la Ballena** (Navarro between Altamarino and

The Museo de la Ballena is one of La Paz's many museums.

Independencia, 9am-1pm Mon.-Fri., 10am-2pm Sat., US$9 adults, US$4 children) is a fun stop for families and those interested in both whales and other marinelife such as dolphins, sharks, and sea turtles. There's a complete skeleton of a gray whale as well as exhibits with history, artifacts, videos, and art related to whales. Kids will enjoy an interactive element where visitors can touch baleen and whale bones. Most of the exhibits are in Spanish, but knowledgeable guides who speak English are available to walk you through the museum for free.

EL SERPENTARIO DE LA PAZ

El Serpentario de La Paz (Brecha California, tel. 612/122-5611, www.

elserpentariodelapaz.org.mx, 10am-4pm Tues.-Sun., US$2.50 adults, US$1.50 children) has reptile exhibits and lectures for guests. The serpentarium focuses on education about conservation and rehabilitation in the region. Lizards, snakes, turtles, reptiles, and fish are all on display for viewers to see. Kids will love the hands-on aspect of getting to hold creatures such as lizards or tarantulas. The aviary provides an opportunity to feed birds and rabbits.

Beaches

The best beaches in La Paz are north of the city, away from the city center and any hotels or large developments. Services at and around the beaches are somewhat limited, but travelers will find stretches of white sand and clear turquoise waters for enjoying a day of snorkeling, kayaking, swimming, and relaxing.

PLAYA PICHILINGUE

East of the ferry terminal, **Playa Pichilingue** is a white sand beach on a calm bay. The shallow and protected waters are good for kayaking or snorkeling. There's a *palapa restaurant* (tel. 612/122-4565, 11am-7:30pm daily, US$6-15) on the beach that serves high-quality seafood like mussels, ceviche, chocolate clams, or lobster. The prices aren't cheap, but the food is good and it's a nice place to watch sunset.

PLAYA BALANDRA

Known for its famous mushroom-shaped rock, **Playa Balandra** is arguably the most beautiful beach in the area. There are a few *palapas* on the beach for shade but no

Beaches and Islands Near La Paz

© AVALON TRAVEL

restaurants or services (there are portapotties that are sometimes open). You can buy some snacks and rent kayaks for US$12 an hour. Because the beach is situated on a bay, kayakers will enjoy paddling around the protected waters to see the famous mushroom rock, as well as exploring nearby mangroves. Go early in the day to snag one of the *palapa* umbrellas and to enjoy the beach in peace before the crowds come in the afternoon. Swimming is also better in the morning as the tide lowers in the afternoon and the water in the entire bay becomes awkwardly shallow—about knee-deep. Beware of stingrays here and be sure to shuffle your feet in the sand when entering the water.

★ PLAYA EL TECOLOTE

Just 1.5 kilometers north of Playa Balandra, **Playa El Tecolote** has the same white sands and clear waters, but a few more services, including restaurants. Tecolote attracts visitors who come to play and swim in the sea and eat and drink barefoot in the sand. This is a popular beach for families because of the sandy bottom and gentle slope into the water, providing shallow

spots for wading and playing. There's plenty of parking for those arriving by private vehicle. Mornings and weekdays are your best chance for peaceful beach time as the winds pick up in the afternoons and weekends can get crowded. At **Palapa Azul** (tel. 612/120-2089, 8am-9pm daily, mains US$8-12) patrons can enjoy chocolate clams, ceviche, and buckets of beers while sitting on the beach enjoying views of the Sea of Cortez and nearby Isla Espíritu Santu. Palapa Azul can also help with arrangements for a fishing charter or to get out to the islands for the day for a cheaper rate than leaving from La Paz. Next door, **El Tecolote** (tel. 612/127-9494, mains US$8-14) offers similar food and drink options.

PLAYA COYOTE

Beyond Playa El Tecolote, the road continues around the east side of the Pichilingue peninsula to Playa Coyote. The beaches on this side of the peninsula turn rocky with gray sand. The kayaking and snorkeling can be good here because of the clear and calm waters, but many tourists prefer white sand beaches like Balandra or El Tecolote.

Playa Balandra is one of La Paz's most popular beaches.

The Islands

No trip to La Paz is complete without a visit to the islands. Teeming with marinelife, they make for an excellent boating day trip for those who want to snorkel, dive, or just enjoy the island bays with white sand beaches. Visitors can arrange for an organized day trip from La Paz, or there are *pangas* that leave from Playa El Tecolote and take travelers for US$55 per person. Tours generally pick up clients in the morning and fees include snorkel or dive equipment, the national park entrance fee, drinks for the day, and lunch.

★ ISLA ESPÍRITU SANTO

The large island 25 kilometers off the coast of La Paz is Isla Espíritu Santo, a designated UNESCO World Heritage Site. It's considered by many to be the most beautiful island in the Sea of Cortez and boasts dozens of bays with white sand beaches and waters full of marinelife.

Most travelers experience Isla Espíritu Santo on a boat day trip from La Paz. These boat trips focus on diving and snorkeling in the waters around the island, because of the rich marinelife that lives around the rock and coral reefs. Visitors will have a chance at seeing and swimming with sea lions, orca, dolphins, manta rays, sea turtles, and blue or humpback whales.

The island isn't inhabited, but tent camping is permitted. This is the only way to spend any substantial amount of time exploring the island since the boat trips stop only briefly to allow some swimming and snorkeling. Camping gives visitors the unique experience of exploring the island and waters by day and enjoy stargazing at night. There are 10 designated hiking paths on the island that are great for getting out in the terrain and encountering mammals, reptiles, birds, and amphibians. Because the islands are protected, camping requires getting a US$4 permit in advance from the **SEMARNAT office** (Ocampo 1045, tel. 612/128-4171, www. semarnat.gob.mx). **Fun Baja** (www.funbaja. com) can arrange for multiday camping trips on the island.

Boats headed to Isla Espíritu Santo leave from La Paz.

Isla Espíritu Santo, Isla Partida, and Los Islotes

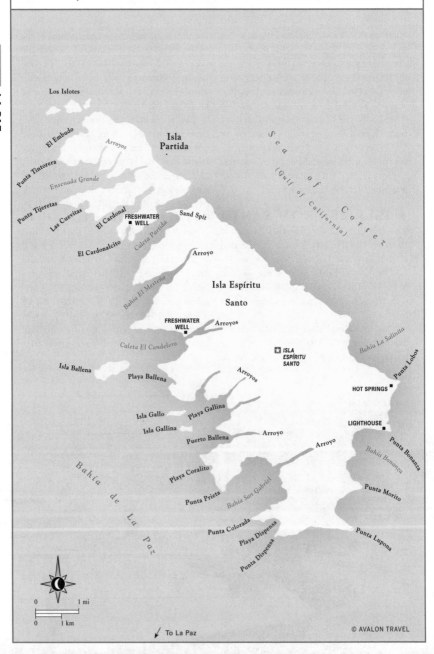

Los Islotes

El Embudo

Arroyos

Isla
Partida

Punta Tintorera

Ensenada Grande

Punta Tijeretas

Las Cuevitas

El Cardonal

FRESHWATER
■ WELL

Sand Spit

El Cardonalcito

Caleta Partida

Arroyo

Sea   o f   C o r t e z

(Gulf of California)

Isla Espíritu

Santo

Bahía El Mesteño

FRESHWATER
WELL ■

Arroyos

Caleta El Candelero

✚ ISLA
ESPÍRITU
SANTO

Bahía La Salinita

Punta Lobos

Isla Ballena

Playa Ballena

Arroyos

HOT SPRINGS ■

Isla Gallo

Playa Gallina

Isla Gallina

Puerto Ballena

Arroyo

LIGHTHOUSE ■

Arroyo

Punta Bonanza

Bahía Bonanza

Playa Coralito

Bahía San Gabriel

Punta Prieta

Punta Morito

B a h í a   d e   L a   P a z

Punta Colorada

Playa Dispensa

Punta Lupona

Punta Dispensa

0   1 mi

0   1 km

↙ To La Paz

© AVALON TRAVEL

ISLA PARTIDA

Connected to Isla Espíritu Santo by a narrow sandbar, **Isla Partida** is a much smaller island, but still has beautiful bays, beaches, dive sites, hiking, and camping opportunities. There are small fishing camps at either end of the island, but otherwise the island in uninhabited. You'll need to bring in your own drinking water and provisions. Just like Isla Espiritu Santo, camping here requires getting a **permit** in advance from SEMARNAT for US$4 (Ocampo 1045, tel. 612/128-4171, www. semarnat.gob.mx).

Los Islotes

At the northern tip of Isla Partida and Espíritu Santo are smaller **Los Islotes** where a large colony of hundreds of sea lions resides. Friendly interaction with the sea lions is highly likely, and these islets are a popular stop on the island day trips for snorkelers and divers who get in the water with the sea lions.

Recreation

With water and land sports aplenty, the options for outdoor activities in La Paz are seemingly endless. Water sports include fishing, kayaking, diving, snorkeling, and stand-up paddleboarding. When you tire of the water, land activities like horseback riding, cycling, yoga, and hiking are all easily accessible.

ORGANIZED TOURS

The best way to fully take advantage of what La Paz has to offer is to go with an organized tour company. Island excursions, fishing charters, whale shark encounters, dive and kayak trips, and whale-watching tours are all available. Most hotels can make arrangements for tours or you can go directly to the tour operators, calling or booking online.

Fun Baja (Carretera a Pichilingue Km. 7.5, tel. 612/106-7148, www.funbaja.com) is highly recommended for snorkeling and scuba diving trips. All of the guides speak English, Spanish, and Japanese. They also have whale shark adventures, whale-watching trips, and day trips to Los Cabos, Todos Santos, and El Triunfo.

Baja Outdoor Activities (BOA) (tel. 612/125-5636, www.kayactivities.com) has extensive options for multiday kayaking trips, fly-fishing, stand-up paddleboarding excursions, whale-watching, and other custom trips.

Mar Y Aventuras, Sea & Adventures (tel. 612/122-7039, www.kayakbaja.com) offers trips for island-hopping, kayak excursions, whale shark adventures. Day trips and multiday trips are available. They also rent kayaks and gear to experienced kayakers.

Espiritu & Baja Tours (Obregon 2130-D, tel. 612/122-4427, www.espiritubaja.com) has the usual snorkeling, whale-watching, kayaking, fishing, and whale shark excursions. They can also provide airport shuttle services for US$30 one-way.

Baja Expeditions (Sonora 585, tel. 612/125-3828, www.bajaex.com) offers sailing trips as well as diving, snorkeling, kayaking, and whale-watching trips. Single day trips and multiple day trips are available.

Baja Adventure Co. (tel. 612/131-4563, www.bajaadventureco.com) provides tailor-made adventure trips. Their custom excursions allow for travelers to choose from the activities that they want to include on their adventure from spearfishing to island outings.

KAYAKING

The islands of La Paz offer some of the best kayaking on the peninsula, with stunning bays featuring clear waters, white sand beaches, and plenty of wildlife. Birds, manta rays, whale sharks, sea lions, dolphin, and whales are all common sights while kayaking.

Most kayakers join organized tours for overnight, multiday trips to explore the islands, as there's too much to see in just a single day trip. Some kayak tour operators will rent kayaks to experienced kayakers who prefer to explore on their own. Those who want to venture out for the day solo can find beaches and mangroves along the mainland of the peninsula.

Baja Outdoor Activities (BOA) (tel. 612/125-5636, www.kayactivities.com) has extensive options for multiday kayaking trips. They offer up to 12-day excursions exploring the peninsula by kayak.

Mar Y Aventuras, Sea & Adventures (tel. 612/122-7039, www.kayakbaja.com) offers trips for island-hopping, kayak excursions, whale shark adventures. Day trips and multiday trips are available. They also rent kayaks and gear to experienced kayakers.

★ DIVING

La Paz is a popular scuba diving destination with abundant marinelife, islands, seamounts, reefs, and shipwrecks to explore. Diving is good year-round, but conditions are best July through October when visibility can reach 30 meters and water temperatures can reach up to 29 degrees Celsius (85°F). Dive sites range from beginner to experienced, and the various outfitters can also accommodate all levels of divers. Popular sites include the sea lion colony at Los Islotes and other island inlets around Isla Espíritu Santo and out at Isla Cerralvo. Shipwrecks include the *Salvatierra*, a ferry that sank in 1976, and the Las Gaviotas wrecks—two wooden boats that were scuttled to create underwater reefs. Advanced divers may head to El Bajo, an underwater seamount where divers go to see manta rays and a chance to catch schools of the hammerhead sharks that used to be prevalent here. Most dive sites in the area are a 45- to 60-minute boat ride from La Paz, and waters can be choppy so remember to take seasickness medicine.

With a fleet of guides that all speak English, Spanish, and Japanese, **Fun Baja** (Carretera a Pichilingue Km. 7.5, tel. 612/106-7148, www. funbaja.com) is great for snorkeling and scuba diving trips. They can also handle diving certification with PADI and SSI courses.

Running a professional top-notch operation, **Dive in La Paz** (tel. 612/149-4410, www. diveinlapaz.com) has gear that's in great condition and captains and guides who are knowledgeable and helpful. Many divers take multiday combination trips diving along with snorkeling with sea lions or swimming with whale sharks.

Based at Club Cantamar, **Baja Diving & Service** (www.clubcantamar.com) has been running dive trips since 1983. They have the largest and most comfortable fleet in La Paz. They offer a variety of dive courses as well as excursions including live-aboard trips.

The **Cortez Club Dive Center** (tel. 612/121-6120, www.cortezclub.com) is a reputable company that has been running dive trips since 1995. They can assist with all levels of PADI courses, from those just learning to dive to those looking to become certified as scuba instructors.

★ SNORKELING

Most of the kayak and dive outfitters in La Paz handle organized snorkeling excursions as well. The most popular snorkeling trip in the region takes visitors out to Isla Espíritu Santo where the highlight is snorkeling with the sea lions at Los Islotes. The tour outfitters will provide snorkeling gear, the park entrance fee, lunch, and beverages. In recent years, since the whale sharks have been more prevalent around La Paz, snorkeling with the whale sharks has become a popular organized tour as well. Those who prefer to snorkel on their own can drive to the beaches along the Pichilingue peninsula where you can snorkel from the beach. You should bring your own snorkel equipment or rent it in town before heading out to the beaches.

WHALE-WATCHING

While the whale-watching in La Paz is not as hands-on as the friendly gray whale

The Steinbeck Connection

The famous American author John Steinbeck traveled through La Paz and the Sea of Cortez in 1940 while on a six-week boating trip around the Gulf of California collecting and examining specimens with his friend, marine biologist Ed Ricketts. Steinbeck made La Paz the setting for his 1947 novel *The Pearl*, and he chronicled his six-week trip with Ricketts in his 1951 book *The Log from the Sea of Cortez*. *The Log from the Sea of Cortez* is considered one of Steinbeck's most important works of nonfiction because it offers detailed insight on both the geographical region and on humanity:

"'...Let us go,' we said, 'into the Sea of Cortez, realizing that we become forever a part of it; that our rubber boots slogging through a flat of eel-grass, that the rocks we turn over in a tide pool, make us truly and permanently a factor in the ecology of the region. We shall take something away from it, but we shall leave something too.' And if we seem a small factor in a huge pattern, nevertheless it is of relative importance. We take a tiny colony of soft corals from a rock in a little water world. And that isn't terribly important to the tide pool. Fifty miles away the Japanese shrimp boats are dredging with overlapping scoops, bringing up tons of shrimps, rapidly destroying the species so that it may never come back, and with the species destroying the ecological balance of the whole region. That isn't very important in the world. And thousands of miles away the great bombs are falling and the stars are not moved thereby. None of it is important or all of it is."

encounters of the Pacific Ocean, it is still a popular activity for the diversity of whales that can be seen. Humpback, pilot, fin, orca, and blue whales can all be spotted around La Paz and the islands. Most whale sighting occurs during day trips out to the islands. **Baja Outdoor Activities (BOA)** (tel. 612/125-5636, www.kayactivities.com) has specific multiday whale-watching excursions. There are some tours that will take visitors from La Paz over to Bahía Magdalena for gray whale watching.

★ SPORTFISHING

The best fishing around La Paz takes places May through November. Anglers will enjoy catching wahoo, dorado, tuna, marlin, and world-record roosterfish. The best and most-consistent fishing is over on the other side of the Pichilingue peninsula near La Ventana and Isla Jacques Cousteau. Most anglers opt to take a one-hour van ride and launch at Punta Arena de la Ventana, rather than going by *panga* from La Paz over to the area.

Because the waters are so calm in the channel of Isla Cerralvo, fly-fishing and kayak fishing are common in addition to traditional fishing. Catch from inshore fishing includes snapper, grouper, sea bass, and mackerel. Many anglers are after the world-record *pez gallo* (roosterfish) in this region.

There are many professional fishing charters in La Paz, with options ranging from *pangas* to big cruisers. Serious fishers should ask around town for recommendations based on their specific wants and needs. One of the most popular choices is **Tailhunter International** (Obregon 755, U.S. tel. 626/638-3383, www.tailhunter-international. com) on the *malecón*. They have a variety of packages for fly-fishing, spearfishing, and sportfishing. **Baja Pirates Fishing Fleet** (U.S. tel. 866/454-5386, www.bajapiratesofla-paz.com) employs knowledgeable and helpful captains. They offer a range of packages from one-day excursions to all-inclusive multiday packages with accommodations and airport transportation included.

BOATING

La Paz is a popular spot for boaters exploring the Sea of Cortez as it has the largest bay along the coast. The city has an impressive selection of marinas, boatyards, boating services, and supplies. **Marina de La Paz** (tel. 612/122-1646, www.marinadelapaz.com), on the west side of the *malecón*, has a launch ramp, fuel dock, convenience store, laundry facilities, yacht maintenance, and dive center.

Next to the Costa Baja resort, **Marina Costa Baja** (tel. 612/121-6225, www.marinacostabaja.com) has 250 slips that can accommodate vessels up to 220 feet. Amenities include wireless Internet, TV, phone, dry storage, showers, parking, and shuttle service to La Paz. **Marina Cortez** (tel. 612/123-4101, www.marinacortez.com) is an ecofriendly option with 50 slips up to 120 feet in length. Amenities here include onboat massage services, grocery delivery, and assistance with immigration and customs paperwork, car rental arrangements, and special tours.

GOLF

There are a few options for golfing in La Paz with rates that are much more affordable than those found in Los Cabos. The peninsula visible across the bay from town, called El Mogote (the antler) has an 18-hole golf course and a putting green at **El Mogote Golf Club of La Paz** (Formerly Paraiso del Mar, Peninsula El Mogote, tel. 612/189-6332, www.mogotegolflapaz.com, US$60 includes a gold cart and club rental). **Costa Baja** (Carretera a Pichilingue Km. 7.5, tel. 612/175-0122, www.costabajagolf.com, US$110, US$85 for tee time after noon, US$65 for nine holes) also has an 18-hole course. Both will provide players with ocean views.

Entertainment and Events

NIGHTLIFE

Compared to other towns in Baja, La Paz has a fairly lively nightlife scene. You won't find the huge clubs and touristy spots that you will in Cabo—the scene here is more laid-back with mostly young locals. Most bars don't open until around 7pm and usually close down around 2am.

For a sophisticated and tranquil evening, **Mezcaleria La Miserable** (Belisario Dominguez 274, tel. 612/157-3217, 7pm-2am Mon.-Sat.) has a large selection of artisanal mescal served in a refined and stylish atmosphere. They have mezcals for sipping, mezcal-crafted cocktails, as well as beers on the menu.

Craft beer aficionados will want to head to **The BeerBox** (Independencia 201, tel. 612/129-7299, www.thebeerboxlapaz.com, 6pm-midnight Mon.-Wed., 6pm-2am Thurs.-Sat.) where there's a large selection of rotating craft beers from Mexico and other parts of the world. The friendly and bilingual staff will help you find the perfect cerveza to enjoy in this intimate space.

The young kids of La Paz congregate at **El Parnazo** (16 de Septiembre 15), a fun and rowdy bar with liter draft beers for US$2. **Clandestino** (Madero 1440, tel. 612/157-3322, 7pm-3am daily) is another bar popular with the locals who go for the cheap beer and live music.

For those looking for a quieter evening, there are a number of movie theaters in town. **Cinépolis** (Blvd. Forjadores 4215, www.cinepolis.com) has numerous theaters and **Cinemex** (Avenida Constituyentes 1975 No. 4120, www.cinemex.com) has a location in town as well. Movies cost US$3 and there are showings in English.

FESTIVALS AND EVENTS
Carnaval

La Paz is home to the largest **Carnaval celebration** (www.culturabcs.gob.mx) on the

Baja peninsula. The six-day festival takes place every February on the *malecón* with parades featuring floats, costumes, and music. There are also fair rides and other family-friendly activities. There's a new theme each year, and all of the floats and costumes are based around it. This is La Paz's busiest time of year, so if you plan on traveling here in February, advanced hotel reservations are required.

Score International Off-Road Races

The famous **Baja 1000** (www.score-international.com) off-road race held annually in November always starts in Ensenada, and every other year it ends in La Paz. It currently comes to La Paz in even years.

Shopping

ARTESANÍA

At the family-run weaving studio **Artesanias Cuauhtemoc** (Mariano Abasalo 3315, tel. 612/141-3018, 10am-3:30pm and 6pm-7pm Mon.-Sat.) visitors can watch the weavers making bedcovers, blankets, and rugs on giant looms. All of the products are 100 percent cotton and are produced on-site on one of the many looms in the studio. There's a small gift shop where they carry their own items as well as handicrafts from mainland Mexico. Bring pesos if you plan on making any purchases as you'll need to pay in cash.

All of the pottery is made on-site at **Ibarra's Pottery** (Guillermo Prieto 625, www.ibarraspottery.mx, 9am-3pm Mon.-Fri., 9am-2pm Sat.), where you can watch the artists molding their creations as they explain the process. The colorful products are also available to purchase at reasonable prices.

Casa Parra Galeria (Madero, tel. 612/124-2528, 11am-8pm Mon.-Fri., 11am-7pm Sat.) stocks a large selection of Mexican folk art, furniture, home decor items, and jewelry. For all things Talavera, head to **Quinta Lupita** (Constitución 422, tel. 612/123-0599, www.quintalupitalavera.com). The shop has serving ware, tiles, sinks, murals, shingles, and more, all in the colorful traditional Mexican pottery style.

BOOKSTORES

For a well-curated selection of books in English, locals and visitors can go to **Allende Books** (Independencia 518, tel. 612/125-9114, www.allendebooks.com, 10am-6pm Mon.-Sat.). Owners Bruce and Kathleen Bennett take great care in supplying quality titles across a wide variety of genres. There's a solid selection of language books, Baja books, field guides, fishing charts, fiction, coffee-table books, and children's books. Pick up something to learn about the region or take home a beautiful illustrated book as a memento of your trip.

MARKETS

The farmers market in La Paz, **Mercadito Madero** (Madero between 5 de Mayo and Constitución, www.facebook.com/lapaz-farmersmarket) takes place on Tuesdays and Saturdays 8am-noon and is a popular spot for locals to do their shopping and socialize. Stands sell fresh local fresh produce as well as artisan breads, baked goods, cheeses, marmalades, and other regional products. All prices are fixed in pesos.

The large public market in town, **Mercado Municipal Nicolás Bravo** (corner of Nicolás Bravo and Guillermo Prieto), is open seven days a week and offers fresh produce, meat, seafood, and dry goods. There are also stands with prepared foods where locals love to enjoy a cheap breakfast or lunch.

Food

Because La Paz is a major city, the culinary scene has a variety of quality Mexican, seafood, and international options. Nicer restaurants and those in the tourist zone will be more expensive than the local taco stands and *mariscos* spots outside the tourist area. Street tacos and the prevalent evening hot dog carts are great for a cheap snack on the go.

MEXICAN

Famous for their traditional Mexican food, ★ **El Zarape** (México 3450, tel. 612/122-2520, www.elzarapelapaz.com, 7:30am-11pm Tues.-Sun., mains US$10-15) has a large Mexican buffet for US$10, or you can order dishes off the menu like *molcajetes*, chiles rellenos, or taco platters. On Sunday they have dancers for entertainment, and there's often live music throughout the week.

For traditional hearty Mexican dishes and large margaritas, travelers enjoy **Los Magueyes** (Allende 512, tel. 612/128-7846, www.losmagueyeslapaz.com, 8am-10pm Tues.-Sat., 9am-6pm Sun., mains US$6-9). The charming Mexican decor creates a welcoming ambience, and the staff is friendly. Don't forget to order flan for dessert.

For an old-fashioned Mexican restaurant with a romantic setting, **Tres Virgenes** (Madero 1130, tel. 612/123-2226, 1pm-10:30pm Tues.-Sun., mains US$15-25) is a favorite for locals and tourists. The outdoor courtyard has a serene garden setting and a fire where they cook the steaks. Dishes like filet mignon, pork shank, and tuna tostadas grace a menu rounded out by a nice selection of wines, many from Mexico. Reservations are suggested.

Enjoy the hip outdoor patio at ★ **Tio Bencho** (Belisario Dominguez, tel. 612/122-6941, 8am-midnight Tues.-Sat., 8am-5pm Sun.-Mon., mains US$6-9) where the tall trees provide shade during the day and light from

hanging lanterns in the evening. The Oaxacan and Guerrero cuisine here is all made from scratch, and the menu includes rich mole sauces, tasty *sopes,* and white, red, and green posole. To drink they serve cocktails as well as Mexican wines and Baja craft beers. After your meal, head next door to La Miserable mescal bar.

With multiple locations, **Rancho Viejo** (tel. 612/128-4647, open 24 hours, mains US$4-10) has an extensive menu of authentic Mexican dishes. The casual atmosphere, flavorful food, affordable prices, and the fact that it's open 24 hours make it a popular choice for locals and travelers alike. The large original venue is on Marquez de Leon, and there's a smaller location on the *malecón.*

For breakfast, head to **Maria California** (Benito Juárez 105, tel. 612/140-0342, restaurantmariacalifornia@gmail.com, 7:30am-2pm Wed.-Mon., mains US$5-9) for great coffee and a large selection of savory traditional Mexican dishes like poblanos in cream sauce, *chilaquiles,* and *huitlacoche* omelettes. The brightly colored Mexican decor, friendly staff, and occasional live music add to the welcoming atmosphere.

Popular with U.S. and Canadian tourists, **Tailhunter** (Obregon 755, tel. 612/125-3311, www.tailhunter.mx, 8am-midnight Sun.-Thurs., 8am-1am Fri.-Sat., mains US$7-11) on the *malecón* has three floors of ocean views. This sports bar serves up traditional Mexican dishes as well as burgers and some Hawaiian dishes. They also arrange for fishing charters and trips.

SEAFOOD

When it's a nice day, head to **Bismarck-cito** (Obregon at Hidalgo, tel. 612/138-9900, 8am-11pm daily, mains US$10-19) for *malecón* and ocean views in the open-air *palapa.* Specializing in seafood, they serve fish, shrimp, and lobster almost any way you could imagine. The original location, **Bismarck** (Degollado and Altamirano, tel. 612/122-4854), has been a landmark in town since 1968.

For fresh seafood in a casual atmosphere, locals go to **McFisher** (Morelos, tel. 612/12-4140, 8:30am-6pm Tues.-Sat., 8:30am-5pm Sun., mains US$5-10). There's a large menu with lots of options for seafood cocktails, tacos, fish filets and shrimp.

Chocolate clams, octopus, tuna sashimi, and ceviche are just some of the seafood dishes you'll get at **Mariscos El Toro Guero** (Mariana Abasalo, tel. 612/122-7892, 10am-7pm daily, mains US$4-8). This casual spot is popular with the locals and a welcome treat for tourists looking for affordable and fresh food.

TACO STANDS AND STREET FOOD

The most popular place in town for fish and shrimp tacos is ★ **Tacos el Estadio** (corner of Independencia and Guillermo Prieto, tel. 612/157-2472, US$1.50-2). This rustic taco stand has been serving up tacos since 1979. Be prepared to wait as this is a popular spot with the locals and lines can form in the afternoon around lunchtime. You'll need to pay with the cashier first and then get in line to get your tacos and dress them with all the usual toppings and sauces. As with most fish taco places, they open in the morning and close early afternoon when the food runs out.

For ceviche and seafood cocktails, **Mariscos El Molinito** (Carretera a Pichilingue Km. 2, tel. 612/128-4747, www.mariscoselmolinito.com.mx, 10am-8pm daily) serves up fresh seafood in a casual atmosphere. The menu is extensive and the prices are cheap, which makes it a popular spot with locals.

INTERNATIONAL

Il Rustico (Revolución 1930, tel. 612/122-3001, 6pm-11pm Mon.-Sat., 4pm-9pm Sun., US$7-10) is the top choice for Italian in La Paz with wood-fire pizzas, pastas, and substantial salads. The lovely outdoor patio has lush trees and hanging lanterns.

For Japanese food in La Paz, **Jiro Sushi** (Obregón 210, tel. 612/146-3617, www.jiro-sushi.com, 1pm-11pm daily, mains US$7-9) has fresh and tasty rolls, sashimi, and

fish tacos from Tacos el Estadio

seafood plates. They have a location on the *malecón* and a second operation in Plaza Náutica.

International foods come together at **Nim** (Revolución 1110, tel. 612/122-0908, www.nimrestaurante.com, 1pm-10:30pm Mon.-Sat., mains US$8-14), where you can enjoy mole chicken or lamb meatballs in tzatziki for dinner and baklava for dessert. There's indoor seating as well as an outdoor patio.

Savor your burgers, pizzas, and salads, alongside craft beer on tap, on the great rooftop patio at **Harkerboard** (Obregón 299, tel. 612/122-7661, www.harkerboardco.com, 7am-2am daily, US$5-10). They also rent out paddleboards, so this is a great place to stop in after a day of SUP for a margarita, a bite of food, and a view of the sunset over the bay.

Locals and tourists in need of a break from Mexican food and seafood head to **Bandido's** (Navarro and Topete, tel. 612/128-8338, 5pm-midnight daily, mains US$5-8) where they barbecue food on a car converted to a grill (where the engine was). Hamburgers, ribs, and chicken burgers are served up in a fun atmosphere with good service.

CAFÉS AND ICE CREAM

For a dose of coffee and baked goods, **Doce Cuarenta** (Madero 1240, tel. 612/125-5991, 7am-9:30pm Mon.-Fri., 7:30am-9:30pm Sat.) is a great place to pop in for a quick cup of coffee to-go or to hang out on the patio and take advantage of the free wireless access. Sandwiches and salads are made from fresh ingredients and come in large portions. The GotBaja? store is located within Doce Cuarenta, where you can pick up free Baja city maps or check out the selection of cheeky T-shirts, mugs, pillows, and other merchandise.

A bit outside of the tourist area, **Café la Choya** (Colima 1650, tel. 612/128-7118, www.cafelachoya.com.mx, 7:30am-2pm and 4pm-8pm Mon.-Fri., 7am-2pm Sat.) is another option for a good cup of coffee. In addition to brewing coffee, they also sell coffee beans from all over Mexico.

You can't visit La Paz without getting a *paleta* at the famous ★ **La Fuente** (Álvaro Obregón, 9am-11pm daily). This La Paz institution is where locals and tourists head on a hot day for a Mexican-style popsicle to help cool down. Grab your *paleta* and head for a stroll along the *malecón*.

Accommodations

UNDER US$50

Popular with backpackers, divers, and budget travelers, **Pensión Baja Paradise** (Madero 2166, tel. 612/128-6097, baja_paradise@yahoo.com.mx, US$28) has clean rooms and comfortable beds. The property provides a cute and funky decor just two blocks away from the *malecón*. There's a communal outdoor kitchen area, air-conditioning, TV with basic channels, good wireless Internet, hot showers, and a coin laundry.

Since 1965 **Pensión California** (Degollado 209, tel. 612/122-2896 pension-california@prodigy.net.mx, US$20) has been a popular spot for motorcyclists and other backpackers. The bold gold and blue building has plenty of character and offers basic and clean accommodations with a friendly staff.

With a great location on the *malecón* in the center of town, **Hotel Posada de la Mision** (Alvaro Obregón 220, tel. 612/128-7767, www.posadadelamision.com, US$37) offers modest and clean accommodations at an affordable price. Rooms have air-conditioning and flat-screen TVs. The junior and master suites (US$60-75) are almost like full apartments with equipped kitchens, living rooms, and separate bedrooms. Master suites have private balconies looking out onto the *malecón* and water. Be aware that there are no elevators here.

US$50-150

With a prime in-town location just up from the plaza, ★ **El Ángel Azul Hacienda** (Independencia 518, tel. 612/125-5130, www. elangelazul.com, US$80-110) affords guests the chance to stay in a remodeled historical hacienda. Swiss-born owner Esther Ammann came to La Paz in 1998 and spent years re-modeling the historic building that was origi-nally the courthouse for Baja California into the hacienda it is today. There are nine regu-lar rooms as well as a suite, all built around a lush and eclectic courtyard. Coffee is ready each the morning in the communal kitchen, and there's an honor bar for guests to enjoy. Towels and coolers are available for guests to use at the beach. They offer discounted rates for extended stays.

Above the offices for Mar y Aventuras is **Posada LunaSol** (Topete 564, tel. 612/122-7039, www.posadalunasol.com, US$85), a hotel with 20 rooms that have air-condition-ing, pillow-top beds, and in-room safes. Suites with kitchens are available. Guests can enjoy the fountain pool, continental breakfast at the café, and bay views from hammocks up on the rooftop terrace. The hotel is owned by the same people as **Mar Y Aventuras** (www. kayakbaja.com), so they can easily book kaya-king or whale-watching adventures for guests.

Popular with anglers because of its location overlooking Marina Palmira, **Hotel Marina** (Carretera a Pichilingue Km 2.5, tel. 612/121-6254, www.hotelmarina.com.mx, US$54) has 89 basic but clean rooms. There's a nice pool area as well as the Dinghy Dock restau-rant and Liparoli bar on-site. The hotel can be noisy, so light sleepers should bring ear-plugs. Anglers who like a more intimate and personal experience stay at **Leo's Baja Oasis** (Ignacio Allende, www.leosbaja.com, US$100) where they can arrange for fishing charters and also freeze and package the fish for you. There's a main house and three additional bungalows that are all open to lodgers. All units have full kitchens, king-size beds, air-conditioning, and wireless Internet. Common areas include a pool, hot tub, barbecue area, and laundry facilities.

An institution in town, **Hotel Perla** (www. hotelperlabaja.com, US$60) has been around since 1940 and offers 110 rooms. The central

El Ángel Azul Hacienda

location on the *malecón* means it is within walking distance to everything in town. It's been updated in recent years and offers basic but clean and modern accommodations. The pool area is small but pleasant, and the wireless signal is strong.

Hotel Seven Crown Centro (Revolución 1090, tel. 612/129-4562, www.sevencrownhotels.com, US$80) also has a central location and offers 54 clean and quiet rooms around a nice courtyard pool. There's a bar and café in the lobby. A second location a few blocks away on the *malecón* has rooms starting at US$68, but doesn't have a pool and the rooms aren't as nice.

La Posada Hotel and Beach Club (Nueva Reforma 115, tel. 612/146-3269, www.laposadahotel.mx, US$137) is a boutique hotel just south of the *malecón* offering spacious and modern accommodations with unobstructed views of the Sea of Cortez. With great service, they also offer a range of amenities with a restaurant, gym, and spa on the property. They can also arrange for you to take a day trip out to Isla Espíritu Santo, whale-watching, or other water activities.

Just north of town, **La Concha Beach Hotel and Condominiums** (Carretera a Pichilingue Km. 5, tel. 612/121-6160, www.laconcha.com, US$95) has a beach location that's still within walking distance to town. It's an older property and the rooms are dated, but the grounds are nice with lawns, palm trees, and a relaxing pool area all within steps to the beach. There's a restaurant and bar on-site as well as an attached dive and snorkel shop that can help you arrange any water activities. Condos, with up to three bedrooms, are in a building next to the hotel and can also be booked for overnight stays.

On the far north end of the *malecón*, **Club El Moro** (Carretera a Pichilingue Km. 2, tel. 612/122-4084, www.clubelmoro.com.mx, US$70-115) has distinct Moorish architecture that sets it apart from other hotels in the area. The rooms could use an update, but are ample

and well-equipped. The suites have kitchenettes. There are multiple options for sleeping arrangements with rooms that can accommodate up to five people. There's a well-maintained courtyard with gardens, palm trees, a pool and Jacuzzi, and *palapas*. An on-site café serves breakfast and lunch.

US$150-250

For a luxury stay, ★ **Costa Baja** (Carretera a Pichilingue Km. 7.5, tel. 612/123-6000, toll-free U.S. tel. 877/392-5525, www.costabajaresort.com, US$250) a few kilometers north of town on the beach offers all the amenities. They have a golf course, beaches, and tennis courts. There's a beautiful infinity edge pool that looks out onto the Sea of Cortez. There are two restaurants on the property, and the neighboring beach club facility has a second pool and a fitness center that hotel guests may use. A free shuttle takes guests between the resort and town or a local taxi will cost you about US$8. The hotel often has special packages and deals if you book directly through them.

Posada de las Flores La Paz (Alvaro Obregón 440, tel. 612/125-5871, www.posadadelasflores.com, US$180) provides guests elegant with modern amenities with Mexican charm and details like traditional mission-style furniture, art, and pottery. Breakfast is included and served daily. Other services cover daily afternoon tea service, a welcome cocktail, and help arranging excursions. There's a pool in the central courtyard, and rooms on the second floor have ocean views. The property was remodeled in 2016.

BED-AND-BREAKFASTS

If you're looking for personal attention and local recommendations, ★ **Hacienda Paraiso** (De las Rosas 300, tel. 612/112-2729, www.haciendaparaiso.com, US$95-145) is the perfect place to stay. Resident owners, Richard and Gloria, are hands-on with their guests, happily booking excursions and day tours to all of the regional attractions. Guest rooms look onto a central courtyard with a large swimming pool and waterfall, a sanctuary providing the perfect backdrop for the hotel. Rooms are nicely appointed with private bathrooms, air-conditioning, ceiling fans, television/cable, and mini-refrigerators. Wi-Fi is available throughout the property. The decor harkens back to old Baja, with Spanish accents and vibrant Mexican tile throughout. A bountiful American-style breakfast, included with the room tariff, is served poolside. For guests with vehicles, there's a huge secure garage for parking that can accommodate even large trailers.

A charming B&B with a prime location, **Casa Tuscany Inn** (Nicolas Bravo 10, tel. 612/128-8103, www.tuscanybaja.com, US$108-143) houses guests a block off of the *malecón* in the central district. There are four rooms with Mexican decor, all centered around a lush courtyard. Owner Carol Dyer is a welcoming host, helping guests with recommendations and suggestions around town.

New in town, **B&B Casa Juarez** (Benito Juárez 443, tel. 612/132-2959, www.casajuarez.mx, US$68-90) is a pet-friendly property with a nice central location, walking distance to restaurants, shops, and the *malecón*. The rooms are bright, clean, and nicely appointed with air-conditioning and wireless access. The quiet central courtyard has a small swimming pool. There are three rooms as well as two apartments that have kitchens and living rooms. Breakfast is included.

For value bed-and-breakfast accommodations, **Casabuena Bed & Breakfast** (Belisario Domingues 3065, tel. 612/122-5538, www.casabuena.net, US$57) is a comfortable spot that's popular with language students, families, and budget travelers. You won't find fancy accommodations here, but there are 13 comfortable rooms, and a simple pool and grilling area. The property is dog- and kid-friendly, and many rooms have multiple beds and kitchens, great for families.

Situated in a restored historic colonial house, ★ **Casa Verde Inn** (Independencia 563, tel. 612/165-5162, www.casaverdeinn.com.mx, US$90-100) has three beautiful and comfortable rooms. The decor is a nice nod to Mexican charm, but rooms still have modern amenities. There's a small courtyard pool for cooling off when temperatures are warm. They also have two guesthouse, in other areas of central La Paz that are equally as well-appointed and available to rent (US$90-100 per night, three-night minimum stay).

Anca Mi Nana (Guillermo Prieto 1050A, tel. 612/123-2499, www.ancaminana.wix.com/ancaminana, US$75) offers three rooms that are beautifully decorated. Beach umbrellas, towels, coolers, and bicycles are provided for guest use. Natalia is a wonderful host who can recommend activities and restaurants in town and arrange day tours. A continental breakfast is served each morning.

Located right on the water, **Casa Kootenay** (Brecha California 1035, tel. 612/122-0006, www.casakootenay.com, US$98-123) boasts a great rooftop deck with lounge chairs and daybeds for enjoying the incredible views of the bay.

Information and Services

TOURIST ASSISTANCE

BCS State tourism (Obregón at Allende, 8am-8pm Mon.-Fri.) has an information booth on the *malecón* with maps and brochures.

Inside the La Paz Cultural Center is the **La Paz Hotel Association** (16 de Septiembre, tel. 612/122-4624, www.golapaz.com, 9am-7pm Mon.-Fri.) where visitors can also pick up brochures and information.

One of the best and free resources for tourists is the La Paz map from **Got Baja?** (Madero 1240, tel. 612/125-5991, www.gotbaja.mx). Copies can be picked up at their location on Calle Madero or at hotels and restaurants all over town. *The Baja Citizen* recently became a glossy magazine (it was once a newspaper). This free English publication comes out every month with good information for both local expats and tourists.

MEDICAL EMERGENCIES

There are two hospitals in La Paz, **Hospital Fidepaz** (Mexico 1 Km. 5.5, tel. 612/124-0400) on the highway, and **Hospital Juan María de Salvatierra** (Ave. Paseo de los Deportistas 5115, tel. 612/175-0503, www.hgejms.gob.mx).

LANGUAGE COURSES

Baja doesn't have many Spanish language courses anymore, but La Paz is a city that still has good language schools. **Se Habla** (Madero 540, tel. 612/122-7763, www.sehablalapaz.com) is a great option for those who want to brush up or learn Spanish for the first time. The tailored language program is designed for each student's specific needs. Courses start at US$275/week with an extra US$225/week for homestay fees.

With a wide variety of options for courses, **El Nopal** (Legaspy 1885, tel. 612/177-4098, www.elnopalspanish.com) has full immersion programs, a 10-month program, family packages, online classes, and a class for locals. They can also include cultural activities like Mexican cooking classes, market visits, and outdoor sports.

Getting Around

CAR

For non-road-trippers who haven't arrived in La Paz in their own car, there are various rental agencies that have locations in the airport and also in downtown La Paz. Most visitors who fly into La Paz's **Manuel Marquez de Leon International Airport (LAP)** (tel. 612/124-6307) or **Los Cabos International Airport (SJD)** rent a car when arriving at the airport to drive around for their time in La Paz. This gives the visitors the flexibility to explore the city and surrounding region. There are plenty of gas stations as well as mechanics and services around La Paz.

TAXI

Taxis are easily found in central La Paz. Fares are around US$5 to get around the center of town, US$8 to get to the closer resorts and beaches just north of town, US$15 to the airport, and US$20 to the ferry terminal or farther beaches like Playa Balandra and El Tecolote. Negotiate the price with the driver before getting in the taxi.

BUS

For adventurous travelers, the *peseros* (*colectivos*) cluster downtown on Revolución de 1910, Aquiles Serdán, Santos Degollado, and Melchor Ocampo. Fares are less than US$1 (no transfers). The system is slightly convoluted, so you'll need to ask the driver which *pesero* to take to get to where you're going. There are routes, but the stops are usually not marked. The *peseros* operate between 6am and 10:30pm.

Vicinity of La Paz

BAHÍA DE LA VENTANA

Forty minutes southeast of La Paz, Bahía de La Ventana shelters the fishing villages of El Sargento and La Ventana. The area has become a premier destination for kitesurfing and windboarding during the months of November to April when the El Norte winds are blowing. Other people come to the area for fishing, stand-up paddleboarding, practicing yoga, and relaxing.

Isla Jacques Cousteau/ Cerralvo

In 2009, the Mexican government officially changed the name of the 29-kilometer-long island off the coast of La Ventana from Isla Cerralvo to Isla Jacques Cousteau. The change was to honor the French oceanographer who led many expeditions in the area and famously referred to the Sea of Cortez as "the world's aquarium."

The change was met with much resistance from citizens in the area, and most people will still refer to the island as Cerralvo. The island is one of the largest in the Sea of Cortez and a popular spot for fishing as well as diving. Palapas Ventana (www.palapasventana. com) runs multiday trips out to the island for diving.

Sports and Recreation
★ KITEBOARDING
AND WINDSURFING

Windsurfers first discovered La Ventana in the 1990s, but in recent years, kiteboarding has become a popular activity as well. Nearly every establishment in town can assist with kiteboarding lessons and rentals including most accommodations in town such as Playa Central and Palapas Ventana.

There are plenty of schools certified by the International Kiteboarding Organization (IKO). Elevation Kiteboarding School (tel. 612/114-0001, www.elevationkiteboarding.com) has customized kiteboarding lessons for all levels, and they provide all of the gear (you'll need to provide your own wetsuit).

Family-run Baja Kite and Surf (tel. 612/155-5775, www.bajakiteandsurf.com) focuses mainly on kiteboarding lessons for different levels and backgrounds starting at US$150 for two hours of instruction. 4Elements Kiteboarding (tel. 612/136-9956, www.4elementskiteboarding.com) is a great for those who are just learning to kiteboard because of their hands-on and patient instructors who are sticklers for safety.

The La Ventana Classic (www.laventanaclassic.com) takes place in January and runs multiple days for kiteboard and windsurf races, SUP races, and parties.

FISHING

Most of the best fishing in this region is around Bahía La Ventana, Isla Jacques Cousteau, Punta Arena de la Ventana, and Bahía de los Muertos. Many fishing charters from La Paz will come over to this region to launch at Punta Arena de la Ventana. This is a prime area for big-game fishing with plenty of marlin, swordfish, dorado, sailfish, swordfish, yellowfin tuna, and large roosterfish.

Food and Accommodations

One of the original restaurants in the area, ★ El Rincon de la Bahía (3pm-9pm Tues.-Fri., 1pm-9pm Sat.-Sun.) is on the beach in La Ventana. Try their specialty, *pescado relleno con camerón* (fish stuffed with shrimp). They also have a full bar.

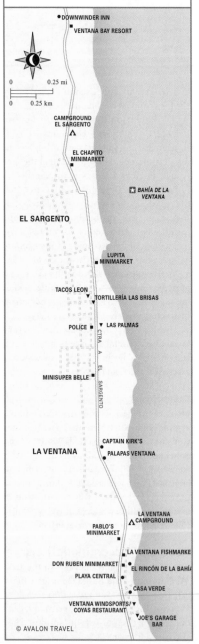

La Ventana and El Sargento

DOWNWINDER INN
VENTANA BAY RESORT

0   0.25 mi
0   0.25 km

CAMPGROUND
EL SARGENTO

EL CHAPITO
MINIMARKET

BAHÍA DE LA
VENTANA

EL SARGENTO

LUPITA
MINIMARKET

TACOS LEON
TORTILLERÍA LAS BRISAS

POLICE
LAS PALMAS

CTRA. A EL SARGENTO

MINISUPER BELLE

CAPTAIN KIRK'S

LA VENTANA
PALAPAS VENTANA

LA VENTANA
CAMPGROUND

PABLO'S
MINIMARKET

LA VENTANA FISHMARKET
DON RUBEN MINIMARKET
EL RINCÓN DE LA BAHÍA
PLAYA CENTRAL

CASA VERDE

VENTANA WINDSPORTS/
COYAS RESTAURANT

JOE'S GARAGE
BAR

© AVALON TRAVEL

Even more than a restaurant/coffee shop/ bar, ★ **Playa Central** (tel. 612/114-0267, www.playacentralkiteboarding.com) has become a gathering place for the kiteboarding community. They regularly have live music as well as events like salsa lessons and open mic nights. November-March they host the La Ventana farmers market on Thursday 9am-noon.

Joe's Garage Bar (tel. 612/114-0001, www.bajajoe.com, 4pm-10pm Mon.-Sat.) has specialty drinks like margaritas and fresh mint mojitos, in addition to 10 beers on tap.

Palapas Ventana (tel. 612/114-0198, www. palapasventana.com, US$60-70 pp) has two casita styles to choose from, regular (for up to two people) and specialty (up to four). The regular *casitas* do not have private bathrooms. All *casitas* have *palapa* roofs and overlook the ocean. They can arrange boat trips, fishing charters, snorkeling tours, stand-up paddleboarding, kiteboarding, and windsurfing. There's a **restaurant** and a **bar** on the property.

Regular rooms and private bungalows are available at ★ **Ventana Bay Resort** (tel. 612/114-0222, www.ventanabay.com, US$120). For an extra US$25 a day, they will include breakfast and lunch in your stay. They also have an IKO-certified kiteboarding school on property as well as a **bar** and **restaurant.**

Boutique resort **Ventana Windsports** (tel. 612/114-0065, www.ventanawindsports. com, US$180-250) has 12 accommodations— nine with one bedroom and three with two bedrooms. The property has plenty of lawn and patio common areas as well as a great room for lounging, a massage pagoda, and an outdoor hot tub. The beach **restaurant** and **bar Coyas** is a favorite for guests at the hotel as well as outside visitors.

For a quiet and peaceful stay in La Ventana, **Casa Verde** (tel. 612/114-0214, www.bajmahal.com) has three *casitas*, three small houses, and four RV spaces with full hookups. Amenities include a common kitchen, *temazcal* sauna, bicycles, kayaks, and SUP boards. They can also arrange for private cooks and nannies during your stay.

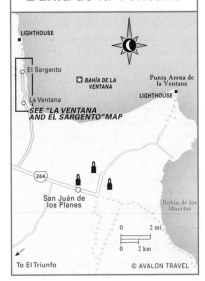

Bahía de la Ventana

612/197-9904, oliver_ms22hotmail.com, www.facebook.com/rvparkelsargento) has spots for up to 16 tents and 14 spaces for RVs with hookups for water and sewer. In addition to *casitas* and houses for rent, **Kurt 'N Marina** (tel. 612/114-0010, www.kurtnmarina.com, US$20) offers beachfront RV spots with full hookups.

BAHÍA DE LOS MUERTOS

There are many theories behind the name Bahía de los Muertos (meaning Bay of the Dead). One theory involves a Chinese ship that landed in 1885 and lost 18 crew members, another theory claims that a group of U.S. farmers died of starvation trying to cultivate the land in the 1900s. A third theory says that *muertos* refers to moorings that were buried underwater to anchor barges for the mines in El Triunfo. Regardless of the origin, when the large development project located here came in to build, they found the name to be off-putting and referred to their resort Bahía de los Sueños (Bay of Dreams). Many people now call the entire bay Bahía de los Sueños. It's a beautiful and relaxing area, popular with snorkelers.

Located in El Sargento, **DownWinder Inn** (Calle Ballenato, tel. 612/156-6244, www.downwinderinn.com, US$60) has six rooms in a garden setting. All rooms have a queen-size bed, refrigerator, and coffeemaker. There's a well-stocked communal kitchen and a rooftop perfect for watching sunrises. They offer free shuttle service to windsurfing and kiteboarding beaches.

Ideally located on the beach, **Captain Kirk's** (Camino de La Ventana Km. 9.1, toll-free U.S. tel. 877/321-5475, www.captainkirks.com, US$120) has accommodations ranging from studio *casitas* to four-bedroom houses. All accommodations have air-conditioning, mini-fridges, wireless Internet, and outdoor patios. Lessons and rentals are available for kiteboarding and windsurfing.

CAMPING AND RV PARKS

The main campground in La Ventana, **La Ventana Campground** (US$7-8), is right in the heart of town on the main beach for kiteboarding and windsurfing. There are restrooms and showers but no hookups.

Campground El Sargento (tel.

Bahía de los Sueños

The grandiose plans at the Bay of Dreams development included a golf course, equestrian center, tennis courts, restaurant, and several *casitas* for a residential community. Most of these plans came to fruition and were built, but most of the facilities have been closed down and the property is now for sale.

Still open for business within the Bay of Dreams development, **GranSueño Resort** (Mexico 286 Km. 56, tel. 335/004-0777, toll-free U.S. tel. 888/812-2162, www.gransueno.com, US$250) has luxury rooms, a stunning pool and private white sand beaches. The remote location provides the perfect backdrop for a relaxing vacation.

Food

A stunning seafront setting and satisfying seafood, **Restaurant 1535** (the former

Giggling Marlin, no tel., US$6-9) offers relaxing patio seating overlooking Bahía de los Sueños. The restaurant has outdoor showers for the many snorkelers who come to the area to snorkel and then enjoy a meal.

RANCHO LAS CRUCES

Set on 4,000 private hectares of a natural sanctuary with 11 kilometers of private beach coastline, Rancho las Cruces (tel. 612/125-5639, www.rancholascruces.com, US$265-295) is an escape that has lured the rich and famous for decades.

Abelardo L. Rodriguez Montijo, the son of a former president of Mexico who started the resort in 1948, had such success that he went on to open Hotel Palmilla (now the One and Only Palmilla) in Cabo in 1957 as well as the Hacienda Hotel. In the Hollywood heyday of Rancho las Cruces, stars such as Bing Crosby and Desi Arnaz were frequent guests at the ranch, and both of their families have inherited private houses that are on the property.

The ranch is named for the three crosses that Spanish conquistador Hernán Cortés placed on land when he came to the area in 1535. Stone replicas of the three crosses now stand on the property. Guests enjoy exploring the 13 different trails for walks and hikes. Boats are available for charter, and the property has swimming pools, tennis courts, croquet courts, shuffleboard, and badminton. The one thing that you won't find here is televisions, as the idea is to escape from daily life. The white hacienda buildings and arched walkways evoke an old Mexico feel, taking guests back to another era.

With its remote location, the resort is all-inclusive providing three meals a day and an evening snack. It's possible to drive in from La Paz but inquire about road condition with the resort before setting out. Many guests arrive by private plane on the private airstrip.

GETTING THERE AND AROUND

Private vehicles are required to get to and around this area. Most travelers fly into La Paz's Manuel Marquez de Leon International Airport (LAP) (tel. 612/124-6307) and rent a car to drive the approximate 45 minutes to this area. Private shuttles from the La Paz airport cost around US$120.

The East Cape and the Sierra de la Laguna

Look for ★ to find recommended
sights, activities, dining, and lodging.

Highlights

★ **El Triunfo:** This old colonial mining town is worth a day trip to explore the old mine ruins, museums, and cafés and restaurants (page 255).

★ **Kiteboarding in Los Barriles:** The El Norte winds and warm waters of Los Barriles attract kiteboarders from all over the world, especially in winter months (page 259).

★ **Sportfishing:** The summer months bring anglers to the East Cape to catch marlin, dorado, yellowtail, roosterfish, and sierra (page 259).

★ **Diving and Snorkeling in Cabo Pulmo:** The coral reef and national park at Cabo Pulmo are home to abundant marinelife and offer some of the best diving on the peninsula (page 269).

★ **Cañon de la Zorra:** The beautiful and remote Cañon de la Zorra is home to a large waterfall and natural pools that make for an exciting day trip (page 279).

★ **Santa Rita Hot Springs:** This is the best spot for soaking in the area (page 280).

East of San José del Cabo, the resorts and crowds of Los Cabos fade away and you're left with the pure natural beauty of Baja California Sur.

The East Cape is home to deserted white sand beaches, coral reefs teeming with sealife, charming colonial towns, and the lush Sierra de la Laguna.

It's a more relaxing and intimate alternative to the glamour and crowds of Los Cabos, but still within close proximity of the airport. The few small towns here are nestled into the foothills of the mountains or dotted along the Sea of Cortez, attracting close-knit expat communities. There are no nightclubs or mega resorts here—in fact quite the opposite. Most of the region is off the grid and quiets down not long after sunset. This is an area prime for families and those who love to get outdoors, whether your idea of being outdoors is relaxing on a pristine beach or hiking to waterfalls in the Sierra. Anglers, kiteboarders, surfers, hikers, divers, and snorkelers will all find plenty to fill their days with here.

Los Barriles is the largest town on the East Cape, and many visitors end up staying here, along with the surrounding communities like Buena Vista and Punta Pescadero.

Cabo Pulmo's coral reef to the south is one of the premier diving and snorkeling destinations in Baja. Inland toward the Sierra de la Laguna are a number of quaint towns that act as gateways to the mountains that shelter scenic hikes, hot springs, waterfalls, and natural pools.

PLANNING YOUR TIME

Although the East Cape is a relatively small area, there's plenty to do here for outdoor enthusiasts. When, where, and how long to go are all largely dependent on the activities you're interested in. A week is enough time to relax, explore most of the area, and fit in a range of activities. Despite the heat, summer is usually the time when anglers come to Los Barriles, Buena Vista, or Punta Pescadero for offshore sportfishing. Summer is also the season for divers and snorkelers who arrive in Cabo Pulmo to enjoy its coral reef abounding with marinelife. In the wintertime, kiteboarders will head to Los Barriles to take advantage of the El Norte winds. If you're planning

---

Previous: the waterfall at Cañon de la Zorra; the town of El Triunfo. **Above:** palm trees on the beach in Buena Vista.

The East Cape and the Sierra de la Laguna

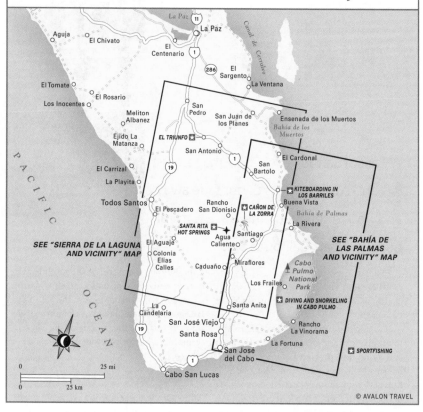

La Paz 11

La Paz

El Centenario 1

286 El Sargento
La Ventana

Aguja
El Chivato

El Tomate
Los Inocentes

El Rosario

Meliton Albanez

Ejido La Matanza

San Pedro

San Juan de los Planes

Ensenada de los Muertos

Bahía de los Muertos

EL TRIUNFO

San Antonio

1

San Bartolo

El Cardonal

KITEBOARDING IN LOS BARRILES

El Carrizal
La Playita

19

Todos Santos

El Pescadero

Rancho San Dionisio

CAÑON DE LA ZORRA

Buena Vista

Bahía de Palmas

La Rivera

SANTA RITA HOT SPRINGS

Agua Caliente

Santiago

SEE "SIERRA DE LA LAGUNA AND VICINITY" MAP

El Aguaje

Colonia Elias Calles

Caduaño

Miraflores

Cabo Pulmo National Park

Los Frailes

SEE "BAHÍA DE LAS PALMAS AND VICINITY" MAP

DIVING AND SNORKELING IN CABO PULMO

La Candelaria

San José Viejo

Santa Rosa

Santa Anita

Rancho La Vinorama

La Fortuna

SPORTFISHING

19

San José del Cabo

1

Cabo San Lucas

PACIFIC OCEAN

Canal de Cerralvo

0   25 mi
0   25 km

© AVALON TRAVEL

a multiday trek into the Sierra de la Laguna, plan on at least 3-4 days for doing so.

GETTING THERE
Car

A car is necessary to take advantage of all that the East Cape has to offer. Travelers who fly into the Los Cabos or La Paz airports should rent one there to use for their time in the East Cape. You'll find Pemex gas stations in all of the small towns, with the exception of Cabo Pulmo.

Air

It's possible to use either the La Paz's **Manuel Marquez de Leon International Airport** **(LAP)** or **Los Cabos International Airport (SJD)** to get to the East Cape. The Los Cabos airport is the more popular choice because there are more flights. Travelers arriving at either airport can rent a car to drive the to the East Cape, which takes 1-1.5 hours, depending on where you're going.

Bus

Autobuses de la Baja California (ABC, tel. 664/104-7400, www.abc.com.mx) has service to Los Barriles from San José del Cabo, Cabo San Lucas, and La Paz. Aguila (tel. 800/824-8452, www.autobusesaguila.com) has the same routes with additional service to Miraflores, Santiago, and Buena Vista.

Best Accommodations

★ **Captain Nemo's Landing:** You can spend the night a teepee or a *casita,* as well as take kiteboarding lessons (page 264).

★ **Rancho Leonero:** The rugged beauty of the East Cape shines through at Rancho Leonero where guests spend their days fishing or relaxing in hammocks poolside (page 266).

★ **Hotel Buena Vista Beach Resort:** The whole family will enjoy a stay at this East Cape hotel where the lush grounds and beautiful beach provide a great backdrop for a range of activities (page 266).

★ **Baja Bungalows:** You'll feel right at home at this peaceful and unpretentious spot in Cabo Pulmo (page 271).

★ **Villa del Faro:** This gorgeous and secluded property is the place to go when you want to take a beach vacation to get away from it all (page 273).

El Triunfo and Vicinity

As highway Mexico 1 winds along the northern foothills of the Sierra de la Laguna between La Paz and Los Barriles, a few small towns pop up along the way. Silver and gold were found nearby in the mid 19th century, which led to the establishment of mining towns in the region. El Triunfo, one of these former mining towns, had been mostly abandoned after the mines were closed nearly 100 years ago. But today, the former ghost town is becoming a must-stop for travelers with its interesting history, chic cafés, and beautiful colonial architecture that's now getting a second life. This entire area is fed by natural springs in the Sierra de la Laguna, providing a lush backdrop for the towns and picturesque drive. Accommodations are scarce in this area, but the small settlements and scenic vistas make for a lovely day trip from both Los Barriles and La Paz.

★ EL TRIUNFO

For decades, it felt like time had forgotten the old mining town of El Triunfo (Mexico 1 Km. 163). What was once the largest and richest

town in Baja Sur during its glory days became a virtual ghost town after the mine closed in 1926. The dusty streets were lined with abandoned and derelict colonial buildings in a hauntingly sad reminder of the town's glorious past. The sleepy settlement was mostly empty except for some local families who had lived here for generations.

But in recent years, a restored interest has brought new life back to El Triunfo. There are some new restaurants, shops and galleries, and plenty of history to explore. Saturday afternoons the town is packed with day-trippers who come to walk around the old mine ruins, eat at the local cafés, and enjoy the historic charms. There are no options for accommodations, but it's an easy (45-minute) drive from La Paz or Los Barriles, making it an interesting and fun day trip.

Sights

THE OLD MINE AND MIRADOR

A trip to El Triunfo isn't complete without a walk through the town's **historic mining ruins.** Access to the area can be found on

Best Restaurants

★ **Bar El Minero:** This bar and eatery is new to El Triunfo and offers a chic indoor space as well as a large outdoor area, home to a weekly Sunday paella fest (page 257).

★ **Campestre Triny:** For an excellent meal, delicious margaritas, and outdoor seating, this spot is a safe bet (page 262).

★ **La Terraza de German:** Enjoy fresh seafood, chicken, and taco dishes on a lovely second-floor outdoor terrace (page 263).

★ **Roadrunner Café & Bakery:** Visitors come here for the best breakfast in town (264).

★ **Lazy Daze Beach Bar:** This casual beach bar is a great place for hanging out and watching the kiteboarders in Los Barriles (page 263).

Calle Libertad (just head toward the tall smokestack). Here, visitors will find old mining equipment, brick ruins, and old smokestacks. The largest smokestack, "La Romana" is 35 meters tall and rumored to have been designed by Gustave Eiffel (of Eiffel Tower fame). Follow the path lined by the white rocks to head up to the *mirador.* At this lookout you'll get a beautiful view of the town and the surrounding mountains. Halfway up the path is a side jaunt to the walled-in Panteon Ingles, a cemetery with 13 white aboveground mausoleums of English citizens who once worked in the mines.

MUSEO DE LA MÚSICA

Housed in a white and amber colonial building on the east side of Mexico 1 is the music museum, the **Museo de la Música** (no tel., 8am-2pm daily, US$1.50).

During the prosperous years of El Triunfo, the town was a cultural center and for music and dance. Pianos and other instruments were shipped from Europe and other parts of

Museo de la Música

the world. Pianist Francisca Mendoza would entertain wealthy patrons with concerts during the El Triunfo's heyday. The Museo de la Música was opened in 2003 to honor that heritage. The late curator of the museum, Nicolás Carrillo, who was known regionally as the "Liberace of Baja," passed away a few years ago, and the museum has declined recently.

SANTUARIO DE LOS CACTUS

Outside of town just a few kilometers north on the highway is the turnoff for the **Santuario de los Cactus** (Mexico 1 Km. 167, no tel., 9am-5pm daily, US$4). This 50-hectare cactus sanctuary is an ecological reserve home to cacti and plants found only in this part of the world. There are a few informational signs along the path that point out some of the unique flora and fauna found in the area. Those interested in learning more in-depth information should take along a copy of Jon P. Rebman's *Baja California Plant Field Guide.*

Entertainment and Events

Every spring the **El Triunfo Festival Artesanal** is a daylong event with *ballet folklórico* dancing and entertainment, booths with arts and regional products. The small town comes alive with bright colors, lively music, and festive crowds.

Food and Accommodations

When it comes to dining options in El Triunfo, it's quality over quantity. There are currently only two places to eat and drink in town (aside from little roadside markets), but they're both excellent options.

Open for breakfast and lunch, **Caffé El Triunfo** (Ayuntamiento, tel. 612/157-1625, 9am-5pm daily) is the only full restaurant in town. They have a wood-burning oven where they bake fresh breads and make pizzas that are a favorite of all who pass through. There's a café in the front (the restaurant is in the back), so if you stop by in the morning, buy a few loaves of bread or some of their famous cinnamon rolls. There are various areas and

outdoor patios for eating, drinking, and relaxing. The owner, Marcus Spahr, previously ran Caffé Todos Santos for 16 years. If you're visiting on a weekend when there are lots of tourists in town, be patient as service can get bogged down when they get busy.

The new, refreshingly chic ★ **Bar El Minero** (Calle Progreso, tel. 612/176-3939, www.barelminero.com, 11am-6:30pm Wed.-Mon., closed July-Sept.) resides in a building that is over 120 years old and once housed the laboratory for the mines. Today the space is beautiful and inviting with upcycled bottle light fixtures, locally crafted wooden tables, and a long bar. The expansive outdoor space has plenty of seating, fire pits, and views of the old smokestacks. El Minero serves craft beer on tap, as well as house-made artisanal sausages, salads, and local cheeses. Chef Felipe studied the culinary arts in San Diego and Tijuana, and his sophisticated understanding of flavor profiles shines through in everything he makes. On Sunday there's a large paella fest that draws locals and visitors for a fun afternoon. Don't visit without dressing up to take your photo with the bronze sculpture of Sofia and Juan Matute in the courtyard.

The only lodging option in town is the small **La Fortelezza** (tel. 624/182-4068, U.S. tel. 916/790-4422, cabolink@yahoo.com, US$50), right across from Caffé El Triunfo. They currently offer two rooms that share a bathroom and have access to a common kitchen and a private patio at night. The property features modern accommodations with Mexican accents. **Rancho LaVenta** (Mexico 1 Km. 144., tel. 612/156-8947, www.rancholaventawines.com, US$75-100), between San Antonio and San Bartolo, is a nearby option if travelers are looking for accommodations closer to El Triunfo than Los Barriles or La Paz.

SAN ANTONIO

This small town doesn't have too much to offer tourists, but it is a hub for local ranchers and farmers. There's a town plaza and a few markets. There's even a Pemex gas station on the south side of town off of the highway. Just north of town is a turnoff from Mexico 1 for La Ventana and Bahía de los Muertos at kilometer 155.5. The road is 22 kilometers long and meets up with Mexico 286 at San Juan de los Planes.

Just off of the highway in San Antonio, travelers will find **Pizza Gourmet** (tel. 612/136-7636, noon-8pm Wed.-Sun., US$6-9) offering pizzas and salads made from fresh ingredients. The friendly atmosphere features an agreeable garden setting. They also have homemade breads and jams (they sell them at the Los Barriles Community Market on Saturday as well). They currently only accept cash.

Between San Antonio and San Bartolo is **Rancho LaVenta** (Mexico 1 Km. 144.5, tel. 612/156-8947, www.rancholaventawines.com, US$75-100), a 350-acre historical ranch that has been in existence since the late 1700s. The ranch offers guests a range of activities from enjoying the spring-fed granite pool and sauna to horseback riding or bird-watching. Owners Liz and Bob Pudwill grow grapes and make wine on the property, and wine-tasting is available by appointment. In addition to red wines, they make a unique mango wine as well as mead from local honey.

SAN BARTOLO

As travelers wind along Mexico 1 north of Los Barriles, they'll find themselves in a lush, semitropical setting with an abundance of mango and avocado trees, palm-filled canyons, and roadside fruit stands populating the highway. The small village of San Bartolo (Mexico 1 Km. 128) is nestled into this fertile region, which is fed by a natural springs from the Sierra de la Laguna. There's a tiny plaza in town and along the highway there are a number of markets, small eateries, and *dulcerías* selling homemade candy. Down in the canyon of San Bartolo are small cement pools that capture the natural springwater and are a popular spot for locals to take a dip in the heat of summer. To get to the pools and springs from town, take Ramon Cota off of Mexico 1.

The springs in San Bartolo can also be reached from Los Barriles by taking an ATV or four-wheeler along the Arroyo San Bartolo, a dry riverbed that runs from Los Barriles to San Bartolo. It's a sandy gravel route frequented by ATV tours and adventurous tourists.

Bar El Minero serves well-crafted food and drink with views of the old mine smokestacks.

Los Barriles and Vicinity

Los Barriles is the largest town on the East Cape and a popular destination for kiteboarders and windsurfers as well as anglers. The dusty streets lined with taco shops, small produce stands, and *tortillerías* are now filled in winter months with retiree snowbirds on ATVs and kiteboarders in search of El Norte winds.

While there's a strip mall and a growing number of expat mansions, at its heart, Los Barriles is still a small laid-back town, especially when compared to Los Cabos. Because there are a number of options for accommodations, restaurants, and activities, Los Barriles can be a great place to stay as a home base for exploring the rest of the East Cape.

Los Barriles and the surrounding communities are situated on the Bahía de las Palmas, a large bay that is 32 kilometers long. The area was discovered by anglers in the 1960s and was a popular spot for fly-in fishing resorts during that time. Anglers are still drawn to the area, especially in the summer months when offshore sportfishing is at its prime.

The coastal areas north and south of Los Barriles are small communities but are constantly growing because of new housing developments. South of Los Barriles, Buena Vista has expat homes and beachfront hotels where fishing and relaxation are the focus. North of Los Barriles, Punta Pescadero also has a few hotels that lure anglers, but the area is generally less developed, in part because of dirt roads that can be rough driving.

LOS BARRILES

The town of Los Barriles has grown from a sleepy fishing village into a friendly and vibrant town over the past number of years due to an influx of American and Canadian expats. While large beachfront homes and a small strip mall have had their influence, you can still get an authentic Baja vibe here at the small markets, and taco stands. It's been a popular destination for anglers since the 1960s and in more recent decades has grown into a world-class destination for windsurfers and kiteboarders. While the town has large grocery stores and a number of services, it's still devoid of nightlife or luxury resorts. Retirees come here to relax and enjoy the slow-paced life while families are drawn to the region for the water sports and friendly feel.

Recreation
★ **KITEBOARDING AND WINDSURFING**

Over the past number of years, Los Barriles has established itself as a world-class spot for kiteboarding and windsurfing. The sandy bottoms and shore break make this is good spot for beginners, while the large swells that pick up in the afternoons bring excellent waves for more experienced riders. November through April the El Norte winds arrive, with consistent wind speeds between 18-25 knots. Playa Norte is considered the best kiteboarding beach in the region. The IKO-affiliated **ExotiKite Kiteboarding School** (tel. 624/145-0064, www.exotikite.com) has been in operation since 1998. They have an experienced staff and all of the equipment and knowledge that you need to learn kiteboarding. In addition to classes, they have a restaurant, SUP center, a store, and can help with accommodations. Another option is **Kiteboarding Baja** (tel. 624/166-0986, www. kiteboardingbajaschool.com), offering private or group lessons for all levels of kiteboarders. They are IKO-certified and also have a location in La Ventana.

★ **SPORTFISHING**

The Sea of Cortez waters on the East Cape are home to an abundance of fish, making this some of the best angling in Baja. In shallow waters, the catch can include cabrillas, jack crevalle, roosterfish, pompano, triggerfish,

Bahía de las Palmas and Vicinity

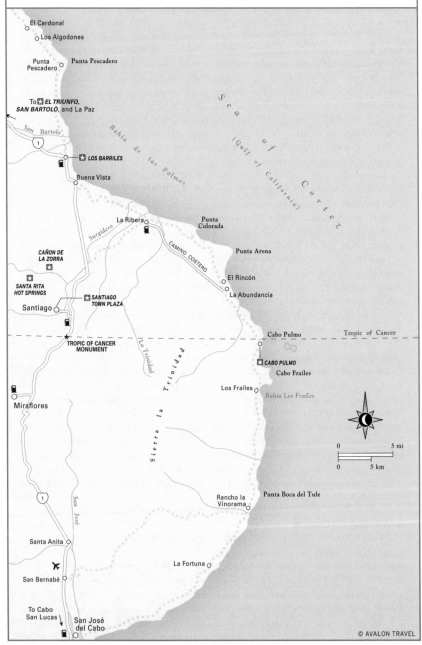

El Cardonal
Los Algodones
Punta Pescadero — Punta Pescadero
To EL TRIUNFO, SAN BARTOLO, and La Paz
San Bartolo
1
LOS BARRILES
Buena Vista
Bahía de las Palmas
Sea of Cortez (Gulf of California)
La Ribera
Punta Colorada
Surgidero
CAMINO COSTERO
Punta Arena
CAÑON DE LA ZORRA
El Rincón
SANTA RITA HOT SPRINGS
La Abundancia
SANTIAGO TOWN PLAZA
Santiago
Cabo Pulmo
Tropic of Cancer
TROPIC OF CANCER MONUMENT
La Trinidad
CABO PULMO
Cabo Frailes
Los Frailes
Bahía Los Frailes
Miraflores
Sierra la Trinidad
0   5 mi
0   5 km
1
San José
Rancho la Vinorama
Punta Boca del Tule
Santa Anita
San Bernabé
La Fortuna
To Cabo San Lucas
San José del Cabo

© AVALON TRAVEL

Los Barriles

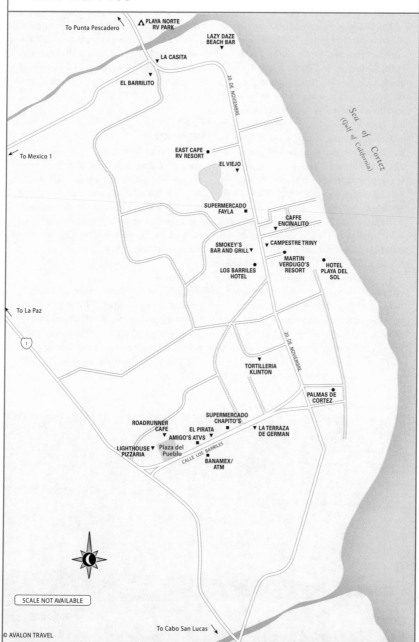

To Punta Pescadero

PLAYA NORTE
RV PARK

LAZY DAZE
BEACH BAR

LA CASITA

EL BARRILITO

To Mexico 1

Sea of Cortez
(Gulf of California)

EAST CAPE
RV RESORT

EL VIEJO

SUPERMERCADO
FAYLA

CAFFE
ENCINALITO

SMOKEY'S
BAR AND GRILL

CAMPESTRE TRINY

MARTIN
VERDUGO'S
RESORT

HOTEL
PLAYA DEL
SOL

LOS BARRILES
HOTEL

To La Paz

20 DE NOVIEMBRE

TORTILLERIA
KLINTON

PALMAS DE
CORTEZ

SUPERMERCADO
CHAPITO'S

ROADRUNNER
CAFE

EL PIRATA

LA TERRAZA
DE GERMAN

AMIGO'S ATVS

LIGHTHOUSE
PIZZARIA

Plaza del
Pueblo

CALLE LOS BARRILES

BANAMEX/
ATM

SCALE NOT AVAILABLE

© AVALON TRAVEL

To Cabo San Lucas

snappers, sierra, ladyfish, and barred pargo. Marlin, sailfish, dorado, and tuna can be hooked in deeper waters.

The waters get deep just offshore here, so it's common to catch roosterfish and jack crevalle from the shore. Punta Pescadero, Punta Colorada, and Punta Arena are three good places for this. If you want to check out the deeper waters, many of the hotels in Los Barriles and Buena Vista have their own fishing fleets or can arrange for a charter for you.

Headquartered at East Cape RV Resort, **Baja's Awesome Sportfishing** (tel. 624/141-0231, www.bajasawesomesportfishing.com) operates two cruisers and can provide all tackle. Rates start at US$600/day for up to four anglers.

Baja on the Fly (U.S. tel. 760/522-3720, www.bajafly.com) is operated by well-known Baja fisherman and writer Gary Graham and his wife, Yvonne. They arrange complete East Cape fishing packages for single anglers or groups, taking care of hotel accommodations as well as guided beach, *panga*, or cruiser trips on private or hotel cruisers. Other activities like diving, kayaking, and whale-watching can be arranged for family members who don't fish.

Entertainment and Events
LORD OF THE WINDS COMPETITION
The annual **Lord of the Winds Competition** (www.lordofthewindbaja.com) is a kiteboarding event that takes place over five days every January. The competition brings riders from around the world who participate in the many kiteboarding and SUP events.

Food
MEXICAN
Serving typical Mexican dishes and combo plates, ★ **Campestre Triny** (20 de Noviembre, tel. 624/124-8067, 2pm-10pm daily, mains US$11-16) has a friendly staff and makes great margaritas. They offer both indoor and outdoor seating. The fresh grilled fish is usually a good bet for an excellent meal. They will also prepare your own catch.

SEAFOOD
El Barrilito (20 de Noviembre, tel. 624/121-5856, lunch and dinner daily, mains US$6-12) has many delicious Mexican and seafood options like *molcajetes,* ceviche, and coconut shrimp served in a casual *palapa* setting. Happy hour is every day 3pm-7pm with

Kiteboarders flock to Los Barriles in the winter.

Smokey's Grill and Cantina

Ruiz Gonzalez, no tel., 10am-8pm daily, mains US$8-15) is the perfect casual spot if you're craving a quick bite of ceviche, *aguachile,* fish tacos, or grilled shrimp. Ask the chef what she recommends if you're looking for the fresh catch or a unique dish.

Don't miss stopping by **Tortilleria Klinton** (Avenida de la Juventud, tel. 624/144-4499, 6am-10am Mon.-Sat., 6am-9am Sun., US$1/dozen tortillas) to watch the women making tortillas and to pick up fresh flour tortillas to take with you.

INTERNATIONAL

Don't let the sports bar atmosphere, expat crowd, or the throng of ATVs parked out in the lot steer you away from **Smokey's Grill and Cantina** (20 de Noviembre, no tel., 11am-10pm daily, mains US$7-12). This restaurant serves large portions of great food made from fresh ingredients. The extensive menu features pastas, sandwiches, build-your-own-burgers, and the option to have them prepare your fresh-caught fish. Don't miss the tasty jalapeño poppers to start. With a half dozen flat-screen TVs, occasional live music, and a fun casual atmosphere, the place is usually packed with locals and tourists who cruise up on their four-wheelers or stumble upon the place during their explorations along the main drag.

If you're craving pizza, head to **Lighthouse Pizzeria** (Plaza del Pueblo, tel. 624/130-2222, noon-10pm Wed.-Mon., pizzas US$8-17). In addition to pizzas, they have hot deli sandwiches, pastas, meatball sandwiches, and salads. It's a casual deli setting with a few tables inside and plenty of outdoor seating as well.

Right on the beach and popular with locals and expats is ★ **Lazy Daze Beach Bar** (no tel., 10am-8pm), serving cold beers, great margaritas and Bloody Marys, and pub fare. This casual spot is an inviting place to come spend the afternoon in the sand playing volleyball and corn hole or watching the kiteboarders. The owner, Rexe, is the mother of motocross superstar Carey Hart (married to the singer Pink) and creates an enjoyable and

half-priced drinks. This is a great place to bring kids, as there's a small playground outside.

Specializing in seafood, ★ **La Terraza de German** (Valentin Ruz, 5:30pm-midnight Thurs.-Tues., mains US$8-12) also has meat, chicken, and taco dishes on the menu, which varies depending on what fresh seafood is available. There's a lovely second-floor outdoor terrace, and all of the food is cooked on a charcoal grill at one end of the patio.

TACO STANDS AND *ANTOJITOS*

Great for a casual breakfast or lunch, **El Viejo** (20 de Noviembre, no tel., 8am-3pm Mon.-Sat., breakfast US$3-5, tacos US$1-2) has a central location downtown with comfortable outdoor seating under the *palapa.* For breakfast, there's a large selection of egg dishes like huevos rancheros or omelettes, in addition to pancakes and *chilaquiles.* The taco selection includes clam, scallop, shrimp, fish, chicken, or beef.

Specializing in seafood, **El Pirata** (Valentin

You'll need a reservation if you want to eat at the new **La Casita** (Santa Teresa, tel. 612/145-0192, noon-10pm Tues.-Sun., mains US$8-16), opened by the same owners as the beloved La Casita restaurant in Todos Santos. They specialize in sushi but also offer a variety of dishes like fresh salads, mango shrimp, New York strip, and pastas.

CAFÉS

For house-roasted, fair trade coffee, head to **Caffé Encinalito** (17 Costa Brava, www.caffeencinalito.com, 7am-2pm daily Nov.-Apr.). Here, customers will find hand-pulled espresso (the beans come from Nayarit, Mexico) served in a sweet outdoor setting with chairs, pillows, and hammocks for lounging. There's free wireless Internet, and they also serve small bites like homemade granola and baked goods.

For some of the best breakfast in town go to ★ **Roadrunner Café & Bakery** (Plaza del Pueblo 5, tel. 624/124-8038, www.roadrunnercafe.com.mx, 7am-4:30pm Mon.-Fri., 7am-2pm Sat.-Sun.). They serve hearty egg dishes and fresh pastries from their bakery, along with great coffee for breakfast anytime.

Fresh salads and sandwiches are available for lunch. There's a classic diner setting inside or a large shady patio outside.

Known for their gooey, cinnamon sticky buns, **Caleb's Café** (20 de Noviembre, tel. 624/141-0531, 7:30am-3pm Tues.-Sat., mains US$4-7) serves breakfast until closing and also has a lunch menu. Located on the main drag in town, it's a good spot for people-watching.

Accommodations
HOTELS

If you've always wanted to spend the night in a tepee, ★ **Captain Nemo's Landing** (North Beach, tel. 624/124-8078, toll-free U.S. tel. 800/657-1664, www.captainnemoslanding.com, casita US$48, tepee US$35, camping US$25) will afford you that opportunity. They also offer regular *casitas* as well as camping. In addition to accommodations, they provide a wide range of activities like kiteboarding lessons, fishing, kayaking, horseback riding, and ATV rentals.

Located centrally in town with 20 rooms, **Los Barriles Hotel** (20 de Noviembre, tel. 624/141-0024, www.losbarrileshotel.com, US$80) offers spacious, basic, neat accommodations that all look over the pool. You won't get beachfront here, but the beach is within

Fair trade coffee is served at Caffé Encinalito.

THE EAST CAPE
LOS BARRILES AND VICINITY

walking distance and there's a nice pool area with a *palapa* bar. The hotel offers secure parking and has a helpful staff and management team.

Just steps from the beach, **Agave Hotel y Cantina** (formerly Casa Miramar Hotel, U.S. tel. 760/275-0339, www.agavehotelandcantina.com, US$115, three-night minimum) in a large house outside of town operates more like a vacation rental with property managers who do not stay on-site. There are nine rooms available, and guests can choose from standard rooms, suites, or a separate beachfront casita. There's a pool on the property, and they can help arrange a number of activities for guests such as ATV or horseback riding.

The Van Wormer Resorts operate two hotels in Los Barriles. **Hotel Playa del Sol** (20 de Noviembre, tel. 624/141-0044, www.vanwormerresorts.com, US$130 meals included) has a great location on the beach just off of the main drag in town. Room rates include three meals a day, and there's a bar on the property as well. The 26 rooms are a bit dated and there are no televisions in the rooms, but there's a nice pool area and beachfront views. Kiteboarding and windsurfing equipment is available for rent, as are bicycles. They have their own sportfishing fleet with cruisers, super *pangas,* and English-speaking captains.

The larger Van Wormer property just south of Hotel Playa del Sol is **Palmas de Cortez** (tel. 624/141-0044, www.vanwormerresorts.com, US$140-160). The hotel offers 50 rooms, an infinity-edge pool, swim-up bar, and hot tub. An optional meal plan can be purchased for US$37/day to include breakfast, lunch, and dinner. There are a number of activities to choose from such as golf, the spa, ATV rentals, and excursions. While it provides some of the nicest accommodations for the area, the property is older and disappoints many who are looking for true resort lodgings like those found in Los Cabos.

Popular with anglers, **Martin Verdugo's Beach Resort** (20 de Noviembre, tel. 624/141-0054, www.verdugosbeachresort.com, US$85-95) is located right on the beach

in Los Barriles. The rooms are small and basic but have air-conditioning and some have fridges and kitchenettes. There's also an RV park and campground (US$17 for dry camping, US$23 for RV with hookup). They have a fleet of super *pangas* and 28-foot super cruisers for fishing.

RV PARKS AND CAMPGROUNDS
In addition to **Martin Verdugo's Beach Resort,** there are a few other options for RV parks and campgrounds.

If you have a big rig, you'll want to head to **East Cape RV Resort** (20 de Noviembre, tel. 624/141-0231, www.eastcaperv.com, US$35, discounts for longer stays) where there's lots of room and 30-amp power. The property is nice with palm trees and vegetation throughout. Wi-Fi is available around the property, and there's a swimming pool and laundry facilities. The location is great for walking to restaurants, markets, and the beach. The owners have two sportfishing boats and can also help arrange day-trip excursions.

Playa Norte RV Park (20 de Noviembre, U.S. tel. 425/252-5952, www.playanortervpark.com, US$22-33) sits on 5 hectares of beachfront property just north of Los Barriles. They have full services like municipal water, power (30 amps), septic, laundry, free wireless Internet, and the waterfront **Gecko Restaurant.** The park features 60 rental sites, 20 of which are waterfront. There's also a designated caravan area. Large pull-through sites will accommodate rigs up to 21 meters long and 10 meters wide. Sites for tent camping are also available. Kids and pets are welcome, and there's even an on-site veterinarian clinic. The Windsurfer's Club is located waterfront for quick beach access.

Services
For medical and dental services, the **East Cape Health Center** (Plaza Libertad 1, tel. 624/124-8203, www.eastcapemedical.com, 9am-5pm Mon.-Fri., 8am-2pm Sat.) is your local clinic. They have a 24/7 emergency phone line.

BUENA VISTA

Just south of Los Barriles is the quieter and smaller community of Buena Vista. There's no town center here as the community is a collection of a few hotels and beachfront houses. Because of the remote location, hotels in Buena Vista offer meal plans for guests. The peaceful area attracts anglers, families, and expats who come to fish and relax.

Outstanding sportfishing and true relaxation await you at ★ **Rancho Leonero** (Km. 103.5, tel. 624/141-0216, toll-free U.S. tel. 800/646-2252, www.rancholeonero.com, US$202-267). This intimate and rustic property is dappled with palm trees, large lawns, and *palapa*-roofed structures that will make you feel like you're spending time in a natural paradise. There are 34 rooms, a pool area, and restaurant and bar. They have a large fishing fleet ranging from super *pangas* to large cruisers. The whole family will enjoy activities ranging from fishing, snorkeling, diving, and stand-up paddleboarding to just relaxing in a poolside hammock. There's also a small gym on the property. Breakfast, lunch, and dinner are all included in your room stay.

The family-run ★ **Hotel Buena Vista Beach Resort** (Km. 105, www.hotelbuenavista.com, US$145-185) offers 40 Mediterranean-style bungalows tucked into lush grounds and set on a beautiful beach. This is a great spot to bring the family to enjoy sportfishing, snorkeling and diving, or relaxing in a beach cabana. The property sits on an underground river of natural hot springs that run out into the Sea of Cortez, creating the soothing tropical paradise. Guests of all ages will enjoy the pool that has a *palapa* swim-up bar, large Jacuzzi, and water volleyball. You can book your room with just breakfast included or with all meals included.

Built in 1952, the historic **Rancho Buena Vista** (Km. 106, tel. 624/141-0177, US$80) is the oldest fishing resort along the East Cape. Situated on a beautiful point, the property was once the premier destination for anglers back in its heyday. Today, the hotel is still in operation but currently a shadow of its former self. Just a portion of the rooms are being used, but the pool is kept in great condition and the bar is open (the restaurant is closed). Rooms are basic but clean with Saltillo tiles and hammocks hanging outside. Today the resort attracts mostly Mexican families.

For more budget-friendly accommodations in Buena Vista, **Ramadas Sol y Mar** (Km. 105, tel. 624/141-0038, www.bajaramada.com, US$37, two-night minimum)

the beach in Buena Vista

offers four well-equipped *ramadas* (yurts). All yurts have views of the Sea of Cortez along with showers, toilets, sinks, mini-fridges, propane stoves, and a double or queen-size bed. Outdoor soaking tubs can be filled with the warm, natural springwater that comes from underground.

PUNTA PESCADERO

Fifteen kilometers north of Los Barriles is the small town of Punta Pescadero with private homes and a few options for accommodations. The area attracts anglers and is a good snorkeling spot as well. The dirt road out to Pescadero can be rough at times, so be sure to ask locally about recent conditions.

The boutique **Hotel los Pescaderos** (Colonia Buenos Aires, tel. 624/121-8786, www.fisheastcape.com, US$107) is a charming spot for anglers and families. Fishing charters here are less expensive than you'll find at the bigger hotels in Los Barriles. There's a pool, restaurant, and bar on the property. The beach is a 5- to 10-minute walk away. Continental breakfast is included with your stay.

The remote **Punta Pescadero Paradise Hotel & Villas** (Camino de Los Barriles al Cardonal Km. 14, tel. 612/175-0860, www.puntapescaderoparadise.com, US$129) has 24 villa-suites with beautiful views of the Sea of Cortez. There's a nice pool, bar, and restaurant. If you stay more than three nights, you have the option of including all meals with your room price. The hotel can arrange for transportation to and from Los Cabos airport, for US$300.

EL CARDONAL

North of Punta Pescadero, El Cardonal is located on the south end of Bahía de los Muertos, 23 kilometers north of Los Barriles. El Cardonal is a small, sleepy fishing village on the Sea of Cortez, with not much of a town to offer travelers, but there are a few accommodations.

With five modern and well-appointed suites for rent, **Las Terrazas del Cortés** (El Cardonal, tel. 612/180-3225, www.lasterrazasdelcortes.com.mx, US$80-100) also has a new pool. They can help arrange for activities like horseback riding, kayaking, and ATV riding. Restaurant **Cielito Lindo** on the property serves traditional Mexican dishes.

El Cardonal's Hideaway (tel. 612/348-9793, www.elcardonal.net, US$79) has six hotel rooms as well as camping and RV space with full hookups. Rooms are basic and a bit dated, but the anglers who frequent the spot don't seem to mind. There's free kayaking as well as a restaurant and bar.

Parque Nacional Cabo Pulmo and Vicinity

Parque Nacional Cabo Pulmo is one of the most popular destinations for scuba diving and snorkeling on the peninsula. With the living coral reef and an abundance of sealife, it's no wonder that the area is a highly protected national park. Divers and snorkelers flock to see the colorful tropical fish, moray eels, octopus, lobster and sea lions. This region has been fighting back large development for years and so far remains occupied mostly by small family-run hotels and dive shops.

The area that surrounds Cabo Pulmo is mostly centered on the nearby beaches and the East Cape coastal road, Camino Cabo Este. The road departs from Mexico 1 at kilometer 93 and heads east to the coast. It then follows the coast along the East Cape and reconnects with Mexico 1 at San José del Cabo. The road is paved for a few kilometers along the northern part until La Ribera, and for a few kilometers out of San José del Cabo along the southern part. There have been plans for over a decade to pave the entire road, but for now, most stretches remain dirt.

CABO PULMO

One of only three coral reefs in North America, the Cabo Pulmo reef is 5,000 years old and the only living coral reef in the Sea of Cortez. The marine reserve was established in 1995 to protect the reef, and in 2005, UNESCO recognized it as a World Heritage Site. There are eight separate fingers of the reef, four close to shore and the other four out in the bay. The reef begins just a few meters off the shore, which makes Cabo Pulmo an extremely appealing dive and snorkel spot. Commercial and sportfishing are banned within the park.

The waters here are teeming with marinelife, and divers and snorkelers have the ability to see sea turtles, dolphin, parrot fish, angelfish, damselfish, mobula rays, sharks, and whales. Large schools of tropical fish provide impressive sights for those who explore this part of the Sea of Cortez.

The little town of Cabo Pulmo is completely off the grid. The rustic, dusty town is inhabited by a small group of Mexicans and expats who operate the dive shops, accommodations, and restaurants in town. There are not many services here (no ATMS or gas stations) and just a handful of small lodging options and restaurants. Travelers who visit are usually divers or those looking for a remote and peaceful escape.

Beaches
LOS ARBOLITOS

Five kilometers south of town, **Los Arbolitos** is the best beach in the area for snorkeling. There aren't many services out here, so if you don't have your own snorkel and mask, you'll need to rent one in town before coming out to Los Arbolitos. There are primitive bathroom and shower facilities. You'll need to pay US$2 to park your car and for access to the facilities.

PLAYA LA SIRENITA

Also known as Dinosaur Egg Beach or Los Chopitos, this beach is difficult to access. **Playa La Sirenita** can only be reached by kayak, boat, or from a walking path from Los Arbolitos. The attractive narrow beach has white sand speckled by rocks. Hidden at the base of a cliff, the beach has protected waters that provide an excellent area for snorkeling around the rocks just offshore.

a tour boat departing from the beach access in Cabo Pulmo

LOS FRAILES

When the winds kick up in the afternoons, divers and snorkelers head to **Bahía de Los Frailes.** Nine kilometers south of Bahía Cabo Pulmo, this sheltered bay provides a calm location for diving. The long beach has a few *palapas* for shade, but otherwise very few services. Snorkeling and diving take place at the northern part of the beach where the rocky point is. Camping is allowed, and this is a popular spot for dry camping and RVers.

El Camino Rural Costero

Laguna Salina

Sea of Cortez
(Gulf of California)

La Ribera

Salinas Punta
Colorada

La Trinidad

Punta Colorada
Punta Colorada

Matanza

Punta Arena

Miramar

Los Mangles

**Parque Marina
Nacional Cabo Pulmo**

Cabo Pulmo

CABO PULMO

La Buquita

San Miguel

Banco
Gorda

Los Frailes

Cabo Frailes

0   2 mi

© AVALON TRAVEL   0   2 km

Recreation
★ SNORKELING

Because the coral reef begins just a few meters from the shoreline, it's possible to snorkel directly from shore at Cabo Pulmo without having to take a boat out to reach the good spots. **Los Arbolitos,** about five kilometers south of town, is the prime spot for snorkeling off of the beach. If it's too windy at Arbolitos, head down to the more protected **Los Frailes** where the snorkeling is good along the point on the north end of the beach.

If you want to go on an organized snorkeling trip, any of the tour operators that run dive trips can accommodate snorkeling trips as well. There are **stands** and information for tours in town where the beach access is (next to La Palapa restaurant). The tour operators can take you out on boats to certain beaches and spots that you can't access on your own.

Snorkeling trips with **Eco Adventures** (tel. 624/157-4072, www.cabopulmoecoadventures.com, US$45-60) last 2.5 hours and include snorkeling equipment, waters, soft drinks, snacks, the national park entrance fee, and a guide. For those with younger kids, they offer a special device with a Plexiglas viewer that allows them to see underwater without using snorkeling gear.

★ DIVING

There's good scuba diving year-round in Cabo Pulmo, but the best seasons are summer and fall when the visibility is best (30 meters or more) and water temperatures are warm. Divers can find themselves surrounded by large schools of fish like snappers, bigeye jacks, and porkfish. Moray eels, sea turtles, octopus, sharks and manta rays are also common sights. Guided drift diving is how most tours operate, with divers drifting along with the current and the captain following with the boat.

In the center of town, **Cabo Pulmo Beach Resort** (tel. 624/141-0726, www.cabopulmo.com) is a PADI-certified dive center. They have well-maintained gear and professional and experienced guides who can handle beginning to advanced divers. They operate a hotel as well, so they offer complete packages including accommodations, food, and diving.

With a stand near the beach access in town, **Cabo Pulmo Sport Center** (tel. 624/157-9795, www.cabopulmosportcenter.com) offers dive tours that start at US$95 for one dive. They also handle snorkeling tours, equipment rental, sportfishing, kayaking, and whale-watching. In case you want to video your underwater adventure, they also rent GoPros.

Cabo Pulmo Divers (tel. 612/157-3381, www.cabopulmodivers.com) and **Cabo Pulmo Watersports** (tel. 624/176-2618, www.cabopulmowatersports.com) are two more options for dive operators.

Food

Because of the remote location, restaurant prices in Cabo Pulmo can be unexpectedly high since everything needs to be brought in. During the summer, restaurants will likely have a weekly schedule where they are closed more days than other parts of the year, but there is always at least one restaurant in town that will be open on any given day.

In the center of the action next to the beach access in town, **La Palapa** (tel. 624/130-0195, noon-9pm, mains US$5-12) is a great place to grab a cold beer and some food after returning from a day of snorkeling or diving. The ocean views and casual atmosphere make it a popular spot for hanging out and enjoying some shrimp or tacos with a margarita.

Nancy Hyzer, the owner of **Nancy's Restaurant** (8am-9pm Mon.-Sat., mains US$7-12) has been a fixture in Cabo Pulmo for 24 years. Her casual restaurant features classic Mexican and fresh seafood dishes like fish guajillo and garlic shrimp. All of the produce comes from a local organic co-op. Nancy also has two *casitas* for rent (US$37-44).

Opposite the road near Nancy's, **El Caballeros** (no tel., 7am-10pm Fri.-Wed., mains US$6-12) is open for breakfast, lunch, and dinner serving homemade Mexican food. This is one of the best spots in town for breakfast and a good cup of coffee. There's also a small store selling an assortment of groceries and snacks.

With a popular Saturday night buffet, **Tito's Bar and Restaurant** (no tel., US$8-11) is also known for serving great margaritas. They're open for breakfast, lunch, and dinner, serving traditional Mexican fare along with cold beer and a selection of mixed drinks. They accept cash only.

Located on the second story of the

When the wind is strong at Cabo Pulmo, snorkelers and divers head to Los Frailes.

turquoise Cabo Pulmo Dive Center, **Coral Reef Restaurant** (mains US$14-17) is open for lunch and dinner. They have a good happy hour, and there are flat-screen satellite TVs for watching sports. Patrons enjoy nice ocean views, but many people feel like the prices are a bit expensive for what you get.

Accommodations

Rustic charm is the standard in Cabo Pulmo, so visitors shouldn't expect to find fancy resorts or large hotels. Accommodations here are small, with only a few rooms available at each property. The entire town is off-grid, relying on solar (and generators as backups), so air-conditioning is not available at most places. If visiting in summer, take this into consideration. Many accommodations offer kitchenettes or access to kitchens, but be sure to buy groceries before getting to Cabo Pulmo where there are no large markets.

Exhibiting the peaceful and unpretentious character that Cabo Pulmo is known for, ★ **Baja Bungalows** (www.bajabungalows. com, US$85-95) is a welcoming and comfortable place to stay. They have a convenient location that's close to the Sea of Cortez, beaches for snorkeling, and local restaurants. They offer snorkel and beach gear for guest use.

Kent and Veronica are wonderful hosts, providing guests with helpful information, personal attention, and great recommendations.

In the center of town, **Cabo Pulmo Beach Resort** (tel. 624/141-0726, www.cabopulmo. com, US$145) has a pool on the property and villas with full kitchens. There's also a dive shop where diving and snorkeling tours are arranged as well as surfing and mountain biking excursions.

With three suites, **El Encanto de Cabo Pulmo** (www.encantopulmo.com, US$105-125) has a convenient location close to dive shops, beaches, and restaurants. Air-conditioning, which can be difficult to find at other places in town, is available here for an extra charge. The colorful and eclectic decor includes folk art that has been collected over the years.

Information and Services

Because it's off the grid and caters to a very small population, services are minimal in Cabo Pulmo. There are no banks or ATMs here and very few places accept credit cards, so it's important to get cash in Los Barriles or La Ribera. The nearest Pemex gas station is in La Ribera. Groceries, a health center, and other services can be found in Los Barriles.

Los Arbolitos is the best beach for snorkeling in Cabo Pulmo.

LA RIBERA

La Ribera is the last town on the Camino Cabo Este with municipal water and power (and paved roads), before heading out to the coast. There are some services like Pemex gas stations, OXXO convenience stores, an ATM, and small markets. The small town is home to local fishers, ranchers, and farmers.

A few large developments are taking shape along the coast. Many locals and preservationists are fighting to halt large developments, and the area is caught in a perpetual struggle between developers wanting to make it an extension of Los Cabos and those who want to preserve the natural beauty and peace of the region. **Costa Palmas** (formerly Cabo Rivera, www.costapalmas.com) is a 400-hectare beachfront development planned to open in 2018 at the same time as the **Four Seasons Resort Los Cabos,** a 285-slip marina, an 18-hole golf course, 7 hectares of orchards and farms, and its own beach and yacht club.

Just east of La Ribera is Punta Colorada, at the southern point of Bahía de las Palmas. The Punta Colorada resort is currently closed.

Food and Accommodations

There isn't much in terms of accommodations in La Ribera, but **Cabanas Vista La Ribera** (Carrera a Cabo Pulmo Km. 13.5, tel. 624/172-7021, www.vistalaribera.com, US$150, three-night minimum) is the nicest option. They have four *casitas*, all nicely decorated with modern features and offering mini-refrigerators, microwaves, and air-conditioning. You aren't right on the sea here, but there's a nice outdoor space with a pool, lounge chairs, and fire pit. All-inclusive dining packages are available for guests through the on-site **restaurant** (11am-9pm daily, US$8-15) that serves Mexican plates and fresh seafood. The restaurant is also open to the public.

For campers and RVers, **La Trinidad** (16 de Septiembre, tel. 624/158-9837, www.

latrinidadrvranch.com, US$25 for RV, US$15 for camping) is an RV Park with a restaurant and bar on property. Their spaces offer full hookups for RVs up to 12 meters in length. They can accommodate tent camping as well. Guests have access to clean bathrooms and showers, wireless Internet, barbecue areas, laundry facilities, and a pool with poolside bar. The **restaurant** (open for lunch Mon.-Thurs. and dinner Fri.-Sat.) boasts some of the best food in the region, and there's often live entertainment.

BOCA DE LA VINORAMA

In between Cabo Pulmo and San José del Cabo is a beautiful and remote stretch of coast, home to a number of great surf breaks, gorgeous empty beaches, and a few services along the way. Those who have 4-wheel drive and a sense of adventure can drive the coastal Camino Cabo Este that goes from San José del Cabo through Cabo Pulmo and up to La Ribera where it meets up with Mexico 1. It's best to check with locals about the condition of the road before deciding to take this route, as the southern part between San José del Cabo and Boca de la Vinorama can be in rough condition. There's a large community of expensive beachfront homes here and a project to pave the roads has lasted from San José del Cabo a few kilometers east. Once the pavement ends, the washboard dirt roads begin. Easier access to this stretch of coast can be had via an inland route that goes through the tiny village of Palo Escopeta.

The inland route meets the coastal road right near **VidaSoul Hotel** (1000 Camino Cabo Este, tel. 624/142-1165, U.S. tel. 323/431-8225, www.vidasoul.com, US$160). The impeccably modern and sleek hotel grew out of what started as a small *palapa* serving beer and tacos to surfers who came to the nearby Punta Perfecta break. There are now 16 rooms in the eco-lodge (they run on solar) with floor to ceiling windows, ocean views, polished concrete construction, and features like rain showerheads, iPod docks, and 400-thread-count sheets. They still serve food and beer in the restaurant on the property at the **Crossroads Bar and Restaurant.** There's a pool on the property and air conditioning in the rooms. The prime beach location and remote site make this a wonderful spot to relax and escape.

Travelers looking for a secluded stay in paradise will find it at ★ **Villa del Faro** (Camino Cabo Este Km. 65, no tel., www.villadelfaro.net, US$190-340). The 5 hectares of lush grounds look out onto stunning private beaches. Tucked into the exquisite oasis are a main house and a number of *casitas* with architecture reminiscent of a mix between a Mexican hacienda and an Italian villa. An afternoon lounging around the pool will make you feel as though you're vacationing at a private mansion along the Italian Riviera. This off-the-grid eco-lodge is a truly magnificent retreat where guests can walk or swim on the secluded beach, hike into the nearby arroyo, or watch the gray and humpback whales go by. There are eight options for accommodations ranging from the large Casa Alberca pool house to the rustic stone cottage right on the beach. The property was originally built as a family's retreat, and the operation is still family-run today. They have a restaurant on-site, and a full breakfast is included with your stay. Table d'hôte dinners are available upon request.

If you're in the area, don't miss a stop at the goat dairy at **Whitt's End Ranch** (www.whittsendorganicgoatdairy.com, 9am-4pm Thurs.-Tues.), an off-the-grid micro farm offering free-range goat milk, cheese, pastured poultry and eggs. You can swing by any day but Wednesday to see the operation and purchase the fresh organic artisan products that are created right on the ranch. The best day to stop by for fresh product is Tuesday, before stock goes out to local markets on Wednesday.

the pool at Villa del Faro

Sierra de la Laguna and Vicinity

Inland from the beaches of the East Cape, travelers will find a very different terrain within the steep mountains and lush green hillsides of the Sierra de la Laguna. The rich mountains are home to waterfalls, hot springs, and plenty of hiking areas. Offering some of the least-explored terrain on the peninsula, the Sierra are a UNESCO-designated biosphere reserve and home to a variety of different ecosystems. There are a few little towns scattered along the foothills that provide some services and access to the mountains.

MIRAFLORES

In the foothills of the Sierra del la Laguna sits the small agricultural town of Miraflores. The town has a source of natural springwater and is extremely lush with mangoes, avocados, and pitayas growing everywhere. There's one paved road in this quaint village, the rest of the roads are all dirt.

The Sierra de la Laguna provides a backdrop for the colonial buildings, a town plaza, a cultural center, and a number of small markets. This is not a town that's centered on tourism—there are no hotels here and very few tourist services. It is however, a lovely glimpse into local life in Baja Sur. The entrance to Miraflores is at kilometer 71 on Mexico 1. There's a Pemex gas station on the highway. The wide paved road will lead you west from the highway into town.

The welcoming restaurant **Los Agaves** (tel. 624/161-2234, 9am-5pm daily, mains US$6-12) is definitely worth a stop if you're passing through Miraflores. The open-air *palapa* serves Mexican dishes like fajitas, enchiladas, and tacos. If the lobster tacos are on special, they are definitely worth a try. Don't miss the piña colada made with locally grown pitaya. Cosme, the friendly owner, is a wealth of knowledge about the area and can direct you to a guide if you want to venture into the Sierra de la Laguna.

Near the entrance of town is the small **Talabartería** (open daily), a tannery and leatherworks shop. Visitors can go inside to see them at work with the leather. They have a small selection of leatherworks for sale like belts, bags, bracelets, and wallets.

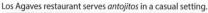

Los Agaves restaurant serves *antojitos* in a casual setting.

Sierra de la Laguna and Vicinity

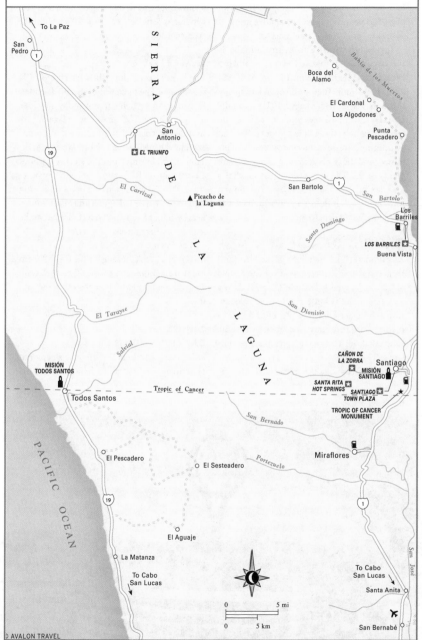

To La Paz

San Pedro

SIERRA

Boca del Alamo

Bahía de los Muertos

El Cardonal
Los Algodones

Punta Pescadero

San Antonio

EL TRIUNFO

DE

El Carrizal

Picacho de la Laguna

San Bartolo

San Bartolo

Los Barriles

Santo Domingo

LOS BARRILES

Buena Vista

LA

El Tarayse

San Dionisio

Salvial

LAGUNA

MISIÓN
TODOS SANTOS

CAÑON DE
LA ZORRA

Santiago

MISIÓN
SANTIAGO

SANTA RITA
HOT SPRINGS

SANTIAGO
TOWN PLAZA

Tropic of Cancer

Todos Santos

San Bernado

TROPIC OF CANCER
MONUMENT

PACIFIC

El Pescadero

El Sesteadero

Portezuelo

Miraflores

OCEAN

El Aguaje

San José

La Matanza

To Cabo
San Lucas

To Cabo
San Lucas

Santa Anita

0   5 mi

0   5 km

San Bernabé

© AVALON TRAVEL

Behind town is a paved road that heads west to the *ejido* (communal land) of **Boca de la Sierra.** There, travelers can park their car, pay US$3 per group, and walk in five minutes to natural pools set in a palm oasis.

Just south of Miraflores in Caduaño is the large and impressive **Parque Acuático Wet Fun** (Mexico 1 Km. 65, tel. 624/188-0518, 10am-6pm Tues.-Sun., open late spring through early fall, kids ages 3-10 US$8, adults US$11). Kids of all ages will enjoy splashing around on huge waterslides, pirate ships, and swimming pools. The grounds are well maintained, and the pools are very clean. There are plenty of shaded areas with tables and chairs for relaxing. No food or beverages are allowed into the park, but there's a grill and snack bar inside with inexpensive prices.

TROPIC OF CANCER

At kilometer 81.5, between Miraflores and Santiago where drivers pass over the Tropic of Cancer (currently latitude 23.26°N) there's a nice new facility built in 2013 worth a quick stop. There are a few sculptures and monuments, a small open-air chapel, and some shops that sell artisan crafts from nearby villages. The Tropic of Cancer, also called the Northern Tropic, is the most northerly line of latitude where the sun appears directly overhead at its culmination. This event only occurs once a year, on the Northern Solstice, which happens between June 20 and June 22 each year.

SANTIAGO

The largest town along the eastern foothills is Santiago. The town was originally founded as a mission settlement and today subsides on agriculture. The small town plaza is surrounded by colonial architecture and a modern church resides on the old mission spot. The water coming from the sierras supplies a large natural lake in town, shaded by palm trees. This is a great starting point for hiking into the Sierra de la Laguna and also home to nearby hot springs and waterfalls that make for interesting and easy day trips.

The town is off of the highway and easy to miss if you aren't looking for the turnoff from Mexico 1 at kilometer 84. You'll head west on a paved road for two kilometers to come into town.

Sights
SANTIAGO TOWN PLAZA
Palm trees and benches line the sleepy but charming town plaza of Santiago. This

the Tropic of Cancer, or Northern Tropic

the Misión Santiago Apóstol Aiñiní in Santiago

picturesque spot is surrounded by beautiful examples of colonial architecture, a post office, Pemex gas station, and a few little markets. It serves as a gathering spot for locals and the venue for events and festivals.

MISIÓN SANTIAGO APÓSTOL AIÑINÍ

In 1721, Padre Ignacio Mario Nápoli set out on an expedition to find a location for a mission between La Paz and Cabo San Lucas. He founded the mission "Santiago de los Coras" in a location he named "Santa Ana" (a few miles south of the town of San Antonio). The project was soon abandoned after the uncompleted church collapsed in a storm, killing many of the people inside. Padre Nápoli eventually rebuilt the mission in 1724 in a new location in the land of the Pericú natives, who called the area Aiñini. The mission was attacked in the giant Pericú Revolt of 1734 and was ruined. The father in residence, Padre Lorenzo Carranco, was killed. Survivors of the attack rebuilt the mission in 1736 (a few

miles south of the 1724 site), but this was eventually abandoned in 1795. A modern church that was built in 1958 still stands on the mission site on the south hill in town. It is often referred to by the mission's first name, **Misión de Santiago de los Coras.**

SANTIAGO ZOO

It seems strange that the small town of Santiago was once the home of Baja California Sur's only zoo. The small facility had endemic animals as well as monkeys, a tiger, a leopard, and a lion. The zoo is currently closed for restoration.

Food and Accommodations

One of the only spots for accommodations in town is the historic **Palomar Restaurant and Bar** (Calzada Maestros Misioneros de 1930, tel. 624/130-2394, restaurant hours 10am-6:30pm Mon.-Sat., 10am-3:30pm Sun., palomarsergio66@hotmail.com, rooms US$38). The current owner, Sergio, is the son of the founder who started the operation in 1966. Palomar has hosted a wealth of Hollywood elite ranging from Barbra Streisand, Harrison Ford, and Susan Sarandon. Santiago used to be home to the best white-winged dove hunting in Baja, a sport that attracted notable figures like Dwight D. Eisenhower, Bing Crosby, and John Wayne, who would arrive via the nearby private airstrip (now closed). Sergio proudly shows off a photo of his mother, Virginia, with Bing Crosby to anyone who asks.

Fruit trees are all around the property—ponderosa lemon, mandarin, almonds, avocado, mango, banana, and coconut. Fruit falls everywhere, giving a lush, overgrown Garden of Eden feel to this peaceful and secluded space. There are five rooms that are very basic but have air-conditioning, and there is wireless Internet on the property. The restaurant and bar open starting at 10am every day. There's also an area for camping.

Another option for accommodations is **Hospedaje San Andres** (24 de Febrero and Francisco J. Mujica, tel. 624/130-2047, US$55),

Santiago to Miraflores

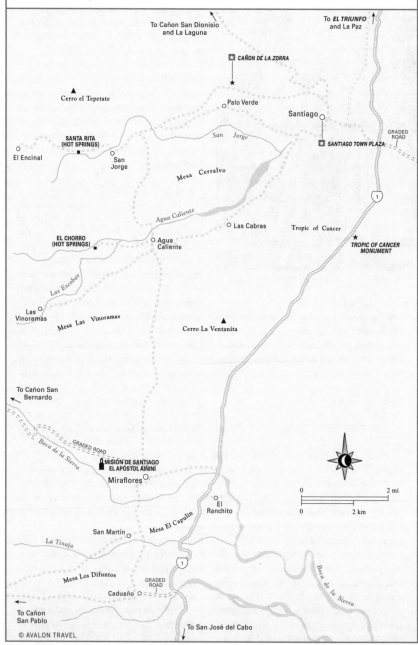

To Cañon San Dionisio
and La Laguna

To *EL TRIUNFO*
and La Paz

✚ *CAÑON DE LA ZORRA*

★

▲ Cerro el Tepetate

○ Palo Verde

Santiago ○

GRADED
ROAD

San Jorge

**SANTA RITA
(HOT SPRINGS)** ■

○ El Encinal

○ San
Jorge

✚ *SANTIAGO TOWN PLAZA*

1

Mesa Cerralvo

Agua Caliente

○ Las Cabras

Tropic of Cancer

★ *TROPIC OF CANCER
MONUMENT*

**EL CHORRO
(HOT SPRINGS)** ■

○ Agua
Caliente

Las Escobas

○ Las
Vinoramas

Mesa Las Vinoramas

▲ Cerro La Ventanita

To Cañon San
Bernardo

Boca de la Sierra

GRADED ROAD

🏛 **MISIÓN DE SANTIAGO
EL APÓSTOL AIÑINÍ**

Miraflores ○

○ El
Ranchito

San Martín ○

Mesa El Capulín

La Tinaja

0 _____ 2 mi

0 _____ 2 km

Mesa Los Difuntos

GRADED
ROAD

Caduaño ○

Boca de la Sierra

To Cañon
San Pablo

To San José del Cabo

© AVALON TRAVEL

which offers basic single or double rooms with air-conditioning, televisions, wireless Internet, and a secure parking lot.

On the road out to Cañon de la Zorra, **Taqueria la Cascada** (no tel., Francisco J. Mujica) serves staples like tacos and carne asada. Right next door is **Tortilleria El Palmar.**

Camping and rustic cabin accommodations are available north and west of Santiago at ranches that are within the Sierra de la Laguna biosphere reserve such as **Rancho Ecológico Sol de Mayo** (tel. 624/130-2055, US$45-75) where access is granted to Cañon de la Zorra, **Rancho la Acacia** (tel. 612/117-1967, US$75 for two-bedroom cabin), and **Rancho Santa Rita** (no tel.US$50) where the hot springs are located.

★ Cañon de la Zorra

Just outside of Santiago is the striking Cañon de la Zorra. The centerpiece of the canyon is an impressive 10-meter waterfall that cascades into natural pools below. It's a great spot for swimming and sunbathing on the rocks. Go in the morning to get the most light as the sun disappears behind the mountains putting the water into shade by early afternoon.

Because the canyon is within the biosphere reserve of the Sierra de la Laguna, a minimal entrance fee must be paid to visit. Access to Cañon de la Zorra is only gained through **Rancho Ecológico Sol de Mayo** (tel. 624/130-2055, US$6) where you will purchase your entry bracelet and be directed to the trail to the waterfall. Ranch owner Prisciliano de la Peña Ruiz is the fifth generation of his family to have lived there on the ranch and if you speak Spanish, he's a wealth of information about the region. Guests can camp at the ranch for US$7. There are also eight *cabanas* for rent (US$47-78) that can hold from two to six people.

To get to the canyon and waterfall from the ranch it's a steep 10-minute hike. There are now steps that have been carved out of the rocks (visitors used to have to use a rope to scale the large rocks to get down to the pools), but even with the steps, it's a moderate hike, and travelers should watch their step.

To get to Sol de Mayo and Cañon de la Zorra, enter the town of Santiago and turn right on Francisco J. Mujica (before you get up to the plaza). Follow the road until the intersection where you'll follow sings for "Sol de Mayo" to make a soft left to go up a small hill. From here, the pavement will end, but the dirt road is in good condition. Continue to

THE EAST CAPE
SIERRA DE LA LAGUNA AND VICINITY

The Palomar Restaurant and Bar has hosted a number of Hollywood celebrities over the years.

follow signs for "Cañon de la Zorra" and "Sol de Mayo" for another 10 kilometers until arriving at Rancho Sol de Mayo.

★ Santa Rita Hot Springs

There are three hot springs areas to visit—Agua Caliente, El Chorro, and Santa Rita. The best is the **Santa Rita Hot Springs** (8am-7pm daily, US$3), set in a lush palm-filled canyon. These natural hot springs have shallow sandy-bottom pools that are nestled in between large boulders and palm trees. It's a beautiful and serene spot to relax for a few hours. The pools are hot, but there's a cold river below where you can cool off if needed. The nearby camping facility has bathrooms and a barbecue area. It's US$6 to camp overnight or US$50 for a cabin. Food and alcohol are not allowed into the hot springs. Santa Rita can be reached either from Cañon de la Zorra or by taking the road in Santiago next to the zoo. You'll head to the *ejido* of San Jorge and then follow signs to Santa Rita. Keep following the power lines overhead. The road is rough, and you'll need a four-wheel-drive vehicle with high clearance in order to make the trek.

SIERRA DE LA LAGUNA

The Sierra de la Laguna is one of the most beautiful and least-explored areas of the peninsula. UNESCO designated the 11,600 hectares of this mountain range a biosphere reserve in 1994. There are more than 900 plant species in the sierra, ranging from cacti to palms. Over 20 percent of them are endemic to the peninsula. As a microclimate, the Sierra de la Laguna receives far more rainfall than any other part of the peninsula, providing a drastic change in scenery from the desert below. The highest peak in the range, Picacho de la Laguna (elev. 2,161 m), is also the highest peak in all of Baja California Sur. The Sierra de la Laguna can be approached either from the East Cape or from the West Cape, depending on the final destination.

The mountains experience heavy rains July through October. November through early spring is the most popular time for hiking. Temperatures can drop below freezing at night during the winter.

There are three access points into the sierra from the eastern side: Cañon San Dionísio from Santiago, Cañon San Bernardo from Miraflores, and Cañon San Pablo from

the road through the Sierra de la Laguna to get to Cañon de la Zorra

Sierra de la Laguna Hiking Trails

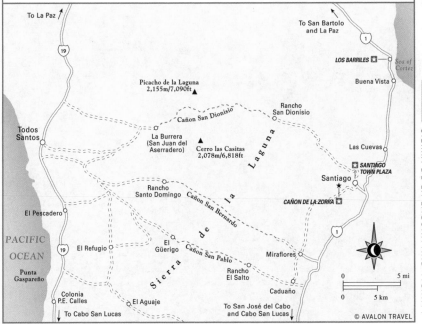

Caduaño. Most hikes use an assortment of trails, canyons, and cow paths that wind through the sierra.

The **Cañon San Dionísio** trail begins at Rancho San Dionísio, in the mouth of the canyon, 23 kilometers from Santiago. Inquire in town about how to get out to the ranch. **Cañon San Bernardo** is the easiest cross-sierra hike, beginning in Boca de la Sierra on the east side of the range and ending with Santo Domingo on the west side. There are permanent water pools that provide drinking water throughout the 22.5-kilometer hike that takes three days to complete.

The most popular overnight hike is to **Picacho de la Laguna,** the lake in the name is now a meadow instead of a pool. This hike is best approached from the western side of the sierras from La Burrera ranch near Todos Santos. This is the only trail in the Sierra de la Laguna that is shown on topo maps. Allow three days for the full round-trip hike.

Trails in the Sierra de la Laguna can be difficult to find and follow. If you aren't an expert or a local who knows your way around, it's better to go with a guide. **Baja Sierra Adventures** (tel. 624/166-8706, www.bajasierradventures.com) leads guided treks through the sierra with a range of day trips and overnight trips.

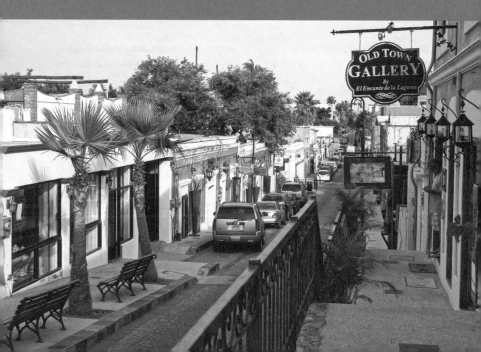

Los Cabos

The iconic rock archway El Arco at the tip of the peninsula marks land's end. This is Los Cabos, the most-recognized destination in Baja.

Los Cabos refers to the region comprising the two cities of San José del Cabo and Cabo San Lucas and the corridor that connects them. This is a Baja completely different from the rest of the peninsula. Yachts fill the marinas and all-inclusive mega-resorts with thousands of rooms line the beaches. Spring breakers flock here for the beach scene and nightlife. Dance clubs and bars are busy until the wee hours of the morning. It's hard to walk down the street in Cabo San Lucas without being prodded to take a boat trip, book a ziplining tour, or buy a T-shirt about tequila shots.

Luxury, relaxation, and fun are the focus here, and Los Cabos does all three things exceptionally well. On the extravagant and lavish side of Los Cabos, jet-setters and celebrities come to escape and play. Rooms at some of the most exclusive resorts can cost at least US$2,000 a night. Golf courses have sweeping views of the Sea of Cortez, spas specialize in indulgent services, and dining can be world-class.

Love it or hate it, this is one of the most popular spots on the Baja peninsula. Because of its worldwide attention, there's no stopping the growth in this region. More and more luxury resorts are planned to open. While it's difficult to call a trip to the area an authentic Mexican experience, it's hard to deny the unique draw that lures over two million visitors each year.

PLANNING YOUR TIME

Most people visit Cabo to enjoy the beaches and take advantage of the all-inclusive resorts. Some tourists don't even leave their hotels during their stay. Depending on how long you need to decompress and relax, a long weekend or a week is plenty. Enjoy day trips to the surrounding areas of the East Cape or Todos Santos.

Many Baja road-trippers who are traveling the peninsula to enjoy the remote settings and natural environment may want to skip Cabo altogether.

Cruise ships coming into the Los Cabos

Previous: sandy beach; historic art district in San José. **Above:** palm trees along Playa Chileno.

Look for ★ to find recommended
sights, activities, dining, and lodging.

Highlights

★ **Plaza Teniente José Antonio Mijares:** The plaza is the heart of the town, surrounded by art galleries, shops, restaurants, boutique hotels, and the mission (page 287).

★ **San José del Cabo's Historic Art District:** Art galleries abound in the historical downtown area of San José del Cabo. On Thursday evenings between November and June the galleries stay open late for the weekly "Gallery Art Walk" (page 290).

★ **Beaches of the Los Cabos Corridor:** The stretch between the two towns of Cabo San Lucas and San José del Cabo is home to some of the most pristine beaches in the area, where visitors enjoy swimming, sunbathing, snorkeling, and just relaxing (page 300).

★ **El Arco:** The signature landmark of Cabo San Lucas is its famous rock archway at the very southern tip of the Baja peninsula where the Pacific Ocean and the Sea of Cortez meet. Travelers can take a boat out to see it up close (page 305).

★ **Lover's Beach:** Accessible only by boat, Lover's Beach is a gorgeous sandy beach on the protected Bahía de Cabo San Lucas (page 308).

★ **Golf:** Golfing has never been more spectacular than at the numerous courses in Los Cabos with beautiful ocean views and a margarita waiting at the clubhouse afterward (page 311).

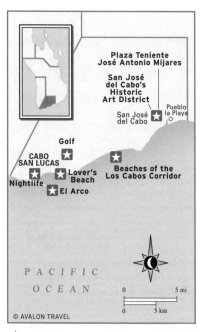

★ **Nightlife:** Spring breakers and the young of heart enjoy clubs where the tequila shots never run out and the party goes until the early morning (page 311).

Best Accommodations

★ **Casa Natalia:** Offering luxury with chic décor, this boutique hotel is just off the plaza and has a pool and restaurant on-site (page 298)

★ **El Delfin Blanco:** Enjoy personal attention, Swedish pancakes, and comfy accommodations for the right price at El Delfin Blanco (page 299)

★ **Hotel El Ganzo:** The understated but hip El Ganzo draws artists, musicians, and trendsetters with its relaxed vibe and chic setting (page 299).

★ **Casa Bella:** This charming hacienda-style boutique hotel in Cabo San Lucas has a prime location near the bustle of town, but also offers a serene and quiet escape (page 317).

★ **The Cape, a Thompson Hotel:** This new resort is making a splash with its sleek urban design, luxurious feel, world-class restaurant, and chic rooftop bar (page 304).

area anchor just out from the marina in Cabo San Lucas and tender passengers to shore (there's no cruise ship port). The drop-off location for passengers is the marina near Sr. Frogs and Soloman's Landing Restaurant.

Many cruise lines only offer a half day in port at Cabo. Excursion companies are well aware of their time parameters and many plan activities to meet the cruise ship timeline. Some cruise lines offer two days in port at Cabo, which means that passengers have the ability to stay out until 9pm on their first evening in port.

GETTING THERE
Car
There are many rental car companies in Los Cabos, most of which are familiar names to U.S. travelers. Even if you do not rent a car at the Los Cabos airport, there are car rental offices in Cabo San Lucas and San José del Cabo as well. Remember that you are legally required to purchase the Mexican auto insurance when renting a car. Liability is the minimum you need, and that will cost US$12 a day. Full coverage can run US$30-50 a day. With many car rental companies, this added insurance will not be included in your initial quote, which can come as quite a surprise when picking up your rental car. With the insurance

added in, expect to pay around US$300-350 a week for a rental car. **Cactus Rent a Car** (tel. 624/146-1839, toll-free U.S. tel. 866/225-9220, www.cactuscar.com) is a local company that will quote you the full price (insurance included) so that there are no unwelcome surprises at pickup. Gas stations and car services are plentiful throughout the area.

Road trippers driving the entire Baja peninsula can reach Los Cabos in a comfortable four days of driving from San Diego. This pace budgets for around six hours of driving a day, straight down the peninsula on Mexico 1. Most road trippers will opt to spend more time making the drive in order to enjoy side trips and to fully experience the activities and offerings of the peninsula along the way. Those who wish to complete the drive from San Diego to Los Cabos in four days could make overnight stops in or around El Rosario, Guerrero Negro, and Loreto.

Air
Most travelers arriving in Los Cabos come by plane. The commercial **Los Cabos International Airport** (SJD, tel. 624/146-5111, www.sjdloscabosairport.com) is near San José del Cabo. Direct flights are available from the United States, Canada, and other areas of Mexico.

Los Cabos

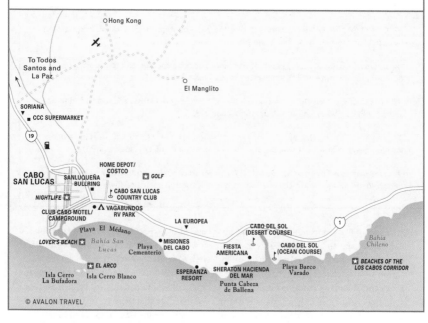

There are shuttles and taxis that run from the airport to your hotel for those who don't plan on renting a car. It takes about 40 minutes by taxi to Cabo San Lucas and will cost about US$80. Many large hotels and resorts have their own airport shuttle service that will be cheaper than a cab. **Ruta del Desierto** (www.rutadeldesierto.travel) is a bus service that will take you to San José or Cabo San Lucas for US$5. You can collect the bus from outside both Terminal 1 and 2 at the airport.

Bus

Aguila (tel. 800/824-8452, www.autobusesaguila.com) and **Autobuses de la Baja California** (ABC, tel. 664/104-7400, www.abc.com.mx) both have services from other cities in Baja California. There are bus terminals in both Cabo San Lucas and San José del Cabo. Tickets can be purchased at the bus station and do not need to be bought in advance, but it's always a good idea to stop by the bus station a day or two before traveling in order to verify the schedule and ticket price.

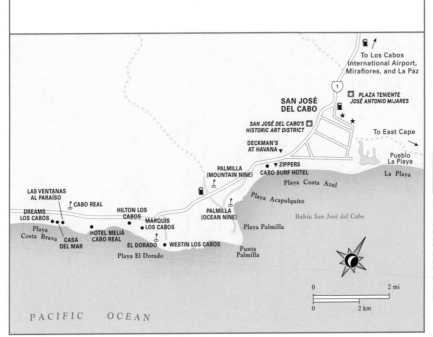

San José del Cabo

For years, San José del Cabo has played the part of low-key counterpart to Cabo San Lucas. The smaller and more laid-back town has a decidedly authentic Mexican feel. While San José has the beaches, resorts, spas, and golfing, it's less developed and more relaxed when compared to its showier and more touristy neighbor. Local life centers around the town plaza and the surrounding streets full of colonial buildings that make up the historic art district. Here travelers will find plenty of renowned restaurants, artisanal shops, and art galleries to enjoy. While there are a few small bars, you won't find any large dance clubs here. Families and couples often prefer this area, where the tranquil town provides a nice dose of culture and the beaches are emptier and more relaxed.

Fishing, golfing, surfing, diving, and snorkeling can be enjoyed nearby. There's also a new marina, Puerto Los Cabos, which is the largest in Mexico and also home to a developing and vibrant community with hotels, restaurants, and plenty of activities.

SIGHTS
★ Plaza Teniente José Antonio Mijares

The heart and pulse of San José is the **Plaza Teniente José Antonio Mijares.** In the center of downtown historic San José, hotels, restaurants, and shops all line the plaza and the surrounding streets. A large Mexican flag flies above expansive plaza that serves as a gathering place for tourists and locals. Town events like music festivals and holiday celebrations all take place here, and on a daily basis, the plaza fills with families in

San José del Cabo

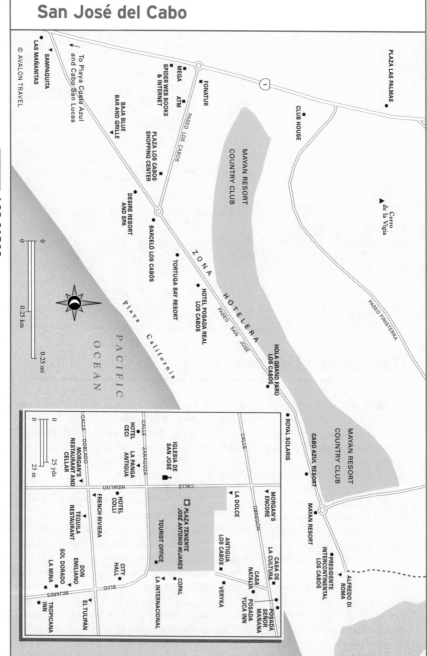

PLAZA LAS PALMAS

CLUB HOUSE

MAYAN RESORT COUNTRY CLUB

Cerro de la Vigía

PASEO FINISTERRA

MAYAN RESORT COUNTRY CLUB

CABO AZUL RESORT

MAYAN RESORT

PRESIDENTE INTERCONTINENTAL LOS CABOS

ALFREDO DI ROMA

PASEO LOS CABOS

MEGA
ATM
SPIDER WEB BOOKS & INTERNET
FONATUR
BAJA BLUE BAR AND GRILLE
PLAZA LOS CABOS SHOPPING CENTER
DESIRE RESORT AND SPA
BARCELÓ LOS CABOS
TORTUGA BAY RESORT
HOTEL POSADA REAL LOS CABOS
ZONA HOTELERA
PASEO SAN JOSÉ
HOLA GRAND FARO LOS CABOS
ROYAL SOLARIS

To Playa Costa Azul and Cabo San Lucas
SAMPAGUITA
LAS MAÑANITAS

Playa California

PACIFIC OCEAN

0   0.25 km
0   0.25 mi

N

CALLE
HOTEL CECI
LA PANGA ANTIGUA
CALLE ZARAGOZA
IGLESIA DE SAN JOSÉ
CALLE

MORGAN'S RESTAURANT AND CELLAR
CALLE DOBLADO
HOTEL COLLI
HIDALGO
PLAZA TENIENTE JOSÉ ANTONIO MIJARES
LA DOLCE
MORGAN'S ENCORE
CASA DE LA CULTURA
OBREGÓN

TEQUILA RESTAURANT
FRENCH RIVIERA
TOURIST OFFICE
ANTIGUA LOS CABOS
CASA NATALIA
POSADA YUCA INN

DON EMILIANO
SOL DORADO
CITY HALL
LA INTERNACIONAL
COPAL
VERYKA
POSADA SEÑOR MAÑANA

LA MINA
EL TULIPÁN
BLVD MIJARES
TROPICANA INN

0   25 yds
0   25 m

Playa California

PASEO SAN JOSÉ

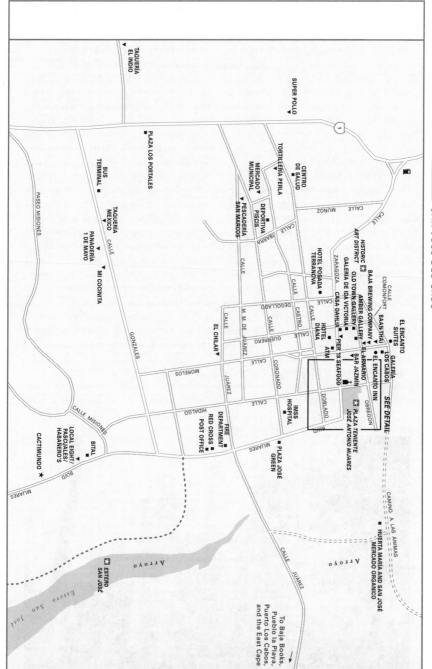

the afternoons. Parents bring their children to play, enjoy ice cream, and to eat tostadas and tamales from small food carts. Just off of the plaza is the large **Boulevard Mijares,** where many restaurants, bars, and shops are located. Dine or drink on the second floor of any of the restaurants or bars lining the boulevard to take in the lively town. The church on the plaza is on the site of the original mission for the area.

Misión San José Del Cabo Añuiti

In 1739, Jesuit Padre Nicolás Tamaral traveled south from the La Purísima mission and started converting the local Pericú. Originally basing his operations on the estuary, Tamaral later moved more inland to a place known as Añuiti. Tamaral worked hard to abolish the practice of polygamy then prevalent among the Pericú. He was unpopular with the locals for this reason, and he lost his life in the Pericú Revolt of 1734. The church that now stands in the plaza was built in 1940 on the old mission site. There's a mosaic over the main entrance that depicts the murder of Tamaral. The church is still actively used today by the San José community. There are daily services in the evening and a mass in English on Sunday at noon. Visitors are welcome, but please be respectful if mass is in progress.

★ Historic Art District

Many of the old historic colonial buildings in downtown San José del Cabo have been renovated into fine art studios and galleries. The vibrant creative scene of the **Historic Art District** includes original paintings, photography, sculptures, and prints from local and international artists. On Thursday nights from November through June, galleries stay open late from 5pm to 9pm for the **Gallery Art Walk** (www.artcabo.com). The art walk has become a don't-miss activity in San José with some galleries offering wine or tequila or the opportunity to see the artist working in their studio. In addition to all of the galleries, a number of local artists who aren't represented will set up booths in the plaza so patrons have the opportunity to buy affordable art from up-and-comers as well. The entire town comes alive, so even those who don't follow the art scene will still enjoy getting out and walking around pre- or post-dinner.

Estero San José

Río San José meets the saltwater of the Sea of Cortez at the **Estero San José.** The estuary

Misión San José del Cabo Añuiti is located on San José del Cabo's plaza.

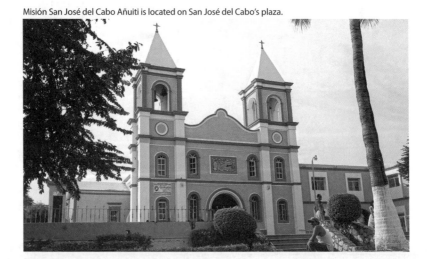

Best Restaurants

★ **El Farallon:** Fine dining, impeccable service, and a champagne bar accompany the incredible views and the waves crashing below (page 316).

★ **Sunset da Mona Lisa:** Get a reservation for sunset to bask in the show over El Arco and the sweeping ocean views (page 303).

★ **El Matador:** This aptly named bullfighting themed restaurant offers high-quality meats with a beautiful patio and live entertainment (page 294).

★ **La Lupita:** Offering unique tacos (like lamb and octopus) and a mezcal menu, this hip restaurant pleases visiting foodies and locals alike (page 294).

★ **Flora's Field Kitchen:** For a unique local experience, visit the garden restaurant where food is made with only the freshest homegrown ingredients (page 295).

★ **Lolita café:** The café features artisan food with a Mexican flare. Healthy eaters will appreciate the wide selection of vegetable dishes (page 297).

is a free attraction since it is a great place to go for a walk anytime to take in the natural habitat left in the area. Birders will enjoy catching sight of the waterbirds that inhabit the estuary like egrets, herons, waterfowl, and osprey. Watch your step as the sidewalks are buckled and washed out after damage from Hurricane Odile. To find the estuary, look for the dirt road turnoff from Boulevard Mijares just inland from the beach.

Puerto Los Cabos Marina

The new and impressive **Puerto Los Cabos Marina** (www.puertoloscabos.com) in San José del Cabo is the home-away-from-home to many of the yachts and boats that come to the Los Cabos region. The 200 slips can hold boats up to 122 meters in length. As Mexico's largest private marina, Puerto Los Cabos is a destination that's home to so much more than just boats. The marina attracts tourists because of a plethora of activities such as Hydro fly boarding, a dolphin experience, an activity center, and a number of restaurants, including The Container Restaurant and Bar. Hotels like the Ritz-Carlton and El Ganzo operate here in Puerto Los Cabos as

well as a Jack Nicklaus and Greg Norman-designed golf course.

Wirikuta Desert Botanical Garden

Just outside the marina, the **Wirikuta Desert Botanical Garden** (www.puertoloscabos.com/the-wirikuta.html, 10am-5pm Mon.-Sat., US$8) is home to over 1,500 varieties of desert plants from around the world. The cacti and plants are arranged in serene geometric patterns that make for beautiful photos. A guide, whom you'll pick up at the entrance, will walk you through the gardens to explain about the plants, and then you're free to wander around on your own. There's a stone sculpture area as well.

BEACHES
La Playita

Now a part of the Puerto Los Cabos development, **La Playita** is a peaceful beach with a beautiful setting. It's great for families because there's a safe roped-off area inside the harbor entrance that's good for swimming or snorkeling. Near the entrance to the marina are nice bathrooms and *palapas*. If you want to spend

Pueblo la Playa

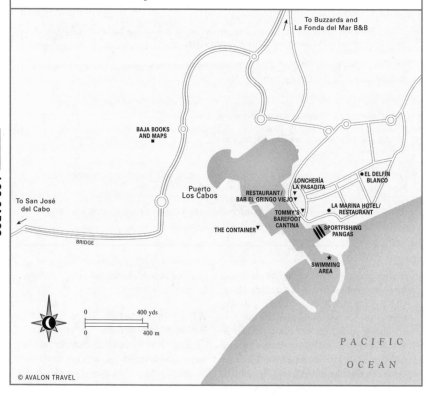

To Buzzards and
La Fonda del Mar B&B

BAJA BOOKS
AND MAPS

To San José
del Cabo

Puerto
Los Cabos

EL DELFÍN
BLANCO

LONCHERÍA
LA PASADITA

RESTAURANT /
BAR EL GRINGO VIEJO

LA MARINA HOTEL/
RESTAURANT

TOMMY'S
BAREFOOT
CANTINA

THE CONTAINER

SPORTFISHING
PANGAS

BRIDGE

SWIMMING
AREA

0   400 yds
0   400 m

PACIFIC

OCEAN

© AVALON TRAVEL

the entire day at the beach, there are nearby restaurants and markets to grab food.

Playa Costa Azul

On the outskirts of San José is **Playa Costa Azul** (Mexico 1, Km. 28.5), one of the premier surfing beaches in the peninsula. It's home to three well-known surf breaks: Zippers, The Rock, and Acapulquito (Old Man's). The Los Cabos Open of Surf is held at Zippers every summer. There are a few restaurants and small hotels here as well as **Costa Azul Surf Shop** (tel. 624/142-2771, www.costa-azul.com. mx), offering board rentals and surf lessons. Swimming isn't advised here, but the beach is popular with joggers and walkers.

RECREATION
Golfing

There are two courses at **Puerto Los Cabos Golf Club** (Bulevar Mar de Cortez, tel. 624/173-9400, www.puertoloscabos.com, US$195): one designed by Jack Nicklaus and the other by Greg Norman. Both courses are only currently nine holes but will eventually be 18 each.

Beginner and expert golfers will enjoy the nine-hole course at **Punta Sur Golf Course** (formerly Mayan Palace, Boulevard San Jose, tel. 624/172-5812, US$63 9 holes, US$98 18 holes) where the prices are more affordable than at other courses in the region.

Which Cabo is for Me?

The name Los Cabos refers to a region comprising three areas: the town of Cabo San Lucas, the nearby town of San José del Cabo and the beach corridor that connects the two. While the area has been so built up that the three appear to blend seamlessly together, each has its own distinct personality:

Cabo San Lucas: Most of the action is in Cabo San Lucas where the tourist areas are teeming with restaurants, souvenir shops, bars, and tour operators peddling you a spot on their next boat to Lover's Beach or ATVing trip in Wild Canyon. This is where the cruise ship passengers disembark to spend the day in port, and with all the large nightclubs and bars, this is where the spring breakers stay to take advantage of the nightlife.

The Corridor: Resort-goers often stay in the corridor. The most expensive and exclusive resorts of the region are found here, as are the most beautiful beaches. Things are spread out in the corridor, which is basically a long string of beachfront resorts. Those seeking more action or nightlife will need to take a taxi into Cabo San Lucas.

San José del Cabo: There's a more authentic Mexican feel to the town of San José del Cabo with its town plaza and historic art district. The vibe is more relaxed and quiet, but you can still find many of the same activities such as golfing, fishing, diving, and surfing. While the town has expanded over the past number of years to accommodate a growing amount of beachfront resorts and timeshares, you can still find fairly affordable accommodations near the historic district in the center of town.

Surfing

Surfers of all levels of experience can find waves at **Playa Costa Azul** (Km. 28.5), one of the premier surfing beaches in the region. There are three breaks here: Acapulquito (Old Man's) has good waves for beginners and longboarders. La Roca (The Rock) is a right break. And Zippers is the most well-known break of Los Cabos, where the Los Cabos Open of Surf takes place every year. **Costa Azul Surf Shop** (tel. 624/142-2771, www.costa-azul.com.mx) offers board rentals, surf lessons, and surf excursion trips.

ENTERTAINMENT AND EVENTS
Nightlife

San José del Cabo doesn't have the nightlife that Cabo San Lucas does. If you're looking for big nightclubs, you won't find them here. But you will find a few friendly bars and a more laid-back scene.

One of the newest hot spots for locals and tourists is **La Osteria** (Alvaro Obregon, tel. 624/146-9696, 6pm-11pm Mon.-Wed., 6pm-3am Thurs.-Sat.). Live Latin, jazz, and Latin rock music is played almost every night. Patrons enjoy margaritas and Mexican wines in the outdoor patio space. The full menu includes dishes like rib eye and *queso fundido.*

Beer lovers will enjoy **Baja Brewing Co.** (Morelos 1227, tel. 624/142-1292, www.bajabrewingcompany.com, noon-midnight Sun.-Wed., noon-2am Thurs.-Sat.), a craft brewery with a restaurant and outdoor patio. Their signature Cabotella ale is joined by their wheat beer, blond ale, stout, red ale, and seasonal creations.

Cuervo's House (Blvd. Mijares 101A, tel. 624/142-5650, www.cuervoshouse.com, 7am-4am daily) is home to Cabo's only piano bar. The large space houses a Mexican restaurant during the day, with the piano bar starting around 9pm. Late night karaoke starts around 2am.

Events

The **Los Cabos Open of Surf** (www.loscabosopenofsurf.com) is a professional surf and music event that takes place every June at the famous Zippers surf spot at Costa Azul. There are both men's and women's competitions that take place over the six days of the event. The event draws large crowds that gather to watch the surfing competitions and the live music performances.

Every November the **Los Cabos International Film Festival** (www.cabosfilmfestival.com) takes place over five days, screening films and bringing together filmmakers, actors, and film viewers from Mexico, Canada, and the US.

SHOPPING

The handicraft market on Boulevard Mijares is home to about a dozen vendors who sell Mexican souvenirs like blankets, hammocks, pottery, and T-shirts. For higher-quality shopping, there are a number of shops around the plaza and art district.

There are plenty of art galleries in town whatever your taste is. **Silver Moon Gallery** (Blvd. Mijares 10, tel. 624/142-6077, 9am-8pm Mon.-Sat.) pioneered the notion of promoting Mexican folk art in the region. They sell pottery from Mata Ortiz, colorful Huichol beadwork, *alebrijes* from Oaxaca, and beautiful silver jewelry.

The chic space at **Santo Cabo** (Obregon, tel. 624/142-1665, www.santocabo.com, 9am-10pm Mon.-Sat.) is filled with handmade locally sourced organic soaps and lotions. They also feature organic produce and baked goods from Flora Farms.

Curios Carmela (Blvd. Mijares, tel. 624/142-1617, 10am-8pm Mon.-Sat., 11am-5pm Sun.) has plenty of Mexican trinkets and souvenirs to take home to everyone on your shopping list. From T-shirts to traditional Mexican arts, they have a wide variety of offerings.

The **San José Mercado Organico** (Huerta Maria, tel. 624/108-4235, www.sanjomo.com) is an organic farmers market that takes place Saturday 9am-3pm northeast of the historic downtown on the road to Las Animas from Calle Centenario. In addition to organic produce, there are arts and crafts, books, and souvenirs for sale. There's also prepared food and local music.

FOOD

Restaurants in touristy areas on Boulevard Mijares, near the plaza, or near the *zona hotelera* will have higher prices. For more authentic food at more affordable prices, head a bit farther out from the center of town.

Mexican

The charming and intimate ★ **El Matador** (Paseo los Marinos, tel. 624/142-2741, www.elmatadorrestaurante.com, 5pm-10pm daily, mains US$20-33) is a family-owned operation with owner Pablo often present. Pablo began bullfighting at the age of 14 and did this professionally until moving to Los Cabos in 1988. There's plenty of bullfighting memorabilia in the restaurant, and the waitstaff dress as matadors. The service is impeccable, going above and beyond to attend to the needs of customers. The quality of the meats—veal, rack of lamb, filet—is unparalleled. There's a lovely outdoor patio and often live entertainment.

For tacos and mezcal, local hipsters and chic travelers flock to ★ **La Lupita** (Calle José Maria Morelos, tel. 624/688-3926, 2pm-midnight Tues., 2pm-2am Wed.-Sat., noon-midnight Sun., tacos US$2-4). The exposed brick, whitewashed walls, wood pallet furniture, and minimal decor create a hip Zen-like atmosphere. The wide variety of tacos includes rib eye, lamb, octopus, and nopal. There's an extensive mescal menu as well as a decent selection of craft beers. Everything is reasonably priced for being in a tourist area. There's a lovely outdoor patio and bar.

Situated on the popular Boulevard Mijares, **Don Sanchez Restaurante** (Blvd. Mijares, tel. 624/142-2444, www.donsanchezrestaurant.com, 5-10:30pm daily, mains US$15-37) serves contemporary Mexican cuisine. This is fine dining complete with artful plating and higher pricing. The service is attentive, and the wine list is extensive. There are a variety of vegetarian options (like chile portobello) in addition to seafood dishes (lobster in white mole) and meats (lamb shank mixiote).

Also on Mijares and operated by the same

Hurricanes

Hurricane Odile, the most intense tropical cyclone making landfall to affect Baja California, hit the Los Cabos region in September 2014. Winds raged at up to 125 mph along with heavy rainfall, causing irreparable damage in some places. Many of the resorts in the region took over a year to rebuild, and there are still signs of damage throughout the area.

Hurricane season runs June-November, with August-October being the most intense months. If you are traveling in the region when a tropical storm or hurricane hits, obey all evacuation orders and avoid driving on washed-out roads or through *vados* as flash floods can be likely. U.S. and Canadian citizens should follow directions from their consulates. U.S. citizens should register with STEP (https://step.state. gov/step/) before traveling outside of the United States in order to receive emails and notifications in the case of an emergency. The **National Hurricane Center** (www.nhc.noaa.gov) has more information on forecasts and being prepared in a hurricane.

owner as Don Sanchez is **Habanero's Gastro Grill and Tequila Bar** (Blvd. Mijares, tel. 624/142-2626, www.habanerosgastrogrill. com, 8am-10:30pm daily, mains US$13-25). Breakfast, lunch, and dinner can be enjoyed on the outdoor sidewalk seating or in the dining room. There's an impressive selection of tequila at the bar and an extensive menu featuring steaks, seafood, pastas, and traditional Mexican dishes.

Traditional Mexican restaurant **Jazmin's** (Jose Maria Morelos 133, tel. 624/142-1760, www.jazminsrestaurant.com, 8am-midnight daily, mains US$11-24) is in the art district downtown, a few blocks away from the plaza. This large restaurant is formed from a collection of different rooms and outdoor spaces with colorful walls, Mexican decor, and strung lights outdoor. They serve typical Mexican dishes.

Housed under a giant *palapa,* **El Herradero Mexican Grill and Bar** (Miguel Hidalgo, tel. 624/142-6350, www.elherraderoloscabos.com, 7:30am-10pm daily, mains US$11-16) serves traditional Mexican dishes for breakfast, lunch, and dinner. The casual and comfortable setting is the perfect background for the flavorful food, live music, and friendly service.

With authentic and affordable Mexican food, **Las Guacamayas** (Paseo de los Marinos, tel. 624/109-5473, 11:30am-10:30pm daily) is a second location to the restaurant in Cabo San Lucas. The large venue has a fun and lively atmosphere the whole family will enjoy.

Seafood

An easy walk from downtown San José, **Mariscos El Toro Guero** (Calle Ildefonso Green, tel. 624/130-7818, noon-6pm daily, mains US$8-10) is where locals and tourists alike go for fresh seafood, large portions, and affordable prices. Enjoy fresh ceviche and seafood cocktails as well as items like baconwrapped shrimp stuffed with cheese.

Another authentic locals' seafood restaurant is **Mariscos La Pesca** (Blvd. Mijares at Benito Juárez, tel. 624/130-7438, 11am-10pm daily, mains US$8-11) with a large outdoor patio and good food and service. Don't miss the tuna tartare.

Street Food

For a more local's experience, head to **Las Cazuelas del Don** (Malvarrose at Guijarro, tel. 624/130-7286, 1pm-10pm Mon.-Sat., mains US$4-6) where diners enjoy grilled steak, fresh fish, and local vegetables cooked in a traditional *cazuela* cooking pot. This family-run restaurant serves delicious and authentic food at affordable prices.

Farm-to-Table

For a farm-to-table experience, head out of town to Las Animas Bajas and ★ **Flora's Field Kitchen** (Animas Bajas, tel. 624/355-4564, www.flora-farms.com, 9am-2:30pm and 6pm-9:30pm Tues.-Sat., 10am-2:30pm Sun., mains US$15-25) where handmade food is crafted with fresh ingredients from the land. All meats are raised on their property (cruelty-free), and all of the produce is local. The beautiful sleek restaurant is set in the lush gardens. They run farm tours a few times daily; check with the restaurant directly for set times. A market, bar, pizzeria, and ice cream cart are also on the property. Reservations are highly recommended.

Also tucked away in the lush farmlands of Las Animas Bajas is **Huerta los Tamarindos** (Animas Bajas, tel. 624/105-6031, www.huertalostamarindos.com, noon-10pm Wed.-Mon., mains US$11-18). The restaurant can be difficult to find, but it's worth the effort. You'll follow the signs along the dirt road before arriving at a large property where a 100-year-old brick building houses the open-air restaurant that looks out over the organic farm. Overgrown vines hang down from the *palapa* roof providing a romantic feel. With the serene outdoor patio seating looking out onto the farm and lush surrounding hillsides, it's easy to forget that you're in Los Cabos. The food is all fresh and meticulously prepared from unique ceviches and fresh seafood to free-range chicken and pork shank with green mole to the house "mezcalita" tamarind and

mescal cocktail. After your meal, don't miss heading up onto the roof to check out the views. In addition to the restaurant, you can take cooking classes or take a tour of the organic farm.

If you want farm-to-table dining without wandering out of town, the sister restaurant to Los Tamarindos, **Tequila Restaurant** (Manuel Doblado 1011, tel. 624/142-1155, www.tequilarestaurant.com, 6-11pm daily, mains US$11-14) uses the same fresh ingredients in dishes served right in downtown San José. There's a lush garden dining patio, a walk-in humidor, and a nice wine list. Tequila shrimp, rack of lamb, lobster bomb (a giant lobster wonton), and beef tenderloin in guajillo sauce are some of the specialties that the restaurant serves.

International

The wine bar and steak house **La Vaca Tinta** (Manuel Doblado, tel. 624/142-1241, 5-11pm Tues.-Sat., 2-9pm Sun., mains US$8-15) has a great selection of Mexican wines on the menu. They grill steaks to perfection and also serve salads, soups, empanadas, and cheese appetizers.

For casual beachside dining **Zippers Bar & Grill** (Carretera Transpeninsular Km. 28.5,

Boulevard Mijares, just off of the plaza, is home to many of San José del Cabo's restaurants.

tel. 624/172-6162, 11am-11pm daily, mains US$15-18) has decent food (a mix of American and Mexican offerings) and live music on most days. It's a spot for tourists and expats, but the views are great and there's a large bar area with televisions. If you're not into watching sports, the restaurant is situated near one of the best surf spots in Cabo, so enjoy a beer while watching the surf instead.

If you are looking for Italian food close to the *zona hotelera*, **La Forchetta** (Plaza del Pescador, tel. 624/130-7723, www.laforchetta.mx, 5pm-11pm daily, mains US$13-16) can provide a break for guests from the all-inclusive food at resorts across the street. Pizza, pasta, raviolis, and Italian staples like chicken parmesan are all on the menu. Make sure to save room for desserts like cannoli or tiramisu. They also have a decent wine list.

For a meal set in a lovely garden courtyard, **Dvur at Casa Don Rodrigo** (Blvd. Mijares 29, tel. 624/142-0418, 11am-11pm Mon.-Sat., mains US$11-17) serves seafoods, meats, salads, and cheese that comes from the family's local ranch. The *dvur* (meaning courtyard in Czech) is located in an old house and creates a beautiful and romantic setting for a lovely meal.

Billing themselves as spontaneous cuisine, **Casianos** (Paseo Mar de Cortes, tel. 624/142-5928, www.casianos.com, 6pm-10pm Mon.-Sat., five courses US$65) is a unique dining experience with no menu. Guests can choose from a three- or five-course meal that the chef will prepare. The multiple courses are served in an intimate setting with friendly and attentive service.

Serving Argentinian barbecue, **Barrio de Tango** (Morelos, tel. 624/125-3023, 6pm-11pm Tues.-Sun., mains US$12-15) is a great place to go for steak. Dining is casual and outdoors here and the place gets busy, so it's best to make a reservation.

Cafés

Located in the art district, ★ **Lolita Café** (Manuel Doblado, tel. 624/130-7786, 9am-9pm Wed.-Sun., mains US$9-12) has plenty of options for healthy eats like their signature egg sandwich with marinated vegetable slices, sun-dried tomato, almond pesto, and chickpea dressing. This is artisan food with a Mexican touch served in a hip and unpretentious setting (don't miss their garden patio in the back). Serving breakfast, lunch, dinner, and coffee.

For a good cup of java, **Coffee Lab** (Benito Juárez 1717, tel. 624/105-2835, www.coffeelab.mx, 7am-7pm Mon.-Sat., US$3-6) is a sleek and stylish coffee shop located in downtown. In addition to great coffee, they serve breakfast, sandwiches, and paninis.

ACCOMMODATIONS
Hotels in Town

Right in the heart of town, **Posada Yuca Inn Hostel** (Obregon 1A, tel. 624/142-0462, www.yucainn.com.mx, US$40-50) offers funky but clean accommodations. Rooms are very basic, but clean and spacious. There's wireless Internet and a communal kitchen for guests to use. Another budget option right in town is **Hotel Colli** (Hidalgo, tel. 624/142-0725, www.hotelcolli.com, US$50), a Mexican hacienda-style hotel that was established in 1972. Hard beds disappoint many guests, but the rooms are clean and comfortable otherwise with air-conditioning, and the plaza, restaurants, galleries, and shops of San José are all just steps away.

Close to the center of town, **Tropicana Inn** (Mijares 30, tel. 624/142-1580, www.tropicanainn.com.mx, US$105) offers traditional Mexican atmosphere with 37 rooms centered around a large courtyard with a heated pool. Rooms are basic, but there's a nice pool area and friendly staff.

Set in the art district in San José, **El Encanto Inn and Suites** (Calle Morelos 133, tel. 624/142-0388, US$118-145) is hacienda-style boutique hotel with Old Mexico charm. Rooms feature Mission-style wooden furniture and crisp white bedding. There are two buildings here—the main inn and another one about a block away. The courtyard pool rooms in the main building, which are a bit more expensive, are worth the splurge to look over the lush courtyard with a lovely pool. This is a pet-friendly property.

For the most luxurious accommodations in town try ★ **Casa Natalia** (4 Blvd. Mijares, toll-free U.S. tel. 888/277-3814, www.casanatalia.com, US$175-230). This boutique property just off of the plaza has a chic décor in neutral colors with bright Mexican accents. The courtyard has a nice pool, and the attached **Mi Cocina** restaurant serves Mexican fare.

Beach Hotels/Zona Hotelera

Situated on 5 hectares of oceanfront property, **Cabo Azul Resort** (Paseo Malecón, tel. 624/163-5100, toll-free U.S. tel. 800/438-2929, www.caboazulresort.com, US$630) is not an all-inclusive resort, but that doesn't keep those who love the resort lifestyle from staying there. Guests will enjoy a three-level infinity-edge pool, with swim-up bar, plus two serenity pools. There's a luxurious day spa, beauty salon, and fitness center. Downtown San José del Cabo is about a 15-minute walk from the resort, but there are enough restaurants and amenities on the property that many guests don't ever leave. Almost the entire property was renovated after Hurricane Odile.

The all-inclusive family resort **Hyatt Ziva** (Paseo Malecón 5, tel. 624/163-7730, www.loscabos.ziva.hyatt.com, US$500) is welcoming to guests of all ages. This massive resort has seven restaurants on property, five swimming pools (including and adults-only pool and a children's pool complete with multiple slides), Cirque du Soleil-style live entertainment, and a plethora of activities to choose from. A full children's center, a variety of sports, and full spa round out the selections.

Design aficionados will want to stay at the slick new **Mar Adentro** (Paseo Malecón, tel. 624/104-9999, www.maradentrocabos.com, US$830) where the modern concept is the brainchild architect Miguel Ángel Aragonés. Distinct water features seem to cover the outdoor area, only to be interrupted by the unique woven "nest" that houses a restaurant. The all-white interiors help to continue the contemporary feel throughout the property. Rooms have private balconies, some with Jacuzzis. The hotel is still in the process of building a spa, beach club, and villas. They are offering discounted soft opening rates until the work is finished.

The family-run **Casa Costa Azul Hotel** (Carretera Transpeninsular Km. 28.5, tel. 624/172-6632, www.hotelcasacostazulcabo.com, US$222-247) is small boutique hotel

the outside patio of Casa Natalia

Day Trips from Los Cabos

Get out of town for a day trip. If you don't have a car or just don't feel like driving yourself, there are many tour operators who will take you to many of these locations:

Cabo Pulmo: Over on the East Cape is a 20,000-year-old coral reef that makes up the Cabo Pulmo national marine park. Divers and snorkelers flock to see the marine life that inhabits one of only three living coral reefs in North America (page 268).

Cañon de la Zorra: Up in the nearby Sierra de la Laguna, a 10-minute hike will get you to a beautiful waterfall. The surrounding pools and rocks provide an unforgettable day of swimming and relaxing in nature (page 279).

El Triunfo: The small old mining town of El Triunfo is having a resurgence. With the old colonial buildings and the new cafés, shops, and restaurants that are opening up, it's becoming a popular day trip for travelers to Baja Sur (page 255).

Todos Santos: The colonial town of Todos Santos on the West Cape is a popular spot for visitors who want to get away from the mega resort crowds for a day (page 326).

with a prime location right on the beach. The 14 rooms are clean with comfortable beds, wooden Mission-style furniture and Mexican accents. A continental breakfast is included in your stay. It's worth the extra money for an oceanview room. There's no elevator so guests on the upper floors will need to take the stairs.

The small **Marisol Boutique Hotel** (Paseo San José 161, tel. 624/142-4040, www.marisol.com.mx, US$75) has eight rooms. You won't find a swimming pool here, but the property is two blocks away from the beach and they provide beach towels, umbrellas, and beach chairs for guests to use. No children under 15 years old are allowed.

Puerto Los Cabos

For budget accommodations, ★ **El Delfin Blanco** (Calle Delfines, tel. 624/142-1212, www.eldelfinblanco.net, US$57) has six separate *casitas* all with air-conditioning and a mini-refrigerator. There's a courtyard with a fountain and plenty of seating, as well as an outdoor kitchen. You'll get personal attention here, unlike an experience at any of the larger hotels and resorts in the area. Don't miss the Swedish pancakes for breakfast.

Creative types looking for a more laid-back vibe will undoubtedly find themselves at ★ **Hotel El Ganzo** (Blvd. Tiburón, tel. 624/104-9000, www.elganzo.com, US$300)

a 69-room hotel in a tranquil area near the marina at Puerto Los Cabos. The hotel is understated, but hip with sleek design and undeniable style. Artists in residence come to leave their mark on the hotel, whether through murals and artwork or to use the underground recording studios. Guests enjoy the rooftop infinity pool, a spa, weekly farmers market, and **Ganzo Downstairs,** the signature restaurant on the property.

The adults-only **Secrets Puerto Los Cabos Golf & Spa Resort** (Ave. Paseo de los Pescadores, tel. 624/144-2600, www.secretsresorts.com, US$1,345) is an "unlimited-luxury" (all-inclusive) romance resort with 500 suites. The property is new and extremely pristine. There are plenty of activities to choose from as well as dining options. There's live entertainment day and night.

Scheduled to open summer 2017, the **Ritz-Carlton Reserve Hotel** (www.ritzcarlton.com) will be coming to the Puerto Los Cabos area. The "Reserve" label for Ritz-Carlton is their more elite sub-brand that brings luxury to one-of-a-kind boutique hotel experiences.

INFORMATION AND SERVICES
Tourist Assistance

The **Los Cabos Tourism office** (tel. 624/146-9628, www.loscabos.gob.mx) is in Plaza San

José. They have brochures and information about the area.

Medical Services

The new state-of-the-art hospital, H+ Los Cabos (Mexico 1, Km. 24.5, tel. 624/104-9300, www.hmas.mx/loscabos) is a large modern facility with a 24/7 ambulance, doctors who can provide specialty care, and the latest modern technology. The Walk in MediClinic (Mexico 1, Km. 28, tel. 624/130-7011) has an emergency room, ambulance and pharmacy. Call 066 for emergencies.

GETTING THERE

The commercial airport for the region, Los Cabos International Airport (SJD, tel. 624/146-5111, www.sjdloscabosairport.com), is located in San José del Cabo, just outside the center of town. A bus service will take you from the airport into town for US$5 or a taxi will cost around US$30.

San José del Cabo is also easy to reach for road trippers. Take Mexico 1 from San Diego all the way down the peninsula.

GETTING AROUND

The downtown San José area is pleasant and easy to explore by foot. If you're planning on staying mostly at a resort or in the downtown area, you can get away with not renting a car.

Bus

The main bus station in San José del Cabo is on Calle González. Aguila (tel. 800/824-8452, www.autobusesaguila.com) and Autobuses de la Baja California (ABC, tel. 664/104-7400, www.abc.com.mx) have services to and from Cabo San Lucas. Ruta del Desierto (www.rutadeldesierto.travel) is a bus service that will pick you up in the San José bus station and go to Cabo San Lucas or the corridor for US$2.

Car

There's a toll road connecting San José del Cabo with the airport, the Corridor, and Cabo San Lucas. Depending on where you are getting on and off the road, the fee will be US$2-4. If you rent a car, the cheapest option will be to do it at the Los Cabos International Airport, although there are rental car offices around San José del Cabo (many along the *zona hotelera*). Remember that you are legally required to purchase the Mexican auto insurance when renting a car.

Taxi

Taxis are available around the downtown area and the *zona hotelera*. A taxi will cost around US$40 to go to Cabo San Lucas. Make sure to negotiate your cab fare in advance.

The Corridor

The 30-kilometer corridor of Mexico 1 between Cabo San Lucas and San José del Cabo is a sprawling stretch of beautiful beaches now populated with posh resorts. This constantly growing area provides a seamless connection between the two Cabos with an endless belt of hotels, restaurants, and shops.

There's no city center here in the corridor. Many of the area's restaurants are those found at the resorts. Visitors stay in this region to relax and enjoy the resort life.

★ BEACHES
Playa Palmilla

Even though Playa Palmilla (Km. 27) serves as the beach for many upscale resorts, it's open for anyone to enjoy. This beach is protected enough for swimming and snorkeling, which makes it a popular spot for families. There are no facilities here other than a few *palapas* for shade on either side of the fishing fleet. Take the Palmilla exit off of the highway and follow signs to the main beach.

Playa Bledito (Tequila Cove)

An artificial breakwater makes swimming possible at **Playa Bledito,** also known as **Tequila Cove.** You can rent a Jet Ski or WaveRunner on the beach here. There's public access through the arroyo at kilometer 19.5 or through the Hilton or Meliá Cabo Real hotels.

Playa Chileno

One of the most picturesque and swimmable beaches in the region is **Playa Chileno** (Km. 14). The protected bay provides a calm area for swimming, and the coral reef out near the point provides one of Cabo's most popular spots for snorkeling from shore. This family-friendly beach is located adjacent to the new Auberge Chileno Bay Resort, but public access is still easily available. Just follow the signs from Mexico 1. There's a dirt parking lot and portapotties.

Bahía Santa Maria

Another good spot for snorkeling is **Bahía Santa Maria** (Km. 12) where you can rent a snorkel and mask from a vendor on the beach if you didn't bring your own. It's best to go in the morning when waters are calm and you have the best chance at reserving one of the beach *palapas.* There are new public showers and clean restrooms. The sand here is very coarse, more like little pebbles, so plan on wearing water shoes if you have sensitive feet. Watch for beach access signs to get to the dirt parking lot.

RECREATION
Surfing

South swells in summer bring consistent breaks in the corridor at spots like Monuments, El Tule, and Acapulquito (Old Man's). There are a few surfing schools for beginners and for board rentals.

Surf in Cabo (tel. 624/117-9495, www.surfincabo.com) can handle everything from beginner lessons to weeklong surf trips to Scorpion Bay for advanced surfers. They can customize special surf events or multi-day trips.

Mike Doyle Surf School (www.mikedoylesurfschool.com) is conveniently located inside Cabo Surf Hotel. They offer board rentals, surf lessons, and clinics.

Diving and Snorkeling

Bahía Santa Maria and Playa Chileno are both good places for snorkelers and beginning divers to enjoy the marinelife amid the coral reef. Offshore from Bahía Santa Maria is the

The Corridor is home to some of the area's most beautiful beaches.

blowhole, where more divers will see larger schools of fish, manta rays, and sea turtles. Divers can take trips to any of the five corridor dive sites with **Dive Cabo** (tel. 624/157-6327, www.divecabo.com). Sites are a 10- to 30-minute boat ride from the Cabo San Lucas marina and a trip will cost US$95 for a two-tank dive.

Golfing

The 18-hole Nicklaus Design **Club Campestre San Jose Golf Club** (free road to the airport, Km. 119, tel. 624/173-9400, toll-free U.S. tel. 877/795-8727, www.clubcampestresanjose.com) is laid out in the foothills of the Sierra de la Laguna with views of the Sea of Cortez.

The multi-themed target-style **Cabo Real Golf Club** (Mexico 1, Km. 19.5, tel. 624/105-6440, questrogolf.com, US$180) was designed by Robert Trent Jones Jr. and has some beautiful views and great staff.

Opened in 1994, **Cabo Del Sol Golf Course** (Mexico 1, Km. 10.3, tel. 866/231-4677, www.cabodelsol.com, US$175-365) is another Nicklaus Design course. There are two 18-hole courses here—the ocean course has incredible views but is more expensive than the desert course.

Palmilla Golf Club (Mexico 1, Km. 7.5, tel. 624/144-5250, www.palmillagc.com, US$145-175) has three nine-hole courses with an interesting layout on the desert and hills as well as some ocean views.

SHOPPING

The Shoppes at Palmilla (Mexico 1, Km. 27.6, www.theshoppesatpalmilla.com) is an international shopping and dining center. This is the only area of the Palmilla property open to the general public. Boutiques, fine jewelry stores, and cigar shops can be found among the restaurants, which range from Chinese to pizza to seafood. Casa Vieja is a clothing store that carries a number of Latin American designers, and Regalito Gifts showcases Mexican souvenirs and locally made products.

FOOD

Many of the resorts along the corridor have restaurants on their properties, so a lot of guests prefer to remain on-site for meals or they explore neighboring resorts. Most restaurants have views of the ocean and many feature outdoor seating.

For oceanfront fine dining at the Sheraton Hacienda del Mar, **De Cortez Grill and Restaurant** (Mexico 1, Km. 10, tel. 624/145-6113, www.decortezrestaurant.com, 5pm-10:30pm daily, mains US$27-42) serves steak, salmon, shrimp, and other grilled specialties. They also have wine-tastings on Thursday 5:30pm-6:30pm. Also at the Sheraton is **Pitahayas Restaurant** (tel. 624/145-8010, www.pitahayas.com) serving Asian fusion cuisine in an enormous *palapa* and outdoor patio. They have over 400 wines from around the world.

At Esperanza, **Cocina del Mar** (Mexico 1, Km. 7, tel. 624/145-6400, US$88 for four-course meal) offers outdoor fine dining featuring fresh fish and seafood dishes inspired by North, Central, and South American cuisines. Many diners create their own three- or four-course meal from items on the menu.

Manta (Mexico 1, Km. 5, tel. 624/163-0000, www.mantarestaurant.com, 6pm-midnight daily, plates US$14-28) is the signature restaurant at The Cape, a Thompson Hotel. The sleek space features walls of windows looking out at El Arco. The menu focuses on smaller plates such as octopus anticucho, beef yakitori, sea bass ceviche, and black miso fish tacos that can be shared or eaten alone. A four-course tasting meal is available for US$66.

At the Cabo Surf Hotel, **7 Seas Seafood Grille** (Mexico 1, Km. 28, tel. 624/142/2666, www.7seasrestaurant.com, mains US$16-35) serves an international menu with mains like shrimp ravioli, beef tenderloin au jus, mango red snapper, and various surf and turf combinations. This is refined beachside dining with ocean views and an upscale open-air *palapa* setting.

Make a reservation for sunset if you go to ★ **Sunset da Mona Lisa** (Carretera Transpeninsular, Km. 6.5, tel. 624/145-8166, www.sunsetmonalisa.com, 6pm-10pm daily, mains US$24-32). The sprawling outdoor patios are perched on the cliffs and offer sweeping views of the ocean and El Arco. Seafood and Italian specialties make up the menu. There are two other areas on the property in addition to the main restaurant: **Sunset Point**, a wine and pizza lounge, and **Taittinger Terrace**, an oyster and champagne bar.

In The Shoppes at Palmilla, **Blue Fish** (Carretera Transpeninsular, Km. 27.5, tel. 624/172-6652, www.bluefishcabo.reakxion.com, mains US$9-12) serves seafood with fresh ingredients and local flavors. The casual menu features tacos, tostada, ceviche, and seafood cocktails.

ACCOMMODATIONS

Golfers will rejoice in a stay at **Casa del Mar Golf Resort & Spa** (Mexico 1, Km. 19.5, tel. 624/145-7700, toll-free U.S. tel. 888/227-9621, www.casadelmar.com.mx, US$200) where seven courses are located within minutes of the resort. Run by Zoëtry Resorts, this boutique property has 32 suites, multiple swimming pools (including one with a swim-up bar), tennis courts, two restaurants on the property, and the Sueños del Mar Spa.

The adults-only **Marquis Los Cabos** (Mexico 1, Km. 21.5, tel. 624/144-2000, www.marquisloscabos.com, US$580-660) is an all-inclusive resort with five restaurants on the property as well as two bars. Resort activities include dance lessons, live entertainment each night, and weekly themed parties. Expect to be welcomed with watermelon mojitos, attentive service, and beautiful suites.

Surfers coming to the region stay at **Cabo Surf Hotel** (Mexico 1, Km. 28, tel. 624/142-2666, www.cabosurf.com, US$265-310) where boutique accommodations are situated right on Acapulquito (Old Man's), one of the best surfing beaches in Los Cabos. There are 36 rooms decorated in a laid-back California style with beautiful views of the ocean.

Over-the-top service is what sets apart **Las Ventanas al Paraíso, a Rosewood Resort** (Mexico 1, Km. 19.5, tel. 624/144-2800, toll-free U.S. tel. 888/767-3966, www.rosewoodhotels.com, $1,470-1,680). Personal butlers will arrange meals and activities for you (both on and off the property). Spa staff will stop by for a 10-minute foot massage on the beach. Complimentary neck massages and signature foam margaritas will be waiting for you upon check-in. Suites and villas are available for rent, and most rooms have rooftop terraces and private hot tubs on the balconies. The food on-site is good with three restaurants to choose from (the tequila and ceviche bar is a favorite among many guests). There's a spa, salon, and state-of-the-art workout facility.

The exclusive **Esperanza, an Auberge Resort** (Mexico 1, Km. 7, tel. 624/145-6400, toll-free U.S. tel. 855/331-2226, www.esperanza.aubergeresorts.com, US$800-1,700) has rooms that come with a personal concierge and suites with private infinity-edge Jacuzzis on the balconies. The resort is à la carte (not all-inclusive) with nothing but breakfast included in the room rate. There are a number of restaurants on the property to choose from for dining. Along with a spa, there are complimentary yoga and fitness classes daily, as well as activities like painting lessons and cooking classes.

If you want to be pampered at one of the most exclusive (and expensive) resorts in the region, **One&Only Palmilla** (Mexico 1, tel. 624/146-7000, toll-free U.S. tel. 866/829-2977, www.oneandonlyresorts.com, US$1,400-3,800) will grant you the luxury of having a butler and personalized service. The historical property is not only one of the most upscale in the region, it's also the oldest. It was started by Abelardo Luis Rodríguez (son of the former Mexican president), who also owned Rancho la Cruces. He opened the One&Only in 1956, and it was a popular spot for the Hollywood celebrities like John

Wayne, Lucille Ball, and former U.S. president Dwight D. Eisenhower. There are two infinity-edge pools—one for adults only and one for families. Foot and head pillows are available for your pool lounge. There are a number of restaurants and bars on the property including **SEARED,** a steak and seafood restaurant from Michelin-starred chef Jean-Georges Vongerichten. The **One&Only Palmilla Golf Club** is a 27-hole course designed by Jack Nicklaus. For those who would like to enjoy some of the activities that Cabo has to offer, private whale-watching tours are available on the One&Only Palmilla yacht, and desert off-roading is offered in a chauffeured all-terrain Hummer. For those traveling with children, there's a kids club as well as in-room babysitters.

The new and modern ★ **The Cape, a Thompson Hotel** (Mexico 1, Km. 5, tel. 624/163-0000, toll-free U.S. tel. 877/793-8527, www.thompsonhotels.com, US$400-875) offers guests a stay with style and impeccable service. This 161-room luxury resort mixes the urban aesthetic of Thompson with a modern mid-century Baja vibe. There are two pools with *cabañas* and a popular rooftop bar with lounge areas. There are three eateries on the property with their signature restaurant being **Manta**. Panoramic corner suites come with breathtakingly impressive views of El Arco, balconies with private plunge pools, and a complimentary bottle of tequila. Rooms on the fifth and sixth floors can be subject to noise from the rooftop bar during the weekend when there's a DJ and the rooftop turns into a club.

A new option for those looking for affordable accommodations in the region is the **Hampton Inn & Suites by Hilton Los Cabos** (Mexico 1, Km. 24.8, tel. 624/105-4000, www.hamptonloscabos.com, US$85). The accommodations are nice, and breakfast is served every morning in the lobby. You won't get beachfront here, but the rooftop pool deck and bar offer some ocean views and a nice relaxing place to hang out. There are plans for a spa.

Currently being constructed on Playa Chileno, **Chileno Bay Resort & Residences,** a property by Auberge (www.aubergeresorts.com) is scheduled to open early 2017. The modern boutique hotel will have 29 rooms and all of the amenities that Cabo travelers have come to expect. They are also building 32 residential beach villas on the 9-hectare property.

In June 2017, Starwood will open its first Los Cabos property, **Solaz Los Cabos** (Mexico 1, Km. 18.5, tel. 624/145-8014, www.solazloscabos.com). The resort will include 131 rooms, three restaurants, a spa, residences, and a private beach club.

GETTING THERE AND AROUND

Because the corridor is very spread out with no city center, it's nearly impossible to walk anywhere. Many resorts provide shuttles into Cabo San Lucas or San José del Cabo or will be happy to arrange for a taxi for you.

Mexico 1 runs parallel to the coast along the corridor, and all of the major resorts and beaches are just off of the highway. Signs and kilometers are well marked so it's easy to drive around the area.

Cabo San Lucas

Cabo San Lucas anchors the region to plenty of activities, shopping, restaurants, nightlife, and a variety of hotels. Its famous El Arco rock archway is the most-photographed landmark in Baja. Water sports and activities are taken to a new extreme here with banana boat rides, parasailing, skydiving, and even camel rides available in addition to the usual diving, snorkeling, fishing, and boating. There are plenty of beaches to enjoy, with Lover's Beach, accessible only by boat, the most famous.

Cabo's marina and downtown are the busy tourist spots, especially when a cruise ship is in town. The nightlife in Cabo is legendary with large nightclubs and bars living up to stereotypical expectations: tequila shots abound and music and dancing go until the wee hours of the morning.

SIGHTS
★ El Arco

As the most prominent and famous feature of the entire peninsula, **El Arco** (also sometimes called *La Finisterra* for Land's End) is the landmark in Cabo. The natural rock arch dramatically singles out the tip of the peninsula and the point where the Pacific Ocean and the Sea of Cortez collide. The arch is visible from points along Playa Médano and the corridor, but one of the best ways to experience it is to take a glass-bottom boat out to see it up close. A walk along the harbor will expose you to a number of companies offering glass-bottom boat trips for US$15. You could also book a private tour with a company like **Roger's** (www.rogerstourboatcabomexico.com). Go in the morning when waters are calmer.

Cabo San Lucas Marina

Cabo's lively **marina** is conveniently located in downtown and lined with shops, restaurants, bars, and hotels. The marina is a hub for tourist activity with snorkeling and diving tours, fishing charters, and boats out to El Arco and Lover's Beach departing from here. There's no cruise ship pier in Cabo, so cruise ships anchor away from land and tender passengers to shore, dropping them off here at the marina. At the north end of the

The famous Land's End arch is one of the most iconic symbols on the entire peninsula.

Cabo San Lucas

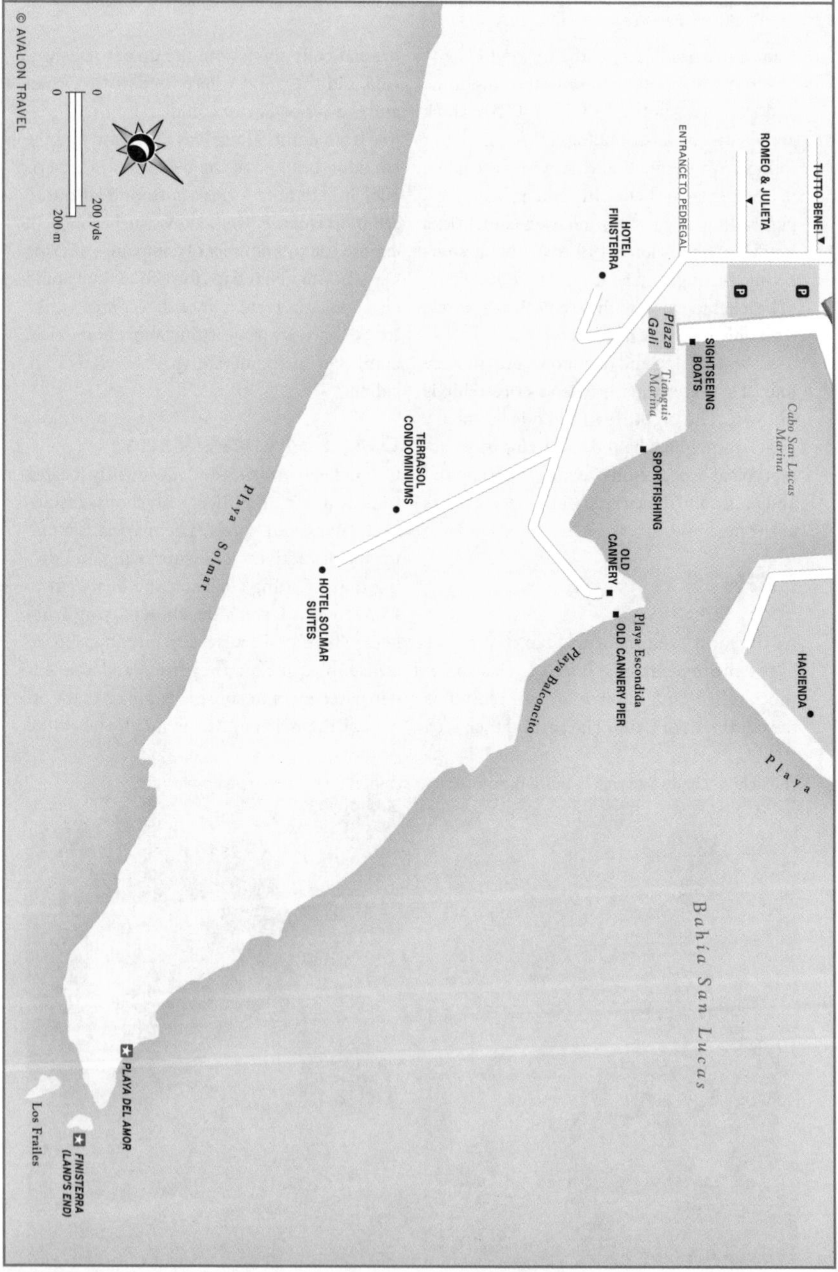

© AVALON TRAVEL

0 200 yds

0 200 m

TUTTO BENE!

ROMEO & JULIETA

ENTRANCE TO PEDREGAL

HOTEL
FINISTERRA

Plaza
Gali

SIGHTSEEING
BOATS

Tianguis
Marina

Cabo San Lucas
Marina

TERRASOL
CONDOMINIUMS

SPORTFISHING

OLD
CANNERY

HOTEL SOLMAR
SUITES

OLD CANNERY PIER

Playa Escondida

HACIENDA

Playa
Solmar

Playa Balconcito

Playa

Bahía San Lucas

PLAYA DEL AMOR

Los Frailes

FINISTERRA
(LAND'S END)

LOS CABOS
CABO SAN LUCAS

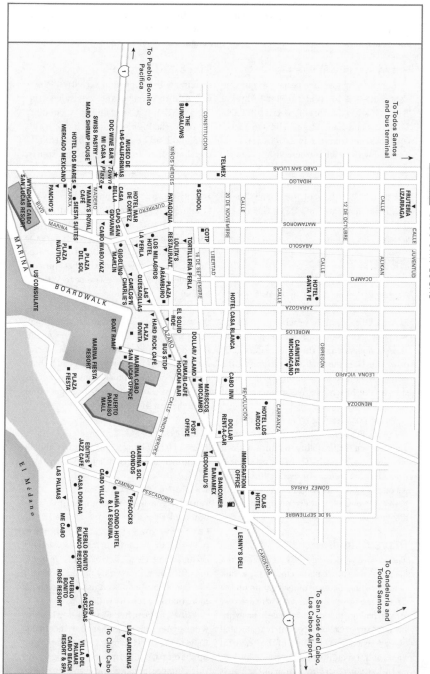

To Pueblo Bonita Pacifica

To Todos Santos
and bus terminal

THE BUNGALOWS

CONSTITUCION

NINOS HEROES

TELMEX

SCHOOL

CABO SAN LUCAS

HIDALGO

CALLE

FRUTERIA LIZARRAGA

CALLE

CALLE

12 DE OCTUBRE

JUVENTUD

MUSEO DE LAS CALIFORNIAS
DOC WINE BAR ▼ Town
MI CASA ▼ Plaza
SWISS PASTRY
MARO SHRIMP HOUSE ▼
HOTEL DOS MARES
MERCADO MEXICANO

PANCHO'S

WYNDHAM CABO SAN LUCAS RESORT

BLVD

ZAPATA

MAMA'S ROYAL CAFÉ

SIESTA SUITES

PLAZA DEL SOL

PLAZA NAUTICA

MARINA

MARINA

BOARDWALK

US CONSULATE

BOAT RAMP

MARINA FIESTA RESORT

PLAZA FIESTA

PUERTO PARAISO MALL

MARINA CABO SAN LUCAS OFFICE

CASA BELLA
CAPO SAN GIOVANNI

HOTEL MAR DE CORTEZ

GUERRERO

CABO WABO/KAZ

GIGGLING MARLIN

CARLOS'N CHARLIE'S

LAS QUESADILLAS

PLAZA BONITA

HARD ROCK CAFÉ

LAZARO

BUS STOP

PATAGONIA

LOLITA'S
TORTILLERIA PERLA

16 DE SEPTIEMBRE

LIBERTAD

20 DE NOVIEMBRE

CALLE

COTP

LOS MILAGROS
HOTEL
LA PERLA

PLAZA ARAMBURO

EL SQUID ROE

FUMARI CAFÉ
HOOKAH BAR

MARISCOS MOCAMBO

DOLLAR/ALAMO

CABO INN

HOTEL CASA BLANCA

MATAMOROS

ABASOLO

OCAMPO

ZARAGOZA

MORELOS

OBREGON

HOTEL SANTA FE

CARNITAS EL MICHOACANO

CALLE

CALLE

ALIKAN

LEONA VICARIO

MENDOZA

REVOLUCION

CARRANZA

HOTEL LOS ARCOS

DOLLAR RENTA-CAR

POST OFFICE

NINOS HEROES

MARINA SOL CONDOS

EDITH'S
JAZZ CAFÉ

CABO VILLAS

CASA DORADA

LAS PALMAS

ME CABO

LAS PALMAS

El Médano

CAMINO PESCADORES

BAHIA CONDO HOTEL & LA ESQUINA

PEACOCKS

PUEBLO BONITO BLANCO RESORT

PUEBLO BONITO ROSÉ RESORT

PUEBLO BONITO RESORT

CLUB CASCADAS

VILLA DEL PALMAR CABO BEACH RESORT & SPA

LAS GARDENIAS

To Club Cabo

McDONALD'S

BANCOMER
BANAMEX

IMMIGRATION OFFICE

OLAS HOTEL

GOMEZ FARIAS

16 DE SEPTIEMBRE

LENNY'S DELI

CARDENAS

To Candelaria and Todos Santos

To San José del Cabo, Los Cabos Airport

harbor is the **Puerto Paraiso Mall,** a large shopping center with a movie theater, stores, and restaurants.

Plaza Amelia Wilkes

Visitors looking for some peace and quiet in Cabo San Lucas will find it at **Plaza Amelia Wilkes** (Lázaro Cárdenas between Calle Cabo San Lucas and Calle Miguel Hidalgo). Set a few blocks up from the tourist area, there's a gazebo with benches where visitors can sit to relax for a bit. Lining the plaza is a small natural history museum, **Museo Cabo San Lucas** (tel. 624/105-0661, 10am-3pm Tues.-Fri., 10am-2pm Sat.-Sun., US$1) that covers the history, archaeology, geology, and biodiversity of the region.

BEACHES
★ Lover's Beach

Accessed almost purely by boat, **Lover's Beach** is a unique two-sided beach out near El Arco. One side of the beach is lined by the Bahía de Cabo San Lucas where swimmers and snorkelers enjoy the calm waters. The other side faces the Pacific Ocean, where the water is too rough for swimming. This rough side of the beach is affectionately called "Divorce Beach."

Water taxis leaving from the marina go to Lover's Beach for US$15 every 45 minutes granting you the flexibility to return to town whenever you're ready. There are no services (including bathrooms) or shade at the beach. As one of Cabo's highlight activities, it can get very crowded, and even more so in the afternoons.

Playa Solmar

The relatively uncrowded **Playa Solmar** is a beautiful, long beach perfect for taking a walk or sunbathing. Because of its location on the Pacific, the waves and currents here are very strong, making this an unsafe beach for swimming. Many of Cabo's large hotels are located along Playa Solmar because of the beautiful views and tranquility of the area.

Unless you're staying at one of the hotels along the beach here, there are no services. Access to the beach is on the road to Hotel Solmar.

Playa El Médano

Buzzing with people and activities, **Playa El Médano** is one of the only safe swimming beaches in Cabo San Lucas, but don't expect a relaxing float or beach day at this wild and loud beach. Spring breakers taking shots, families enjoying water sports, and vendors selling jewelry and knickknacks all crowd together here. Any kind of water activity can be booked on this beach, from kayaking to hydroboarding. Beachfront *palapa* restaurants and bars are close by, including **Mango Deck,** which anchors the spring break scene. Playa El Médano is the closest beach to town and stretches from the east side of the harbor entrance to Villa del Palmar.

If walking from downtown, walk around the marina to the end and go left at the channel entrance. There's also access via Av. del Pescador or Camino Hotel Hacienda. There's no parking lot and street parking can be hard to find, especially on weekends or during spring break, so walking or taking a cab is often the best solution.

RECREATION

There's no lack of tour operators in Cabo for a seemingly unlimited number of activities.

Extreme Adventures

Whether you want to mountain bike, hydroboard, fly in a small plane, zipline, or sail, **Cabo Adventures** (tel. 322/226-8413, www. cabo-adventures.com) can make your activity dreams come true. They have a large booking office in downtown Cabo on Paseo de la Marina. They offer discounts when you book more than one activity with them.

Wild Canyon (tel. 624/144-4433, www. wildcanyon.com.mx) takes tourists outside Cabo to the "Wild Canyon" where they've set up a large park with ziplines, ATVing, camel rides, bungee jumping, and even a small zoo.

Authentic and Affordable Cabo

Anyone familiar with Cabo 30 years ago will tell you about the good old days when the town was nothing but a quaint fishing village surrounded by beautiful beaches. That was before the highway was paved, the commercial airport opened, the cruise ships came to visit, and the endless string of mega-resorts populated the beaches. While the resorts, golf courses, and nightlife of Cabo may not appeal to many Baja travelers, the beauty of the region is undeniable, and it has a proximity to many other interesting sights. Peninsula road-trippers may want to stop in for a few days without dealing with all-inclusive resorts or tourist traps. There are still ways to enjoy authentic Mexican charm; you just have to work harder to find it.

Stay small and in town. Stay in the downtown areas of San José or Cabo San Lucas, where you'll find boutique hotels, bed-and-breakfasts, and budget accommodations with plenty of Mexican soul. This will also put you walking distance of historical plazas and shops and restaurants—helping you feel more of the local culture. Conveniently enough, these small, authentic accommodations are often also the cheapest choices when compared to the large hotels and all-inclusive resorts.

Take advantage of public beaches. All of the beaches in Los Cabos (and the rest of the peninsula for that matter) are public property. That means that you don't have to stay at an expensive beachfront resort in order to use the beach there. The properties all legally have to provide public access to the beach, so even if the resort hasn't allowed for access along the side of the hotel, most will let you to go through the resort to get to the beach.

Get off the beaten path. Get out of the heavy tourist areas to eat at more authentic restaurants and pay lower prices. Don't be afraid to ask the locals for their favorite places to eat. The prices decrease significantly when you eat outside of the tourist areas.

Avoid peak hours. The marina and downtown area of Cabo San Lucas become mayhem during the day when cruise ship passengers are on shore. The area becomes much more relaxed after 5pm when the cruisers are back on the ship.

Get out of town. Day trips to explore the peninsula will give you a less-touristy experience (page 299). Quaint colonial towns, vast deserted beaches, cascading waterfalls, natural hot springs, and premier coral reef diving are all just an hour or so away.

Diving and Snorkeling
DIVE AND SNORKEL SITES

The Bahía de Cabo San Lucas was designated a protected underwater national marine park in 1973, marking it as an area abundant with sealife. The bay provides relatively calm waters for diving.

Lover's Beach and **Land's End** are the best spots for snorkeling in Cabo San Lucas. You can snorkel off of the beach at Lover's Beach on your own or with a guide. The waters won't be perfectly calm, but they should be clear enough to spot some tropical fish. Winds will pick up later in the afternoon. For snorkeling off of Land's End, there are a number of boat and tour operators who can take you out to swim with the sea lions and fish near El Arco. Many of the outfitters out

of Cabo San Lucas will take snorkelers over to Bahía Chileno and Bahía Santa Maria along the corridor, where the waters are calmer.

The **Sand Falls** are one of Cabo's most famous and unique dive sites. Close to Lover's Beach, 30 meters below the surface, is a river of sand that flows between rocks and over the edge of a canyon, creating an unusual sand fall. The sand rivers are not always flowing, and are usually the most active when stormy weather makes the seas more turbulent (the opposite of normal optimal diving conditions). Even if the falls aren't active, there's still abundant sealife around the site such as rays, zebra eels, and grouper.

For diving, Land's End is also a great option. This is a unique site because it allows divers to experience both the Pacific Ocean and the Sea of Cortez at the same time. Barracuda, tuna, baitfish, and rays can be spotted. The site is also home to a colony of sea lions who love to swim and play with divers. Nearby **Pelican Rock** is a reef that drops off a deep wall down to 150 meters. There are devil rays, moray eels, porcupine fish, and puffer fish. There are two coral reefs at **Neptune's Finger,** which is also home to one of the largest sand falls. Tropical fish, sea turtles, and manta rays can be seen here.

OUTFITTERS

Most hotels and resorts can arrange for a dive or snorkel trip and equipment rental. Morning outings are the most popular as that's when the seas are calmer and better for diving.

Dive Cabo (tel. 624/157-6327, www.divecabo.com) offers daily snorkel and dive trips. Their small groups are guided by experienced leaders. They offer PADI courses and free 30-minute "scuba refreshers" prior to your dive. They also provide a free underwater photography service so you can take home a memento from your dive.

Aqua Los Cabos (tel. 624/143-9286, www.aqualoscabos.com) hosts snorkel and dive trips around the Los Cabos region and as well as excursions up to Parque Nacional

Cabo Pulmo. They have courses and trips for all levels of divers.

Fishing

Cabo was initially a small fishing village, and sportfishing remains a popular draw for the region today. There are a number of fishing charters and services in the area. Marlin, billfish, red snapper, yellowtail, grouper, sierra, and roosterfish are all common in the region. Marlin and sailfish are caught on an optional catch-and-release program in Los Cabos to support local conservation efforts. One species is permitted per boat. Ask ahead to see if your fishing charter includes the fee for cleaning your fish or if you'll need to pay it yourself when back on shore (US$2-30 depending on the size of the fish). Fishing licenses are required when angling from a boat in Mexico and fishing charters usually provide one for you, but check ahead of time to make sure it's included.

A reputable and long-established fishing charter in the region is **Pisces Sportfishing** (tel. 624/143-1288, toll-free U.S. tel. 877/286-7938, www.piscessportfishing.com). They are located on the Cabo marina and have a huge fleet with a wide variety of options for charters. Also located at the marina is **Picante**

Glass-bottom boats take tourists out to see the famous arch.

Sportfishing (tel. 624/143-2474, www.picantesportfishing.com) with a large fleet of yachts and experienced charter captains.

Cabo Fishing and Tours (toll-free U.S. tel. 866/261-3872, www.cabofishings.com) can arrange fishing charters for first-time anglers, families, and serious anglers. They have party packages that start at US$450.

Offering a variety of packages that include lunch, transportation, fishing licenses, and live bait, **Sushi Time Sport Fishing** (tel. 624/147-5162, www.sushitimefishing.com) has a fleet of six super *pangas*. All reservations must be made through the website.

Boating

Cabo Sails (tel. 624/111-3900, www.cabosails.com) is a sailing charter company specializing in private sailboat charters that can accommodate 2-20 guests. They also have snorkeling, whale-watching, and sunset tours. Another option for sailing and boating is **Cabo Sailing Ocean Adventures** (toll-free U.S. tel. 800/209-1669, www.cabosailing.com). From sunset cruises to whale-watching to snorkel tours, they can arrange for private or group excursions.

In addition to the usual whale-watching and snorkeling trips, **Pez Gato** (tel. 624/143-3797, U.S. tel. 619/446-6339, www.pezgato.com) also offers sunset cruises like the "jazz and wine cruise" and a "fiesta dinner cruise" with open bar.

★ Golf

There are several world-class courses in Cabo that attract golfers from all over the world. The courses wind through beautiful desert and mountain terrain with stunning views of the Sea of Cortez. November through May is ideal for golfing because the temperatures are mild and there's very little rain. Summer months can be too hot and bring tropical storms, but because of this, the prices are discounted in summer, so budget golfers are lured to the region during this time. Greens fees can be around US$300 during peak time.

Teeing off during twilight hours will be close to half the regular price.

The **Cabo San Lucas Country Club** (tel. 624/143-4654, www.cabocountry.com) features a Dye-designed 18-hole golf course. Set among cacti and bougainvillea, this is the only golf course in the area that has views of Cabo's famous El Arco.

For an exclusive golfing experience, **Diamante** (tel. 624/172-5811, www.diamantecabosanlucas.com) offers two courses. The Dunes Course meanders through untouched sand dunes and was ranked 38th in *Golf Magazine*'s Top 100 Courses in the World. The new El Cardonal course was designed by Tiger Woods and offers long-range views of the Pacific Ocean.

With a stunning setting, **Quivira Golf Club** (toll-free U.S. tel. 800/990-8250, www.quiviragolfclub.com) has dramatic ocean views set among granite cliffs and sand dunes.

Horseback and Camel Rides

It's possible to do both horseback riding and camel riding on the beach in Cabo. If you want to go horseback riding and get off of the beaten tourist path, **Cuadra San Francisco** (Mexico 1, Km 19.5, tel. 624/144-0160, www.loscaboshorses.com) is a world-class equestrian center where travelers can go for longer horseback rides along the beach as well as onto the trails of nearby hills and canyons. They can accommodate riders of all levels. Camel riding is offered through a couple of tour companies in the region like **Cabo Adventures** (tel. 322/226-8413, www.cabo-adventures.com) or **Wild Canyon** (tel. 624/144-4433, www.wildcanyon.com.mx).

ENTERTAINMENT AND EVENTS
★ Nightlife

The unofficial Cabo spring break headquarters is **Mango Deck** (7am-11pm daily, www.mangodeckcabo.com), the happening place on Playa Médano for entertainment and drinks. Get there early in the day to grab a deck chair and listen to the emcee who will guide you through the day's worth of entertainment and contests. When you're thirsty, there are two-for-one drink specials, or flag down "Big Johnson," the tequila man with a holster full of tequila and shot glasses. They serve breakfast, lunch, and dinner in case you need to soak up some of the alcohol.

A standard on the Cabo bar scene for over 30 years is **The Giggling Marlin** (Paseo de la Marina, tel. 624/143-1182, 9am-1am daily, www.gigglingmarlin.com). They're most famous for their gimmick where visitors can hang upside down by their feet, like a caught fish, next to a large marlin for a shot and a unique photo op. There's a fun and friendly staff, and they serve decent food, including salsa made tableside.

Probably the most popular and classic late-night Cabo spot is **El Squid Roe** (Lázaro Cárdenas, tel. 624/155-9630, www.elsquidroe.com, 10am-5am daily) located on the main strip. If you're looking for dancing, loud music, drinking, and fun, this is your place.

For an evening of live music, drinks, and food, head to Sammy Hagar's **Cabo Wabo Cantina** (Vicente Guerrero, tel. 624-143/1188, www.cabowabo.com, 9am-3am daily). They make their own blue agave tequila and serve

Cabo Wabo Cantina

Mexican food (US$19-30). The atmosphere provides one of the liveliest spots in Cabo, whether day or night.

For those who enjoy a more subdued nightlife scene away from the large clubs

For a night of dancing and drinking, tourists head to El Squid Roe.

and spring breakers, **Bar Esquina** (Ave. El Pescador, tel. 624/143-1890, www.bahiacabo. mx) offers a more elegant and sophisticated ambience. Located in the Bahia Hotel & Beach Club, they have live music, like a jazz band or Spanish guitar, almost every night. This is also a favorite dinner spot with a full menu featuring Mediterranean and Mexican fusion.

Rámuri Cerveza Artesanal Mexicana (Lázaro Cárdenas, tel. 624/105-0163, www. cervezaramuri.com) is a microbrewery serving its own Belgium and German-influenced craft beers. Visitors can take a tour of the brewery or enjoy pub-style food like burgers, wings, and gourmet pizzas at the restaurant. If the weather is nice, patrons can savor their beer and food outside on the rooftop beer garden where there are a number of flat-screen televisions.

SHOPPING

There's no lack of souvenir shopping in Cabo. Across the street from the Giggling Marlin, **Plaza de los Mariachis y de la Salsa** (Paseo de la Marina, tel. 624/143-4596, 8am-4pm daily) has a smattering of souvenir shops as well as a few open-air bars. Silver, colorful Talavera pottery, beaded jewelry, and other typical Mexican souvenirs can be found in the small shops here.

Mega souvenir shop **Hacienda Tequila** (Paseo de la Marina, 9am-9pm daily) sells sombreros, shot glasses, T-shirts and, as the name suggests, a large selection of tequila. There's a large **"flea market"** on Melchor Ocampo, a few blocks up from the marina where visitors will find a large market of stalls full of souvenirs and curios (but don't expect any vintage or antique finds here as the name may suggest).

For some more authentic shopping, **Zen-Mar Mask Store** (Lázaro Cárdenas, tel. 624/143-0661, 9am-6pm daily) sells a large selection of masks, rugs, Catrina figurines, and other decor from Oaxaca and other areas of mainland Mexico. The store has been there for 35 years.

Edith Jimenez (the owner of The Office and Edith's restaurants) turned her hacienda-style home into a unique shop, **La Coyota** (Leona Vicario, tel. 624/143-0714, 9am-5pm daily) where everything you see is for sale. It's not in a touristy neighborhood, but those looking for hand-blown glassware, pottery, crosses and sacred hearts from mainland Mexico, and other authentic decor will find that it's worth the trip.

For some serious shopping, interior

There are plenty of options for souvenir shopping in Cabo San Lucas.

decorators and in-the-know design aficiona-dos go to **Artesano's** (Mexico 1, Km. 4.1, El Tezal neighborhood, tel. 624/143-3850, 9am-2pm Mon.-Sat.) where you'll find a giant warehouse full of rows of colorful pottery, glassware, outdoor furniture, handwoven baskets, and more.

In downtown Cabo near the marina, **Puerto Paraiso Mall** (Lázaro Cárdenas 1501, tel. 624/144-3000, www.puertoparaiso. mx, 9am-10pm daily) is a large modern mall with stores like Kenneth Cole, Sunglass Hut, and Tommy Bahama.

There are plenty of large grocery stores for those staying at condos. There's also a **Costco** (San José del Cabo 1659, tel. 624/146-7180, 9am-9pm Mon.-Sat., 9am-8pm Sun.).

FOOD

Eat with your toes in the sand at casual beach restaurant, **The Office** (Playa El Médano, access to Av. Del Pescador, tel. 624/143-3464, www.theofficeonthebeach.com, 7am-10pm daily, mains US$8-14), which has become a Cabo staple for most tourists. The prices are reasonable and the atmosphere is fun with live music, lively crowds, and flowing drinks. From burritos and coconut shrimp to burgers and steak, the menu is diverse and the spot is great for hanging out during the day to watch the people going by, drink, and eat.

Mexican

For authentic Mexican food in a charming courtyard setting, **Mi Casa** (Ave. Cabo San Lucas, tel. 624/143-8245, www.micasarestaurant.com.mx, 11:30am-10:30pm Mon.-Sat., 5:30pm-10:30pm Sun.,US$12-25) is right on Plaza Amelia Wilkes. They serve traditional Mexican dishes from the heart of the mainland like rich moles, *chile en nogada*, and seafood cocktails. They now have a second location in San José del Cabo.

For elegant outdoor dining at Playa Médano, **Hacienda Cocina y Cantina** (tel. 624/163-3144, 8am-10pm daily, haciendacocina.com, mains US$16-24) is a casual but sophisticated option. Views look out at El Arco

Shoppers can find authentic artisanal masks and souvenirs at Zen-Mar Mask Store.

and the menu features Mexican specialties from regions in mainland such as Oaxaca, Puebla, Guerrero, and Veracruz. Tequilas, local craft beers, handcrafted cocktails, and wine top off the selection.

Traditional Mexican food is served in large portions at the family-owned and operated **Maria Jimenez Restaurante Mexicano** (Calle Narcizo Mendoza, tel. 624/105-1254, 2pm-10pm Tues.-Sun., mains US$10-14). There's a casual but festive atmosphere with mariachi bands. They currently only accept cash.

With almost 200 options available, patrons head to **Pancho's** (Hidalgo and Emiliano Zapata, tel. 624/143-2891, www.panchos.com, 8am-10:30pm daily, mains US$11-14) for the tequila tastings as much as the Mexican food. The service is friendly, the portions are large, and the restaurant is conveniently located in downtown.

At **Maria Corona** (16 de Septiembre, tel. 624/143-1111, www.mariacoronarestaurant. com, 3pm-11pm daily, mains US$9-14) every

Tuesday patrons enjoy a live show featuring traditional dancers and music. Traditional Mexican dishes are served with the spectacle that tourist enjoy—such as guacamole made tableside and Mexican coffee lit on fire.

From the same owners as The Office, **Edith's** (Camino a la Playa El Médano, tel. 624/143-0801, www.edithscabo.com, 5pm-11pm daily, mains US$17-36) serves Baja California cuisine with a Guerreran influence, creating a fusion of steaks and seafood along with local flavors and ingredients. Owner Edith has been with this restaurant since arriving in Cabo from Jalapa in 1977 when she was 15 and working as a waiter (she changed the name to Edith's in 1994).

For signature moles and authentic traditional Mexican dishes that have been passed down for generations, head to **Los Tres Gallos** (20 de Noviembre, tel. 624/164-5869, www.lostresgallos.com, 8am-10pm daily, mains US$12-14). There's a cozy atmosphere with a charming outdoor patio as well as an open kitchen so you can watch them cooking.

The place to go for breakfast is **Mama's Royal Café** (Calle Hidalgo, tel. 624/143-4290, www.mamasroyalcafeloscabos.com, 7am-2:30pm Mon.-Sat., US$6-9). From *huevos charros* (a deluxe version of huevos rancheros) to eggs Benedict and a large selection of omelettes, the dishes are rich and savory. The bright and colorful setting is casual with plenty of Mexican charm.

Seafood

The seafood dishes are what keep patrons coming back to **Misiones de Kino** (Vicente Guerrero Guerrero at 5 de Mayo, tel. 624/105-1408, www.misionesdekino.com, 3:30pm-11pm Mon.-Sat., mains US$10-14). There's indoor seating as well as a small and intimate courtyard with romantic outdoor lighting. The seafood pastas are a favorite and shrimp lovers won't want to miss their shrimp served in a special garlic sauce.

Don't let the very casual, no-frills setting at **Mariscos las Tres Islas** (Revolución de 1910, tel. 624/143-3247, 8am-10pm daily, mains US$8-12) fool you—this is some of the best and freshest seafood around. The catch of the day is always fantastic at this locals' spot. Wash it down with a mango margarita.

The eclectic and quirky **Maro's Shrimp House** (Ave. Hidalgo, tel. 624/143-4966, noon-10pm daily, mains US$14-17) is decorated with college sports team pennants and the signatures of patrons. As the name suggests, they're known for their shrimp, and the lobster comes in a close second. For being a tourist restaurant downtown, the prices are reasonable for the value.

Don't miss the seafood combination platter at **Las Mariscadas** (Calle Cabo San Lucas, tel. 624/105-1563, 1pm-10pm daily, mains US$7-11), where you'll enjoy casual dining under a large open-air *palapa*. From coconut mango shrimp to ceviche to grilled octopus, the food is delicious at reasonable prices, and the staff is friendly and welcoming.

Taco Stands

Tacos Guss (Lázaro Cárdenas, tel. 624/105-1961, US$5-7) serves classic Mexican street food (*huaraches, tortas,* tacos, and quesadillas) in a casual sit-down restaurant. This is a popular place so the lines can be long and it can be difficult to get a table after you've ordered, but most patrons think it's worth the wait. You can always take the food to go.

For a California-style burrito made with fresh and healthy ingredients, head to **Burrito Surf** (Mariano Matamoros and Nino Heroes, tel. 624/143-0098, www.burritosurfcabo.com, 11am-9pm Mon.-Sat., US$5-8). They also have salads, burrito bowls, and quesadillas.

With a convenient location downtown, seafood lovers will want to head to **Tacos Gardenias** (Paseo de la Marina, tel. 624/355-4871, www.tacosgardenias.com, 8am-10pm daily) where the menu features fish tacos, shrimp *molcajetes,* and seafood cocktails.

For *carnitas,* the best place to go in the area is **Los Michoacanos** (Mexico 19, tel. 624/146-3565, 7:30am-6pm daily, US$4). You can order *carnitas* by the kilo, which comes along with tortillas and all the salsas and fixings. Don't miss trying the *chicharrón* as well. They have four locations (all called Carnitas Los Michoacanos) throughout Los Cabos, but the main location is on the highway on the road to Todos Santos, across from the Soriana.

If you follow celebrity and TV chefs, you'll definitely want to head to **Asi y Asado** (Km. 3.8, tel. 624/105-9500, www.asiyasado.com, 10am-9pm Mon.-Sat., 11am-7pm Sun.) where Guy Fieri visited on his show *Diners, Drive-ins and Dives*. He called the octopus in the octopus taco "so fresh, it tastes like the sea." They have an extensive toppings bar with cucumbers, salsas, radishes, and coleslaw.

International

On the property of The Resort at Pedregal, ★ **El Farallon** (Camino Del Mar 1, tel. 624/163-4300, 5:30pm-10:30pm daily, mains US$30-75) provides guests with an exquisite dining experience. Fresh fish, shrimp, lobster, and steak are all on the menu for main courses, in addition to the set family-style appetizers served beforehand. Built right into the side of the mountain with the crashing waves below, the atmosphere and views are spectacularly memorable. There's also a champagne terrace carved out of rock where diners can choose from over 15 types of champagne to try with a selection of salts.

Solomon's Landing (Paseo de la Marina, tel. 624/154-3050, www.solomonslanding-cabo.com, 7am-11pm daily, mains US$18-25) is a popular spot for expats, tourists, and cruise ship passengers. They're conveniently located on the marina with well-prepared food (the extensive menu has sushi, seafood, pastas, and more) and a fun and lively atmosphere.

For Italian dining featuring huge portions and friendly service, locals and tourists head to **Salvatore's** (Emiliano Zapata, tel. 624/105-1044, 11am-3pm and 6pm-10pm daily, mains US$13-16). The pork shank is slow-cooked and tender and savory, served with a side of alfredo. The lasagna is a famous

dish here because it's delicious and large enough for two people to share.

Mediterranean specialties like stuffed tenderloin scaloppini and pasta carbonara are served up at **Alcaravea** (Zaragoza and 16 de Septiembre, tel. 624/105-1844, noon-11pm Mon.-Sat., mains US$9-16). They have a French chef who makes rich and savory sauces that top items like filet mignon and the catch of the day. The set lunch special includes a choice of entrée and a dessert, and at US$7 is one of the best deals in Cabo.

ACCOMMODATIONS

For those looking for a more authentic and intimate experience than the resorts, there are a few options for boutique hotels and budget accommodations in the downtown and marina area. Only resorts and large hotels will be found along the beaches and water's edge. To get beachfront, you'll need to go out of downtown to Playa Médano or to Playa Solmar. The beach at Playa Médano is buzzing with energy, people, and activities, since it is one of the few swimmable beaches in Cabo San Lucas. Playa Solmar, in contrast, is a beautiful and more deserted beach, great for enjoying a walk on the sand, but the strong waves and currents here make it an unsafe place for swimming.

Resorts on Playa Solmar are over on the Pacific Ocean side of Cabo and have beautiful expansive beaches to look at. The sand is coarse, and the surf and currents are strong here and definitely not for swimming. If you're looking for a resort on the beach where you can swim in the ocean, head to a hotel on Playa Médano, but be ready for the crowds.

Many of the large resorts in Cabo will let you book room and airfare at the same time.

Downtown and Marina

For budget accommodations, **Baja Cactus Hotel & Hostel** (Lázaro Cárdenas, tel. 624/143-5247, US$22-50) offers both shared dorm rooms and private suites. There's wireless access throughout, a common area with games, and a communal kitchen. Continental breakfast is provided.

For boutique hotel accommodations in a resort town, head to ★ **Casa Bella** (Hidalgo 10, tel. 624/143-6400, www.casabellahotel. com, US$213-253). This 14-room hotel has plenty of Spanish character with arched windows and rooms centered around a lovely lush courtyard with a small pool. A stay here will evoke a more authentic "old-world" Mexican charm than you'll get at any of the typical Cabo resorts. A free continental breakfast of fruits, pastries, coffee, and tea is included in your stay. The staff is very friendly and helpful and can make arrangements for excursions like fishing trips, golfing, and whale-watching. The prime location is quiet and relaxed, just off of the plaza and walking distance to the lively downtown and marina area.

Off the beaten path, **Norman Diego's The Mexican Inn** (16 de Septiembre and Abasolo, tel. 624/143-4987, www.themexicaninn.com, US$150-170) has six basic rooms decorated with Mexican accents. Rooms have TVs and DVD players (a DVD collection is available to borrow at the front office). There's a common area where free continental breakfast is served in the mornings (cooked breakfast available for an extra price).

With plenty of charm **Los Milagros** (Matamoros 116, tel. 624/143-4566, www. losmilagros.com.mx, US$85-125) features a calming colonial courtyard with Talavera tiles, wrought-iron tables with mosaic work, paired with overgrowing bougainvillea. There are plenty of spots to sit and relax around the gardens and courtyard, and even a small dipping pool. There's a sun terrace on the upper level. The rooms are basic but clean and feature Mexican accents with Saltillo floors and colorful Talavera tiles.

Cabo Inn Hotel (20 de Noviembre and Leona Vicario, tel. 624/143-0819, www.caboinnhotel.com, $48-73) has a wide range of rooms available from standard rooms with twin beds to rooftop *palapa* suites. This colorful and funky property has a courtyard, rooftop patio, small dipping pool, and full communal kitchen and barbecue. The on-site restaurant, **Hole in the Wall,** serves breakfast and lunch.

With affordable prices and a location in the heart of the action downtown, **Siesta Suites** (tel. 624/143-2773, toll-free U.S. tel. 866/271-0952, www.cabosiestasuites.com, US$72) is walking distance to nearly everything in Cabo. Rooms are large and clean, and the property is pet-friendly. There's a great deck where guests mingle and enjoy happy hour Wednesday through Friday.

The colonial-style **Hotel Mar de Cortez** (Lázaro Cárdenas 140, tel. 624/143-0032, www.mardecortez.com, US$80) is a budget hotel in a historical building in downtown Cabo. The rooms are basic (no TV or minifridge), but the location is ideal and there's a nice pool in the courtyard. American-style breakfast is included in the stay. The restaurant is also open for lunch, and there's a sports bar with happy hour noon-3pm and again at 5-7pm daily.

With a great location right on the marina, **Marina Fiesta Resort & Spa** (Paseo de la Marina, tel. 624/145-6020, www.marinafiestaresort.com, US$180-220) is walking distance to everything in downtown. There are now two ways to book—bed-and-breakfast (with just breakfast included with your room) or all-inclusive, which requires a fournight minimum stay. The swimming pool has a large *palapa* swim-up bar. The friendly staff pay a lot of attention to detail and customer satisfaction.

For an authentic Mexican experience, **El Nido at Hacienda Escondida** (Libertad and Miguel Angel Herrera, tel. 624/143-2053, www.cabobedbreakfast.com, US$160-180) is a bed-and-breakfast nestled into a charming hacienda building. There are six rooms in total, with two of them on the ground floor and the other four "*palapa* rooms" with *palapa* roofs and that are open on one side to the mountains. There's a rooftop deck, Jacuzzi, and a restaurant and cantina on the property.

At **The Bungalows Hotel** (Miguel Angel Herrera, www.thebungalowshotel.com, US$165-185) all rooms have kitchenettes, airconditioning, pillow-top mattresses, handmade desert soaps, and bathroom amenities. A delicious, full gourmet breakfast is served in the morning. They're happy to help arrange for activities and rental cars and recommend restaurants and things to see. The location is great, out of the touristy area, but close enough to walk to downtown and the marina.

Playa El Médano

The high-end, family-friendly resort **Villa del Arco Beach Resort and Spa** (Camino Viejo a San Jose Km. 0.5, tel. 624/145-7200, toll-free U.S. tel. 800/831-1191, www.villagroupresorts.com, US$885-1,085) has 217 suites all with kitchenettes or full kitchens, air-conditioning, and private balconies. There are two outdoor pools with waterfalls, right on Médano beach with views of El Arco. One is home to a full-size replica of Spanish galleon that serves as a bar. They have two room packages when booking—all-inclusive or room only.

The ultramodern **ME Cabo by Meliá** (Playa El Médano, tel. 624/145-7800, toll-free U.S. tel. 888/956-3542, www.melia.com, US$290-325) is a popular place for 20 and 30-somethings who want a nice hotel on the beach and close to the nightlife of downtown. The pool area has numerous cabana lounges and a DJ playing music. Weekends can be rowdy with music coming from the bar areas until late at night.

All-inclusive **Casa Dorada** (Ave. Pescador, tel. 624/163-5757, US$715) has a number of restaurants on the property, with **12 Tribes** being a favorite among guests. Médano beach and two large pools provide plenty of space for sunning and relaxing. Be aware that wireless Internet isn't free here, you'll have to pay for it. Casa Dorada tends to draw an older clientele, and the property is relatively quiet at night, so you'll need to go into town nearby if you're looking for a nightlife scene.

Boutique **Bahia Hotel & Beach Club** (Ave. Pescador, tel. 624/143-1890, www.bahiacabo.mx, US$310) is set a block away from Médano beach and two blocks away from the marina. There's a pool area and poolside bar. **Bar Esquina** on the property is a popular spot for both locals and tourists and serves handcrafted food and cocktails.

For an all-inclusive experience, **Hotel Riu Palace** (Camino Viejo a San José del Cabo Km. 4.5, tel. 624/146-7160, toll-free U.S. tel. 888/748-4990, www.riu.com, US$1,040 for three-nights, all-inclusive double occupancy) provides 24-service in a relaxing environment right on the beach. Three-night minimum required. There are two freshwater swimming pools, a spa and wellness center, and plenty of organized activities like volleyball, gymnastics, windsurfing, kayaking, and golf. There's entertainment in the evening at the restaurants, bars and clubs on the property. You'll need to get up early (before 7am) if you want to get a pool lounge facing the ocean. A three-night minimum is required. There are no "spring breakers" allowed at Riu Palace any time of year, but right next door is the **Riu Santa Fe** (Camino Viejo a San José del Cabo Km. 4.5, tel. 624/163-6150, www.riu.com, US$688 three nights, all-inclusive double occupancy) that attracts a lot of 20-somethings with more of a party vibe.

In the process of opening on Médano Beach is **Cachet Corazon** (www.corazondelcaboresort.com), the first resort destination project for Cachet Hotel Group. The first tower, Cachet Beach, featuring 77 rooms. The second tower Cachet Delux is scheduled to open at the beginning of 2018. The resort will feature Cachet Hotel Group's revolutionary technology platform, enabling features such as "Personalized Hotel Rooms" allowing guests to design their room and upgrade add-ons such as choosing designer bedding, bath and body products, and beauty essentials.

Set back from the beach on the other side of the highway from Playa El Médano in a neighborhood called El Tezal is **Los Patios Hotel** (Mexico 1, Km. 4.5, tel. 624/145-6070, www.lospatioshotel.com, US$45). This affordable option is a newer property, and rooms are nicely appointed with air-conditioning, in-room safes, hair dryers, coffeemakers, and private terraces with hammocks. The hotel still has plenty of Mexican charm with bright colors and Mexican decor accents. There's a heated pool, a Jacuzzi, and a restaurant on-site. The downfall is that you'll need to take a taxi or bus to get to the beach or other parts of town.

Also in El Tezal is **Casa Contenta** (Calle Modelo, tel. 624/143/6038, www.cabocasacontenta.com, US$200-225), a bed-and-breakfast situated in the house of a former mayor of Cabo. This beautiful residence has been turned into a clean, comfortable, and spacious luxury hotel where guests will enjoy personal attention and a relaxing and rejuvenating stay.

Playa Solmar

Playa Solmar is a more secluded and empty beach than the busy Playa Médano. Swimming here is not advised with the strong surf and currents.

A luxurious stay at **The Resort at Pedregal** (Camino del Mar 1, tel. 624/163-4300, www.theresortatpedregal.com, US$990) will provide you with all of the standard upscale resort amenities. The staff are genuine, welcoming, and friendly, providing outstanding service. Daily guacamole, salsa, and Coronitas are delivered to your room between 4pm and 5pm as a perfect pre-dinner snack. The famous **El Farallon** restaurant is on the property where guests can enjoy exquisite seafood dishes with waves crashing in the background. Although the resort is private and secluded, the entrance of the property (you can take a golf cart, as you'll need to go through the signature tunnel) is just a short walking distance to the marina.

There are five Solmar properties in Cabo, **Solmar Resort** (Ave. Solmar 1, toll-free U.S. tel. 800/344-3349, www.solmarcabosanlucas.com, US$164 for bed & breakfast, $274 for all-inclusive double occupancy) is one of their intimate oceanfront resorts. Guests can book either an all-inclusive plan (which includes all food, drinks, and activities), or a bed & breakfast plan which just includes breakfast. From the property guests can hike to Lover's and Divorce Beach (only reachable by boat for most travelers). For a more exclusive experience, Solmar offers their **Grand Solmar Land's End Resort & Spa** (Ave. Solmar 1-A, tel. 624/144-2500, www.grandsolmarresort.com, US$450). This property features the highly acclaimed **La Roca** restaurant.

Once the legendary Hotel Finisterra, **Sandos Finisterra Los Cabos** (Paseo de la Marina, toll-free U.S. tel. 888/774-0040, www.sandosloscabosresort.com, US$340) is now a renovated all-inclusive resort. There are beautiful beach views and a large pool area, anchored by their famous tall *palapa* pool bar in the middle. There's no swimming on the beach here as the waves of the Pacific are too fierce, but the resort has *palapas* and lounges on the beach to enjoy the views. Unlike at many other resorts in the Los Cabos area, finding a chair near the pool or on the beach is not a problem here.

Opening late 2017 is **Hard Rock Los Cabos** (www.hardrockhotels.com), an all-inclusive resort that has 600 rooms, six restaurants, and multiple pools. There are both family-friendly and adults-only sections. Live music performances, a full-service spa, a workout facility round out the services offered at this resort.

Also expected is the 200-room, beachfront **Nobu Hotel** (www.nobuhotels.com), which is scheduled to open in 2017. The luxury accommodations will have a contemporary and elegant style with inspiration coming from the local beach as well as Japan. The resort will also feature a signature **Nobu Restaurant and Bar.**

Camping and RV Parks

Vagabundos del Mar Trailer Park (Mexico 1, Km. 3, tel. 624/144-7223, www.vagabundos-restaurant.com, US$18) has 85 spaces with full hookups, including water and 15- or 30-amp power. The restaurant on the property, while not fancy, is open daily for lunch and dinner from noon and has good food and an extensive menu.

Set in a gated residential community, **Villa Serena RV Park** (Mexico 1, Km. 7.5, tel. 624/145-8244, www.villaserenacabo.net, US$23) has access to the pool, restaurant, lounge, and other services in the community.

INFORMATION AND SERVICES
Tourism Assistance
Los Cabos Convention and Visitors Bureau (Lázaro Cárdenas Edificio Posada, tel. 624/143-4777, 9am-5pm daily) can provide tourist help and assistance with hotels, restaurant, and local events.

The U.S. Consulate
The United States has a **consular agency** in Cabo San Lucas (Tiendas de Palmilla, Km. 27.5 Local B221, tel. 624/143-3566). They can provide emergency services for U.S. citizens as well as routine services such as notarial services, reports of birth abroad, and applications for U.S. passports. This location is unable to provide visa-related information or services.

Medical Services
There are plenty of clinics in the area with English-speaking doctors. Open 24/7, **AmeriMed** (Lázaro Cardenas, tel. 624/143-9670, www.amerimed.com.mx) is equipped to handle emergency services, has a bilingual staff, and accepts insurance policies. Dial **066** for emergencies.

GETTING AROUND
Most visitors who stay in Cabo San Lucas get around by walking or taking a taxi. Most taxis in Los Cabos are large vans that can fit 10 passengers or more. A taxi around town should cost under US$8, but always ask about the fare before getting in. Larger hotels and resorts will have taxis waiting outside the lobbies.

Todos Santos and the West Cape

Look for ★ to find recommended
sights, activities, dining, and lodging.

Highlights

★ **Todos Santos Historic Center:** Brick and pastel adobe colonial buildings line the streets and town plaza. Wander the picturesque streets while checking out art galleries, artisanal shops, restaurants and cafes (page 327).

★ **Sea Turtle Rescue:** From December through April, head to the beach to see hatchlings released. Stay for a period of time to help volunteer in the efforts (page 327).

★ **Surfing:** The breaks in this region have lured adventurous surfers for decades. Novice surfers head to Playa Los Cerritos, while experts hunt out the waves at La Pastora or San Pedrito (page 331).

★ **Gallery-Hopping in Todos Santos:** This artist town is one of the best spots in Baja California for perusing galleries and exploring the colorful art scene (page 333).

★ **Playa Los Cerritos:** The most popular beach in the region offers the swimmable waters and mild waves attracting novice surfers (page 339).

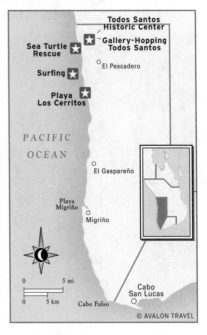

Just an hour's drive up Mexico 19 from Cabo San Lucas, travelers will find a place where the mega-resorts, nightclubs, and commotion melt away to reveal only the pristine beaches and undeveloped landscapes.

The West Cape prides itself on being the intimate and serene alternative to Los Cabos.

Once thought of as a side trip from Cabo, the West Cape has now become a popular destination in its own right. Small boutique hotels and B&Bs offer a relaxed alternative to the major resorts of Los Cabos. Deserted beaches and quaint towns replace the Cabo golf courses and rowdy tourist zones.

Surfers, artists, snowbirds, and chic jet-setters all find themselves in the West Cape, either passing through or taking up residence. Many expats have made a home here, and with the proximity to the Los Cabos airport, many travelers make their way here as well. While the area is developing rapidly, locals remain hopeful that the region will retain its authentic small-town charm.

The beaches in this area are beautiful with white sand shores and dramatic pounding waves that draw surfers from around the world. The currents can be strong and the surf rough, so be aware that most beaches on the West Cape are not for swimming.

Anchoring the region is Todos Santos, a designated *Pueblo Mágico*—only one of three on the entire Baja peninsula. This title was awarded from the Mexican government because of the historical and cultural value the town offers. Todos Santos was noticed by expat artists a number of decades ago, and the art scene remains strong with numerous galleries in addition to the artisanal shops, restaurants, and bars that now reside in the restored colonial buildings throughout town.

To the south of Todos Santos, the small fishing village of El Pescadero has now grown into another tourist area with plenty of hotels and restaurants to accommodate the expanding number of travelers. Most of the action

Previous: Todos Santos town plaza and church; beach *palapas* at Rancho Pescadero. **Above:** Guests will find a beautiful setting at Villa Santa Cruz.

Todos Santos and the West Cape

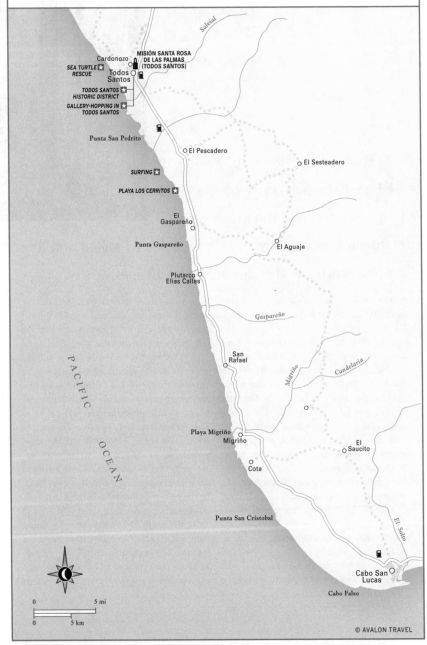

© AVALON TRAVEL

Best Accommodations

★ **Villa Santa Cruz:** Every detail is incredibly curated at this intimate and magical B&B on the beach at Todos Santos (page 338).

★ **The Hotelito:** Beautifully designed, this bright and modern hotel offers cozy accommodations and welcome margaritas by the pool (page 336).

★ **Hotel California:** A popular choice, Hotel California has eclectic décor, comfortable beds, and an on-site restaurant and bar (page 337).

★ **La Bohemia Hotel Pequeño:** Mixing outdoor adventure and comfy lodging, this bed-in-breakfast aims to give guests unforgettable experiences (page 337).

★ **Rancho Pescadero:** This mini-resort in El Pescadero has become a hip spot for jet-setters looking for a more relaxed alternative to Cabo (page 343).

takes place on or around Playa Los Cerritos, one of the best beaches in the region for surfing, swimming, and relaxing.

While the climate for most of the year is pleasantly moderate, August and September are extremely hot and also hurricane season. Many businesses, including some hotels, shut down during this time, so it's best to make arrangements in advance. December through March is the busiest time of year with holidays, the Todos Santos Music Festival, and the film festival.

PLANNING YOUR TIME

As the West Cape is just an hour drive from Los Cabos, the region can be a day trip for those who are staying in the Cabo area. However, most people come to the West Cape to relax and enjoy the beautiful beaches and the quaint town of Todos Santos, so they stay for at least a long weekend, if not longer. There are plenty of boutique luxury hotels, B&Bs, and eco-lodges to choose from.

There are more things to do in Todos Santos than in El Pescadero. Surfers and beachgoers are often attracted to staying in El Pescadero, while those looking to explore shops, restaurants, bars, and galleries

opt to make Todos Santos their base for the region.

If you're interested in exploring the nearby Sierra de la Laguna, plan on spending at least four days up in the mountains.

GETTING THERE
Car

The best and easiest way to explore the West Cape is with a car. The nearest airport is in Los Cabos, an hour's drive from the West Cape. Most travelers fly into Los Cabos and rent a car at the airport to drive north up Mexico 19 to get to the West Cape. There's a new toll road bypass from the airport to north of Cabo San Lucas, so drivers can easily skip the traffic and congestion of both San José del Cabo and Cabo San Lucas. A new four-lane freeway opens up north of Los Cabos, so driving from then on is fast and easy.

FUEL AND SERVICES

There's a gas station in Todos Santos as well as one in El Pescadero. Outside you are of the two towns, there are no gas stations or services for cars in the West Cape. Most major car repair and services will need to be done in Los Cabos.

Best Restaurants

★ **Los Adobes de Todos Santos:** Enjoy great food and ambiance at Los Adobes. Start with a traditional soup on the menu (page 333).

★ **Tequila's Sunrise Bar & Grill:** Offering traditional Mexican food and good service, this fun spot keeps patrons coming back (page 333).

★ **Café Santa Fe:** Don't miss the lobster ravioli at this delicious Italian restaurant right on the historic plaza of Todos Santos (page 334).

★ **El Mirador:** Stunning views are the real draw for this spot. Sunset is the best time to stop in (page 335).

★ **Hortaliza Hierbabuena:** Farm-to-table dining is taken literally at this unique dining experience where the open-air restaurant is situated in the middle of lush vegetable gardens (page 341).

Air

Flights arrive at the **Los Cabos International Airport** (SJD) daily from the United States and Canada. Alaska Airlines, America West, American Airlines, Delta Airlines, Southwest Airlines, and Sunquest Vacations all have international flights to the Los Cabos airport. It's about an hour by car from the airport to the West Cape.

Bus

Aguila (tel. 800/824-8452, www.autobusesaguila.com) and **Autobuses de la Baja California** (ABC, tel. 664/104-7400, www.abc.com.mx) have service directly to Todos Santos and El Pescadero from Cabo San Lucas and other cities in Baja. There are no bus services within El Pescadero or Todos Santos, so travelers will need to walk or rely on the limited taxi service.

Todos Santos

Todos Santos is a designated *Pueblo Mágico* (only one of three on the entire Baja peninsula)—a moniker given by the Mexican government for places that have significant offerings in terms of natural beauty, cultural riches, or historical relevance. Travelers only need to spend a few moments in the central historical district to understand why the town was chosen for this special honor. Todos Santos oozes charm with its restored colonial buildings, town plaza, palm-lined streets, and the stunning beaches nearby. The town has become a popular spot for visitors looking for an escape from the large resorts and glamour of Cabo.

The modern history of the town begins in the 18th century when the Jesuits discovered freshwater springs here and built a *visita* for the La Paz mission. They eventually founded a separate mission in 1733—Misión Santa Rosa de las Palmas. The mission was secularized in 1840 and only a few ruins remain today. In the 19th century, Todos Santos became the sugarcane capital of Baja with eight sugar mills supporting a thriving industry. Most of the springs dried up in the 1950s, and the sugarcane industry soon faded out.

The town was bleak for a number of decades until the springs came back to life in 1981 and the freeway was paved in the mid-1980s. A thriving agricultural industry developed (and continues to this day), providing markets and Cabo restaurants with organic produce. American and Canadian artists discovered Todos Santos in the 1980s and helped to revitalize the town, turning it into a chic and bohemian destination for expats and travelers. Today, the art scene is still thriving, and many travelers spend time visiting the numerous art galleries around Todos Santos.

While Todos Santos is considered to be a coastal destination, the center of town is not directly on the beach. Beach communities and some boutique hotels have started to populate the coastline, but most of the action is in town, about two kilometers away from the beaches. Surfers will want to head out to the waves, but the beaches in this area are not safe for swimming because of the heavy surf and riptides. It's beautiful to walk along the beach and watch the sunset over the Pacific, but save the swimming for the hotel pool.

Although the plaza is missing the hustle and bustle that most plazas have, it is home to the historic church and old theater. Most of the tourist action in Todos Santos takes place on the surrounding streets. It's pleasant to spend the afternoon walking around the town, admiring the brick and colorful

adobe colonial buildings that have now been restored as boutique hotels, art galleries, artisanal shops, cafés, and upscale restaurants. Ecotourism is also important for Todos Santos, and the sea turtle rescue projects are a popular draw for volunteers.

SIGHTS
★ Historic Center

The large town plaza is lined with colonial buildings including the **Teatro Márquez de León, Iglesia Nuestra Señora del Pilar**, and the Café Santa Fe restaurant, housed in one of the largest adobe structures still remaining in town. But unlike in other Mexican towns, the plaza in Todos Santos is not the epicenter of activity. The surrounding streets are much busier with active businesses and people milling about. A stroll around the streets to the north and east of the plaza will reward travelers with galleries, shops, restaurants, bars, and hotels.

★ Sea Turtle Rescue

Tortugueros Las Playitas (tel. 612/145-0353, U.S. tel. 213/265-9943, www.todostortugueros.org) is a nonprofit that helps to restore the Pacific leatherbacks, a critically endangered sea turtle on the verge of extinction. The

the Todos Santos town plaza at twilight

Todos Santos

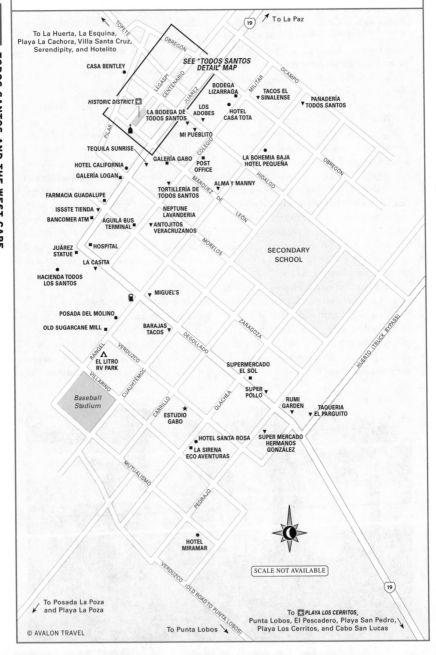

To La Huerta, La Esquina,
Playa La Cachora, Villa Santa Cruz,
Serendipity, and Hotelito

To La Paz

TOPETE

OBREGÓN

OCAMPO

SEE "TODOS SANTOS
DETAIL" MAP

CASA BENTLEY

LEGASPI

CENTENARIO

JUÁREZ

MILITAR

BODEGA
LIZARRAGA

TACOS EL
SINALENSE

PANADERÍA
TODOS SANTOS

HISTORIC DISTRICT

LA BODEGA DE
TODOS SANTOS

LOS
ADOBES

HOTEL
CASA TOTA

PILAR

MI PUEBLITO

TEQUILA SUNRISE

COLEGIO

GALERÍA GABO

POST
OFFICE

LA BOHEMIA BAJA
HOTEL PEQUEÑA

OBREGÓN

HOTEL CALIFORNIA

GALERÍA LOGAN

ALMA Y MANNY

HIDALGO

FARMACIA GUADALUPE

MARQUEZ DE

TORTILLERÍA DE
TODOS SANTOS

ISSSTE TIENDA

BANCOMER ATM

AGUILA BUS
TERMINAL

NEPTUNE
LAVANDERIA

ANTOJITOS
VERACRUZANOS

LEÓN

JUÁREZ
STATUE

HOSPITAL

LA CASITA

MORELOS

SECONDARY
SCHOOL

HACIENDA TODOS
LOS SANTOS

MIGUEL'S

POSADA DEL MOLINO

ZARAGOZA

OLD SUGARCANE MILL

BARAJAS
TACOS

DEGOLLADO

HUERTO (TRUCK BYPASS)

RANGEL

VERDUZCO

EL LITRO
RV PARK

VILLARINO

CUAUHTÉMOC

Baseball
Stadium

SUPERMERCADO
EL SOL

CARRILLO

OLACHEA

SUPER
POLLO

RUMI
GARDEN

TAQUERIA
EL PARGUITO

ESTUDIO
GABO

HOTEL SANTA ROSA

LA SIRENA
ECO AVENTURAS

SUPER MERCADO
HERMANOS
GONZÁLEZ

MUTUALISMO

PEDRAJO

HOTEL
MIRAMAR

SCALE NOT AVAILABLE

19

To Posada La Poza
and Playa La Poza

VERDUZCO (OLD ROAD TO PUNTA LOBOS)

© AVALON TRAVEL

To Punta Lobos

To PLAYA LOS CERRITOS,
Punta Lobos, El Pescadero, Playa San Pedro,
Playa Los Cerritos, and Cabo San Lucas

Pacific Leatherback Sea Turtles

The leatherback sea turtle is the largest of all living turtles. Its name comes from its unique back, covered only by skin instead of the hard shell other turtles have. Adults can grow up to two meters in length and weigh up to 2,000 pounds. It's estimated that they live around 45 years in the wild. The leatherback is the world's most migratory sea turtle and can travel up to 16,000 kilometers a year.

Leatherbacks mate at sea, and the females come ashore at night to nest. They dig a hole in the ground and deposit around 80 eggs, filling the nest before returning to sea. Incubation is about 60 days, and once the eggs hatch, the baby sea turtles make their way into the ocean where they must learn to fend for themselves without any help from their parents. Female hatchlings will roam the seas until they reach sexual maturity when they will return to the same nesting area to produce their own offspring. Male leatherbacks spend the rest of their lives in the ocean without returning to land.

The leatherback population is rapidly declining in many parts of the world. There are only about 2,300 females of the Pacific leatherback sea turtle remaining, making it the most endangered marine turtle subpopulation.

organization collects the eggs and places them in their incubation greenhouse, which helps to keep the eggs warm and safe from predators. Once the eggs hatch, the hatchlings are released into the ocean. Hatchling releases happen between November 15 and April in the evenings around sunset at **Las Tunas Sanctuary** (the Tortugueros website and Facebook page will have specific information during hatchling release season). Hatchling releases are open to the public and free of charge for anyone who wants to watch the young sea turtles venture out into the ocean for the first time. Tortugueros Las Playitas accepts volunteers to help with nest relocation, recording data, incubation supervision, and caring for hatchlings. Volunteers are responsible for paying for their own airfare, transportation, accommodations, and meals.

La Poza

This freshwater lagoon is a bird-watchers' paradise, home to over 100 species of birds. Egrets, herons, gulls, ducks, pelicans, and sandpipers are just some of the birds that can be found at **La Poza**. This picturesque spot features sand dunes on one side of the lagoon, providing a barrier to the ocean, and palm trees on the other side. Stay out of the lagoon, as the waters are deeper than they look and large waves are known to have come crashing over the dunes. The easiest way to get to the lagoon is to follow the signs for Posada La Poza.

Misión Santa Rosa de las Palmas

In 1724 Spanish Jesuit Padre Jaime Bravo founded Todos Santos as a *visita* for the La Paz mission. Because of the freshwater springs and prime location, the *visita* eventually became a full mission under Padre Sigismundo Taraval in 1733. **Misión Santa Rosa de las Palmas** was destroyed the following year during the great revolt of the Pericú natives. A second mission was built and eventually relocated to another spot one mile south in 1825. Its population decreased until the mission was eventually secularized in 1840. The original mission site, just north of town, is now a car repair business (ruins of the mission walls were expanded upon to create the repair shop) and a church that was built in 1970. The **Iglesia Nuestra Señora del Pilar** on the town plaza occupies the second 1825 mission site. Newer construction was added to the original foundation and walls.

BEACHES

The beaches of Todos Santos are stunningly beautiful with white sand, crashing waves, and often complemented by sand dunes and palm trees speckling the landscape. However, the beaches in this area (aside from Playa Los Cerritos in El Pescadero) are not for swimming. The strong currents and forceful waves create dangerous situations for swimmers. Beaches are great for sunbathing, taking walks, or enjoying sunsets, but not for a swim. Most of the beaches are accessed by little dirt roads heading west from town. There are no services at the beaches so take umbrellas, water, and food if you plan on spending the day. The following beaches are listed in order from north to south.

Playa La Pastora is a sandy beach popular with surfers because the right point break will be breaking when other surf spots are not. The long stretches of sand are beautiful for taking a walk, but strong waves mean that swimming is not an option here. Because La Pastora is a little more difficult to get to than other beaches in the area, you'll likely have the beach mostly to yourself. Access is via Topete which turns into Horizonte and then the coastal road, going north about three kilometers out of town.

Playa La Cachora is great beach for whale-watching, walking along the shore, and horseback riding—but not for swimming. This is one of the beaches in the area where the sea turtles come to lay their eggs. From town, take Topete west to La Cachora.

Playa La Poza (Las Pocitas) is known for the freshwater lagoon, La Poza, which is a fantastic spot for bird-watching. Surf fishing can be good here early in the morning. Sunbathing and relaxing for the day are popular activities, made more convenient by the access to the restaurant at nearby Posada La Poza. From town, follow the signs for Posada La Poza.

Punta Lobos is where local fishers depart on their *pangas* for bigger catches out in the Pacific. This can be a great spot to buy fresh fish from their daily catches when they come back into shore in the afternoon. If it's whale season and the fishing is slow, you may be able to arrange with one of the *pangueros* (you'll need to speak Spanish) to take you out whale-watching for a few hours. There's a colony of sea lions near the south point of the beach. For surfers, the point/reef breaks on south swells. Access Punta Lobos by heading south on Vidal in town or from Mexico 19 at kilometer 54.

the beautiful beaches of Todos Santos

Playa San Pedro (Playa Las Palmas) is a small and secluded beach accessed by walking through a grove of palm trees. There are rocky points at both ends of the beach providing a protected area in between. If the sea is calm, this can sometimes be a good swimming spot. Hiking and bodysurfing are other popular activities here. There's a small lagoon and an abandoned old ranch from sugarcane days. There are no concessions and the location is remote, so take snacks and a picnic lunch if you plan on staying for the day. To access the beach, look for a small turnoff from Mexico 19 at kilometer 57 across from the research station. There's a gate that closes at 6pm, so plan to be out by then.

Playa San Pedrito at the north end of Playa Pescadero is popular with body boarders, anglers, and surfers. There's a rocky point at the north end of the beach that produces decent waves on west and north swells. The point is also a good spot for fishing. The turnoff for the beach is just south of the El Pescadero Pemex gas station on Mexico 19 at kilometer 62.

SPORTS AND RECREATION
★ Surfing

The lure of big breaks and near-empty waves along the West Cape has attracted adventurous surfers to the area for decades, although empty waves are becoming increasingly difficult to find. Todos Santos is an area for experienced surfers who have their own boards and know what they're doing. Beginners will want to head down to El Pescadero where surf lessons and board rentals are readily available at Playa Los Cerritos.

Playa La Pastora has an exposed point break with right and left breaks, but is mostly known for bigger rights on northwest swells. This is a popular spot because it can be breaking when other spots are not. There's a rocky bottom, so this is not a spot for beginners. Access is via Topete, which turns into Horizonte and then the coastal road, going north about three kilometers out of town.

To the north of La Pastora on the coastal road, **Punta Márquez** and **Punta Conejo** require some serious off-road exploring to reach. You can camp along the shore if you bring all of your own supplies. Make sure to set up on the bluff and not below in the sandy *vado*, where you could be at risk for flash floods. You'll likely find a small community of surfers and families who come to camp here for a few days while enjoying the surf and serene beaches. These spots are also accessible from Bahía Magdalena to the north.

Named for the colony of sea lions, **Punta Lobos** breaks on south swells. Local fishers launch their *pangas* here and the beach has a rocky point and lighthouse. It can be accessed from Vidal in town or from a turnoff at kilometer 54 on Mexico 19.

Down near El Pescadero, **Playa San Pedrito** is a solid beach break that's best on west and north swells. Between San Pedrito and El Pescadero around kilometer 59 are consistent right reef and beach breaks. Many paddle out from the sandy beach as there are sea urchins on the reef.

Yoga

Yoga classes are a favorite pastime of many residents and visitors of Todos Santos, and there are a number of options. Some hotels, such as **The Hotelito** (Rancho de la Cachora, tel. 612/145-0099, www.thehotelito.com), **Casa Bentley** (Calle Pilar 99, tel. 612/145-0276, www.casabentleybaja.com), and **Villa Santa Cruz** (Camino a la Playitas, tel. 612/143-9230, U.S. tel. 760/230-5557, www.villasantacruzbaja.com) hold classes or can arrange for a private instructor. **Baja Yoga & Ayurveda** (tel. 612/131-6387, www.bajayoga-ayurveda.com) offers yoga and Ayurveda retreats, seminars, and private classes from October to July.

Organized Tours

Todos Santos Eco Adventures (tel. 612/145-0189, www.tosea.net) offers a multitude of single-day and multiday excursions to swim with sea lions and whale sharks, venture into the Sierra de la Laguna, go whale-watching, try rock climbing, or take a cultural visit to a local ranch. Some of their trips are around the Todos Santos area, and some of the excursions take you to other locations in Baja Sur to have your adventure.

Leading similar adventures for wildlife excursions and water sports is **La Sirena Eco-Adventures** (tel. 612/145-0353, www.lasirenakayaksurf.com) a branch of Tortugueros Las Playitas, who run the sea turtle rescue. They also have vacation rentals available.

ENTERTAINMENT AND EVENTS

Bars

While there are a number of little bars in town that provide a great option for grabbing a few drinks, there are no nightclubs or swanky lounges in Todos Santos like those found in Cabo. The bar scene here is much more casual and subdued, with most places closing down around 10pm.

A number of hotels have popular bars such as **La Copa Bar** (Calle Legaspi 33, tel. 612/145-0040, 3pm-11pm daily) at The Todos Santos Inn, where visitors will find a classy saloon-style setting and a nice selection of wine. Over at Hotel California's **La Coronela** (Benito Juárez, tel. 612/145-0525, 9am-10:30pm daily) a decent selection of wines and flavored margaritas grace the menu. You can enjoy the bar inside or sit outside in the courtyard patio.

If you're really in the mood for margaritas, head across the street from Hotel California to **Tequila's Sunrise Bar & Grill** (Benito Juárez, no tel., 11am-9pm daily). The damiana margarita is a specialty and definitely worth trying. The funky decor features retro-inspired margarita signs and plenty of messages from patrons who have been inspired to leave their mark on the wall with Sharpies.

For a sports bar that serves cold beer and a great burger, don't miss **Shut up Frank's** (Santo Degollado 13, tel. 612/145-0707, 10am-10pm daily). This low-key and friendly spot is popular with both the expat locals and

tourists passing through. With plenty of big-screen TVs, it's one of the best places to catch a game in town.

Outside of town on the road to La Paz is **The Distillery Tasting Room and La Fuente Winery** (Mexico 19 Km. 50, tel. 612/145-0213, www.thedistillery.mx, 11am-7pm Thurs.-Sun.). The boutique distillery makes tequila, vodka, and moonshine, and the adjoining winery offers wines like trebbiano and ruby cabernet. They have a tasting room as well as an outdoor picnic area. Distillery tours can be arranged with a week's notice.

Festivals and Events

Created by Peter Buck of R.E.M. and hosted at the Hotel California, the **Todos Santos Music Festival** (www.todossantosmusicfestival.com) has become one of the town's most popular annual events. The festival takes place in January each year and benefits a local charity group.

The **Open Studios Tour** (www.artistsoftodossantos.com) is a few days each February where the artists of Todos Santos open their studios up to the public. People can visit with the artists in their studios to get a behind-the-scenes experience about their process. The **Festival de Cine** (www.todossantoscine.org) takes place in March and features films by local and international filmmakers.

SHOPPING

For Mexican crafts and souvenirs, there are a number of shops and artisan stalls around town. Colorful Talavera pottery, wood-frame hammocks, Mexican blankets and ponchos, and silver jewelry are common as well as other trinkets.

If you're looking for a quality Mexican souvenir to take home, try **Manos Mexicanos** (Topete and Centenario, tel. 612/145-0538, 10am-5pm Mon.-Sat.). The selection includes local crafts, soaps, jewelry, and home decorations as well as handcrafted pottery by artist Rubén Gutierrez.

In a storefront adjoining the hotel,

Emporio Hotel California (Juárez between Morelos and Márquez de León, tel. 512/145-0217, 10am-7pm daily) has an eclectic assortment of books, jewelry, clothing, decorative home accessories, and artwork by local artists.

For a dose of bohemian dresses, chic kaftans, and ethnic jewelry, don't miss Nomad Chic (Juárez and Hidalgo, tel. 612/105-2857, www.nomadchic.mx, 11am-5pm daily). Owner Linda Hamilton stocks contemporary designers not easily found in other stores. She also designs her own line of apparel, jewelry, and accessories, inspired by travels around the world.

For a unique gift or souvenir from the region, La Sonrisa de la Muerte (Centro C/ Militar and Hidalgo, no tel., www.smuerte.com, 10am-5pm daily) is an art and graphics gallery with handpicked prints from young Mexican artists. In addition to prints, this hip little shop sells items like T-shirts, bags, stickers, and cards.

Bibliophiles will love a trip to El Tecolote Bookstore (Juárez and Hidalgo, 9am-5pm Mon.-Sat., noon-3pm Sun., reduced hours during the summer) with a curated selection of new and used books. The assortment includes fiction, coffee-table books, Baja-specific titles, as well as maps, DVDs, music, and cards.

La Bodega (Calle Hidalgo, tel. 612/152-0181, labodegadetodossantos@gmail.com, noon-7pm Tues.-Sat.) carries bottles of wine only from Mexico, with many of the wines coming from Baja's famous Valle de Guadalupe. The boutique shop has wine-tastings on Monday and Wednesday for US$9. For an extra US$6 you can get a sampling of tapas from Mi Pueblito right next door to accompany your wines. In addition to wine, La Bodega sells high-quality olive oil, including their own label coming from the well-known Rancho Córtes in Valle de Guadalupe.

★ ART GALLERIES AND STUDIOS

One of the top galleries in town, and a must-visit for anyone who appreciates art, is Galería de Todos Santos (Juárez, tel. 612/145-0500, www.galeriatodossantos-com.webs.com, 10am-4:30pm Mon.-Sat., 11am-4pm Sun.). The gallery has been carrying a variety of artists and mediums since 1994. The light and airy space features pieces from local and international artists.

Featuring the work of artist Gabo and his son, Gabriel Rodriguez, Gabo Galería (Calle Márquez de León, tel. 612/145-0514, 11am-4:30pm Mon.-Sat.) is popular with those who appreciate abstract art. Gabo is a popular Mexican artist whose work can be seen all over town in various hotels and public spaces.

Artist Jill Logan has her work on display at her gallery Galería Logan (Juárez and Morelos, tel. 612/145-0151, www.jilllogan.com, 11am-4pm Mon.-Sat.). Her colorful and bold paintings are a favorite among tourists and locals.

For a more hands-on approach to the Todos Santos art scene, Todos Artes (tel. 503/219-5918, www.donnabillickart.com/todos-artes) hosts destination art workshops with instruction from guest artists. Various mediums and projects are explored.

FOOD
Mexican

For a trifecta of great food, setting, and ambience, head to ★ Los Adobes de Todos Santos (Calle Hidalgo between Juárez and Colegio Militar, tel. 612/145-0203, www.losadobesdetodossantos.com, 11:30am-9pm Mon.-Sat., 11:30am-5pm Sun., mains US$10-13). Tucked away in a courtyard behind a 100-year-old adobe building, the outdoor dining patio looks over a beautiful and well-manicured cactus garden. Start with one of the traditional soups on the menu, and for your entrée, enjoy a hearty meat or seafood dish prepared in authentic Mexican style.

Good service, delicious traditional Mexican food, and great margaritas (try the damiana flavor) keep patrons going back to ★ Tequila's Sunrise Bar & Grill (Benito Juárez, no tel., 11am-9pm daily, mains US$9-15). It's a fun environment with flat-screen

TVs and signatures of patrons all over the walls. The shrimp chiles rellenos and the Mexican combination plate are favorites among patrons.

For casual *palapa* dining, **Miguel's** (Degollado and Rangel, tel. 612/145-0733, 8am-9pm Mon.-Sat., mains US$6-10) is the place to go for cold beer and tasty authentic Mexican dishes. Surfboards line the ceiling and the restaurant just recently upgraded from dirt floors. Miguel himself is usually there to wait on customers. The chiles rellenos stuffed with shrimp are a well-deserved favorite dish of anyone who visits. Finish up with the flan for dessert (Miguel's wife makes it).

The fresh guacamole, nachos, and fish tacos are what keep people coming back for the traditional Mexican cuisine at **Mi Pueblito** (Calle Hidalgo, tel. 612/145-0889, mipueblitobcs@gmail.com, 8am-9pm Mon.-Sat., 8am-4pm Sun.). There's inside and patio seating and most of the staff speak English. There's another smaller location across the street right next to La Bodega wine shop. They partner with La Bodega to serve tapas during Monday and Wednesday evening wine-tastings.

What originally started as a small tamale stand has now been upgraded to an open-air restaurant at **Alma y Manny** (Marquez de Leon, 9am-9pm daily). With a selection of homemade tamales, tacos, chiles rellenos, and traditional Mexican breakfasts, the spot has become a favorite of local Mexicans and expats. The plastic chairs and *palapa* roof create a casual setting for enjoying a deliciously authentic and affordable meal.

Seafood

In a friendly and unassuming setting, **Fonda El Zaguán** (Juárez, tel. 612/145-0485, www.fondaelzaguan.com, noon-8:30pm Mon.-Sat., mains US$8-11) serves not only fresh fish and seafood but also has some meat and poultry options on the menu. Main dishes are served with fresh garden vegetables and rice. If you don't want to eat in the dining room, there are sidewalk tables that are perfect for enjoying a glass of Baja wine and people-watching.

Focusing on small plates and fresh ingredients, **La Casita Tapas and Wine Bar** (Degollado and Calle Militar, tel. 612/145-0192, www.lacasitatapaswinebar.com, noon-10pm Tues.-Sun., mains US$8-13) is known for sushi and seafood dishes like coconut shrimp. The wine menu includes a good selection of Baja and international wines, and they also serve delicious sangria. This is a great family-friendly restaurant that's a favorite of both locals and visitors.

Taco Stands

Street food enthusiasts, taco lovers, and foodies in general will enjoy **Taqueria El Parguito** (Santos Degollado and Del Huerto, no tel., 11am-3pm daily). Their shrimp and fish tacos are popular with anyone looking for a cheap and quick meal. Like any fish taco stand, the setting is casual and they close when they run out of fresh seafood—so it's best to plan to go on the early side.

Owner Pepe and his team at **Tacos y Mariscos El Sinaloense** (Calle Colegio Militar at Obregon, tel. 612/173-2989, 10am-6pm Wed.-Mon., US$2-5) win over crowds with their friendly service and marlin fish tacos. They serve a variety of seafood tacos and ceviches at affordable prices.

For a tasty, cheap, and quick meal, **Carnitas Barajas** (Santa Degollado and Calle Cuauhtemoc, no tel., 8am-11pm daily, US$2-6) has *carnitas* by the taco, half kilo and kilo. They also have fish, shrimp, and carne asada tacos as well as *papas rellenas* (stuffed potatoes). The service can be aloof, but the food and price make up for it.

If you're in the mood for fresh ceviche, **Mariscos el Compa Chava** (Del Huerto, no tel., 10am-7pm daily, US$4-7) is the place to go. In addition to seafood cocktails and ceviche, they have cooked fish and shrimp dishes—all served with homemade sauces in a breezy *palapa* setting.

Italian

For decades, a mandatory dining experience in Todos Santos has been ★ **Café Santa Fe** and travelers. Owners Magda Valpiani and Angelo Dal Bon came from Italy in 2006 and also run Caffè Todos Santos. Fresh ingredients are skillfully prepared into dishes such as artisanal pizzas, the daily fresh catch, and homemade pasta dishes.

International

On the grounds of the Todos Santos Inn, **La Copa Cocina** (Legaspi 33, tel. 612/117-2426, www.todossantosinn.com, 5pm-10pm Thurs.-Tues., mains US$15-20) serves gourmet tacos, sliders, sushi, and other California-inspired tapas. The extensive wine list and beautiful outdoor garden help to create a romantic setting.

For a dining experience accompanied by incredible views, ★ **El Mirador** (Old Punta Lobos Road, tel. 612/175-0800, www.guaycura.com, 1pm-9pm daily, mains US$16) is the place to go. Sunset is the best time to go to really take advantage of the vista offered by this large *palapa* on the beach outside of town. The food is average and prices are a bit high, but many people return just for the views.

It doesn't look like much from the outside, but don't let appearances fool you at **Rumi Garden** (128 Santos Degollado, tel. 612/145-1088, www.rumigarden.com, noon-9pm Wed.-Mon., mains US$10). Once you get past the monolithic looking exterior, the inside unfolds into a colorful dining area with a garden and fountain. With authentic dishes like pad thai and shrimp curry made with organic ingredients, this is a favorite spot for locals and tourists.

For a unique twist on fresh Asian fusion cuisine, try **Michael's at the Gallery** (Juárez, tel. 612/145-0500, 6pm-10pm Fri.-Sat., US$13-16). The ambiance is memorable, as the restaurant is located on the veranda of a gallery space. Reservations are required as the restaurant is only open limited hours for Friday and Saturday.

Cafés

Serving breakfast, lunch, and dinner, **Caffè Todos Santos** (Calle Centenario 33, tel. 612/145-0300, 7am-10pm Tues.-Sun.,

Café Santa Fe has some of the best Italian food on the peninsula.

(Calle Centenario 4, tel. 612/145-0340, www.cafesantafetodossantos.com, noon-9pm Wed.-Mon., closed Sept. and Oct., mains US$15-22). Paula and Ezio Colombo opened the restaurant in late 1990, and with Ezio's northern Italian background, they bring uncompromised flavors of Italy to Baja. The food is carefully crafted with produce grown in their own organic garden and fresh fish and meats. The results always seem to exceed expectations. The atmosphere is Italian bistro meets Mexican paradise with checkered floors and white tablecloths in the open-air dining room looking out onto the tropical *palapa* patio. The service is always great here, and some of the servers, like Carlos, have been working at the restaurant for two decades. Don't visit without trying the fish carpaccio and the lobster ravioli.

Tucked into a lush garden setting, **Tre Galline** (Calle Centenario 33, tel. 612/145-0300, angelodalbon@gmail.com, 5pm-10pm daily, mains US$12-15) is another Italian restaurant that's become a favorite for locals

US$8-11) is a longtime favorite in town. It's now owned by the proprietors of Tre Galline, so in addition to great pastries and breakfasts, they're serving well-made Italian food for lunches and dinner.

In addition to coffee and baked goods, **La Esquina** (tel. 612/145-0851, www.laesquinats.com, 7am-7pm Tues., Wed., Fri., Sat., 9am-10pm Mon. and Thurs., 9am-3pm Sun., US$4-7) serves breakfast and lunch with healthy food choices like made-to order sandwiches, soups, and organic salads. This is a popular hangout for locals, and they regularly host community events like fund-raisers, movie screenings, and live music. There's a farmers market on Wednesday 9am-noon.

ACCOMMODATIONS

Accommodations in Todos Santos can be expensive compared to other parts of the peninsula. Many hotels are seasonal, closing for the hot, humid summers in August and September. Accommodations that remain open during that time may offer cheaper rates, but be sure to ask if they have air-conditioning in the rooms. There are no large resorts here; accommodations consist mostly of B&Bs and boutique hotels with only a few rooms. Reservations should be booked in advance for this region, especially around Christmas and New Years when the area is extremely popular and room rates will go up for a few weeks.

Under US$50

Catering to surfers and backpackers, **Hotel Miramar** (Mutualismo y Pedrajo 102, tel. 612/145-0341, US$30) has basic and clean rooms with TV and wireless Internet. Some rooms have air-conditioning, and there's a clean pool on the property. The hotel is located outside of the town center in a neighborhood that can be somewhat noisy with the local sounds of neighbors, dogs, and roosters, so bring earplugs if you're a light sleeper. There's a large parking area for guests who have cars.

On the south side of town, **Hotel Santa Rosa** (Agustin Olachea, tel. 612/145-0394,

www.hotelsantarosa.com.mx, US$35) has eight rooms with kitchenettes. Accommodations are sparse, but there's a small swimming pool and Jacuzzi. Rooms have TV with cable as well as air-conditioning. Discounts are available for stays of one week or longer.

US$50-150

The rooms are spacious and comfortable at **Serendipity** (Las Tunas, tel. 612/178-0104, www.serendipityventures.com, US$120-160), a hacienda-style bed-and-breakfast. In addition to having a pool, the property runs down to the beach and all rooms have ocean views. They have a renowned full to-order breakfast in the mornings. The B&B is two kilometers outside of town and a short drive to the center.

For a stay in a Portuguese-style castle try **Casa Bentley** (Calle Pilar 99, tel. 612/145-0276, www.casabentleybaja.com, US$110-140). This boutique hotel is set on lush grounds with palm trees and century-old mango trees. The building is made of incredible stonework, featuring multi-level patios, and features a pool fed by waterfall. The location is easy walking distance to the town center.

The Spanish colonial-style **Posada del Molino** (Col San Vicente, tel. 612/169-2095, www.posadadelmolinots.com, US$90-110) has an old mill on the premises, left over from the town's sugarcane era. With Mexican-style decor, each studio has a fully equipped kitchenette.

With a design that strikes a balance between cozy and modern, ★ **The Hotelito** (Rancho de la Cachora, tel. 612/145-0099, www.thehotelito.com, US$135) is a small property with four well-crafted rooms. Owner Jenny Armit has taken care to finish modern rooms with bright paint colors and designer furniture touches. Each has its own private garden. Services include a 48-foot saltwater pool and welcome margaritas. The beach is a 10-minute walk from this property on the edge of town.

Although housed in an old historic

building, **Hotel Casa Tota** (Calle Álvaro Obregon, tel. 612/145-0590, www.hotel-casatota.com, US$123-143) features modern rooms with amenities like plasma TVs and room service. There are 15 rooms, a roof deck, swimming pool, and hot tub. There's an on-site store where they sell their own blends of tequila and mescal.

US$150-250

The fact that it wasn't actually the inspiration for the famous Eagles song (although many rumors claim that it was), doesn't seem to diminish the popularity of ★ **Hotel California** (Benito Juárez between Morelos and Marquez de Leon, tel. 612/145-0525, www.hotelcaliforniabaja.com, US$150-185). They have 11 rooms with down comforters, air-conditioning, and patios. Eclectic decorations and artwork come from around the world. Founded in 1947, the hotel has a lock on the town of Todos Santos with its **La Coronela** restaurant and bar and **Emporio** gallery and store. The landmark is home to the annual music festival and remains a stop for many tourists passing through town, whether they come to dine, drink, shop, or stay.

With three guesthouses and four luxury suites, **Hacienda Todos los Santos** (Benito Juárez, tel. 612/145-0547, www.tshacienda. com, US$130-190) also boasts beautiful lush grounds and a nice pool area. The modern rooms are luxuriously appointed with comfortable beds, high ceilings, and large bathrooms. Breakfast is included in your stay, and the property has a great location a few blocks away from the center of town.

The historic brick building that now houses **The Todos Santos Inn** (Calle Legaspi 33, tel. 612/145-0040, www.todossantosinn.com, US$145-225) was once the home of a sugar baron in the mid 19th century during the town's sugar mill days. The hotel offers terrace rooms, junior suites, and garden suites. All rooms come with free breakfast. The popular **La Copa Cocina** restaurant offers enchanting outdoor dining in the courtyard and also has an accompanying wine bar.

With the mission of creating an unforgettable experience by way of accommodation and facilitating exploration is ★ **La Bohemia Hotel Pequeño** (Calle Rangel 108, tel. 612/145-0759, www.labohemiabaja. com, US$146-183). Owners Erin and Andrew Wheelwright are outdoor adventurers who used to run a glamping business in Santa Barbara before moving to Todos Santos. The well-curated bed-and-breakfast has six rooms

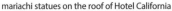

mariachi statues on the roof of Hotel California

with whitewashed walls and tasteful decorations. Gardens and hammocks help guests relax during their stay, and there's a main *palapa* for yoga, mescal tastings, and social gatherings. The hotel serves as a delightful base camp for getting out to explore Todos Sandos and the surrounding sierras. They can help arrange explorations like hiking to waterfalls, surf lessons, whale-watching, and cycling.

One of the few accommodations actually located on the beach in Todos Santos is the magical bed-and-breakfast ★ **Villa Santa Cruz** (Camino a la Playitas, tel. 612/143-9230, U.S. tel. 760/230-5557, www.villas-antacruzbaja.com, US$195-250). Americans Matt and Jessica Canepa opened the B&B in 2011 and overlooked no detail in building the property from the ground up. While you're enjoying your welcome margarita, you'll get a tour of the exquisite villa and grounds. Decorated with authentic wood and wrought-iron Mexican furniture and accented with colorful artisan pieces, the villa looks like something out of a movie (the floating glass staircase is uniquely superb). The pool is perfectly heated to 87 degrees and comes complete with a large hot tub, lots of comfortable chaise lounges, and a hammock. There's a large *palapa*, replete

with a comfy sleeping loft, that sits up on the sand dunes overlooking the magnificent, and fairly empty, beach. The famous La Pastora surf spot is a 10-minute walk south from here. There are beach towels, coolers, beach chairs, and sunscreen all available for guest use. There's also a cask of tequila (first shot is on the house) as well as wine and beer (all available on the honor system). At night, tiki torches illuminate the outdoor areas and candles are lit throughout the villa, giving everything an ethereal glow. You can enjoy the hot tub under a blanket of stars and the sound of crashing waves in the background, or there are fire pits set up on the roof for enjoyment as well. Sleep with the French doors open to enjoy the lulling sound of crashing waves throughout the night. In the morning, you'll awake to find a basket of hot coffee and tea outside the door, which you can leisurely enjoy on your balcony before heading downstairs for a full breakfast served in the outdoor dining area.

Guests at **Guaycura** (Calle Legaspi at Topete, tel. 612/175-0800, www.guaycura. com, US$175-228) get the enjoy the central location of the hotel in town and also have access to Guaycura's **El Faro Beach Club,** outside of town on the beach with a swimming

the pool area at Villa Santa Cruz

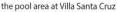

pool and **El Mirador restaurant**. There's a shuttle that will take guests from the hotel in town to the beach club. The hotel in town has 14 elegantly decorated rooms and a rooftop bar that has great views at sunset time.

Located directly on the lagoon, **Posada La Poza** (Col. La Poza, tel. 612/145-0400, tel. U.S. toll-free 855/552-7692, www.hotelposadalapozatodossantos.com, US$195-235) has eight boutique suites that are well appointed with air-conditioning, orthopedic mattresses, and high-quality linens. To augment its lagoon location, binoculars and bird books are available in all rooms, and it's a great spot for bird-watching. There's a heated saltwater pool and hot tub for guests to enjoy. Spa services are available, and **El Gusto restaurant** is located right on the property.

INFORMATION AND SERVICES

There's a Pemex gas station in town at the intersection of Degollado and Militar. There are **Bancomer** and **Banorte** branches for withdrawing money from ATMs. There are small markets but no large grocery stores. There's no official tourist office in Todos Santos, but most hotels and businesses are willing to give recommendations and answer questions.

While there are no large hospitals in the area, the **Centro de Salud** (tel. 612/145-0095) located at Degollado and Juárez and is open 24/7. Call **066** for any emergencies.

GETTING THERE AND AROUND

Todos Santos is about an hour's drive north of Cabo San Lucas. There's a new four-lane highway, making the drive extremely easy even for those not accustomed to navigating Baja. **Aguila** (tel. 800/824-8452, www.autobusesaguila.com) and **Autobuses de la Baja California** (ABC, tel. 664/104-7400, www.abc.com.mx) buses have service directly to Todos Santos from Cabo San Lucas and other cities in Baja. There is no local bus service in town. The central historic district is very compact, and the best way to explore it is on foot. There are very few taxis in Todos Santos, so if you plan on exploring the region, it's best to have your own vehicle or rent a car when you fly into Los Cabos.

El Pescadero

The beach community of El Pescadero 13 kilometers south of Todos Santos used to be a small remote fishing and agricultural village. The area has grown rapidly over the past number of years and now supports an assortment of boutique hotels, eco-lodgings, and even a mini-resort. There is a handful of restaurants and bars, as well as a Pemex gas station. The actual town of Pescadero is on the eastern side of Mexico 19, but most of the hotels and attractions for tourists are to the west, down near the beaches.

Bordered by the Sierra de la Laguna to the east and the Pacific to the west, the area boasts a number of surf breaks that have helped bolster its popularity with bohemian types. Most of the action in Pescadero centers around Playa Los Cerritos. The beach is popular for beginning surfing, boogie boarding, and one of the few spots in the West Cape safe for swimming. In the past decade, many new hotels and restaurants have opened up near Cerritos, catering to surfers and savvy travelers looking for a more tranquil alternative to Cabo.

SIGHTS
★ Playa Los Cerritos

For years, **Playa Los Cerritos** was referred to as one of the best beaches in Baja. Word got out, and the once tranquil beach is not constantly buzzing with surfers, tourists, vendors, and a growing number of beachfront developments. Although the beach has changed, it remains a favorite for many Baja travelers. The waves are great for beginner surfers and this is one of the few beaches on the West Cape safe for swimming as well. Access to the beach (without having to pay for parking) is now only available in two areas on the far north and south sides of the beach.

SPORTS AND RECREATION
Surfing

Playa Los Cerritos is a popular spot for beginner surfers because of the beach breaks, sandy bottom, and easy fun waves. There's a break at the point that more experienced surfers will enjoy. Farther south of El Pescadero, at kilometer 73 is Punta Gaspareño, a right point break that breaks on west or northwest swells.

Surfers of any level will want to check out **Mario's Surf School** (tel. 612/142-6156, www.mariosurfschool.com). Mario has over 10 years of experience as a surf instructor and is great about showing the ropes to beginners or taking out more experienced surfers on excursions to some of the more advanced breaks in the region. Private lessons start at US$60 per hour.

Costa Azul Surf Shop (tel. 624/142-2771, www.costa-azul.com.mx, 8am-6pmMon.-Sat.,

9am-5pm Sun.) offers surf lessons for US$150 for two hours as well as surf excursions for all levels. They have surfboard rentals for US$20 a day and also rent paddleboards, skim boards, body boards, and snorkeling equipment. The shop sells surf wear, accessories, and clothing.

Down on Playa Los Cerritos, there are many outfitters renting boards right on the sand. There are also surfboards available for rent on the beach at **Cerritos Beach Club & Surf** (tel. 624/124-6315, www.cerritosbcs. com).

Yoga

Near the main entrance to Playa Los Cerritos, **Baja-Zen** (tel. 612/142-5038, www.baja-zen. com) yoga studio and retreat center has a beautiful facility, offers daily public yoga classes, and can also arrange for private classes. They have simple but nice accommodations for those participating in a yoga retreat.

The luxury hotel **Rancho Pescadero** (www.ranchopescadero.com) offers daily morning yoga classes as well as private classes (US$75 per hour for up to six guests). In addition to classes, they have specialty weeks at the resort with a more intense yoga focus.

Surfers, swimmers, and sunbathers enjoy Playa Los Cerritos.

El Pescadero and Vicinity

To La Pastora,
El Carrizal, and
Las Playitas

To San Pedro
and La Paz

19

MISIÓN SANTA ROSA
DE LAS PALMAS
(TODOS SANTOS)

Playa la
Cachora

San
Ignacio

La
Poza

Todos Santos

Cerro La
Calera

Cerro
La Poza

LIGHTHOUSE

Cerro Salado

Punta
Lobos

GRADED ROAD

Puerto
Campechana
Puerto
Algodones

PLAYA SAN PEDRITO
(PLAYA LAS PALMAS)

Cerro San
Pedro

CAMPO
EXPERIMENTAL

Punta
San Pedro

Cerro Los
Viejos

19

Agua   Grande

Playa
San Pedro

0   1 mi
0   1 km

San Juan

CARLITO'S
PLACE

GRADED

RANCHO
PESCADERO

El Pescadero

ROAD

HORTALIZA
HIERBABUENA

BAJA
BEANS

GRADED
ROAD

Cerro
Tecolote

Cerro
El Gavilán

PESCADERO
SURF CAMP

Cuatro
Vientos

HACIENDA
CERRITOS

GRADED ROAD

Punta Pescadero

CERRITOS
BEACH HOTEL
DESERT MOON

19

CERRITOS BEACH
AND TENNIS CLUB

PLAYA LOS CERRITOS

© AVALON TRAVEL

MAYA VILLA
RESORT

To Cabo
San Lucas

FOOD

On the dirt road out to Rancho Pescadero resort, visitors will find ★ **Hortaliza Hierbabuena** (tel. 612/149-2568, www. hierbabuenarestaurante.com, noon-9pm Thurs.-Mon., mains US$10-14) where farm-to-table dining comes alive at its finest. The open-air restaurant is surrounded by lush vegetable gardens that supply the restaurant with fresh produce. The menu changes with what's in season and growing in the garden. They're known for their wood-fired pizzas, and other entrées like flank steak, fresh fish of the day, and baked eggplant, are all made from ingredients grown on the property and locally sourced. There's a separate bar area where they serve up drinks like the "Sandiatini" (vodka, watermelon juice, and mint) and the "Baja Surprise" (hibiscus liqueur, citrus juices, tequila) as well as a wide variety of freshly squeezed juices. If you want to take home some of the fresh flavors, they sell bundles of vegetables and herbs picked from the gardens.

The large roadside *palapa* at **Jungle Pescadero** (Mexico 19 Km. 69, tel. 624/143-7401, 11am-7pm Tues.-Sun., mains US$8-11) is a popular local hangout serving margaritas in mason jars. For food they offer shrimp in a variety of styles and fish filets. There's a corn hole game and fire pit on-site. With a kid's menu and a playground, this is a great spot for families.

For unique Asian-inspired seafood creations, **Carlito's Place** (just east of Mexico 19, tel. 612/155-4492, 1pm-9pm daily, US$12-18) is so popular that people drive up from Cabo just to dine here. The prices can be expensive, but those who love sushi and fresh seafood say that it's worth it. The best way to experience Carlito's is to splurge and have the chef's choice with Carlito making custom dishes for your enjoyment. Don't miss the stuffed pepper appetizers.

Right in the middle of the action on Playa Los Cerritos, **Cerritos Beach Club & Surf** (tel. 624/129-6315, www.cerritosbcs.com, 8am-6pm daily, mains US$12-24) makes the most of a prime beach location and often has live music. Many complain that it's become somewhat of a tourist trap with mediocre food and expensive prices (even by U.S. standards), but it remains a popular spot with tourists because of the setting. It stays open for breakfast, lunch, and dinner.

New at Playa Los Cerritos, the rooftop restaurant and bar **Free Souls** (tel. 624/191-4666, info@thefreesoulsproject.com, 12:30pm-10pm Tues.-Sun., mains US$9-15) has captivated patrons with its cool vibe. The menu has a wide range of items, but a solid choice is the Mediterranean-style pizzas cooked in a wood-burning oven. The rooftop has great views at sunset and a saltwater infinity-edge swimming pool looks out onto the beach and Pacific. Expect U.S. prices on drinks and food here.

With good strong coffee and tasty baked goods, **Baja Beans** (Mexico 19 Km. 19, tel. 612/130-3391, www.bajabeans.com, 7am-3pm Tues.-Sun.) has made quite a splash since opening in 2011. This combo bakery, café, and roasting company has plenty of outdoor seating in the large garden. It's a popular gathering spot for locals and visitors and even more so on Sunday mornings when there's a large market with music and handicrafts.

Hortaliza Hierbabuena restaurant

ACCOMMODATIONS

Many of the accommodations in this area are centered on Playa Los Cerritos. There are also a number of vacation rentals in the area that can offer lodgings from individual rooms and *casitas* to large houses. Budget accommodations are increasingly difficult to find here as more and more resorts and higher-end inns are taking foothold.

Under US$50

Choose from one of the *casitas* or bring your own tent for camping at **Pescadero Surf Camp** (Mexico 19 Km. 64, tel. 612/134-0480, www.pescaderosurf.com, US$10-45). There's a pool with a swim-up bar (BYOB), as well as a large outdoor kitchen and barbecue area. Located about two miles from the beach, it's

a bit too far to walk to the ocean, but with the affordable price, this is a great budget option for the area. They offer boogie board and surfboard rentals as well as surf lessons for US$60.

US$100-150

Brought to you by the same owners as Pescadero Surf Camp is **Cerritos Beach Hotel, Desert Moon** (tel. 612/134-0480, www.cerritosbeachhotel.com, US$150). Just steps away from Playa Los Cerritos, the hotel is popular with surfers and beachgoers. The modern minimal rooms are all well appointed with kitchens and have beach views. There's a restaurant on-site serving dishes like pizza and wings, and there's also a pool with a poolside bar.

US$150-250

A short walking distance to Cerritos beach, **Olas de Cerritos** (Mexico 19 Km. 66, tel. 612/159-0396, www.olasdecerritos.com, US$170) offers the use of beach chairs, umbrellas, boogie boards, and surfboards to guests. There's a nice pool and communal *palapa* area. A cold breakfast and coffee are served every morning, and pots and pans are available for those guests who wish to cook their own breakfast.

If you don't mind roughing it a bit in exchange for location and views, **Mayan Village Resort** (Mexico 19 Km. 67, U.S. tel. 858/551-8852, www.mayanvillageresort.com, US$185) offers beachfront eco-*cabañas*. Each cabana is an individual *palapa* structure right on Playa Los Cerritos. Bathrooms are shared (separate for men and women), and there's no wireless Internet. Also right on Playa Los Cerritos is **Cerritos Surf Colony** (U.S. tel. 858/551-8852, www.cerritossurfcolony.com, US$200-250). This sister property to Hacienda Cerritos offers private, thatched-roof villas right on the sand. The pool has a swim-up bar, and there's a restaurant and snack bar on the property.

Located right on Playa Los Cerritos but south of most of the activity and crowds is the **Cerritos Beach Inn** (Mexico 19 Km. 68, tel. 612/183-1077, www.cerritosbeachinn.com, US$125-250). Newly opened, this property features a swimming pool, rooftop deck, and outdoor cantina. Oceanfront rooms cost double the price of desert/mountain view rooms.

Over US$250

Looming over the cliff of Punta Pescadero on the north side of Playa Los Cerritos is **Hacienda Cerritos** (Mexico 19 Km. 65, U.S. tel. 503/926-8131 www.haciendacerritos.com, US$350). This boutique hotel has fewer than 12 rooms, all set in the large mansion with pools and incredible ocean views surrounding. The property has fallen into some disrepair after damage from Hurricane Odile in 2014 that was not fixed. Wireless access is available only in common areas. The hotel bar, which has beautiful ocean views, is open to the public, so you don't have to stay at the Hacienda to enjoy a margarita with a vista of the Pacific.

North of Cerritos on Playa Pescadero, ★ **Rancho Pescadero** (Mexico 19 Km. 62, U.S. tel. 910/300-8891, www.ranchopescadero.com, US$275-450) is a boutique resort with chic and luxurious amenities and a relaxed vibe. There are 28 rooms, but the hotel still has a very personal feel to it. Staff members remember the guests' names and give a lot of personal attention. Signs around

Hacienda Cerritos looks over Playa Cerritos in El Pescadero.

the property remind guests of events, activities, and classes in a casual and chummy way. "We are so glad you've chosen to hang with us!" begins the welcome note in the binder up in the room. All of the rooms have air-conditioning, a safe, binoculars, board games, and a welcome basket with snacks and useful items like bug repellent, a flashlight, and matches for use during your stay. The bathrooms are fully stocked with toiletries from Teva and Los Cabos Soap Co. In the morning, you can expect a breakfast basket to be waiting outside of your door with continental breakfast (fruit and pastries) as well as coffee or tea. All stays include free welcome drinks at the poolside bar. The property feels very Zen-like with minimalistic adobe-style structures with *palapa* roofs and palm trees all around the property. Fire pits are scattered around with seats that look like they've been carved out of giant boulders. Down at the beach, guests will find a number of *palapa* umbrellas with Adirondack chairs as well as *palapa cabañas* with daybeds for lounging. More fire pits are situated along the sand so that guests can enjoy evening beach bonfires. The resort has a number of activities and items available for free use: bikes, surfboards, fishing poles (they will cook any fish that you catch), and yoga class every morning at 10am (all levels welcome). The Rancho Pescadero spa offers a variety of facials and massages in oceanfront rooms for total relaxation. There's a restaurant on the property that's known for having great food and drinks. No kids under 18 are allowed at the resort.

SERVICES

El Pescadero is home to the only gas station and OXXO convenience store between Cabo and Todos Santos. They are conveniently located on Mexico 19 in the actual town of El Pescadero. Buses stop across the highway from the gas station. Ask at your hotel for tourist information and local recommendations.

Rancho Pescadero offers some of the most luxurious accommodations on the West Cape.

The West Cape

The stretch between El Pescadero and Cabo is filled with beautiful undeveloped landscapes and empty beaches, making for a scenic drive. Adventurous travelers looking for access to the empty beaches can find unmarked turn-offs along Mexico 19. Signals of pending development are popping up in the form of real estate signs littering the landscape and the rumors that the locals will tell you. For now, enjoy the relatively empty beaches and the peaceful views of the Pacific. The area is remote, and there are no accommodations and very few services here. Most travelers stay in El Pescadero or Todos Santos and explore this area on day trips.

TURTLE RESCUE

About 20 kilometers northwest of Cabo San Lucas is the coastal village of San Cristóbal where visitors will find the sea turtle rescue nonprofit **Asupmatoma AC** (tel. 624/143-0269, www.asupmatoma.org). They offer people the chance to camp for the night and participate in either collecting and relocating newly laid turtle eggs or releasing hatchlings into the ocean (US$6 pp). Egg relocation happens between July 15 and September 15, and hatchling releases take place between September 15 and December 15. Those who just want to participate in the turtle hatchling release without spending the night are able to do so as well (US$2 for children 10 and under, US$3 for adults).

PLAYA MIGRIÑO

The beautiful shore at Playa Migriño is a great spot for whale-watching and catching the sunset. While the beach is not for swimming, surfers may be interested in the right point and hollow beach breaks that receive lots of swell. Unfortunately the peace and quiet of the location are often disrupted by ATV tours coming through. There are unmarked turn-offs on the west side of Mexico 19 at both kilometer 94 and kilometer 97. The turnoff at kilometer 94 requires a high-clearance vehicle. The beach is about two kilometers from the highway.

Playa Migriño on the West Cape

Cabo Falso to Playa Migriño

© AVALON TRAVEL

guide on an ATV tour such as with **Cactus ATV Tours** (tel. 624/146-4650, www.cactusatvtours.com) and **Amigos Cabo Moto** (tel. 624/143-0808, www.amigosactivities.com).

For those who want to drive to La Candelaria on their own, there is access from Cabo San Lucas on a dirt road called Camino a la Candelaria just to the east of the small Cabo San Lucas airport. For true off-road enthusiasts with good high-clearance, four-wheel-drive vehicles, there is a way to get to La Candelaria through the riverbed at Playa Migriño. The route is unmarked and extremely sandy and rocky. It should not be attempted in the rainy season.

SIERRA DE LA LAGUNA

The mountains of the Sierra de la Laguna biosphere reserve can be accessed from either the East Cape or the West Cape. The approach depends on the final destination. The sierras are filled with lush canyons, waterfalls, and plenty of opportunities for single-day or multiday hikes. While the namesake lake of the Sierra de la Laguna has dried up and is now a meadow, a trip to this area is a beautiful adventure to a rarely explored region. It's one of the popular spots in the range accessed from the West Cape. Treks to the *laguna* of the Sierra de la Laguna can be made through multiday hikes from Todos Santos. **Todos Santos Eco Adventures** (tel. 612/145-0189, www.tosea.net) offers guided hikes and treks with pack animals.

SPORTS AND RECREATION
ATV Tours

Both with convenient highway locations on Mexico 19, **Cactus ATV Tours** (tel. 624/146-4650, www.cactusatvtours.com) and **Amigos Cabo Moto** (Mexico 19 Km. 106, tel. 624/143-0808, www.amigosactivities.com, 9am-7pm daily) offer ATV, Rzr, and horseback riding adventures to various destinations around the region.

LA CANDELARIA

In the foothills of the Sierra de la Laguna is the small ranching oasis town of La Candelaria. Because ATV tours have been coming up to the town in recent years, it's become known as a spot to purchase pottery from local residents. There's not much of a town in La Candelaria and you have to know how to get there and what to look for once you arrive, so the best way to access La Candelaria is with a

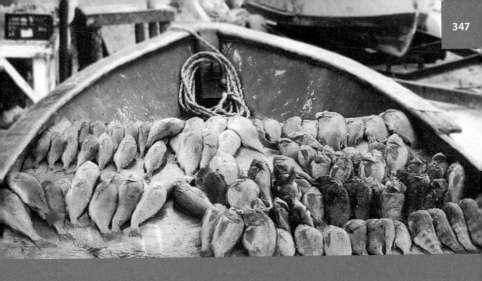

Background

The Landscape

GEOGRAPHY

The entire Baja peninsula is 1,300 kilometers (806 mi.) long, from Tijuana in the north to Cabo San Lucas at the southern tip. As the northwestern region of Mexico, the Baja peninsula is separated from mainland Mexico by the Golfo de California (Gulf of California), more commonly referred to as the Mar de Cortés (Sea of Cortez). The Pacific Ocean borders the western side of the Baja peninsula.

There are four main desert areas that make up 65 percent of the peninsula—the San Felipe Desert, the Central Coast Desert, the Vizcaíno Desert, and the Magdalena Plain Desert. There are 23 mountain ranges on the peninsula with the highest peak being Picacho del Diablo at 3,095 meters (10,154 ft.) in the Sierra de San Pedro Mártir.

CLIMATE

While the climate varies by region and season, what attracts most travelers to Baja California is the warm, sunny weather. The southern part of the peninsula is the warmest, drawing snowbirds in the winter. Summers in Baja Sur can be extremely hot and humid, especially along the Sea of Cortez. The Pacific side of the peninsula generally has much cooler temperatures. In the late summer and early fall, tropical storms (called *chubascos*) and hurricanes can hit southern Baja, bringing high winds and heavy rains.

In northern Baja, the areas along the Pacific coast are temperate year-round, while temperatures inland and on the Sea of Cortez can be extremely hot in the summer. The northern mountains of the San Pedro Mártir and Sierra de Juárez remain cool in the summer and can get very cold in the winter, receiving snow on the high peaks.

ENVIRONMENTAL ISSUES

Most of the Baja peninsula remains undeveloped due to the desert and mountain terrain and a lack of freshwater. But recent years have seen rapid growth in the development around the Los Cabos area for tourism as well as real estate. Cabo Pulmo has often been a place of contention between developers and environmentalists over the years. So far, large developments have been fought off by those wanting to protect the natural coral reef. In recent years, the danger of mining developments in the Sierra de la Laguna have threatened to contaminate the springs of the mountain range providing water to many of the towns on the East Cape. Wildcoast (www.wildcoast.net) is an active nonprofit working to preserve the environment in Baja California (Norte).

a burro in the Baja desert

Previous: fresh-caught fish; cardón cactus.

PLANTS

There are over 4,000 plant species and sub-species on the peninsula with over 600 species endemic to Baja. For the most descriptive information on the flora of Baja California, pick up a copy of the *Baja California Plant Field Guide,* by Jon P. Rebman and Norman C. Roberts. The animal life is just as diverse with over 100 types of mammals inhabiting the peninsula, two dozen of which are considered to be endemic.

Cacti

There are 120 species of cactus in Baja, and many of them flower after rains, which can paint the desert with a vibrant splash of color for a few weeks. The most dominant, and perhaps most recognizable, cactus of the Baja landscape is the *cardón* or elephant cactus. It's also the largest cactus and can reach heights of up to 20 meters (65 ft.), and can weigh up to 10 tons. Some of the older plants are believed to be over 200 years old. Other common types of cacti found on the peninsula include varieties of the barrel cactus, cholla, and *nopal* (prickly pear). The *nopal* is an edible cactus and commonly found on menus around the region.

Agaves

There are over 20 species of agave growing on the peninsula. Many are edible, so the agaves have always been a source of food, drink, and fiber. Agaves live many decades before they flower, earning them the name "century plant" (although flowering actually happens between years 30 and 60). The flower stalk emerges from the cluster of basal stems.

Cirios (Boojum Tree)

Perhaps the most unique and striking plant on the peninsula is the *cirio* or boojum tree. Many travelers remark that it looks like something out of a Dr. Seuss book. The shape resembles a tall tapered candle (hence the Spanish common name, *cirio,* meaning candle) with spiny branches covering the entire trunk. Mature *cirios* may have several wide stems at the top as well. The *cirios* are almost endemic to Baja California, with just a small number of them found in Sonora as well. They are plentiful throughout the central desert in Baja. If you are driving on Mexico 1, they can be found starting just south of El Rosario.

Trees

Trees found along the peninsula are often very

cactus in bloom

specific to their regions. Many Baja travelers consider it a surprise to see conifers such as cypress, cedar, Sierra lodgepole pines, and white fir in the mountain ranges on the northern part of the peninsula. There are seven different varieties of palm trees in the oases farther south on the peninsula. This includes the date palm, which was brought over from Europe by the Jesuit missionaries to be cultivated. It naturalized throughout the region in places like San Ignacio, Loreto, Mulegé, and Comondú.

ANIMALS
Land Mammals

There are over 100 types of mammals on the peninsula, with over 20 endemic species. Coyotes, mountain lions, foxes, bobcats, and raccoons are fairly prevalent. The desert bighorn sheep and the endangered peninsular pronghorn (*berrendo*) are among the endangered species on the peninsula.

Gray Whales

Each October, gray whales in the eastern Pacific Ocean start a two- to three-month migration from the Bering Sea to the warm waters of Baja California. At 16,000-22,000 kilometers (9,900-13,700 mi.) it is thought to be the longest annual migration of any mammal. The whales spend the winter in Laguna San Ignacio, Laguna Ojo de Liebre, and Bahía Magdalena where they breed and give birth. The whales can grow up to 15 meters (50 ft.) and can weigh up to 40 tons.

Other Marine Mammals

In addition to gray whales, blue whales, pilot whales, humpback whales, and orca can all be spotted along the peninsula. Dolphins are prolific in the Pacific Ocean and Sea of Cortez. The endangered *vaquita,* a small porpoise, can still be found in very small numbers in the northern Sea of Cortez. California sea lions can be found living in colonies around islands in the Sea of Cortez.

Fish

To the delight of anglers and divers, thousands of species of fish ply the waters of both the Pacific Ocean and the Sea of Cortez. Yellowtail, marlin, amberjack, corvina, roosterfish, dorado, wahoo, bluefin tuna, halibut, snapper, and sea bass are just some of the species that lure anglers who come to fish the prolific waters. There are a number of tropical

the unique Boojum Tree

fish, eels and rays, including the Pacific manta rays that can have wingspans of up to seven meters (23 ft.).

Shellfish including shrimp, clams, oysters, mussels, scallops, and lobster are all found in large numbers, making them popular dishes at restaurants and food carts. There are over 60 types of sharks around the peninsula, including the whale shark, which can be found increasingly in the warm waters of the Sea of Cortez in areas like La Paz and Bahía de los Angeles.

Birds

With over 400 species of birds, Baja can be a birders' paradise. Coastal birds such as pelicans, blue-footed boobies, frigate birds, egrets, and gulls are commonly spotted. Inland lakes and streams are home to freshwater birds such as ducks, geese, herons, sandpipers, teal, and storks. In the desert, falcons, hawks, owls, hummingbirds, sparrows, roadrunners, and turkey vultures can be sighted. Mountain birds like eagles, red-tailed hawks, pheasant, woodpeckers, and wren are common to the Sierras. The California condor is currently being reintroduced into wild in the San Pedro Mártir, which can be a treat to see.

Reptiles and Amphibians
SEA TURTLES

There are five types of sea turtles found in Baja: the leatherback, green, hawksbill, western ridley, and loggerhead. All are endangered, and it's illegal to hunt them or their eggs. There are a number of conservation groups in Baja Sur helping to protect the sea turtles and promote their reproduction.

SNAKES

Of the 35 snakes (*serpientes*) on the peninsula, about half are nonvenomous (*culebras*), and the other have are poisonous (*víboras*). There are 18 species of rattlesnakes, including the Baja California rattler, red diamondback, and western diamondback.

Pelicans

History

INDIGENOUS HISTORY

Historians agree that there have been people living on the Baja California peninsula for over 11,000 years. In the north were several groups belonging to the Yuman language family: the Kiliwa, Paipai, Kumiai, Cucupá, and Quechan. The Cochimí inhabited the central and southern part of the peninsula. The groups were adaptive to their environments and led mostly hunter-gatherer lifestyles. The Guachimis came from the north and were the people who created most of the impressive Sierra de la Guadalupe cave paintings.

SPANISH EXPLORATION

California existed as a myth for Europeans long before it was finally discovered by explorers in the early 16th century. Following Hernán Cortés' conquest of mainland Mexico, he sent three ships to explore Baja California in 1532. The peninsula was believed to be an island at this time. The ships of that first expedition disappeared without a trace. Cortés sent a follow-up expedition in 1533 that landed in La Paz, but most of the men in the expedition were killed by the indigenous people. In 1539, another expedition sponsored by Cortés was led by Captain Francisco de Ulloa and explored the entire perimeter of the Sea of Cortez as well as the Pacific Coast up to Isla Cedros. It was Ulloa who is credited with naming the Mar de Cortés.

The Mission Era

The Jesuits were the first missionaries to inhabit the peninsula. Padre Juan Maria Salvatierra established the first mission in all of Alta Baja California at Loreto in 1697. The Franciscans and the Dominicans came after the Jesuits to settle the peninsula. In total, there were 27 missions as well as supporting *visitas* (visiting stations) founded on Baja. Uprisings by the indigenous people were very common, the most famous being the Pericú rebellion in 1734, which ended in extensive damage, the destruction of four missions, and the death of two padres. The history of each mission and the GPS points of the current sites (or ruins) can be found in David Kier's book, *Baja California Land of Missions.*

INDEPENDENCE FROM SPAIN

At the end of the 18th century, the Age of Enlightenment and liberal revolutions sparked the movement for independence from Spain. The revolt against the Spanish crown began on September 16, 1810, when Miguel Hidalgo shouted the *Grito de Dolores*, the cry for revolution, from the mainland city of Dolores, Guanajuato. September 16 is still considered Mexican's independence day, and the reigning president reenacts the *grito* every year on the evening of September 15. It took more than a decade, but Mexico officially gained its freedom from Spain in 1821 after the Mexican War of Independence.

THE MEXICAN-AMERICAN WAR

The Mexican-American War (1846-1848) had a major impact on Baja California. President James K. Polk believed the United States had a "manifest destiny" to spread across the continent from the Atlantic to the Pacific Ocean. In 1844 Polk made an offer to Mexico to purchase the lands between the Nueces River and Rio Grande (in what is now Texas). The offer was rejected and U.S. forces invaded Mexico, starting a string of battles that would lead to the Mexican-American War and end with Mexico losing one-third of its territory. In the Treaty of Guadalupe Hidalgo ending the war, Mexico gave into the United States and received US$15 million for the land that is now California, Nevada, Utah, and parts of Colorado, Arizona,

Spanish Missions

- Nuestra Señora de Loreto Conchó (1697-1829)
- San Francisco Javier Biaundó (1699-1817)
- San Juan Bautista de Malibat (Ligüí) (1705-1721)
- Santa Rosalía de Mulegé (1705-1828)
- San José de Comondú (1708-1827)
- La Purísima Concepción de Cadegomó (1720-1822)
- Nuestra Señora del Pilar de la Paz Airapí (1720-1840)
- Nuestra Señora de Guadalupe de Huasinapí (1720-1795)
- Nuestra Señora de los Dolores Apaté (1721-1768)
- Santiago el Apóstol Aiñiní (1724-1795)
- San Ignacio de Kadakaamán (1728-1840)
- San Jose del Cabo Añuítí (1730-1748 and 1768-1840)
- Santa Rosa de las Palmas (Todos Santos) (1733-1748)
- San Luis Gonzaga Chiryaqui (1737-1768)
- Santa Gertrudis (1752-1822)
- San Francisco de Borja Adac (1762-1818)
- Santa María de los Ángeles (1766-1774)
- San Fernando de Velicatá (1769-1825)
- Nuestra Señora del Rosario de Viñadaco (1774-1829)
- Santo Domingo (1775-1839)
- San Vicente Ferrer (1780-1833)
- San Miguel Arcángel (1787-1834)
- Santo Tomás de Aquino (1791-1849)
- San Pedro Mártir de Verona (1794-1811)
- Santa Catalina Virgen y Mártir (1797-1839)
- El Descanso (San Miguel la Nueva) (1810-1834)
- Nuestra Señora de Guadalupe (1834-1840)

New Mexico, and Wyoming. In the original draft of the treaty, Baja California was included in the land to be sold to the United States, but it was eventually left to Mexico because of its proximity to Sonora.

THE MEXICAN REVOLUTION

Because of Baja's remote location in relation to the rest of Mexico, the peninsula was somewhat insulated from political turmoil

Missions (1697-1856)

Tijuana
EL DESCANSO (1817-1834)
SAN MIGUEL (1797-1834)
Ensenada
UNITED STATES
MEXICO
SANTO TOMÁS (1791-1849)
GUADALUPE (1834-1840)
SANTA CATALINA (1797-1840)
SAN VICENTE (1794-1824)
SANTO DOMINGO (1769-1772)
SAN PEDRO MÁRTIR (1794-1824)
EL ROSARIO (1766-1767)
SAN FERNANDO VELICATÁ (1769-1772)
Sea of Cortez
CALAMAJUE (1766-1767)
SAN FRANCISCO BORJA (1762-1818)
PACIFIC OCEAN
Guerrero Negro
SANTA GERTRUDIS (1752-1822)
SAN IGNACIO (1728-1840)
GUADALUPE (1720-1795)
SANTA ROSALÍA DE MULEGÉ (1683-1685)
(Gulf of California)
LA PURÍSIMA (1720-1822)
COMONDÚ (1708-1827)
LORETO (1697-1829)
Loreto
SAN JAVIER (1699-1817)
LIGÜÍ (1705-1721)
SAN LUIS GONZAGA (1740-1768)
DOLORES (1721-1768)
0   50 mi
0   50 km
La Paz
LA PAZ (1720-1749)
TODOS SANTOS (1733-1840)
FRANCISCAN
DOMINICAN
JESUIT
Cabo San Lucas
SANTIAGO (1721-1795)
SAN JOSÉ DEL CABO (1730-1840)
© AVALON TRAVEL

that took place in Mexico in the 19th century. But Baja California played an important part in the Mexican Revolution (1910-1920) which radically changed government and culture in Mexico. The revolution set out to end the dictatorship of President Porfirio Díaz, called for democracy, and demanded the return of lands taken unfairly from Mexican villages. Led by Francisco Madero and aided by Pancho Villa and Emiliano Zapata, rebel armies of workers and peasants rose up to fight against Díaz and his dictatorship. Baja California played a key role in the revolution in the Magonista Rebellion of 1911. This early uprising was organized by the Partido Liberal Mexicano (PLM) against the presidency of dictator Porfirio Díaz. The rebel army took control of both Mexicali and Tijuana. The success of the uprising encouraged rebel troops in other regions to join in the fight of the revolution.

The Mexican Constitution of 1917 is largely looked upon as the end of the Mexican Revolution even though a few more years of instability followed. The Constitution returned lands to the peasants in the form of cooperatively owned *ejidos,* which are still in effect today.

STATEHOOD

Northern Baja California became the 29th state of Mexico in 1952. With its sparse fishing villages and small towns, Baja California Sur remained a territory, unable to meet the population requirements to become a Mexican state. When the Transpeninsular Highway (Mexico 1) was finally completed in 1974, it opened up commerce and tourism to the southern part of the peninsula and Baja California Sur became a state later that year.

Annual Festivals and Holidays

JANUARY

- New Year's Day, January 1, is a national holiday.

- Día de los Reyes (Day of the Kings), January 6, is a Catholic holiday honoring the three kings who brought gifts to baby Jesus. The day is celebrated with a round cake called a *rosca de reyes* inside which is hidden a plastic figurine of baby Jesus. Whoever receives the baby Jesus in their piece of cake has to make tamales for friends and family on Día de la Candelaria.

FEBRUARY

- Día de la Candelaria, February 2, is a religious holiday celebrating the Virgen of La Candelaria. Whoever received the figurine of baby Jesus on Día de los Reyes traditionally hosts a tamale party for friends and family.

- Constitution Day, February 5, is a national holiday.

MARCH

- Birthday of Benito Juárez, March 21, is a national holiday.

APRIL

- Semana Santa (Holy Week) is the week before Easter and a popular time for Mexican nationals to take their vacation.

- National Children's Day, April 30, is an observed holiday.

MAY

- Labor Day, May 1, is a national holiday.

SEPTEMBER

- Mexican Independence Day, September 16, is a national holiday celebrating Mexico's independence from Spain.

NOVEMBER

- Día de los Muertos, November 1-2, is All Saints' Day, celebrating those who have passed away.

- Revolution Day, November 20, is a national holiday.

DECEMBER

- Día de Nuestra Señora de Guadalupe (Day of the Virgin of Guadalupe), December 12, is a feast day for this patron saint.

- Las Posadas, December 16-January 6, are traditionally religious processions reenacting Mary and Joseph trying to find accommodations before the birth of Jesus. Today, they have become a time for holiday parties.

- Navidad (Christmas Day), December 25, is a national holiday.

Government and Economy

ORGANIZATION

The 28th parallel divides the two states of Baja California Sur and Baja California (Norte). Mexicali is the capital of Baja California (Norte) and the state is divided into five *municipalities*: Tijuana, Rosarito, Ensenada, Tecate, and Mexicali. The northern state of Baja California was accepted as a state of Mexico in 1952.

The capital of Baja California Sur is La Paz. There are also five municipalities: La Paz, Los Cabos, Mulegé, Loreto, and Comondú. Baja California Sur was officially accepted as a state of Mexico in 1974 after the Transpeninsular Highway was completed.

POLITICAL SYSTEM

There are 31 states in Mexico that form a representative democracy. There are three branches to the government: executive, legislative, and judicial. Mexican presidents serve a six-year term with no reelection. The legislature is comprised of two houses, the Senate and the Chamber of Deputies.

The three main political parties in Mexico are: Partido Acción Nacional (PAN), Mexico's conservative political party; Partido Revolucionario Institucional (PRI), Mexico's centrist political party; and Partido de la Revolución Democrática (PRD), Mexico's leftist political party.

ECONOMY

Tourism is one of the driving factors in Baja's economy. Regions such as Los Cabos and the northern border zone around Tijuana heavily rely on tourism from the United States and Canada. Baja's other industries include fishing, agriculture, and manufacturing at *maquiladoras* in the northern border regions. The North American Free Trade Agreement (NAFTA) entered into effect in 1994 and opened the door for large car and electronics manufacturers to develop factories in northern Baja and easily import the items produced into the United States. Because of the close ties with the United States, the economy of Baja California is closely tied with that of its northern neighbor.

Economic inequality is a large problem in Mexico. The whole Baja California peninsula is in the higher wage zone for the country, but the minimum is still low, starting at US$5 per day for unskilled workers.

People and Culture

The population of the Baja peninsula is around four million, with most inhabitants living in the northern state of Baja California, and more specifically in the cities of Tijuana and Mexicali. Most of the rest of the peninsula remains sparsely populated. There are very few true indigenous people left on the peninsula today, and most Baja residents are a mix of Spanish and Indian cultures as well as descendants from Europe and Asia. In more recent decades, the peninsula is home to a growing number of U.S. and Canadian retiree expats.

RELIGION

The Spanish missionaries first brought Catholicism to the peninsula, and it remains the dominant religion. Catholic holidays hold the same importance (or more) than secular national holidays. Missions and churches are prevalent everywhere on the peninsula, and although church and state are separate,

Catholicism plays a large part in Mexican culture. One of the most important figures in Mexican Catholicism is the Virgin of Guadalupe, or Our Lady of Guadalupe, a title for the Virgin Mary associated with an apparition at the Basilica of Our Lady of Guadalupe in Mexico City. Representations of the Virgin of Guadalupe are prevalent throughout the peninsula.

LANGUAGE

Latin American Spanish is the primary language spoken in Baja California. Mexicans who work in the tourism industry in large cities do speak at least some English. All travelers heading to Baja should learn at least a few basic greetings and phrases, which will go a long way in providing a better travel experience.

VISUAL ART

Baja California Sur has a lively art scene in cities like San José del Cabo and Todos Santos where the expat community has attracted foreign and local artists who have open galleries. In the north, Rosarito and Tijuana have a vibrant art scene that can be experienced from colorful street art to local galleries.

MUSIC

Mexico has a vibrant tradition of music. Mariachi music is probably the first thing that comes to mind for most people, and mariachi groups can be found throughout the peninsula, especially in the larger, more touristy towns. The ensemble usually consists of a trumpet, violin, guitar, and vihuela (five-string guitar), and performers are distinguished by their silver-studded *charro* suits. Another popular type of music in Baja is Norteño. Norteño music is mostly easily identified for its use of the accordion and polka-like sound. European migrants brought the accordion, along with the waltz and polka, to northern Mexico (hence the designation Norteño) in the late 19th century.

DANCE

The folk dancing of Mexico, the *ballet folklórico,* can be seen in various places along the peninsula. The highly choreographed dance includes both men and women and is characterized by lively music and bold movements. The women wear colorful traditional Mexican dresses with ruffled skirts they hold while they dance which are an integral part of the spectacle.

Essentials

Transportation

GETTING THERE
Air

Baja has commercial airports in Tijuana, Loreto, La Paz, and Los Cabos. Tijuana and Los Cabos are the two largest airports with regular international flights. It can be cheaper to fly to the airports in Baja Sur from the Tijuana airport, and thanks to a new pedestrian bridge that connects San Diego to Tijuana's Rodriguez airport, this is now easy to do. Ticketed passengers can park their cars in short- or long-term parking lots in San Diego and walk across the **Cross Border Xpress** (www.crossborderxpress.com) pedestrian bridge to take them directly to the Tijuana airport. The cost is US$12 one-way.

Bus

Greyhound (tel. 800/890-6821, www.greyhound.com.mx) has cross-border bus service between Los Angeles, Long Beach, and San Diego in the United States and Tijuana and Mexicali in Mexico. Service costs between US$12 and US$42 one-way depending on exact origin and destination.

Car

Because the peninsula makes for such a popular and exciting road trip, most travelers choose to explore Baja by car. Mexico recognizes U.S. and Canadian driver's licenses, so an international license is not required.

MEXICAN AUTO INSURANCE

Mexican auto insurance is required by law when driving in Mexico. Even if you have U.S. insurance that covers you in Mexico, this is not sufficient, and you must additionally get a Mexican insurance policy. This is because Mexico does not recognize U.S. insurance and requires that you be financially responsible for any physical and bodily injuries caused by an accident. Therefore, all drivers must have at least liability coverage from a Mexican insurance provider. Mexican auto insurance policies are available for short trips by the day or can be purchased to cover you for the year. Liability-only policies are the minimum required by the law and will cover damages you may cause to other property or people. Full coverage will additionally cover damages that happen to your own vehicle. While the law does not require full coverage, it's always recommended. There are a handful of Mexican auto insurance vendors on the U.S. side of border towns, but it's better to get a policy in advance with a reputable company. There are a number of options for this. **Discover Baja Travel Club** (3264 Governor Dr., San Diego, U.S. tel. 619/275-4225, toll-free U.S. tel. 800/727-2252, www.discoverbaja.com) has been in business for over 25 years. Daily or yearly policies are available by going online to print at home, or you can call them or go into their office in San Diego.

TEMPORARY VEHICLE IMPORTATION PERMITS

Temporary Vehicle Importation Permits are not required for driving in Baja California, but if you are planning on crossing over to mainland Mexico, they are mandatory. Your car can be impounded permanently if you are caught driving in mainland Mexico without the permit. Temporary vehicle import permits can be obtained at the border crossings between the United States and Mexico or in La Paz at the Pichilingue ferry terminal.

Previous: date palm oasis; San Ysidro's El Chaparral border crossing.

Sea

Passenger and car ferry service is available to Baja from mainland Mexico. **Baja Ferries** (tel. 612/123-6397, toll-free tel. 800/337-7437, www.bajaferries.com) is the most popular option with two routes from mainland—one from Mazatlán and other from Topolobampo, both arriving in La Paz. The other option is **Ferry Santa Rosalía** (tel. 800/505-5018, www.ferrysantarosalia.com) with service between Santa Rosalía in Baja to Guaymas, Sonora, in mainland.

If you have your own boat and are crossing into Baja by sea, there are port captain offices in Ensenada, Guerrero Negro, Bahía Magdalena (at San Carlos), Cabo San Lucas, San José del Cabo, La Paz, Puerto Escondido, Loreto, Mulegé, Santa Rosalía, Bahía de los Angeles, and San Felipe. You must complete a crew list document and get FMMs at your first port of entry for all passengers on the vessel. If you will be entering Mexican waters for sportfishing, but not making landfall, you must obtain a **nautical FMM** (www.gob.mx).

BORDER CROSSING

There are six official border crossings into Baja California from the United States.

- San Ysidro/Tijuana (24 hours daily)
- Otay Mesa (24 hours daily)
- Tecate (5am-11pm daily)
- Calexico/Mexicali West (24 hours daily)
- Calexico/Mexicali East (3am-midnight daily)
- Algodones/Andrade (6am-10pm daily)

Southbound crossings into Mexico are generally very quick. The northbound crossing back to the United States takes more time. Tijuana is the busiest land border crossing in the world, and northbound travelers should expect waits of up to a few hours when crossing at peak times.

GETTING AROUND
Car

Most travelers choose to explore Baja by car—whether flying into an airport and renting a car or driving their own into Mexico. Most of the highway consists of the two-lane Mexico 1,

San Ysidro border crossing

Expedited Reentry to the United States

There are two methods that grant expedited entry to the United States. The first and fastest way to cross the border is to become SENTRI-qualified as a part of the Trusted Traveler program. SENTRI lanes may be used by those with a SENTRI, NEXUS, or Global Entry card. However, in order to use the SENTRI vehicle lane, the car you are in must be SENTRI-approved as well.

The other program is called the "Ready Lane" for travelers with an RFID-enabled identification such as a U.S. Passport Card, Enhanced Driver's License, Trusted Traveler Card (SENTRI, NEXUS, Global Entry), or the new Border Crossing Card (BCC) or new Permanent Resident Card (PRC). Not all border crossings have SENTRI or Ready Lanes. For more information visit the **U.S. Customs and Border Protection website** (www.cbp.gov).

with little to no shoulder and inconsistent road conditions. Drive slowly and safely, and you'll have a wonderful time exploring the peninsula.

DRIVING PRECAUTIONS

It's extremely important to only drive during the daylight in Baja. Driving at night is dangerous for a number of reasons. There are no streetlights on the highway and cows and other animals come to sleep on the warm asphalt at night, causing many accidents with unsuspecting drivers. It's not uncommon for cars in Mexico to not have functioning brake lights, blinkers, or headlights, which can also be dangerous. It's important to keep all of this in mind when planning your road trip as the days are shorter in the winter, giving you less drive time.

It's important to never speed when driving in Baja. *Topes* (speed bumps) and *vados* (dips where the river crosses the road) are often unmarked, and road conditions can deteriorate without any notice, causing a number of potholes in the road. There are no shoulders on the road for many parts of Mexico 1, which is another good reason to take it slow.

You'll encounter many trucks along Mexico 1. They'll often help you out with passing by putting on their left blinker to tell you when it's clear for you to pass. But be careful to read the situation correctly so as not to misunderstand their signal as an indication that they will be passing or making a left-hand turn themselves.

OFF-HIGHWAY TRAVEL

Although Mexico 1 has been paved all the way to Cabo since 1974, much of Baja driving still consists of traveling on dirt roads. The condition of the unpaved roads can vary greatly and can change quickly, so it's always best to ask around locally about road conditions before taking an off-highway adventure. Mexican auto insurance will cover travel on dirt roads (the road must lead to a destination), but will not cover you when off-roading.

KILOMETER MARKINGS

The major highways in Baja use kilometer markings. People use these kilometer markings when giving distances and directions. You'll find that many businesses use their kilometer marking as their address. In Baja California (Norte), the kilometers start at 0 in Tijuana and ascend as you head south. There are a few spots where the kilometers reset, until getting to the state line at Guerrero Negro. At the state line in Guerrero Negro, the kilometers start at 220 and descend heading south, again resetting a few times in various cities.

ROAD SIGNS

All speed limits are posted in kilometers. Many Baja road signs are accompanied by symbols, allowing even non-Spanish speakers to understand. Here are some common phrases seen on road signs:

- *Alto*: Stop
- *Tope*: Speed Bump
- *Vado*: Dip
- *Ceda el Paso*: Yield
- *Despacio*: Slow
- *Entrada*: Entrance
- *Salida*: Exit
- *Curva Peligrosa*: Dangerous Curve
- *Desviación*: Detour
- *No Tire Basura*: Don't Throw Trash
- *Conserve Su Derecha*: Keep to the Right
- *No Rebase*: No Passing
- *Un Solo Carril*: Single Lane Ahead
- *Conceda Cambio de Luces*: Dim Your Lights
- *No Deje Piedras Sobre el Pavimento*: Don't Leave Rocks on the Road
- *Este Camino No Es De Alta Velocidad*: Not a High-Speed Road

FUEL

Mexico's gas industry has been state-owned and operated since 1938, but just opened up to deregulation in 2016. The ubiquitous Pemex (Petroleos Mexicanos) gas stations, which were once the only stations on the peninsula, will now be joined by other brands of gas stations, and the prices that were once fairly fixed will now vary from station to station.

There are two types of regular gas, Magna (87 octane) with the green handle, and Premium (93 octane) with the red handle. Diesel will be available at a separate pump with a black handle. Ultra low sulfur diesel (ULSD) is available through the northern state of Baja California, but not currently in Baja California Sur.

The price for gas will always be shown at the pump. When you pull up to the station, you'll need to let them know how much gas you want and of what type. It's normal to refer to the grade of gas by the color of the handle. *Lleno con verde* (full with green) is a common request when pulling up to the pump.

Gas stations in Mexico are full service, so the attendant will pump the gas for you. They will often clean your window as well. You should give them a few pesos (US$0.50) as a tip for the service. Even though stations are full service, it's always a good idea to get out and watch them at the pump to ensure that the attendant isn't trying to take advantage of

The toll roads in northern Baja from Tijuana to Ensenada are large, well-maintained roads.

you. Make sure that the pump is zeroed out before they pump gas, and don't let them top off your tank.

It's always a good idea to fill up on gas when you see a station when traveling the central part of the peninsula as gas stations can be few and far between. As Mexico is on the metric system, gas is sold by the liter. It's always best to pay in pesos for gas as doing the peso to dollar conversion can get tricky on top of trying to figure out the liter to gallons. It's becoming more common for gas stations on the peninsula to accept foreign credit cards, but you should never rely on this. It's always best to have pesos ready to pay for your gas.

TRAFFIC OFFENSES

In general, the same rules apply in Mexico as they do in the United States. You must wear your seat belt, license and registration must be current, no speeding, no drinking and driving, no cell phone usage while driving, and you must have at least liability coverage for Mexican auto insurance. The fines for these infractions vary from region to region but can be very expensive (the ticket for parking illegally in a designated handicap spot in Los Cabos is US$450).

In large cities that you're unfamiliar with, it can be challenging to navigate the busy areas of town, especially knowing when to stop at intersections, as stop signs can often be difficult to see. It's also important to know that in urban areas you must stop for pedestrians in the crosswalk.

If you're pulled over by a police officer, remember to be polite and courteous. If you are in a large city in northern Baja (Tijuana, Rosarito, Ensenada, Tecate, or Mexicali), you are able to take your ticket and pay the fee by mail from the United States. The instructions will be on the ticket. If you are in any other area of the peninsula, you will need to follow the police officer to the local station to pay the fine. If the officer is asking you to pay on the spot, he is illegally asking you for a *mordida* or bribe. Giving him the bribe is illegal on your behalf and can get you into big trouble. It also perpetuates a cycle of police officers targeting foreigners in the hopes of getting some case. Don't do it.

ROADSIDE ASSISTANCE

The **Angeles Verdes** (Green Angels) have come to the rescue of many Baja road-trippers who experience a breakdown or troubles on the road. The green trucks are sponsored by the Secretary of Tourism and can assist if you get into an accident, have a flat tire, run out of gas, or break down. They offer free labor, service, and towing. Gas and spare parts are available for a charge. The service of the Green Angels is free, but tips are appreciated.

The Green Angels patrol the roads on a regular basis. If you break down, pull over to the side and lift your hood to signal that you need help. If you have cell phone service, you can call 078, which will get you the 24/7 bilingual tourist assistance, who will send roadside assistance.

MILITARY CHECKPOINTS

Road-trippers will encounter a number of military checkpoints on Mexico 1 throughout the peninsula. The soldiers will be dressed in full army fatigues with large guns, and may seem intimidating at first, but they are there to keep you safe and are just checking that you aren't transporting drugs or arms. They will likely ask you where you are coming from and where you are going. They may ask to look through your vehicle. Tell them that you are on *vacaciones* (vacation). It's best to be polite and respectful, and you'll be on your way in no time.

MAPS

If you can get a copy of the currently out-of-print ***Baja California Almanac*** (www.baja-almanac.com), this is the only map you'll need for a road trip on the peninsula. The *Baja Almanac* is considered the ultimate map for Baja and by far the most detailed and accurate navigation tool. Even older editions will still be useful.

CAR RENTAL

There are car rental companies in Tijuana, Ensenada, Mexicali, Loreto, La Paz, Los Barriles, Todos Santos, San José del Cabo, and Cabo San Lucas. Larger cities, especially those with airports, generally have more options and cheaper rates.

Some car rental companies in San Diego will allow you to take the rental car to Mexico, but make sure in advance. Understand that you'll need to purchase Mexican auto insurance through them, which will be an additional charge. If renting a car in Baja, be aware that the insurance is not included in the rate at which you rent the car.

Bus

There are a number of businesses that provide bus service between the towns on the peninsula. **Autobuses de la Baja California** (ABC, tel. 664/104-7400, www.abc.com.mx) and **Aguila** (tel. 800/824-8452, www.autobusesaguila.com) are two large companies with routes between most cities on the peninsula. Buses tend to be large and modern, with air-conditioning and confortable seats. It's generally not necessary to make a reservation in advance, but it's a good idea to stop by the bus depot a day or so ahead of time to check out the schedule and current fares. It takes about 30 hours to travel the full peninsula between Tijuana and Cabo on a bus.

Taxi

Taxis can be found around larger cities, especially in the central tourist areas, at taxi stands, and at larger hotels. There are no meters in taxis in Baja, so always negotiate the fare with the driver before getting in the taxi. Uber is now available in Tijuana, and can be found as far south as Ensenada.

Motorcycle

More and more riders are being lured by the adventure of cruising on their motorcycle down the Baja peninsula. Specifically motorcycle mechanics are less common than auto mechanics, so it's wise to be self-sufficient in this aspect. There are a number of guided motorcycle trips on the peninsula if you don't want to travel alone. **Adventure Rider Motorcycle Forum** (www.advrider. com) has some of the best information about riding on the peninsula.

Bicycle

Bicycling along Baja's Mexico 1 is a dangerous feat that should not be attempted by any cyclists who are not experts. The lack of shoulders and guardrails on the windy highway coupled with the fact that there are large trucks and many drivers that speed make for a dangerous situation for any cyclist. The **Baja Divide** (www.bajadivide.com) is a new self-guided route that links 2,000 miles of dirt roads from Tecate to Cabo for cyclists looking to explore the Baja peninsula, without having to take the harrowing highway option.

Visas and Officialdom

PASSPORTS AND VISAS

As of 2009, a passport is required for travel in Baja. If you are crossing in and out of Mexico by land, you can use a passport card. If traveling by air, a passport book is required.

There is a lot of confusion about the visa situation for U.S. and Canadian travelers headed into Mexico. A visa is not required for U.S. and Canadian citizens. However, a *forma migratoria múltiple* (FMM) tourist permit is mandatory for all non-Mexican citizens traveling in Baja. Many people will refer to the FMM as a visa, which causes an extreme amount of confusion about the issue. An FMM is required for all U.S. and Canadian citizens every time they enter Baja, regardless of where they will be going and how long they will be staying. The previous exceptions for trips under 72 hours and/or within the border zone no longer apply. For trips seven days or less, there is no charge for the FMM.

Visas are required for citizens traveling to Mexico from certain countries. For a full list, see www.gob.mx.

FMM TOURIST PERMITS

All U.S. and Canadian citizens are required to have a *forma migratoria múltiple* (FMM) tourist permit every time they enter Baja. The previous exceptions for trips under 72 hours and/or within the border zone no longer apply. To be clear, the FMM tourist permit is not a visa, although many people refer to it as a visa, creating much confusion about the topic.

If crossing by land, travelers must stop at the border to complete the FMM form, pay the US$25 fee, and then have the form stamped with the date of entry. You must present your passport book or passport card when getting your FMM. FMM tourist permits are valid for up to 180 days. If you will be spending seven days or less in Baja, free FMM tourist permits are available as well.

Travelers arriving in Baja by commercial flight from outside of Mexico will have the cost of their FMM included in their plane ticket and will be provided with all of the paperwork to clear when arriving in Baja at the airport. Travelers crossing by sea into Baja must stop at the port captain's office to have their FMM stamped. If you will be entering Baja by boat and will not be stopping on land, but will be in Mexican waters, you must get a nautical FMM, which is a separate process. For more information go to www.gob.mx.

EMBASSIES AND CONSULATES

There is a U.S. Consulate in Tijuana and a U.S. Consular Agency in San José del Cabo. They can help with passport and visa services, provide assistance for U.S. citizens arrested in Mexico, register births and deaths of U.S. citizens, and perform notarials.

U.S. CONSULATE – TIJUANA

Paseo de las Culturas, Mesa de Otay
Delegación Centenario C.P. 22425
Tijuana, Baja California
Tel. 664/977-2000
7:30am-4:15pm Mon.-Fri.
Emergency after-hours tel. 619/692-2154
ACSTijuana@state.gov
mx.usembassy.gov

U.S. CONSULAR AGENCY – SAN JOSÉ DEL CABO

Tiendas de Palmilla, Carretera Transpeninsular Km. 27.5, Local B221
San José del Cabo, Baja California Sur, C.P. 23406
Tel. 624/143-3566
9am-2pm Mon-Thur.
Emergency after-hours tel. 619/692-2154
ConAgencyLosCabos@state.gov
mx.usembassy.gov
Canada has a Consular Agency in Cabo San Lucas.

CANADIAN CONSULAR AGENCY – CABO SAN LUCAS

Plaza San Lucas
Carretera Transpeninsular Km. 0.5, Local 82
Col. El Tezal 23454 Cabo San Lucas, Baja California Sur
Tel.624/142-4333
9:30am-12:30pm Mon.-Fri.
lcabo@international.gc.ca

There is a **Mexican Consulate** (1549 India St., San Diego, info@consulmexsd.org, tel. 619/231-8414, 8am-6pm Mon.-Fri.) in San Diego that can assist with visas, permanent and temporary residency for Mexico, special import permits, and questions about Mexican customs.

CUSTOMS
Entering Mexico

Travelers crossing into Mexico are allowed to bring items for personal use, as well as up to US$75 of new merchandise (per adult) duty free when crossing by land. If crossing by air,

US$300 of new merchandise is permitted duty free. Adults may bring up to three liters of liquor or beer and up to six liters of wine. You may carry up to US$10,000 cash without paying duty.

Many people find themselves wanting to bring items to donate to orphanages and other charitable causes in Baja. However, bringing large amounts of used clothing and other items will be subject to paying duty. Firearms are illegal in Mexico and may only be possessed with a proper permit for hunting.

Returning to the United States

Travelers may bring up to US$800 worth of new merchandise into the United States from Mexico every 30 days without paying a duty. Adults may bring back one liter of alcohol and 200 cigarettes. Some foods are allowed into the United States from Mexico; however, most fruits, vegetables, nuts, and meat products are prohibited. The specific list changes often, so check with www.cbp.gov for a complete run-down.

Recreation

HUNTING

Many hunters come to Baja to hunt quail, dove, pheasant, waterfowl, and deer in northern Baja in regions around Mexicali, the Río Hardy, Tecate, and south of Ensenada. Hunting season runs from the beginning of September and extends through the end of February for certain species.

Guns and ammunition are highly regulated in Mexico, and permits can be expensive (US$350 for the year). Most hunters rent guns by the day from the hunting outfitter they are using. A hunting license and game tags are required. All non-Mexicans must be accompanied by a licensed Mexican hunting guide while in the field. **Baja Hunting** (www.bajahunting.com) can assist with permits and arrangements.

HIKING AND BACKPACKING

Baja is a peninsula that has captured the hearts of many hikers and explorers. From the high mountains of the northern sierras to the sands of the *desierto central,* the peninsula offers a wide variety of options. One thing that's common throughout the peninsula is the lack of well-marked trails, if there are any trails at all. **Mexico Maps** (www.mexicomaps.com) has topographic maps available for the entire peninsula.

You will need to be prepared for self-sufficient camping, and please be respectful by carrying out all of your trash and to abiding by low-impact camping principles. Make sure to bring plenty of water and a first-aid kit, in addition to the usual hiking and camping essentials.

FISHING

Sportfishing is popular all over the peninsula, and anglers come for the thrill of catching yellowtail, dorado, tuna, roosterfish, and more. Mexican fishing licenses are required when fishing on the water. Everyone who is on board a boat with tackle, whether or not they are fishing, must have a fishing license. They are available by the day, week, month, or year. You can obtain a fishing permit in advance through the **Mexico Department of Fisheries (PESCA)** (2550 Fifth Ave. 101, San Diego, CA, tel. 619/233-4324) in San Diego or through **Discover Baja Travel Club** (www.discoverbaja.com). If you are paying to take a fishing charter, they will often take care of the fishing permit for you, but be sure to ask in advance. Fishing permits are not required if you are fishing from shore.

BOATING

Recreational boating is an enjoyable way to experience Baja and grants access to remote beaches and places that other travelers can't easily get to. Temporary Import Permits (TIPs) for boats are now required for Baja. The permits are good for 10 years. You can start the process online at www.banjercito.com.mx.

There are port captain offices in Ensenada, Guerrero Negro, Bahía Magdalena (at San Carlos), Cabo San Lucas, San José del Cabo, La Paz, Puerto Escondido, Loreto, Mulegé, Santa Rosalía, Bahía de los Angeles, and San Felipe. You must complete a crew list document and get FMMs at your first port of entry for all passengers on the vessel. If you will be entering Mexican waters for sportfishing, but not making landfall, you must obtain a nautical FMM (www.gob.mx).

KAYAKING

Most kayaking in Baja takes places over on the Sea of Cortez where the waters are calmer and can be crystal clear in certain areas. Bahía Concepción, La Paz, and Loreto are popular areas for sea kayakers. Kayaking on the Pacific side of the peninsula is for more experienced kayakers. Bahía Magdalena is a popular spot for kayaking on the Pacific. In larger towns like Loreto and La Paz, kayaks will be available for rent, but many serious kayakers bring their own kayaks so that they can explore more freely in areas where there are no rentals.

SURFING

From Tijuana to Cabo, Baja is full of surf breaks on the Pacific side of the peninsula. While spots in the far north around Rosarito and Ensenada and at the south, down in Cabo and Todos Santos, are more popular, there are plenty of empty waves along the center of the

peninsula in between. Surf shops, rentals, and lessons can be found in cities in the north and south. Most surfers who are looking to surf in more remote areas bring their own boards and are prepared for self-sustained camping in order to surf any of the spots in the middle of the peninsula.

WINDSURFING AND KITEBOARDING

Kiteboarding and windsurfing season on the peninsula is November-March. La Ventana south of La Paz and Los Barriles on the East Cape are two of the most popular spots for windsurfing and kiteboarding. A large community has built up around the sport in these two areas, and there are a number of companies that give lessons and have rentals available in both locations.

SNORKELING AND SCUBA DIVING

The peninsula has a diverse marinelife, which makes for interesting snorkeling and diving in both the waters of the Pacific and the Sea of Cortez. On the northern Pacific side, Rosarito and Ensenada both have some diving sites and dive shops that can assist with trips and equipment. The water is cold here and wetsuits will be necessary. Farther south and on the Sea of Cortez side of the peninsula, the waters are much warmer, and tropical conditions can be found for diving and snorkeling. Loreto, La Paz, Cabo Pulmo, and the Los Cabos region are the most popular dive and snorkel areas in Baja California Sur. The living coral reef at Cabo Pulmo makes it a particularly unique destination for diving.

Food and Accommodations

FOOD
Food and Water Safety

The most frequently asked question among first time Baja travelers is "Is it safe to drink the water?" The tap water in Mexico contains different bacteria than that found in the water in the United States and for this reason can cause upset stomachs for travelers. It's safe to drink the water and ice that will be served at large restaurants and hotels in big tourist cities, as they will serve purified water. You should brush your teeth with bottled water to be safe. When in remoter areas, always ask for bottled water.

As when traveling in any developing country, it's a good idea to carry some Imodium with you. Most towns in Baja have pharmacies where they can give you something like Lomotil over the counter if needed.

Where to Eat

Foodies from around the world are flocking to northern Baja where Tijuana and Ensenada are leading the way in an incredible culinary scene. The fresh local seafoods, meats, and Mexican flavors are being combined with Asian and Mediterranean influences. This new Baja California style of cooking is now catching on all over, with "Baja California"-style restaurants opening in places like New York and Chicago. Los Cabos also has a number of nice restaurants, many trying to compete with the ingenuity and creativity coming out of northern Baja. Expect much higher prices at the restaurants in Cabo than you'll find in northern Baja.

Throughout the rest of the peninsula, fresh seafood, rich traditional Mexican dishes, and savory *antojitos* like tacos and tamales are the staples. Don't miss picking up a bag of fresh tortillas, either *harina* (flour) or *maíz* (corn), whenever you pass a *tortillería*.

What to Eat
ANTOJITOS/STREET FOOD

Antojitos, little whims, are traditional Mexican fast-food dishes such as tacos, *tortas*, tamales, tostadas, and quesadillas. You can find these served on menus at many casual sit-down restaurants (either à la carte or served as a meal with rice and beans on the side) and also at street food carts.

SEAFOOD

Because the peninsula is surrounded by water, *mariscos* are practically a dietary staple in Baja. You can enjoy seafood at all different price ranges and settings. At street carts and cheap *mariscos* stands, you'll find items like fish tacos, ceviche (raw fish "cooked" in lime juice), and *cocteles de mariscos* (seafood cocktails where the seafood is served chilled in a tomato-based broth). A favorite among locals are *almejas gratinadas* (clams au gratin), where the clam is topped with cheese and

---

Seafood Guide

- *almejas* - clams
- *atún* - tuna
- *camarón* - shrimp
- *cangrejo* - crab
- *caracol* - sea snail
- *erizo* - sea urchin
- *jurel* - yellowtail
- *langosta* - lobster
- *mejillones* - mussels
- *ostiones* - oysters
- *pargo* - red snapper
- *tiburón* - shark

La Cuenta, Por Favor

Mexicans consider it rude to bring the check to the table before it's asked for. When you eat at a restaurant in Mexico, you are welcomed with a warm hospitality that invites you to come eat, drink, relax, and enjoy. They would never dream of kicking you out in order to turn tables. Many foreigners may be frustrated with this at first, but most come to enjoy it. When you're ready for the check, you'll have to ask for it: *la cuenta, por favor.*

served on the grill. At sit-down restaurants, you'll find items like *pescado del día* (fish of the day), *camarónes* (shrimp), *langosta* (lobster), and *pulpo* (octopus).

MEAT

Carne is a large part of Mexican food, whether served by itself or as part of a dish. You'll find *pollo* (chicken), *puerco* (pork), and *res* (beef) on many menus as well as less-traditional meats like *chiva* (goat) and *borrego* (lamb).

SALSAS

No meal in Mexico is complete without adding some kind of salsa. Many restaurants and food stands make their own, adding to the unique flavors of the food. Pico de gallo (also called *salsa fresca* or *salsa bandera*) is a combination of chopped tomatoes, onions, cilantro, and jalapeño. *Crema* (a thinned sour cream), guacamole, and other salsas are common as well. If you don't like hot flavors, ask how hot the salsas are before trying them; you don't want to be caught off-guard by a habanero salsa!

BEVERAGES

A standard selection of sodas can be found around the peninsula. Coca-Cola here is made with cane sugar instead of corn syrup, giving it a different taste and making it somewhat of a sought-after beverage over the years. *Aguas frescas* (literally fresh waters) are infused waters, served around Mexico. The most traditional flavors are *jamaica* (hibiscus), *horchata* (rice milk), and *tamarindo* (tamarind), although hip restaurants will serve other refreshing and creative flavors. *Limonada* is

Mexico's version of lemonade. It is made with simple syrup and *limones,* which are limes in Mexico. You can order it *natural,* made with still water, or *mineral* with sparkling water.

ALCOHOLIC BEVERAGES

Even those uninitiated with Mexico are likely familiar with the margarita and tequila. Mexico makes a number of good beers, and beers like Tecate, Dos Equis, and Pacífico, that can be found all along the peninsula. In northern Baja there's a growing craft beer scene as well. Baja's wine region, the Valle de Guadalupe, has helped wine become more popular around Mexico, and you'll see wines from the region on the menus of nicer restaurants throughout the peninsula.

ACCOMMODATIONS

There are a wide variety of accommodations found on the peninsula. The options depend on your destination and personal preference.

CAMPING AND RV PARKS

There are plenty of places to camp on the peninsula ranging from isolated sites with no services to fancy RV parks with full hookups. There's a large community of snowbird RVers who spend their winters in Baja California Sur to take advantage of the warm weather.

MOTELS

Budget motels are found all over the peninsula and in some places are the only option for accommodations. It's common at many of the affordable motels and hotels for them to ask for a deposit of a few hundred pesos as collateral for the TV remote control.

BED-AND-BREAKFASTS AND BOUTIQUE HOTELS

There are more and more boutique hotels and B&Bs opening up on the peninsula. In Baja Sur, travelers can find these more intimate accommodations in Loreto, La Paz, Todos Santos, San José del Cabo, and Cabo San Lucas. In northern Baja, there are a number of B&Bs in the Valle de Guadalupe, just outside of Ensenada.

RESORTS

For those who love resorts and luxury, Los Cabos is the place to go. There are no resorts in Baja outside of the Los Cabos area, even though there a number of establishments that may have the word "resort" included in their name.

VACATION RENTALS

Vacation rentals abound all along the peninsula, and these can be a good option for travelers planning to stay for an extended period of time or for locations where there are very few options in terms of hotels or motels. It can also be convenient to have access to a full kitchen to avoid having to eat all meals out at restaurants. **Vacation Rentals by Owner** (VRBO, www.vrbo.com) and **Airbnb** (www.airbnb.com) both have rentals along the peninsula.

Travel Tips

TIME

Many foreigners may experience frustration with the fact that things happen at a much slower pace in Baja than at home. It's not abnormal for service to be slower than you are used to and for everything in general to take longer. Punctuality amongst friends may fall to the wayside in Mexico, but you should be on time for any business-related matters. Most professionals are aware of foreigners' adherence to punctuality and put in the extra effort to be prompt.

POLITE INTERACTIONS

Mexican people are far more polite and less direct than stereotypical U.S. citizens. They always exchange niceties and ask about your well-being and your family before getting to the matter at hand. You should begin all conversations with at least a polite *Hola, buenos días* (or *buenas tardes,* depending on time of day) before delving into matters.

A cultural difference that foreigners may find frustrating is that Mexicans have a hard time delivering bad news or saying "no." They often consider it rude and will skirt the issue, which can lead to much confusion and irritation. Mexicans will rarely give you a "no" for an RSVP; they are far more likely to say "yes" and then not show up, as they consider this to be more acceptable than declining from the beginning. Likewise, if you are waiting on something they don't have, the common response will be that they will have it *mañana,* tomorrow. Many foreigners have learned to accept the fact that in Mexico *mañana* doesn't necessarily mean tomorrow, it just means not today.

If you sense that you are not getting a direct answer, it's best to rephrase the question or to ask again in a different manner, to make sure that you are getting the whole story.

TIPPING

You should tip a few pesos to the attendants at the gas station, the baggers at the grocery store, and parking lot attendants. At restaurants, 10 percent is standard, and you should give 15 percent for a fancy fine dining experience. Just a few pesos will be sufficient as a tip at taco stands and food carts.

WHAT TO PACK

If it's your first time road-tripping down the peninsula, here are a few items to bring along:

Electronics: A GPS unit will be your most valuable tool for navigating the peninsula. Street names and addresses don't exist in many areas, so using GPS coordinates is often the most reliable way to find your destination. There are stretches of the peninsula where you won't get music on the radio so an auxiliary cable and portable music player are a good idea. Camera and cell phone are a must for most Baja travelers. Expensive larger electronic items like laptops should be left at home unless you absolutely need them. The more you bring along, the more you need to keep track of, and most hotels on the peninsula don't have safes. Mexico uses the same outlets as the United States and Canada, so you don't need to bring along a converter for your chargers.

Toiletries and First Aid: Don't forget items like sunscreen, aloe vera, bug spray, and hand sanitizer in addition to your usual toiletry items. Most Baja hotels do not provide toiletries like shampoo, conditioner, or lotion, so you should bring your own from home. Hair dryers are another item not usually provided by hotels, so you should bring one from home if you need one for daily use. Pack a small first-aid kit with Neosporin and Band-Aids. You can get the generic version of most over-the-counter medications and items at any pharmacy on the peninsula, but if there's a specific medication or product you like to have on hand, bring it from home. Most Baja travelers carry Pepto-Bismol and Imodium A-D to help soothe an upset stomach. An extra roll of toilet paper is always valuable to have on hand for pit stops and because many gas station and public restrooms will not provide it.

Personal Items: Bring sturdy footwear for hiking and sandals for the beach. Water shoes can come in handy for hikes where you'll be crossing streams and for swimming in natural pools or rivers. Swimsuits, sunhats, sunglasses, and beach towels are necessary for beach time. Pack clothing that can be layered for hot days and cool nights. Leave expensive jewelry at home. Bring along plenty of reading material as English books and magazines can be difficult to find and expensive.

Sports Equipment: The equipment you bring with you depends on your interests and the size of your vehicle. Most sports enthusiasts secure gear on the top of their car with sturdy straps. You'll be able to rent equipment like kayaks, surfboards, stand-up paddleboards, bicycles, fishing rods, snorkels, and scuba gear in more developed towns. Many road-trippers bring along their own coolers, beach chairs, and umbrellas. Camping equipment will all need to be brought with you.

Vehicle: Be sure to have a standard emergency road kit, tow straps, flashlight, jack, and spare tire at the very minimum. Duct tape and a tire repair kit can help if you're in a desperate situation. It's always a good idea to carry a gas can and extra water.

ACCESS FOR TRAVELERS WITH DISABILITIES

Baja California is a region that can be difficult to explore independently for visitors with disabilities. Uneven sidewalks (if there are sidewalks at all), stairs without ramps, and dirt roads and floors can make getting around in a wheelchair nearly impossible in most areas. Buses and shuttles are generally not wheelchair accessible. Check in advance with your hotel to ask about accessibility and to make any special advance arrangements. Large resorts in the Cabo region will be the most likely to have wheelchair access and the ability to accommodate travelers with disabilities.

There are very few provisions in Baja for blind or hearing-impaired travelers. A few new intersections in Tijuana now have audio assistance for the blind, but they are rare exceptions on the peninsula.

TRAVELING WITH CHILDREN

Baja is a great place to travel with children and there are plenty of activities for kids of all ages and interests. Many hotel rooms along the peninsula are equipped with multiple beds to suit families. There are a few adults-only resorts in Cabo, and some of the exclusive boutique accommodations in places like Todos Santos or Valle de Guadalupe many not accept children, so it's best to check ahead. Otherwise, kids are warmly welcomed along the peninsula.

TRAVELING WITH PETS

Many road-trippers travel with their dogs as there are a number of motels and campsites that are pet-friendly in Baja. You should carry current vaccinations and registration for your dog. Mexico requires that travelers have a "certificate of health" from a veterinarian dated within 72 hours of entering Mexico.

TRAVELING ALONE

Solo travelers heading to the southern cape region or to the northern region of Baja shouldn't have any hesitation in doing so. Driving the peninsula alone or heading to remote areas requires a firm grasp of the Spanish language and sufficient automotive skills in the case of a breakdown. Many solo travelers who are driving down the peninsula look for other travelers to caravan with.

SENIOR TRAVELERS

A large number of senior travelers are attracted to Baja California because of the warm weather and affordable prices. Retired snowbirds arrive in Baja California Sur each winter to enjoy the sunny days and laid-back quality of life. There are a growing number of retired expats all over the peninsula who have made Baja their full-time or part-time home.

GAY AND LESBIAN TRAVELERS

LGBT travelers should have no problems traveling in Baja. Larger cities like Tijuana, La Paz, and Los Cabos will have more options for nightlife and entertainment.

Health and Safety

MEDICAL ASSISTANCE AND EMERGENCY EVACUATION

Travelers will find knowledgeable doctors and modern medical facilities in nearly every sizable town in Baja. Large modern hospitals operate in larger cities and clinics and Red Cross facilities are available in smaller towns.

There are a number of companies that provide emergency evacuation from Baja. **Medical Air Services Association** (MASA, tel. 800/423-3226, www.masamts.com) and **Aeromedevac** (Mex. tel. 800/832-5087, toll-free U.S. tel. 800/462-0911, www.aeromedevac.com) are two such services. It's always a good idea to purchase extra travel insurance when traveling to help cover any medical payments or emergency evacuation.

SUNBURN AND DEHYDRATION

The Baja sun can be intense and is prone to catching travelers off-guard. Sunburns and dehydration are common afflictions for unsuspecting tourists who have spent too much time out in the sun and heat. Sunscreen and hats should be worn outside. Always make sure you have plenty of drinking water and are staying well hydrated.

STINGS AND BITES

Stingrays and jellyfish are often the culprits for any stings in the ocean. Although the

Emergency Phone Numbers and Resources

These numbers can be dialed from any cell phone or landline in order to reach emergency services in Baja:

- **911/066:** While historically 066 has been the emergency services phone number in Mexico, the entire country is switching to 911 as their emergency phone number. The state of Baja California Norte adopted 911 at the end of 2016. Baja California Sur will adopt 911 as an emergency number by the end of 2017. 066 is expected to continue to work in Baja through the year 2017 as the switch to 911 is being rolled out.

- **078:** Tourist assistance hotline. Travelers can call from anywhere in Baja California (Norte) and Baja California Sur to get 24/7 bilingual assistance from roadside assistance to emergency services or travel information.

- **074:** Roadside assistance

stings may hurt, they are not life-threatening. When entering the water from the shore, always do the "stingray shuffle" to frighten off any unsuspecting rays hiding under the sand. Seek medical attention for any allergic reactions.

On land, scorpions are common throughout the peninsula. They like to hide in cool, dark places like under rocks or in piles of wood. Always shake out towels, blankets, clothing, and shoes that have been outside and may have become a hiding spot for scorpions. A scorpion sting is painful, but rarely dangerous for adults. If your child is stung, seek medical attention.

CRIME

Mexico has been in the news the past decade for drug cartel-related violence. The violence, which was never targeted at tourists, has significantly declined in recent years. That said, it's always a good idea when traveling to be aware of your surroundings and to avoid drawing attention to yourself. Expensive electronics and flashy jewelry should stay at home. Don't leave items in your car that could be a target for petty theft.

Tourist Information

MONEY

The Mexican currency is the peso, abbreviated MXN or sometimes MN. It uses the same symbol as the U.S. dollar ($), which can cause some confusion at times. Establishments in Mexico are legally required to post their prices in pesos, but you'll sometimes find at tourist-centered restaurants and at some hotels, that the prices are listed in U.S. dollars. Mexico has a 16% IVA (sales tax) that is also supposed to be included in the listed price of items, but sometimes isn't.

Dollars or Pesos?

While U.S. dollars are accepted in some tourist areas of Baja, it's always advisable to pay with pesos so that you get the best exchange rate. There are a number of exchange houses in large cities, but these days most travelers get cash out of the ATMs in Baja for the best exchange rate. Be aware that you'll pay a fee at the ATM and will possibly pay another fee with your bank in the United States, depending on how your bank operates with foreign transaction fees.

Foreign credit cards are commonly accepted in larger cities in the north and in the Los Cabos region, but it's always best to have enough cash on you in case businesses don't take cards or the machine is not working (which is common). There are many small towns in the middle of the peninsula where credit cards are not accepted and there are no ATMs, so you'll need to have cash. Always remember to call your bank ahead of time to let them know you will be using your debit or credit card in Mexico, so that they can put a travel alert on your account. Travelers checks are not widely accepted, so it's best to have credit cards or cash.

Bargaining is accepted, and expected, in markets and at street stalls. Start by asking how much the item costs (¿Cuanto cuesta?) and then counteroffer with a lower price (go down to about half of the initial asking price). You can go back and forth from there until you settle on a mutually acceptable price. Always be polite and kind while bargaining. Never insult the merchandise or the vendor in attempt to get a lower price. For brick-and-mortar stores, the set price will likely be posted.

COMMUNICATIONS
Phones and Cell Phones

Because of the growing numbers of cross-border travelers and citizens, many of the large U.S. phone carriers have plans that will give you data, minutes, and texting in Baja. Always make sure to call your carrier to find about your options before traveling. There will be places on the peninsula where no cell phone service is available.

Phone numbers in Baja follow the same format as numbers in the United States, with a three-digit area code followed by a seven-digit number. There's no standard format for hyphenating the phone numbers in Mexico, so they may at times look different than presented in this book. The area code for Mexico is 52. For dialing a Mexican phone number from the United States, you will need to dial 011-52 before the area code and phone number.

Internet Access

Many hotels along the peninsula now offer wireless access. The service is not guaranteed and the signal is not always strong enough to extend everywhere around a property. But it's usually sufficient for light Internet use and will be available at least in the lobby area. More restaurants are also offering wireless Internet, especially in larger cities. Internet cafés are few and far between along the peninsula because of the prevalence of wireless Internet access.

WEIGHTS AND MEASURES

Mexico is on the metric system for weights, volumes, temperature, and distances. Driving directions and speed limits are given in kilometers. Gas is sold in liters, and temperature is measured in degrees Celsius.

TIME ZONE

The state of Baja California (Norte) is on Pacific Standard Time, while Baja California Sur is an hour ahead on Mountain Time. You'll adjust your clock when you pass the state line in Guerrero Negro. Daylight savings time takes effect in the two states at slightly different times, usually a few weeks apart, just to add to the confusion.

TOURIST OFFICES

Most large cities in Baja have at least one tourist office where travelers can speak to someone in English and gather brochures and information about the region. The **Baja California (Norte) website** (www.discoverbajacalifornia.com) has helpful information, as does the **Baja California Sur website** (www.visitbajasur.travel).

TRAVEL CLUBS

Whether you are a first-time tourist or a seasoned Baja traveler, there are a number of advantages to joining a Baja-specific travel club. They offer up-to-date information, travel discounts, services and assistance, and premium Mexican auto insurance. **Discover Baja Travel Club** (3264 Governor Dr., San Diego, U.S. tel. 619/275-4225, toll-free U.S. tel. 800/727-2252, www.discoverbaja.com, US$39/yr.) is conveniently located in San Diego where you can stop in to get your auto insurance, prepaid FMM tourist permit, fishing license, and Baja books and maps, before heading south.

MAPS

The **Got Baja?** (www.gotbaja.mx) series of maps are available for a number of cities in Baja California Sur like Cabo, La Paz, Todos Santos, and Loreto. The free maps can be found around the city and are helpful for identifying sights, restaurants, bars, and hotels. For driving the peninsula, the currently out-of-print *Baja California Almanac* (www.baja-almanac.com) is considered the ultimate map of Baja and by far the most detailed and accurate navigation tool. Even older editions are still useful.

Resources

Spanish Glossary

abarrotes: groceries

aduana: customs

aguas termales: hot springs

alberca: swimming pool

antojitos: literally "little whims," casual Mexican dishes like tacos or *tortas*

bahía: bay

BCN: the state of Baja California (Norte)

BCS: the state of Baja California Sur

calle: street

callejón: alley

campestre: literally "country," used to refer to outdoor country restaurants

canon: canyon

cardón: a large cactus native to northwestern Mexico

caseta: tollbooth or guard shack

cervecería: brewery

cerveza: beer

colectivo: taxi van that picks up several passengers at a time, operating like a small bus

efectivo: cash

ejido: communally held land

farmacia: pharmacy

federales: nickname for the federal police

FMM *forma migratoria multiple:* tourist permit required for non-Mexican citizens traveling in Baja

Green Angels: a group providing free roadside assistance

gringo: a foreigner in a Spanish-speaking country who is not Latino or Hispanic

INM *Instituto Nacional de Migración:* unit of the Mexican government that controls migration

malecón: waterfront promenade

mariscos: seafood

mercado: market

mordida: literally "bite," a bribe

palapa: structure with a thatched roof

PAN *Partido Acción Nacional:* Mexico's conservative political party

panga: aluminum fishing boat

Pemex: the government-regulated gas stations in Mexico

playa: beach

PRI *Partido Revolucionario Institucional:* Mexico's centrist political party

PRD *Partido de la Revolución Democrática:* Mexico's leftist political party

punta: point

SAT *Servicio de Administración Tributaria:* unit of Mexican government that controls customs

SECTUR *Secretaria de Turismo:* Secretary of Tourism

tienda: store

tinaja: pool or spring

tope: speed bump

ultramarine: mini market/liquor store

vino: wine

ABBREVIATIONS

Av.: Avenida

Blvd.: Boulevard

Col.: Colonia

Km.: Kilometer

s/n: *sin número* (without number, used for addresses without building numbers)

Spanish Phrasebook

Spanish commonly uses 30 letters—the familiar English 26, plus four straightforward additions: ch, ll, ñ, and rr, which are explained in "Consonants," below.

PRONUNCIATION

Once you learn them, Spanish pronunciation rules—in contrast to English—don't change. Spanish vowels generally sound softer than in English. (*Note:* The capitalized syllables below receive stronger accents.)

Vowels

a   like ah, as in "hah": *agua* AH-gooah (water), *pan* PAHN (bread), and *casa* CAH-sah (house)

e   like ay, as in "may:" *mesa* MAY-sah (table), *tela* TAY-lah (cloth), and *de* DAY (of, from)

i   like ee, as in "need": *diez* dee-AYZ (ten), *comida* ko-MEE-dah (meal), and *fin* FEEN (end)

o   like oh, as in "go": *peso* PAY-soh (weight), *ocho* OH-choh (eight), and *poco* POH-koh (a bit)

u   like oo, as in "cool": *uno* OO-noh (one), *cuarto* KOOAHR-toh (room), and *usted* oos-TAYD (you); when it follows a "q" the u is silent; when it follows an "h" or has an umlaut, it's pronounced like "w"

Consonants

b, d, f, k, l, m, n, p, q, s, t, v, w, x, y, z, and ch   pronounced almost as in English; h occurs, but is silent—not pronounced at all

c   like k as in "keep": *cuarto* KOOAR-toh (room), Tepic tay-PEEK (capital of Nayarit state); when it precedes "e" or "i," pronounce c like s, as in "sit": *cerveza* sayr-VAY-sah (beer), *encima* ayn-SEE-mah (atop)

g   like g as in "gift" when it precedes "a," "o," "u," or a consonant: *gato* GAH-toh (cat), *hago* AH-goh (I do, make); otherwise, pronounce g like h as in "hat": *giro* HEE-roh (money order), *gente* HAYN-tay (people)

j   like h, as in "has": *Jueves* HOOAY-vays (Thursday), *mejor* may-HOR (better)

ll   like y, as in "yes": *toalla* toh-AH-yah (towel), *ellos* AY-yohs (they, them)

ñ   like ny, as in "canyon": *año* AH-nyo (year), *señor* SAY-nyor (Mr., sir)

r   is lightly trilled, with tongue at the roof of your mouth like a very light English d, as in "ready": *pero* PAY-doh (but), *tres* TDAYS (three), *cuatro* KOOAH-tdoh (four)

rr   like a Spanish r, but with much more emphasis and trill. Let your tongue flap. Practice with *burro* (donkey), *carretera* (highway), and Carrillo (proper name), then really let go with *ferrocarril* (railroad)

Note: The single small but common exception to all of the above is the pronunciation of Spanish y when it's being used as the Spanish word for "and," as in "Ron y Kathy." In such case, pronounce it like the English ee, as in "keep": Ron "ee" Kathy (Ron and Kathy).

Accent

The rule for accent, the relative stress given to syllables within a given word, is straightforward. If a word ends in a vowel, an n, or an s, accent the next-to-last syllable; if not, accent the last syllable.

Pronounce *gracias* GRAH-seeahs (thank you), *orden* OHR-dayn (order), and *carretera* kah-ray-TAY-rah (highway) with stress on the next-to-last syllable.

Otherwise, accent the last syllable: *venir* vay-NEER (to come), *ferrocarril* fay-roh-cah-REEL (railroad), and *edad* ay-DAHD (age).

Exceptions to the accent rule are always marked with an accent sign: (á, é, í, ó, or ú), such as *teléfono* tay-LAY-foh-noh (telephone), *jabón* hah-BON (soap), and *rápido* RAH-pee-doh (rapid).

BASIC AND COURTEOUS EXPRESSIONS

Most Spanish-speaking people consider formalities important. Whenever approaching anyone for information or some other reason, do not forget the appropriate salutation—good morning, good evening, etc. Standing alone, the greeting *hola* (hello) can sound brusque.

Hello. *Hola.*
Good morning. *Buenos días.*
Good afternoon. *Buenas tardes.*
Good evening. *Buenas noches.*
How are you? *¿Cómo está usted?*
Very well, thank you. *Muy bien, gracias.*
Okay; good. *Bien.*
Not okay; bad. *Mal or feo.*
So-so. *Más o menos.*
And you? *¿Y usted?*
Thank you. *Gracias.*
Thank you very much. *Muchas gracias.*
You're very kind. *Muy amable.*
You're welcome. *De nada.*
Goodbye. *Adios.*
See you later. *Hasta luego.*
please *por favor*
yes *sí*
no *no*
I don't know. *No sé.*
Just a moment, please. *Momentito, por favor.*
Excuse me, please (when you're trying to get attention). *Disculpe* or *Con permiso.*
Excuse me (when you've made a mistake). *Lo siento.*
Pleased to meet you. *Mucho gusto.*
How do you say ... in Spanish? *¿Cómo se dice ... en español?*
What is your name? *¿Cómo se llama usted?*
Do you speak English? *¿Habla usted inglés?*
Is English spoken here? (Does anyone here speak English?) *¿Se habla inglés?*
I don't speak Spanish well. *No hablo bien el español.*

I don't understand. *No entiendo.*
My name is ... *Me llamo ...*
Would you like ... *¿Quisiera usted ...*
Let's go to ... *Vamos a ...*

TERMS OF ADDRESS

When in doubt, use the formal *usted* (you) as a form of address.

I *yo*
you (formal) *usted*
you (familiar) *tu*
he/him *él*
she/her *ella*
we/us *nosotros*
you (plural) *ustedes*
they/them *ellos* (all males or mixed gender); *ellas* (all females)
Mr., sir *señor*
Mrs., madam *señora*
miss, young lady *señorita*
wife *esposa*
husband *esposo*
friend *amigo* (male); *amiga* (female)
sweetheart *novio* (male); *novia* (female)
son; daughter *hijo; hija*
brother; sister *hermano; hermana*
father; mother *padre; madre*
grandfather; grandmother *abuelo; abuela*

TRANSPORTATION

Where is ...? *¿Dónde está ...?*
How far is it to ...? *¿A cuánto está ...?*
from ... to ... *de ... a ...*
How many blocks? *¿Cuántas cuadras?*
Where (Which) is the way to ...? *¿Dónde está el camino a ...?*
the bus station *la terminal de autobuses*
the bus stop *la parada de autobuses*
Where is this bus going? *¿Adónde va este autobús?*
the taxi stand *la parada de taxis*
the train station *la estación de ferrocarril*
the boat *el barco*
the launch *lancha; tiburonera*
the dock *el muelle*
the airport *el aeropuerto*

I'd like a ticket to ... *Quisiera un boleto a ...*
first (second) class *primera (segunda) clase*
roundtrip *ida y vuelta*
reservation *reservación*
baggage *equipaje*
Stop here, please. *Pare aquí, por favor.*
the entrance *la entrada*
the exit *la salida*
the ticket office *la oficina de boletos*
(very) near; far *(muy) cerca; lejos*
to; toward *a*
by; through *por*
from *de*
the right *la derecha*
the left *la izquierda*
straight ahead *derecho; directo*
in front *en frente*
beside *al lado*
behind *atrás*
the corner *la esquina*
the stoplight *la semáforo*
a turn *una vuelta*
right here *aquí*
somewhere around here *por acá*
right there *allí*
somewhere around there *por allá*
road *el camino*
street; boulevard *calle; bulevar*
block *la cuadra*
highway *carretera*
kilometer *kilómetro*
bridge; toll *puente; cuota*
address *dirección*
north; south *norte; sur*
east; west *oriente (este); poniente (oeste)*

ACCOMMODATIONS

hotel *hotel*
Is there a room? *¿Hay cuarto?*
May I (may we) see it? *¿Puedo (podemos) verlo?*
What is the rate? *¿Cuál es el precio?*
Is that your best rate? *¿Es su mejor precio?*
Is there something cheaper? *¿Hay algo más económico?*

a single room *un cuarto sencillo*
a double room *un cuarto doble*
double bed *cama matrimonial*
twin beds *camas gemelas*
with private bath *con baño*
hot water *agua caliente*
shower *ducha*
towels *toallas*
soap *jabón*
toilet paper *papel higiénico*
blanket *frazada; manta*
sheets *sábanas*
air-conditioned *aire acondicionado*
fan *abanico; ventilador*
key *llave*
manager *gerente*

FOOD

I'm hungry. *Tengo hambre.*
I'm thirsty. *Tengo sed.*
menu *carta; menú*
order *orden*
glass *vaso*
fork *tenedor*
knife *cuchillo*
spoon *cuchara*
napkin *servilleta*
soft drink *refresco*
coffee *café*
tea *té*
drinking water *agua pura; agua potable*
bottled carbonated water *agua mineral*
bottled uncarbonated water *agua sin gas*
beer *cerveza*
wine *vino*
milk *leche*
juice *jugo*
cream *crema*
sugar *azúcar*
cheese *queso*
snack *antojo; botana*
breakfast *desayuno*
lunch *almuerzo*
daily lunch special *comida corrida* (or *el menú del día* depending on region)
dinner *comida* (often eaten in late afternoon); *cena* (a late-night snack)

the check *la cuenta*
eggs *huevos*
bread *pan*
salad *ensalada*
fruit *fruta*
mango *mango*
watermelon *sandía*
papaya *papaya*
banana *plátano*
apple *manzana*
orange *naranja*
lime *limón*
fish *pescado*
shellfish *mariscos*
shrimp *camarones*
meat (without) *(sin) carne*
chicken *pollo*
pork *puerco*
beef; steak *res; bistec*
bacon; ham *tocino; jamón*
fried *frito*
roasted *asada*
barbecue; barbecued *barbacoa;*
al carbón

SHOPPING

money *dinero*
money-exchange bureau *casa de*
cambio
I would like to exchange traveler's
checks. *Quisiera cambiar cheques de*
viajero.
What is the exchange rate? *¿Cuál es el*
tipo de cambio?
How much is the commission? *¿Cuánto*
cuesta la comisión?
Do you accept credit cards? *¿Aceptan*
tarjetas de crédito?
money order *giro*
How much does it cost? *¿Cuánto*
cuesta?
What is your final price? *¿Cuál es su*
último precio?
expensive *caro*
cheap *barato; económico*
more *más*
less *menos*
a little *un poco*

too much *demasiado*

HEALTH

Help me please. *Ayúdeme por favor.*
I am ill. *Estoy enfermo.*
Call a doctor. *Llame un doctor.*
Take me to ... *Lléveme a ...*
hospital *hospital; sanatorio*
drugstore *farmacia*
pain *dolor*
fever *fiebre*
headache *dolor de cabeza*
stomach ache *dolor de estómago*
burn *quemadura*
cramp *calambre*
nausea *náusea*
vomiting *vomitar*
medicine *medicina*
antibiotic *antibiótico*
pill; tablet *pastilla*
aspirin *aspirina*
ointment; cream *pomada; crema*
bandage *venda*
cotton *algodón*
sanitary napkins *use brand name,* e.g.,
Kotex
birth control pills *pastillas*
anticonceptivas
contraceptive foam *espuma*
anticonceptiva
condoms *preservativos; condones*
toothbrush *cepilla dental*
dental floss *hilo dental*
toothpaste *crema dental*
dentist *dentista*
toothache *dolor de muelas*

POST OFFICE AND COMMUNICATIONS

long-distance telephone *teléfono larga*
distancia
I would like to call ... *Quisiera llamar*
a ...
collect *por cobrar*
station to station *a quien contesta*
person to person *persona a persona*
credit card *tarjeta de crédito*
post office *correo*

general delivery *lista de correo*
letter *carta*
stamp *estampilla, timbre*
postcard *tarjeta*
aerogram *aerograma*
air mail *correo aereo*
registered *registrado*
money order *giro*
package; box *paquete; caja*
string; tape *cuerda; cinta*

AT THE BORDER

border *frontera*
customs *aduana*
immigration *migración*
tourist card *tarjeta de turista*
inspection *inspección; revisión*
passport *pasaporte*
profession *profesión*
marital status *estado civil*
single *soltero*
married; divorced *casado; divorciado*
widowed *viudado*
insurance *seguros*
title *título*
driver's license *licencia de manejar*

AT THE GAS STATION

gas station *gasolinera*
gasoline *gasolina*
unleaded *sin plomo*
full, please *lleno, por favor*
tire *llanta*
tire repair shop *vulcanizadora*
air *aire*
water *agua*
oil (change) *aceite (cambio)*
grease *grasa*
My ... doesn't work. *Mi ... no sirve.*
battery *batería*
radiator *radiador*
alternator *alternador*
generator *generador*
tow truck *grúa*
repair shop *taller mecánico*
tune-up *afinación*
auto parts store *refaccionería*

VERBS

Verbs are the key to getting along in Spanish. They employ mostly predictable forms and come in three classes, which end in *ar, er,* and *ir,* respectively:

to buy *comprar*
I buy, you (he, she, it) buys *compro, compra*
we buy, you (they) buy *compramos, compran*
to eat *comer*
I eat, you (he, she, it) eats *como, come*
we eat, you (they) eat *comemos, comen*
to climb *subir*
I climb, you (he, she, it) climbs *subo, sube*
we climb, you (they) climb *subimos, suben*

Here are more (with irregularities indicated):
to do or make *hacer* (regular except for *hago,* I do or make)
to go *ir* (very irregular: *voy, va, vamos, van*)
to go (walk) *andar*
to love *amar*
to work *trabajar*
to want *desear, querer*
to need *necesitar*
to read *leer*
to write *escribir*
to repair *reparar*
to stop *parar*
to get off (the bus) *bajar*
to arrive *llegar*
to stay (remain) *quedar*
to stay (lodge) *hospedar*
to leave *salir* (regular except for *salgo,* I leave)
to look at *mirar*
to look for *buscar*
to give *dar* (regular except for *doy,* I give)
to carry *llevar*
to have *tener* (irregular but important: *tengo, tiene, tenemos, tienen*)
to come *venir* (similarly irregular: *vengo, viene, venimos, vienen*)

Spanish has two forms of "to be":
to be *estar* (regular except for *estoy,* I am)
to be *ser* (very irregular: *soy, es, somos, son*)

Use *estar* when speaking of location or a temporary state of being: "I am at home." *"Estoy en casa."* "I'm sick." *"Estoy enfermo."* Use *ser* for a permanent state of being: "I am a doctor." *"Soy doctora."*

NUMBERS

zero *cero*
one *uno*
two *dos*
three *tres*
four *cuatro*
five *cinco*
six *seis*
seven *siete*
eight *ocho*
nine *nueve*
10 *diez*
11 *once*
12 *doce*
13 *trece*
14 *catorce*
15 *quince*
16 *dieciseis*
17 *diecisiete*
18 *dieciocho*
19 *diecinueve*
20 *veinte*
21 *veinte y uno* or *veintiuno*
30 *treinta*
40 *cuarenta*
50 *cincuenta*
60 *sesenta*
70 *setenta*
80 *ochenta*
90 *noventa*
100 *ciento*
101 *ciento y uno* or *cientiuno*
200 *doscientos*
500 *quinientos*
1,000 *mil*
10,000 *diez mil*

100,000 *cien mil*
1,000,000 *millón*
one half *medio*
one third *un tercio*
one fourth *un cuarto*

TIME

What time is it? *¿Qué hora es?*
It's one o'clock. *Es la una.*
It's three in the afternoon. *Son las tres de la tarde.*
It's 4 a.m. *Son las cuatro de la mañana.*
six-thirty *seis y media*
a quarter till eleven *un cuarto para las once*
a quarter past five *las cinco y cuarto*
an hour *una hora*

DAYS AND MONTHS

Monday *lunes*
Tuesday *martes*
Wednesday *miércoles*
Thursday *jueves*
Friday *viernes*
Saturday *sábado*
Sunday *domingo*
today *hoy*
tomorrow *mañana*
yesterday *ayer*
January *enero*
February *febrero*
March *marzo*
April *abril*
May *mayo*
June *junio*
July *julio*
August *agosto*
September *septiembre*
October *octubre*
November *noviembre*
December *diciembre*
a week *una semana*
a month *un mes*
after *después*
before *antes*

(Courtesy of Bruce Whipperman, author of *Moon Pacific Mexico*.)

Suggested Reading

TRAVELOGUES

Berger, Bruce. *Almost an Island: Travels in Baja California*. Tucson: University of Arizona Press, 1998. With his rich and descriptive writing, Berger recounts his three decades spent traveling in Baja California.

Hazard, Ann. *Agave Sunsets: Treasured Tales of Baja*. San Diego: Sunbelt Publications, 2002. This collection of spirited Baja tales will introduce you to colorful characters and erase barriers between Mexican and gringo cultures.

Hill, Herman, and Silliman, Roger. *Baja's Hidden Gold: Treasure Along the Mission Trail*, 2nd ed. Oaxaca: Carpe Diem Publishing, 2014. A collection of the stories of Herman Hill, a prospector, dreamer, and adventurer seeking gold in Baja California.

Mackintosh, Graham. *Into a Desert Place*. New York: W.W. Norton & Co., 1995. One of the most widely read Baja books chronicling the journey of a British self-described "couch potato" who walks the entire coastline of the Baja peninsula.

Smith, Jack. *God and Mr. Gomez*. Santa Barbara: Capra Press, 1997. A comedic account of the author's experience purchasing land and building a house along Baja's northern coast.

Steinbeck, John. *The Log from the Sea of Cortez*. New York: Penguin USA, Viking, 1951. This classic book recounts Steinbeck's journey by boat into the Sea of Cortez with marine biologist Ed Ricketts.

HISTORY AND CULTURE

Crosby, Harry W. *The Cave Paintings of Baja California: Discovering the Great Murals of an Unknown People*. San Diego: Sunbelt Publications, 1998. Crosby is viewed as the ultimate authority on the rock art of Baja California, and this book provides detailed descriptions and color photographs of most of the sites.

Kier, David. *Baja California Land of Missions*. El Cajon, CA: M&E Books, 2016. This comprehensive guide covering the history and information about all of the Spanish missions in Baja California is an invaluable tool for any Baja traveler.

Niemann, Greg. *Baja Legends*. San Diego: Sunbelt Publications, 2002. The useful book explains some of the most prominent Baja establishments, personalities, and legends region by region.

NATURAL HISTORY AND FIELD GUIDES

Hupp, Betty, and Malone, Marilyn. *The Edge of the Sea of Cortez*. Tucson: Operculum, LLC, 2008. For beachcombers who love exploring tidepools, this guide will help with identifying shells, sea creatures, and birds found along the shore.

Rebman, Jon, and Roberts, Norman C. *Baja California Plant Field Guide*, 3rd ed. San Diego: Sunbelt Publications, 2012. This must-have field guide is the definitive book for identifying Baja's diverse flora.

Swartz, Steven L. *Lagoon Time: A Guide to Gray Whales and the Natural History of San Ignacio Lagoon*. San Diego: Sunbelt Publications, 2014. This firsthand account looks into the natural history of Laguna San Ignacio and provides a guide to gray whale behavior.

SPORTS AND RECREATION

Church, Mike and Terry. *Traveler's Guide to Camping Mexico's Baja*, 5th ed. Rolling Homes Press, 2012. This indispensible guide gives all of the most accurate information for all of the campsites and RV parks on the peninsula.

Kelly, Dave and DeeDee, and Nugent, Ed. *Hiking Loreto*, 2nd ed. Over 60 hikes and 20 mountain bike rides in the Loreto area are detailed in this book.

Parise, Mike. *The Surfer's Guide to Baja*. Surf Press Publishers, 2012. This guide gives detailed directions and maps to the best surf spots along the peninsula.

Internet Resources

Many establishments in Baja now have websites or at least Facebook pages where you can find information about hours and location. For general Baja travel, there are a number of online forums and even Facebook groups, but always double-check the information that you find as it's not always accurate. The websites below have reliable and accurate information about travel in Baja.

Baja.com
www.baja.com
This website covers information about Baja and also offers vacation rentals.

Baja California State Tourism
www.discoverbajacalifornia.com
The state tourism website for Baja California (Norte) gives specific and helpful information about hotels, sights, and restaurants for each region.

Baja Insider
www.bajainsider.com
This comprehensive website covers valuable information for Baja residents and visitors.

Best Time to Cross the Border
http://traffic.calit2.net
This website provides the current wait times at Baja border crossings as reported by the CBP

as well as historical data and graphs. They also have an app you can download on your smartphone.

Discover Baja
www.discoverbaja.com
Not only do they offer Mexican auto insurance, but this website is a wealth of information about travel regulations and the best places to go and things to do in Baja.

INAH
http://inah.gob.mx
INAH is responsible for protecting Baja's cultural sites like rock art and the Spanish missions.

INM
www.gob.mx
The Mexican migration website, where non-Mexican citizens can obtain FMM tourist permits online.

Los Cabos Tourism
http://visitloscabos.travel
The Los Cabos tourism website has helpful information about hotels and events.

Smart Traveler Enrollment Program (STEP)
https://step.state.gov

The U.S. Department of State runs the Smart Traveler Enrollment Program (STEP) as a free service that allows U.S. citizens traveling abroad to enroll their trip with the nearest U.S. embassy or consulate.

U.S. Customs and Border Protection
www.cbp.gov
Has customs information about items allowed back into the United States from Mexico.

U.S. Embassy
https://mx.usembassy.gov
The website for the U.S. embassy in Mexico City has information about services for U.S. citizens.

ONLINE NEWSLETTERS

There are a few Baja websites that send out regular online newsletters with helpful travel information. **Discover Baja** (www.discoverbaja.com) and **Baja.com** (www.baja.com) offer newsletters that travelers can sign up for to receive monthly emails with quality articles about all areas of Baja.

For events and news for specific regions, **Rosarito Town Crier** (www.rosaritotowncrier.com) covers cultural events in the Rosarito area. **The Baja Western Onion** (bajawesternonion.com) focuses on Todos Santos and the West Cape. **The Ventana View** (www.theventanaview.wordpress.com) promotes events and news around La Ventana, and **The Baja Pony Express** (www.thebajaponyexpress.com) covers updates about the East Cape area.

Index

List of Maps

Photo Credits

Also Available

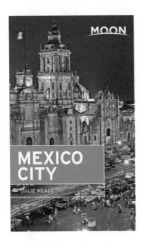

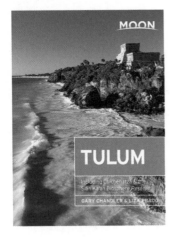

MAP SYMBOLS

▦▦▦	Expressway	○	City/Town	✈	Airport	⌐	Golf Course
▦▦▦	Primary Road	◉	State Capital	✗	Airfield	℗	Parking Area
▦▦▦	Secondary Road	⊛	National Capital	▲	Mountain	▲	Archaeological Site
-------	Unpaved Road	★	Point of Interest	✛	Unique Natural Feature	⚑	Church
——	Feature Trail	•	Accommodation			⛽	Gas Station
- - - -	Other Trail	▼	Restaurant/Bar	〰	Waterfall	⬡	Glacier
·········	Ferry	•	Other Location	⚑	Park	▨	Mangrove
▤▤▤	Pedestrian Walkway	■	Other Location	⬡	Trailhead	▧	Reef
▥▥▥	Stairs	Λ	Campground	✘	Skiing Area	▤	Swamp

CONVERSION TABLES

°C = (°F − 32) / 1.8
°F = (°C x 1.8) + 32
1 inch = 2.54 centimeters (cm)
1 foot = 0.304 meters (m)
1 yard = 0.914 meters
1 mile = 1.6093 kilometers (km)
1 km = 0.6214 miles
1 fathom = 1.8288 m
1 chain = 20.1168 m
1 furlong = 201.168 m
1 acre = 0.4047 hectares
1 sq km = 100 hectares
1 sq mile = 2.59 square km
1 ounce = 28.35 grams
1 pound = 0.4536 kilograms
1 short ton = 0.90718 metric ton
1 short ton = 2,000 pounds
1 long ton = 1.016 metric tons
1 long ton = 2,240 pounds
1 metric ton = 1,000 kilograms
1 quart = 0.94635 liters
1 US gallon = 3.7854 liters
1 Imperial gallon = 4.5459 liters
1 nautical mile = 1.852 km

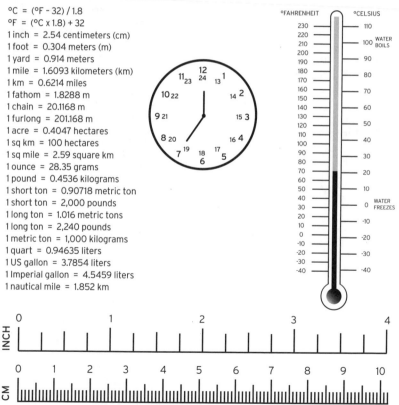

MOON BAJA

Avalon Travel
An imprint of Perseus Books
A Hachette Book Group company
1700 Fourth Street
Berkeley, CA 94710, USA
www.moon.com

Editor: Kimberly Ehart
Series Manager: Kathryn Ettinger
Copy Editor: Ashley Benning
Graphics and Production Coordinator:
  Lucie Ericksen
Cover Design: Faceout Studios, Charles Brock
Interior Design: Domini Dragoone
Moon Logo: Tim McGrath
Map Editor: Albert Angulo
Cartographers: Austin Ehrhardt and Brian Shotwell
Indexer: Greg Jewett

ISBN-13: 978-1-63121-406-6
ISSN: 1098-6685

Printing History
1st Edition — 1992
10th Edition — April 2017
5 4 3 2 1

Some photos and illustrations are used by permission and are the property of the original copyright owners.
Front cover photo: Danzante Island, Loreto © Richard Jackson, soulcatchingimages.com
Back cover photo: hotel view in Los Cabos © Carlos Sanchez Pereyra/ Dreamstime.com
Interior images

Printed in Canada by Friesens

All recommendations, including those for sights, activities, hotels, restaurants, and shops, are based on each author's individual judgment. We do not accept payment for inclusion in our travel guides, and our authors don't accept free goods or services in exchange for positive coverage.

Although every effort was made to ensure that the information was correct at the time of going to press, the author and publisher do not assume and hereby disclaim any liability to any party for any loss or damage caused by errors, omissions, or any potential travel disruption due to labor or financial difficulty, whether such errors or omissions result from negligence, accident, or any other cause.